This is a limited and numbered edition
This copy is number 255

THE HISTORY AND ANTIQUITIES OF

THE DEANERY OF CRAVEN,

IN THE COUNTY OF YORK.

THE

Ḣistory and Antiquities

OF THE

ḊEANERY OF ĊRAVEN,

IN THE

COUNTY OF YORK.

Volume II

BY

THOMAS DUNHAM WHITAKER, LL.D., F.S.A.,

Vicar of Whalley, in Lancashire.

Ṫhird Ėdition,

WITH MANY ADDITIONS AND CORRECTIONS

EDITED BY A. W. MORANT, F.S.A., F.G.S., &c.

AND WITH

A CHAPTER ON THE GEOLOGY, NATURAL HISTORY AND PRE-HISTORIC ANTIQUITIES,
BY L. C. MIALL, F.G.S., PROFESSOR OF BIOLOGY IN THE YORKSHIRE COLLEGE.

E. J. MORTEN (Publishers)
Didsbury, Manchester
and
THE CRAVEN HERALD
38 High Street, Skipton
Yorkshire

This Edition First Published 1878
JOSEPH DODGSON
Leeds

CASSELL, PETTER AND GALPIN
London

Republished 1973
E. J. MORTEN (Publishers) E & L Ass.
10 Warburton Street, Didsbury
Manchester, England
and
THE CRAVEN HERALD
38 High Street, Skipton
Yorkshire

Foreword © R. Geoffrey Rowley, Skipton 1973

Printed in Great Britain by
The Scolar Press Limited Menston, Yorkshire

PARISH OF SKIPTON.*

HAVE reserved for this parish, the most interesting part of my subject, a place in Wharfdale, in order to deduce the honour and fee of Skipton from Bolton, to which it originally belonged.

In the later Saxon times Bodeltone, or Botltune† (the town of the principal mansion), was the property of Earl Edwin, whose large possessions in the North were among the last estates in the kingdom which, after the Conquest, were permitted to remain in the hands of their former owners.

This nobleman was son of Leofwine, and brother of Leofric, Earls of Mercia.‡ It is somewhat remarkable that after the forfeiture the posterity of this family, in the second generation, became possessed of these estates again by the marriage of William de Meschines with Cecilia de Romille. This will be proved by the following table :—

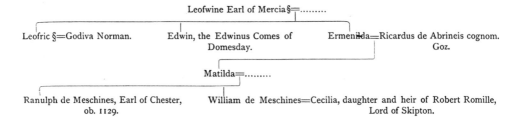

But it was before the Domesday Survey that this nobleman had incurred the forfeiture ; and his lands in Craven are accordingly surveyed under the head of TERRA REGIS. All these, consisting of LXXVII carucates, lay waste, having never recovered from the Danish ravages. Of these—

[* The parish is situated partly in the wapontake of Staincliffe and partly in Claro, and comprises the townships of Skipton, Barden, Beamsley, Bolton Abbey, Draughton, Embsay-with-Eastby, Haltoneast-with-Bolton, and Hazlewood-with-Storithes ; and contains an area of 24,789 a. 2 r. 38 p. in Staincliffe, and 5,330 a. 1 r. 13 p. in Claro. The population of the parish in 1871 was found to be 8,473, living in 1,721 houses. Enclosure Acts were passed for Tarn Moor 7th George III., for Halton Green 7th George III. and 13th George III.]

† Thus ƿicanbottle is translated by Dr. Hickes *Aula* Wicensis. " Thesaurus Ling. Sept." vol. i. pref. p. 5.

‡ See Dugdale's " Warwickshire," first edit. p. 87.

§ An Inspeximus Harl. MSS. 2,085 recites, " quod comes Leuricus tenuit feodum mil. in Clyderhow." This is by far the most ancient notice I have met with of Clitheroe, and proves that place, as Domesday proves Skipton, to have been a portion of the demesnes of the Earls of Mercia.

ꝯ Ịn *Bodeltone* . comes Eduuiñ ħƀ . vi . cař ꞇræ ad ǥld.

ƀ In Altone . vi . cař . In Embesie . iii . cař inland . 7 iii . cař soca.

.III.c′   .III.c′   .IIII.c′   .VI.c′   .X c′

ƀ In Dractone . Scipeden . Sciptone . Snachehale . Toredderbi.

.II.c′   .III.c′

§ Bedmesleia . Holme.*

These constitute the present parish of Skipton [which contains 25,755 acres]. The remainder lay in Gargrave, Staintone, Adingham, Otterburne, Scostrop, Malgun, Conistone, Helgefeld, Aneley, and Hangclif; and have been already noticed. Such, therefore, was the fee of Earl Edwin, which constituted, in the next place, the first fee of Skipton, soon afterwards augmented by a moiety of the possessions of Roger de Poitou, which altogether make up the *present* fee, consisting, in the whole, of ii knights' fees, iii carucates, ii oxgangs; whereof xiiii carucates made a knight's fee.†

After the forfeiture of Earl Edwin, the first grantee of his lands in Craven was Robert de Romille,‡ a Norman adventurer of ancient family. In his choice of a situation for the seat of his barony, Romille had nothing but the face of Nature to direct him. There had, unquestionably, been a Saxon manse at Bolton, for the occasional residence of the lord; but it was now dilapidated; and though the sequestration of that favoured place would have attracted a monk, and its beauties a man of taste, yet it wanted two of the first ingredients in the residence of an ancient baron—elevation and natural strength. These Romille found on the brink of a perpendicular rock at Skipton, which furnished an impregnable barrier to the north; while a moderate declivity to the south, equally rocky, and therefore incapable of being undermined, afforded sufficient room for the enclosure of a spacious "bailley," the ramparts of which would command the plain beneath.

The erection of this castle elevated the place at once from a poor dependent village to a respectable town. In times of turbulence and disorder, the inhabitants of the adjoining country would crowd for protection under its walls. Many privileges also would be granted by the lords, many advantageous offices enjoyed by their immediate dependents; and all

---

[* Manor.—In Bodeltone (Bolton) Earl Edwin had six carucates of land to be taxed. Berewick.—In Altone (Halton) six carucates. In Embesie (Embsay) three carucates inland, and three carucates soke. Berewick.—In Dractone (Draughton) three carucates, Scipeden (Skibeden) three carucates, Sciptone (Skipton) four carucates, Snachehale (Snaigill) six carucates, Toredderebi (? Thorlby) ten carucates. Soke.—Bedmesleia (Beamsley) two carucates, Holme (Holm) three carucates.]

[† Skypton.—Villa cum castro est in manu regis tamquam dominicum suum; et sunt in eadem xii car. terræ quarum sex et di. sunt in dominico regis, et v et di. tenentur de rege; et qualibet car. prædictarum v et di. redd. per ann. ad finem wap. iii*d*. ob. q.; unde summa est per ann. xx*d*. ob.—Kirkby's "Inquest," A.D. 1284.

Emmesay cum Esteby.—In eadem villis sunt xi car. terræ quæ tenentur de rege, et redd. per ann. ad finem prædictum vii*d*. ob.—Kirkby's "Inquest," A.D. 1284.

Stretton cum Torleby.—In eadem villa sunt x car. terræ quæ tenentur de rege et domino castri, quarum una car. dudum assignata fuit per predecessor' comites albem' ad missas celebrandas imperpetuum in capella castri de Skipton; et pro residuis ix car. nullum fit servitium de quo fit mentio in prædictis inquisitionibus.—Kirkby's "Inquest," A.D. 1284.

Skybdon.—In eadem villa sunt iii car. terræ quæ tenentur de rege in bondagio; quarum quælibet car. redd. per ann. ad prædictum finem iii*d*. ob. q. Summa xi*d*. q.]

‡ "Romille, Romilli, Rommilly, Romilley, famille ancienne et considerable en Bretagne et en Normandie. Le premier dont en a connoisance par les histoires en Robert de Romille qui se trouve compris dans le catalogue des seigneurs renommes Normandie qui accompagnerent leur duc Guilliaume le Batard dans sa conquete d'Angleterre en 10C6."—Voyez "L'Histoire de Normandie," par Gabriel de Moulin, p. 48 de la fin du livre.

these causes would account even for a greater increase of population than appears at that time to have taken place.   It may be observed, that though Skipton never had a municipal government, excepting that of a reeve, and was never represented in parliament, the town is generally styled in charters a burgh, and its inhabitants burgenses.

No reader, I suppose, will feel himself satisfied with Camden's etymology of the word—

"In the very middle (of Craven)," says that antiquary, "stands Skipton; hid, as it were, with steep precipices, lying quite round, like Latium, in Italy, which Varro thinks was really so called from its low situation under the Apennines and Alps."

Either this reference to Varro was impertinent, or Camden must be understood to mean that the verb "skip" anciently meant "to be hid," which assuredly it never did.   But in Domesday, and in all the early charters I have seen, the word is spelt Sciptone, Sceptone, or Scepetone; evidently from the Saxon "scep," a sheep.   Skipton, therefore, is the Town of Sheep; a name which it must have acquired from the vast tracts of sheep-walk which lay around it before its Norman lords appropriated the wastes of Crokeris and Elso to the range of deer.

The feudataries holding under the family of Romille at two different periods, first de veteri feoffamento, that is, at the marriage of Matilda, daughter of Henry I., and afterwards in the end of Henry II.'s time, are found in the Black Book of the Exchequer.*

"Carta de feodo de Scipton q'd tenet Alexander fil. Gerini.
De feodo de Scipton q'd tenet Alex. f. Gerini fuerunt XIII † milites feoffati temp. Regis H. (primi.)
Wil'mus de Wan'vil t. f. IIII, et quintum feodum tenet Gervasius de Wan'vil.
Joh'es de Argentoen duo feod. mil.
Rad. de Chailli duo feod. mil.
Wil'mus fil. Clerenbald I feod. mil. et dim.
Wil'mus Maleleporar. Steph. de Bulmer I feod.
Wil'mus Vavasor dim. feod. mil.
Hæc duodecim ‡ feod. sunt de antiquo feoffamento."

With respect to the specific manors held by these persons, who were probably Normans, the companions of Romille, or their immediate descendants, little can now be retrieved with certainty.   The fee of Mauliverer consisted of Bethmesley, Hawkswick, and East Malham; that of Bulmer included Burnsal and its dependencies, together with Areton; that of Vavasour, Addingham and Draughton.   William, son of Clarenbald, I conjecture, and can only conjecture, to have been the first William de Rilleston.   Of the rest I know nothing.

"De eodem feodo de Scipton q'd tenet Alex. fil. Gerini XIII milites post obitum Reg. H. sunt de D'nico feoffati heredes.
Ada' fil. Swani tenet I feod. mil.
Reinerus Flemenge I feod. mil. et dim.
Hereveius de Reineville dim. feod. mil.
Osbert Archidiacon. tenet XI carucatas ter. qu. XIIII car. faciunt feod. mil.
Pet. de Martun XII car.

----

* "Lib. Nig. Scacc." i. 322, 323. [Alice de Romilli gave four dwellings in Skipton to the Canons of Bolton.—Burt. "Mon." 119.]
† *Sic.*
‡ *Sic.*

Sigilla veterum Dominorum de Skipton.

Walter fil. Wil'mi x car.
Roger. Tempestas III car. et II bov.
Uctred de Cunegestone VI car.
Simon de Muntalt III car.
Roger de Fasinton IV car. et dim.
Walt. fil. Gamel III car.
Ric. fil. Ric. III car.
Helto fil. Wil'mi de Arches III car.
Roger Mitun I car.
Edward Camerarius* x bov. t're.
Ric. de Brocton I car.
Galfr. —— Mori I car.
Walter Axel I car.
Hugo Nepos Episcopi dim. car.
Ranulph Paileve dim. feod. mil.
Hic octo feoda mil. sunt de nov. feodis de D'nico."

These evidently refer to the second fee of Skipton, which principally consisted of the lands of Roger of Poitou.

But to return—

Robert de Romillè left a single daughter and heiress, Cecilia, whose marriages and issue, together with the descent of this castle and barony in their line, will be rendered more intelligible by the following table than a regular narrative—

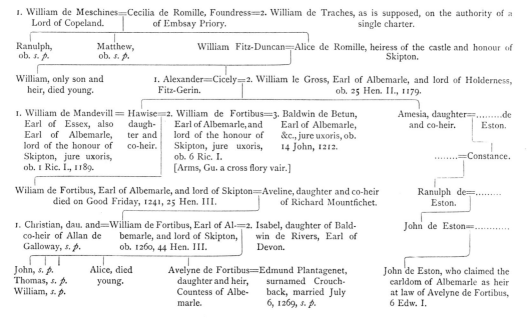

The wardship of Aveline, during her minority, was granted by Henry III., A. R. 43

---

* *Chamberlain*, a name of office most probably acquired in the service of the Romilles, and yet remaining in a respectable condition of life at Skipton.

2 M

[1258-9], to his son Edward, who for the sum of 1,500*l.* assigned the castle and barony of Skipton to Alexander, King of Scotland.*

On the demise of Edmund Crouchback, Edward I. is said to have used the following artifice to obtain possession of this barony, with the other lands appertaining to the earldom of Albemarle.†

There was one Stratton, a priest, who had great influence over the Countess Aveline. This man was engaged by the king to procure a grant of her inheritance upon very unequal terms; but, failing in his purpose, he is accused of having forged a charter, to which he affixed the countess's seal after her decease.

Of this foul transaction the king was probably ignorant. He might, and I have no doubt did, enjoin Stratton to use all the influence which his situation of confessor gave him over the conscience of Aveline to accomplish his purpose; while the bold and officious priest, failing in his plan, and despairing otherwise of his expected reward, might have recourse to a forgery of his own contrivance.

The general character of this magnanimous prince induces me to hope and believe whatever within the bounds of probability is favourable to his memory.

But an obscure lord of a manor in Craven presumed to contest the barony of Skipton with his sovereign. In 9th of this reign [1280-1] John de Eshton impleaded Edward I. for the lands of the earldom of Albemarle, deriving his title from Amice, daughter of William le Gros, and sister of Hawise; which Amice was mother of Constance, mother of Raghunt (called in the pedigree Ranulph), who was father of John the father of John de Eshton, the demandant. This case affords a remarkable instance either of the equity of Edward's temper, or of the prevalence of law over sovereign power when its claims were at the highest. The king, unable to evade the claim of his competitor, condescended to come to an agreement with him; and, in consideration of a hundred pound lands, of which the manor of Apletrewick was part, John de Eshton released the earldom and barony of Skipton by deed, the original of which, in Dodsworth's time, was remaining in Skipton Castle.‡

From this period till the 1st of Edward II. [1307-8] the barony of Skipton was vested

---

* Dugdale's "Bar. Angl." in Albemarle.

† Ibidem. See also "Mon. Angl." vol. i. p. 791.

‡ I have sought in vain for this release among the mouldering remains of the family evidences at Skipton; but among the MSS. in the Heralds' Office, in the box entitled "Skipton Box," is a confirmation from Edward I. to John de Eshton of several manors, &c., assigned as the consideration for this release; and, among the rest, "Hamlettum de Apletrewick quod est membrum Castri de Skipton cum capitali mess. et VI car. terre qu. extendit ad XVI. XII. VI. Et Hamlettum de Broghton quod est membrum cast. p'dict' quod extendit ad XIII. II. X. exceptis sectis lib'm hom'm facient. Sect. ad curiam de Skipton. Et Lacum de Eshton qui extendit ad XXX. Et insuper III Acr. bosci de Elishow versus Aston, quas terras eidem Joh. concessimus pro jure hereditario quod habere clamabat in comitatu Albemarle, et in omn. terris quæ fuerunt Alicie de Fortibus." But the several steps of this transaction are retrieved from a valuable paper among the MSS. at Bolton Abbey.

[This account is partly corroborated by the following extract from the Plea Roll of 35th Edward I.: "Thomas de Multon et Thomas de Lucy qui dicunt se esse hæredes Avilinæ, quondam filiæ Willelmi de Fortibus, patunt quod dominus rex r̄spectum habeat ad jus suum, quod habent in maneriis de Cokermewe in com. Cumberland, Skipton in com. Ebor., et Roddeston in com. Northampton. Petitio mittitur hic, &c. Et Johannes de Cestria, qui sequitur pro domine rege, et servientes regis dicunt pro rege quod in Parliamento regis tento anno IIII regni sui quidam Johannes de Eston petiit præmissa, simul cum aliis terris de quibus dicta Avelina obiit seisita, &c. Qui quidem Johannes illa tenementa remisit domino regi pro C lib. terræ quas idem dominus rex idem concessit in manerio de Thorneton prope Pyckeringe, et Skipton in com. Ebor., &c. Ideo Johannes de Eston, consanguineus et hæres dicti Johannis sum' per vicecomitem, etc., antequam procedatur, etc." (Abbrev. Placit. 261).—Surtees Society, Kirkby's "Inquest," p. 145 n.]

in the Crown;* but in the 21st Edward I. [1292–3] I find a grant for the wife and family of William Lord Latimer, who was then on the king's service in Gascony, to reside in Skipton Castle, with allowance of fuel out of the woods there for her necessary use.†

One of the first acts of Edward II. was to bestow this valuable inheritance on his minion Piers de Gaveston, whose enjoyment of it was very short.‡ The next alienation transferred it to a family who, with the exception of a single attainder, have held it five hundred years, during the longer part of which they have resided at Skipton Castle, in great wealth and honour.

The curious reader will not be displeased with a sight of the original grants under which this noble patrimony has so long been held.

1st. "Rex concessit Roberto de Clifford et her's de corp' suo procr's 100*l.* terræ de manerio de Skipton, in Craven, per extent' inde faciendam, una cum feodis mil. et advocationibus ecclesiarum ad illas 100*l.* spectant." §

2nd. "Rex. Sciatis quod cum nos nuper per cartam nostram dederimus et conc' dil'o et fid' nostro Rob. de Clifford centum libratas terræ cum pert. in manerio nostro de Skipton, in Cravene, &c., et insuper concessimus eidem Roberto Castrum nostrum de Skipton, in Cravene, et alias centum libratas terræ in man. p'dict' habend. et tenend. ad terminum vitæ suæ; ac idem Rob. nobis dederit et concess. omnes terras et omnia tenem. sua in Munemuthe et valle de Munemuthe, &c. Nos in excambium præd. ter. et ten. concessimus eidem Roberto quod ipse p'dict. castrum et C libratas terræ quæ tenet ad terminum vitæ suæ habeat et teneat sibi et hered. suis de corp. suo legitimè procreatis per eadem servitia quæ comites Albemarlie, nuper d'ni castri et man. p'dictorum, facere debuerant et consueverant, 5to die August', a. r. 4° [1310.] Apud Nottingham."

3. After reciting the last charter :—

"Nos volentes eidem Roberto uberiorem gratiam facere in hac parte, concessimus quod ipse habeat et teneat sibi et heredibus suis de corpore suo legitimè procreatis, castrum, manerium, terras, et ten'a p'dicta, cum feodis militum, advocationibus ecclesiarum, capellarum, abbatiarum, prioratuum, ac etiam cum homagiis, libertat', et omnibus aliis ad p'dictu' castrum, manerium, &c., spectantibus, adeo integrè sicut præfati comites temporibus suis tenuerunt. Teste Rege apud Nov. Castrum super Tynam 7 die Sept. a. p'dict."

4th. Next follow three mandates to the feudataries of Skipton Castle, to yield due obedience to Robert de Clifford :—

"Et Mandatum est militibus, liber. hom. et omn. aliis tenentibus de castro et man' de Skipton, in Craven, quod eidem Rob. tanquam domino suo sint intendentes et respondentes."

"Et mandatum est Gulielmo le Vavasur quod eidem Roberto de homagio et fidelitate suâ sit intendens et respondens in formâ p'dictâ. Eodem modo mandatum est Henrico filio Hugonis, Margaretæ de Nevill, Ranulpho de Nevill, Henrico de Kygheley. Per breve de priv. Sigill."

These grants may properly be accompanied by an original survey of the several manors and other premises conveyed under them, and compared with a second valuation made three centuries after, by order of Francis Earl of Cumberland.

[* SKYPTON.—Villa cum castro est in manu regis tanquam dominicum suum; et sunt in eadem XII car. terræ, quarum sex et di. sunt in dominico regis, et V et di. tenentur de rege; et quælibet car. prædictarum V et di. redd. per añn. ad finem wap. III*d.* ob. q.; unde summa est per ann. XX*d.* ob.—Kirkby's "Inquest," A.D. 1284.

In 1308, 1 Edw. II., the king grants to Piers Gavaston and Margaret his wife, amongst other manors, "Castrum et manerium de Skipton in Craven, cum membris et aliis pertinentiis suis, in Comitatu Eborum." If the said Piers and Margaret should die without heirs of their bodies, then the manors, &c., to revert to the king or his heir.—Rymer's "Fœdera."]

† Dugdale's "Bar." in Latimer.

‡ Pat. Rot. Edw. II. a. r. 1*mo* N° VI. Rex concessit Petro de Gavestone et Margaretæ uxori ejus manerium de Skipton cum membris.

§ Pat. a. 3 Edw. II.

20 Octobris, } A Declarac'on or Report off yᵉ value of yᵉ honor or maner of Skypton, in Craven . . . . upon &
1612.   } conteyning in . . . at yᵉ s'val townes, hamletts, granges, places, and p'fits hereunder mentioned,
which weer granted to Rob't lord Clifford, by King Edward II. anno regni sui quarto, ass yᵉ same
weere p'ticulerly rated by extent* thereof, made anno regni sui 3 to CCl. *per annum,* and what yᵉ same
be now w'rth *per annum.*

SKIPTON.

The castle, court-yard, building, and gardin, then valued at IIs.   Sat. adhuc IIs.

Two corne-milles, then at XIIIl. VIs. VIIId. now XXXl.

Arrable land,† 235 acres then at Xd. now VIs. an acre, LXXl. Xs.

Pasture ground, 12 acres, then at IVd. now Vs. the acre, LXs.

Two oxegangs of land and medow, then in demeyne at VIIIs. now at XLs.

Arrable land in Galflat, 2 acres, then at VIIId. now at Vs. the acre, LXs.

Medow 68 acres, then at IIs. VId. now at VIIs. the acre, XXIIIl. XVIs.

Medow dispersed in the fields, then at XLs. now VIIIl.

One toft and acre of land, then at Vs. now at VIIIs. IVd.

Two burgages,‡ then at Vs. now Xs.

Nyne tofts, then at XXIVs. now XXXs.

The parke, adjoining to yᵉ castle, rated then, besydes the fedyng of the deare, to LXs. ys now w'rth,
besyde the same feiding, 10l.

Incomes p'ceived for ageistmenth § & escape of beastes tempore cl'o and ap'to,‖ then rated ⎫
at XXVIs. VIIId. now yieldeth nothing by reason the grounds are enclosed, and ⎬ Nihil.
kept in sev'altie.   ⎭

The fine or rent for Lytsters,¶ then rated at XXs. of long time had yielded nothing ; and now Xs.

The fulling mille,** then rated at Xs. now but VIs.

The rent of freeholders in Skypton then extended to XXXVIIs. IId. now decaied, by reason of dissolution of
monasteries,†† &c., and cometh but to XVIIIs. VIIId.

White Rents, now called Wapentake Fines, then extended to LIs. VIId. now by reason supr', cometh but to XXXs.

The free rents of forrein freholders, then XLVIs. Xd., decaied by reason supra,†† and now yieldeth but
XXVIs. VIIId.

The profits of the weekely market and two faiers in the yere, then valued at XVIl. XIIIs. IVd. doth not now yield
so much as XVIl. XIIIs. IVd.

The profit of the court for the burgh of Skypton, then XLs. yieldeth no more now, XLs.

The profit of the Knighth Court ther, als' the Lib'tie Court, then Xl. XVs. is now, *per annum,* XVl.

The Free Chappell and Landes belonging, then extended at LXXXVIs. VIIId. was, by ⎫
inquisition, found concealed upon the statute of chantries, and came to the kinge's ⎬ Nihil.
hands, and the late erle p'chased them againe.   ⎭

Grounds improved from the grant of the co'mons and wastes, w'rth, *per annum,* XLs.

Wood sales in Cawder, extended to IIIs. and so may contynue, IIIs.

Wood·sales in the Haw extended to IIs. now may be VIs. VIIId.

---

* [*Extent,* the estimate or valuation of lands, which, when made to the utmost value, is said to be the full extent ; whence come our
" extended rents " or " rack-rents."—Jacob's " Law Dictionary."]

† In the reign of Edward II. arable land bore a rent of 10d. and pasture only 4d., because corn was dear and cattle cheap ; but
the proportions are now reversed.

[‡ Burgage is a tenure proper to borows, whereby the inhabitants by ancient custom hold their lands or tenements of the king, or
other lord, at a certain yearly rent.   It is a kind of soccage, says Swinburn.—Blount's " Law Dictionary."]

[§ *Agistment,* the taking in of other men's cattle into pasture-land at a certain rate per week, and the profit of such feeding.]

‖ *Clauso and aperto,* that is, when the common fields were in corn and fenced off, and when they were in fallow and open.

[¶ *Litster,* a dyer.]

** See " Hist. of Whalley," p. 366, where I had inferred the existence of a woollen manufactory in England, temp. Edward II.,
from that of Fulling Mills.   This, however, did not follow : our ancestors might purchase their cloth from the Flemings unscoured.

†† I do not understand this.   The dissolution of monasteries certainly contributed to depopulate *their domains ;* which, from tillage,
were generally converted into pasturage ; but it does not appear what effect this could have upon the freeholders of the neighbouring
towns.

Pannage was extended in Cawder* to xIId. and now, and of long time past, *nihil.*

Summa ccxcIIIl. xs. vIId.

SKIBDEN.

One toft, then valued at Ivd. now xxd.

One other toft, then valued at IIs. now IIIs. Ivd.

Land and medow, xxIV oxegangs, then rated at xxIVs. *per annum,* and is now worth, ev'y oxegang, xxxs. xxxvIl.

The customes, s'vices, and other boines then paied and done by the ten'ts of thes tofts and oxeg' were extended to xl. xIIIs. *viz.* For carriage of wood, IIs. Vitailes at xxIVs. For plowing and harrying vIIIs. Shering of corne, xxxvIs. Thatching, xIId. Freedom of tolles, IIs. Mille Ferme, xxxIxs. Tallage, Lxxxs. M'chett† and Leirwet,† fines and p'quisites of Halmote,‡ &c., xxs. For Nutt'g§ at Hawe, all which are decaied and lost, saving some s'vice in bringing wood to the castle, and mawing of hey, worth by est'n, *per annum,* xvs.

Summa, xxxvIIl.

HOLME.

One capitall mess', ten't, one acr', two lathes,‖ and a stable, then of no value, by reason of decaie, and now worth, *per annum,* vIs. vIIId.

Of arrable land, 287 acr' then at xd. now being medow or pasture, vIIs. *per* acr. cl. Ixs.

Of medow, 80 acr' then at IIIs. Ivd. and now at xs. the acre, xLl.

Some little corn's and p'cels of ground, then val'd at Lxs. and can be demed no more, being almost wasted with the water of Ayre, Lxs.

Ageistment and escape of beasts in those grounds then lying open, extended to xIIIs. Ivd. and now yeldeth nothing, by reason all are enclosed.

Summa, cxLIIIl. vs. vIIId.

STIRTON and THORLEBY.

The rents of freeholders then extended to xIId. and now a sparrehauke, or IIIs. Ivd.

One toft and two oxegangs of land, tout xII acres, then vIIIs. is now worth every acre vIs. LxxIIs.

Demayne land, xxII oxegangs, then rated ev'y oxegang at vIs. *per annum,* which was after divided into ten'ts and v dwellyngs, vIII oxegangs and a close geven the Free Chapel, and, upon inquisition of Concelm' upon the Statute of Chantries, those v mess' and vIII oxegangs of the land, and the close called Turne Ing, were founde for the kynge, and the late erle p'chased the same agayne; so 14 oxegangs remayn'g, being but of small content, valued at ev'y one xxxs. cometh to xxIl.

The tallage¶ for vIII bondmen then extended to xxxs. now yieldeth *nihil.*

The p'fits of the Halmote, with M'chett and Leyrwhett, then IIIs. Ivd. now no p'fit; but of the Halmote *coib. ann.* xs.

Grounds improved on the co'mons since the grant, w'rth, *per annum,* xxs.

Summa, xxIxl. xIIs.

---

* The Parks de la Caudre and Heye are first mentioned in a charter of William de Forz, Earl of Albemarle, A.D. 1257. Calder, or Cawder Park, stretched along the skirts of Romille Moor, and near the confines of Bradley, where a farm, belonging to the Earl of Thanet, still retains the name. Yet the Licentia imparcandi was not granted before the 40th of Edward III. [1366-7]. It is as follows, "Edwardus, &c. Sciatis nos de gra' n'ra speciali concessisse Rogero de Clifford, quod ipse quingentas acras terre de terris suis propriis in Brenhill et Lysterfield infra Boscum de Calder et villam de Skipton includere, et parcum inde facere, &c. Dat. ap. Westm. 30 die Nov. a. r. 40."—Dugd. MSS. in Mus. Ashmole. Oxon.

† "Merchett et Leyrwyte." Much has been written on the Mercheta Mulierum, which I shall not repeat. I shall only say, that there is a very innocent sense in which the terms are used by our old English (not Scottish) lawyers—namely, that of a fine paid by a prædial slave for leave to marry his daughter. Bracton, l. 2, tit. 1, cap. 8.—Leirwite, or Legerwite, was a fine paid by the same to their lord for incontinence. From leʒep, *concubitor,* and pɪʒe, *mulcta.*

["Marchet." Blount says that by the custom of the Manor of Denever, in the county of Carmarthen, every tenant at the marriage of his daughter pays xs. to the lord, which in the British language is called "Gwabr-merched"—*i.e.,* a maid's fee.]

"*Lairwite, Lecherwite,* or *Legergeldum,* a fine or custom of punishing offenders in adultery and fornication; which priviledge did anciently belong to the lords of some mannors, in reference to their villains and tenants."—Blount's "Law Dictionary."]

‡ *Halmote,* the court of a copyhold manor; a court baron; called also healgemot or halimote.

§ "Pro nucibus colligendis," as it is expressed in a later inquisition. This, however trifling it may seem, was an ancient rustic service, which, in the forest of Pendle, gave name to the family of Nutter. The mother of Archbishop Tillotson was of this family.

[‖ *Lathe,* a barn or granary.]

[¶ "*Tallage* was a certain rate, according to which barons and knights were taxed towards the expenses of the State, and inferior tenants by their lords on certain occasions."—Bailey.]

ELSO and CROOKRISE.

> The lodge, then called Helsten, now Elso, nigh Crookrise, extended to xxvis. viiid. is now worth xls. Another lodge there, called Crookrise, xxvis. viiid. is now worth lxs. Agistment then xxxiiis. those grounds now being enclosed, beside feeding for the deare, xiiiil.
>
> Wood, then xs. now xxs.

BARDEN FOREST.

> Drebley Lodge, then extended to xxvis. viiid. now vil. xiiis. ivd.
>
> Barden Lodge, xiiis. ivd. now lvis. viiid.
>
> Launde Lodge, xs. now viil.
>
> Gamelswath Lodge (now Gamsworth), then xxviiis. viiid. now xl.
>
> Holgil Lodge (now Howgill), then xxiiis. now vil.
>
> Ungayne Lodge, with Eskewath and Dersailes (? now Dowshill), xiiis. ivd. now xl.
>
> Agistment in Barden, xvil.
>
> Wood sales then extended to xxl. and so resteth, because the woods are sore decaid, &c.

HOLDEN cum GILGRANGE.

> Lodges and Park adjoining, then viiis. now xll.
>
> Other lands, Pannage,* &c. xxxviis. vid.
>
> Total Value, in 1612, 749l. 3s. 2d. ob.

It would be indelicate to inquire minutely into the present rental of these demesnes; and it might be injurious to individuals to guess at their real value. The comparison would else be curious.

> In the lord's hands.
>
> > The Old Parke, adjoining to the castle.
> >
> > The Parke George.
> >
> > Crookrise and Skirackes (Elso).

BARDEN.

> The Parke wherein the tower standeth.
>
> The great rough Park, in two.

The honour of Skipton was divided into three bailiwicks, namely, of Ayredale, Malghdale, and Kettlewell Dale, to each of which a principal gentleman of the district was always appointed, and the whole was placed under the control of a receiver, to whom the bailiffs annually accounted. To the bailiff of Ayredale were subjected the foresters of Elso and Crokeris, and of the parks of Skipton. The forest of Barden seems to have been independent. Under this bailiwick also, were included the inferior præpositure of Sighelsden and Thorlby. The foresters annually accounted for the profits of waifs (Estrahuræ, Estrays) agistment, pannage, husset, bark, croppings, beestock, and turbary. The bailiffs accounted for free rents, profits of courts military and wapentake, of which 18 were held annually, *de tribus septimanis in tres septimanas*, or nearly so. The bailiwick of Ayredale comprehended Skipton, the seat of the barony, Stretton, Thoralby, Bradeley, Fernehill, Neweton, Okeworth, Moreton, Ridlesden, Wath and Wombwell, Kigheley, Lacok, Glusburne, Collinge, Conondely.

The bailiwick of Kettlewell Dale comprehended Eastby, Draughton, Berwick,

---

[* *Pannage*, the money taken by the agistors of a forest for the food of hogs, such as mast of beech, acorns, &c.]

Coningeston, Brynshale, Thorpe, Hawkswicke, Sutton, Halton super Montem, Rilston, Hetton and Doxhill, an obscure hamlet near Hartlington.

The bailiwick of Malghdale contained Conyngeston Cald, Ayreton, Broghton, Elslak, Calton, Essheton, Gayregraf, Scowsthorpe, Malghun, Hanlithe, Kigheley, Morton, Utley, Stoke, Bracewell, Helifeld, Rilston and Otterburn. Several of these names appearing under two different bailiwicks, it is to be supposed that different parts of such townships were under different jurisdictions.

Skipton itself was under the government of burgh-reves,[*] appointed half-yearly. It had a town hall and a tolbooth, the former repaired, according to ancient custom, by the tenants of Sighelsden, in one of which every burgh-reve, during his administration, held nine " burgh-cortys."

Such, under the earlier Cliffords, and probably long before, was the administration of the burgh and honour of Skipton.[†]

The forest of Skipton, which, excepting Holden, comprehended all these parks and demesnes, consisted of that rocky and central part of Craven, which extends east and west from the Wharf to the Are, and is bounded on the north and south by the two great openings which connect those valleys.

The whole may be estimated at an area of six miles by four, or 15,360 acres. With respect to its subdivisions, the name of Elso [‡] is now forgotten. But Aylso, Aylshow, or Elso, which means the Hill of Elsi, or Aylsi, a well-known personal name [§] in the Saxon times, was that portion of the forest now called Skirackes, divided from Crookrise by the aperture in the hills from Skipton to Rilston, and stretching thence to the boundaries of Flasby, Eshton, and Holme. Crookrise, which means nothing more than the " Crooked Rise," or ascent, is still known, and rears its bold and craggy front to the north of Embsay. These rugged districts are now stripped of their woods, though the Compotus of Bolton, and the foregoing survey, represent them, in the reigns of Edward the First and Second, as far from destitute of timber. Modern incredulity, surveying the naked state of our moors and mountains at present, will scarcely be convinced by evidence, that they were ever clothed with wood. The soil, it is said, was shallow, the cold extreme, the winds (more injurious than any other cause to the growth of young plants) unbroken by fences, and the whole tract

---

[* *Burgh-reve*, the governor or bailiff of a town : the same as the German burgraff or burgrave.]

† The particulars of this account have been extracted from the Compotus of Thomas Lord Clifford for 1434.

‡ The last instance in which I meet with the word is in Harrison's "Description of Britain," prefixed to the first edition of Holinshed, where it is called " Elsewood."

From a paper of Henry VIII.'s time, among the MSS. at Skipton, I find that the following singular toll was anciently levied in Skirack and Crookrise :—

" Note, that theise customes hayh ben used tyme out of mynd, by ye report of Rob. Garth, forster ther ; the whych sayeth, that he, in all his tyme, and his father afore him in y^t office, always hayth taken the sayd customes :

" First, That ev'y bryde cumynge that waye shulde eyther gyve her lefte shoo or IIIs. IVd. to the forster of Crookryse, by way of custome or gaytcloys."

The rest only relate to tolls taken for the passage of sheep, cattle, and wool.

The commutation was so high, that I suppose the penalty would generally be paid in kind ; and by this ungallant custom the poor brides of Craven would be reduced to tread the rugged ways of Crookrise in the situation of the light-footed sons of Thestius.

"————το λαιον ιχνος αναρβυλοι ποδος,
Τονδ' εν πεδιλοις."　　　　EURIP. in Fragm.

§ At the foundation of Kirkstall Abbey, the rector of Leeds was Ailsi. Ex cart. orig. in Bib. Bodl.

ranged by wild animals, which were often excluded from the surface of the earth by snow, and compelled by hunger to browse on every bush and twig within their reach. Nay, independently of this last impediment, artificial plantations of the hardiest trees, which are carried but midway up the skirts of these acclivities, dwindle and grow deformed; while the native woods, which flourish in the valleys, as they ascend along the sides of the hills, show, at every step, their growing abhorrence of exposure, become poor and stunted, and gradually leave the undisputed possession of the heights to ling and bentgrass. Much of this is true; but it must be remembered, that if the principle of vegetation in forest trees operated on these wastes at all, it might operate many centuries without interruption; that woods, which are long in arriving at maturity, are equally slow in their decay; and that the parent plants might have acquired strength and closeness enough to protect their undergrowth of seedlings long before there was a deer or sheep to browse them.

From a passage in one of the earliest charters relating to Bolton Priory, it appears that the Forest of Skipton was enclosed with a pale;[*] the Chaces of Blackburnshire were fenced in the same manner. The Saxon forests, as far as I know, lay open, and the practice of enclosing these immense tracts must have been introduced by the great Norman lords. Musing on this circumstance, I was struck by a passage of Columella, from which it appears that the idea was familiar to the ancient princes of Gaul: *Hoc autem modo licet etiam latissimas regiones tractusque montium claudere, sicuti Galliarum; locorum vastitas patitur.*[†] The subject is treated by that writer in a very lively and elegant manner. The materials of the fence were cleft pales (*Vacerræ*) of oak, cork-tree, &c. Care was taken to enclose a supply of perennial water; as also great plenty of mast-bearing and bacciferous trees, particularly the arbutus. The animals nourished in these enclosures were the stag, the wild boar, the fallow-deer, the roe, and the oryx; which last, from the account given of his inverted mane by Pliny, can have been no other than the aurochs, or wild bull, still found in the Lithuanian forests. Beans, yet in use for the winter fodder of deer, are particularly recommended. On the whole, I propound it as a subject of curious speculation, whether the practice of enclosing forests were not continued in France from the era of classical antiquity to the Middle Ages, and whether the Norman lords, when they became possessed of tracts equally wild and extensive in this country, did, by enclosing them, anything more than follow the example of their ancestors. The forests of the French nobility at the time of the late revolution, were uniformly open, but so have been our own during four or five centuries.

In the Compotus of the Forests of Skipton and Barden for the year 1437, is the following article :—

"Foreste—De ligno, proficuo corticis sive crop. quercuum ib'm prostratarum, nec de pannagio porcorum, neque de cera sive de melle, nil rec'r. hic quia nullum tale proficuum per tempus compotûs contigebat."

I have elsewhere observed, that in the old economy of the forests, the wild bee-stocks were always an object of attention. In the vast extent and undisturbed solitude of the

[*] Haia de Crokeris.
[†] Columella de R. R. l. 9, c. I.   Ed. Steph. MDXLIII.

ancient woods, these objects of pursuit must have been much more numerous than at present; so numerous, indeed, that in the great forests of France, and even in our own country, officers were appointed specifically for the purpose of pursuing them, and securing the wax and honey. These were called Bigres, or Bigri, possibly a corruption of Apigeri.

"It. avons droit de tenir en la dit Forêt ung Bigre lequel peut prendre Mouches (Bees) miel & cire pour le luminaire de notre eglise."—Carta, dat. 1642. "It. ai droit de envoyer mon Bigre lequel doit etre juré de bien & fidelement *querre* les Abeilles & le miel."—Alia Cart. dat. 1479.*

And in a charter of our Richard the Second, which I quote to show that the name and practice were both known in England,

"In Foresta de Bord. unum Bigrum ad luminare ecclesiæ."—See Du Cange *in voce* Bigrus.

The following narrative, which I give in its original form, exhibits, together with many interesting particulars relating to these domains, a lively picture of baronial manners in the close of the 15th and beginning of the 16th centuries.

From the records of a cause† depending before the President and Council of the court at York from 32 Henry VIII. [1540–1] to 2 Elizabeth [1559–60] it appears that the Nortons of Rilston contested the right of the Cliffords to hunt within that township, on the plea that it was not included within the forest of Skipton.

In order to support the claim of the superior lord, the following persons were examined :—

"Thomas Garth, of Bolton Canons, keeper of the king's woods there,‡ of the age of 74 years, deposeth, That he hath been at general views and ranges taken in the forest of Skipton, and saith, that Thomas Garth, his grandfather, was Master Forster there in King Richard's time, when this deponent was very young. He also knew Henry Popeley, Forster in my lord's father's days, and went with him when he went to range and view the deer ; also he went a ranging with Henry Radcliffe, which was Master Forster after Popeley ; and then Henry Martin ; and then master Anthony Clifford ;§ then master Thomas Clifford ; and then Sir Roger Bellingham ; and after him was the Prior of Bolton : and such times as he was with them they began at the 'Round Topt Esh,' within the same forest, to Eshton ; then to Hetton, from Hetton to Rilston, then to Cracoe, then to Thorpe, then to Burnsal, and so into the heart of the forest of Skipton."

"Robert Kitchen, of Skipton, of the age of 70 years, deposeth, That he hath been at divers views and ranges of the deer in the forest of Skipton, at the commandment of master Henry Popeley, forster to my lord's father that now is. They began to range at the Round Topt Esh, and from thence to Flasby, and so to Eshton, thence to Rilston, and so to Burnsal."

"Launcelot Marton, of Eshton, Esq., saith, That he was a boy, and, together with his father, he did see the keepers of Skipton Forest hunt and chase deer out of the grounds of Rilston ; and also myne old lady Clifford ‖ divers times, to bring deer forth of Rilston, without any let : and this deponent saw old lady Clifford, mother to my lord of Cumberland that now is, hound ¶ her greyhounds within the said grounds of Rilston, and chase deer, and have them away at her leisure, both red and fallow, till now of late that master Norton hath walled his grounds of Rilston, where the Forsters were wont to walk, and to draw my lord of Cumberland's deer into his ground, he hath made a wall on an high rigge, beside a quagmire, and at the end of the wall he hath rayled the ground, so that it is a destruction to my lord's deer, so many as come." **

"Robert Kitchin, of Skipton, yeoman, æt. 60, deposeth, That he was one of the Forsters of the Old Park of Skipton twenty-three years; hath hunted and chased out the deer in Rilston Lordship to every other place where he would in the forest

---

* See also Du Cange *in voce* Abollagium, which he defines "Jus quod habet Dominus feodi in apum examinibus, quæ reperiuntur in sylvis vasallorum." The Bigres had a right to cut down trees, in order to get at the honey.

† Skipton MSS.

‡ This was in the short interval between 1539, when the priory of Bolton was dissolved, and 1542, when the site and demesnes of the house were granted to the first Earl of Cumberland.

§ Whose name appears on the steeple at Carlton. He is omitted in the pedigree of the family.

‖ I am not sure whether this is meant of the widow of "Black-faced Clifford," or the second wife of her son. The "old lady Clifford," next mentioned, is evidently the first wife of Henry the Shepherd.

¶ Hound is used as a verb, by Alan Ramsay, in the "Gentle Shepherd;" "Then bad me hound my dog." And, not unfrequently, in the dialect of Craven at this day.

** There are still remaining considerable traces of this work near Norton Tower. See Rilston.

2 N

of Skipton; he did see my old lady Clifford hunt in Rilston Lordship, and set the hounds and greyhounds, and kill two bucks there, and carry them off ; and Thomas Garth, keeper at that time, had the shulders for his fee; and there was with her, at one course, Sir Thomas Tempest, knight, Sir Thomas Darcy, knight, Master Viewers,[*] and many others ; and this deponent saith he hath walked there an hundred times as Forster and Keeper of the Old Park."

"Thomas Roberts, of Embsay, was servant to Robert Garth, keeper ; and kept his master's room ; and did many times walk in the grounds of Rilston ; and from the grounds into the forest ; he did see my lord that now is set his course (in or to) Rilston, and hound greyhounds at the deer there ; and my lord Latimer[†] hunted in Litbank and Houden, and Robert Garth had the schulders for his fee."

"At one time master John Norton gate leave of my old lord for a morsel of flesh for his wife's churching ;[‡] and the said Garth hunted and killed a grete fatt stagg; and so one half thereof went to Berden, and master Norton had the other half; and Garth had the shulders and the ombles : and he saith, that Robert Langton servant to the said master Norton, went with this deponent to Barden, to know whether the said master Norton should have the whole stagg or the half; and so he had but the half."

"John Steyninge, of Crookrise, Keeper, many times, both day and night, hath chased out of Rilston into the forest of Skipton all the deer that he could find there ; he hath seen my lord that now is, with his company, hunt in Rilston, and hound thirty brace of deer, both horned and not horned, and kill all they might, both red and fallow, because they would not abide out of that ground."

These are original representations of some very curious and animated scenes, in which the ladies seem to have taken as bold and forward a part as their lords.

But such "mighty huntings" certainly contributed to a general ferocity of manners ; for where is the wonder if two neighbouring and rival noblemen, with boundaries ill defined, and game which disdained any boundaries, inspired by the ardour of pursuit, and backed by troops of armed followers, should sometimes be provoked to convert those images of war into the dreadful reality ?

Here, however, the Cliffords were in the centre of their territories, and would probably regard the opposition of Mr. Norton as the rebellion of a petty vassal.

Of the anxiety of the Cliffords to preserve the deer in the forests I have traced the following vestiges in the family records—

15 Henry VII. [1499–1500]. "W'm Gyzeley of Thornton is bound in the penalty of 40l. conditioned to save harmless the deer and woods of Henry lord Clifford.   Counterpart of the bond to remain in the custody of Henry Popeley, Master Forester of Craven."

38 Henry VIII. [1546–7]. "James Horner of Beamesley enters into recognizances, with two sureties, to be of good abearing to my lords Deere within Cravyn."

Date omitted. "Charles Car of Thornton, gent., W'm Lyster of Mydhop, W'm Malham of Elslack, Esqrs., enter into a bond of 100l. conditioned that Car shall not molest the deer."

18 Elizabeth [1575–6]. "Tho. Frankland, of Michels Ing, gent., for killing and destroying deere, as well tame as wild and savage, in Littondale and Longstroth', to yield himself as prisoner into the castle of Skipton, there to remain during the *Earles pleasure*, and until the said earle shall declare his pleasure for the enlargement and deliverance of the said Frankland out of the said castle."

The imprisonment of West, the Grassington deer-stealer, by the first earl, I have mentioned elsewhere. Happily for us, the equal operation of law has put an end to such arbitrary proceedings.

To these details little needs to be subjoined on the subject of the demesnes of Skipton. It may be proper, however, to add that the old Park, which lay immediately contiguous to the castle northward, is now enclosed, and that it had one deep and beautiful dell

---

* Evers ?

† John Nevile, Lord Latimer, first husband of Queen Catharine Parr.

‡ Hence it appears that thanksgivings after childbirth were anciently celebrated with feasting. For this custom I have a still older authority. "In 11bus Hogsheveds vini albi empt. apud Ebor. erga purificationem Dominæ, tam post partum Mag'ri mei nuper de Clifford, quam post partum Mag'ri mei nunc de Clifford, LXVIJ. VIIId." Master is here used in the Scottish sense for the heir apparent of the family. From this article alone it appears that Black-faced Clifford had an elder brother, who died in his infancy. Compotus Tho. Dom. Clifford, A° 15 Henry VI., or 1437.

immediately beneath the walls, of which I will not say how it has of late been mutilated, and how defiled.* The Hawe Park, retaining some vestiges of the ancient ridings, is now a bushy pasture; of Park George the dimensions, or particular site, are not remembered; Cawder is become a grazing-farm; Crookrise and Elso, with the exception of some enclosures on their skirts, have continued in their primitive state of bog and fell. But the forest of Barden is too interesting to be passed over without a distinct and particular account.

BARDEN

is the valley of the wild boar, from Baɲ, *Aper,* and Dene, *Convallis ;* and it was well adapted to the habits of that animal, from the deep solitude of its ancient woods, and the profusion of acorns which they must have shed.

Though unnoticed in Domesday, it is mentioned in the original donation of Bolton by Alice de Romille; and in a charter, perhaps still older, I meet with the attestation, " Ric. Sclao (Senescallo) de Bardani."

In the Compotus of Thomas Lord Clifford, A.D. 1437, are some very curious articles, accounted for by Henry Yonge, the forester of Barden, as, 1st,

" Pro Husset prostern. pro averiis pascend. et sustentand. in tempore hiemis, IV*l.* III*s.* VIII*d.*"

Husset is, undoubtedly, the old French *Houset,* or Holly; and it appears, from the magnitude of the sum—at least 50*l.* in our money—and from the word *Averia,* that the croppings of this evergreen constituted, at that time, a principal article of winter fodder for cattle, as well as for sheep. It is recommended by Evelyn for the same purpose.

Secondly, at the bottom of the account stands the following article—

" De aliquo proficuo corticis sive crop. querc. ib'm prostrat. neque de cera sive de melle provenient. de Bestoks, nec de pannag. porcor. nil rec*r.* hic quia nullum tale proficuum per tempus hujus Compotus contingebat."

" Bestoks," being only accounted for by the foresters, were undoubtedly the produce of wild swarms discovered in the stocks or trunks of trees. The word is *Islandic,* and has therefore been propagated in Craven from the Danish times.†

The following memorandum on the rights of this, and, consequently, the other forests or chases within the honour of Skipton, supposing all which it asserts to be true, will prove that, however arbitrary the old nobility might be within their own domains, they made some compensation to their dependents, by allowing no partners in tyranny—not even their sovereign.

" BARDEN had all the officers of a Forest, as Verdurer,‡ Forester, Regarder, Agister, and Woodward. Also a Swain-mote Court, where the Forest-laws were executed, and offenders punished accordingly. It was within no constablery—had

---

[* Dr. Whitaker evidently alludes to the Springs Canal, cut for the purpose of conveying limestone from the quarry in the Hawe Park to the Leeds and Liverpool Canal.]

† See pp. 304-5. And see Mr. Lye's excellent note on " Junius," *voce* Stock, Isl. Stockaby. " Vet. Hollandis alveare dicebatur, Stock der Bien, quod hodieque Suecis nuncupatur Bistack, a Stock Truncus, quo cavo apes mella sæpissime condunt."

‡ In a paper of Earl George's time, I meet with an " Arbryer" of Barden. The word is new to me, but it seems to be formed from Arborarius.

no muster-rolls for service; the inhabitants being only subject to the power and authority of the lord. The kings and queens of this realm never claimed to appoint constables, or other officers, nor demanded any subsidy, or other tax or imposition within the same. None were ever pressed out of this forest for service of the kingdom, nor any provision required therein. The inhabitants were always a free people, exempt from galds and assessments for highways, bridges, &c., yet have always had contribution from the wapontake for their own bridge. This forest was, in ancient times, a parish of itself,* until the dissolution of abbies, that the lord purchased Bolton Abbey, and then, for his own ease, being bound to find a curate at Bolton, he caused the tenants to repair thither, to hear divine service, to christen their children, and bury their dead. The forest of Barden is also a privileged place, and no arrest, but by the officer of the same, can be made within it. Neither could any doggs be kept within the said forest, but according to assize, and a ring kept for trial of the same."†

In the Hawe, and another high pasture at the S.E. extremity of Barden, a considerable space of ground is covered by remains of a very singular appearance. First, a long tract, resembling a street, and stretching from N.W. to S.E., has been levelled with much toil, and on either side are the vestiges of numerous enclosures, large and small. These are formed sometimes by rude and massy stones rolled from the adjoining ground, sometimes by broad and slender stones pitched on edge, and standing from two to three feet above the surface. The lands adjoining, now covered with ling, bear evident marks of the plough. Contemplating these appearances, I quickly discovered the remains of an abandoned and forgotten village, of high antiquity; for some of the enclosures have evidently been garths or homesteads, in the centres of which remain the outlines of the ancient dwelling-houses: adjoining, are the groundworks of larger buildings, proved to have been cow-houses by the inclination of their rude pavements, while the adjoining tofts, of much larger dimensions, stretch beyond. At my request, the areas of what appeared to have been dwelling-houses were dug into; and in the middle of the floors, the universal situation of the "ingle" in ancient times, relics of peat-ashes were discovered. Within one of these areas stands an oak, computed to be 500 years old. The stonework remains of its original height, and must have supported slender crooks or poles, forming a roof for the thatch. Appearances and evidence concur in assigning a high antiquity to these remains. The oldest thatched buildings in Barden, supported on crooks, have yet regular walls. No garden-plants remain, though it is well known that if left to themselves some will survive several centuries. The villages mentioned in Domesday as dependent upon Bolton, though ruinous at that time, by which can only have been meant that they were in a state of partial dilapidation, are all in existence at present; and from these circumstances the most probable inference is, that in these appearances we see the skeleton of a village of high Saxon antiquity, probably destroyed by the Danes, but at all events so completely depopulated in the reign of the Conqueror that it did not even then retain a name.

Similar appearances are found in the Stank near Bolton, and in Longstrother, but the ancient villare of the kingdom has been so wonderfully preserved that they are very rare.

This forest stretches nearly four miles on the banks of the Wharf, from the confines of Burnsal to those of Bolton. Of this the upper part, which has long been divided into farmholds, carries back the imagination at least three centuries; for the buildings are thatched, and generally supported upon crooks, while the inhabitants, a plain and homely

* *I.e.*, with the other forests and demesnes, it constituted the castle parish of Skipton.
† Bolton MSS.

The Rev.d J. Griffith. del.

S. Rawle fecit.

Bardin Tower.

Barden Tower.

race, of ancient manners, subsist in retired tranquillity, under the protection of a noble family, by husbandry and pasturage.

The lower part of the township appears to have been wholly occupied in parks and chases. We have already seen that Barden, in the 4th of Edward II. [1310-11] had six lodges for the accommodation of the keepers and the protection of the deer—viz., Dreblay, Barden, Laund, Gamleswath, Holgill, and Ungayne. In the time of Thomas Lord Clifford, A.D. 1437, two other lodges had been erected in Barden—Over Fyshscrythes and Nether Fyshscrythes. These were probably on the banks of the Wharf, and so called, as containing some accustomed haunts or seats of the old fishermen, ꞃcꞑỹꝺe in Saxon being *sella*. In times of lawless rapine, when poaching was a kind of petty war, as it is now a system of stealth, these lodges of the foresters were often small square towers, constructed for defence; and may be considered as castles of the lowest form. But the retired habits of Henry Lord Clifford, leading him to prefer the retreat of Barden to the bustle of his greater houses, he seems to have enlarged the second of these lodges for the reception of himself and a modest train of followers;* and here he spent the greater part of an innocent and peaceful life. His son, a very different character, is found occasionally residing here, and till the later days of the third Earl of Cumberland, it never seems to have been wholly neglected by the family. From the inventory taken A.D. 1572, after the death of the second earl, it appears that the hall and kitchens at Barden Tower were furnished, but the bed-rooms empty. From this circumstance I conclude, that the family at that time resorted thither for the pleasures of the chase, dined at the tower, and returned to Skipton in the evening. In this inventory, the chapel is mentioned for the first time. One very curious item must not be omitted :—

"It'm, the old chariett, with II p'r of wheeles bound with iron, and cheynes belonging thereto, xxx*s*. It'm, one charrett, with all apperteyninge."

Coaches are generally understood to have been introduced about ten years after this time, by an Earl of Arundel. What sort of vehicle was the ancient chariot in use before?

Barden seems to have been neglected by the two last earls; and, when the Countess of Pembroke succeeded to her inheritance, was become a ruin.

The following contract, bearing date June 2, 1657, will show upon what terms it was repaired :—

"Articles of agreement between the Right Hon. Anne countesse dowager of Pembroke, &c. on the one part; and Thomas Day the elder and Thomas Day the younger on the other part.

"It is hereby required, that the said parties shall pull down so many of the walls of Barden tower as the said Right Hon. Countesse hath lately appointed, and shall build both the walls of the house and the chapell adjoining in such sorte as hath bene sett out; and shall pull down all yᵉ ould walls about the said house and chappel as shall be thought fit, and shall repair all such windows, arches, doors, and other places about the said house and chappel as shall be thought fit and necessarie by yᵉ said Countesse, and shall raise a parpointe wall of a yard high for battlements round about yᵉ said house.

"In consideration of the work abovesaid, the said Countesse is to pay to the said parties the sum of 100*l*.

"The said work is to begin in March, and to be ended at Michaelmas, which shal be in the yere 1657."

---

* It appears, however, from an old Compotus at Londesborough, that in 1517, wages were paid to more than fifty servants at Barden. But this was a modest train for a baron of those days.

This restoration is recorded in an inscription still remaining over the principal entrance :—

> THIS BARDEN TOWER WAS REPAYRD
> BY THE LADIE ANNE CLIFFORD COVNTE
> SSE DOWAGER OF PEMBROOKEE DORSETT
> AND MONTGOMERY BARONESSE CLIFFORD
> WESTMERLAND AND VESEIE LADY OF THE
> HONOR OF SKIPTON IN CRAVEN AND HIGH
> SHERIFESSE BY INHERITANCE OF THE
> COUNTIE OF WESTMERLAND IN THE YEARES
> 1658 AND 1659 AFTER ITT HAD LAYNE
> RVINOVS EVER SINCE ABOVT 1589 WHEN
> HER MOTHER THEN LAY IN ITT AND WAS
> GREATE WITH CHILD WITH HER TILL
> NOWE THAT ITT WAS REPAYRD BY
> THE SAYD LADY. ISA. CHAPT. 58. VER. 12.*
> GOD'S NAME BE PRAISED !

Three years before the date of the last transaction I find this indefatigable lady, who had a right to style herself "a repairer of breaches," restoring the park of Barden. This appears from the following :—

> "Contract between the Right Hon. countess dowager of Pembroke, and Elizabeth, countess of Cork, dated May 20, 1654, touching the deer that are or shall be driven into Barden Parke.
>
> "That as soon as a certain number shall be taken, as well of those already come in as of such deer as shall hereafter be driven into the said parke of Barden, which was lately walled in by the said countess of Pembroke, the said number so taken shall be and remain in the said parke of Barden, and be employed to the use and behoofe of the said countesse of Pembroke, until such time as there shall be a parke walled in and made staunch at Bolton or Stedhouse by the countesse of Corke ; and then yᵉ one half of yᵉ said number of deer shall be redelivered by the said countesse of Pembroke, or her appointment, to the countesse of Corke, or her appointment."

The heiresses of the elder and younger line of the Cliffords having succeeded to their respective portions of the family estates, the deer, which had hitherto ranged at large over both, were now to be appropriated and enclosed. From this transaction, therefore, we are enabled to fix the era at which the ancient forests of Craven were finally depopulated of their old and stately inhabitants ; and as the park of Bolton was the retreat provided for one moiety of them, we have here a positive proof that the stags which yet adorn its summits are lineal descendants of that wild race which anciently spread from Skipton to Longstrother, at once the pride, the chase, and the luxury of Romille and Albemarle, of Percy and Clifford.

The manor and chase of Barden, containing by survey 3,232 acres, were separated from the other demesnes of Skipton, thus : In the 9th of James [1611–12], Earl Francis levied a fine, and suffered a recovery of Barden, by which the estate tail created by Earl George was barred, and the uses declared to be to Henry Lord Clifford and his lady for their lives, remainder to their right heirs. However, the profits of Skipton and Barden were levied, first by the king's and then the Parliament's garrison in the castle, from the

---

* "Thou shalt build up the foundations of many generations, and thou shalt be called the Repairer of the Breach, the Restorer of Paths to dwell in." A text which Spelman has applied, with greater propriety, to the immortal Alfred. (Spelman, "Life of Alfred.")

beginning of the siege, till, by the interest of Philip Earl of Pembroke with his masters, the Lady Anne was permitted to enter ; Lord Corke being then under sequestration, and unable to prosecute his claim to Barden. But in 1661 and 1662, his lady having made entries upon the premises, to strengthen her claim, surrendered her reversionary right in the whole honour of Skipton to the Crown, and had it re-granted in ampler form. Notwithstanding all this, the Countess of Pembroke actually kept possession of Barden * till her death in 1676, when the Earl of Burlington brought an action of ejectment against the Earl of Thanet, and finally prevailed.† This decision closed the great family contest, which had sometimes slumbered, but never slept from the death of Earl George in 1605.

Since the last transaction, Barden Tower has been occasionally resorted to by the Burlington family. In the year 1774 I saw it entire. The lead and timbers of the roof have since been taken away, and it has now put on that picturesque form which only dilapidating remains have the privilege of assuming. The chapel, however, a plain convenient building, apart from the tower, is still kept in repair, and used for public worship.‡ As the mouldings in the timber are evidently of the age of Henry VIII., it was probably the work of Henry Lord Clifford, the shepherd ; and, before the Dissolution, would be served by the chaplain of St. John, in the castle, as it is now by the minister of Bolton, to whose charge it has been added, though no part of the Saxon cure.

[Barden Bridge has the following inscription :—

> THIS BRIDGE WAS
> REPAYRED AT THE
> CHARGE OF THE
> WHOLE WEST RIDING
> 1676.

It was repaired again, and new parapets placed, in 1856.]
From the demesnes of Skipton I now go on to

The House of Clifford,

As connected with CRAVEN.

Of this illustrious family, which had long flourished in the marches of Wales, and afterwards obtained a settlement in Westmoreland, the first who acquired an interest in Craven was Robert, son of Roger de Clifford and Isabella,§ co-heiress of the Viponts.

---

* Barden Case, int. Bolton MSS.

† Yet I find that all was not quiet ten years after; for in a letter of Lord Burlington to his agent, in 1686, are these expressions, " since my l. Thannet goes this silent way, I must desire that you will, without noyse, putt into Barden Tower a trusty person that may secure that place."

[‡ In 1860 the Duke of Devonshire caused the chapel to be reseated and much improved.]

[§ Edw. II., in the third year of his reign, 1309–10, granted to Robert Clifford, the messuage, with the appurtenances next the church of St. Dunstan's in the West, in the suburbs of London, which was formerly Malcuilne de Herley, and came to the hand of Edw. I., by reason of certain debts, which house John Earl of Richmond held at the pleasure of Edw. II. At the death of Robert Clifford, Isabel his wife let the mansion to students of the law (Apprenticiis de Banc , for ten pounds *per annum.*—Stow's " London."]

William de Veteripont=Maud or Matilda, dau. of Hugh de Morsvill, of Kirkswald,
co. Cumberland, Lord of the Honour of Knaresborough.

Robert de Veteripont=Idonea, dau. and heiress of John de Busley, *alias* Burley, Lord
ob. 12 Henry III. (1227-8). | of the Honour of Tickhill, co. York. She died 19th Hen. III.
Arms: Gules 6 annulets | (1234-5). Buried at Roche Abbey. *Arms:* Gules a bezant,
or, 3, 2, & 1. | but shown upon all the Clifford tombs gules a 5-foil or.

Christian=Thomas FitzRalph,   John de Veteripont=Sibilla, dau. of William Lord Ferrers, Earl of Derby.
Baron of Greystock   ob. ante 26 Henry III.
Castle.   Buried in Shap Abbey.

Robert de Veteripont=Isabella FitzPiers, one of the four co-heiresses of Richard,
a ward for some time after his father's | son of John FitzPeter, *alias* FitzGeoffrey, Baron of Bark-
death. He followed the fortunes of | hamstead, Chief Justice of England and Ireland.
Simon de Montfort. Ob. 48 or 49 | *Arms:* Quarterly or and gu. a bordure vair.
Henry III.

Isabella Veteripont=Mar. c. 1269, Roger de Clifford.   Idonea, or Ivetha, Veteripont=1. Roger de Leyburne,
dau. and co-heiress, | Buried in Anglesea, 10 or 11   dau. and co-heiress, ob. 8 | ob. 12 Edw. I.
ob. c. 1291. | Nov. 1283. He acquired with   Edw. III. (1234-5) *s.p.*, leaving =2. John de Crumb-
his wife Appleby and the   Robert Lord Clifford, grand- | well, outlived his
hereditary sheriffdom of West-   child of her sister Isabella, her | wife.
moreland.   heir.

Harl. MSS., 6177, and "*Skipton Book of Recordes.*"]

The castles of Appleby and Brougham were the purparty of Isabella; and in one of these her son must have been born about the year 1274. The situation of his estates on the confines of the western marches, the military character of his family, and the period of turbulence and war which followed the death of Alexander III. of Scotland, contributed to form him for an active and strenuous life. He was only nine years old at the death of his father, and about thirteen at the demise of Roger his grandfather, a long-lived and famous baron in the reign of Henry III., and the earlier years of his son.

"From his infancy," * said Sir Matthew Hale, "he was educated in the schoole of Warre,† under King Edward I. as good a master, for valour and prudence, as the world afforded; for by the record of the plea of the 14th Edward I. it appears, that when he was not above 19 yeares of age, *stetit in servicio regis juxta latus suum*, the great businesse of the claime of the king of England in the superiority of Scotland, and the disposition of the crowne of Scotland, then being in agitation, which, doubtless, was a time of high action, and fitt to enter a young counsellor, courtier, and soldier. And this king, who knew well how to judge of men fitt for action, was not wanting to supply this young lord with employments befitting the greatnesse and towardnesse of his spirit. In the 25th of his reign, he appointed him governor of Carlisle, to represse the insolence of the Scotts, which he did with much fidelitie and courage. In the same yeare, he appoints him chief justice of his forrests beyond Trent. At the several parliaments holden in the yeares 28, 30, 32, and 34 Ed. and likewise twice in 1st Ed. II. and twice more in 6th Ed. II. he was summoned as one of the peers of the realme; and 26 Sept., 26 Ed. I., summoned, with the rest of the barons, to bring in his service of horse and armes upon the king's expedition into Scotland, as appears by the Close Rolls of those yeares. And as it appeares by the honours and possessions conferred upon him from time to time by this Edward, the wisest of English kings,‡ so he retained the like favour with his sonne Edward of Carnarvan, who, in the first yeare of his reign, granted him the office of Earl Marshall of England. And by a French charter, dated at Carlisle 24 Sept., 25 *regni sui*, the king, having entered Scotland, and seized the lands of his opposers, grants unto him and his heirs the castle of Carlavrock in Scotland, and all the lands thereunto belonging, which were Robert Maxwell's, and all the lands in Scotland which were William Douglas', the king's enemy, upon Mary Maudlin-day, 26 Edw. I., at which time he (Douglas) was taken and imprisoned; and this was in satisfaction of 500*l. per annum*, land in Scotland with an agreement, that if it did not arise to soe much, it should be made good out of other lands in Scotland, and if it exceeded to defaulk.§

* In the following narrative, for several of the first generations of the family, I shall principally follow Sir Matthew Hale's "Memoirs of the Cliffords," and shall give his own words, as far as possible, within inverted commas.

† "In 1297, Lord Robert Clifford entered Annandale with the power of Carlisle, and slew 308 Scots near Annan Kirke, chasing them into a Mareys."—Holinshed, vol. i. p. 830. In 1301, he signed the famous letter from Edward I. to Pope Boniface, claiming the seigniory of Scotland, by the title of Chatellain of Appleby.—Id. p. 837. In 1306, immediately after the coronation of Robert Bruce, he entered Scotland, with the Earl of Pembroke, and defeated Bruce at St. John's Town.—Id. 842.

‡ Something is wanting in the MS. at this place.

§ This, as it might have been foreseen, came to nothing. The skirts of Kirne Table were as strong and as well guarded in the 13th century as in the 16th.—See the "Border Minstrelsy."

" But these acquisitions of lands in Scotland were not such as our Robert could build much upon : as they were gotten by power, soe they could not be preserved or kept, without difficulty. Peace or warr between the two nations might be fatal to these his purchases. The latter might make the retaining of them difficult, or casual, and the former might occasion a restitution of such prizes. Robert, therefore, not willing to build any great confidence on these debateable acquisitions, in the beginning of the reign of Edward II. cast his eye upon a more firme possession at a reasonable distance from Scotland ; and this was the castle and honour of Skipton.*

" Now wee come to the domestical relations of this Robert de Clifford. He married Matilda, one of the daughters and coheirs of Thomas de Clare, by whom he had two sonnes, Roger and Robert ; and in the great battle of Striveling [or Bannockburn] fought between Robert de Bruis and the Scotts, of the one p'tye, and the English on the other [on 25th June, 1314], this Robert de Clifford, together with divers other of the nobilitie of England, were slaine ; for soe the history records it : Nobilis Baro Rob. de Clifford, cum multis aliis viris nobilibus, in hoc funesto conflictu peremptus est. His body, together with that of Gilbert de Clare, the great Earl of Gloucester, the companion of his death, was sent by the Conqueror unto Edward II. at Berwick, to bee interred† with the honor due unto them ; but where burried appeares not. Hee lived about 40 yeares, and was a person eminent for his services to this kingdom, and his deserved favour with both Kings, Edward I. and Edward his sonne. And though hee were upon all occasions engaged in foreign differences, especially with the Scotts, yet wee find him not much entangled with broils at home ; but hee always soe kept the king's favour, that he lost not the love of the nobility and kingdom, and by that meanes had an easye access to the improvement of his honours and greatnesse. He was employed upon all occasions in offices and services of the greatest trust, both military and civill, having the advantage of a most close education in his youth, under a prince most eminent for both. Hee lived an active life, and died an honourable death in the vindication of the rights‡ of his prince and country." §

[Arms on the picture, Clifford quartering Vipont and impaling or three chevrons gu. for Clare.]

ROGER LORD CLIFFORD, SECOND LORD OF THE HONOUR OF SKIPTON.

" Hee came of age about the 13th yeare of Edward II.‖ and shortly afterwards was summoned to parl't by writt. This time now began to bee very tumultuous between the king and his barons, by reason of the insolencies of Hugh Spencer, father and sonne. The discontented nobility having formerly bridled the king in the time of Peerce Gavaston his former favourite, entered again into a confederacy among themselves ; and upon the popular pretence of reforming things amisse, they raised a considerable army, and put ye earle of Lancaster, a man in reputation for a good patriot, in the head thereof. Our young lord, Roger, haveing lost a wise father too early to be seasoned with his principles, and being rich and honourable, was drawn into this confederacy under these popular pretences. The king, on the other hand, prepared to represse the power of his barons, and at last (for this onely conduceth to our purpose) at Borough-bridge in Yorkshire, the barons are beaten, the earle of Lancaster and many of his party taken, and amongst these our young Roger de Clifford. And, the third day after this victory, a kind of military Court was erected at Pontefract, where the king in person, Edmund earl of Kent, Aymer earl of Pembroke, John earl of Surrey, David earl of Atholl, and John earle of Angoss, pronounced judgment of death against the earl of Lancaster, and, amongst others, against this Roger lord Clifford ; soe that all his lands were seized into the kinges hands, as forfeited ; but by reason of his great wounds, being held a dying man, ye execution was respited for that time ; and after the heat of the fury was over, his life was spared by ye said king soe as he died a natural death in ye 1st yeare of Edward III. [1327.] He dyed childless, and unmarried, Robert de Clifford being his brother and heire.

" This young baron miscarried in the prime of his youth. His father left him under the disadvantage of infancy, and a troublesome time ; the latter gave him opportunity to be a confederate in a faction, and the former made him more obnoxious to it ; want of experience, and a popular pretence, won him to the party of Lancaster, and there hee fell."

[Arms on the picture, Clifford quartering Vipont.]

ROBERT DE CLIFFORD, THIRD LORD OF SKIPTON.

" This Lord [born on All Saints Day, 1305], at the attainder of his brother, was within age, but noe lands came unto him, for his mother held the third part for her dower, and the king, by reason of this extraordinary attainder of his brother Roger, took the profits of the other two parts ; but, had the attainder beene ever so lawful, there had been small cause to seize either the honor of Westmorland or Skipton, they being both descended to this Roger in tayle, the reversion in the

[* In the 8th Edw. II., 1314–15, Robertus de Clifford was found to have been possessed of Skipton in Craven, the castle, manor, and hamlet, with the free chapel of St. John the Evangelist, and the market there.]

† Had the body of Robert de Clifford been sent to Carlisle, I should have concluded that it had been buried at Shap. But from Berwick the distance was not much greater to Bolton than to Shap, and the circumstance of a charge in the Compotus of Bolton for sarcophagi (stone coffins), in this year, strengthens my conjecture, that the first of the Cliffords was really interred there.

‡ Did then the upright Sir Matthew Hale really think this most unjust and unprovoked war a vindication of the *rights* of England? Surely the words must have dropped from his pen in a moment of inadvertence.

§ Rob. de Clifford was one of the four knights of Aymer de Valence, Earl of Pembroke, whose portraits were painted on the magnificent tomb of their lord in Westminster Abbey. But the traces of these curious figures are now become very obscure. A century ago, it should seem from Dart, that they might have been copied.

[‖ He was born 2nd Feb. 1299 (Collins, vi. p. 514). He was summoned to Parliament from 6th Nov., 13 Edw. II., 1319, to 15th May, 14 Edw. II., 1321.]

2 O

crowne, for at that time treason forfeited not intayled lands; but in the time of Edward II. the contestation was too high between the king and his nobility, and the many indigent persons of the king's party that were to bee gratified, gave noe leave to this dispute, to the losse of such a bootie.

"But, not many yeares after, Edward II. was deposed, and his sonne lifted into the throne, and that, principally, by meanes of y⁰ discontented nobilitie that were of the Lancaster party. Therefore, in the first place, the judgment given at Pontfrait by Edward II. against the earle of Lancaster, was reversed as erroneous, 1st, because he was not arraigned, or put to answere, and was not to bee concluded by the kinges recording his offence; and, 2ndly, he had not his tryall by his peeres, according to Magna Charta. I find not yet the reversall of the judgment against Clifford, but in the Parliament holden 4th Edward III. [1330–1] there was a general act of restitution of all that were in the company of the Earle of Lancaster, and all their lands restored.

"Touching lands in Scotland given to his father by Edward I., little fruit thereof came to the grantee, or his posterity: only, Edward Baliol claiming the crowne of Scottland, and by the help of the young king of England, against David de Bruis obteyning it, this Edward, in the first year of his reign, granted unto this Robert, and his heyres, for his service done, and to be done, the castle of Douglasse, and all the lands which were James Douglas' then seized into this king's hands for the rebellion of James. This Robert had, by Isabell his wife, daughter of Barkley,* Robert, Roger, and Thomas.† He dyed on Thursday after the Feast of the Ascension, which was May 20, 17 Edward III. [1343].‡ Isabel, his wife, over-lived him, and enjoyed, during her life-time, the castle and manor of Skipton, whereof there is a large extent made after her death, the value being then computed to arise to 107*l.* 15*s.* 9*d.* She over-lived her son Robert (who was therefore never seized of Skipton), and died July 25, 36 Edward III. [1362].

"We cannot say much concerning this man's life. He rose with the rising sun, King Edward III., by which means he had the opportunity to recover the inheritances which his elder brother's misfortunes, and the troubles of those times, had for a while lost. He was a favourite with both the Edwards, of England and Scotland. He prudently matched his young sonne in his life-time to a family of power in the north, and dyed after he had lived lord of Skipton in possession twenty-eight yeares."

[Arms on the picture, Clifford quartering Vipont and impaling gu. a chevron between ten crosses patty arg. for Berkeley.]

ROBERT DE CLIFFORD, FOURTH LORD OF THE HONOUR OF SKIPTON.

"This lord was but of the age of thirteen yeares at his father's death, and in ward to the king. He married Euphemia, daughter of Ralph Lord Nevill [of Middleham], who over-lived him, and married, 2nd, Sir Walter Heslerton. This Robert Lord Clifford dyed before the 25th yeare of Edward III. [1351–2],§ without issue, and within age."

[Arms on the picture, Clifford quartering Vipont and impaling gu. a saltire arg. for Nevill.]

ROGER LORD CLIFFORD, FIFTH LORD OF SKIPTON.‖

[Was brother to Robert, the fourth lord.] "In the 40th Edward III. [1366–7] the king grants to this Robert licence to impark 500 acres of his own lands in Brenhill and Listerfield in the wood of Calder, within the town of Skipton, and to retain the same, so imparked, to himself and his heires. Hee married Mawde de Beauchamp, daughter of Thomas de Beauchamp, Earle of Warwicke, by whom he had two sonnes, Thomas, his oldest, whome, in his life-time, he married to Elizabeth, daughter of Thomas Lord Rosse and Hamlake, and William, who died without issue 6th Henry V. [1418–19].¶

[* She was only daughter to Maurice Lord Berkeley, of Berkeley Castle, in the county of Gloucester, and she brought a portion of a thousand pounds and fifty marks. She re-married Sir Thomas Musgrave, Knt., and died 25th July, 1362.—Collins, vi. 515.]

[† Query—Had he also a son John, whose monument is in York Cathedral?—

✠ 𝔥𝔦𝔠 𝔦𝔞𝔠𝔢𝔱 𝔡𝔬𝔪. 𝔍𝔬𝔥𝔞𝔫𝔫𝔢𝔰 𝔡𝔢 𝔆𝔩𝔦𝔣𝔣𝔬𝔯𝔡 𝔮𝔲𝔬𝔫𝔡𝔞𝔪 𝔱𝔥𝔢𝔰𝔞𝔲𝔯𝔞𝔯𝔦𝔲𝔰 𝔦𝔰𝔱𝔦𝔲𝔰 𝔢𝔠𝔠𝔩𝔢𝔰𝔦𝔢, 𝔮𝔲𝔦 𝔬𝔟𝔦𝔦𝔱 𝔵𝔵𝔵𝔵 𝔡𝔦𝔢 𝔪𝔢𝔫𝔰𝔦𝔰 𝔪𝔞𝔦𝔦 𝔐𝔆𝔆𝔆𝔏𝔵𝔵. 𝔣𝔦𝔫𝔦𝔢𝔫𝔱𝔢 𝔳𝔦𝔞𝔪 𝔲𝔫𝔦𝔟𝔢𝔯𝔰𝔢 𝔠𝔞𝔯𝔫𝔦𝔰 𝔢𝔰 𝔦𝔫𝔤𝔯𝔢𝔰𝔰𝔲𝔰. 𝔆𝔲𝔧𝔲𝔰 𝔞𝔫𝔦𝔪𝔢 𝔭𝔯𝔬𝔭𝔦𝔱𝔦𝔢𝔱𝔲𝔯 𝔇𝔢𝔲𝔰. 𝔄𝔪𝔢𝔫.

(Arms chequy...on a fess...three eopards' faces...).—Drake's "York," 501.]

[‡ Collins says he died 20th May, 1340 (vi. 515); and the date on the picture is 18 Edward III., 1344.]

[§ Collins says 1362, 35th Edward III. The picture gives 36th Edward III.]

[‖ He was born in 1333, and first served in 1345, when Jacob Anartfeld was murdered in Flanders. In August, 1350, he was at the sea-fight with the Spaniards near Winchelsea. In 1355 was in the expedition in Gascony with his father-in-law, Thomas Earl of Warwick. In 1356 he was employed in the defence of the Marches of Scotland. He was first summoned to Parliament in December, 1357. In 1359 and 1360 he was in the wars in France. He was a Warden of the Western Marches of Scotland in September, 1367, and again in 1370. In 1377 he was constituted Sheriff of Cumberland and Governor of Carlisle. Lord Clifford was in the army with which Richard II. invaded Scotland in August, 1385, and had a retinue of 60 men-at-arms and 40 archers. In October, 1386, he was examined at Westminster as a witness for Sir Richard Scrope, in the Scrope and Grosvenor controversy.

He married Maud, daughter of Thomas Beauchamp, Earl of Warwick, and left issue Thomas, his son and heir, and Sir William Clifford, his second son, who married Ann, daughter and co-heiress of Thomas Lord Bardolf, and died without issue in 1419. He also had three daughters— Mary, the wife of Sir Philip Wentworth, of Wentworth, co. York; Margaret, who married Sir John Melton; and Katharine, the wife of Ralph Lord Greystock. He died 13th July, 1389.—"Scrope and Grosvenor Controversy," ii. 469, &c.]

[¶ There is great uncertainty as to the parentage of Sir Lewis de Clifford, shown on the large table of the descent of the Barony of Clifford as being the son of Roger de Clifford, the fifth lord of the honour of Skipton.

Sir N. Harris Nicholas, in his "Scrope and Grosvenor Controversy," ii. 427 says: "Dugdale, and all other genealogical writers who have

" This Roger, at the time of his death, was seized of the honor of Skipton, and the king's fees thereunto belonging, all particularly expressed in the inquisition. He died the 14th of July, 13th Richard II. [1389]. *

" Much cannot be said of this Roger, because there is little extant upon record, or in history, concerning him. He lived in the busy time of Edward III. and of Richard II., and it seems he was a man given to military imployments, the differences with France and Scotland not suffering men of spirits to be still, without action ; † but what imployments he undertook appears not, only that he retained Sir Robert Mowbray, for peace and warr, at ten pound *per annum* salary. This was the way of great men in those times, to retain persons of valour in their imployment, which continued them great and powerful in their countries, and ready for the service of their prince and country."

So far Sir Matthew Hale; but the two following indentures of military service will prove not only that Roger de Clifford retained others beside Mowbray, but that he was himself retained by a nobleman of still higher rank. The chain of feudal dependance reached from the cottage to the throne.

" Cest endent', fait entre Mons. Roger de Clifford seign'r de Westmerland d'un p't, & Mons. Ric. de Fleming d' autre p'te, testmoigne q' le dit Mons. Ric. est dem . . . . ove le dit Mons. Roger pur un an entier pur la guerr. Et prend' pur luy meme dux Archiers ben armez & covenantable mountez & arrayez a sept Chevaulx vint livres des q'x s'ra pay en man pur un quart'r. Et pur un autr' quartr quant il s'ra a la mere p. mandement le dit Mons. Roger. Et issi de quart'r en quart'r selone ceo q' il est arme de guerre en la Compagnie le dit Mons. Roger prenant gages pur luy & ses gents co'e attent al jour q' il s'ra comand p. les l'res le dit Mons. Roger de luy approcher a le mere, et s'ra luy mesmez ove un Archer a bouch de Court & . . . . archiers et quatre garcons a gagez co'e autrez de leur estate sont. Et seront ces Chivaulx a fenis & aveins az costiges le dit Mons. Roger & prendr' pur la ferrur d' icelles gages usuelles. Et le Mons. Richard don'a a dit Mons. Roger pur luy & pur ses gents de les compagnez de guerre co'e autr' de son estate donneront a leurs S'n'rs ou Mestres en les parties ou ils guerront. Et si case q'l soit perdus p' fait de guerre en la service le dit Mons. Roger due restore luy s'ra fait co'e reason demand & av'a eskippeson & reskippeson pur luy mesmez, ses gents & sept' chevalx avant ditz. Don a Burgh'm ‡ le disme jour de July l'an du regne le Roy Edw. tierce puis la conquest quarrantissime tierce.

" Cest Indenture fait p'entre le noble & puissant S. Mons. Esmon Conte de la Marche d' un pt' & Mons. Roger de Clifford sen'r de Westm'ld d' autre p't, testmoigne q' le dit Mons. Roger est demies ove le dit Conte de lui servir de Guere en les p'ts, d'Irlande ove cynk Bachilers, trent & quatr Esquiers, quartante Archiers a Chival armes de Palet, Hawb'gon, Arks, Setts,

noticed him, assert that he was a younger son of Roger, fifth Lord Clifford, by Maud, daughter of Thomas de Beauchamp, Earl of Warwick ; but this is proved to be impossible by the fact that Thomas, the *eldest* son of the said Lord Clifford and Maud de Beauchamp, was only about twenty-five years old at his father's death in July, 1389, so that he was born after 1364, whereas the deponent (Sir Lewis) must have been born at least as early as 1336, because he says he was more than fifty years old in 1386, which the notices that are recorded of his life corroborate."

Sir Lewis Clifford was probably a younger son of Robert, third Lord Clifford, who died in 1344, by Isabella, daughter of Maurice Lord Berkeley, whose eldest son, Robert, fourth Lord Clifford, above-mentioned, was born in 1331 ; but in the inquisition on the decease of the said Robert Lord Clifford, in 1344, three sons only are mentioned—namely, Robert, Roger, and Thomas. Froissart, however, supports the conjecture that he was the son of Robert, third Lord Clifford, by Isabella de Berkeley, for, in speaking of Sir Lewis in 1385, he calls him "brother to the lord," the Lord Clifford in that year being Roger, the fifth baron, second son of Robert, third lord, and heir to his brother Robert, fourth Lord Clifford. The resemblance which his arms bore to those of the Barons Clifford, they being merely differenced by a bordure gules, also renders it likely that he was closely connected with them.

Sir Lewis in 1352 fought under Sir John Beauchamp near St. Omer, when the English were defeated, and Beauchamp, Clifford, and others taken prisoners. In 1363 was in Acquitaine ; in 1367 in Spain ; in July, 1373, he was in the army with which the Duke ot Lancaster marched through France to Bordeaux ; and in June, 1376, was present at Westminster at the publication of the will of Edward the Black Prince.

In June, 1385, his services in the field were dispensed with, and he was commanded to remain in attendance on Joan Princess of Wales, the king's mother, who made him one of her executors. He also fulfilled a similar trust for the following persons :—Guichard d'Angle, Earl of Huntingdon, in 1380 ; Sir Thomas Latimer of Braybroke, in 1401 ; Anne Lady Latimer, in 1402 ; and Isabel Duchess of York, in 1392. The Princess of Wales having died in 1385, he served against the Scots, and defended Carlisle when besieged by the French. Froissart says he was in Spain in 1386, but he was in Westminster in October of that year, and made his deposition on behalf of Sir Richard Scrope. In 1389 he was one of the parties to the letter to the Pope respecting the excesses of the Court of Rome, and in the next year he was one of the ambassadors sent to negotiate a peace with France. In 1393 Sir Lewis was elected a Knight of the Garter. In 1404, Henry IV. revoked the grant of his predecessor of the manor of Ryseburgh to Sir Lewis for life. He died during this year, and his will was proved 5th December. He is said to have married Eleanor, daughter of John Lord la Warr, and by her to have had a daughter, who married Sir Philip La Vache, and a son, William Clifford. He also appears to have had another son, Lewis.

Sir Lewis Clifford in the early part of his life joined the Lollards, but about 1402 he withdrew rom them. His will is exceedingly curious, and is printed in Dugdale's "Baronage," i. 341.]

[* Roger de Clifford ch'r and Matilda uxor ejus were found possessed of the castle, &c., of Skipton in Craven, the forest of Berden, the chace of Holden, Sylesdon, Swarthowe, Brouthweyt, Skybedon, Thorleby, Stretton or Cheteland, and the advowson of the Priory of Bolton in Craven.—Inquisition, 13th Richard II., 1389-90.]

[† He also went with the Earl of Arundel to sea at the time he was sent in aid of the Duke of Brittany against the French. He was Sheriff of Westmoreland, joint guardian of the West Marches of Cumberland and Westmoreland in 1370, Sheriff of Cumberland and Governor of Carlisle Castle, 1376.—Collins' "Peerage," vi. 515. He was summoned to Parliament from 15th December, 31st Edward III., to 28th July, 12th Richard II., 1388.—Courthorpe's "Historic Peerage."]

‡ Brougham Castle.

Espee & Bokeler bien & covenantablement mountez & arraiez co'e apent' a lour degrees a lour Costages p'pres pur un an entir comenceant l'an le jour q' le dit Mons. Roger s'ra premierment venu & areve en la terre d' Irlande p' maundement du dit Conte. Et le dit Conte trouvera a dit Mons. Roger eskipeson pur luy & ses gents en alant devers la dit terre & retournant. Et prendera le dit Mons. Roger du dit Conte gages accustomes pur luy & touts ses gents suisdit, pur le temps q'e demurra a la mier sur dit service & a sa volente de mesmes pur aler ou q'l luy plerra s'il ne soit par novel bargaine, & prendera le dit Mons. Roger de le dit Conte per sons Corps de mesme & per cheschun de ses dits Archiers . . . . armes diz marks per le dit an p'r toutes lour Coustages dont le dit Mons. Roger s'ra payes p'r un quart'r di an. en Londres a la feste de Noel prochein venant & p'r dits autr's quart' devant sons passage et apres le primer di' an. fyny il s'ra payez de quart' en quart.

"Et en droit de prisoners priz & autres gaynes de guerres pris ou gaynes per le dit Mons. Roger & ses gents le dit Conte ent avera pur sa p'te sicome ad este usee en le dits partes avant ces heures en tel case. Don a Londres le 25 jo'r de Sept'r l'an du regne le Roy Richard second puis le Conq. tierce."

[Arms on the picture, *Clifford* quartering *Vipont* and impaling gu. a fess between six crosses crosslet or for *Beauchamp*.]

THOMAS LORD CLIFFORD, SIXTH LORD OF THE HONOUR OF SKIPTON.

"This Thomas, sonne and heir of Roger lord Clifford, being of the age of 26 yeares at the time of his father's death, had his livery Sept. 6, 13th of Richard II. [1389], and touching him there is not much to be said, for he lived not much above two yeares after his father's death.

"He married (*ut supra*) Eliza, daughter of Thomas lord Rosse, in the lifetime of his father, and because there was a neare degree of consanguinitie between them, that might require the help of a dispensation, it was agreed (8th May, 47 Edward III. [1373]) that each shall contribute to the charges of such prosecution, if need bee.

"Roger lord Clifford farther agreed to settle 100*l. per ann.* upon the young couple, and the heires of their bodies.

"This Thomas was thrice summoned to the Parliaments held in the 13, 14, & 15 Richard II. and accordingly there sat. He had issue John, his only sonne, and dyed in the parts beyond the seas on the 6th day after the Feast of St. Michael, 15 Richard II. [1391], leaving John, his heire, of the age of three yeares, and a daughter, Mawde de Clifford, who was second wife to Richard Plantagenet, earle of Cambridge. His widow* survived John her son, and dyed the 26th, or, as others, the last of March, 2d Henry VI. [1424], as appears by the inquisitions after her death,† Thomas her grandchild and heir, born on Monday next after the assumption of the Virgin, 2d Henry V. [1414], being then of the age of nine yeares and 47 weekes."

[Arms on the picture, *Clifford* quartering *Vipont* and impaling gu. 3 water-bougets arg. for Ros.]

JOHN LORD CLIFFORD, SEVENTH LORD OF THE HONOUR OF SKIPTON.

"This lord, being in ward to the king, the wardship, as appears, was granted to Elizabeth his mother, who during his minority took care for a convenient match for him ; and a treaty was accordingly had between her and Henry Peircy, earl of Northumberland, for a match between him and Eliza, only daughter of Henry Peircy, sonne of the said earle. And this was accordingly solemnized, when this John was not much above 15 yeares old ; for the said earle and his son, Sir William Greystock, &c., became bound to Eliz. in 1,000 marks, which by her indentures, dated May 22nd, 5th Henry IV. [1404], reciting the said marriage, is defeazanced. Hee was a souldier, and hee lived under a martial prince, who, by indenture dated February 8, 4th Henry V. [1417], retained him in his service for the warre of France for one yeare : the contract was to this effect, that this lord, with 50 men at armes well accoutred, whereof three to bee knights, the rest esquires, and 150 archers, whereof two parts to serve on horseback, the third on foote, should serve the king from the day hee should bee ready to set sayle for France, taking for himself 4*s.* for every knt. ; for every esquire 1*s.* ; for every archer 6*d. per diem.*

"This was the usual meanes whereby the kings in those times furnished their armyes with men of value ; and it was counted no dishonorable thing for persons of honour upon this kinde of traffick to make themselves an advantage : indeed, it was in those martial times the trade of the nobility and great men."

[He was a Knight of the Order of the Garter, and was elected 3rd May, 1421.—Beltz's "Memorials," p. clviii.]

"He dyed‡ March 3d, 9th Henry V. [1422], as appears by inq. Elizabeth, his wife, over-lived him, and married, 2dly,

---

[* Maud, in her long widowhood, resided much at Coningsborough Castle, and probably held it in dower. Her last will is entered in Archbishop Kemp's Register. It was made at the monastery of Roche whilst she lay sick at Coningsborough. She directed that she should be buried at Roche Abbey, in the chapel of the blessed Virgin Mary, before the image of the same, in the south part of the said monastery, and a stone of alabaster to be laid over her grave. She gives to her niece, Beatrix Waterton, a gold cross ; to her cousin Thomas Lord Clifford, a bed ; to her god-son "filiolus" John Clifford, twelve silver dishes ; to Alice Bolton, who was the wife of John Bolton, citizen and alderman of York, 20*l.* to the marriage of one of her daughters ; to Richard Fairfax, one hundred shillings to the repair of her house at Braithwell, which he is to have for his life, and at his death to be disposed of for the good of her soul. She mentions also her god-daughter Matilda, and her cousin Alice, Countess of Salisbury. She names as executors William Scargill, Edmund Fitzwilliam, and William Stafford, Rector of Hooton Roberts. In a codicil she gives her collar of gold to her niece Joan, Lady Clifford, and 10*l.* to her niece, Dame Beatrix Waterton. The will is dated on the Feast of the Assumption (15th August), 1446, and was proved on the 4th September in the same year.—Hunter's "South Yorkshire," i. 113.]

[† The inventory of her goods and debts is printed in "Test. Ebor." iii. 85.]

‡ He was killed at the siege of Meaux, and I have discovered, from the Chronicon de Kirkstall, in the British Museum, that he was interred "*apud Canonicus de Boulton.*"

[In the choir of Bolton Abbey portions of the stone slab, with matrices of the brasses of inscriptions and shields within the Garter, still remain.]

Ralph earl of Westmoreland. She died October 16th, in the 14th of Henry VI., Thomas lcrd Clifford, her sonne and heire, being 22 yeares of age."

[Arms on the picture, *Clifford* quartering *Vipont* and impaling or a lion ramp. az., *Percy* quartering gu. 3 pike fish hauriant arg. *Lucy.*]

THOMAS LORD CLIFFORD, EIGHTH LORD OF THE HONOUR OF SKIPTON.

In the life-time of his father, King Henry V., by letters patent, dated May 7, A. R. 3° [1415], granted to Sir William Harrington, and others, the custody of the honour of Skipton for two years next after the decease of John Lord Clifford, in case his heir were within age. His mother seems to have obtained the wardship, for by indenture between her and Thomas Lord Dacre, of Gillesland, dated August 1, 2° Henry VI. [1424], the parties covenant for the marriage of this lord with Joan daughter of the Lord Dacre : and it was likewise agreed that 1,100 marks should be given as her marriage portion. This nobleman, by several conveyances, vested almost all his lands in feoffees in trust.

"The scope of these several conveyances* was partly to prevent wardships, under which his family had suffered greatly, and partly to prevent forfeitures, which now began to bee a reasonable care, for discontents were breeding apace in the kingdome. The title of the House of York began to bud, and these probably were the reasons why this wary lord, who knew that he must have a share in these broiles, though he knew not the event, tooke care to lodge his estate in the hands of trustees, who either must not be engaged in the difference, or at least might pass through them without danger to the estate, which was only lodged in them as trustees.

"Hee followed, as neare as hee could, the pattern of Robert, the first Lord of Skipton, that while hee kept in favour with the king, yet lost not his interest in the nobility. For he appears actually the king's servant in the 24th Henry VI. when the king granted to Maude Countesse of Cambridge, and to this Thomas, by the style of *Dilecto Servo n'ro Thomæ de Clifford,* an annuity of 100*l.* out of the issues of the County of York, by authority of Parliament.

"Afterwards, 27 April, .25 Henry VI., he granted to this Thomas Lord Clifford, Henry Vavasor, and the heire of the body of Thomas, the bailiwicke of Stannercliffe in the county of Yorke."†

I now take leave of my venerable guide, Sir Matthew Hale, and shall principally compile my account of the later generations of the Cliffords from sources unknown to him.

The first of these documents which I have met with, has been preserved by Dodsworth, and has an air of ancient simplicity, which gives it a title to be transcribed at length.

"Be it knowne to all men, yatt for as much as itt is meritorie and medeful for every true Cryten man to testify and bare true wytnes in every true matter or cause ; therefore we, William Ratcliffe, being the age of $^{xx}_{v}$ ‡ yeres, Nicholas Whitfield of $^{xx\text{-}xviii}_{iiii}$ § yeres, and John Thorn of $^{xx}_{iiii}$ yeres, will record and testify for verrey trawthe, that the lord, Sir Thomas Clifford, maryed Elizabeth, his doghter, unto Rob'te Plumpton, the eldest son and heyre of Sir William Plumpton, when she was bot of six yeres of age, and they were wedded at the chappell within the castell at Skypton, and the same day one John Garthe bare her in his armes to the said chappell. And also itt was agreed at the same tyme yt if the foreseid Rob'te dyed within age, that then the said lord Clifford should have the second son of the s'd Sir William Plumpton unto his sec'd doghter. And they were bot III yeres marryed when ye said Rob'te dyed ; and when she came to ye age of XII yeres she was marryed to William Plumpton, second son to the foreseid Sir William, and ye seid Sir William promised the seid lord Clifford y't they shuld not ligg togedder till she came to the age of XVI yeres, and when she cam to XVIII yeres she had Margarete, now lady Roucliffe. And how as evydenc' hath bene imbeseled, or what as hath been doon syns, we cannot tell, butt all y't ys afore rehersed in thys bill we wyll make yt gode, and yf nede be depely depose afore ye kynge & hys counsell, y't yt is matter of trawth in anye place wher we shal be comanded, as farr as is posible for any such olde creatures to be carryed to.

"In witness whereof, we ye said W'm, Nicholas, & Jhon, hath sett our seales the XXVIth of October, in the XIX yere of the reane of kynge Henrie ye VIIth." [1527].

---

* I have two original conveyances in trust made by the Radcliffes to this Lord Clifford, and others, for the same purpose.

† From a transcript of the MS. entitled "Titles of Honour and Pedigrees, especially touching Clifford," among the books bequeathed by Sir Matthew Hale to Lincoln's Inn. This fragment is valuable on its own account, as it is the only specimen of Hale's historical style which has been published, and appears to me superior to that of his moral and religious works.—See Burnet's "Life of Hale," p. 100.

‡ That is, fivescore.

§ Fourscore and eighteen.

The Compotus of Thomas Lord Clifford, for the year 1437, affords some curious particulars, which I shall first exhibit in the words of the Roll itself, and afterwards comment upon them.

" Sojorina.—In solutione D'ne comitisse Cantabrigiæ in part. solutionis pro sojorinâ D'ni & D'ne consortis sue, ac aliorum generosorum & feminarum generosarum valettorum & garcionum dicti D'ni, in hospitio dicte D'ne existent. temp. hujus Comp. XX*l.*

" Et in solutione eidem comitisse in parte pro sojorina dictorum D'ni & D'ne ac familie sue in dicto hospitio a die pentecost LX*l.*

" In sol. pro II Hogsheveds vini ad Cunesburgh in purificatione D'ne tam post part. nup. magistri de Clifford quam post partum Mag'ri nunc de Clifford."

Maud, Countess of Cambridge, and aunt to this lord, had Conisburgh Castle in dower. Here her nephew and his family seem to have resided with her during the greater part of this year, and, what is very singular, paid for their board. Here too Black-faced Clifford must have been born ; for the feast of his mother's purification would not have been kept at any other place than that of her confinement. Besides, the Countess of Cambridge was his godmother ; for in her will she bequeaths " Joh. Clifford filiolo meo XII Discos argenteos." *

It is an extraordinary fact, that Richard Duke of York, and John Lord Clifford, his bitterest enemy, should have been born in the same castle ; and it may seem at first sight equally extraordinary, that such an alliance between the two families should not have united their interests and inclinations ; but second marriages have often a contrary effect. What circumstances of family disagreement might have happened after the death of the Earl of Cambridge, and whether his widow's holding the great honour of Conisburgh so long in dower, might not occasion a gradual alienation and dislike between the two families, it is now impossible to discover.

In this year, Lord Clifford appears to have paid only two visits at Skipton, once in January, on his way to Conisburgh, I suppose from his Westmoreland estates, and once in summer, when he made a longer stay.

These facts are proved by the following articles in the Compotus :—

" Allocat. eidem Computanti (W'm Garth) virtute præcepti corporalis in camerâ dicti Domini infra castrum de Skipton die Jovis XXIII die Januar. in transitu suo usque Conisburgh C*s.*

" Vetus parcus XX*s.* & non plus, eo quod magna pars herbagii ejusdem parci depasturata fuit per equos Domini & D'ne Comitisse Cantab. & aliorum de consilio dicti Dom. ib'm existent. in Augusto."

What account can be given of the following items ?

" In solutione uxori Hen. Favvell nuper de Berden subita interfecti eidem concess. per consilium D'ni XLV*s.*

Et in solutione matri dict. Hen. ad satisfaciendum sibi de debitis quæ idem Hen. sibi debuit C*s.*

Et in sol. Ri. Pudsay ad sat. sibi de denariis sibi debitis per dict. Henr. XXIII*s.*

Et in sol'ne fratri ejusdem Hen. de deb. sibi deb. XIV*s.* S'ma IX*l.* II*s.*"

It seems not unsuitable to the manners of that ferocious age to conclude, that Fawell had been slain by the hand of the lord himself. An accidental death in Clifford's service would scarcely have drawn down so profuse a liberality to his family, besides that, the word *interfecti* certainly implies something more.

* Townley MSS.

It might be a random shot or stroke while hunting in Barden; but the value of the " Blodwite," at least 100*l.* of our money, seems rather to point at manslaughter.

The strong and almost disloyal terms in which another article of this account is expressed, show what the great families even then thought and felt on the subject of wardship.

" Item. allocat (allowed) eidem (that is, to Garth the Receiver) pro quadam annuitate eidem per D'nam Eliz. matrem D'ni nuper concessam & per dictum D'num pro assiduo & diligenti labore suo apud Ebor. in deliberatione & p's' (preservatione) dicti Domini extra manus regias post mortem dictæ D'ne I*s.*

" In liberatione facta mense Febr. pro expensis forinsecis D'ni versus London xx*l.*

" In solutione D'no in denariis mense Septembre per manus Hug. Kirke servientis dicti D'ni XIII*l.* VI*s.* VIII*d.*"

Thus it appears that Lord Clifford came from Westmoreland in January, stayed a short time at Skipton in his way to Conisburgh, was at London in February, at Skipton again in August (where his and the countess's horses eat up almost all the herbage of the Old Park) and spent the rest of the year at Conisburgh. There appears to have been no household at Skipton Castle in his absence, and the demesne lands were mostly in lease.

I do not find that, after all deductions for repairs, wages, &c., he received in clear money from the honour of Skipton more than CXIII*l.* VI*s.* VIII*d.* The total sum received was CCLXIX*l.* VIII*d.*

This Lord Clifford was slain in the battle of St. Albans, May 22nd, 33rd Henry VI. [1455], and was interred with his uncle, Henry Percy, Earl of Northumberland, and the other noblemen who fell on that occasion, in the Lady Chapel of the monastery. He was born on the Monday after the Assumption of the Virgin, A° 2do Henry V. [1414],[*] and was therefore killed in the 41st year of his age. By a subsequent agreement it was awarded that, at the costs of the Duke of York, the Earls of Warwick and Salisbury, 45*l.* of yearly rent should be amortised for ever to the Monastery of St. Albans for suffrages and obits for the souls of Henry Earl of Northumberland, Thomas Lord Clifford, &c. Also, that the Earl of Warwick should give to the Lord Clifford the sum of M marks, to be distributed between the said Lord Clifford, his brethren, and sisters." [†]

[Arms on the picture, Clifford quartering Vipont and impaling gu. three escallops arg. for Dacre.]

[In the 8th Henry VII. (1492–3) Sir Robert Clifford (third son of Thomas Lord Clifford) and William Barley were sent into Flanders by those who were plotting for Perkin Warbeck, believing him to be Richard Duke of York, and son of King Edward IV.

Sir Robert visited Margaret Duchess of Burgundy, and was introduced to the supposed duke, and, in the words of the chronicler Hall (p. 465), "beleved surely that he was extracted of the blood royall, and the very sonne of Kyng Edward the IIII., and thereof he wrote a lettre of credite and confidence into England to his company and fellowes of his conspiracy; and to put them out of all doubte he affirmed y^t he knew him to be Kinge Edwardes sonne by his face and other ligniamentes of his body." King Henry VII., finding that Lord Clifford had gone into Flanders, caused the coasts to be watched, that he might seize him,

---

[*] Inq. *p. m.* Joh. de Clifford.

[†] Holinshed, vol. ii. p. 1292, ed. 1.

or any other suspected persons going or returning; and he sent to Philip Archduke of Burgundy, and his counsellors, Sir Edward Poynings, Knt., and William Warram, Doctor of Laws, to assure them that Perkin Warbeck was born of obscure parents, and an impostor. The duke and his advisers promised not to aid him.   King Henry then sent messengers to Flanders to entice Sir Robert Clifford and Barley to return to England, promising to them frank and free pardon.*   In the 10th Henry VII. [1494–5] Sir Robert returned to England, and met the king in the Tower of London, where he charged Sir William Stanley with being a supporter of Warbeck; and on the 16th February, 1495, he was beheaded in the Tower. Hall states, in his "Chronicle," p. 468 : " I will shew the opinion that at that time ranne in mens heddes of this knyghtes goynge into Flaunders.   Some men holde this opinion, that Kyng Henry for a polecy did send him as a spye to Flaunders, or els he would not have so sone receaved him into his grace and favour agayn.   Neverthelesse this is not like to be true by diverse reasons and apparant argumentes.   Firste, after that attempt begonne by Syr Robert he was in no small danger him selfe, and by that was not a little noted, and hys fame blemished, but also hys frendes were suspected and had in a gealosy.   Secondarely, he was not after y^t in so great favour, nor so estemed with the kyng as he had been in tymes past, because he was blotted and marked with that cryme and offence.   And therefore he, bearing his favour to the House of Yorke, entendynge in the beginning to administer displeasure to King Henry, sayled to the lady Margaret, being seduced and brought in belefe y^t Perkyn was the very sonne of Kynge Edward.   But to my purpose, when Syr Robert came to the presence of the kyng he knelyng on his knees most humblye beseched hym of grace and pardon, whiche he shortely obteyned."]

JOHN LORD CLIFFORD, NINTH LORD OF THE HONOUR OF SKIPTON,

who was born April 8, 1430,† held the titles and estates five years, eight months, and seven days.   His hands were early dipped in blood, for he was engaged in the civil war of the Houses almost three years before his father's death.   After the second battle of St. Albans the king was brought to meet the queen in Clifford's tent.   This nobleman, partly from the heat of youth, and partly in the spirit of revenge for his father's death, pursued the House of York with a rancour which rendered him odious, even in that ferocious age.   His supposed slaughter of the young Earl of Rutland ‡ in, or perhaps after, the battle of Wakefield, has left

[* According to Stow, certain persons were, in 1495, sent to Calais to entice him over, "promising him and William Barley pardon for all their offences, and *high rewards*.   They that were sent did so earnestly apply their business that they brought to pass all things at their own desires ; for they learned who were the chief conspirators, and persuaded Sir Robert Clifford to give over the enterprise."   At the coming of Sir Robert to the king's presence, he besought of him pardon, and obtained in it, and therewith opened the manner of the conspiracy, and who were the aiders, fautors, and chief beginners of it."   The Privy Purse expenses of King Henry VII. bring to light the bribe which Clifford received for his treachery:—

"20th Jan. 1495.   Delivered to Sir Robert Clifford by thand of Master Bray, 500*l.*

To William Hoton and Harry Wodeford, for bringing of Sir Robert Clifford, in rewarde, 26*l.* 13*s.* 4*d.*"

This payment was a reward given to the persons who had so successfully negotiated with Sir Robert Clifford.— "Excerpta Historica," pp. 100, 101.]

† So say Lady Pembroke's MS. memoirs.   But, if he were so old, the wine drunk at his mother's purification was not paid for till four years after.   See note ‡ at the bottom of p. 306.

‡ Still it is by no means certain that Rutland fell by *his* hand.   Leland only says, "that for slaughter of men at Wakefield he was called the boucher."   Shakespeare spoke the language of his own age when he called him Clifford of Cumberland : he should have said of Westmoreland.   But the great poet despised such minutiæ.

a deep stain upon his memory; and his own untimely end, which happened the next year, is remembered without regret. On the day before the battle of Towton, and after the rencontre at Ferrybridge, having put off his gorget, he was struck in the throat by a headless arrow, out of a bush, and immediately expired. In the MS. memoirs of the family at Appleby, this is said to have happened at Deindingdale, a place unnoticed in any map;* but a respectable friend,† resident near the place, has discovered the evanescent and almost forgotten name of Dittingdale in a small valley between Towton and Scarthingwell. Here, therefore, John Lord Clifford fell. The place of his interment is uncertain, but the traditional account of the family is probably true that his body was thrown into a pit with a promiscuous heap of the slain.‡ Dittingdale is so near the field of Towton that it proves, at least, the advanced posts of the two armies to have been close to each other on the evening preceding the battle.

John Lord Clifford was attainted 1st Edward IV. [1461–2], and, in the fourth year of that reign [1464–5], the castle, manor, and lordship of Skipton, and manor of Marton, were granted in tail-male to Sir William Stanley, Knight. In the 7th of the same reign [1467–8] is a deed of resumption with a saving to the grant made to Sir William Stanley, which I do not understand; and in the 15th of this reign [1475–6] the castle, manor, and demesnes of Skipton, and manor of Marton, were once more granted to Richard Duke of Gloucester, and were held by him to his death.§

In the 1st of Henry VII. [1485–6] the attainder of John Lord Clifford was reversed, together with those of all the other adherents of the House of Lancaster, and the estates of the family restored to Henry his son. The original petition for this restitution will not be uninteresting to the reader—

"In most humble and lowly wise beseecheth yo'r highnes yo'r true subject and faithfull liegman Henry Clifford, eldest sonne to John late Lord Clifford, that when the same John, amongst other persons, for the true service and faithful legiance w'ch he did and owed to king Henry the Sixt, yo'r uncle, in the parliament at Westmynster, the fourth day of November, in the first yeare of king Edward the Fourth, was attainted and convicted of high treason; and by the same act y't was ordained, that the said John, late lord, and his heires, from thenceforth should be disabled to have, hould, inherite, or enioy, any name of dignity, estate, or preheminence, within the realmes of England, Ireland, Wales, Calice, or the Marches therof, and should forfaite all his castles, manors, landes, &c. he desireth to be restored. To the w'ch petic'on the king, in the same parliam't, subscribeth,

"Soit faite come est desier."

In the interval of turbulence and disaster which preceded this restitution, I meet with no evidences among the archives of the family to throw light on any of the dark transactions of the age.

---

* It is mentioned by Holinshed.

† The Reverend Francis Wilkinson, A.M., Vicar of Bardsey.

‡ Yet, as he was certainly killed fourteen or fifteen hours before the great engagement began, his body might have been removed for interment at Bolton. But the following night was an interval of busy and anxious preparation, and the event of the battle left the surviving followers of Clifford no leisure to celebrate his obsequies. "Nec fuit posthac lamentis aut fletibus locus." (Ammian. Marc.) Lord Clifford must have been accompanied to Towton by the *flower of Craven;* yet, though one-half of the Lancastrian army was cut off, I cannot discover a Craven name among the slain.

§ The reader may be tempted to smile at the terms of this grant: "The king, in cons'on of ye laudable and commendable service of his dere b'r Richard duke of Gloucester, as *for the encouragement of piety and virtue* in the said duke, did give and grant, &c., the honor, castle, manors, and demesnes of Skipton, with the manor of Marton, &c. &c."— Pat. Rolls, 15th Edward IV. [1475-6].

2 P

[John Lord Clifford married Margaret Bromflet. She brought with her the title of Baron de Vesci, and the quarterings of Atton, St. John, and Bromflet. The following table shows her descent :—

William Atton⹋.........
Lord Vescy, 2 Ric. II. *Arms:* Or a cross
sa., for some time before 1375 charged with
5 bulls' heads arg. for Vescy (" Scrope and
Grosvenor," ii. 348). But the family arms of
Atton, as quartered by the Cliffords, were,
barry of six or and az. on a canton gu. a
cross patonce or.

Katherine,
dau. and co-heiress,
mar. Ralph Euers.

Elizabeth,
dau. and co-heiress,
mar. 1st, Wm. Placie;
mar. 2nd, Sir John
Coiners, of Stock-
borne, Knt.

Anastasia Atton⹋Sir Edward St. John, Lord St. John.
dau. and co-heiress. | *Arms:* Arg. on a chief dancetty gu. an
annulet between two mullets or.

Sir Thomas Bromflete⹋Margaret St. John,
Lord Vescy, ob. 9 Henry VI. (1430-1). | dau. and heiress.
Arms: Sa. a bend fleur-de-lisé or.

Sir Henry Bromflet⹋1. Joanna, dau. and co-heiress of Thomas Holland, Earl of
died 16 Jan. 1468, *s.p. m.* His | Kent, and widow to Edmund of Langley, Duke of York.
will is dated 26 May, 6 Edw. IV., | ⹋2. Eleanor, dau. of Henry Lord FitzHugh.
1466. Abstract in "Testamenta
Vetusta," i. p. 302.

1. John Clifford, Lord Clifford.⹋Margaret Bromflet, dau. and heiress.
She married secondly Sir Lancelot Threlkeld, Knt. | She brought into the Clifford family
the title of Baron Vescy, and the
Londesborough estates. Died 15
April, 1493; buried at Londesborough, co. York. Her monument
there. She was 26 years of age at
her father's death.

Henry Lord Clifford⹋Anne, dau. of John St. John.

Compiled from Harl. MSS., 1487 *and* 6177.]

A single charter only remains of the 12th of Edward IV., which is a " dede of arbitration between Lancelot Threlkeld, Knight, and lady Margaret his wyfe, the ladie Clyfford, late the wyfe of John lord Clyfford, on the one part; and William Rilston, one of the executors of the will* of Henry de Bromflet lord Vescie, deceased ;" in which the

[* ABSTRACT OF THE WILL OF HENRY LORD VESCY.

Dated 26th May, 6th Edward IV., 1466.

"My body to be buried in the church of White Friars in London, of which, and of all that order in England, I am the principal founder. I will that my lordships and advowsons in the County of York, which are by deed entailed, viz. Lonesborough, Brompton, Aton, Malton, Wellome, Sutton, Wyesthorpe, Wykham, Bromflete, and Bardelby, remain to Margaret my daughter, and the heirs of her body ; also I will that my lordships of North Cave, Clyff, and Clyff-Wighton, Burneby, Fangfosse, Ellerker, Brantingham, Farflete, Weton, Esthorp, Lonesburgh, Holme, Brompton, and Gatesforth, in the said county, shall be sold by my executors, and likewise I desire my executors to sell my lordship of Wymington, in the County of Bedford, and all my other lands in the counties of Bedford and Bucks, with a tenement in Kingston-upon-Hull, together with all my lands and messuages in London, Sussex, and Northampton, and the money received for the same I will may be disposed of for the weal of my soul, in chauntries and other works of charity, viz., to find six priests perpetually to sing for my soul, and for the souls of my father and mother, in such places as I have before determined."

He died 16th January, 8th Edward IV. ; will proved 30th January, 1468.—" Testamenta Vetusta," vol. i. 302.]

said Launcelot and Margaret promise "to be good maister and ladie to the said William, and to move the children of the said John late lord Clifford to be lovyng and tendre to yᵉ said William." The mention of Henry Clifford, the heir, by name, would then have been dangerous, which accounts for the plural "children," when one only could have any material interest in the transaction. This lady, who brought the barony of Vescy into the family, survived the death of her first husband thirty years, and the restoration of her family seven. Having been interred at Londesborough, where she died, a plain brass, on a flat stone, near the altar of that church (the oldest memorial of the family now remaining), thus commemorates the widow of "Black-faced Clifford" :—

Orate p aīa Margarete D'ne Clyfford et Vescy, olim sponse nobilissimi viri Joh's d'ni Clifford et Westmland, filie et heredis Henrici Brownflet quondã d'ni Vescy, Ac eciã matris Henrici dñi Clyfford, Westmland, et Vescy, que obiit rbᵒ die mens' April. Anno Dñi MᵒCCCCᵒ. nonogesimo iiiᵒ cuj corp sub hoc marmoreo est humatū.*

Of Henry Lord Vescy, who introduced that Christian name into the Clifford family, the following curious petition to Henry IV., soon after his assumption of the Crown, was lately discovered among the family evidences at Londesborough. George, the abbot, here mentioned, was Flaccet, a creature, as appears, of the king, who was raised to that dignity in 1402, and in one of whose apartments, the Jerusalem Chamber, Henry died.

"To the Kyng, owre liege Lorde.

"Humble besechethe youre highnesse Henry Bromflete knyght, lord Vessy, that whereas he was possessed of certeyn goodes as of his own p'pre goodes, that is to wete, XI. c li. in money *nowmered* in XI baggs, and silvʳ plate gilt . . . . value . . . . all which money, plate, evidences, *escripts*, and muniments, were conteyned in a flat *bourden* chist,† VI Card-voiaunce,‡ a casket, p'æsages,‡ baggs, cases of lethir, and in two clothes, oon of wollen *an* other of lynnyn ; all which goodes the saide Henry, for his most surtie and saufgarde therof put and layde in a secrete place, to be kept within the church of the monestary of Westm'r : all which goodes in the said church saufly remayned by the space of a quart' of a yere, or more. And at such tyme as it pleased youre highnesse rightwisly to take uppon you the crown of England ; and also at such tyme as my lorde chancellor of England that nowe is, hadde by writyng, under his sele, takyng the *othe* and assurance of the allegiaunce of yoʳ saide besecher to youre said highnesse ; and on youre behalf charged and straitly commanded that *noman* upon peyn of the lawe dewly and straitly to be executed for eny malice, invie, hatrede, or false suggestion, ymaginacon, and mocon of eny invidious p'son or p'sons, do robbe, take, and dispoile any goods of the saide lorde Vessy, as by the saide writyng evidently it may appere. At which tyme, that is for to say, the Setirday in Estre weke, in the furst yere of your noble reyne, that William bisshop of Salesbury that nowe is, accompanied wʰ George the abbot of Westm'r that nowe is, then beying archedekyn of the said monestary, and other with theym accompanied, all the saide money, plate, evidencs, escripts and muniments, as is afore specified, wrongfully toke away, and bere away, and theym caried unto suche places as it pleased the said bisshop and nowe abbot, contʳary to the . . . . and pre'lege of the said monestary, agenst all lawe, reson, and consciens. All which goods the said bisshop, and now abbot, from youre said besecher yit kepyn and reteyn, except certeyn of the said evidences, whych were delyv'ed by the means of sade lorde chancellor of England. Wherfore please it youre highnesse of youre speciall ryghtwisness and gᵃce, the p'misses tenderly considered, and that yoʳ said besecher stondeth gretely chargeably to the execucon of the p'fo'm'ng of the last wille of S' Thomas Bromflete, knyght, his fader ; to the which wille the said Henry trewly to be p'fo'med, he bounde hymself to his said fader, and therto straitly charged himself, the which can not be p'fo'med w'out dewe restitucon of the said goodes to youre said besecher nowe be hadde. That it please yor saide highnesse, by the advise of yoʳ noble Councell to rewill § and compelle aswell the said bisshop, as nowe abbot, to make dewe restitucon and satisfaccon of all the saide goodes to youre said besecher ; and we shall contynually p'y to God for yoʳ moste noble roiall *astate*."

[* Dr. Whitaker had not copied this inscription correctly, and had also given the date 1491 ; it is now printed from a rubbing, kindly furnished by the Rev. Richard Wilton, Rector of Londesborough.]

† An ancient form of the adjective, as *treen* mould, &c., in Spenser.

‡ Qu. the meaning of these words.

§ *I.e.* rule.

HENRY LORD CLIFFORD, TENTH LORD OF THE HONOUR OF SKIPTON, AND FIRST BARON DE VESCY OF THAT NAME,

on the accession of Henry VII., emerged from the fells of Cumberland, where he had been principally concealed for twenty-five years, with the manners and education of a shepherd. He was at this time almost, if not altogether, illiterate, but far from deficient in natural understanding; and, what strongly marks an ingenuous mind in a state of recent elevation, depressed by a consciousness of his own deficiencies. On this account he retired to the solitude of Barden, where he seems to have enlarged the tower, out of a common keeper's lodge, and where he found a retreat equally favourable to taste, to instruction, and to devotion. The narrow limits of his residence show that he had learned to despise the pomp of greatness, and that a small train of servants could suffice him who had lived to the age of thirty, a servant himself.* I think this nobleman resided here almost entirely when in Yorkshire, for all his charters which I have seen are dated at Barden.

His early habits, and the want of those artificial measures of time which even shepherds now possess, had given him a turn for observing the motions of the heavenly bodies; and having purchased such an apparatus as could then be procured, he amused and informed himself by those pursuits, with the aid of the canons of Bolton, some of whom are said to have been well versed in what was then known of the science. It is pleasing to find these religious so rationally employing themselves, and so well qualified to afford their illiterate but curious patron a liberal occupation, which alone could prevent him from sinking into sordid habits.

Among the lovers of science or of virtue that visit Bolton and Barden, there are few who will not feel their interest in those beautiful scenes increased by the remembrance of such an intercourse.

I suspect, however, this nobleman to have been sometimes occupied in a more visionary pursuit, and probably in the same company.

For, in the family evidences, I have met with two MSS. on the subject of alchemy, which from the character, spelling, &c., may almost certainly be referred to the reign of Henry VII. If these were originally deposited with the MSS. of the Cliffords, it must have been for the use of this nobleman. If they were brought from Bolton † at the Dissolution, they must have been the work of those canons whom he almost exclusively conversed with.

---

* Yet in the 8th Henry VIII. "howshald wages" are paid to more than sixty servants at Barden. S'm. tot. xxvs. xviid. Wages from vs. to xxvs. each. Yet this was a slender train at that time for a baron.—"Londesbro' Papers." In 1521 two tons of wine were sent from Newcastle to Barden.—*Ibid.*

† Among the Bolton MSS. I have since met with another volume of the same age, and in a similar hand, which consists partly of alchemy and partly of astronomy. This strengthens my conjecture. A specimen of the latter MS. will be given under Bolton. Among Thoresby's MSS. ("Ducat Leod." p. 538), I met with another relic of the literary intercourse which took place between Henry Lord Clifford and the canons of Bolton—"A Treatise of Natural Philosophy," in old French. It was given to the priory of Bolton by Henry Lord Clifford, father of the first Earl of Cumberland, and after its dissolution reverted to the family, as appears by some verses made by the second earl before his marriage with the Lady Eleanor, daughter of Charles Brandon, Duke of Suffolk, by Mary Queen of France. These, if extant, would confer upon the writer as good a title to a place in the catalogue of noble authors, as Lord Rivers, Lord Vaux, and others, whose fame is built on a single ballad.

Notwithstanding the absurdity of this pretended science, I make no apology for inserting a specimen of the work before me, especially as a history of the manners of our forefathers cannot but be defective without some account of their follies.

Thus much, however, may be said in favour of alchemy, that, however subservient to fraud or superstition, it was never, like modern chemistry, degraded into the handmaid of atheism.

> " Keeppe thys lessone well in your my'de,
> That our pryncipall ys symple beyinge,
> Mony in no'bre and on in kynde,
> Sevyne thyngs y'r dowthe in owr p'ncipall dwell
> Most p'cyows whoo cane them fynde,
> I have soo sworne I may nott telle,
> In thys book I schew to yow wryttynge
> As my breyne doone ev'ycheon.
> Assi'litude to ev'ry thynge—
> Howbeytt ytt ys noo moo bott oon
> That in hyme hathe booth sowll and lyffe
> Ytt ys hee tow and one in kynde
> Mareyde togey'r as mane and wyffe.
> Keeppe thys secret well yn thy mynde,
> Owr sulphur ys owr masculyne,
> Owr erthe ys in owr wattur cleer,
> Owr m'cury ys owr femynyne,
> Owr sulphur ys in lyme as fyre,
> As erthe ys yn owr wattur clere.
> Now have yee iiii elements off myght,
> Ryght soo ys aer in ow'r fyre.
> Howbeytt ther apeyrs bot tow in sycht,
> Wattur and erthe yee may well see.
> Thys may not be towght to ev'y mane.
> Fyre and aer ys as qualyte.
> Hee wer accursyde that soo wolde done.
> How schold yow have servans then
> To tyll yowr lands and dryffe your plughe
> Yff ev'y mane to ryches came?
> Then none for oth'r owght wolde dowghe." *

All the precepts, however, of this profound work might have been imparted to the profane vulgar without much risk of the evils incident to a state of universal wealth. But there might be another and a better reason for reserve, lest the philosopher should happen to take into his confidence such an acute and penetrating knave as the canon's yeoman in Chaucer, whose tale is perhaps the finest satire upon chemical jugglers to be found in any language.

In these peaceful employments, whether rational or otherwise, Lord Clifford spent the whole reign of Henry VII.† and the first years of his son. But in the year 1513, when almost 60 years old, he was appointed to a principal command over the army which fought

---

* Has not the alchemy of modern commerce produced something like the same effect?

[† This does not appear to be correct, for in the 13th Henry VII., 1497-8, the King of Scotland invaded England, ravaged the borders, and laid siege to Norham Castle. Richard Fox, Bishop of Durham, furnished the castle with both men and munitions, and sent to the king, who ordered the Earl of Surrey to take command of an army to proceed to drive the Scots from the kingdom. The earl, who was then in Yorkshire, marched forward, and the chronicler Hall (p. 481, ed. 1809) states, that " after him followed other noble men oute of all quarters of ye north, every one bringyng as many as

at Flodden,* and showed that the military genius of the family had neither been chilled in him by age, nor extinguished by habits of peace.

The enumeration of his followers on this occasion, in the old metrical history of Flodden Field,† is so local and exact, that it would be unpardonable to omit it in a History of Craven :—

> "From Penigent to Pendle Hill,
> From Linton to Long Addingham,
> And all that Craven coasts did till,
> They with the lusty Clifford came;
> All Staincliffe hundred went with him,
> With striplings strong from Wharlèdale,
> And all that Hauton hills did climb,
> With Longstroth eke and Litton Dale,
> Whose milk-fed fellows, fleshy bred,
> Well brown'd with sounding bows upbend;
> All such as Horton Fells had fed
> On Clifford's banner did attend."

He survived the battle of Flodden ten years, and died April 23, 1523, aged about 70. I shall endeavour to appropriate to him a tomb, vault, and chantry,‡ in the choir of the church of Bolton, as I should be sorry to believe that he was deposited when dead at a distance from the place which in his life-time he loved so well.§

In the Memoirs ‖ of the Countess of Pembroke he is described as "a plain man, who lived for the most part a country life, and came seldom either to Court or London, excepting

they coulde gather for the defence of their naturall countrey and region. Emongest whome the chiefe rulers and leaders were these whose names ensue :—

Raufe earle of Westmerland	Of Knyghtes :—
Thomas lord Dacres	Sir William Percy
Raufe lord Nevell	Sir William Boulmer
George lord Straunge	Sir William Gascoyne
Richard lord Latymer	Sir Raufe Bigod
George lord Lumley	Sir Raufe Bowes
John lord Scrope	Sir Thomas a Parr
Henry lord Clifford	Sir Raufe Elerker
George lord Oge	Sir Jhon Constable
William lord Conyers	Sir Jhon Ratclyffe
Thomas lord Darcy	Sir Jhon Savell
Thomas Baron of Hylton	Sir Thomas Strangneys."]

[* He was appointed to a command in the centre of the "forwarde," or vanguard. Hall tells us that, "the Erle and his counsayll with greate deliberacion appointed his battayles in order with wynges and with ryders necessarie. Fyrste of the forwarde was Capitayne the lorde Howarde, Admyrale of Englande, with suche as came from the sea, and with him Syr Nicholas Applyarde, Syr Stephen Bull, Syr Henry Shyreburne, Syr William Sydney, Syr Edwarde Echyngham, lorde Clifforde, the lorde Conyers, the lorde Latymer, the lorde Scrope of Upsale, the lorde Egle, the lorde Lomley, Syr William Bulmer, with the Power of the Bishoprycke of Durham, Syr William Gascoyne, Sir Christopher Warde, Syr Jhon Everyngham, Syr Thomas Metham, Syr Water Gryffith, and many others." The officers of the wings on the right and left of the forward, the rereward and its two wings are also then detailed.—Hall, pp. 558—559. Richard Tempest was in the rerewarde.]

[† Said to have been written by one Richard Jackson, schoolmaster, of Ingleton, about fifty years after the battle.]

‡ 1521. Payd to my lord's chaplyan at Bolton hys quarᵗˢ wayge XXVIs. VIIId To the chanon of Skipton, XVIs. VIId.—"Londesboro' Papers."

§ By his last will he appointed his body to be interred at Shap, if he died in Westmoreland; or at Bolton, if he died in Yorkshire.

‖ Appleby MSS.

when called to Parliament, on which occasion he behaved himself like a wise and good English nobleman. This Lord Clifford never travelled out of England." He married first, Anne, daughter of Sir John St. John of Bletsho, cousin-german by the half blood to Henry VII.; and, secondly, Florence, daughter of Henry Pudsay, of Bolton, Esq., who, in the 20th of Henry VII., was first married to Sir Thomas Talbot of Bashall; and after the decease of her second husband, to Richard, third son of Thomas Marquis Dorset, son of Elizabeth Widvile. Her first jointure was 10 marks; her second, 150*l.*, which she continued to receive in the 3rd and 4th of Philip and Mary [1556–7]. The gradual advancement of this lady is remarkable: her father was an esquire, her first husband a knight, her second, a baron; her last, the grandson of a queen. She survived her father-in-law—who was slain at Towton—97 years; and having conversed with many of the principals in the war between the Houses, must, in the middle of the next century, if her memory remained, have been a living chronicle, fraught with information and entertainment.

Her husband was succeeded by his son—

HENRY LORD CLIFFORD, FIRST EARL OF CUMBERLAND, ELEVENTH LORD OF THE HONOUR OF SKIPTON,

born in 1493, with whom he had lived on bad terms for several years.

In the same memoirs I meet with the following curious letter to a privy councillor from the old lord, on the subject of these disagreements:—

"I doubt not but ye remember when I was afore you with other of the king's highnesses councel, and ther I shewed unto yow the ungodly and ungudely disposition of my sonne Henrie Clifforde, in suche wise as yt was abominable to heare yt; not onlie disobeyinge and despytynge my comaundes, and threatening my servaunts, sayinge that yf ought came to mee he shold utterlie destroye al, as apeireth more likelie in strikyng, with his own hand, my pore servaunt Henrie Popeley, in peryl of dethe, w'ch so lyeth, and is lyke to dye; bot alsoe (he) spoiled my houses, and feloniously stole away my propre goods, w'ch was of grete substance, onlie of malyce, and for maynteinyng his inordinate pride and ryot, as more speciallie dyd apere when he dep'tyd out of ye corte and com into ye contrie, aparellyd himself and hys horse in cloth of golde and goldsmyths wark, more lyk a duke than a pore baron's sonne as hee ys. And moreover I shewyd untoe yow at that tyme, his daylie studyng how he myght utterlye destroy me hys pore Fader, as wel by slaunders shamful and daungerous, as by daylie otherwyse vexyng and inquyetynge my mynde, to the shortenynge of my pore lyfe. And notwithstand'g ye p'misses I by ye kynge's comaunde, and yo'r desier, have sithens geffen unto him XL*l.* and over that my blessyng upon hys gude and lawful demeanor, desyring alsoe y^t hee shuld leave ye daungerous and evyll consaille of certain evyll disposyd p'sons, as wel yonge gents as oth'rs, w'ch have before this geffen hym daungerous conseille, whose conseilles he dailie followeth; and wher I shewed unto ye kynge's grace and yow, that yf his shamful disposiciouns were not lokyd upon, and something promysed by his Hyghness, to bring hym to drede (as ye begynning of all wisdome ys to drede God and hys prynce), hc sholde bee utterlie undone for ev'r, as wel bodilie as ghostlie, as apeiryth at large, not onlie by ye encrese of hys evyl disposiciouns, but also sekyng further to grete lordes for meintenaunce, wherein he hath taken more boldness, sayinge, that he shal cast downe one of my servants that be nigh unto mee, though they bee in my p'sence; and yet moreover he in his countree makyth debate betweine gentilmen, and troblith divers housys of religioun, to bring from them thcr tythes, shamfully betyng ther tenaunts and s'vants, in such wyse as some whol townes are fayne to kepe the churches both nighte and dcye, and dare not com att ther own housys."*

This complaint, however reasonable, was not likely to be received by the council of a young monarch like Henry VIII. with the attention it deserved. Henry Clifford had been

---

* Was it owing to the carelessness or contrition of the son that he suffered a copy of this letter to remain among the family papers? Probably to the former.

educated along with that prince,* and of course presumed on his friendship and protection. Indeed the extravagances of a gay and gallant young nobleman, cramped in his allowance by a narrow father, under the influence of a jealous stepmother, were likely to meet with more than sufficient indulgence from the world.

The method which this high-spirited young man took to supply his necessities is characteristic of the times; instead of resorting to Jews and money-lenders, computing the value of his father's life, and raising great sums by anticipation, methods which are better suited to the calm unenterprising dissipation of the present age, Henry Clifford turned outlaw,† assembled a band of dissolute followers, harassed the religious houses, beat their tenants, and forced the inhabitants of whole villages to take sanctuary in their churches.

He is said, however, to have been reclaimed in good time; and there is great reason to hope that his father lived to see the effects of his reformation; for I can scarcely suppose him to have continued this irregular course of life long after his marriage; and he was a father by his second lady at twenty-four. Besides, there is no hint in this letter at his misconduct as a husband. On this account I am inclined to fix the date of it about 1512 or 1513, when Henry Clifford was from twenty to twenty-one.‡

Within two years after his accession to the estates and honours of the family, this nobleman was advanced to the dignity of Earl of Cumberland;§ and I trust that few

---

* Appleby MSS.

† I hope it will be thought no extravagant conjecture that Henry Clifford was the hero of the "Not-browne Mayd." That beautiful poem was first printed about 1521, and from the use of the word *spleen*, which was introduced into the English language by the study of the Greek physicians, it could not have been written long before. Little, perhaps, can be inferred from the general qualification of an outlaw's skill in archery, "Such an archere as men say that ye be," compared with the circumstance of the Earl of Cumberland's providing himself with all the apparatus of the bow in the following account: but when "the Man" specifically describes *Westmarland* as his *heritage*, we must either suppose the whole story to be a fiction, or refer it to one of the wild adventures of Henry Clifford, who really led the life of an outlaw within ten years of the time. The *great Lynage* of the lady may well agree with Lady Percy; and what is more probable than that this wild young man, among his other feats, may have lurked in the forests of the Percy family, and won the lady's heart under a disguise, which he had taken care to assure her concealed a knight? That the rank of the parties is inverted in the ballad, may be considered as nothing more than a decent veil of poetical fiction thrown over a recent and well-known fact. The barony of Westmoreland was the inheritance of Henry Clifford alone.

[‡ In the 14th Henry VIII., 1522-23, Henry Lord Clifford was summoned, with the Earls of Northumberland, Westmoreland, and Derby, Lords Dacre, Lumley, Scrope, Latimer, Ogle, Darcy, Conyers, &c., to be ready within eight hours' warning, with all their retainers, to proceed against the Scots.—Hall, p. 649, 650.

And again in the next year Lord Clifford was at Alnwick with the Earls of Surrey, Northumberland, and Westmoreland, and many of the lords above mentioned, together with 40,000 men, ready to give battle to the Scots under the Duke of Albany; but he, with his army, retired into Scotland.—Hall, p. 666.]

[§ The following note is interesting as showing the occasion of the meeting at which Lord Clifford was created Earl of Cumberland:—"You shall understande, the Kyng in his freshe youth, was in the chaynes of love with a faire damosell called Elizabeth Blount daughter to Sir Jhon Blunt Knight, whiche damosell in syngyng, daunsyng, and in all goodly pastymes exceded all other, by the whiche goodly pastymes she wan the Kynges harte: and she again shewed hym suche favor, that by hym she bare a goodly manne child, of beutie like to the father and mother. This child was well brought up, like a Princes child, and when he was VI yere of age, the Kyng made hym Knight, and called hym lorde Henry Fitz Roy, and on Sondaie beyng the XVIII daie of June, at the Manor or place of Bridewell the saied Lorde, ledde by twoo Erles, was created Erle of Notyngham, and then he was brought backe again by the saied twoo Erles, then the Dukes of Norffolke and Suffolk led hym into the great chamber again, and the Kyng created hym Duke of Richemond and Somerset; and the same daie was the lorde Henry Courtenay Erle of Devonshire, and cosyn germain to the Kyng, created Marques of Excester, and the lorde Henry Brandon, sonne to the duke of Suffolk, and the Frenche Quene, the Kynges sister, a childe of twoo yere old, was created Erle of Lincolne, and Sir Thomas Manners, lord Ross, was created Erle of Rutlande, and sir Henry Clifford was created Erle of Cumberlande, and the lorde Fitz Water Sir Robert Radclif was created Viscount Fitz Water, and Sir Thomas Bullein threasorer of the Kynges household was created Viscount Rocheforde, and at these creacions were kept greate feastes and disguisynges."—Hall's "Chronicles," edit. 1809, p. 703.]

readers will be displeased with the following original account of his journey, attendants, expenses, &c , upon that occasion.*

" My lord's coste from Skipton to London, and att London, att his lordeshipp creat'on in Com' anno XVII Hen. VIII.

My lord's expence, ┐ First paid for my lord's expence, and 33 his servants, riding from Skipton to London, as apperith by riding to London. ┘ the houshould booke, VIII*l*. XV*s*. I*d*.

Costs of my lord's ┐ Item, paide for the expence of my lord's house att London, for five weeks and one daye, in June and house att London. ┘ July, A° XVII Hen. VIII. with horses meat and fewell, and all other charges, with all other necessaryes thereunto belongyng, with ——— III*s*. XI*d*. wyne III*s*. cheries II*d*. rishes IV*d*. thred I*d*. sakket IV*d*. ; XLVI*l*. VII*s*."

With respect to these particulars, it may be observed,

1st, That the Earl of Northumberland, according to the household book of 1509, only sixteen years from this time, travelled with thirty-six horse, which is a good scale of the comparative magnificence of the Percies and Cliffords.

Supposing my lord to have rode from Skipton to London in five days, the expense of each man and horse would be about 10*d*. per day. A nobleman of the same rank travelling to town without his family at present would be content with six horses, two postillions, and two outriders. Modern habits have certainly gained in elegance what they have lost in cumbrous parade.

2nd, About 9*l*. a week suffices for an establishment of thirty-four men and as many horses in London ; and what wonder, when my lord's wine for five weeks cost only three shillings and four pence, and his desserts two pence ? Rushes were used instead of carpets at Derby House. These "strewments," according to Erasmus, were receptacles of all manner of filth, human and canine. I know no change of habits which contributed more to neatness than the substitution of naked floors to rushes, where nothing can be concealed. Carpets have contributed still more to the same end. If you call a spitting clown into your library or dining-room, he will always forbear to discharge his saliva upon a covering which he considers as rich and ornamental. Our rush-strewn churches in the country are still subject to the old annoyance.† Sakket, I suppose, was sacking, intended to be stuffed with straw for the servants' beds, as we are not to suppose that, though they slept on straw (*vide infra*), they were bedded precisely like horses.

" Household stuff bought and remaining.

Item, for 12 napkins dy'p', VII*s*. VIII*d*.
Item, 4 y'ds ditto, for a towell, III*s*. V*d*.
Item, 10 yerdes dyap' for burd clothes (table-cloths), XIII*s*. IV*d*. (I suppose of superior quality.)
Item, for 2 table clothes for the hall, V*s*. VIII*d*.
Item, for sewyng, VIII*d*.
Item, for galypots and cupps, VIII*d*.

Summa, XXX*s*. VI*d*."

Hence we see that the modern luxury of napkins at table was in use as early as 1525.

" Item, paid for liv'ais (liveries) for my lord's servants, XV*l*. IX*s*.
Item, for liv'ay hose (livery hose) III*l*. XVIII*s*. IV*d*.
Item, for silver, gold, and satten, for the', XVII*s*. IV*d*.

---

* This account was copied by Dodsworth from the original in Skipton Castle, which cannot now be found.
† *Vide* Du Cange *in voce* Saccellus.

2 Q

Item, to Lancelot Marton and Lionel Marton, for two coates, 1l. IIs.
Item, to the p'son of Giseley, for his liv'ey, XIIIs. IVd.
Item, paid to the brotherer (embroiderer) for ye coinsant (cognisance), 1l. Xs.
Item, paid to Rob. Secretary, for his liverey, Xs.

Summa, XXIVl."

On this occasion the new earl was to appear in the first style of fashion. Accordingly, his old liveries were discarded, and his train arrayed anew, in laced coats faced with satin, and embroidered with the cognisances of the family.

Lancelot Marton was lord of Eshton, and one of his gentlemen.

A livery for the parson of Guisely, who seems to have been chaplain to the household, sounds oddly in modern ears; but the scarf, the modern livery of chaplains, was then unknown. In the statutes of some colleges in Oxford, the habit of the fellows, for which a stated allowance was made, is called the *liberatura.**

Then follow some trifling payments, amounting to XIl. XVIs. IVd., of which nothing deserves notice but the following, " P'd to my lord at dise, XLs." This was probably high gaming in 1525.

" Item, delivered to Leonard Whitfeld, when my lord rode to Pishaw Parke, IVl."

This, I suppose, is Pishoberry, in Herts. I do not know to whom it belonged.

" My Lord's Robes and Apparell.

For 16 yerdes of Russet velvet, doble, after 1l. 11s. 8d. the yerd, XXVIl. IIs. VId.
Item, for 12 yerdes damask, black, after 7s. 6d., IVl. Xs.
Item, for 2¾ yerdes black satten, after 8s., 1l. IIs.
Item, for a girdle to my lord, 1s. Vd.
Item, for 3 yerds of black carsey, for hoise to my lord, VIIs. VId.
Item, a roll buckram, for lynyng my lord's fotecloth, 1s. VIIId.
Item, 8 yards black velvet for the fotecloth, IVl.
Item, to Edw. Radclyffe for byenge sherts to my lord, 1l. IIIs. IVd.
Item, for velvett shoes to my lord, IIs.
Item, for 16 yerds of black satten, at 8s., VIl. VIIIs.
Item, for 25 yerdes of velvett cremisyn for my lord's robes, at 13s. 4d. the yerde, XVIl. IIIs. IVd.
Item, for 2½ yerdes of tawney satten, at 7s. 8d., XVIIIs. IId.
Item, to Rauf Warren, for 3 yerdes black satten, 1l. IVs.
Item, for 2 French capps to my lord, VIIIs. VIIId.
Item, for my lord's sweard, to the cutler, XIIIs. IVd.
Item, for furringe of my lord's robes, as apperith by a bill of the parcells, VIIIl.
Item, paid for a pair of black shoes, and a paire of black slipp's, for my lord, b't by Edw. Radcliffe, 1s. VId.
Item, paid for a chape of silver, gilted, for my lord's swerde, IIIs.
Item, paid for a horne to my lorde,
Item, paid for flewynge the said horne with two ounces and three } XVIIIs.
    quatrons silver, aft' 6s. 8d. the ounce, and 4d. les at all,
Item, paid for a grene sasshe, &c., IIIs. IVd.
Item, 2 doz. strand heeds, bought by Tho. Martin, VIs.
Item, half a doz. brode heds, 1s.
Item, a shotynge glove, IVd.
Item, a dozen and a halfe brede arrow shafts, IIIs.
Item, paide to my lord the 18th of July, for a white frontelett brodered and wrought with gold, for my lady, IIl. Xs.
Item, paid to Ridley, my lord's taylor in London, for makyng my lord's robes, and other app'ell, IVl."

Some trifling particulars are omitted, which make the sum LXXXVIIl. Vs. IIId.

* In the statutes of the cathedral of Carlisle, dated 37th Henry VIII., is this title : " De vestibus ministrorum quas liberatas ' vocant."

The robes of an earl, it appears, were of crimson velvet and ermine, his dress-shoes of velvet, the "chape" of his sword [? scabbard] silver gilt.

Under this head are included a (bugle) horne, tipped with silver, at 6*s.* 8*d.* the ounce—almost as high as silversmith's work at present; a pair of shooting-gloves, and two sorts of arrows : all which show the nature of my lord's amusements.

Strand heeds—I suppose, as opposed to brede arrow heeds—were some sort of arrows sold in the Strand. Here is also a charge of 2*l.* 10*s.* for a white embroidered frontlet, as a present to my lady (Margaret Percy) on his return to Skipton. She might complain, with some reason, that he had been sufficiently profuse in the decoration of his own person, and very economical with respect to hers.

> "Almonses and offerands.
> The first day the terme in almons, 11*d.*
> Item, 22d day of Juyne, my lord's offering to our Lady of Pew, 1*s.* VIII*d.*
> 22d of Juyne, in almons, 1*d.*
> Item, to Laurence Hammerton, that he had giffen by my lord's commands, 11*d.*
> Summa, 11*s.* 1*d.*"

Very sparing indeed!

Our Lady of Pew had her shrine somewhere near Westminster Hall,[*] for there the new-made serjeants were wont to make their offerings : "And then they goo to ower Lady of Pewe, and ther they offer, and then they come into the hall."—Dugdale, "Origines Juridiciales," p. 116.

> "Payment of old debts, summa, XXXI*l.* XV*s.* 11*d.*
> Paid to my lord's consaill the first tyme that they were at the Serjeant's Inn, III*s.* IV*d.*
> Item to my lord's consaill on St. Peter's day at Derby-Place, 1*l.*
> Item, for copy of the bill against the p'son of Marton, VIII*d.*
> Item, in reward to Mr. Fitzjames and Master Fitzherbert, jugg's (judges), IV*l.*
> Item to the freres box and ushers att my lord's appearance in the King's Escheker, 1*s.* IV*d.*
>
> Rewards of learned men.
> To Mr. Bolland, of Theschequer, VI*s.* VIII*d.*
> With some trifling items omitted,   Summa, IX*l.* XI*s.* III*d.*"

The earl seems to have filed a bill against the parson of Marton, on what account I know not. The large rewards paid to the judges, one of whom was the celebrated Sir

[* "By this Chapel of S[t]. Stephen (in Westminster) was sometime one other smaller Chapel, called Our Lady of the Piew. To the which Lady, great Offerings were used to be made ; amongst other things I have read, that Richard the Second upon the coming of the Rebel Wat Tyler, with his Rout of Kentish Men in Armes to London, went first to Westminster, to the High Altar there, and offered and after that confessed himself to an Anchorite. And then betook himself to this Chapel of Our Lady in the Pew, and there said his devotions and then went to Smithfield to meet this Fellow and his Company.

"After the Overthrow of Wat Tyler, and other the Rebels, in the fourth of his reign, he went to Westminster and there giving thanks to God for his Victory, made his offering in this chapel, but as divers have noted, namely John Pigot in the year 1452 on the 17th of February by negligence of a scholar appointed by his Schoolmaster to put forth the Lights of this Chapel, the Image of Our Lady, richly decked with Jewels, precious stones, Pearls, and Rings, more than any Jeweller could judge the Price (for so saith mine Author) was with all this Apparel, Ornaments, and Chapel itself burnt : But since again re-edified by Anthony Earl Rivers, Lord Scales, and of the Isle of Wight, Uncle and Governour to the Prince of Wales, that should have been King Edward the Fifth, &c.

"There is a warrant from Richard the Third, to this tenor : Sir John Cave, Priest, Keeper of Our Lady of Pew : An Annuity of ten marks until the time he be better promoted."—Stow's "Survey of London," edit. 1720, book vi. pp. 54, 55.

"Anthony Earl Rivers, in his will dated 23 June, 1483, directs that his heart be carried to Our Lady of Pue adjoining to St. Stephen's College at Westminster, there to be buried by the advice of the dean and his brethren."—Test. Vetust. 380.]

Anthony Fitzherbert, were, I hope, not to pervert justice, but for extra-judicial opinions, which they might lawfully give. The begging friars appear to have had boxes in the most public places, like the poor's boxes in modern churches.

"Item, for botehire to Durham Place, when my lord was commanded to wait upon the duke, VIII*d*.

(Next follow 21 items for boat-hire alone, one of which was when Mr. Blenkinsop went with my lord's water to the phecic'on, IV*d*.)

Summa, II*l*. IV*s*. IX*d*."

It was the Duke of Richmond, natural son of Henry VIII., upon whom the Earl of Cumberland was "commanded" to wait. The duke was warden, and the earl deputy, of the Western Marches, under him.—Clifford MSS. in Off. Arm.

"Costs.

Item, paid to Thomas Johnson, for his costs and a horsehire from London to my lord chamberleyne, for borroweing of robbes, I*s*. VI*d*.

Item, in a reward to a skinner for a sight of my lord of Northumberland's robes, IV*d*.

Item, for strey to bedds, VIII*d*.

Item, to Pemberton for hawkmeat, I*s*. VIII*d*.

Item, for repairing stolls and trestrills at my lord Darbies place, IV*d*.

Item, to a phesicion at Westminster for seying my lord's water, IV*d*.†

Item, stray for bedds, &c., IV*d*.

With other items,   Summa, II*l*. XIII*s*. IV*d*.

Item, in reward to Clarencieux for the fees of the heralds at my lord's creac'on, X*l*.

Item, in reward to the gentlemen ushers of the king's chamber, II*l*. X*s*.

Item, in reward to a frere that keeped my lord's l'res patent, IV*d*.

Item, to a servant of thabbot of Waltham that brought a buk to my lord, III*s*. IV*d*.

Item, to a freire that song masse afore my lord, IV*d*.

Item, to a servant of my lord of Westm'land that broght my lorde a hound, III*s*. IV*d*.

Item, paid to the clerke and churchwardens of St. Bennet's for chappell stuff borrowed of them, III*s*. IV*d*.

Item, to my lord Derbies minstrells, III*s*. IV*d*.

Item, in a reward paid by my lord to a phesician of Cambridge, the 17th of June, I*l*.

Item, p'd to Pemberton for a falcon, I*l*.

Item, for bying wyne to my ladie, I*l*.

Item, velvet to my ladie, VII*s*.

Item, to by gere with, to maistres Dorothy, I*l*.

Summa, XXX*l*. IX*d*."

The Abbot of Waltham's park was famous for its fat venison; in allusion to which, Fuller * has recorded an incident which happened to two fat biped bucks of that place, greatly to the amusement of Henry VIII.

The Earl of Cumberland lodged at Derby Place, now the Heralds' College, which is immediately adjoining to St. Bennet's Church, where he borrowed the apparatus of an altar for masses in the house.

The medical profession had practitioners at that time as high and low as at present. The regular Cambridge doctor, whom my lord consulted on his journey, received just sixty times as much as the poor caster of urine. [See † above.]

The price paid for a falcon, which was probably half as much as the best horse in the earl's stables had cost him, shows the high estimation in which hawking was then held. A sum equivalent to 20*s*. then, is now much better laid out in a good fowling-piece.

* History of Abbeys, "Church History," p. 317.

What are the articles of luxury and amusement which this great nobleman, returning from London after his creation, carries with him into the north ? A hound and a falcon, a bugle-horn, and a sheaf of arrows. Every groom in his stables, every keeper in his parks, would have made the same choice. Yet what could he have done better ? We should forbear to blame men for not anticipating the knowledge or the elegance of future times. The few who rise above the habits of their own age are to be admired. The many who content themselves with the ancient level are entitled to excuse.

The three last articles under this head are for my lady in the country. Maistres Dorothy was probably my lady's woman.

> " Burd-wages, coste of my lord's servants.
> Item, delivered to Stephen Tempest, for the cost of my lord's servants at Grenewich, I*s*. X*d*.
> Item, p'd to Laurence Hammerton, and his servant, for the burd-wages for five days, after six-pence upon the day every of them, V*s*.
> Item, p'd to George Blenkinsop for his burd-wages, II*s*. VI*d*.
> Item, p'd to Christ. Wharton, Rob. Bellingham, Anthony Hoton, Stephen Tempest, Roland Thompson, Tho. Blenkinsop and his sonne, for the burd-wages the said five days, XVII*s*. VI*d*.
>
> Summa, I*l*. VI*s*. X*d*."

Most of these, if not all, were gentlemen attending upon the earl.

The court was probably at Greenwich during these five days, when they received the sum of sixpence *per diem* each for board-wages. Laurence Hammerton was of Hellifield Peel, and Stephen Tempest of Broughton ; the rest are Westmoreland names. Blenkinsop was of Helbeck, near Brough.

> " Item, paide to my lord Rich. Gray for my lady Clifford's payment at Whitsunday, LXXV*l*.
> Item, ...
> Item, p'd to Mr. Garter, upon Thursday, the . . day of July, A⁰ 17 Henry VIII. for the first payment of his reward, VI*l*.
> Item, p'd by Thomas Marton to Sir Ric. Tempest, knight, by my lord's commandment, XVII*l*. VI*s*.
>
> Summa, LXXXXVIII*l*. XVI*s*. III*d*."

The first of these articles was a half year's jointure due to old Lady Clifford (Florence Pudsay),* widow of Henry Lord Clifford the Shepherd, and step-mother of the new-created earl, who was then married to Lord Richard Gray, younger son of Thomas Marquis Dorset.

As all these payments were made in London, or on the way thither, I conclude that Sir Richard Tempest of Bracewell was in the earl's train with his neighbours.

> " Item . . . .
> Item, paid to the pope's collector for the licence of marriage † between John Scrope, sonne and heire apparent to the lord Scrope, and ladie Katherin Clifford, daughter of Henr' earle of Cumberland, II*l*. XIII*s*. IV*d*.
> Summa of all the payments and costs aforesaid, CCCLXXVI*l*. IX*s*."

This is one of the most satisfactory details of the manners and expenses of the reign of Henry VIII. I have ever met with ; and I have only to add to the foregoing remarks that the earl's journey to London was undertaken precisely at that season of the year in

---

* Vide Bolton juxta Bowland.

† This was a lucrative branch of the legatine power, which, not many years after, was transferred, by statute, to the Archbishop of Canterbury, and is now exercised under him by the Master of the Faculties.

which all families of fashion at present are hastening into the country.   But in the dreadful state of the roads at that time, a state which continued, with little amendment, till the introduction of post-carriages and horses, together with their concomitants the toll-bars (not half a century ago), winter journeys to London were formidable undertakings.   I am not sure that increased facility of access to the capital is to be considered as a national benefit.

For the earldom and the Garter, the latter of which was conferred upon him seven years after the former, this nobleman made every return which became a grateful man and a dutiful subject; and when attacked in Skipton Castle by Aske and his fellow-rebels, amidst a general defection of the dependents of his family, bravely defended it against them all.*

[Froude, in his " History of England," 4th edition, vol. iii. p. 140–142, in describing the events which occurred in the insurrection called the Pilgrimage of Grace, says that towards the end of 1536 "Skipton Castle alone in Yorkshire now held out for the Crown."

With the defence of this place is connected an act of romantic heroism which deserves to be remembered—

" Robert Aske, as we have seen, had two brothers, Christopher and John.   In the hot struggle the ties of blood were of little moment, and when the West Riding rose, and they had to choose the part which they would take, 'they determined rather to be hewn in gobbets than stain their allegiance.'   Being gallant gentlemen, instead of flying the country, they made their way with forty of their retainers to their cousin the Earl of Cumberland, and with him threw themselves into Skipton.   The aid came in good time; for the day after their arrival the earl's whole retinue rode off in a body to the rebels, leaving him but a mixed household of some eighty people to garrison the castle.   They were soon surrounded; but being well provisioned, and behind strong stone walls, they held the rebels at bay, and but for an unfortunate accident they could have faced the danger with cheerfulness.   But unhappily the earl's family were in the heart of the danger.   Lady Eleanor Clifford, Lord Clifford's young wife, with three little children, and several other ladies, were staying, when the insurrection burst out, at Bolton Abbey.   Perhaps they had taken sanctuary there; or possibly they were on a visit, and were cut off by the suddenness of the rising.   There, however, ten miles off among the glens and hills, the ladies were, and on the third day of the siege notice was sent to the earl that they should be held as hostages for his submission.   The insurgents threatened that the day following, Lady Eleanor and her infant son and daughters should be brought up in front of a storming party, and if the attack again failed they would 'violate all the ladies, and enforce them with knaves' under the walls.   After the ferocious murder of the Bishop of Lincoln's chancellor, no villany was impossible; and it is likely that the Catholic rebellion would have been soiled by as deep an infamy as can be found in the English annals but for the adventurous courage of Christopher Aske.   In the dead of the night, with the Vicar of Skipton, a groom, and a boy, he stole through the camp of the besiegers.   He crossed the moors, with led horses, by unfrequented paths, and he 'drew such a draught,' he says, that he conveyed all the said ladies through the commons in safety, 'so close and clean that the same was never mistrusted nor perceived till they were within the castle;' a noble exploit, shining on the by-paths of history like a rare, rich flower.   Proudly the little garrison looked down, when day dawned, from the battlements upon the fierce multitude who were howling below in baffled rage.   A few days later, as if in scorn of their impotence, the same gallant gentleman flung open the gates, dropped the drawbridge, and rode down in full armour, with his train, to the Market Cross at Skipton, and there, after three long 'Oyez's!' he read aloud the king's proclamation in the midst of the crowd—'with leisure enough,' he adds in his disdainful way—and that done, he returned to the castle."

[* " Aske and his followers being now in Pomfret, Lancaster, the herald came (Oct. 20), with a proclamation from the Earl of Shrewsbury, requiring it to be read.   But Aske, sitting in state, and having the archbishop on the one hand, and the Lord Darcy on the other, desir'd first to know the contents, which being told, he said it should not be proclaimed. Nevertheless, he gave the herald a safe conduct as long as he ware his coat.   But the rebels not contented thus, requir'd Henry Clifford, Earl of Cumberland (being then in his castle of Skipton) to join with them; but he by letters assures the king, that though 500 gentlemen (retained at his cost) had forsaken him, he would yet continue the king's subject, and defend his castle (in which he had great ordnance) against them all.   Sir Ralph Evers also kept Scarborough Castle with no less courage against the rebels; he and his company having no sustenance but bread and water for the space of twenty days that they besieged him."—The " History of England under Henry VIII.," by Edward Lord Herbert of Cherbury, edit. 1870, pp. 598, 599.]

The above information appears to have been taken by Mr. Froude from the examination of Christopher Aske (Rolls House MS. first series, 840); but from the following table it seems a very doubtful tale, for Eleanor Clifford was not married until 1537, consequently after Christopher Aske's supposed feat.

This table will show the relationship of the Askes with the Earl of Cumberland at the time of the siege of Skipton Castle, in 1536 :—

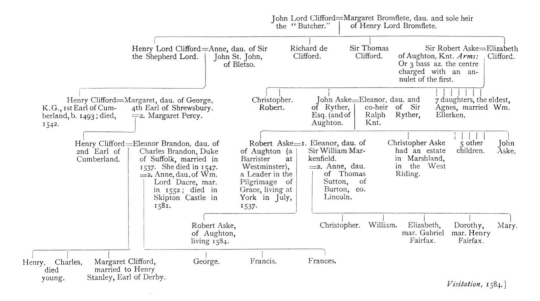

Visitation, 1584.]

A little before this time he built the great gallery of Skipton Castle, for the reception of his high-born daughter-in-law, the Lady Ellenor Brandon; and a short time before his death received, as a reward of his courage and loyalty, a grant of the priory of Bolton, with all the lands thereto belonging, in the parish of Skipton, together with the manors of Storithes, Heslewood, Embsey, Eastby, Conondley, &c., and the manor of Woodhouse (part of Appletrewick), which last belonged to the dissolved priory of Marton. This acquirement, so desirable in point of situation, and especially as these lands had for the most part been amortized* by the ancient lords of Skipton, was equal in value to the whole of the Clifford's fee. But this was not all; by the marriage of this earl with Lady Margaret Percy, on the demise of her brother Henry, Earl of Northumberland, in consequence of a settlement, confirmed by Act of Parliament 27th Henry VIII. [1535–6], the whole Percy fee, equivalent in extent to half of Craven, became vested in the Cliffords, and nearly completed their superiority over the whole district.

[* *Amortization* is an alienation of lands, &c., in mortmain, to any corporation or fraternity and their successors, &c. The right of amortization is a privilege or licence of taking in mortmain. In the statute *de libertatibus perquirendis*, an. 27th Edward I. st. 2, the word *amortisement* is used.—Jacob's "Law Dictionary."]

This earl, so fortunate in his life, was cut off by a premature death April 22, 1542, about the age of forty-nine; and was interred in the vault at Skipton.

By the inquisition after his death the whole amount of his vast estates was found not to exceed 1,719*l.* 7*s.* 8*d. per annum.*

The will of this nobleman contains these curious and interesting particulars :—

" I WILL that C m'kes be bestowed on the highways in Craven, and C m'kes w^{th}in Westmoreland.—It', I will that ev'y curate w^{th}in Westmoreland and the deanery of Craven, and elsewhere wher I have any land in England, doe cause a masse of requiem and dirige to be songe or saide for my soul w^{th}in every y^r p'ish church, and they to have for doing therof VI*s.* VIII*d.* or soe much therof as my ex'ors shall think fitt, the remaynder to be given to the poore.

" I^{tm}, wheras ye kyng, for paym't wherof the right hon. prynce my l^d duke of Suffolk & Jhon l^d Scroope standeth bounden, was pleased that I should have & enjoye to me and myne heires & assignes the scyte of ye late dissolved Priory of Bolton in ye Channons, wth other lands & ten'^{ts} to the said priory belonging ; I will y^t my son Henry l^d Clyfford shall have ye saide scyte & lands to him & his h'rs for ev'r, soe y^t my s^d son pay ye arr's of ye monyes due to the kyng, & discharge ye s^d duke & John l^d Scrop.—I^{tm}, I giff to my son Ingelram a chest of plate sta'ding in my cha'ber, and one chayne of gold.—It^m, I wyll & requyre my ex'ors, that a yerlie obit be hade & mayde for ever in the churche of Skypton ; and on C*s.* land, which I have late purchased in Crakehou, shal defraye ye charge.—It', I make my well-bel^d son-in-law John lord Scrop, Sir Tho. Tempest of Bracewell, k^t. &c. my ex'ors."

He was succeeded by his son,*

HENRY LORD CLIFFORD, SECOND EARL OF CUMBERLAND, TWELFTH LORD OF THE HONOUR OF SKIPTON,

who, falling upon tranquil times, enjoyed his honours without disturbance, but without renown. On the insurrection, however, of the Earls of Northumberland and Westmoreland, he assisted the Lord Scrope in fortifying Carlisle against them; and, on the 8th of January following [1570], died at Brougham Castle. He was buried at Skipton.

When only sixteen years old he was made Knight of the Bath,† at the coronation of Queen Anne Bullen; and by the interest of Henry VIII., a firm and constant friend of the family, in 1537, married, at Brandon House Bridewell, the Lady Ellenor Brandon, daughter of Charles Brandon, Duke of Suffolk, by Mary Queen Dowager of France, daughter of Henry VII.

[* In August, 30th Henry VIII., 1538, Edward Clifford was attainted and executed at Tyburn, for counterfeiting the king's sign manual.—Hall's " Chronicle," p. 826. Query, Who was he ?]

† The red ribband is better bestowed at present than any other Order. It was usually given at that time, not to officers of tried merit in the army or navy, but to mere boys, the sons of the great nobility.

[On Friday, the 30th May, 25th Henry VIII., 1533, " at diner served the kyng all suche as were appointed by his highnes to be knightes of ye bath, which after dyner were brought to their chambers, and that night were bathed and shreven according to the old usage of England, and the next day in the mornyng the kyng dubbed them accordyng to the ceremonies therto belongyng whose names ensueth—

The Marques Dorset.	Sir Wyllyam Wynsore.
The Erle of Darby.	Sir Fraunces Weston.
The lorde Clyfforde.	Sir Thomas Arrondell.
The lorde Fitzwater.	Sir Jhon Hulstone.
The lorde Hastynges.	Sir Thomas Pownynges.
The lorde Mountaigle.	Sir Henry Savell.
Sir Jhon Mordant.	Sir George Fitzwyllyam.
The lorde Vaux.	Sir Jhon Tyndall.
Sir Henry Parker.	Sir Thomas Jermey."

Hall's " Chronicle," edit. 1809, p. 800.]

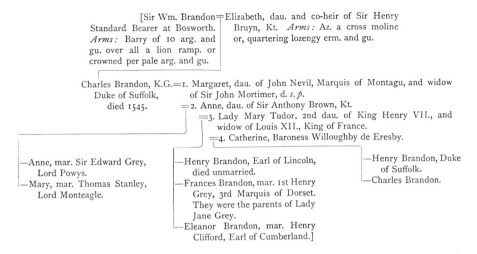

[Sir Wm. Brandon=Elizabeth, dau. and co-heir of Sir Henry
Standard Bearer at Bosworth. | Bruyn, Kt. *Arms:* Az. a cross moline
Arms: Barry of 10 arg. and | or, quartering lozengy erm. and gu.
gu. over all a lion ramp. or
crowned per pale arg. and gu.

Charles Brandon, K.G.=1. Margaret, dau. of John Nevil, Marquis of Montagu, and widow
Duke of Suffolk, | of Sir John Mortimer, d. *s. p.*
died 1545. | =2. Anne, dau. of Sir Anthony Brown, Kt.
=3. Lady Mary Tudor, 2nd dau. of King Henry VII., and
widow of Louis XII., King of France.
=4. Catherine, Baroness Willoughby de Eresby.

—Anne, mar. Sir Edward Grey, —Henry Brandon, Earl of Lincoln, —Henry Brandon, Duke
   Lord Powys.   died unmarried.   of Suffolk.
—Mary, mar. Thomas Stanley,   —Frances Brandon, mar. 1st Henry   —Charles Brandon.
   Lord Monteagle.   Grey, 3rd Marquis of Dorset.
                                   They were the parents of Lady
                                   Jane Grey.
                              —Eleanor Brandon, mar. Henry
                                 Clifford, Earl of Cumberland.]

Probably not long after this marriage, but certainly before the death of the first earl in 1542, is to be dated the following letter, which merits preservation, not for anything in the matter, for it is merely a letter of compliment, but for the easy politeness and elegance of the expression :—

" Noble Lo'!

"Since your great occasions of business and the foulnes of the wayes depryved me of my expected hapynes of seeing you and my cosine until the next spryng, I can noway better satisfy myself, then by saluting you as offten as I can send, or hear of anye messenger; for your worth hath made me so much yours, as I desier nothyng more then to have the means to manyfest myself for ever,

" Your most constant Frynd and Cosine

" E. Derby.

" I desier yʳ Lo' to present my most affectionate wishes unto my Lo' yʳ father."

Directed, " *To the Right Ho. my good L. & Cosine Clifforde.*"

The writer was Edward, third Earl of Derby, who succeeded to the title in 1521, and died in 1572; was the first of the family who was interred in the new chapel of Ormskirk. A winter journey from Skipton to Latham would not at that time have been very agreeable to a princess of the blood, who probably travelled on horseback.

This royal alliance brought with it a train of expenses, which compelled the earl to alienate the great manor of Temedbury, co. Hereford, the oldest estate then remaining in the family; but after the death of this lady, which happened in 1547, he withdrew into the country, grew rich, and became a purchaser. Soon after this event the earl fell into a languishing sickness, and was reduced to such an extreme state of weakness that his physicians thought him dead. His body was already stripped, laid out upon a table, and covered with a herse-cloth of black velvet,* when some of his attendants, by whom he was greatly beloved, perceived symptoms of returning life.† He was once more put to bed, and,

---

* A curious passage in the Paston Letters shows that it was usual to cover the bodies of the nobility when laid out, and before they were chested, with the richest herse-cloths that could be obtained.

† To compare great things with small, there is something in this scene which reminds me of the apparent death and sudden revival of Tiberius, as related by Tacitus, " XVII cal. Apr. interclusâ animâ creditus est mortalitatem explevisse. Et multo gratantum concursu ad capienda imperii primordia C. Cæsar egrediebatur : cum repente adfertur redire Tiberio

by the help of warm clothes without and cordials within, gradually recovered. But, for a month or more, his only sustenance was milk sucked from a woman's breasts, which restored him completely to health, and he became a strong man.*

In 1552 or 1553 he married, at the church of Kirk Oswald, secondly, Anne, daughter of William Lord Dacre, a very domestic woman, who was never at or near London in her life. She survived her lord above ten years, and proved an excellent guardian to her son, in whose presence she died at Skipton Castle in 1581.

The character given of this earl by his grand-daughter states, "that he had a good library, was studious in all manner of learning, and much given to alchemy." After his first lady's death he came to court only three times : once at the coronation of Queen Mary; a second time at the marriage of his daughter to the Earl of Derby; and lastly, to visit Queen Elizabeth soon after her accession. His lady and all his children, excepting George Lord Clifford, were with him at his death. Five years before that event, it appears, from the following letter, that he was negotiating a marriage between his son George, then only seven years old, and the daughter of the Earl of Bedford :—

"After my most hartie comendac'ons to yo' good L.

"According to my form' l'res sent unto y' l. I have now wrytten my l'res of request to my very good l. the Vicount Mountague, and my brother Leonard Dacres, to joyne wth such other of yo' good l. ffrendes as yo' l. shall lik to ......and appoint to......of the mariage motioned by my very good l. therle of Lecestre, between yo' l. daughter and my sonne and heire, and likewise sent certeyn articles for there better p'ceding in that behalf accordingly. And understanding yo' good l. daugther to remayn at Ca————, I will, wth yo'r l. favor, in the meane tyme be so bold to wryte unto my kynsman Sir Jervise Clifton, to mak a jorney......to have a sight of yo' sayd daughter, whose oppynyon and report I dare asmoch credit as eny frends I have in this North p'ties. And if it shall lik yo' good l. to use the semblable to my sonne, the same shall be right hartely welcome, asknoweth almightie God, who send yo' good l. the helth and hono' I desier to my self. From my castell of Appulby in Westmerland this......of Januarii 1565.

"Postscript. I have wrytten unto my lord of Lecester to open the matter to the Quenes ma^te for her highnes assent to be had to the same mariage."

In the last illness of this nobleman [Francis], the old Earl of Bedford, anxious to obtain the wardship and marriage of his heir, addressed the following letter to Queen Elizabeth :—

"Maye it pleas y'r most excellent Majestie to be advertized, that, heretofore, as it is wel knowne to manie, ther hath bene communication betwene my lo. of Cumbrelande and me for the marrynge of his son to one of my d'rs ;† and beying now informed that he is in some danger, I doe presume to bee a suiter to y'r highness, that I maye have the wardship of his son, if it stande with y'r Majesties pleasure, and therby I shal think myeself most bounden (as I have every way good cause) to your Highness. And thus I beseech God to send unto your Majestie a most prosperous hethful raigne, to God's glory, and your hearts desire, &c.　　　　"*From Russell Place, this 3rd of January*, 1570."‡

This was only five days before the earl's death. It is almost unnecessary to add that the petition was granted, and the marriage took effect. From these nuptial bargains of the great, where the tempers, understandings, and inclinations of the young parties were equally disregarded, little domestic happiness could be expected, and less was seldom attained than in the instance before us.

---

vocem ac visus, vocarique qui recreandæ defectioni cibum adferrent." (Annal. VI. *sub fin.*) But there was a striking difference between the situation of a virtuous and beloved nobleman in the arms of faithful attendants, and a detested tyrant, surrounded by assassins. Accordingly, the one was restored and the other suffocated.

　*　Appleby MS.

　[† His youngest daughter, the Lady Margaret, was married to George Clifford, third Earl of Cumberland, on the 24th of June, 1577.]

　‡　Appleby MS. [and Collins's " Peerage," vol. i. p. 271.]

GEORGE LORD CLIFFORD, THIRD EARL OF CUMBERLAND, AND THIRTEENTH LORD OF THE HONOUR OF SKIPTON.

From this period I shall, in a great measure, make the Cliffords their own biographers; and shall extract the materials of their history from the celebrated family portrait in Skipton Castle,* the long inscription on which was drawn up by Lady Anne Clifford, Countess of Pembroke, assisted, according to tradition, by the celebrated Sir Matthew Hale.

DIAGRAM EXPLANATORY OF THE DESCRIPTION OF THE CLIFFORD PICTURE.

This picture is 8 feet 4 inches high, exclusive of the frame: each end is of the breadth of 3 feet 10 inches. A frame goes round the middle part entirely, and likewise round each end, of the breadth of 5 inches, [and the two smaller pictures are hinged so as to fold over the centre picture as a triptych]. This frame is adorned with flower-de-luces, harps, roses, and crowned roses. The middle part contains the picture of George Earl of Cumberland, who stands on your right as you look at the picture; on his right hand is the countess his lady, holding in her left hand the Psalms of David; on her right hand stands her eldest son, Francis; and on his right her other son, Robert.

[* It seems that the picture formerly in Skipton Castle, and now at Hothfield, was only a copy, and that the original, which is now in perfect preservation, has always been at Appleby Castle, where is also preserved what is most probably, from its appearance, the original manuscript from which the inscriptions were copied. It is thus headed:—"These inscriptions are thus written in the Greate Picture at Appleby Castle made for the Right Honourable George Clifford, Third Earle of Cumberland and the Lady Margaret his wife, Countess of Cumberland, and their children, with his two sisters, and her two sisters, and the descent of the said Earl, both by the Cliffords, Vipounts, and their wives." On the 9th June, 1684, Ralph Thoresby relates in his diary that he "rid to Skipton, where for six hours he was hard at work transcribing the pedigrees of the ancient and noble family of the Cliffords, Earls of Cumberland, with others they married into, from the inscriptions upon the folding pictures in the castle."—Thoresby's "Diary," ii. 433.]

[* The earl is dressed in full armour of blue steel, studded with large gilt stars with eight points; and over it a brown tunic with short sleeves. He wears a blue sash with the George suspended from it, and the Garter is buckled round his left leg. His sword is suspended by a gold-lace belt. Upon his head is a broad-brimmed, low-crowned hat. His helmet and gauntlets are upon a table near him.

The countess is dressed in a rich brown brocaded gown, the edges studded with jewelled buttons: it is open in front, exposing a white satin brocaded petticoat. The sleeves of the gown are loose and open, showing a light white brocaded sleeve beneath. Around her neck is a lace ruff. Her hair is short and dark, with a peak on the forehead. She wears a pearl necklace, and round her shoulders is a long chain of pearls, looped up. Her right hand, upon the thumb of which is a ring, points to her two sons.

The child Francis stands with his left hand resting upon an antique-shaped inscribed shield, marked F in the diagram. His right arm is akimbo. He wears a blue frock, brocaded with gold and having tight yellow sleeves trimmed at the cuffs with linen, embroidered with black ants and edged with lace. His collar is similar to his cuffs. He wears a gold chain, from which hangs a jewel and a large pearl. His hair is short, and he has a girdle, with a loose ring, through which is passed and hangs a pocket-handkerchief fringed with lace.

The other child is similarly dressed. His left arm rests upon his brother's shoulder, and his right hand holds his cap, which has a plume of white ostrich-feathers.

On the right side of the countess's head are three books on a shelf, marked, " A written hand book of Alkimee, Extractions of Distillations, and excellent Medicines. All Senekae's Workes, translated out of Latine into English. The Holy Bible; the Old and New Testament." A little on the left of the earl's head is his coat of arms with full quarterings [marked G], encircled with the Garter, and surmounted with an earl's coronet, above which is the following inscription † [on the tablet marked A] :—

"This is the picture of GEORGE CLIFFORD third earle of Cumb'land ; ‡ in the male line of his family the 14th Baron Clifford of Westmerland, and Shereiff of that Countye by inheritance ; and in the same descent the 13th Lord of the Honor of Skipton, in Craven, and also Lord Vipont and Baron Vescy. He was borne sonne and heire apparant to Henry Earl of Cumberland, by his second wife Anne daughter to Will'm Lord Dacres of the North ; he was borne in his Father's Castle of Bromeham, in Westmorland, the 8th of August, in Anno Domini of our Lord and Saviour Christ Jesus 1558. At the age of eleven years and five months, lieing then in the house called Battell Abbey, in Sussex, he cam to be earl of Cumb'land, by the decease of his father, who died in the said castle of Bromeham, about the 8th or 10th of January, 1570,

[* As the description of the picture given by Dr. Whitaker is exceedingly meagre, a complete account, with copies of all the inscriptions and shields of arms, is here substituted.]

[† All the inscriptions are written very neatly, and though exceedingly small are quite legible.]

[‡ Lodge, Norroy King of Arms, in his " Portraits of Illustrious Personages," gives one of George Clifford, copied from the picture in the Bodleian Library at Oxford, and in a memoir he states that he was educated in the University of Cambridge, " where he studied in Peterhouse, under the care of Whitgift, afterwards Archbishop of Canterbury—or rather, devoted his attention so earnestly to the mathematics as to abstract it wholly from all other studies. Thus it happened that the ardent spirit of adventure and the boundless activity which afterwards distinguished him took first a nautical turn, acquired an increased force by assuming a peculiar direction, and enhanced the charm of curiosity by adding to it the interest of science."

He was in great favour with Queen Elizabeth, and was one of the peers who sat in judgment on Mary Queen of Scots, and was created a Knight of the Garter in 1592. When, on account of age, Sir Henry Lea, K.G., resigned, the queen appointed him to be her own peculiar champion at all tournaments Sir William Segar has preserved, in his treatise of "Honour, Military and Civil," an account of the pomp and parade of his admission into that romantic office.

At an audience with Queen Elizabeth after one of his voyages, she dropped one of her gloves, which he took up and presented to her on his knees. She desired him to keep it for her sake, and he adorned it richly with diamonds, and wore it ever after in front of his hat at public ceremonies. This little characteristic circumstance is commemorated in a very scarce whole-length portrait of the earl engraved by Robert White.]

as the yeare begins on New-year's day.* When he was almost 19 yeares old he was maried in ye church of St. Mary Overs, in Southwark, June 24, 1577, to his virtuous and onely wife the lady Marg't Russell, 3rd daughter and youngest child to Francys 2nd earle of Bedford, by his first wife Margarett St. John, by whom he had two sonnes and one daughter, Francys and Robert, who being successively Lords Clifford, died yong, in their Father's life tyme ; and the lady Ann Clifford, who was just fifteen years and nine months at her Father's death, being then his sole dau'r and heire. Hee performed nine viages by sea in his own person, most of them to the West Indies, with great honour to himself, and servis to his Quene and country, having gained the strong town of Fiall, in the Zorrous Islands,† in the yeare 1589, and in his last viage the strong forte of Portereco in the year 1598.‡ He was made K't of the Garter by Quene Eliz. and Councellor of State by King James. He died in the Dutchy House, in the Savoy, London, the 30th of October, 1605, being then of the

[* In England, in the seventh and so late as the thirteenth century, the year was reckoned from Christmas Day ; but in the twelfth century, the Anglican Church began the year on the 25th of March, which practice was also adopted by civilians in the fourteenth century. This style continued until the reformation of the calendar by stat. 24 Geo. II. c. 23, by which the legal year was ordered to commence on the 1st of January in 1752. It appears, therefore, that two calculations have generally existed in England for the commencement of the year, viz. :—

1. The historical year, which has, for a very long period, begun on the 1st of January.

2. The civil, ecclesiastical, and legal year, which was used by the Church and in all public instruments until the end of the thirteenth century, began at Christmas. In and after the fourteenth century it commenced on the 25th of March, and so continued until the 1st of January, 1752.

The confusion which arose from there being two modes of computing dates in one kingdom must be sufficiently apparent ; for the legislature, the Church, and civilians referred every event which happened between the 1st of January and the 25th of March to a different year from historians.

Remarkable examples of the confusion produced by this practice are afforded by two of the most celebrated events in English history. King Charles I. is said by most authorities to have been beheaded on the 30th of January, 1648 ; while others, with equal correctness, assign that event on the 30th of January, 1649. The revolution which drove James II. from the throne is stated by some writers to have taken place in February, 1688 ; whilst, according to others, it happened in February, 1689. These discrepancies arise from some historical years, though both would have assigned any circumstance after the 25th of March to the same years—namely, 1649 and 1689.

To avoid as far as possible the mistakes which this custom produced, it was usual to add the date of the historical to that of the legal year, when speaking of any day between the 1st of January and the 25th of March ; thus :—

January 30, 164$\begin{cases}8 \\ 9\end{cases}$ *i.e.,* the civil and legal year, *i.e.,* the historical year.

Or thus :—   January 30, 1648-9.]

† The Azores.

[‡ His first voyage was made in 1586, with three ships and a pinnace—the *Red Dragon*, 260 tons, 130 men, commanded by Capt. Robert Weddington ; the bark *Clifford*, 130 tons, 70 men, Capt. Christopher Lister ; the *Roe*, Captain Hawes ; and the pinnace *Dorothy*, which had formerly belonged to Sir Walter Raleigh (and, Lodge states, was on this occasion commanded by him). They sailed to America to Rio del Plata, took a few prizes, and returned to Plymouth in August in the same year.

In 1588 he commanded a ship called the *Elizabeth Bonaventure* in the fleet which destroyed the Spanish Armada, and distinguished himself equally by his bravery and his skill in the various engagements by which that great work was accomplished, particularly in the last action, which was fought off Calais.—Lodge.

Queen Elizabeth, on the 4th of October, 1588, flattered the earl by giving him a royal commission to go to the South Seas, and lent to him the *Golden Lion*, one of her royal fleet. He victualled and furnished it at his own charge, and took with him a considerable number of English gentlemen, but the voyage was a failure : he was baffled by contrary winds and storms, did not reach the South Seas, and only took one prize— a Spaniard.

In 1589 the earl obtained permission from the queen to make a third attempt, and she again lent him a ship belonging to the Royal Navy— this time the *Victory*, commanded, under his lordship, by Capt. Lister, which ship, with two small ships, the *Megg*, the *Margaret*, and a carvel, composed the fleets. He sailed from Plymouth on the 18th of June, and reached the Azores. He took the town of Fyal, and stripped it of fifty-eight pieces of iron ordnance, and in the course of this cruize sent home twenty-eight ships of various burthen, worth more than £20,000. In a desperate engagement between the *Victory* and a Brazil ship he received several wounds, and was severely scorched. A rich West Indian prize of which Capt. Lister was in charge was wrecked upon the coast of Cornwall, and nearly all the crew drowned. The sufferings of the earl and his men from want of provisions, especially water, during his return voyage are perhaps unparalleled. Edward Wright, a famous mathematician, who sailed with the earl, wrote a narrative of the voyage, and states that the men who died of thirst exceeded in number those who had perished otherwise during the voyage. On the 2nd of December the survivors landed in Bantry Bay.

Not discouraged by his past failures, the earl in 1591 fitted out another fleet consisting of five ships—the *Garland*, one of the Royal Navy, 600 tons burthen ; the *Golden Noble*, the *Allegarta*, the *Sampson*, a ship of the earl's, and a pinnace called the *Discovery*. This voyage, which was to the Mediterranean, was very unfortunate, and soon completed. Two rich Spanish ships were taken, but were soon afterwards retaken, and some of the English made prisoners.

In 1592 a fifth expedition was determined upon, but this time no ship from the Royal Navy was taken. The earl hired from the merchants a vessel of 600 tons called the *Tiger*, which, with the *Sampson* and the *Golden Noble*, together with two small vessels, completed the fleet. The ships were detained for nearly three months by contrary winds, and the earl did not sail, but transferred the chief command to Capt. Norton, with instructions to sail for the Azores. He fell in with three large ships, one Spanish and the others Portuguese, which he took with the assistance of other vessels. When the prize-money was settled, the earl's share, under the pretext of his personal absence, was declared to be only £36,000 ; but as he was at the sole cost of fitting out his fleet, he probably did not gain much.

In his sixth voyage, in which the earl commanded in person, the vessels were the *Golden Lion*, the *Bonadventure*, from the Royal Navy, the *Anthony*, of 120 tons, the *Pilgrim*, 100 tons, the *Chaldon*, and the *Discovery :* they sailed in 1593. After having taken two valuable French ships, the earl was seized with a severe illness, and was obliged to return to England. The *Anthony, Pilgrim,* and *Discovery*, under the command of William Monson (afterwards a celebrated admiral), proceeded to the West Indies. They reached the island of St. Lucia, seized pearls to the value of £2,000 at Marguerite, and obtained 2,000 ducats ransom for the town which they took. They afterwards fought and took seven Spanish ships, and reached England in safety on the 15th of May, 1594.

In 1594, before the return of the last expedition, the earl had sailed with a seventh fleet, consisting of the *Royal Exchange*, 250 tons, Capt. George Cave ; the *Mayflower*, Capt. Wm. Anthony ; the *Sampson*, Capt. Nicholas Deinton ; a carvel, and a pinnace. They fell in with two of the best carracks of the King of Spain—one of 2,000 and the other of 1,500 tons burthen. After a serious engagement, in which Capt. Anthony was killed and Capt. Cave mortally wounded, and several men lost, the Spaniards were beaten ; but they set their ships on fire to prevent the English getting the treasure, consisting of pearls, jewels, silks, &c., and the crews (about 1,100 men) perished, only two men being saved. The

age of 47 yeares and 3 months wanting 9 days. His bowells and inner partes was buryed in the sayd Chappell of the Savoy, and his bodey was honorably buried among his ancesters in the Vault of Skipton church, in Craven, in Yorkshire, the 13th of March following. By his death the title of Earl of Cumberland cam to his only Brother S'r Francis Clifford. But the ancient right to his Baronies, Honors, and Ancient lands, descended then to his onely daughter and heire the lady Ann Clifford, for whos right to them hir worthy mother had, after, great Suits at Law with his brother Francys Earle of Cumberland. This Earle George was a man of many natural perfections, of a great wit and judgment, of a strong body,* and full of agility, of a noble mind, and not subject to pride or arrogancy, a man generally beloved in this kingdome. He died of the Blody Flix, caused, as was supposed, by the many wounds and distempers he receyved formerly in his sea viages. He died penitently, willingly, and christanly, the 30 of October 1605. Job the 7th vers the 1st ; Eccl cap. 8 vers 6. His onely daughter and heire, the Lady Ann Clifford, and the Countess hir mother, weare both present with him at his death.

"This is the picture of the LADY MARGERET RUSSELL, Countess of Cumb'land, 3d daughter and youngest child to Francis Russell, second earle of Bedford, by his first wife Margrett, daught. to Sir John St. John, of Bletnesho. Shee was borne in the Earle hir father's house, in the Citty of Exeter, in Devonshire, formerly a priory, about the 7th of July, in the yeere of our Lord and Saviour Christ Jesus, 1560 ; hir moother dyeng 2 yeares after of the small-pox, in Whoborn-house, in Bedfordshire, which was once an Abbey. Shee was maried, about the age of 17 yeares, to Georg Clifford Earle of Cumberland, in St. Mary Overs Church, London, by whom she had 2 sonnes, Francys and Robert, successively Lords Clifford, who died both yong, before they were 6 yeares old, and one onely daughter, the Lady Ann Clifford, who was afterwards sole heire to both hir parents. This Countess and hir husband were Cozen Jermans twice removed by the blood of the St. Johns ; For his great-grandmoother Anne St. John, wife to Henry Lord Clifford, was great aunt to hir moother Margaret St. John, they being both of the house of Bletneshoe. In the year of our Lord God 1593, all hir husband's lands in Westmorland was made to hir in Joincture, by Act of Parliam't. Shee lived his wife 28 yeares and upwards, and his widow 10 yeares and 7 months, in which tyme of hir widowhood, espetially in the 3d and 4th yeares thereof, shee had great Suits at Law with her Brother-in-law Francis, then Earle of Cumberland, for the right of her onely daughter's inheritance. In which business she was much opposed by the King and the great ones of this kingdome, yet by industry and search of records of this kingdome she brought to light the then unknown Title which hir daughter had to the Ancient Baronies, Honors, and Landes, of the Viponts, Cliffords, and Vescyes. (Ro. 1, cap. 4, vers. 22. The last words thereof, Esay 38 cap. vers. 16.) Soe as what good shall accrew to hir daughter's posteritie, by the sayd Inheritance, must, next under God, be attributed unto hir. (Prov. 31, vers. 28–29.) Shee was of a greate naturall witt and judgment, of a swete disposition, truly religious and virtuous, and indowed with a large share of those 4 morall virtues, Prudence, Justice, Fortitude, and Temperance. The death of hir two sonnes did so much afflict hir as that ever after the booke of Jobe was her dayly companion. Shee died in her castle of Bromeham, in Westmorland, in hir widowhood, 24th of May, 1616, in ye Chamber wherein hir husband was borne into this world, when she was 56 yeares old, wanting 6 weekes, and that very day 25 yeares after the death of hir sonne Robert Lord Clifford. Shee outlived all hir brothers and sisters. Hir bowels and inward partes was buryed in the Church called Nine Kirks, hard by wheare she died, and hir body was buryed in Apleby church in Westmarland,† the 11th of July following. (Rev. chap. 14, vers. 13.) And when this worthy Countess Dowager of Cumberland died, hir only dau'r Anne Clifford Countess of Dorsett did then lie in Knowle House, in Kent. But when hir said Moother was buryed was she present at hir buriall in Apleby church in Westmerland. For then she lay in Bromeham castle, in that County. But that Countess of Cumb'land's only Grandchild, the Lady Marg't Sackvile, then did lie in Horsley House, in Surrey, both when her grandmother ye countess of Cumb'land died, and when she was buried."

---

fleet returned to England in August, 1594. The eighth, ninth, and tenth voyages were made in 1595 and 1596, but were unsuccessful. He built a ship of 900 tons at Deptford, called the *Scourge of Malice.*

The eleventh and last voyage, commenced in March, 1596, was by far the most important. The fleet consisted of twenty sail, several of which were his lordship's own ships ; the earl commanded in person, and his lieutenant-general was Sir John Berkeley. At the Canary Islands, about 600 men under Sir John Berkeley were landed upon Lancerota, but not finding anything of value, sailed for Dominica, afterwards for the Virgin Islands, and then for Porto Rico, which they took ; but the earl nearly lost his life, for having slipped off the causeway leading to the fort into the sea, and being encumbered by the weight of his armour, was very nearly drowned. It was the intention of the earl to keep the island and city of Porto Rico in his hands, but a violent flux attacked his men, and out of about 1,000 first landed, about 500 died, and there were not enough left to both hold the island and navigate the fleet home : it was therefore determined to force a ransom from the Spaniards and to return to England, which they did.

The above sketch of the voyages of the Earl of Cumberland is chiefly compiled from the collection of "Voyages and Travels," by John Harris, published in 1705, vol. i. pp. 686—693. The writer concludes with a description of the character of the earl, in which he says that "he was a man of admirable abilities, both in civil and military affairs. He knew how to fight, and as well how to govern, and had virtues capable of rendering him illustrious both in war and peace. He was so excellent a person that it can hardly be said what was wanting *in* him ; but still there was a very considerable thing wanting *to* him—namely, a great gale of good fortune. . . . . He did not come off in his enterprises so well rewarded as he deserved to be. Considering the vast expenses he was at in building, hiring, and furnishing of ships, perhaps his voyages did not increase his estate."]

* This is proved by his weighty suit of tilting-armour, now at Appleby Castle, of which the helmet alone is almost insupportable to modern shoulders. But he must have been of a stature well adapted to bearing great weights, for the whole suit measures only five feet nine inches from the cone of the helmet to the ground. The perpendicular pressure, however, may have occasioned some contraction in the leathern ligaments of the joints. [This suit of armour does not appear to have belonged to the earl ; it is beautifully embossed, but is marked with the cypher ₱P.]

[† Her monument in the south side of the chancel of Appleby Church consists of an altar-tomb, upon which is a marble recumbent effigy of the countess, of life-size, beautifully executed and quite perfect. She is represented clad in a bodice fastened down the front with small buttons, a

Under the picture marked B* upon the diagram, and which measures within the frame 8¾ in. by 7⅛ in.—

"This is the Picture of LADY FRANCES CLIFFORD wife to Phillip Baron Wharton of Wharton Hall in Westmerland to whom she was maryed in St. Mary Overs Church in Southwark at the sam place and day where her brother Georg. Earle of Cumberland was maried to yᵉ Lady Margarett Russell. Shee was borne Ano. Dm. 1556, in hir Father's Henry Clifford E. of Cumberland, his Castle of Skipton in Craven, she being his first child by his 2nd wife, Ann, daughter to Wm., Lord Dacres of the North; she had by this Lord Wharton 2 sonnes and 3 daughters, viz.:—Georg. eldest sonn (a gallant man), who was borne in Bromeham Castele, slayne in a private cumbate at Islington nere London, 1609. Sir Thomas Wharton, 2nd sonne, a grand scholler, who died 2 yeers before his father, leaving issu by his wife, the Lady Phelodelpha Cary, daughter to yᵉ E. of Monmouth, 2 sonns Phillipp, now Lord Wharton, and his brother Sir Thomas Wharton—both of great hope but hir eldest and deerest childe Margarett Wharton, borne in Skipton Castle, is now widdow to the Lo. Wootton, a woeman of great goodnes and worth. This Lady Wharton was a woeman of great witt, and much esteemed for virtue, she died in hir husband's house, at Wharton Hall, in Westmorland, being about 36 yeares old, the 16th day of Aprill 1592, and was buryed in Kirkbysteven Church in that Countie. And that day 30 yeers after in Aske in Richmondshire, died hir then onely sonne, Sir Thomas Wharton 2 years before his Father."

Upon the picture is a shield of arms: Sa. a maunch arg. within a bordure or, charged with eight pairs of lions, gambs in saltire gu. *Wharton.* Impaling *Clifford* quartering *Vipont.*

Under the portrait of Anne Countess of Warwick, marked C on the diagram, and measuring 8⅞ inches by 7¼ inches, is this writing—

"This is the Picture of LADY ANN RUSSELL Countes of Warwick 2 child and eldest daughter to Francys Russell 2 E. of Bedford, by his first wife, born in hir Fathers house of Cheynis in Buckinghamshire about the latter end of December Anno Dm. 1548. Maried in the Q. Chappell at Whitehall (hir Matie. being present) to Ambrose Dudley, E. of Warwick the XIᵗʰ of Nov. 1556, which E. died at Bedford House in the Strand 22nd of Feb. 1590. And 14 yeares after shee died his widow in her owne house at Northall in Hartfordshire the 9th of February 1604 having never had child. She was buryed at Cheynis in Buckinghamshire, wher she Founded an Almehouse: she served Q. Eliz. most part of hir life, was deeply beloved and favoured by hir, whom she outlived not a full yeere. She was a most virtuous and religious lady, and yet an Excellent Courtier; shee was a moother in affection to hir younger brothers and sisters, and to theire children, espesially to the Lady Ann Clifford. This Ann Countess of Warwick, and hir twoe yonger sisters, Elizabeth Countess of Bath, and Margarett Countes of Cumbirland, whose Pictures are all 3 heere, was the 3 sisters of the greatest for honor and goodness of any 3 sisters that lived in theire tyme in this Kingdom."

gown, a cloak or mantle drawn over the head, and confined by a coronet (which is of brass); round her neck is a plaited ruff. At her feet is a lamb, sculptured out of a separate piece of marble.

On the south side of the altar-tomb is this inscription—

HERE LYETH INTERRED THE BODY OF THE LADY MARGARET
COVNTESS DOWAGER OF CVMBERLAND YOVNGESTE CHILDE TO FRAN
CIS RVSSELL SECONDE EARL OF BEDFORD, MARRYED TO GEORGE
CLIFFORD THIRD EARL OF CVMBERLAND, SHE LYVED HIS WIFE XXIX
YEARES, AND DYED HIS WYDOWE AT BROVGHAM CASTLE THE XXIIIITᴴ OF
MAY MDCXVI TENN YEARES AND SEAVEN MONTHS AFTER HIS DECEA
SE. SHE HAD ISSVE BY HIM TWO SONS, FRANCIS AND ROBERT WHO
BOTH DIED YOVNGE, AND ONE DAVGHTER THE LADY ANN CLIFFORD
MARRIED TO RICHARD SACKVILLE THIRD EARL OF DORSETT
WHOE IN MEMORY OF HER RELIGIOVS MOTHER ERECTED THIS MONVMENT Aᴼ Dꝫ
              MDCXVII.

On the north side—

WHO FAYTH, LOVE, MERCY NOBLE CONSTANCIE
TO GOD, TO VIRTVE, TO DISTRESS TO RIGHT
OBSERV'D EXPRES'T SHEW'D, HELD RELIGIOVSLY
HATH HERE THE MONVMENT THOV SEEST IN SIGHT.
THE COVER OF HER EARTHLY PART, BUT PASSENGER,
KNOW HEAVEN AND FAME CONTAYNES THE BEST OF HER.

On the west end is a shield of *Clifford* and quarterings impaling *Russell* and quarterings, nine coats in each three; three and three. First, *Clifford.* 1 and 9, *Clifford.* 2, *Augmentation coat.* 3, *Bromflete.* 4, *Vescy.* 5, *Flint* (*the charges three flint-stones*). 6, *Vipont.* 7, *Atton.* 8, *St. John.* The impalement—1 and 9, *Russell.* 2, *De la Tour.* 3, *Mustyan.* 4, *Froxmore.* 6, *Wyse.* 7, *Sapcote.* 8, Arg. on a cross gu. five mullets or. The shield is surmounted by an earl's coronet, and has for supporters—dexter, a red wyvern; and sinister, a red lion.

At the east end—Upon a lozenge, quarterly of eight, *Russell* and quarterings as above, except that the arms of *Russell* only occur once.]

[* This and the other small portraits are represented hanging upon the wall in gilt frames.]

On this little picture is a shield of arms : Arg. a lion ramp. gu. *Dudley* impaling
Russell.

Under this picture, marked c, and lying upon a shelf, are three books, lettered "The
Holy Bible, the Old and New Testament," "All Senekaes Works translated out of
Latine into English," "A written hand booke of Alkumiste Extraction of Distillations
and excellent Medecines."

The inscription under the portrait of Elizabeth Countess of Bath, marked d on the
diagram, and measuring 8⅝ inches by 7¼ inches, is—

"This is the Picture of the LADY ELIZABETH RUSSELL, Countess of Bath 6 child and 2 daughter to Franciz Russell,
E. of Bedford, by his first wife. She was borne in hir Father's House at Moer-Parke, in Hartfordshire, September,
Ano. Dm. 1558. She was maried to Willim Bourchier, E. of Bath, in Sᵗ. Maryes Church at Exeter 7° Aug. 1583, by
whom she had one daughter, hir first child, and 3 sonnes, wch first child was the Lady Francys Bourchier, one of excellent
witt and goodnes. She died a mayd at Sutton in Kent and was buried at Cheneys in Co. Buck., the two eldest sonns
died infants, but the 3ᵈ sonn Edw. lived to be E. of Bath, who was born Ano. 1590, died the 2ᵈ of March 1637, leaving
behind him only 3 daughters his sole heires, viz. the ladys Eliz. Dorothy . and Anne, all 3 Honorably maried. This
Countess died yᵉ 24 or 25 of March 1605, some 18 yeers 3 monethes before hir husband, who also died July the 12, 1623,
and was buried by hir in the church there at Tavestock, and all their sonns also, she was a virtuous and good woman and
lived for the most pte a country life, all hir children being borne in Tavestock Hous. She was 46 yeers and 7 months old
when she died."

On this little picture is a shield of arms: *Bourchier* impaling *Russell.*

Under the small portrait, marked E on the diagram, and measuring 9¾ inches by 8¼
inches, is the following inscription—

"This is the Picture of the LADY MARGARETT CLIFFORD, Countess of Darby, eldest child to Henry Clifford 2 Earle
of Cumberland and by his first wife Elianor Brandon yongest daughter to Charles Brandon, Duk. of Suffolke, by Mary
the French Queene, which Lady Margrett was the only child of hir mother that lived any tyme, for hir twoe brothers by
hir mother died infants. Shee was borne in hir father's Castle at Bromeham, in Westmurland, Ano. Dm. 1540; hir
mother dieing there about seaven yeares after, in November 1547, but was buryed at Skipton in Craven, which high-born
Lady Elianor was grandchild to K. H. 7th, and his wife Elizabeth, and neece to K. H. 8 and Cozen-Jerman to K. E. 6,
Q. Elizabeth and to James the 5th K. of Scotland, she being Cozen-Jerman twice removed to yᵉ E. of Cumberland, hir
husband by the blood of yᵉ St. Johns. The Lady Margaret Clifford was the Lady Elian. Grace hir onely childe, was
maryed in the King's Chappell at Whithall, the K. and Q. being present, to Henry Stanley, Lo. Strang, afterwards E. of
Derby, the 7th of February 1555: and lived his wife 38 yeers and his widow about 3 yeeres, and had by him twoe sonnes
Fardinando and William successively Earles of Darby, which Wm. was father to James now E. of Darby. This great
Countess deceased in hir house at Clarkenwell London, when she was about 56 yeres old the 29ᵗʰ of September 1596:
and was buryed presently after in the Abbey Church at Westminster, in St. Edmund's Chappell there. Shee was a virtuous
and noble kind-harted lady, and full of goodness a deere lover of hir brother by the halfe-blood George, Earle of
Cumberland, and his worthy wife and theire children."

Upon the picture are two shields of arms, each within the Garter—

1. Barry of ten arg. and gu., over all a lion ramp. or; quartering, counterquarterly 1 and
4 az. a cross moline or, 2 and 3 lozengy erm. and gu.; and impaling *France* and *England*
quarterly.

2. Arg. on a bend az. three stags' heads cabossed or, *Stanley.* Impaling *Clifford,*
quartering *Vipont.*

The eldest son holds in his left hand a scroll [or rather an antique-shaped shield,
divided into four spaces, marked F on the diagram] containing the following inscription :—

"Theese are the pictures of the two eldest children of Georg Clifford Earle of Cumberland, which he had by his
worthy wife the Lady Margarett Russell Countess of Cumberland.
"Theire first-borne child was Francis lord Clifford whom his Moother was delivered of in his Father's Castle at
Skipton, in Craven, in Yorkshire, on Friday yᵉ 10th of Aprill, Anno D'ni 1584. His Father being then theare; which

Francys Lord Clifford, after he had lived five years and eight months, died in the same Castle theare, the 10th or 11th day of December, 1589, and was presantly after buryed in the vaut of Skipton Church, amongst many of his Father's Ancestors, the Cliffords and others. When this yong Lord Francys Clifford and his Brother Rob't lay in Channell-row, by Westminster, with theare Father and Moother, the Spring before this yong Lord's death, 1589, he was admired by those who knew him for his goodnes and devotion, even to wonder, considering his childish yeares. His Brother Robert and the Countess theire Moother was in Skipton Castle at his death, wheare the sayd Countess was great with childe with her onely daughter, whom she was delivered of, in that Skipton Castle, the 30th day of January following: shee that was the Lady Ann Clifford, and cam after to be the onely childe to hir parents. When this Lord Francys died, his said Father was then beyond the seas, in Munster, in Ireland, wheather he was driven on land by extremity of tempest, and great hazard of life, ten dayes before the death of his said sonne, when that Earle was then in his returne from the Ile Azores, in the West Indies."

"Theire second-borne Childe was Mr. ROBERT CLIFFORD, whom his mother was delivered of on a Wednesday, the 21st of September, Anno D'ni 1585, in Northall Hous, in Hartfordshire, wheare she and hir husband Georg E. of Cumb'land then laye. Which Mr. Robert Clifford, by the death of his elder brother Lord Francys, cam to be Lord Clifford, the 10th or 11th of December, 1589. And as theare was neere a yeare and six months between their births, so was theare neere a yeare and six months between their deaths; and they both dyed when they cam to the age of five yeares and eight months old, and in the same severall houses wherein they were both borne; for this Robert Lord Clifford died in Northall House, in Hartfordshire, on a Whitson Monday, the 24th of May, 1591. After his death, he being opened, his bowells and inward p'ts was buryed in the church at Northall, in Hartfordshire; but his dead body was buryed in the Vaut of Chenys Church, in Buckinghamshire, with his Moother's Ancestors, the Russells Earles of Bedford, and others. He was a childe endowed with many perfections of nature for so few yeares, and likely to have made a gallant man. His sorrowfull Moother, and hir then little daughter and onely childe, the Lady Ann, was in the house at Northall when he died: which Lady Ann Clifford was then but a yeare and four monethes old, whoe, by the death of hir sayd brother Lo. Ro. Clifford, cam to be ye sole heire to both hir Parents. And when this yong Lord Rob't died, his Father Georg E. of Cumb'land was in one of his viages on the seas toward Spaine and the West Indies."

"These 8 Pictures conteyned in this frame are copies drawne out of the Originall Pictures of theese Hon'ble Personages, made by them about the begening of June, 1589, and were thus finished by the appointment of Ann Clifford, Countess of Pembrooke, in memoriall of them, in Anno D'ni 1646. When theese originalls were drawne, did Georg Clifford E. of Cumb'land, with his worthy Wife and theire two sonnes, lie in the Lord Phillip Wharton's house, in Channell Rowe, in Westminster, wheare the said worthy Countess conceyved with childe, the 1st of May, Anno D'ni 1589, with hir onely daughter the Lady Ann Clifford, who was borne the 30th of January following, in Skipton Castle, in Craven, in Yorkshire; shee afterwardes being the onely child of hir Parents, and is now Countess of Pembrooke. (Psa. 139.)"

[The pedigree and shields which form the borders upon either side of the centre picture have to be read commencing at the bottom corner of the left side, and are thus :—

RICHARD FITZ PUNT, a Norman, cam into England with W^m. the Conqueror and seated himselfe in this Kingdom, being the Originall of the Family of all the Cliffords in England, for his sonne, sonn tooke upon him first the name of Clifford, by reason he was seized of the Castle in Herefordshire called Clifford Castle.
A blank shield.

WILLIAM FITZ PUNT, sonn of Richard, Father of Richard whoe first tooke upon him the surname of Clifford, but wee cannot find by Record the matches of this William or his Father or theire Coate Armour, they being obscured by the length of tyme.
A blank shield.

WALTER DE CLIFFORD, Sonn of W^m. Fitz Punt, Sonne of Richard Fitz Punt, whoe came into England wth William the Conqueror, was now called Walter de Clifford, Lord of Clifford Castle, in Herefordshire in Wales, which Castle and the lands about it cam to him with his wife Margaret de Tony, by whom he had divers children, as appears by the Booke of Records. Amongst them theare was most remarkeable Walter theire eldest sonne, who succeeded him in his Lands and Honors. Richard, theire second sonne, whoe was called in the Records Lord of Frampton in Glostershire, from whom succeeded lineally all the heirs males of the Cliffords of Frampton ever since. And Mr. Anthony Clifford, now of Frampton, is the direct heire male of that lyne. Also the fayre Rosamund Clifford was daughter to this Walter, first Lo. Clifford and his wife, as appeares by many recordes : shee was unfortunate by being beloved of King Henry the 2, by whome she had 2 or 3 base children.
This Walter Lord Clifford and his wife were Grandfather and Grandmother to that Roger de Clifford, called Roger the Elder, who was Father to Roger de Clifford the younger, whoe married Isabella Veteripount. This Walter de Clifford dyed ——.
Shield of arms : Chequy or and az., over all a bendlet gu. Impaling arg. a maunch gu.

WALTER LORD CLIFFORD, Sonne of Walter Lord Clifford and brother to Rosamund Clifford, maried Agnes daughter to Roger de Condy, by whom he had Walter Lord Clifford, Roger Clifford, Symon, Gyles, and divers daughters. His eldest sonne Walter was the last heire male of the Cliffords, that were Lords Marchers of Wales. And Roger de Clifford his second sonne was after called Roger de Clifford the Elder, Father of that Roger de Clifford the Younger who maried Isabella de Vipount, whose inheritance in Westmerland first brought the Cliffords into the North. He dyed the —— day of ——.
Shield of arms : Chequy or and az., over all a bendlet gu. Impaling arg. a fess between three martlets gu.

2 S

WALTER DE CLIFFORD, third and last heire male of the Cliffords of Clifford Castle in Wales, whoe maryed Margarett de Brews Lady of Cantrescliff, by whome he had but one onely Child that lived to any age, whoe was Maud de Clifford who was maried to Wm. Longspee third Earle of Salsbury and last heire male of the Longspees that weare Earles of Salsbury, soe as she and hir husband weare neere akin, for she was cosin German once removed to his Father. And from that mariage did proceed Margaret Longspee whoe maried Henry Lacy, Earle of Lincoln, by whom she had one onely daughter Alice, whoe maried to Thomas Plantaginet E. of Lancaster, and they both dyed without issue. Soe the generation of this Mawd de Clifford ended by hir first husband in her Grandchild Alice Countes of Lancaster; but from the daughter shee had by hir second husband John Clifford did descend the Talbotts Earles of Shrewsbury, and many other noble Familyes. This Walter third Lord Clifford died the —— yeare of H. 3. This Walter his yonger brother was called Roger de Clifford the Elder, in regard for his sonn was called Roger de Clifford the yonger, which Roger de Clifford the younger maried Isabella de Veteripont.

Shield of arms : Chequy or and az., a bendlet gu. Impaling az. semy of crosses crosslet a lion ramp. or.

This ROGER DE CLIFFORD, though a yonger sonne to Walter de Clifford, second Lord Clifford, and Agnes Cundy his wife, yet in Records is he called Roger de Clifford the elder, because his sonne was called Roger de Clifford the yonger, for distinchon sake. This Roger de Clifford the elder was nephew to Rosamund Clifford, and the sayd Roger's elder brother was Walter third Lord Clifford of Clifford Castle, and the last heire male owner of that Castle in the Marches of Wales.

Shield of arms : Chequy or and az., over all a bendlet gu. Impaling arg. a fess gu. between three mullets sa. for Ewias.

On the small scroll marked J upon the diagram—

To this Roger de Clifford did his Father and Moother, Walter second Lo. Clifford, and Agnes Cundy his wife, to whom he was second sonne, give and gran. the Mannor of Temedbury lying pt. in Herefordshire and pt. in Worstershire, to him the sayd Roger, and Sibell de Ewias his first wife, and the heires of his body, which sayd Mannor was also confirmed to him by his Neece, Maud de Clifford, daughter and sole heire to his elder brother Walter de Clifford, which Mannor of Temedbury continued in the posterity of the sayd Roger and his first wife till Quene Elizabeths tyme, when Henry Clifford second Earle of Cumberland and lineall heire to this Roger sold it away.

This Roger called the Elder had two wives. His first wife was Sibell de Ewias daughter and heire of Robert Lord Ewias of Ewias Harold Castle in Herefordshire, and widow to Lord Robert Tregoss. His second wife was a Countess of Lorayne, by whom he noe children, but the eldest over-lived him some yeares. The sayd Roger Lord Clifford the Elder had by his first wife, Roger de Clifford called the yonger, whoe maried Isabella dᵃᵘʳ. and co-heire of Robert de Veteripont, Lord of Westmerland, which mariage brought first the Cliffords to be Lords and Shereifes of Westmerland, as may appeare by the Scrole on the other side of the Picture (marked H).

Then proceeding upwards again—

RICHARD PLANTAGINET sirnamed of Conesborough E. of Cambridg after the decease of his first wife Ann Mortimer, did marry for his wife Mawd de Clifford daughter to Thomas Lord Clifford of Westmerland, and sister to John Lord Clifford of Westmerland, but she died without issue. And he was beheaded about the 3 H. 5.

Shield of arms : France and England quarterly within a bordure arg. charged with lions gu. Impaling *Clifford* and *Vipont* quarterly. N.B.—The arms of Clifford now beare a *fess* gu. for the first time.

WILLIAM FITZWILLIAM E. of Southampton maried Mabell Clifford eldest daughter of Henry Lord Clifford of Westmerland by his first wife and sister to Henry first Earle of Cumberland, by whome he had 2 sonnes that died in the life tyme of theire Father and Moother, soe this Earle and Countess died about the latter end of H. 8 without issue.

Shield of arms : Lozengy arg. and gu. a mullet for diff. Impaling *Clifford* and *Vipont* quarterly.

HUGH LOWTHER of Lowther in Westmerland Esq., sonn and heire of Sir John Lowther Kt., married Ann Clifford yongest daughter and onely child by the second wife of Henry Lord Clifford of Westmerland, and sister to Henry Clifford first Earle of Cumberland, from whom is descended the now Sr. John Lowther of Lowther Kt. Baronet, being the 5th in descent from them both, wch. Hugh and Ann died about the latter end of H. 8.

Shield of arms : Or, six annulets sa. 3, 2, and 1. Impaling *Clifford* and *Vipont* quarterly.

SIR RICHARD CHOLMLEY of Whitby in Yorkshire, Knighted at the Battaile of Lieth in Scotland the 34 H. 8. maried the Lady Katherin Clifford eldest daughter to Henry Clifford first Earle of Cumberland and widow to John Lord Scroope of Bolton, by whome this Richard had divers children. Soe as the now Sr Hugh Cholmley and Sr. Henry Cholmely his brother are the —— in descent from them whoe died about the midle of Quene Elizabeths Raigne.

Shield of arms : Gu. a garb or in chief two helmets ppr. Impaling *Clifford* and *Vipont* quarterly.

HENRY CLIFFORD first E. of Cumberland did marry for his first wife Margrett one of the daughters of Gilbert Talbot E. of Shrewsbury, but she died within a little while after hir mariage without issue. But hir sister's daughter after was second wife to his eldest sonn, Moother to George Earle of Cumberland. This first E. Henry married Margarett Percy for his second wife and died the 34th yeare of H. 8.

Shield of arms : *Clifford* and *Vipont* quarterly. Impaling gu. a lion ramp. in a bordure engr. or.

HENRY CLIFFORD second E. of Cumberland did in the life tyme of his Father marry Elianor Brandon daughter to Charles Duke of Suffolk and Mary the French Quene, by whome he had but one daughter that lived, the Lady Margarett Clifford, whoe after was maryed to Henry E. of Darby. This Henry Earle of Cumberland married for his second wife Ann Dacres, by whom he had George Earle of Cumbland and other children.

Shield of arms, surmounted by an Earl's coronet : *Clifford* quartering *Vipont ;* and impaling barry of ten arg. and gu., over all a lion ramp. or for *Brandon*.

SR. FRANCIS CLIFFORD Kt. 4th E. of Cumberland, in the life tyme of his brother George E. of Cumberland, about the yeare 1589, did marry Mrs. Grizell Hewes daughter of Thomas Hewes of Uxbridg, and widow to Edward Nevill Lord Aburgavenny, by whom he had divers Children, whereof Henry Clifford, borne 1592, was 5 E. of Cumberland and the last Earle of that family. This Countes died the 16 of June 1613, and hir husband died 21st of January 1641.

Shield of arms, surmounted by an earl's coronet: Chequy or and az. a fess gu. Impaling per fess or and arg. a lion ramp. regard. sa. for *Hewes*.

HENRY CLIFFORD, Earle of Cumberland, in the life tyme of his Father did marry, the 25th of July, 1610, the Lady Francys Cecile, daughter to Robert E. of Salisbury, by whom he had divers Children, but none lived anye tyme, but theire onely daughter and heire Elizabeth Clifford wife to the E. of Cork. This Henry died the 11th of December, 1643, in York City, and his wife died there the 14th of February after.

Shield of arms, surmounted by an Earl's coronet: Chequy or and az. a fess gu. Impaling barry of ten arg. and az. on six escus sa. 3, 2, and 1, as many lions of the first for *Cecil*.

RICHARD BOYLE now Earle of Corck in the life tyme of his Father did marry the Lady Elizabeth Clifford, daughter and at length sole heire to Henry Clifford, Earle of Cumberland, by which Lady the sayd Earle of Corck hath now living 5 Children, 2 sonnes and 3 daughters.

Shield of arms : Per bend embattled arg. and gu. Impaling chequy or and az. a fess gu.

JOHN TUFTON now Earle of Thanett did in the life tyme of his Father, 21 April 1629, marry the Lady Margarett Sackvile, eldest daughter and coheire of Richard Sackvile Earle of Dorsett, by his wife the Lady Ann Clifford, which E. of Thanett hath 7 children by the sayd Lady Margarett his wife now liveing, 5 sonnes and 2 daughters.

Shield of arms: Sa. an eagle displ. erm. within a bordure arg. for *Tufton*. Impaling quarterly or and gu. over all a bend vair, for *Sackville*.

JAMES COMPTON now E. of Northampton did the 5 of July, 1647, marry the Lady Isabella Sackvile, second daughter and coheire to Richard E. of Dorsett by his wife the Lady Ann Clifford.

Shield of arms : Sa. a lion pass. arg. between 3 helmets for *Compton*. Impaling *Sackville*.

This is the uppermost shield on the left side of the picture.

The right-hand border, beginning at the bottom, contains the following inscriptions and arms :—

ROBERT DE VETERIPOUNT the first Lord and Baron of Westmerland, to whom King John, the 4th of October in the 5th yeare of his raigne, gave his lands in the sayd County, with the Shreifwick to him, and his then espoused wife, Idonea de Buly, and theire heires, in whose lynes it hath continued ever since. He died the 16th of Henry the third, and she died the 19th of Henry the third.

Shield of arms : *Vipont* impaling gu. a five-foil or.

JOHN DE VETERIPONT second Lord and Baron of Westmerland, and Shreife of the same County by inheritance. He maried Sibella, daughter of William Earle Ferrers, whoe, some antiquarves think, was afterwards created Earle of Darby. He died 26 yeare of Henry the Third.

Shield of arms : *Vipont* impaling arg. six horseshoes sa.

ROBERT DE VETERIPOUNT third Lord and Baron of Westmerland, and last heire male of the Veteriponts of Westmerland. He maried Isabella Fitz Geoffrey, and had by her two daughters, whoe were his coheires; the elder of them carried away the inheritance of the Veteriponts to the Family of the Cliffords. This Robert de Veteripont died the 49th of Henry the Third.

Shield of arms : *Vipont* impaling, quarterly or and gu. a bordure vair.

ROGER DE CLIFFORD, the yonger sonne to Roger de Clifford the elder, maried Isabella de Vipount, eldest daughter and coheire to Robt de Vipont Lord of Westmerland and Shreife of that County by inheritance, by whome he had Robert, his eldest sonne, 9 yeares of age at his death. The issue of Idonea his sister fayling, all Vipont's inheritance in Westmerland cam to Isabella and hir issu. This Roger was slayne in the King's wars in the North Parts of Wales, the 11th of King Edward the First.

Shield of arms : *Clifford* impaling *Vipont*.

Upon a small scroll of parchment near the gauntlets and sword point, and marked II upon the diagram, is this writing—

As is said on the other side, Roger de Clifford the younger, by his mariage with Isabella de Veteripont, brought himself, and consequently his posterity, by the blessing of God, to inhabit in Westmerland and in the Northern parts, for many generations. For from the 8 of Aprill in the yeare 1269, when he married hir, till the 30th of October, 1605, when Georg. Clifford Earle of Cumberland dyed without issu male, which was 326 yeares, did this Roger and his issue male continue to be Lords, Barons, and High Shreife of the County of Westmerland, except where some were wards and others attainted for treason some little tyme. But by the death of the sayd Georg. Clifford E. of Cumberland, the issue of his body fayling, the inheritance of all the said Lands and honors came to his sole daughter and heire, the Lady Ann Clifford, whoe was afterwards Countess of Dorsett, and afterwards Countess of Pembrooke and Montgomery, though the said lands and honors were wrongfully detayned from her many yeares by hir Unkle the Earle of Cumberland and his sonne; the last of which dyed the 11th of December, 1643, and then her Inheritance cam back to her agayne. This Roger was slayne upon St. Laurence' Daye, in the Ile of Anglesey, the tenth yeare of Edward the First, 1283, and was buryed there.

Then proceeding upwards—

ROBERT LORD CLIFFORD of Westmerland maried Maude de Clare, Aunt and one of the heires of Thomas de Clare, Steward of the Forrest of Essex, descended from the Earles of Glocester, by whome he had twoe sonnes, successively Lords Cliffords of Westmerland.

To this Robert did King Edward the Second grant Skipton Castle and the lands about it. He was slayne the 8 Edw. 2 at the Battaile of Striveling, in Scotland, and she died the first of King Edward the Third, the same yeare hir eldest sonne Roger died.

Shield of arms: *Clifford* and *Vipont* quarterly. Impaling or three chevs. gu. for *Clare.*

ROGER LORD CLIFFORD of Westmerland, called Lo. Shevaler of Apleby, was attainted of treason the 15th of Edward 2. But he was returned to his honours and lands the first of Edward the Third. In which yeare this Roger died without lawfull children, hee being never maried, by which means his Brother Robert cam to succeede him in his lands and honors.

Shield of arms: *Clifford* quartering *Vipont.*

ROBERT LORD CLIFFORD of Westmerland maried Isabella daughter of John de Vallibus, by whome he had twoe sonnes that was successively Lords Clifford of Westmerland, and other children. He dyed the 20th of May the 18th of Edward the Third, leaving his sonne and heire Robert 13 yeares of age, and shee died the 36 of Edward the Third, a little before his eldest sonne Robert.

Shield of arms: *Clifford* and *Vipont* quarterly. Impaling gu. a chev. between ten crosses patty arg. for *Berkeley.*

ROBERT LORD CLIFFORD of Westmerland maried Eufamia, daughter of Ralph Nevill, Lord of Midleham Castle in Yorkshire, but they both dyed without issue, soe as he left his Brother Roger to succeed him in his lands and honors. This Robert Lord Clifford died 36 Ed. 3.

Shield of arms: *Clifford* and *Vipont* quarterly. Impaling gu. a saltire arg. for *Nevile.*

ROGER LORD CLIFFORD of Westmerland maried Maud daughter of Thomas Beauchamp Earle of Warwick, by whome he had Thomas, his eldest sonne, 26 yeares old at his Fathers death, and other children. He lived 27 or 28 yeares Lord Clifford, and died the 13th July the 13th of King Richard the Second. And she died the last day of February, in the 4th yeare of King Henry the 4th.

Shield of arms: *Clifford* and *Vipont* quarterly. Impaling gu. a fess between six crosses crosslet or for *Beauchamp.*

THOMAS LORD CLIFFORD of Westmerland maried Elizabeth daughter of Thomas Lord Ross of Hamlake, by whome he had John Lord Clifford and Maud Clifford Countes of Cambredg, and other children. He lived Lord Clifford not passing 3 or 4 yeares. Hee was slayne beyond the seas the 4 of October the 15th of Richard the Second, in the warrs in the North parts of Jermany, leaving his eldest sonne but 2 or 3 yeares old at his death, his wife Elizabeth died about the 3 yeare of King Henry the 6th.

Shield of arms: *Clifford* and *Vipont* quarterly. Impaling gu. three water bougets arg. for *Ross.*

JOHN LORD CLIFFORD of Westmerland, Kt. of the Garter, maried Elizabeth daughter of Henry Percy, surnamed Hotspur, who was sonn to the first E. of Northumberland, by which Elizabeth he had Thomas Lord Clifford, his eldest sonne, and other children. This John was slayne beyond the seas in the King's warrs in France the 9th of Henry the 5th, leaving his sonne and heire Thomas about 7 yeares and 3 weeks old. And this Elizabeth was after maried to Ralph second E. of Westmerland; she died the 15th of H. 6.

Shield of arms: *Clifford* and *Vipont* quarterly. Impaling or a lion ramp. az. quartering gu. three pike fish hauriant arg. for *Percy* and *Lucy.*

THOMAS LORD CLIFFORD of Westmerland maried Jeane daughter of Thomas Lord Dacres of the North, by whom he had John Lord Clifford, and other children. This Thomas was slayne in the first Battaile at St. Albanes, May 22nd 34 H. 6, and was buryed in the Abbey Church theare with his Unkle the E. of Northumberland, leaving his sonne John 20 yeares and 7 weekes old.

Shield of arms: *Clifford* and *Vipont* quarterly. Impaling gu. three escallops arg. for *Dacre.*

JOHN LORD CLIFFORD of Westmerland maried Margarett, daughter and sole heire to Henry Bromflete Lord Vescy, who brought the Title of Vescy to the hous of Cliffords. For by hir this John had Henry Lord Clifford, and other children. This John was slayne on Palme Sunday at the Battaile of Tawton in Yorkshire, the first of Edward the 4th.

Shield of arms: *Clifford* quartering *Vipont.* Impaling or a cross sa. for *Vescy.*

HENRY LORD CLIFFORD of Westmerland and Vescy in the first yeare of Henry the 7th was restored by Act of Parliament from Attainder of his Father, John Lord Clifford, which Henry maried to his first wife Ann St John, Cozen-Jerman by the halfe-blood to King Henry the 7th, by whom he had issue Henry Clifford first E. of Cumberland and other children. This Henry died the 15th yeare of H. 8, Aprill 22nd.

Shield of arms: *Clifford* and *Vipont* quarterly. Impaling arg. on a chief dancetty gu. two mullets or for *St John.*

HENRY CLIFFORD first Earle of Cumberland, his first wife being dead without issue, maried for his second wife Margarett Percy, daughter to Henry E. of Northumberland, by whom he had his sonn Henry Clifford, afterwards E. of Cumberland, and divers other children. He died in the 33 yeare of H. 8, April 23. Shee died some two yeares after him.

Shield of arms, surmounted by an earl's coronet: *Clifford* quartering *Vipont* and impaling *Percy* and *Lucy* quarterly.

HENRY E. of Cumberland maried to his second wife Ann Dacres, daughter to William Lord Dacres of the North, by whom he had his sonne Georg. who was after E. of Cumberland, and divers other children. And by his first wife he had Margarett Countess of Darby. This Earle Henry dyed in his Castle at Bromeham in Westmerland, in January, 1570. And his wife died in Skipton Castle, 1581, in July.

Shield of arms, surmounted by an earl's coronet: *Clifford* quartering *Vipont* and impaling *Dacre.*

GEORGE CLIFFORD E. of Cumberland maried the Lady Margarett Russell, da. to Francis E. of Bedford, the 24th June, 1577, in St. Mary Overs Church, by whom he had twoe sonnes that died young, and one daughter, the Lady Ann Clifford, his sole heire. This E. George died in the Duchy House in the Strand, Savoy, London, the 30th of October, 1605. And his wife died in Bromeham Castle in Westmerland, the 24th of May, 1616.

Shield of arms, surmounted by an earl's coronet: *Clifford* and *Vipont* quarterly. Impaling arg. a lion ramp. gu. on a chief sable three escallops of the field for *Russell.*

RICHARD SACKVILL Lord Buckhurst did marry Lady Ann Clifford daughter and sole heire to George late E. of Cumberland, 25 of February, 1609, as the yeare begins at New Yeares Tyde in her Mothers the Countess Dowager of Cumberland's House in Austin Friers London, and within twoe dayes after his mariage he came to be Earle of Dorsett by the death of his Father. He had divers children by the sayd Lady, but none of them lived but the Lady Margarett and the Lady Isabella.   He died in Great Dorsett Hous,[*] London, 28 March, 1624.

Shield of arms, surmounted by an earl's coronet : Quarterly or and gu., over all a bend vair.   *Sackville* Impaling *Clifford* and *Vipont* quarterly.

PHILLIP HARBERT E. of Pembrooke and Montgomery, being then a widdower, did marry the Lady Ann Clifford, Countess Dowager of Dorsett, the 3 day of June, 1630, in Cheyny's Church in Buckinghamshire, which Lady Ann Clifford was sole daughter and heire to hir deceased Father and Moother, George Clifford Earle of Cumberland.

Shield of arms, surmounted by an earl's coronet : Per pale az. and gu. three lions ramp. arg.   *Harbert.*   Impaling *Clifford* and *Vipont* quarterly.

This is the uppermost shield on the right side of the picture.]

[The left-hand picture represents the Lady Anne Clifford when young.   She is standing near a table, upon which is an hour-glass ; there is also a piece of music, upon which her left hand rests ; the table is covered with a scarlet cloth, ornamented with gold lace and fringe ; a lute is leaning against the table.   The Lady Anne is dressed in a white satin gown with long peaked body and tight slashed sleeves; the skirt is embroidered down the front and along the bottom edge, as also are the body and sleeves, with red roses and blue corn-flowers with gold stalks and green leaves.   She has a narrow lace collar round her dress at the neck and a laced ruffed collar; a necklace of pearls, and a long gold chain enriched with jewels is looped at the neck.   Her brown hair is short, and brushed from her forehead ; it is ornamented with pearls.   On the floor at her right side are four books, marked " Camden's Britannia," " Abraham Ortemus, his Maps of the World," " Cor. Agrippa of the Vanity of Scyences," " The Feighned History of Don Quixote ;" against these books rests a pair of compasses. Near the left side of her head is suspended an antique shield, marked M on the diagram, and inscribed —

" This is the Picture of the LADY ANN CLIFFORD at 15 yeares of age, daughter and sole heire of George Clifford, Earle of Cumberland, by his worthy wife Margaret Russell, Countess of Cumberland, of whom hir Moother conceyved with child in Channell Row House in Westmt., the first day of May Ano. Dm. 1589.   And was delivered of hir the 30th of January following in Skipton Castle in Creaven, wheare she and her sonn Robert Lo. Clifford then lay ; and wheare hir first childe Fran. L. Clifford died 11th December before.   The E. his Father did lie at Bedf. House, London, when his sayd onely daughter was borne, and about the end of that March following he cam to Skipton to them, being the first tyme he saw his daughter Ann, who proved after to be his onely heire.   About ye 2 of that Aprill, 1590, they all went out of Skipton Castle towards London, whither they cam the 17th of that Month.   And ye begening of that Aprill was the last tyme that Coun. and her sonn Ro. L. Clifford weare ever in Skipton Castle, for he died in Northall House in Hartf., May 24, 1591.   This Lady Ann Clifford was about 9 weeks old when she was brought out of Skipton Castle towards London, wheare and in the sothern pts. she continued to live for the most pt. till shee was maried.   When she cam to be 5 yeers and 8 months old, which weare just the age hir 2 brothers died at, she had a most desperat sicknes, so as she was given over for dead (as also 1604), and in hir childhood shee narrowly escaped death by water and fier and other great dangers, for God miraculously preserved hir life.   When shee was 15 yeares and 9 months old, hir Father died in Savoy Hous, London, the 30 of Oct. 1605 ; and presently after hir Moother comensed great suits at Law for hir sayd onely daughter's right to the Baro. of Clifford, Westmerland, and Vescy, and for the Shreifwick of that County, and for Skipton Castle, and ye ancient lands belonging to it, whearin that Countess shewed much wisdome and resolucion.   The 22nd of July, 1607, this yong La. with the Count. hir Moother cam from London to Apleby Castle in Westmoland, to ly theare for a while, it being the first tyme the La. Ann Clifford cam into Westmd., or so far Northward.   And then they went into Brougha. and Brough. and Pendragon Castles in that County.   The 8 of that Octob. 1607, they cam out of Apleby Castle in Westmerland towardes London, and they weare nevear both together in Apelby Castle after.   The 22 day of that October, 1607, they cam to the geats of Skipton Castle, but weare denied entrance into it, by reason of the suits in Law betweene them and Fran. then E. of Cumbe. ; it being the last tyme that the sayd Countes Dowagr of Cumberland was neer that Castle or in hir Almes House theare, which she founded.   This Lady Ann Clifford in hir childhood at severall tymes lived

[* " Dorset House, Fleet Street, was the town house of Thomas Sackville, Baron Buckhurst and Earl of Dorset ; it was formerly the Inn or London house of the Bishops of Salisbury, alienated to the Earl of Dorset's father by John Jewel, Bishop of Salisbury.   The house was divided into ' Great ' and ' Little Dorset House.'   Great Dorset House was the jointure house of Cicely Baker, Dowager Countess of Dorset, who died in it, October 1, 1615.   The loyal Marquis of Newcastle inhabited part of it at the Restoration.   The whole structure was destroyed in the Great Fire of 1666 and not rebuilt."—Cunningham's " Handbook of London," p. 159.]

much in Lillford House in Northampt., with old Mr. Elmes and his wife, who was Aunt to hir Moother, by the blood of the St. Johns, wheare this La. A. C. was seasoned with goodness and the love of a private country life, which ever after continued in hir.   In hir youth she lived much in Clarkenwell House, London, and in Northall House in Hartfordshire, with hir Father and Moother, and some littell tyme at Grafton House in Northamptonshire with hir Father, the sommer before his death.   After his death she lay with hir Moother for the most pt. at Sutton House in Kent, and in Austin Friers in London, wheare shee was maried 3 yeares and 4 months after the death of hir sayd Father.   Shee was blessed by the education and tender care of a most affectionate, deare, and excellent Moother, who brought her up in as much Religion, goodnes, and knowledg, as hir seakts and yeares weare capabell of.   Shee was also happy by being beloved in hir childwhood by Q. Elizab., and in hir youth by Q. Ann.—Pro. c. 10, v. 21 ; c. 20, v. 24.

"The Lady Ann Clifford being 19 yeares and a mounth old was maryed in hir Moothers the Countes Dowager of Cumblands howse at Austin Friers in London, in hir presence to Richard Sackvile Lord Buckhurst 25 of February 1609 as the yeare begins the First of January.   He cam to be E. of Dorsett within 2 dayes after his mariadg. by the death of his Father Robt. E. of Dorsett, whoe died the 27th day of that month in Little Dorsett House in Salesbury Court, London. This Lady was maryed 15 yeares and a month to Richard E. of Dorsett, who died of a Bloody Flux in Great Dorsett House London, the 28th of March 1624, his dead body was not opened at all, but buryed the 7th of Aprill next ensewing in the Vaut of Witheham Church in Sussex with his sonn the little Lord Buckurst, and many of his ancesters—the Sackvills and others, He being 35 yeares old at his death, and his Lady 34 yeares and 2 months over, whoe with hir 2 daughters weare then leying at Knowle House in Kent, by reason of the indisposition of hir body at that tyme.   This Ann Countes of Dorsett had divers children by hir sayd Lord, but none of them that lived any tyme but three (vizt.) Margrett hir first borne childe of whom shee was delivered in Great Dorsett House, London, the second of July 1614.   Thomas Lord Buckhurst, of whom shee was delivered in Knowle House in Kent, the 2 of February he died in the same house 26 of July following, and the Lady Isebella Sacvile, borne in the sam house of Knowle in Kent the 6th of Octob. 1622.   This Countess of Dorsett had onely one childe in the life tyme of hir Moother, the Countes of Cumberland Dowager, whoe cam purposely out of Westmorland to London to be at the birth of this Childe, and lay then at hir house in Austen Fryers in London for a while, yet by accident she was not present at hir daughter delivery, being then in the Tower of London about buisenes ; but she was at the Christning ye 30th of July and was Godmother to hir grandchild whoe bare hir name.   The 4th of August following ye sayd Countes of Cumberland took her last leave in Great Dorsett House London of her onely grandchilde, the La. Margt. Sackvile, as she had done the day before of hir Father, Richard Sackvile, Earle of Dorsett, in the same hous and never saw either of them after and that same 4th day was the last tyme she saw hir only daur. the Countes of Dorsett at London or in the Southerne pts. yet afterwards they saw on another in Westmerland.   The 5th day did this Ann, Countess of Dorsett, with hir then onely child the Lady Margt. Sackvile, being then about a month old, and hir Father Rich. E. of Dorsett remove from London to Knowle House in Kent.   The 8 of that August 1614, did that Margt. Russell Co. Dowager of Cumberland remove from her hous at Austin Friers in London, Northwards towards Westmorland, which was the last tyme she ever was in London, for the 22nd of that month shee cam to lye in hir Castle of Brougheham in Westmerland, wheare she died about a yeare and 9 months after.   The 6 of March before hir death did hir onely daur. come to that Excellent Moother of hirs, to Bromeham Castle in Westmerland to lye theare with hir for a while, it being the first tyme of hir coming into that Country or any pt of hir inheritance, after shee was first maryed.   The second day of that Aprill 1626 about halfe a mile from that Castle in the open ayre theare she tooke hir last leave of hir sayd worthey Moother, and they never saw one another after for then she went from thence towards London and so to Knowle in Kent, to hir Husband, and theire only childe being then there.   And the sayd Countess of Cumberland died in Brougham Castle in Westmland the 24th of May folowing:—Rev. chap. 14, vers. 13.   This Countes of Dorsett, whilest she was wife to R. Erl. of Dor. lived for the most pte. at Knowle House in Kent, and some tymes at Bolebrooke House in Sussex, and at Little Dorset House and Great Dorsett House, London.   In the yeare 1615 shee began to be in troubles about the lands of hir Inheritance in the North which continued with hir for divers yeares, soe as the 18th and 20th dayes of January 1617, shee was brought before K. James about that award made by him concerning all the Lands of hir Inheritanc, wherein God gave hir grace to deny that King to yeld or consent to that award which was the means that preserved the Lands of hir Inheritance to hir, and disposeing by the mercifull providence of Allmighty God.—Isa. c. 30, v. 21 ; c. 43, v. 2.   Psa. 32, v. 8.   Deut. c. 23, v. 5.

"This Lady Ann Countes Dowager of Dorsett, cam to be a widdow the 28 of March 1624 by the death of hir first Husband, Ri. Sackvile, E. of Dorsett : shee and hir twoe daughters at that tyme lyeing in Knowle Howse in Kent, where the 19th day of the mounth following hir first childe, the Lady Margret. Sackvile, lay at the point of death with the infection of the small-pox, and soe did the Countes her Moother of the same disease, theare the Mounth after being May, but by the mercifull providence of God they were both delivered from death.   The Mounth following June 9th, 1616, the sayd Countes with hir two daughters Margret and Isabella removed from that Knowle House in Kent, in which house the sayd Countes never did lye after.   But then from thence they 3 went to lye at Chenys House in Buckinghamshire wheare and hir Joynture House of Bolebrooke in Sussex, and in Tutle Street House in Westminster, and twoe other howses in the Pallace theare, shee continewed to lye for the most part of her widdohood saving that she once lay in Wooburne House in Bedfordshire with her eldest daughter for a few nights.   The 6 of May 1626 when shee then laye with hir two daughters in Bolebrooke Hous in Sussex, shee theare escaped a great danger by Theefes that then intended to rob hir and hir house. The 30th of March 1627 shee and hir eldest daughter went together into Knowle House in Kent for a while, which was the last tyme this Countes was ever in that house.   Hir first Childe, the Lady Margt. Sackvile was maryed in the Chapell of Great St. Bartholomew in hir presenc to John Lo. Tufton, 21st of Aprill 1629 who cam to be E. of Thanett 2 yeeres and 2 months after by the dath of his Father.   This Countes of Dorsett was not in any pt of hir inheritance all the tyme of hir being now a widdow, for hir Unkle of Cumbland kept posecion of those hir lands theare by power of K. James his Award, yet did she cause claymes to be made to it in a legall manner to preserve hir right thearein. She lived now a widdow six yeeres 2 months and 6 dayes at the end of wch tyme she was maried to Phillip Harbert 11. E. of Pembrooke and Mongomery in Chenys Church in Buckinghamshire. This Countes had many Enymyes in the tyme of hir now widowhood from whose evell and crafty devises it pleased God to delivir hir.—As Job, chap. 5, vers. 11th, 12, 13, 14, 15, 16, 17. Cor. chap. 1. Psal. 221. Dewte. 23, vers. 5. Psal. 76, vers. 9 and 10. Psal. 97, vers. —— Psal. 64, vers. 2, 3, 4. Esay. chap. 50, vers. 20. Prov. chap. 19, vers. 20; chap. 21, vers. 24."

Suspended by a ring to the escutcheon upon which the above long inscription is written, is a lozenge-shaped shield emblazoned with the arms of *Clifford* and *Vipont* quarterly.

Above her head, supported upon iron brackets, are two shelves, containing the following books neatly arranged and lettered :—

Epectetus his Manuall.—Boetius his Philosophicall Comfort.—All ye works in vers of Samuell Daniell tutor to this young lady.—The Holy Bible, the Old and New Testament.—St. Augustine of the Cittie of God.—Eusebius his History of the Church.—All the works of Dr. Jossowagh Hall.—Sir Phillip Sydney's Arcadia.—All Edmond Spencer's Work.—Ovid's Metamorfices.—John Downham his Christian Warfare.—All Du Barras his Works.—All Jeffrey Chawcer's Workes.—The French Academy 1 Part.—The French Academy 2 Part.—French Academy 3 Part.—The Courtier by Co. Castilio.—Godfrey of Boloigne.—The Variety of Things by Loys de Roy.—The Chronicle of England in proes by Samuell Daniell, Tutor to ye young Lady.—Lo. Michaell Montaigne his Essaies.—The Epitome of Gerrard's Herball.

Above the book-shelves are two small portraits in plain black frames. The one marked κ on the diagram is that of Samuel Daniel, who is represented as having a short beard and a high linen collar. The portrait measures within the frame 7 inches by 6⅛ inches ; underneath the frame is a tablet, inscribed—

" Samuel Daniel, Tutour to this Young Lady a man of an Upright and excellent Spirit as appeared by his Workes was borne in the yeare of our Lord 1563. He dyed at Redge in the parish of Beckinton in Somersetshire about the 9th of October in the yeare 1619 and lyeth buried in the Chancell of the sayd Church, leaving no issue."

The small portrait marked L on the diagram measures 6⅞ inches by 5⅞ inches, and is that of Mrs. Ann Taylor. She is represented in a close black cap tied under her chin, and a black gown with large falling linen collar. The inscription beneath is—

" Mrs. Anne Taylour Governesse to this Young Lady a Religious and good Woman was daughter to Mr. Cholmley and was borne in his house in the Old Bailey in London in the yeare ...... She had diverse children by her husband Mr. William Taylour who all dyed before her and without issue."

The right-hand picture represents the Countess Dowager of Pembroke and Montgomery. She is shown as a very masculine-looking woman, standing turned towards the centre picture. She is dressed in a black gown with loose sleeves slashed and lined with white, turned back and edged with lace ; and her stomacher is edged with two rows of pearls. She wears a large falling collar double edged with lace, a large pearl drop at her neck, and a double row of pearls for necklace : she also wears a pearl girdle. Her hair is brown and long, with long ringlets at each side of her head ; and she has a black veil. Her right hand rests upon two books, marked " Charons Booke of Wisdome translated out of French into English," and " The Holy Bible, the Old and New Testamt," placed on a table. On her left thumb is a ring. At her feet is a black cat, lying down facing to the front ; and a little white greyhound is jumping up towards her left hand, which is at her side. On the scroll marked P on the diagram is the inscription as printed on page 353. Over her head are two shelves, upon which are a number of books, laid carelessly, and labelled on the edges.

On the upper shelf are—

Mr. George Sandes his translation of the Psalmes and other pts of ye Bible into vers.—Phillipp De Cominos in English.—More his Mapp of Mortallity.—All Benjamine Johnson's his Works.—Mr John Dunn his Poems, whoe was after Deane of Pauls.—The Age of Man's Life by Henry Cuff.—George Herbert his Devine Poems.—Barklayes Argenies.—Antonius his Meditacons.—Dr King Bpp. of London his Sermons.—Mr William Astin his Book of Meditations and Devotions.—All Dr Dun. Deane of Pauls his Sermons.—Amianus Mercilanus.

On the lower shelf—

Mr. George Strowde his Booke of Death.—Plutarches Lives in French.—Plutarches Mortals of French.—An Appologie of the Providence and Power of God.—Dr George Hackwell.—Sr Foulke Grevill, Lord Brooke his works.—Gurcherdines History in French.—Sr Henry Wootton his Booke of Architecture.*

Upon the wall are two small pictures in gilt frames. The upper, marked N in the diagram, is the portrait of Richard Sackville, Earl of Dorset, her first husband. Above the frame is a shield of the arms of *Sackville*, impaling az. a fess betw. three swans' heads erased ...... *Baker ;* all within the Garter. Upon the picture are two shields with an earl's coronet over each. The first bears *Sackville* impaling *Howard ;* and the second *Sackville* impaling *Clifford* and *Vipont* quarterly.

Underneath the picture, on a tablet, is this inscription :—

"This is the Picture of RIC SACKVILLE Lo. Buckhurst and E. Dorsett, eldest sonne to Robt. Sackville Lo. Buckhurst and E. of Dorsett, that lived any years by his first Wife the Lady Margt. Howard. Which E. Richard was borne in Charter House, London, now called Suttons Hospital the 26 of March 1589, his Moother dyeng twoe yeares and five months after at Bolebrooke House in Sussex, yet shee was Moother of two children after his birth. When he was 19 yeares old and a month over died his Grandfather Thomas Sackville Lord Buckhurst and E. of Dorsett, Lord High Treasurer of England and Kt. of the Garter suddenly in the Councell Chamber at Whitehall the 19 April, 1608. This Richard maried the Lady Ann Clifford, daughter and sole heire to George E. of Cumbland 25th of February, 1609, in hir Moother the Countes Dowager of Cumbland house Austin Fryers, London, in hir presenc. And within twoe dayes after the sayd mariage his Father died in Little Dorset House in the sayd towne. This Richard E. of Dorsett was maried 15 yeares and a mounth to the sayd Lady Ann Clifford, and had by hir three sonns, which died in theire infancy, and two daughters, Margt. Countess of Thannet, borne the 2 of July in Great Dorset House 1614 ; and Isabel Countess of Northampton, borne at Knowle House in Kent 1622. He travelled beyond the seas in France and the lowe Countries most part of the yeare 1611 : and about the begning of Aprill 1612 he returned agayne into England to his wife and lived 12 yeares after. And in August and September 1616 he was for a while with his wife at Browham Castle in Westmerland and in Naworth Castle Cumberland. He died in Great Dorsett House London of a Bloody Flix 28th of March 1624, Christianly and Penitantly, and was buried at Whitheham Church in Sussex, the 7th daye of the month following.—Job 7 vers 1—He was by nature of a juste minde sweet disposition and very valliant in his own pson and attayned to be a great scholler for his ranke, when he lived at the University at Oxford. He was so bountifull to souldiers, schollers, and others, which were in distress that therby he much empaired his Estate. He was a zealous Patriot to this Kingdome and the onely builder and one of the Chiefe Founders of the Hospitall at East Grinsted in Sussex, and truly religious in his latter tymes."

The other small portrait, marked O, is that of Philip Herbert, her second husband. Above the head are two shields of arms, each within the Garter : *Herbert* per pale gu. and az., over all three lions ramp. arg. impaling *Vere ;* and *Herbert* impaling *Clifford* and *Vipont* quarterly. Beneath the picture is a tablet inscribed—

[(* Notes on some of the books shown upon the picture.)—" Christian Warfare," by John Downham, in four parts ; London, 1634, folio. He also published "Spiritual Physick to cure the Diseases of the Soul," in 1600 ; and "Guide to Godliness," 1622. "The Courtyer," by Baldessar Castiglione, done into Englysh by Thomas Hoby ; London, 4to, 1561. "The Theatre of the Whole World," by Abraham Ortelius ; London, folio, 1606. "Of the Vanitie and Uncertaintie of Arts and Sciences," by Henry Cornelius Agrippa, englished by James Sanford ; London, 4to, 1569. "A Paraphrase upon the Psalms of David, &c.," by George Sandys ; London, 1636 ; Dryden pronounced Sandys to be the best versifier of his age. "Differences of the Ages of Man's Life," by Henry Cuff ; 8vo, London, 1607 ; reprinted in 1633 and 1640. "The Temple, Sacred Poems and Private Ejaculations," by George Herbert, B.A., 1631. "John Barclay: his Argenis ; or the Loves of Poliarchus and Argenis ;" translated by Kingsmill ; folio, London, 1625 ; the poet Cowper pronounced this to be the most amusing romance ever written. "Antoninus's Meditations," 1634. "Certain Devout, Godly, and Learned Meditations," by William Austin ; London, folio, 1635. "Ammianus Marcellinus ;" the Roman historie translated into English by Philemon Holland ; London, folio, 1609. This was Dr. Hakewell, the 3rd edition of whose chief work was published in 1635, and called, "An Apology or Declaration of the Power and Providence of God in the Government of the World."]

"This is the Picture of PHILLIPP HERBERTT E. of Pembrooke and Montgomery, and Kᵗ. of the most noble Order of the Gartar, 2 sonn to Henry Herbertt E. of Pembrooke, by his 2 wife Mary Sidney, onely daughter to Henry Sidney Knight of the Gartar and onely sister to the famous Sr. Phillipp Sidney, and Sr. Robert Sidney E. of Leicester. This Phillipp Herbert was borne in his Fathers house in Wilton in Wiltshire the 10th daye of Octob. in 1584 in which house his sayde Father dyed the 10th of January in 1601 : And his Mother dyed twenty yeares and 8 monthes after in hir widowhood of the small-pox the 25th of Septemb. 1621 being about sixty-one years old, in the House called Montacute House, Aldersgate Street, London : hee was deerly beloved of King James from his first coming into England till his death, which King made him E. of Montgomery the 4th day of May 1605 and Kt. of the Gartar the 20th of May 1608, and also bestowed many guifts and Favours on him. Hee was maried in the sayd Kings Chappell at Whitehall in his precnce to his first wife the Lady Susan Veer the 27th of December 1604 whoe was youngest daughter to the deceased Edw. E. of Oxford, and shee died of the smallpox in the same house of Whithall the 2 day of February 1629 : soe as she dyed a yeare and more befor hir sayd Husband came to be E. of Pembrooke. His Brother Wm. Harbertt E. of Pembrooke died suddenly in Bynards Castle, London, of an Apperplexye 10th of Apprill 1630, by whos death the sayd Phillipp Harbertt his onley Brother came to be E. of Pembrooke, and the 3 June following did the sayd Phil. Harb. E. of Pembrooke and Montgomery marry the Lady Ann Cliff. Countess Dowager of Dorsett and sole daur. and hire to George E. of Cumbland, in Chenys Church in Buckinghamshire, after she had bin a widow 6 yeares 2 months and 6 dayes and he a widdower one yeare and 4 months and 3 dayes."

[Upon a parchment scroll depending from the table, and marked P on the diagram, is this inscription:—

"This is the Picture of the Lady Ann Clifford, now Countess of Pembrooke, Dʳ. Whoe when shee was Countess Dowager of Dorsett, and had lived six years and two months a widow, was maryed in Chenys church, in Buckinghamshire, the 3d day of June, 1630, to hir second husband Philip Herbert Earle of Pembrooke and Montgomery, Lord Chamberlayne of his Majesties household, and Kt. of the most noble Order of the Garter, hee being then of the age of 45 yeares and 8 months wanting 7 dayes, and she being of the age of 40 yeares and fower months.

"Shee lived most part of yᵉ time whilst shee was his wife, first in yᵉ Court at Whitehall, and after at Baynard's Castle in London, Ramsbury, and Wilton, in Wiltshire ; but espetially in Ramsbury Hous and in Baynard Castle.

"And whilest the sayd Countess then laye in the sayd Castle in London, dyed Henry Clifford Earle of Cumb'land, in one of the Prebende's houses in Yorke yᵉ 11th of December, 1643 ; And his wife, the Lady Frances Cecill, Countess Dowager of Cumb'land, died in yᵉ same hous yᵉ 14th of February following. By reason of which Erle's death without issue male, did yᵉ landes in Westmerland and Craven, which of right belonged to this Countess of Pembrooke, and was detayned from hir by the sayd Erle and his Father many yeares, revert and come peaceably to the sayd Countess, though the misery of yᵉ then Civill warrs kept hir from having the profitt of theese landes for a good while after.

"The 5th of July, 1627, was this Countess of Pembrooke's youngest daughter by hir first husband, the Lady Isabella Sackvile, maried in Clerkenwell Church, in London, to James Compton Erle of Northampton."•]

[* The Countess Anne was born on the 30th of January, 1590, at Skipton Castle. Her father and mother, from unhappy dissensions, separated in her childhood. She was left to the care of her mother, who entrusted her education to Samuel Daniel, a poet and author (born 1563, died October, 1619). From him she acquired a taste for history and poetry, and a fondness for literary composition, which she indulged to a great extent.

On the 27th February, 1609, she was married to Richard Sackville, third Earl of Dorset, "a man of lively parts and licentious life, and probably a polite and negligent husband." They had one son, who died in his infancy, and two daughters—Margaret, who married John Tufton, Ear of Thanet ; and Isabella, who married James Compton, Earl of Northampton. The Earl of Dorset died on the 28th of March, 1624, being just 35 years of age.

On the 3rd of June, 1630, she married for her second husband Philip Herbert, Earl of Pembroke, "a person distinguished only by the brutality of his manners and the most ungrateful disloyalty. She had abundant cause of private offence from each. The first was a spendthrift, and quarrelled with her because she prevented him from dissipating her estate ; the second was a tyrant, and distracted her by the savageness of his humour. Yet she speaks well, and even kindly, of both." Lord Clarendon says of Philip Herbert that, "being a young man, scarce of age, at the entrance of King James, he had the good fortune, by the comeliness of his person, his skill, and indefatigable industry in hunting, to be the first who drew the king's eyes upon him with affection ; which was quickly so far improved that he had the reputation of a favourite. Before the end of the first or second year he was made Gentleman of the King's Bedchamber and Earl of Montgomery. . . . . He pretended to no other qualifications than to understand horses and dogs very well, and to be believed honest and generous, which made him many friends and left him then few enemies. He had not sat many years in that sunshine when a new comet appeared in court—Robert Carr, a Scotsnan, quickly after declared favourite ; upon whom the king no sooner fixed his eyes but the earl, without the least murmur or indisposition, left all dóors open for his entrance, which the king received as so great an obligation that he always after loved him in the second place, and commended him to his son at his death as a man to be relied on in point of honesty and fidelity, though it appeared afterwards that he was not strongly built, nor had sufficient ballast to endure a storm." He died on the 23rd of January, 1650. By his first wife, Susan, daughter of Edward Vere, Earl of Oxford, he had seven sons and three daughters ; but not any by his second wife, the Countess Anne. She had separated herself from him for some time, and after his death retired to her estates in the north, and occupied herself in restoring her castles and improving her estates. She died at Brougham Castle on the 22nd of March, 1675, in the 86th year of her age.

There are portraits of the countess when young, painted by Mytens, in the collection of his grace the Duke of Dorset, at Knowle ; and also of Philip Herbert, Earl of Pembroke, painted by Vandyke, in the collection of the Earl of Pembroke at Wilton, both engraved in Lodge's "Portraits of Illustrious Personages."

In Skipton Castle there are also two portraits—one when she was young, and the other taken in her old age. There is also another of her in her old age at the Duke of Devonshire's house, Bolton Hall.]

2 'l'

Such is the account which this lady has transmitted to posterity of her ancestors, herself, her nuptial alliances, and her immediate descendants. But paint and canvas, when neglected, soon give way to the operation of damp. Even now the compartment which contains her own youthful portrait is nearly destroyed. Many of the marginal inscriptions are become almost illegible; and unless the press and the graver had united to perpetuate these perishing remains, another century might have doubted whether such a monument of the Cliffords was ever in being. [This refers to the Skipton copy now at Hothfield.]

The idea of combining so much family history and so numerous a group of figures upon canvas was, I think, original. The principal portraits are given in the annexed engraving. The miniatures could not be reduced.

The foregoing narration leaves me little to add with respect to that part of the family to which it extends but a few gleanings and reflections.

George Earl of Cumberland was a great but unamiable man. His story admirably illustrates the difference between greatness and contentment, between fame and virtue. If we trace him in the public history of his times, we see nothing but the accomplished courtier, the skilful navigator, the intrepid commander, the disinterested patriot. If we follow him into his family, we are instantly struck with the indifferent and unfaithful husband, the negligent and thoughtless parent. If we enter his muniment-room, we are surrounded by memorials of prodigality, mortgages and sales, inquietude, and approaching want. He set out with a larger estate than any of his ancestors, and in little more than twenty years he made it one of the least. Fortunately for his family, a constitution originally vigorous gave way, at forty-seven, to hardships, anxiety, and wounds.* His separation † from his virtuous lady was occasioned by a court intrigue; but there are families in Craven who are said to derive their origin from the low amours of the third Earl of Cumberland.

Among the evidences of the family I have met with a MS. journal of the first voyage, fitted out at his expense, but which he does not seem to have accompanied in person. It appears to have been followed by Hacklyit, and is entitled as follows :—

"A Vyag pretendyd to the Indya, set foorth by the good earle of Cumberland, with two shyps and a pinnys, Mr. Wytheryngton beyng Captyn of the Athmerall, and Mr. Lysster of the Vys Athmerall."

It seems to be the work of an ordinary pilot or inferior officer, and contains little which will be deemed either interesting or useful. The following passage, however, may be commended to the captain and crew of a modern slave-ship—

"Nov. 5, our men went on shor and fet rys abord, and burnt the rest of the housys in the negers towne ; and our bot went doune to the outermoste pointe of the ryver, and burnt a toune, and brout away all the rys that was in the toune."

---

* "He was sick of a bloody flux a month before his death ; his wife and child were present a few hours (only) before."—Countess of Pembroke's MS. Memoirs.

† "But as good natures, through human frailty, are often misled, so he fell to love a lady of quality, which did by degrees draw and alienate his affections from his so virtuous and loving a wife ; and it became the cause of many sorrows."—*Ibid.*

After this humane and honest employment on the Saturday, mark the next article, " The 6th day we sarvyd God, being Sunday !!! " Surely the barefaced irreligion of the present day is more tolerable than such sanctified iniquity.

I conclude this account with the following entry of this earl's interment in the parish register of Skipton.

" 1605, Oct. 29, departed this lyf George earle of Cumbreland, lord Clifforde, Vipounte, and Vessie, lord of the honor of Skipton, in Craven, knyght of the most noble order of the Garter, one of his highness privie counsell, lord warden of the citie of Carlell and the West Marches, and was honorably buried at Skipton, the XXIX of December, and his funerall was solemnized the XIIIth day of Marche next then following."

From the family evidences at Bolton I have selected the following original compositions of this great man. There are many others in that collection bearing his name, but they are either written by a secretary, and merely subscribed by the earl, or, if indited wholly by himself, relate to subjects of little general interest.

" MY VERY GOOD LORD,

" I have bene, as your Lo. well knowethe, longe tyme a suter to her Maiesty to bestowe sume suche benefit upon me as myght manyfest to the worled her good opinion, and macke me the better able to dooe her such servis as at any tyme she should have cause to com'and me, wᶜʰ not longe sence she did, as I then thought, but beinge of late in the cuntri, where I should have receved the benefyt of hir gifte, I founde not any, but were ether unable or unwillynge to disburse presente muny, soe that I am assured not to be relived by that meanes, wᶜʰ I then hoped, & her Mai. mente ; wherfore I noue most earnestly desier that it would please hir Majesti to lende me tenne .thousande pound. I will paye it agayne by a thousand pounde a yeare, and for the assurance ether paune suche land as your Lo. shall lycke, or putt soe many jentellmen in bonde as shall be thought suffitient, and also resine up agayne her late gifte, wᶜʰ wilbe more benefit to her then the lone of the mony canbe, and more profitt to me then tooe suche sutes, my dayes of payement beinge soe neare, and the forfetures greate, wᶜʰ I shall faule into, if I be not relived by your Lo. good meanes in this, as I thyncke, my resonable sute, wᶜʰ I will not move, till I knoue your good lykynge, by whom in this, as in everi other thynge, I will be derected. Thus hopinge for your Lo. beste advice and furtherance, I proteste never to be forgetfull of any favor you shall bestoue upon me."

" From the Courte, this XXIII of September.

" Your Lo. most assured Frynd,
" GEORGE CUMBRELAND."

Directed—

" To the ryght honorable my
    very good Lord the Lord Burghley,
    hey tresorer of Inglande."

Indorsed, seemingly in Lord Burleigh's hand—

" 23 Sept. 1586.
    E. of Cumberland
      To borrowe Xᵐ li. of her Mai'ty."

" To the ryght honorable Francis Walsy'gham, knyght, hir maiestyes schyfe secritary.

" SIR,   " XXIX October, 1588.

" Beinge at Plymouthe to water, I harde of a hulcke beten in by foule wether, by Hope, a toune XXIII myle from thence. She was one of the Spanyshe flyte, and it was reported the Ducke was in hir, and great store of treasure ; wherfore I ridde thither, with Mr. Cary and Mr. Harris, whoe then were w'th me, to knowe the truthe of it, where we founde no such thynge as was reported of the Ducke ; but a shippe suche and soe furnished as by an examination taken by hus and sent herew'th you may perseve. Mr. Cary stayeth at the place, to kepe hir from spoylynge of the cuntry-men till here youre further derection. Thus muche the have intreted me to macke knowne to you, and thus in hast I co'mitte you to GOD. From Malborowe, this XXIX of October.   " Your lovynge frynde,

" GEORGE CUMBRELAND."

An original despatch to Secretary Walsingham, relating to the defeat of the Spanish Armada, in which this nobleman bore so considerable a part, will be considered as no small curiosity. By the Ducke, I suppose, is meant the Spanish admiral, the Duke of Medina Sidonia, who, in one of those rumours which at such times are flying in every direction, was said to have been driven on shore near Plymouth.

" To the ryght honorable my very good Lo. the Lo. Hygh Tresorer of Ingland.

" My good Lo',   "20 *Feb.*

" Upon a letter from her mai. co'mandyng me to repare with my fleete to the rode of Callis, and to bryng w'th me all such shipps as I should fynd fitt to dooe hir servis ther, I comanded tooe shipps in the harbor of Porchmouth, and three at the Cowes, good shipps, and laden w'th nyne companyes of soulgerrs, out of France, to returne w'th me. Sir He. Poure, their coronell, writte me word that before ther cu'mynge from the Dounes the Spanyards aryvall at Callis was knowne, yett they were suffered to procede. Soe, doubting least I should dooe amisse, I have stayed them, to remayne where they be till further derection cum for them, w'ch I pray your lo. maye be sent, soe that they depend upon it. My selfe am nowe gooeinge towardes Douer, wher, if hir mai. have any thynge to co'mande me, I wil be redy to obey it. Your lo. to co'mand,

" George Cumbreland."

" To my very good Lo. the Lo. High Tresorer of Englande.

" My very good Lo',   "1 *Sept.* 1594.

" Since I last moued your lo. to favor my lo. Tomas,* in his sute, Sir Jo. Forteskew hath delte with her maie. in it, who, after muche speeche (as he sayethe), concluded, not unwyllingle, to grante what my lo. desiered (but in fee-farme), and, for any thynge I can perceve, grew in 'to that eumer by Sir Jo. soe movynge it to hir, wher in he hath donne my lo. a myghty displeasure ; for I assure your lo. in that kynde it will not by worthe any thynge. To releeve this harme I hope it will not be harde sethe it may be may do apparante to hir ma. to be as I informe your lo. and that in grantynge the fee-simple she gevethe but 120*l.* and 2 or 3 pound for the lyfe of my lo. of Arundayll and his sunne, then w'ch hir mai. connot (gevynge any thynge to suche a man) geve lesse, and that she meanes to him sumthynge is well sene by this sayd already, so as I well hope your lo. favor nowe showed will easely effecte my lo. desier macke me muche bound to you for it, and him to you in loue, whom, I assure your lo. for his firme disposition, and true honesty, is as well worthe hauynge as any man lyvethe. If your lo. when you ar w'th the quine, will but offer speeche that my lo. admeraw may be cauled to you, he will faule in to my lo. To. cause, is instructed well in it, and will (I dout not) macke very playne to be but a very tryflynge demand, out of which your lo. if soe you lyke, may tacke best occation to favor him ; if not, I pray your lo. co'mand me to wayte upon youe at your leasuer, and lett me knowe what other cource you will derecte, for my lo. meanethe hooly to depend upon your derection. Your lo. to co'mand,

" George Cumbreland."

" My lo. admeraule is alredy instructed."

" To the ryght honorabl. the Lo. Tresorer of Ingland.†

" My good Lo.   " 24 *Nov.* 1596.

" If want of health had not stayed me, before this I had waited upon your lo. and let yout knowe boothe what I perseve my lo. of Darbye's cources ar, and alsoe therrs whoe advise, follow, and depend upon him ; to longe and intricate it would be to troble your lo. w'th nowe, soe I will forbere till more fittyngly I may attend you ; but heryng that your lo. hath apoynted Mr. Ireland to be w'th you this day, I thought good to desier your lo. to euse him w'th kynd speeches, and not to seeme but that you beleve he hath dealte most honestly in thes cources w'th his lo. ; els I feare me, in a desperate eumer, he may perhapps dooe what hardly agayne may be helped. And I dare assure your lo. this conveance effected, though but as it is, other thynges after will easely be effected to your lo. conttentment. Thus, hartely thanckyng your lo. for your care of him whoe cares not for him selfe, I ende, ever your lo. to co'mand,

" George Cumbreland."

" To my very good Lo. the Lo. Tresorer of Ingland.

" My good Lo.   "26 *April,* 1597.

" As ever I have found your lo. willyng to dooe me kindnes, soe I besiche you (nowe in the tyme when muche it may pleasure me boothe in my reputation and estate) to geve me your best furtherance. I here hir mai. will bestowe the Ile of Wyght upon sum suche as shall ther be resident. To w'ch condicion willyngly I woulde, as is fittyng, tye myself : not w'th such eumerrs to sea-journeys as heretofore have caried mee ; but, by just discorage, setell myselfe to what shall neither gett envi, nor geve coler for falce informations. I protest to your lo. desier of inablyng myselfe for hir maie's servis cheeflyest drew me w'th greedyness to follow thos cources all this yeare, as your lo. knowes ther hath bene lycklyhoud of my imployment, and generawlly spoken of. Now I here it is otherwye determyned, to w'ch I willingly submitte meselfe, but soe sensible of the disgrace, as if hir mai. dooe not showe me sum other token of hir favor, I shall as often wyshe myselfe dead as I have houres to lyve. For my fittnes to govern that island I leave to your lo. iudgment ; but this I vooe, he lyves not that w'th more duty and care shall kepe and defend it then I will ; and if by your lo. good meane it may be obtayned I shall thyncke hir mai. deales most gratiusly with me, and ever acknowledge myselfe most bound to your lo. whom I com'tte to God, and rest your lo. to command,

" George Cumbreland."

---

* I suppose Lord Thomas Howard. It does not appear what was the particular of his suit.

† This letter seems to refer to the great dispute which happened after the death of Ferdinando Earl of Derby, in 1595, between his three co-heiresses and William his brother and successor in the title, with respect to the property of the Isle of Man. In the conclusion, Earl William, who was then very young, is censured by his kinsman " as not caring for himself." He became in due time, however, a very prudent man, and survived to the year 1642.

This last letter shows how long the sentiments of chagrin and disappointment, so strongly expressed in the following speech, had been brooding in the mind of the speaker.

"A Copie of my Lord of Combrlande's Speeche to ye Queene,
"upon ye 17 day November, 1600.

"This knight (Fairest and Happiest of all Ladies) removyng from castell to castell, now rowleth up and downe, in open feild, a field of shaddow, having no other m'rs but night-shade, nor gathering anie mosse but about his own harte. This mallancholly, or rather desperat retirdness, sommons his memorie to a repetition of all his accions, thoughtes, misfortunes, in the depth of which discontented contentedness upon one leaf he writes, *utiliter consenesco,* and musters up all his spirite to its wonted corradge : but in the same minut he kisseth night-shade, and imbraceth it, saying, *Solanum Solamen.* Then, having no companye but himselfe, thus he talkes w'th himselfe : that he hath made ladders for others to clymbe, and his feet nayled to the ground not to stirr. That he is lyke him that built ye ancker to save others, and themselve⁻ to be drownd. That when he hath outstript manie in desert, he is tript upp by Envy, untill those overtake him that undertooke nothing. He, on the confidence of unspotted honour, leveld all his accions to nurse these twinnes, Labor and Dutie, not knowinge which of these was eldest, both running fast, but neither formost. Then, casting his eyes to heaven, to wonder at Cinthia's brightness, and to looke out his own unfortunate starr : with deepe syghes he breathes out a twofold wishe, that the one may never waine while the world waxeth ; that the other may be erring, not fixed. Howe the two haith troubled ye sacred eares, mine with glowing and tingling, are witnesses ; but they shall confess that their eyes shall prove their being lyers, being as farr from judgm't as they are from honnor. There is no such thing as night-shade ; for wher can there be miste or darkenes where you are, whose beames wrappes up cloudes as whirlewindes dust ? Night-shade is falne off, shrinking into ye center of the earth, as not daring to showe blackenes before your brightnes. I cannot excuse my knightes error, nor care that he knows it, to thinke he could cover himselfe obscurely in anie desolate retirdness wher your highnes beautie and vertue could not find him out. These Northeren thoughtes, that measures honnor by the acre, and would have his crest a plase, he controwles so far in his truer honnor, that (he ?) contempes them. He now grounds all his accions neither upon hopes, counsell, nor experience, he disdaines envy, and scornes ingratitude. Judgem't shall arme his patience ; patience confirme his knowledge, which is that, yourselfe being perfection, knaves measures number and tyme to cause favour wher it shold, and when you please, being onely constant and wyse in waiging with true stedines both the thoughtes of all men, and their affections ; upon w'ch he soe relies that whatsoever happen to him you are still yourselfe (wonder and happynes), to w'ch his eyes, thoughts, and actions are tyed, w'th such an indissolvable knott, that neather death, nor tyme, that triumphs after death, shall or can unloose it. Is it not, as I have often tould ye, that, after he had throwne his land into ye sea, ye sea would cast him on the lande for a wanderer ? He that spines nothing but hopes shall weave up nothing but repentance. Let him cast his accompts sinc he was first wheeld about with his will wheele ; and what can he reckon, save only he is so manie years elder ? Haith not he taken his fall, wher others take their rysing, he having ye Spanish proverbe at his backe that should be sticked to his harte, 'Adelante los Abenstados.' 'Let them hold the purses with ye mouth downeward that hath filled them with mouth upwards.' He may well entertaine a shade for his m'rs that walkes in the world himselfe like a shaddow, embracing names instead of thinges, dreames for trouthes, blind prophesais for seeing verities. It becomes not me to dispute of his courses ; but yet none shall hinder me from wondring to see him that is not to be, and yet to be that never was. If ye thinke his body too straighte for his hearte, ye shall find ye worlde wyde enoughe for his body."

In this speech, which seems to have been delivered by the earl under the character of a pensive and discontented knight, at one of those romantic spectacles so fashionable in the reign of Elizabeth, he hints, in a doleful strain, at his services and disappointments. He had (for what great courtier ever had not?) many enemies. He had been superseded in some naval command ; and had probably been refused the government of the Isle of Wight. When he complains that he had thrown his land into the sea, he obviously alludes to the great waste he had made of his estates in equipping ships, and even squadrons, at his own expense. Queen Elizabeth, "the fairest of all ladies, Cinthia's brightness, &c.," had now attained to the age of sixty-seven !

FRANCIS, FOURTH EARL OF CUMBERLAND.

The following accurate and technical account of the great contest for the honour of Skipton, &c., which took place after this nobleman's death, is abstracted from a report of Sir Matthew Hale among the family evidences, and offered as much more satisfactory than any statement of the author :—

" By the death of George earl of Cumberland, there fell a great division in the family. The earldome went to Francis, as heire male of the body of Henry the first earle of Cumberland, and the titles of baronage descended to the lady Anne his daughter; also the lands (excepting the new purchases made by this earle and his ancestors, not comprized within the entayle of Edward II. for Skipton), though intended by the late earle to accompany the earledom, yet did not, but in truth descended to the lady Anne by virtue of the sayde entayle, for the reversion continuing still in the crowne, all those severall experiments by the late earle and his ancestors could not alter nor unhinge the entayle, nor soe much as trouble or displace it.

" The occasion, progress, and successe of this debait, suit, and controversie follows briefly.

" The late earle Henry, father of George, not taking notice of the old entayle of Skipton, did by his will limitt the same, or the greater part thereof, in several manners. Earle George succeeding, and, as is the use of great persons of plentifull estates, looking no higher than the will of his father, and finding an entayle there limitted of these manors, in the 33d Eliz. takes care by fine and recovery, with all the advice and circumspection that may be, to barr that intayle, but never soe much as dreamed of the former guift of that honr in tayle, saveing the reversion in the Crowne, which by the statute 34 Hen. VIII. could in noe sort by fine and recovery, or any other meanes, be barred, unless first the reversion were taken out of the Crowne; for had this beene as much as suspected, Sir Rich. Hutton, who was a learned man, and counsell and party in these settlements, would have taken care for the removing of this reversion out of the Crowne before these recoveries suffered.

" But oftentimes it falls out that the vanity of men in studying to preserve their name, though to the totall disherison of their owne children, is crossed, or proves unsuccessfull to the end designed.

" And soe it happened here; for when Francis, now Earle of Cumberland, upon ye view of soe fair evidences, made noe question of enjoying these landes; presently a title is started for ye Lady Anne by virtue of the ancient intayle, which was most effectually prosecuted by that excellent woman Margarett Countesse Dowager of Cumberland. After the death of Earl George information to an office is preferred in the court against Francis Earle of Cumberlande and others, setting forth ye guift of ye manor of Skipton to Rob. de Clifford and ye heires of his body, by King Edward II, and deriving the same down to the ye Lady Anne Clifford, as heire in tayle, the reversion continuing in ye Crowne. The Defendants answered: 1st, That the grant of Skipton was resumed by authority of Parliament, 5to Edw. II. 2d, That the confirmation by Ric. II. amounts to a new grant of the fee simple. 3d, That by the Act of Attainder, 1st Edw. IV. and ye Act of Restitution, 1st Hen. VII., it was turned into a fee simple. 4th, That it was settled as a fee simple, by the fine and recovery of George Earle of Cumberland, upon the now Earle.

" To this the Attorney replies, The resumption of 5 Ed. II. was repealed by Parliament 15 Ed. II.

" They rejoine, deny, &c.

" Presently, upon this suit, and before the hearing, Earl Francis taking the alarme, and thinking to mend his condition by a grant, or at least to make sure of the reversion of the title in the Crowne, 4th June 5th Jac., obtains a grant to him and his heires of the honor and manor of Skipton, &c., and the reversion thereof.

" This, though it passed nothing in possession, yet it passed the rev'on out of the Crowne, though it came too late.

" After this there was an Inq. 24th Apr. 7th Jac. whereby are found the Letters Pat. of K. E. II. to Robert de Clifford and ye heires of his body ye fine of recovery of 33 Eliz. the deed of 3d Jac. and the titles on either side, drawne downe to Francis Earle of Cumberland, by his remainder limitted upon the recovery, and to ye Lady Anne, by the entayle of Edw. II.

" But into that office there was shuffled a clause, without any collor of evidence, that K. H. VI. did grant unto Thomas Lord Clifford, his heires and assignes, the rev'on of the said castle and manor of Skipton; which was therefore inserted to support the fine and recovery by George Earle of Cumberland, and the conveyance made thereof to Earle Francis. Upon the return of this Inq. exception was taken thereto in the Court of Wards; and upon solemne argument before the two Chief Justices and Chief Baron, assistants to that Court, Hil. 1 Jac. 7. it was agreed that all the lands in Yorkshire, contained in the settlement of 33 Eliz. except the manor and castle of Skipton, were well settled upon Earle Francis, and ye heires male of his body. 2d, Because exception was taken to that clause, the court directed a special livery to be sued with a *salvo jure*, so that either p'ty might try their title. In pursuance of which order, 16 June, 1615, a triall at barr of the Com'on Pleas was had in an *ejectione firmæ*, wherein the Plaintiff setts forth her title by the guift in tayle made unto Rob. Lord Clifford, &c. &c.

" Against which they, pretending that Henry VI. granted the reversion in fee to Thomas Lord Clifford, produced not the record thereof, but endeavoured to prove it by circumstances; viz., the favour of that Lord with Hen. VI.; the feoffments made thereof by him to uses, 26th Hen. VI., &c. To this it was answered, that it is a dangerous p'sident to prove a matter of record by such p'sumption.

" After the evidence on both sides, a reference was moved by the Court, and a juror withdrawn.

" 14th March, 1617, the King took upon him the awarding of this difference, and ordered that a conveyance be made by the Lady Anne, then Countess of Dorsett, and the Earle her husband, of the said honor, &c., to Francis Earle of Cumberland, for life; remr to his first and other sons in tayle, remr to the Countesse for life, remr to her first and other sons, remr to her drs; and 20,000l. to be paid by the Earle of Cumberland to the Earle of Dorsett.

" To this award the two Earls subscribed; but, notwithstanding the potency of the Earle of Cumberland, the will of the King, and the importunity of a husband, the Countess refused to subscribe or submit to it. Afterwards, the Earle of Dorsett dying, she, in 1628, made her entries into the lands; which she renewed in 1632, and hath since enjoyed them, the rather for that Francis and Henry Earles of Cumberland dying without issue male, the pretence of title which he could make under the award ceased.

" Thus ended that great controv'sie touching ye honr of Skipton."

Francis fourth Earl of Cumberland was born in Skipton Castle, A.D. 1559, and died in the same apartment more than eighty years after. He seems to have been an easy, improvident man, but otherwise comparatively blameless.

His niece contents herself with observing of him, that he and his estate were governed by his son Henry Clifford for the last twenty years of his life.

She had an excellent hand at drawing characters ; but the best painter of the face, or of the mind, is confounded by absolute vacuity.

The date of his death, not interment,* is thus recorded in the Register of Skipton :—

"1640, Jan. 28th of this month, departed this life the right honorable Francis earle of Cumberland, lord of the honnor of Skipton, in Craven ; and was solemnly buried in the valte of Skipton church, with his most noble ancestors." † (His body was not embalmed.)

His countess was interred at Londesborough, with the following epitaph, which I subjoin, as it has not been published before :—

Here lieth in
rest the body of
the right honorable
Lady, the lady Grisold,
Countess of Cumberland,‡
daughter of Thomas Hughes of
Uxbridge, in yᵉ countie of Middlesex,
Esq. She was first married to Edw.
Nevill, lord Abergavennie, and after
to Sir Francis Clifford, knight, earl of
Cumberland, by whome she had issue
George Clifford, that died a child,
Henry now lord Clifford,
Lady Margaret, married to Sir Thomas
Wentworth, of Wentworth-wood-
house, in yᵉ countie of York, knight and baronet,
and lady Frances, maried to Sir Gervaise
Clifton of Clifton, in yᵉ countie of
Nottingham, knight and baronet.
This noble Lady, being of the age
of .... years, departed this
mortal life at Londsbrough,
on the 15th day of April,
in the year of our
Lord 1613.

---

* Yet in the accounts at Londesborough is this entry, relating to the funeral of Earl Francis :—"1640, Jan. 14, For opening the vaut, and for frankincense, 5s.—Jan. 20, Doctor Padua, who came to my ould Lord in his sickness, 4*l.*—Jan. 22. To the ringers at my lord's buriall, 1*l.*"

† After the death of his lady, Earl Francis resided almost always at Skipton; yet in 1617 he entertained his patron King James at Brougham, and musical amateurs may inquire for

"The Ayres that were sung and played at Brougham-castle, in Westmerland, in the King's Entertainment : given by the Right Honorable the Earle of Cumberland, and his Right Noble Sonne the Lord Clifford. Composed by Mr. George Mason and Mr. John Earsden, London, printed by Thomas Snodham; cum privilegio, 1618," fol.

‡ She resided wholly at Londesborough after her lord's accession to the title, not enduring to go to Skipton or Brougham while in litigation with her niece.—"Lady Pembroke's Memoirs."

HENRY, FIFTH AND LAST EARL OF CUMBERLAND.

Earl Francis was succeeded by Henry Lord Clifford, fifth and last earl of the family, born at Londesborough, 28th or 29th February, 1591, who had the misfortune to see the beginnings of the great rebellion, and the happiness to be taken from the calamities which followed.

"Earl Henry," says the Countess of Pembroke, "was endued with a good natural wit, was a tall and proper man, a good courtier, a brave horseman, an excellent huntsman, and had good skill in architecture and mathematics.* He was much favoured by King James and King Charles, and died of a burning fever, at one of the prebends' houses in York, Dec. . . 1643." †

Of this nobleman Lord Clarendon speaks in these terms : " The Earl of Cumberland was a man of great honour and integrity, who had all his estate in that country, and had lived most among them, with very much acceptation and affection from the gentlemen and the common people ; but he was not in any degree active, or of a martial temper ; and rather a man not like to have any enemies, than to oblige any to be firmly and resolutely his friends.

" The great fortune of the family was divided, and the greater part of it carried away by an heir female ; and his father had so wasted the remainder, that the earl could not live with that lustre his ancestors had done."

In both the last assertions the great historian is mistaken ; for it was not till the death of this nobleman‡ that the partition of the family estates took place ; and it was not his

* She might have added, in poetry, or, at least, in versifying, for he turned into rhyme Solomon's Song, &c., which were remaining at Londesborough long after his decease.

† His lady survived him little more than three months, and was interred in York Cathedral. Her tomb has been engraven, and her epitaph printed by Drake. [Here lyeth in rest the body of the right honourable FRANCES CECIL, Countess of *Cumberland*, daughter of the right honourable *Robert* earl of *Salisbury* (lord high-treasurer of *England*, and knight of the most noble order of the *Garter*, and Master of the Court of Wards and liveries). She married the right honourable *Henry* lord *Clifford, Bromfleet, Vetrepont*, and *Vessey*, earl of *Cumberland*, and lord-lieutenant of the county of *York* under King CHARLES the first, the last earl of that ancient and most noble family of CLIFFORD, by whom the said lady had issue the right honourable the lady *Elizabeth Clifford* (married to the right honourable *Richard* lord *Boyle*, baron *Clifford* and earl of *Burlington* in *England*, earl of *Cork* and lord high-treasurer of *Ireland*), also, three sons, viz., *Francis, Charles*, and *Henry*, and one daughter more, the lady *Frances Clifford*, who all died young. This noble lady being of the age of forty-nine years and eleven months, departed this mortal life at *York*, on the 4th day of *February*, in the year of our Lord *1643.*—Drake's "York," p. 505.]

‡ The magnificent and costly manner in which the old nobility were habited, may be proved from the following account of a single suit made for Lord Clifford in 1632.

"For 13 yards of bezar-culler broade tabie, at 22*s.* the yerd, 14*l.* 17*s.*—For a yard and ⅓ of tafety, for lyning the doublett, 1*l.* 4*s.*—For 395 oz. ¾ of gould and silver lace, plated, clouded, and whipt, in compass, rouning by measure to 38 dozen, at 5*s.* 6*d.* the oz., 108*l.* 17*s.* 4*d.*—For 6 dozen of buttons, gould and silver, 1*l.* 5*s.*—For 6 yards of gallon lace, and 1 of collers, 6*s.* 5*d.*—For 18 oz. and ½ of collored silk, 1*l.* 17*s.*—To Macalla, for canvas and stiffening callicoe to interlyne the cloake, holland for the hose, fustian for pocketts, hookes and eyes, &c., 1*l.* 9*s.*—For making suite and cloake, 9*l.* 10*s.*—For a p'r of perle-culler stockings, 1*l.* 16*s.*—For a paire of garters and roses, and 3 dozen of pointes suitable, all of rich gold and silver thrid, without mixture ; one pair of gloves trim'd suitable, and a hatband stringed, suitable, all of rich gold and silver thrid, without mixture : one pair of gloves trim'd suitable, and a hatband stringed, 13*l.*—For 1 long button, a loope for the cloake, with gold and silver head, 2*s.*—The whole charge of this suite, and the furniture, is 154*l.* 4*s.* 9*d.*"

The following particulars relating to the latter years of the earl, together with his death, funeral, &c., will not be unacceptable to the curious reader : "To the door-keepers at Parlyam'ᵗ House, on the 17th day of my lord of Strafford's tryall, 10*s.*—Mem. The 12 Maii that his lord'p came from Parlyam'ᵗ the earl of Strafford suffered.—1641, Apr. paid to the Yeoman Usher of the Parly'ᵗ House for his lo'ps fees at his entrance as earle into the house, *viz.* Usher of the Black Rod, 4*l.* 10*s.*—Upper Clerk, 4*l.* 10*s.*—Yeoman Usher, 26*s.*—Under Clerk, 20*s.*—Total, 11*l.*—May. For wateridge to the Tower, when his lordship went to take leave of my lord of Strafford the day afore he was executed, and for wyne & beare at Bridgefoote with Sir Gervase Clifton, and boat-hyre back, 6*s.*—July. To his lordship, in gold, for a benevolence to my lord Primate of Ireland, lately dispossest of all his estate by the rebells, 5*l.*—Disburst by my lady's journeye from Londesborough to London, being *eleven* days in the way with 32 horses, 68*l.* 18*s.* 4*d.*

"1643. Disbursed since the 11th day of Dec'ʳ. the yeare aforesaid, on wᶜʰ day it pleased God to take the soule of my most noble lo. out of this miserable, rebellious age, I trust, to his eternall joyes !

"Dec. 12. Imprimis, To the Gov'ʳ of Yorke's clarke, for a pass for a trumpeter, & a servant of my lo. to go to Hull, 2*s.* 6*d.*—

father only, but his uncle, who wasted the great property of the Cliffords. At all events, he was happily removed from times little suited to tempers like his; and was interred at Skipton, amidst the roar of arms,* when his castle was held for the king against all the assaults of the rebels.

I have thrown together in this place the most interesting letters in the correspondence of this nobleman and his father; of which a much larger collection remains in the family archives at Bolton Abbey, extending from the year 1611 nearly to the death of the last earl, in 1643. The first is addressed to Lord Clifford, then a hopeful young nobleman at Paris, from John Taylor, the faithful and confidential secretary of Earl Francis.

"My Most Honorable Lord,

"I beseche the God of heaven and earth to bless and direct you in all y'r waies, and sende yo' home well in dewe tyme, that yo' then see with y'r owne eyes, and judge accordingly of men's deservings.

"I praise God, albeit the wynde was awhyle contrary, yet I gott to London in eight daies, and delivered my l'res to my l. tres'r. His l. used me very nobelly, and seemed very glad of my so spedy and safe retorn. I found him in the garden at Whytehall, and many of the l'ds w'th him: e'ch one p'tic'l'rly enqueared of y'r l., to all whom I presented yo'r service.

"This done, my l. tre'r w'thdrewe himself aparte w'th me from the company, and read his l'res, and curiously enqueared many questions of me touchyng yo'r l'p's health, yo'r dyett, and all yo'r exercises, and w'thall what yo' did studdy or read, to which last I was able to speak least; yett soe farr as I could I did: then of y'r jurney intended. Lastly, we came to speak of my l. ambassador, of whome I did not spare to speak (besides y'r p'ticular obligation unto him) that my poore opinion was, he didd his prince and cuntrey much hon'r in living so nobelly and discreetly, w'h he could not do but at an extraordinary charge. He herd me willingly; and yett the times were unseasonable, for the newes were not then comed of my la. Arbella's taking, and so bothe kinge an councell were then muche trobled.

"Yo'r l'p knowes I profess plain dealing w'th dewtie, and protest against flattery; owt of w'ch grounds I must needs tell y'r l'p I fynd an opinion now very generally received by moste men heare of good hope and expectation of yo'r sufficiency, w'ch proceedeth from those that have observed y'r courses their. In good faith I do heare this song song muche to my comfort whensoever I am in company wheare y'r name is spoken of.

"My lo. and la. Wotton lye at Greenwiche; they arc bothe well, and very kind and carefull over y'r l'p. I heare no speech of his discontinuance, as was their reported. Sir Tho. Wharton is expected heare this . . . My la. his sister, tells me, they have begoon to live at too great . . . already. They were all at Londesbrowghe, and, as I heare, were very nobelly entertained theare.

"I understand all are well at Londesbrowghe. I had a l're from my lo. but it concerned Mr. Wentworth only. The

---

To George Middleton, on account of several things bought at Hull, towards the funerall of my lorde, the sum of 40*l.*—To the paynter, for making exchuchons, 2*l.* 1*s.*—To the coachmaker, for making the chariott for carrying the corps to Skipton, 4*l.*—Dec. 13. For one of the vergers for ringing the Minster bell, being double fees for a nobleman, 1*l.* 8*s.*—33 yards of black cloath for coachman and footmen, 16*l.*—Dec. 15. Mr. Beomant of York, for 3 whole pieces, of black, 24*l.* 15*s.* 6*d.*—Mr. Squuyre, for fine cloth, 9*l.* and coarse 5*l.* 3*s.*, 14*l.* 3*s.*—Ditto, bought at Hull, cloath, 27*l.* 17*s.* 4*d.*—Several sorts of ribbon, 4*l.*—For royal paper, for eschuchons, 12*s*—Mr. Adgar Taylor, 27½ yards of velvett at 26*s. per* yard, for a black pall for covering the corpse, 35*l.* 15*s.*—J. Plaxton, on account of wine to be bought at Skipton, 15*l.*—Mr. Deane the surgeon, in part for embalming the bodye, 10*l.*—29 yards of searge, for my la. Wotton's mourning, 4*l.*—For a mason, for mending and blacking the sceling in my lo. chamber, 3*s.*—To my lo. Fairfax servants, for a safe conduct to London, 10*s.*—For 4 stone of tow, to putt into the coffin, and between the coffin and the charriot, to keep it from shaking, 10*s.*—To Mr. Horseman, for escucheons, 5*l.* 17*s.*—To the poor at my lord's gate when the body went from the house, 3*l.*—Dr. Vadguer, (Padua?) for coming 6 dayes to his lordship in his sickness, 5*l.*—Disbursed in the journeye between York and Skipton, for all my lord's servants, horse-meat and man's meat, and others, and poore of every parish, w'th rewards to ye souldyers by the way, of foot and horse, w'ch guarded the corpse, the sum of 28*l.* 2*s.*—To the souldyers and gunners of the garrison, at enterring my lord, 10*l.*

"Bolton, 12 July 1644. Agreed w'th Rich. Barnvis for all that piece of ground at Bolton, called the Hambilton, as it now putteth out to be eaten and foiled by the princes horse as they passed thro' this county, &c. 20*l.*"

From the inventory of this earl's effects, taken in May, 1644, it appears, that he had at Skipton and Bolton 47 horses, of which 32 had been plundered by the Rebels. Of the rest, Bay Barbary had been "given by my lord to my Lord Newcastle. White . . . taken by General Goring for what my lord of Corke pleases, and Shotten Herring, taken by Prince Rupert on the same terms, as by note under his hand appears."

* The entry of his interment, in the parish register, is in the following words: "1643, Dec. The last of this month was interred in the valte in the church at Skipton, Henry earle of Cumberland, lord of West'd, l'd Vipont and Vessey, Aitoune, and Bromfleet, and l'd of the honor of Skipton in Craven."

2 U

father and sonn are now bothe heare. Y'r l'p's l're gave them good satisfacc'on. I think his sonn goes down. This order of barronetts proceeds ; divers are created already. Mr. Wentworth* is ranked in the first place for Yorkshire, w'ch is a great favor.

"The ho'rable course y'r l'p held with me their, and the co'mandment y'o laied upon me to conceale nothing from yo', makes me presume to let y'r l'p trewly see what my brother writes unto me of things at home, by sending unto yo' his own l're, w'ch I would not have done to any body livyng but by co'mand ; when y'r l'p have p'used I pray yo' burn it. It shall well appeare, I will labor, by all the means I can possible devise, to drawe all to better order.—In the mean time, I beseche y'r l'p be not greeved, nor trobled therat.† —Mr. S'jeant will helpe me.

"I came hither in good time for the terme business, and I hope we shall keep all in an orderly course.

"My owld ladies spoile of the woods greeves us moste—she will obey no order.‡

"Methinks the Hunters § are not so wholly p'ecuted as p'haps y'r l'p could wishe. I doubte I shall see nothinge in that good order I wishe until God sende y' retorne.—Sir John Yorke is heare, and justifyeth his doings, purposing, as it seems, to maintain suites against my l.||

"Y'r ladie went from hence, w'th my la. of Darbye, on Whitsun Munday, very well.

"My lo. Suffolke was dispached downe before I returned, reasonably well to his own contentment. The k. renewed patent of the 1000 a yeare out of the Exchecq. for tenn yeares mo'e. But I heare he must live w'thin his govern't. My lo. Cooke and he fell out bitterlie the daye before he went downe. It is sayed he gave my lo. Cooke the lye, and redobled it.

"Men speake muche of the change of the Northern government,¶ and moste conclude the cawse to be by reson my lord did so seldom come their. It is too much spoken of heare, and too litle thought of at home.

"I was in good hopes this shipping would have proved well ; but I find it quite contrary : it comes but to 88o*l.* in all, out of which 500*l.* was presently payed for the halfe yeare's rent of the patent. The remainder is all the relief I have to work upon towards the debts, interest-moneye, and all other occasions heare. Not one penny comes from the country, and yet my lor. charged me to pay the 40*l.* to my ladie of Conisby, and 45*l.* to my la. of Darbye ; bothe whiche sho'd have come out of the countrey, and divers thinges besides.

"No order or care taken wheare I should have meanes to furnish y'r allowance, nor any mention thereof. God is my Judge, I do all I can for my lief to keep things in some order till y'r retorne. I have too far stretched my creditt, whereof litle or no regard is had. I shall acquaint my lo. treas'r herewith, so far as it may be fitt, for prevention sake, in modest termes.

"I had a fine lief whilst I was w'th y'r l'p in France ; but I am now baited like a beare.

"And so, w'th my daly praiers to God for the contenewance of his grace and blessing upon you, and the remembrance of my owne humble duty and service, I take my leave.   &c. &c. &c.

"*From London this* 12*th of June,* 1611.   "JOHN TAYLOR.

"I forbeare to write muche of my la. Arbella and Mr. Seimer's escape, and her apprehension and impr't in the Tower, because my lo. Cumb. hath advyse thereof. And so of my la. of Shrewsbury's impr't for the same matter. We may thank God and frends that she was not sent to Londesbr' at first."

What a lamentable picture of the affairs of a great family! Bills, pensions, interest, and even the allowance of a favourite son on his travels unpaid and unprovided for ; half the estate in danger of being torn from the earl by an heir female, while he was over-living the income of the whole ; a law-suit with Sir John Yorke, about one of the few manors which were unclaimed by his niece ; and the lieutenancy of the northern counties threatened to be taken from him for indolence and inattention to his charge! On Lord Clifford's return, however, he was associated with his father in this trust, and associated himself in the management of his fortune ; so that, after a short time, matters both public and private were in a better train.

Mr. Taylor's account of his reception at Whitehall, and the consternation of the Court on account of the escape of the Lady Arabella is curious and original. It seems to have

---

* The father of the Earl of Strafford.

† Probably Mr. Serjeant Hutton, afterwards a judge, who was much in the confidence of the family.

‡ Margaret Countess Dowager of Cumberland, who resided at Brougham, which she had in settlement. I am sorry to find that either rapacity or revenge could prompt so good a woman to such a conduct. Yet much might be forgiven to a mother who saw her daughter about to be deprived of estates which she believed her own.

§ The Hunters : these were, I believe, the deer-stealers in Longstrother, &c., who, taking advantage of the imbecility of Earl Francis, carried on their depredations with a security very galling to the young lord. In another place (among the Skipton papers) I find the earl complaining of these "lewd persons ;" but he probably did little more than complain.

|| This refers to the suit about free-warren within the manor of Appletrewick.

¶ The Lieutenancy of the Middle Shires, as they were called—*i.e.*, Westmoreland and Cumberland.

been the intention of the Court to commit that unfortunate lady to the care of the Earl of Cumberland, at Londesborough. A man of less vigilance could not have been chosen for the purpose; and his faithful servant had reason to be thankful that he escaped that perilous and ungrateful office.

"GOOD MADAM,

"I have understood by so many wayes how well you have affected the match betwene my lord Clifford and my daughter; as I think it my part no longer to delay my thanks for the same : for when I consider what he is in himselfe, both by birth and vertue, what love he hath and deserveth to have of all men, I must needs conceave he must be more to you, to whom he is the onely sonne; and therefore my thanks the greater, in that you have bene so desirous to plant him into my stock whome you have cause to hold so deere. More I cannot say, madame, at this tyme, but that I will love him, and cherish him as the aple of one of myne eyes. To yourselfe I will wishe long life, that wee may bothe see some branches of him to our comfort in our old dayes. And so remayne your ladyship's assured loving friend,

"*Salisbury-house, this 28th of July.*" "R. SALISBURY.

This is a letter of compliment from Robert Cecil, Earl of Salisbury to Grisold Countess of Cumberland on the marriage of his daughter with her son, Lord Clifford. The wish of long life was not granted to either, the lord treasurer dying within one year, and the countess within two years after.

"MY GOOD L.

"Such is ye comfort your owne vertew yelds me (as all men's reports bring to me, and particularly Mr. Beecher, who cannot too much commend you), besides ye honour you bring my house, as I know not what to write to you to make you know how much I love you. This onely I will say, that your father (excepting nature) cannot hold you dearer. Of y^r expense at ye tyme of yo'r journeys this sommer, and such other particularitys, I need write nothing, because you arr so well able to govern yo'self, and are uppon ye place where you see more than I can do. My advise is therefore this, that you do avoyd occasion of heate by violent exercise or stay in ye whottest clymate * in ye hottest seasons; and that you remember your complexion is cholerick, and therefore wyne to be moderately drunk. I have now don, and therefore do conclude, that this bearyr shewes his love to yo'r p'son by this journey, y^t I find his care of yo'r fortune by his pauses here; and for myself can tell you, that I am your affectionate father-in-law, "R. SALISBURY."

These directions, worthy the good sense of Robert Cecil, were evidently dictated by the information he had received from Mr. Taylor, with respect to the behaviour and pursuits of his son-in-law. A general decay in this nobleman's faculties at the age of fifty leads me to suspect that he continued to indulge himself too liberally in the use of wine. It was owing to this circumstance that, when his assistance was wanted by Charles I., he was become nearly useless.

"To the Right Honorable my very good Lord and Cosine the Lo. Clyfford.

"NOBLE LORD,

"By so fitt a messenger I can not omitt the testimony of a well-wishinge mind to the good success of your hopeful courses. For the more rare it is in theas daies to finde younge noblemen enclyned to vertowe and industrye, the greater cause have all worthy mindes to encourage and honor them.

"The respect which I owe to your howse by honor, to your frendes by bonde, and to yourself by sympathy, is such, as I assure you, that nothinge can be more welcome to me than an apt occasion to witness that goode will which wantes but opportunity to express affection.

"In this place we enjoye all happiness, under the most worthy kinge that did ever live, and holde ourselves secure by observinge that all princes in the world, at this day, are desirous, in a kinde, to make his m'ty an indifferent umpier in their differences.

"We lacke nothinge here but mony; and that lacke also growes out of the bownty of the kinge, which is vertuous so longe as it is proportioned to means sutable; but furder it hath no warrant amonge philosophers.

"At this instant we have nothinge newe that is worth your knowledge; wherfor presuminge that this bearer, y'r father's faythful and trewe servant, will acquaint your lo. with the ordinary state of thinges as now they are, I recomend your lo. with your noble and towardly endeavours, to the gratious protection of God; and ever rest, your lo. lovinge cosine and assured frende, "H. NORTHAMPTON.

"*May v, 1611.*"

---

* Lord Clifford was probably setting out for Italy from Paris in the beginning of summer, the worst season which could have been chosen for the purpose.

I am not a little gratified by having retrieved this composition of an accomplished nobleman, the son of a more illustrious father, Henry Howard, Earl of Surrey, who fell a sacrifice to the brutal tyranny of Henry VIII., sixty-five years before this time.

Henry Howard, Earl of Northampton, was called the most learned among the nobility, and the most noble among the learned. Such an exhortation to virtue and industry from so venerable a peer could not but have a powerful effect on the mind of his young correspondent.

The modern reader, who has formed his opinion of James I. from Whig writers, will do well to weigh this testimony from a contemporary and excellent judge, given in circumstances when there was no temptation to flatter. James was thoughtless and profuse, but generally well-meaning; and it would become posterity to reflect at what time the English nation enjoyed more uninterrupted happiness than under the reign of a monarch whom they unreasonably contemn because he refused to sacrifice that happiness at the bloody altar of military glory.

With respect to prerogative, however, it must be allowed that a Howard who had seen and felt the last years of Henry VIII. was not likely to be very captious.

" My Loveing Sonne,

"The newes of y'r safe retorne to Paris from that longe journey, w'ch wee dayly expecte and praye for, would be to yo'r mother and me, and soe to yo'r sisters and other frendes here, the most welcome tydinges that could possibly come unto us. I hope manie dayes will not passe over before we receive advertisement thereof.

" Mr. Wentworth* is an earnest, and seemeth to be a very affecc'onate suiter to y'r sister: he hath beene here altogether for these three weekes past, and remaines here still: yo'r sister is lykewyse therewith well pleased and contented. His father and I are agreed of all the conditions; we shall onely want and wish yo'r compaine at the marriage, which is, I thinke, not lyke to be long deferred. God blesse them!

" I was verie well pleased to see, by yo'r last l're, howe carefull yow were for the good of our estate, to have things reduced to order and conformitie, whereof I am not unmyndefull; and to thend yow may the better see that something is donne, I have thought good breefely to lett you know, that, by a commission † granted to some knights and gentlemen, rather to satisfy oth'rs than myself, I have lately cawsed a full review and examination to be taken, what monies were owinge and dewe unto me at my brother's death, or since, and howe the same have been answered unto me.

" Upon this, we have fallen further into consideration howe my estate standes, and p't'c'ly what may be necessary to be donne for reliefe. Wherein, albeit we could not at this p'sent proceed to a full resolution, yet doe we see what is fitt to bee done, and are determined to putt it in execution so farr as wee maye, and that ere longe. I have directed John Taylor to acquaint yo' w'th o'r proceedings more at large, whom I am dispatchinge to London to intend my businesses there. Yo'r wyfe is well in Lancashyre. And soe, with God's blessinge and o'rs to yo'rself, I commend yow in my prayers to God, and will ev'r remaine,   " Yo'r verie lovyng and affectionate father,
    " *Londesbrough, this* vth *of October*, 1611."   " Fr. Cumbreland.

" To my verie loving son the lord Clifford, at Paris.
    " My Deere and Loving Son,

    " Y'r last letter, of the first of January, by that accompte, came to my hands heare before o'r Christmas was ended, w'ch much increased o'r joy and comfort. Nothing was therein unpleasing unto us, sav'g only that by some late advises, which I had but a lyttle before receaved from my lord tres'r by letters, I found that yo'r soe wisshed, and by us all soe much desired, p'sent retorne, and soe certenly expected at this next Candlemas, was, by his especiall desire and dyreccion, countermanded, or deferred for a moneth longer, or thereaboute.

    " Only as you doe soe now knowe, it is alsoe fitt for us to submytt our desires, (especially beinge but for a verie short tyme) to his bett'r judgem't whoe best knowes the fittest tymes and seasons for you. I wrote unto him last terme, that, as

---

* Afterwards Earl of Strafford. How far love could soften the native sternness of this great man, or whether the gaiety of youth could in any degree suppress it, must be left to conjecture. But there is always much disguise in courtship. The entry of Wentworth's marriage in the parish register of Londesborough, which has fallen into the hands of a gentleman at a distance from the parish to which it belongs, is as follows: "Thomas Wentworth, son and heier of Sr William Wentworth, Knight Barronett, and the La. Margarett, eldest daughter to the Right Honora^ble Francis earl of Cumberland, and Grisell his countess, maryed the xxiid of October 1611, being Thursday."

† This is the last vestige I have met with of the regal style assumed by the old nobility in appointing a council, granting commissions, &c., for the management of their affairs. A modern peer, writing to his son on the same subject, would say, "I have desired my friend Sir John ——, Mr. ——, and Mr. —— to look into my accounts," &c. &c.

well in reguard of yo'r charge soe increasinge, as for some other respectes, I desired to see you shortly in England ; but yet left all to his disposal ; to which he retorned me a verie loving and noble answer, and p't'ly some reasons of yo'r stay for a lyttle whyle. It seemes yo'r charge haith of late increased much, w'ch I know you are sensible of so far as hon'r will p'mitte : soe are your mother and I, for yo'r future good, devisinge by all the meanes we can think of how to lessen ours heare. And it pleaseth us bothe well to see by some of yo'rs that you have a feeling for the releeving and rayseing o'r estate, whereunto wee doubt not you will put your helping hande at yo'r retorne. Wee are thus contented even to restrayne and confine ourselves within a lesser compass for yo'r goode. Wee are lykwyse exceedingly well pleased and well satisfied to see by bothe your owne lett'rs soe good a begynnyng of love and kyndnes setled betwene you and yo'r brother-in-law. Yo'r sister thinkes herselfe much bownd to you for entertayning her husband soe kyndely, which he haith hyghly co'mended in his letters to hir ; and besides your mother and I doe both of us much thank you for it. Co'mend me very kyndely to the lord ambassador there ; and forgett me not to Mr. Beecher. Tell that gentleman whom you call in yo'r letters yo'r good friend mounsier Benjamin, that I doe very specially take notice of his lovinge kindnesses towards you, which, at yo'r dep'ture, I hope you will reco'mend ; and I shall desire him to transfer them over to yo'r brother Wentworth. Yo'r mother longes not a lyttle to see you. Soe, with God's blessings unto you and yours, to whose infinite mercy and goodness we daylie co'mend you in ou' prayers, that his holy hand and blessed proteccion may alwaies keepe and defende you in all your waies ; there will I leave you. And soe am, from Londesbr', this 13th of Januarie, 1611, your very loving father,

" Fr. Cumbrelande."

Such was the religious language which a great nobleman scrupled not to use two centuries ago in writing to his son. And I doubt not that it was a faithful transcript of his feelings. If anything can excite the spirit of devotion in a parent, surely it must be the situation of an only son, beset with all the temptations of youth and rank, and all the dangers of foreign travel.

" To the Ry't Ho'ble my very good Lo. the lord Clifforde.

" My Lord,

" The king will by no meanes dispense w'th your runninge at tilt ; and, for my payrt, if I might advyse you respecting the state of your father's bussinesse, I would by no meanes have you excuse your selfe, for that I am sure would better please your enemies. So, promissinge to your lo. all rednisse in me to value to his m'ty your cair to do him honnor and servise at this marriage, I rest your lo. assured friend,

" Ro. Rochester."

Robert Carr, then Viscount Rochester, was afterwards better or worse known by the title of Earl of Somerset. The marriage here alluded to seems to have been that of the Earl of Essex with Lady Frances Howard, procured by the king's mediation, and celebrated, according to the fashion of the times, with tilts and tournaments. It was Carr's criminal intrigue with this lady which occasioned the death of Overbury, and his own disgrace. The advice, however, which he gave his young correspondent was good : the great cause of the baronies and estates of the family was now, by reference, before the king ; and Rochester well knew that his master's interest and affections could in no way be so surely engaged as by the splendid appearance of Lord Clifford at a public spectacle.

" To the Right Honorable Lorde the Lord Clyfforde.

" My Noble Spaniard,[*]

" Though distance of place have for a tyme seperated us, yet are you not forgotten by your poor frends heer, in whose memories you doo not only live, but have also a tryumphant seat in our hartes, w'ch never cease to wish the good of you and yours. The state of the Court, with marriages and masquerades, I leave to the reporte of honest and wyse Mr. John Tayler. Concluding this, w'th kissing your l'p's and your noble ladie's handes, by whom to be commanded I should repute it a glory.   " Your l'p's to doo you service,

" *Whitehalle, 29th of November,* 1613."   " E. Wotton.

" To the Right Honorable my very good Lorde the Lorde Clifforde.

" My Very Good Lorde,

" Your letter, brought me by your footman, hath allmost made me falle into one of the seaven deadly sinnes : I mean that of pryde, finding myself to enjoy so great a portion of your favor ; the w'ch I will studie to conserve, by my much

---

[*] Why " Noble Spaniard ?" I suppose it was fashionable at that time to affect the manners of Spain. Lord Clifford certainly understood and loved the language, for several of the old Family Books of Account have marginal notes by him in Spanish.

honouring you, and by my redynes upon all occasions to do you service ; her'of I pray your l'p to rest assured.　Mr. Tailer can informe your l'p of the news of these partes, w'ch makes me forbear to trouble you w'th them.　I humbly kisse your handes, and rest your l'p's unfayned frend and servant,　　　　　　　　　　　　　　　　　"E. WOTTON.

　"*Whitehalle*, 16*th of December*, 1614.

　"I humbly present my service to your noble lady."

　　　　　　　　　　　　"To the Right Honourable the Lorde Clifforde.

"NOBLE LORDE,

　"How sorrowful wee weare for the doleful newes, your l'p may easely gesse by our loves to your house.　Wee may not repine at God's doings, who doth every thing for the best, though to flesh and blood sometymes, through weaknes, it may seeme otherwyse.　Bee of good comfort, sweet lorde, and let wisdome worke that effect in you w'ch length of tyme dooth in all, I mene diminution of greef.　So shall the tyme of your ladies greatnes bee the lesse irksome to hir, who I doubt not will bring comfort to you and your hous, by bringing you many sonnes.　Of this no more.　One thing I wish, that my lorde your father, woold now take occasion to lessen his expenses of housekeeping, whereof (as your l'p knoweth) ther is som need ; and that your l'p, in your sportes, wil drawe as lyttle company as you may, wherein you shall both keep decorum, and ease your charges.　So wishing to my l. your father, yourself, and your lady, the comfort w'ch this world can affoord, I rest your l'p's to do you service,　　　　　　　　　　　　　　　　　　　"E. WOTTON."

Edward Lord Wotton was one of the executors of the will of George Earl of Cumberland, and therefore well acquainted with the affairs of the family.　The last letter, which does equal honour to the head and heart of the writer, was occasioned by the death of the infant son of Henry Lord Clifford ; a stroke peculiarly afflictive, as the continuance of the baronies and principal estates in the line of Earl Francis depended upon male issue from his son.

This nobleman was a man of great talents and address, who had recommended himself to James I. in Scotland.　He was elder brother of Sir Henry Wotton, a name which has long been familiar to scholars, but is better and more generally known of late in consequence of the republication of " Walton's Lives," with copious and edifying notes, by Dr. Zouch, to whom, as I have not the happiness of being personally known to him, I take this opportunity of making my acknowledgments for the pleasure and improvement which I have received from that elegant work.

　　　　　　"To the Right Hon'ble my singulare good Lord and Cousen the Earle of Cumberland.

"NOBLE LORD,

　"Your owen tyme shall satisfye me, for the ending of that business is betwene us in controversy.　A few months will breede but a smaule alteration in a matter that hathe been so long in concluding ; I wish it had bene souner ended for boeth our sakes ; but since that tyme past cannot be recauled, we must make of necessyte a vertu.　For the satisfaction that shall ryse to both of us, I cannot doubt but it must nedes be good, when the mediators shall be sutche as ourselves, boeth born with honor and justisse in our mynds, or else we are not worthy of the stile wee are cauled by ; besydes, the neereness of blood and freendshippe, can but promise a noble proceeding, and an honorable and kind ending.　The case of my lord Sheffield's infortunate chance is very lamentable, yett doeth he bare it with a noble courage and resolution.　In theas partes there is nothing new worth your knowledge ; only the two armyes in the Loe Cuntryes hathe bidden adew one to the other till the next spring.　Your lo. is determyned not to be heare till Easter Terme ; but I thinke yow will be cawled up sowner if that goe forwarde is intended, or at least sayd to be intended ; I meane a parlement.　This is all I can tell yow for the present, but that there is a maske towards * for this Christenmas.　And soe, with my best wishes, I rest your lo. true frend and cousin to dispose of,　　　　　　　　　　　　　　　　"H. NORTHUMBERLAND.

　"*This* 13*th of December*, 1614."

Henry Percy, ninth Earl of Northumberland, was convicted of misprision of treason in 1606, on account of the Powder Plot, of which it does not appear that he had any knowledge, and sentenced to be imprisoned in the Tower for life.　He was, however, released in the year 1621, and died in 1632.　No place is mentioned in the date of this letter, but it is

---

* That is, "going forward," a sense in which the word is used by Shakespeare.

evident from the foregoing statement that it was written in the Tower, where he must have been allowed to receive and answer letters relating to his private concerns.

The principal subject of the letter seems to have been the long arrears due from the Cliffords for the ancient rents of the Percy fee, in Craven. These amounted to about 250*l. per annum,* and had been originally paid to the Crown; but Queen Mary, when she restored the titles and estates of the family to Sir Thomas Percy, grandfather of this earl, granted these rents to him. They were therefore payable from that time, by the Cliffords, to the Earls of Northumberland. But I find in the Skipton papers that Earl George was at one time twenty years in arrear; and I strongly suspect that this sum, or a great part of it, remained unpaid in 1614, and drew from the earl this dignified though delicate expostulation. The case of my Lord Sheffield's unfortunate chance was as follows :—In the beginning of this month (December, 1614), Sir John, Edmund, and Philip Sheffield, sons of this nobleman, were unhappily drowned in crossing the Humber at Whitgift Ferry.

Eight years' confinement had not so far detached this nobleman from the concerns of the world, but that he could write about the meeting of parliament, and even of the gaieties of the court, as if he had not been precluded from partaking either of the one or the other. He merited better treatment; and having shared with the Earl of Cumberland in the dangers of the Armada, and, with him, received the Garter from his royal mistress, after such services, and such testimonies, he should not have been condemned to perpetual imprisonment merely for admitting to some subordinate office a kinsman with whose criminal conduct he seems to have been unacquainted. The tranquillity expressed in this letter is strongly conclusive in favour of his innocence.

"S'R CHRISTOFER PICKERINGE,*

"I have beene moved by some hon^{ble} persons, who wish well to all us the partyes, and desire a generall peace amongst us, to lett my ladie of Cumberland, my sister-in-lawe, knowe : That whereas all differences that were betweene my lord of Dorsett and my niece his wife of thone p'ty, myselfe and my sonne of thother, were generally referred to the award of my lord Hoobert, and the rest of the Judges of the Com'on Pleas, who by their wisdomes have already in their award expressed how all the saide differences shalbe composed : I am soe farr from spleene or malice, as if she be of the same mynd, I can be well contented in like sorte upon equall & fayre termes, to referr all things whereupon any question can be stirred upp betweene her la'p and me to the full and finall order alsoe and award of the said Judges ; wherein I desire w^{th}all not to be mistaken, as if I did this out of any necessity or distrust of my owne right, or meanes to right myselfe otherwise, in case shee refuse, but onely as *knowinge whose wife shee* was, for *whose sake I must ever* honor her, and preferring peace farr before warr. And because I knowe not any whome shee will heare more willingly, or I maye trust more safely, then yor selfe ; I shall desire yo^u to deliv^r soe much unto her from me, & returne mee her la'ps answere ; for wh^{ch} I will thanke you, and alwayes rest   "Yo^r assured lovinge friend,
       "13 *March,* 1615."   "F. CUMBERLAND.

"To the Right Hono'ble his very good Lo. the Earle of Cumberland.

- - - - - - - - - - - -

"The many honorable favoures I have receaved since my coming home and my two sonnes before my coming, from my honorable lady of Comberland, induced me, in my returne fro' Carliel, to see her honor, which I had not formerly done. The performance of which my duty she was pleased to take in good p't. At my dep'ture I tould her ladyship that I did intend (God willinge) to ride over and do my duty unto your l'pp ; wishing that it would please God that all differences between your honor and her lady'pp weere well composed ; w'ch reconcyliation was also generally wished and expected in the South partes, and would, no doubt, be sone brought to pas, if som that made profitt of your honnors differences, and loved to fish in trobled waters, weere not the impedementes of it.

"Her honor desired and enjoyned me to say playnely, what was generally spoken herof, and what the woorld conceaved of her. I was loth, but, being co'manded, used words to this effect : Your lady'pp is heald to be very honorable, much

* I cannot discover who this person was ; for Sir Christopher Pickering, last of the Pickerings of Killington in Westmoreland, certainly died early in the reign of Elizabeth. See Burn and Nicholson's "Hist. of Cumberland and Westmoreland," vol. i. p. 261.

devoted to religion, very respective unto ministers and prechers, very charitable unto the poore ; yeat, under favour, som do tax your honor to be too much affected to go to law.—That is, sayd my lady, that I am contentious and overruled by busy wrangling fellowes.

"(I did humbly crave pardon for my plainnes.)—Sir, I do like you much the better for your free speakeing : and, if my l. of Cumberland will make me any honorable offers, I will deceave the woorld or them that think me given unto law and contention.

"I tould her how great an honor it would be unto her to shew love and good affection unto your l'pp's house.—Sir, I do proteste, that, next myselfe, daughter, and sister, I do wish well unto my lo. of Cumberland, my lo. Clifford, and his lady, and will not think the better of any that shall exasperate me against them ; and, if you have cause to attend my l' of Cumberland, commend me hartyly unto his l'p, my l. Clifford, and his lady.—I then asked her la'pp whether I should acquaint your l'pp with the speach that had past betwene her lady'pp and me.—I pray you do so ; for what I speake I wish his l'p should know.—Her lady'pp seemed much offended with my l. Dorcett for so' speaches his l'pp used in publique.— Right hon'ble, I am persuaded her lady'pp will inclyne to peace. Shee tould me that shee would com unto Apleby-castell the next weeke. .   .   .   .

"*Barwyes-halle,*   "Your l'pp's ever at command,
"*25th August,* 1615."   "JO. BOWYER.

I have inserted this fragment, not merely to show what was said and thought of Margaret Countess of Cumberland by her enemies, but with how little asperity she supported her daughter's claims against the male line of the family. Of Sir John Bowyer I know nothing more than that he had lately purchased Barwise Hall, and was labouring to ingratiate himself with Earl Francis. The account of this interview is both candid and curious ; but it may be observed that there is no topic on which a man dilates with more complacency than on the freedom with which he has offered advice to a superior ; and more especially when that advice was in favour of another superior, to whom he is relating his achievement.

"RIGHT HONORABLE AND MY VERIE GOOD L^DS,

"Haveing seene the copie of a letter directed to my l. of Walden, the deputie lieuetenants, and justices of the peace in the countye of Westmerland, signed by some of your l'ps of the fourth of this instant, for preventing of any violent or unlawfull courses that might be moved between my lord of Dorsett's servants and myne, about the possession of the castles of Browham and Apleby in that countye, upon the death of the late countesse dowager, my sister-in-lawe, grounded as it seemes upon an information made of great force and vyolence practised and donne against them ; and being desirous, as becomes me, to give your l'ps satisfaction, and soe to acquite myself of that imputation : I have presumed, by these, to make a true report to your l'ps (as I am credibly informed) how the case standeth. But first, as touching my right of entrye, not obscure, but evident, and soe by way of pleadings admitted by the late countesse in her lyfe-time, approved and confirmed, first by office, and since by the general award made between his l'p and me by the judges of the Com'on Pleas, upon a reference by both our consents, I shall desire yo^u wilbe pleased, and give my counsell leave to make that manifets unto yo^u ; and then I must be an humble suitor to you^r good l'ps, and, if need be, to his ma^ty also, to afford me the benefitt of lawes, whereof I never doubted.

"And as touchinge the manner of my entrye, wherein for many respects, myself, under his ma^ties gracious favour, holdinge the place of one of his lieuetenants there, I was the more cautious and carefull not to give offence, and soe commanded my people whom I employ in that business to proceed temperately and peaceably ; expecting, indeed, no resistance in the possession at all, bycause the whole matter was fully settled by that award and our own consents ; besides, I was informed that my l. of Dorsett was very nobly minded still to make good the award on his parte, and endeavoured by all good meanes to draw my niece his wife to joyne with him in the assurances already agreed upon and p'fected by our counsell accordinge to the same award ; wch I was the rather also induced to beleeve, in that my lord of Dorsett, neither before her death nor since, for anythinge I knowe yet, hath given any warrant to detaine the possession from me.

"And withall, I may safely protest to your l'ps, I was free from thinking the course any way distastefull to him, haveing but lately before by my sollicitor received a motion from him, tending to his own satisfaction, thoe p'tly in another kind, in case his wife would not be drawne to consent ; whereunto in regard I see the fault was only hers, I returned him a friendly and reasonable answere, such as I thought would have given good content. The two houses of Browham and Apleby were the places pointed at in yor l'ps letters, and wherin the force and violence is supposed to be done.

"And first, touching Browham, the chief house, where she lived and dyed, in wch all the goods she hadd of any value were, I held the deceased corps in that reverence, as I forbidd them utterly to meddle with that house ; nor have they attempted to enter thereunto at all.   And for the other, where neither shee, nor any for her, did inhabite for these two yeares last at the least, but such as entered after her death without warrant ; I understand, my people entered peaceably, and had the possession thereof without vyolence, and quietly hould it for my use, as I am advised by my counsell I may lawfully doe : yett, not satisfied with the report of my owne people, least they should varry from the truth in their owne excuse, soe soone as I understood what information hadd beene delivered to your l'ps, I thought it fitt to send my sonne, the better to know the truth, not only from my servants, but from the justices there likewise, who I heard were called thither at the first by some of my ladies' servants to vewe the supposed force ; from whom I received a certificate wch I will make bould herew'th to present to yor l'ps : and as I heare more from them, soe shall I be bould to informe yor l'ps further.   In the meane time, I shall only desire that I may still enjoy yor honorable favo^{rs}, for wch I shall alwaies remaine

"At yor l'ps commandment,

"F. C.

"*Skipton*, 12° *Junii*, 1616."

Margaret Countess of Cumberland, who held the Westmoreland estates in jointure, was just now dead at Brougham Castle, which, notwithstanding the present opposition made by the agents and servants of Lady Dorset, appears to have been shortly after yielded to Earl Francis, as he entertained the king there in the following year.

"S<small>ONNE</small> H<small>ARRIE</small>,

"I could no longer deferr to send unto yow, though I rather desyred to have seene yow, out of w'ch respect I staied the longer at Hodstocke and Woodhowse, that I might be nearer yo'r l'res.

"Upon Sonday last I receaved a letter, by packett, from his ma'tie, for my repaire to London against this Christemas.

"We are much bounde unto his ma'tie, in that he is so graciously pleased to respect us and our howse.   But if this my journey doe but onely concerne the conclusion of our business w'th my l'd of Dorsett, I could wish to be excused, if it could be, w'thout giving the least distaste to his ma'tie.—Yow knowe I growe much into yeares, and am something infirmited, and nott so well able to endure travell as formerly nowe this winter season.   And againe, whatsoev' may concerne the effecting of this business w'th my l'd of Dorsett, I referr the same wholly unto yow, and I shalbe willing at anie time to make what farther confirmac'on shalbe thought convenient.   Notwithstanding, if suche be his ma'stie's pleasure to have me there, I will most willingly obey his comand.   And nowe that I have acquainted yow herew'th, I shall desyre yow to consider of e'ch p'ticular, and to advyse therof w'th some of our frendes, that I may be spedily advertised from you what yow conceyve is most expedient to be donne ; and, in the meane tyme, I shal be preparing my businesses here, and afterwards to doe as I shal be advysed from yow.

"F<small>R</small>. C<small>UMBRELAND</small>.

"28*th Nov.* 1616."

This letter has been selected as the only specimen of Earl Francis's own composition. He had usually recourse to a secretary ; and no wonder, when he had in his faithful servant John Taylor a scribe who was not unqualified for secretary of state.   The letter expresses a pleasing sense of gratitude to the king, and shows how early the writer had resigned himself to the direction of his son.

"S<small>ONN</small>,

"I have till now expected y'r l'res, according to your promis at y'r departure ; so did Geo. Minson y'r directions touching the musick, whereupon he mought the better have writt to doctor Campion.*   He is now gone to my L'd President's, and will be redy to do as he heares from yo'.

"For my own opinion, albeit I will not dislyke y'r device, I fynde plainly, upon better consideration, the charge for that entertaynment will grow very great, besyde the musick ; and that, instead of less'ning, my charge in gen'all encreaseth, and newe paim'ts come on, w'ch, without better providence hereafter, cannot be p'formed.

"Yf now we fayle, the suytes being ended, the fawlte is o'r own ; therfore we must, bothe of us, look to o'r own courses For myselfe, bothe you and y'r wyfe know how willing I was, as well for my comforts as for good husbandry, to have had us lyve togeth'r ; but y'rselves, or rather, I may say, my daught'r, yo'r wief, have, without any cawse at all, devyded y'rselves from me ; wherof I have with patience hitherto, and nothing to my profitt, expected the yssew.

"Synce she went to Skipton, I have been contented to allowe in the time of y'r absence VIII*l*. above y'r own allowance, for her weekly charge ; but I fynde, by the accounte, they have exceeded that proportion above 200*l*., which I may well wonder at.

"You know the portion had from my l. tres'r was 6000*l*., and for this he requyred, and I granted, 600*l*. a yeare for y'r present maintenance.   How far out of my fatherly affection I have exceeded this, yo' maye both of you see.

"Hee sente, lyke a wyse fath', to vew the houses and landes to be assigned for you, and on w'ch yo' were to lyve during my tyme, as appeares by the articles of conveyance, and allowed therin : yett now it seames no place will serve but my own principall house, w'ch I hould neither fitt for yo' to use continewally, nor me to want.

"My chefest care is to leave yo' a good and free estate.   When the debts and portions are payed, yo' maye lyve

---

* Dr. Campion, I think, was a musical composer of those days.   See note †, p. 359.

2 V

plentifully ; but, in the mean time, yo' shall doe well to observe where and howe some of y'r noble ancestr's have lived in their fathers' time, whose matches were not inferior to y'rs.

" I mean shortly to lye at Skipton-castle myselfe ; and therefore yo' must resolve unto wh'ch of y'r own houses you will remove for a time.

" Neither lett it troble yo' that I wryte so playnly, for so yo' do that w'h maye be fitt on y'r partes, be well assured that both yo' and y'rs shall fynd me a carefull and loving father in all, and most glad to see you bothe joyn in one and the same course, for the good of y'rselves, y'r children, and y'r house, in w'ch I shall tak no small comfort, and esteem yo' both deare unto me.

" FR. CUMBRELAND."

The first part of this letter refers to the preparations making for the king's reception at Brougham ; the probable expenses of which seem to have produced a sudden fit of economy in the mind of the good earl, who expostulates with Lord Clifford on his, or rather his lady's, mismanagement, in a strain of dignity which he seldom ventured to use. With respect to Skipton Castle, however, he was as good as his word, for he seems to have resided principally there during the remainder of his long life. The whole letter appears, from the handwriting, to have been composed by faithful John Taylor, who has expressed his lord's sentiments with great propriety and vigour. The date of it must be fixed early in the year 1617.

" To the Right Honorable my veri good Lo. Frauns' Earle of Cumberlande, at Londesbrough, or elsewhere.

" RIGHT NOBLE EARLE,

" Having taken the p'sent opportunity to visitt this p't of the countri so nere yo'r lo. (yf you be at Londesbrough) I could doe noe lesse then as kindley as my heart can conceive, to salute you, and to learne of yo'r good health and happiness, wishing w'thall, that, if it maie stande w'th yo'r lo'p's occasions, I might see you here before my remove to Southwell, intended before the ende of this moneth ; for although it be not long since we beheld one another, yet such was then the employm't of us both, as hardly wee could enjoye one another's companie or conference.

" Gladly would I heare by or from y'r lo. what good newes out of Scotland, or at least the confynes thereof ; and, namely, in what solemnitie his ma'tie departed out of Berwick thither ; as likewise whether o'r English officers relinquished their places (as is here reported) to the nobles and gentles of North Brittaine ; and whether the quene's highnesses fearful dreme, signified to his ma'tie (for so ru'neth the rumor here), be like to shorten the p'gresse. But, among and above the rest, whether his resolution be constant and p'manent of holding his courte sett downe in the......heretofore designed. God's holie name be blessed for the peace like to be in France, and sende all well elsewhere abroad in his mai'ys absence. I am the more bold thus to wearie, if not wrong your l'p, presuming that my lo. Clifford, yo'r honorable intelligencer, hath and will weekly acquaint yo'r lo'p how the world goeth east, west, north, and south. Thus, hoping to be rather excused than accused for these jdle lynes, I betake yo'r good lo. with all your noble ones, to the speciall and continuall p'tec'on of the Almighty.

" Yo'r lo. moste loving and faithfull,
" TOBIAS EBORACEN.

" *At Pocklington, this* XVII*th of Maye,* 1617."

This pleasing letter from Dr. Tobias Matthew, the witty and eloquent Archbishop of York, proves the earl to have lived on most friendly terms with his metropolitan. I do not know whether any historian has mentioned " the queen's highness fearful dream, or whether it shortened the progress ;" but James was not likely to despise such a warning. The king and court were sumptuously entertained in this progress at Brougham Castle, by Earl Francis, who was indeed obliged to the royal interposition for that and the best part of his other estates.

" To the Right Hon'ble the Lo. Clifford, one of his Ma'ties Lieutenants for the Midle Shires, his very good Lo.

" MY VERY GOOD LO.

" Our blessed soverayne hath advanced y'u to the highest degree of honor in these Midle Shires, and sent me from my domestique service in his ma'ties court, not only to guide the stern of this diocese, but to bear a part in the temporall affaires of these Northerne Shires. By our religious, vertuous, and courteous combinac'on, wee shall more easily and comfortably undergoe the burdens jointly and severally laid upon us. And to the end I may in all sincerity make myself knowne unto y'u, I doe here and now confesse and p'test that I ever shal be, in matters of justice and equity, for all men indifferently; in matters of privat quarrell or faction, for no man, whatsoever condic'on he be of; in matters of hon'ble respects, for all noble p'sons and publique officers; in matters of courteoucy, for those most that shall deserve me best : and that I may see good daies, I shall follow the advice of the kingly pp'fet—by my utmost endeavours I shall labour to 'keepe my tongue from evill, and my lips that they speak no guile;' I shall 'eschew evill and doe goode;' and I 'shall seek peace and ensue it.' According to these rules and maxims I have resolved to order all my p'ceedings; and if yo'r lo'p shall approve them in me, and observe them with me, our unity shall both be honest and stedfast. I doe assume that yo'r judicious and ingenuous nature will fairly enterpret this declarac'on of my goode affection towards y'u. And so, wishing all happiness unto y'u, I rest yo'r l'p's in the Lord, at co'maund,

" ROB'T CARLIOL.

" *Rose-castle, Aprilis* 25, 1618."

After so many specimens of good breeding, and easy expression, in the correspondence of noblemen by birth, this pedantic letter of a lord by office may produce a diverting contrast. In truth, I have seldom seen a more disgusting piece of egotism and consequence. The writer, Dr. Robert Snowden, appears, from other parts of this correspondence, to have behaved very injudiciously and unskilfully as a magistrate; and, having addicted himself to the party of Lord William Howard, thwarted the measures of Sir Richard Hutton, and the gravest of his brethren, who were seriously desirous of reducing the country to order. In the epistle before us, the bishop, though nothing more than an ordinary justice of peace, writes as if he thought it a condescension to act with the lord lieutenant of the county, one of the first noblemen in the kingdom. But recent honours are apt to turn weak heads; and this prelate's lawn had not yet lost its first starching. He was consecrated in November, 1616, and died in 1621.

Copy of a letter of Lord Henry Clifford to His Majesty.

" MAY IT PLEASE YOUR MOST SACRED MA^STY,

" I am not able to express the boundles joy my hart conseved, when, cumming to Carlisle, I found your ma^sty had continewed the sequestration of the justices of peace, which report here in this place had restored to thir former othority. This I aprehend as a comfortable signe of your so gracous remembrance of me in my absence; as all my endevors shall ever labor wth comfort in your maj^ties commandes and services.

" The business of this place hath be'n of more waight than many expected by the singular industry of Sr William Hutton, whoe sent all those to prison wch now are goeinge to the gallows. For all your graisous and public favors to me, yet have I received the most unsufferable and continuall affrontes by the sherif of this county, and others of this county, all the time of this service, as none could have endured but I, who can bear any thing rather than make the least interruption in your service. My humble sute shall therefore be to your ma^sty, that you will accept of none of ther apologies till I shall attend you in person, for I have b'en a public spectacle of paisance, to the great grief of my enemies.

" Your ma^sty will finde that one of the prisoners, by the sherif's negligence, hath made an escape after conviction out of the Judgment Hall, while the other prisoners wer arrained, so as noe judgement was given upon him, but Sr Tho. Tillesly and I have set a heavy fine upon his head, wch I humbly pray your ma^sty not to remitt till I attend you, wch shall be very speedily.

" I beseech the Almighty God to send your Ma^styl many hapy dayes, and that I may be but worthy of your graisous opinion, wch is the greatest comfort of

" Your Ma^styes," &c.

" For his Ma^ts speciall affayrs.

" To the Right Honorable my very good Lord, the Ld Clifford, one of his Maties l. lieutenants for the county of Westmerland.

" MY GOOD LORD,

" I acquainted his Ma^ty wth the contents of yor l'ps letters forw^th upon theyr receipt. In answer whereunto, he directed me to let yo^u know, that there is given for the observing yor time set for the geoale delivery at Carlisle, and that Ld William Haward is to stay his jorny till that service be dispatched; and further, that you shall receave some additionall directions from the l^ds of the Counsaill touching the Middle Shires; his Matie seemes to be unsatisfied, for that the proclamacons were not sufficiently published, and made knowen to the contrey in due time, and bad me give it y^r l'p in particular recomendacon, that his service, and the government of those parts comited to yo[r] l[p], should be religiously and zealously tendred and observed in the first place, and that no animosities or opposic'ons betweene p'rticuler persons should in any wise give hinderance or prejudice hereunto.

"So, with my due respect unto yo[r] l'p, I take leave, and rest

"Yo[r] l[p] most assured to do you service,

"*Whitehall, Ap.* 21, 1618."   "ROBERT NAUNTON."

"MY NOBLE LORD,

"For the busines whereof your lo'p hath written to me, I referre your lo'p to S[r] Robert Naunton's letter, from whome I have understood the particulars, and his Ma[ty] hath given him order for the answeare, w[ch] your lo'p will now receave. I am glad to see your lo'p so vigilant for his Ma[ties] service, whereof I ever assured myself; and shall omitt no opportunitie to nourish his Ma[ties] good opinion of your care and forwardness to advance his service; as in all other occasions wherein you shall have use of me, I'll ever shew myself

"Your lo[ps] faithful servant,

"*Whitehall,* 22 *of April* 1618."   "G. BUCKINGHAM.

"MAY IT PLEASE YOUR LORDSHIP,

"From my lord deputy you will receive the articles from my lord of Corke, fully finished. The care and resolution his l'p hath exercised throughout this treaty, in pursuance of your l'p's directions, will appeare, by the safety and advantadge he hath gayned for your l'p, upon the payment of 7000*l.* in case you have a forme ordring that condition notably, for the quietness of your l'p, and fredome of your estate during your life. And now that all things are here accomplished, according to your owne propositions, there is yet an election left, to take or leave the whole business, according to your owne wisdome. He who hathe bene least able to serve you in that w'ch hath past, desyreth, w'th most intyre affectionns, your l'p may nowe fall upon the safest and happiest resolution, most conducing to the contentment of your noble daughter, and the future satisfaction of your l'p. Nether can I discharge my dewtie to ether as becomes me, w'thout a perfect representation of what I conceave fitt for your l'p to understand for the directing your finall resolutionn in this important and weighty affayre. I pass by the remoteness of the place, cutting off a great part of that comfort indulgent parents promise to themselves by frequent enjoying and visiting their children and grandchildren. But that a branch sprung from honorable and famous ancestors should be grafted into a newly planted and barely rooted stocke of honor, that a consyderable part of ancyent possessions acquired and p'served by noble atchevements, shold be suffred to divolve and be mingled w'th a hastily gotten and suspitiously kept Fortune, I confess, in my judgment requires very good conditionns to followe after, such as might probably render a more comfortable life for the future to your swete daughter here then in another place. But, my lord, the comforts and blessings of marradge are not so plentifully sowen upon this land, that wee may promiss she shall assuredly gather them; for it passeth under observation here, that from thoss nine daughters of his now living and bestowed in marradge, the comforte fatherhoode and old age promiss to themselves from these children is not reaped by him; and howe much the quiet and composed condition of your daughters swete and gentile affectionns may be perturbed and disordered by a harsh and incivill conversation, or what disanimation and distemper the discovery and prosecution of my lord of Corke, by the quicke and impartiall sight of my lord deputy, may bring w'th it, I most humbly submit to your l'p's more serious consyderation; for if the day of retribution never come when the rest of his estate shal be questioned, yet it is not to be doubted but there will be a tyme given for the complaints of the Church; for I am very confydent, since the suppression of the abbeys, no one man in ether kingdome hath so violently, so frequently layde prophane hands, hands of power, upon the church and her possessions (even almost to demolition where he hath come), as this bold earle of Corke. Of that 6000*l. per annum* estated nowe upon his sonn, I take full a third part to be spiritual deduction. Lismoore, his principall house and seate, with lands worth near 2000*l. per annum,* the possessionns of the bishop of Lismore, reserving a free rent of 20*l. per annum* for the bishop, torne from that sea by the poure of S'r Walter Rawley. Yughall (nowe to be the jointure-house of your swete daughter) a colledge consisting of a warden and eight personnes, all p'sentative and endowed, in valeue 800*l. per annum,* depopulated by himself (the incumbent warden yet living), and turned into a laye possession. And the better to support thess dignityes of the church he hath, *in commendam,* nere one hundred spirituall livings, some impropriations, divers vicaridges, w'ch he supplyeth by small stipendaryes.

"My Lord, I have breifly pointed out all thoss things, w'ch, by a better hand, are more cleerely and fully expressed to your l'p. In dischardge of the obligationns and service I shall ever beare to your l'p, and her who is so neare you, I could say no less. Your wisdome and better interpretationns of my honest and faithfull intentionns will, I hope, excuse me, if I have sayde to much. There remaynes no more for me but to contineue my prayres to the Guide of all hartes that the resolution you nowe take in the conclusyon maye bring w'th it the blessed frutes of tranquellitye and constant comfort to your daughter, and quietness and honor to your l'p. In which no freind you have in the whole world shal take more treuer contentment then your l'p's most humble affectionate servant,

"*Dublin, Decemb.* 9, 1633."   "C. WANDESFORDE.

"MY NOBLE LORDE,

"My due respects and my wife's towards y'r lordship, and my lady y'r daughter, shall never be a wantinge. Her owne worth and mereit (were all other regardes set aside) would enforce as much from us, as in trueth they doo gaine her much honor and affection from all. I knowe not what to saye concerninge my lord of Corke. His disposition and his causes are such, as it is a most difficulte thinge for a man that respects honor and justice to keepe but faire quarter w'th him. I should to much trouble y'r lo'p to instance in particulers. But for his greate cause now dependinge in yᵉ Starchamber here, as justice must be done, so my desire is, that no suche blemish may fall upon him as might descende unto his posteritie. To w'ch ende, for my lady Dungarvan's sake, I shall ever be ready to contribute my best assistance. There remaines nowe to be perfected the conveyance yᵗ is to settle 6000*l. per annum* on my lord Dungarvan, without leavinge a power (as it now is) in my l'd treasurer, E. of Corke, to revoke it. I had a copy of a great conveyance formerly made of all his landes : it lay by me a good while ; but what for yᵉ extreme length of it, what my manifold and much pressinge busines in yᵉ Terme and parliament tymes, what my lord chiefe justice his absence in yᵉ vacation, I could perfect nothinge as yet. And I made yᵉ less hast for other considerations. For first, I know not yᵉ valew of yᵉ lands to be estated ; it were fitt one from y'r lo'p should, by view or enquiry, be satisfied of that. Secondly, The title would be looked into ; w'ch is not so fitte to be done by me, especially at this tyme, as yᵉ matter now standes betwene yᵉ kinge and his lo'p. Thirdly, I perceive he intends Youghall and Lismore to be part of that value, which are yᵉ most questionable parts of his estate : and in such sort questionable as that if my lo. Dungarvan have them not, I thinke all yᵉ rest will prosper better. So as this businesse does require that an understandinge able man be sent from y'r lo'p to see it perfected as it should be, beinge of so great consequence as it is to y'r lo'p's posterity. Mr. John Tailers yeares, and such a journey, would not well agree together, otherwise I should heartily have wished to have had his assistance herein. But y'r lo'p wantes not others yᵗ are fitte to be imployed about it. For as much as concernes my part both in this and all thinges else w'ch y'r lo'p shall co'mande me, I shall faithfully and readily expresse myselfe, my lorde, y'r lo'p's most humble servant,

"*Dublin Castle*, 24 ᵗobris, 1634." "GEO. RADCLIFFE.

"To the Right Hon'ble and my most honoured Lord the Lo. Clifford.

"MY LORD,
"Mr. Errington returninge homewarde, w'th a purpose in his way to wayte uppon your lo'p, I have taken the bouldnes agayne to kisse your gracious hands for that favour, w'ch, when I have acknowledged, I must ever acknowledge, and, by a daily sacrifice, make up in tyme what my devotion wants in merit towards you. The first and solemne act of yᵗ, I hope, y'r l'p hath allready read in that letter, w'ch, by the addresse you gave me, I directed to S'r Thomas Finch three weekes since. This is but the same renewed, save that my hart gathers strength as it goes, and hastens to y'r presence, lyke cattle, tyred, to their home. I attend but your lo'p's co'maundement, w'ch may give me leave to acquaynt my lady w'th busines, unles your lo'p will thinke fitt yourselfe to give her the first notice, and so receave me from her hand immediately, rather than by my owne donation. Either way her la'p will, I know, be pleas'd to license my acceptance of that good which God and your goodnes have prepared for me w'thout her trouble. To deserve this hapynes is a worke disproportionable to my weaknes, to serve you, to love you, and to honour you, must be (my lord) that lower sphere wherein my thoughts and indeavours are to move, and shall be the wholle imployment of my life.
"What is here worth your knowledge Mr. Errington can much better acquaynt your lo'p with than I whoe came, but this day, from the conversation of trees and beasts at Moor-parke, where I learne rather to forget then understande yᵉ world, which hath bin, I confesse, soe ill a frende to me I could have given up w'th yᵗ, had not your lo'p ben pleased to bringe me agayne in favour w'th myselfe by your favour bestowed uppon your lo'p's unworthiest but faythfull servant,

"*Sharington-house, the* 24*th of May*." "HEN. LUCAS.

After an interval of fifteen years in the correspondence of the family, we meet with Henry Lord Clifford negotiating a marriage between his only daughter and Richard Viscount Dungarvan, eldest son of the first Earl of Cork, whose conduct and character are here represented in so unfavourable a light that it will be necessary, by an impartial statement, to take off the impression which so eloquent and forcible a letter as that of Wandesford must have made upon the reader's mind.

Wandesford * and Radcliffe were the devoted adherents of Strafford, and, though very able and honest men, saw with their master's eyes, and were tinctured with all his prejudices. Now it appears that this nobleman, before he became Deputy of Ireland, had used his influence to promote the match in question ; but no sooner was he entered upon his government than he grew jealous of the Earl of Cork, whose wealth and talents rendered him formidable; and laboured to defeat the scheme of a marriage with his niece, which would have added to a new family, what alone they wanted, the splendour derived from an alliance with some ancient and illustrious house.

* Wandesford was Master of the Rolls, and afterwards Lord Deputy in Ireland, and founder of the Castlecomer family. There *was* a very fine portrait of him by Vandyke at Houghton.

It was Strafford's object, therefore, to represent, through his agents, the earl's title to his great estates as suspicious, if not sacrilegious : but the truth was this :

Richard Boyle, the founder of this distinguished house, was the younger son of a good family in England ; and, with something less than the ordinary provision of a younger son, resolved to be the artificer of his own fortune in Ireland. I am here his apologist, not his biographer, and shall not stay to relate what were the earlier steps of his prosperity. Suffice it to say, that there were at that time vast tracts of land in the counties of Waterford and Cork torn from the Church by Sir Walter Raleigh and others ; which the possessors, partly from their own necessities, partly from the insecurity of the tenure, were willing to dispose of at low rates. These were purchased, planted, and improved, by our young adventurer, who thus laid the foundation of that great fortune which his descendants still enjoy in that country. Now, though after forty years' possession, the title to church lands, thus acquired, might not be the most eligible to ground a settlement upon, yet a purchase for a valuable consideration, even from a *malæ fidei* possessor, was a much more excusable mode of acquisition than direct acts of violence and rapine, with which the Earl of Cork is charged by Mr. Wandesford. This is all that can be said upon the subject.

I have subjoined the third letter, though I know nothing of the writer, because it seems to refer to some matrimonial alliance which never took place, and is written in a very elegant and engaging manner. The mention of Moore Park will probably bring to the recollection of many readers that upright statesman of a corrupt court, Sir William Temple, who spent many days at that place, " in conversation with trees and beasts," in order to " forget a world which he understood " but too well.

" To the Right Hon'bel and my very good Lord and Cosin the Lorde Clifforde, at Skipton Castell.

" NOBLE LORD,

" I give y'u many thankes for y'r letter, and for y'r care of yᵉ businesse in yᵉ countrye w'che may so much concerne us all. I am sorye yᵉ countrye is soe ill provided for defence ; but soe much yᵉ more care must be had to helpe yᵉ beste yᵗ may be for our three poore Northerne shires. It will be fitter to fitte them w'th such lighte armes as they have bin accustomed to use and beare, then loade them with heavier, which, mingled w'th some other, may stande in good steade, and archerye* to be kepte on foote. His m'tie takes very well y'r lo'p's diligence and discreete care, as y'u will understande by his owne gracious letter ; y'u will likewise understande, by Mr. Secretary, the care is heere taken of providing those partes better, if anie storme should come. His m'tie hath bin pleased to speake with me about makinge some necessaryes for an army at Sheffelde, as spades, pickeaxes, carriages for feelde-pieces, and such like, where, perhappes, they may be both cheaper, and save carriage from hence. And I thinke it were not amisse that y'r lo'p, by y'r example, would invite yᵉ nobility and gentry of yᵉ Northe to sette on work country smithes to make playne pecees and pistolles, w'th restes for muskettes, and such like ; though they be but homely worke, they may stand in good stead. Lead cannot want soe near Derbyshire, and his m'tie is carefull to sende some proporcion of powder to Hull † shortly, as your lo'p will understande. All yᵗ I can say is, yᵗ I hope yᵉ beste ; but it is all wise men's partes to provide for the worst. Soe, w'th my best wishes unto y'r lo'p, I remayne y'r lo'p's most affectionate cosin to serve y'u,

" *From Alberye my Alpine Celle*, 31 *July*, 1638."

" ARUNDELL & SURREY.

" MY LORD,

" I have, upon all occations, ever found your lo'p so favorable to me as I doubt not but you will excuse my long silence, knowing how I have been diverted, by want of health, from the performance of many respects unto my friends, and from the attendance of divers businesses, w'ch I shall now studie to redeeme, if the increase of strength will permitt me ; but in this season I find myself recover slowly.

" The businesses of those counties under our liftenancies have not here so quicke dispatches as I could wishe ; but, by your lo'p's care, they are now in a way to be brought into better order for armes then I expected to have seene them. The royall army of 30ᵐ that was to waite upon his ma'tie into our Northern partes, is reduced to 6ᵐ, and these not to be taken

---

* Is not this the latest instance of the use, or intended use, of archers in an English army ?

† Part of his own stores, which were afterwards seized by the Parliament, and turned against him.

out of the trained bands, but levied by presse. To thes 6ᵐ the trained bands of the North are to be added upon occation, and those of the remoter shires to be joined unto them, as neede shall require. The lessening the army doth not allter the king's purpose of being att Yorke by the tyme appointed, where I hope to meete your lo'p, although you are desired, by his ma'tie, to reside neerer unto the borders for a while. When this resolution was taken, I doubted it might be inconvenient for your lo'p : and all the service I could do you in it was to have it left unto your own choice to be at Carlile* or Appleby, w'ch should best like you. If I knew in what I might be here useful to your lo'p, I should most willingly undertake anything w'ch might witnesse my being your lo'p's most affectionate coussen and faithful servant,

"A. NORTHUMBERLAND.

" If it may be no trouble to your lo'p, I desire to have my service presented to my lady and to my lord your father.
" *London, Feb. 5, 1638.*"

" MY LORD,
" Your noble professions of favours to mee hath been receved with as mutch fayth and joye, and both hath ever made me hapy. I see how mutch I am oblidged to your lo'p in your extraordinary favors to Sir William Widdrington,† and the great honor you would have dun him, and yett more, my lo., the unwillingnes your lo'p hadd to take him frome mee, knowing how greate a prejudice it woulde bee to mee. For all this, what can I doe more than give your lo'p thanks ; and in returne, my lord, because I woulde have no blame lighte of your lo'p, or your place, I have acquainted his ma'tie, whoe co'manded mee to lett your lo'p knowe, frome him, that it is his sacred ma'ties pleasure, thatt nott one man that is engaged to mee shall bee employde elsewhere. And so, wishinge your lo'p all succes in your designes, I reste, your lo'p's most faythful, to serve you,

" W. NEWCASTLE.

" *London, the 7th of Martch, 1638.*"

" To the Right Honorable my very good Lord Clifford, Lord Liftenant of the Northerne Shires.
" NOBLE LORDE,
" I recived, yesternight late, yo'r dispach, w'th that of the advertisemente.........of the desperate resolutions of yᵉ Scottish Covenanters, w'ch I acquainted his ma'tie w'thall, whoe hath that care of this kingdome, wh'ch becomes soe good a kinge, and doth not soe much trust theyre greate professions never to invade this kingdome, as to leave so important frontiers to theyre courtesye. My lo. of Essexe is cominge swifter then I can. If yo'r lo'p see him at Newcastle, I am sure y'u will use him as yᵉ lo'd generall. And I hope to see you soone after him. I must intreate y'r lo'p, have a greate care to rayse y'r troope of horse of stronge and able ones, w'ch I doubte those partes will hardly provide, for his ma'tie hath a principall care the horse be good, as the parte of the army in w'ch he reposeth most trust. His ma'tie takes your lo'p's watchfulness in very gracious parte. Soe, w'th my best wishes to y'r lo'p, I remayne, y'r lo'p's most affectionate cosin,

" ARUNDELL & SURREY.

" *Arn-house, 19 March, 1639.*"

" To the Right Honorable my very good L'd the L'd Clifford, Governor of Newcastle, att Newcastle.
" MY LORD,
" Your l'p's letters of . . . 12th of March are all come safely . . . . hands ; by which I understand, that by y'r lo'p's care the trained bands in those Northerne counties are in better order then I expected they would have beene : for the appointing a coronell and captains to them, I never heard any thing but from my lord marshall ; and I have ever beene of opinion, that a coronell would be unnecessarie to soe small a number of men ; and in divers of our Southern counties, that have syx tymes as many men, there are not any coronells belonging to them. The joyninge the troupes of Cumberland and Westmerland to those of Northumberland, and forming them all into a regiment, would, I conceave, have proved very inconvenient, in regard these forces are for the defence of the severall counties, and are not to be drawne out of the same, but upon extraordinarie occasions. I could have wished that the mayor of Newcastle had forborne to give y'r lo'p a cause of offence, espetially at this tyme ; for all disputes of this nature happen nowe very unseasonable. The kinge holds constant to his day for begining his journie North . . . . . unallterable, though yet the . . . . . are not out for levyinge the foote. I wishe unto y'r lo'p all good fortune, and much honor by your new imployments, and myselfe often occations to expresse my being your lo'p's affectionate cousen and servant,

" A. NORTHUMBERLAND.

" *London, Mar. 18, 1638.*"

" To the Right Hono'ble my very good Lord and Cosen the Lord Clifford, these. *Carlisle.*
" NOBLE LORD,
" I write nowe only to lette y'u knowe, that nowe this eveninge thinges are soe farre agreede heere as this night the marquesse Hamilton goes by land towardes Edenburge, to receive his ma'ties castell there for the kinge's use ; and I think generall Ruffen will be left there to co'mande. On Thursday the Scottish army breakes, and on Friday or Saterday ours will doe soe allsoe. The kinge co'mandes me that the Yorkshire regimente, w'th y'u, goe hoame ; and I shall tomorowe, send money for them by my cosen S'r Francis Howarde : and noe forces are to be left there but only S'r Fra's Willoubye's ;

---

* He chose Carlisle ; for in Burnet's "Memoirs of the Dukes of Hamilton," p. 118, I find the following passage in a letter of the king, dated April 2d, this year, " Carlisle is possessed by my lord Clifford, with 300 men."
† Afterwards Lord Widdrington, killed in Wigan Lane.

and the kinge is pleased y'r lo'p should come hither, and to lett my lo. of Neddesdale, and ye rest of ye Scottishe nation, knowe y^t all is quiette ; and tomorowe I shall send a dispach from ye Scottishe lordes of ye freeinge ye seege of ye Tyene. The lo. Barrimoore's regimente is sent to be stayed. Soe, w'th my best wishes unto y'r lo'p, I remayne y'r lo'p's most affect'te cosin to c'omande,   " ARUNDELL & SURREY.

" *Campe, Wednesday 17th June,* 1639."

" To ——— Willoughby.

" SIR,

" I have receyved yo'r l're, and whereas yo'r former messingers have been stopped, that course was not taken on our side when all passage from us to England was barred, and l'res intercepted for that purpose (as it seemed) that all intelligence of the state of o'r affayres might be kept from o'r neighbour country, and they held by a blind mistake, builded upon badd information, to invade us their frends, whoe would rather choose death then minde any evill to o'r bretheren and neighbours. Receive y'r trunck, and w'th them this frendly advertizem't. Yo'r father hath been hitherto upon very hon'ble employments, and I am hartely sorye that he should nowe, in ye ende, have undertaken in such an unjust quarrell ; a man of conscience will consider the equity of the cause before he engages himselfe ; w'ch makes me doubt, though it be reported for certeyne, that he is an undertaker in this busines. The cause we mayneteyne is the libertie of o'r religion, confirmed by o'r nationall oath, the constitution of o'r national assemblies, and the lawes of the kingdome, and the liberties of o'r cuntrie. And I wish men would consider what it is to enforce uppon free people, by power of armes, what doth not stand w'th their confession of faith, the judgement of their nationall church, their greate oath, and the lawes of the kingdome. If neyther religion nor justice, nor the long peace betwixt two neighbour nations, nor the love towardes the fruite of their own loynes, can move them to refuse soe impious, soe inhumane, soe unjust an employment ; then wee doubt not but ye God of heaven (whoe hath owned o'r buisines by many clere evydences of his devyne assistance in the whole course thereof), will pleade o'r cause throughly agaynst the unmercifull people, and make ye evyll they intended for others retorne upon themselves, whoe have averred, upon o'r oath, in o'r informat'on, that wee minde not to invade England, w'ch wee know groaneth under their owne burthens. But since men are brought to lye upon o'r borders, to looke over us in a menacing way, wee could doe noe lys then send some to wayte uppon o'r borders, that wee receave no wronge ; and yett wee may affirme, upon o'r oath, that wee minde no invasion. If wee be invaded, or, by the keeping of garrisons on yo'r side, wearied and wasted w'th wayting on, wee will bee forced upon thoughts w'ch have not yet entred into o'r mindes to visitt you w'th farr greater numbers than you expect. Noe farther. I am yo'r affecc'onate frend to serve you,

" *Edinburgh,* 13 *Apr.* 1639."   " ROTHES.

" For the Earle of CORKE.

" MY D. D. BROTHER,

" I can send y'u noe intelligence from hence but y^t w'ch y'r owne sence and experience must keepe y'u from receiving as news, w'ch is, y^t quiet is a more pleasing enjoyment for ye very present yⁿ a hurry, and is much more tending to everlasting rest yⁿ a toss in crouds of company can be ; and therefore I have now for a while gott ye advantage ground of y'u, for whom I have so reale and intyre an affection to be able to looke upon y'u in ye noyse and confusion of London and ye court, w'ch are certainely as great hindrances to ye converse y^t our soules are capable of w'th God, and w'thout w'ch they are uncapable of beinge happye, as such throngs are forbiding to ye freedome of discourse where friends doe acquaint one another w'th those thoughts of their harts w'ch they reserve as secrets from ye rest of ye world ; and, upon that accoumpt, those things are to be avoyded as ye great interrupters of our happyness, of w'ch there is much more to be tasted in this world, in spight of al its emptynes and uncertainties yⁿ can be immagined by those who allow not y^mselves leasure to entertaine their owne thoughts upon those objects for w'ch a power of thinking was given us by y^t God, who is seene, and heard, and knowne by us onely by ye exercising of our thoughts upon and w'th him, who wil not leave us alone, if we seperate ourselves from other companyes to wayte upon him w'thout distraction, nor be w'th us w'thout giveing us cause to say y^t no company nor noe friendship can be compared to his.

" This is, indeed, to entertaine y'u at a too uncourtly rate ; but I as hartely wish y'u may be a great lord in ye court of heaven as I litle care to have y'u have any imploym't in earthly courts ; and therefore my stile is suteable to my designe, though not to ye fashion, w'ch wil certainly never be fit for a Christian to conforme too ; let us countenance an owneing of God in al our conversation, and make it as shameful in visits to talke of vanety as its now esteemed to speake of religion : and till the fashion be thus reformed, I wish I may keepe out of it.   " Y'rs,

                                                                    " K. R." *

" GOOD MR. GRAHAM,

" This Monday the tenants are very sad, for they cannot procure this 150*l.* to pay on Wedsonday next at York ; they are gone to other places to try what they can doe. For God-sake, send some speedy stopp from Goldsmiths' Hall to the comitty at York, for they are so very ferce that they will straine every third day, till they have the 800*l.* and the use ; and as they order the matter, every straining comes to twenty pownd, with charges and feese ; and soone as you gitt any stopp, send it by the very next post, for we send every Monday to Cave, to see for some releif from you. The Docter writ to you the last night, what ill case my lord's estate is in. If my lord's fine be not paid, there is no mercy with these men ; though Plaxton is gon to-day to Sr Henry Chamly and Mr. Stockdale, to procure the comitty to give some time till we heare from

                              * Katherine Viscountess Ranelagh.

Goldsmiths' Hall, and to gitt theire hands, that the money that is paid here may be allowed above, as part of payment : if wee gitt any such note for this 150*l.* you shall be sure to have it next post after. The sequestrators came on Thursday last, and they and theire soldiers lay here till Monday. I never saw so great distraction in hous and towne in my life ; little rest taken by any but children neither night nor day: the soldiers came into the hous to carry Docter prisoner to London, because he would not be bownd to pay 300*l.* in two daies, and threatened to sequester him too ; which they had done, if he had not had his discharge to shew out of Goldsmiths' Hall. All the tennants are so frightened, that they will keepe theire rents in their hands to loose their owne cattle when they are strained ; which way then can I sett meat before my lord's children ? The 7 of June Mr. Lane thretens to be here againe the very next post after my lady is come. Her hon^r should be pleased to send orders to Mr. Cary to pay that 4 score and 17 pownd, or else the straining will come to twenty pownd charges, as this hath done, and make the tennants stark madd. The berar being in haste, I can say no more, but that I am your very loveing friend,   " S. BALL.

"*May the* 27. 1650."

"Why doth nobody goe to Colonel Mathy Alured? The sequestrators say, they will let out all the deare out of the park when the first of June is past ; for then, they say, half the estate is confiscat, and they will enter on it ; so, if we have no order from you on next Fryday, what will become of us on Satterday ?"

This series of letters, except the last, which is added as a monument of the distress to which the loyalists were reduced under the usurpation, refers to the last and most unquiet period of Lord Clifford's life. As lieutenant of the northern counties, and governor of Newcastle, it was impossible for him not to take a part in the two disgraceful expeditions against Scotland, in the years 1638 and 1639. But he was now grown inactive, and probably did little more than his office compelled him to do. Yet I do not find him accused of having any share in the infamous surrender of Newcastle, and am inclined to hope that he was absent at the time.

The Earl of Arundel's letters are sufficient to rescue him from Lord Clarendon's imputation, that he was almost wholly illiterate. They display no great ability, and no gross deficiency : but he was a man better adapted, by his understanding and habits, to collect a museum than to command an army ; and he was perhaps the first person in England (though he has since been followed by a host of feeble amateurs) who understood much of the arts, and little of the languages of antiquity. A character, however, like that of Peireske,* priding itself on a minute and pedantic acquaintance with ancient literature, united to a passion for virtù, would ill become a man of birth and fortune ; but a vehement passion for the one, without a *tincture* of the other, is a combination of impotence and desire, which cannot but render the subject of it contemptible. The greatest master of ancient languages and manners, in a private station, may be allowed a more circumscribed acquaintance with the works of ancient art, while the man of rank must be indulged in a more superficial knowledge of languages ; and such, after all, might be the attainments of the Earl of Arundel.

To Algernon Earl of Northumberland, who followed Lord Arundel in the command of the northern army, the noble historian allows an understanding no more than moderate. If this account be true, it was a moderate understanding well cultivated, and under the guidance of great discretion and self-command; for by a conduct which his friends would call dexterous, and his enemies temporising and selfish, by deserting his master when it grew dangerous to support him, by lending to the Parliament his counsel in the House, and not his services in the field, by withdrawing from them likewise, when their conduct became outrageous ;

[* Nicholas Claude Fabri de Peiresc was a French antiquary and naturalist. He formed large collections of Oriental and other manuscripts ; he first verified Harvey's discovery of the circulation of the blood. He died 24th June, 1637.]

2 W

above all, by keeping at a distance from those detestable counsels which brought Charles to the block, this earl preserved his life and fortune through all the changes of those perilous times, and appeared at the Restoration with the countenance of a man whose errors were lost in the guilt of others, and who even made a merit of rebellion, untainted with regicide.

The letter from the Earl of Rothes is a mixture of cant and hypocrisy, though in some places very well expressed. No man of common discernment will fail to infer the intention of the Covenanters to invade England, from the vehement asseverations with which it is here so needlessly disclaimed:

"But God had owned their business by many cleere evidences of devyne assistance;" that is, divine approbation may be inferred from success : the language of every fanatic.

Yet, if this were true, there could be no such thing as prosperous wickedness in the world. Had Lord Rothes lived a little longer, he might have been puzzled with his own argument, when urged upon his covenanting brethren after the victories of Montrose on one side, and Cromwell on the other. *Victrix causa Deo placuit*, says Sir Henry Wotton, is but the gospel of a poet.*

I have allotted the last place in this collection to an excellent letter from Katherine Viscountess Ranelagh, the accomplished sister of Robert Boyle, who generally resided in her house, and survived her only a single week. It contains such admonitions as all men of the world require, and few receive.

After the epistolary correspondence of the last Earls of Cumberland, my readers may not be displeased with some miscellaneous particulars relating to their personal habits and domestic economy (if it can be so called), extracted from their own account-books.† Of

---

* "Remains," p. 378.

† Of the nuptial or other festivals of this family, I have met with few memorials ; but the following memoranda, taken from the evidences of the Cliffords, and relating to the finery and good cheer of the Neviles of Chevet,[1] are extremely curious.

"The Marriage of my Son-in-law GERVYS CLIFTON and my Daughter MARY NEVILL,[2] the 17th Day of January, in the 21st Year of the Reign of our Sovereign Lord King Henry the Eighth (1530.)

First, for the Apparell of the said Gervys Clifton and Mary Nevill :

21 yards of russett damask, every yard 8s.; 7l. 14s. 8d.—Item, 6 yards white damask, every yard 8s.; 2l. 8s.—Item, 12 yards of tawney camlet, every yard 2s. 8d. ; 2l. 9s. 4d.—Item, 6 yards of tawney velvet, every yard 14s. ; 4l. 4s.—Item, two rolls buckram, 6s.—Item, 3 black velvet bonnetts for women, every bonnet 17s. ; 2l. 11s.—Item, a frontlet of blew velvet, 7s. 6d.—Item, an owncе of damask gold, 4s.—Item, 4 laynes for frontletts, 2s. 8d.—Item, an egge of pearl, 1l. 4s. 10d.—Item, 3 pair of gloves, 2s. 10d.—Item, 3 yards of kersey, 2 black, 1 white, 7s.—Item, lining for the same, 2s.—Item, 3 boxes to carry bonnetts in, 1s. Item, 3 pastes, 9d.—Item, a pair of white lusarts,[3] 2l.—Item, 12 whit heares, 12s.—Item, 12 black conies, 10s.—Item, a pair of myllen sleves, white sattin, 8s.—Item, 30 white lamb skins, 4s.—Item, 6 yards of white cotton, 3s.—Item, 2 yards ½ black sattin, 14s. 9d.—Item, 2 girdles, 5s. 4d.—Item, two ells white ribbon for tippets, 1s. 1d.—Item, an ell of blue satten, 6s. 8d.—Item, a wedding-ring of gold, 12s. 4d.—Item, a myllen bonnett, dressed of *ogletts*, 11s.—Item, a yard of right white satten, 12s.—Item, a yard of white satten of Bridge, 1s. 4d.—Total, 30l. 16s. 1d.

The Expence of the Dinner at the Marriage of the said GERVIS CLIFTON and MARY NEVILL.

Imprimis, three hogsheads of wine, one white, the one red, and one clarett, 5l. 5s.—Item, 2 oxen, 3l.—Item, 2 brawns, 1l.—Item, 12 swans, every swan, 6s. ; 3l. 12s.—Item, 9 cranes, every crane 3s. 4d. ; 1l. 10s.—Item, 16 heron sews, every one 12d. ; 16s.—Item, 10 *bytters*, each 14d. ; 11s. 8d.—Item, 60 couple of conies, every couple 5d. ; 1l. 5s.—Item, as much wild fowl and the charge of the same, as cost 3l. 6s. 8d.—Item, 16 capons of grease, 16s.—Item, 30 other capons, 15s.—Item, 10 piggs, every pigg 5d. ; 4s. 2d.—Item, 6 calves, 16s.—Item, other calfe, 3s.—Item, 7 lambs, 10s.—Item, 6 weathers, every

---

[1] Near Wakefield. This branch, the only remnant of the great name of Nevile, still subsists ; but the estate of Chevet was sold about 40 years ago.

[2] Sir John Nevile, of Chevet, high sheriff of Yorkshire 19 Hen. VIII., married Elizabeth daughter of ——, and widow of Sir Thomas Tempest ; and had issue, Elizabeth, married to Roger Rockley, esq. and Mary, married to Sir Gervase Clifton.—Thoresby's "Ducatus Leodiensis," p. 183.

[3] The word will be explained under the Furrura of Bolton.

these I have seen four, all moderate-sized folios, for the years 1606, 1634, 1637, 1638, and part of the year following. At the date of the first of them, the rental of the Craven and Londesborough estates was little more than 2,000*l. per annum.* Westmoreland was in jointure to the dowager countess. Yet the expenditure of this year was no less than 7,990*l.*

weather 2*s.* 4*d.* ; 14*s.*—Item, 8 qrs. of barley malt, every qr. 14*s.* ; 5*l.* 10*s.*—Item, 3 qrs. of wheat, every qr. 18*s.* ; 2*l.* 14*s.*— Item, 4 doz. chickens, 6*s.*—Besides butter, eggs, vergus, and vinegar.

In Spices as followeth:

Two loaves of sugar, weighing 16lb. 12 oz. at 7*d.* per lb. 9*s.* 9*d.*—Item, 6 lb. of pepper, every pound 22*d.* ; 11*s.*—Item, one pound ginger, 2*s.* 4*d.*—Item, 12lb. currants, every pound 3*d*½. ; 3*s.*—Item, 12lb. of proyens,[1] every pound 2*d.* ; 2*s.*— Item, 2lb. of *marmalet*, 2*s.* 1*d.*—Item, two *goils*[2] of sturgeon, 12*s.* 4*d.*—Item, a barrel for the same, 6*d.*—Item, 12lb. of dates, every pound 4*d.* ; 4*s.*—Item, 12lb. of great raisins, 2*s.*—Item, 1lb. of clove and mace, 8*s.*—Item, 1 qr. of saffron, 4*s.*—Item, 2 pound of *tornself*, 4*s.*—Item, 1 pound of isinglass, 4*s.*—Item, 1 pound of bisketts, 1*s.*—Item, 1 pound of carraway seeds, 1*s.*—Item, 2 pounds of comfits, 2*s.*—Item, 2 pounds of *sorts*[3] of Portugal, 2*s.*—Item, 4 pounds of liquorice and anniseeds 1*s.*—Item, 3 pounds of green ginger, 4*s.*—Item, 3 pounds of *sucketts*, 4*s.*—Item, 3 pounds of orringe buds, 4*s.*—Item, 4 pounds of orringes in syrup, 5*s.* 4*d.*——Sum total, 61*l.* 8*s.* 8*d.*

Sir JOHN NEVILL⎰ The Marriage of my Son-in-law ROGER ROCKLEY and my Daughter ELIZABETH NEVILL, the 14th of Chevit, knt. ⎱ day of January, in the 17th Year of our Sovereign Lord King Henry the Eighth, 1526.

First for the Expence of their Apparell:

For 22 yards of Russet satin, at 8*s.* per yard, 8*l.* 16*s.*—Item, 2 mantilles of skins for his gown, 2*l.* 8*s.*—Item, 2 yards ½ of black velvet for his gown, 1*l.* 10*s.*—Item, 9 yards of black sattin for his jackett and doublet, at 8*s.* per yard, 3*l.* 12*s.*— Item, 7 yards of black sattin for her kertil, at 8*s.* ; 2*l.* 16*s.*—Item, a roll of buckram, 2*s.* 8*d.*—Item, a bonnet of black velvet, 15*s.*—Item, a frontlet to the same bonnet, 12*s.*—Item, for a smock, 5*s.*—Item, for a pair of perfumed gloves, 3*s.* 4*d.*—Item, for a pair of other gloves 4*d.*

Second Day.

Item, for 3 yards of black satin, for lacing her gown, at 8*s.* ; 1*l.* 4*s.*—Item, for 22 yards of tawney camblet, at 2*s.* 2*d.* per yard, 2*l.* 11*s.* 9*d.*—Item, 2 yards of black velvet for her gown, 1*l.* 10*s.*—Item, a roll of buckram for her gown, 2*s.* 8*d.*— Item, for 7 yards of yellow satten-bridge [Bruges-satin], at 2*s.* 4*d.* ; 1*l.* 6*s.* 4*d.*—Item, for a pair of hose, 2*s.* 4*d.*—Item, for a pair of shoes, 1*s.* 4*d.*——Sum, 26*l.* 8*s.*

Item, for Dinner, and the Expence of the said Marriage of ROGER ROCKLEY and the said ELIZABETH NEVILL.

Imprimis, 8 qrs. of barley malt, at 10*s.* qr. 4*l.*—Item, 3 quarters and ½ of wheat,[4] at 14*s.* 4*d.* per qr. 2*l.* 16*s.* 8*d.*— Item, 2 hogsheads of wine, at 40*s.* per hogshead, 4*l.*—Item, 1 ditto of red wine, at 40*s.* ; 2*l.*——Total, 39*l.* 8*s.*

For the First Course at Dinner.

First, brawn with mustard, served alone, with malmesey—Item, frumetty to pottage—Item, a roe roasted for standart —Item, peacocks, two of[5] a dish—Item, swans, two of a dish—Item, a great pike on a dish—Item, conies roasted, 4 of a dish—Item, venison roasted—Item, capon of grease, 3 of a dish—Item, mallards, 4 of a dish—Item, teals, 7 of a dish— Item, pyes, baken with rabits in them—Item, baken oringe—Item, a flampett—Item, stoke fritters—Item, dulcetts, 10 of a dish—Item, a tart.

Second Course.

First, *marterns* to pottage—Item, for a standart, cranes, 2 of a dish—Item, young lamb whole roasted—Item, great fresh sammon *gollis*—Item, heron sewes, 3 of a dish—Item, bytters, 3 of a dish—Item, pheasants, 4 of a dish—Item, a great sturgeon goil—Item, partridges, 8 of a dish—Item, stints, 8 of a dish—Item, plovers, 8 of a dish—Item, curlews, 8 of a dish —Item, a whole roe baken—Item, venison baken, red and fallow—Item, a tart—Item, a *march-pane*—Item, gingerbread— Item, apples and cheese, stewed with sugar and sage.

For Night.

First, a Play, and streight after the play a Mask ; and when the mask was done, then the Bankett, which was 110 dishes, and all of meat ; and then all the gentilmen and ladyes danced ; and this continued from Sunday to the Saturday after.

The Expence of the Week for Flesh and Fish for the same Marriage.

Imprimis, 2 oxen, 3*l.*—Item, 2 brawnes, 1*l.* 2*s.*—Item, 2 roes, 10*s.* and for servants going, 15*s.*—Item, in swans, 15*s.*— Item, in cranes, 9, 1*l.* 10*s.*—Item, in peacocks, 12 ; 16*s.*—Item, in great pike, for flesh dinner, 6 ; 10*s.*—Item, in conies, 21 doz. 5*l.* 5*s.*—Item, in venison, red deer, hinds 3, and fetching them, 10*s.*—Item, fallow deer, does 12 ; ...... —Item, capon of grease 72 ; 3*l.* 12*s.*—Item, mallards and teal 30 doz. 3*l.* 11*s.* 8*d.*—Item, lamb, 3 ; 4*s.*—Item, heron sewes, 2 doz. 1*l.* 4*s.*— Item, in bitters, 12 ; 16*s.*—Item, in pheasants, 18—1*l.* 4*s.*—Item, in partridges, 40 ; 6*s.* 8*d.*—Item, in curlews, 18 ; 1*l.* 4*s.*—

---

[1] Prunes. [2] Gula, or Jola. [3] Sorts, *i.e.* species, or spices. [4] *I.e.* of wheaten malt. [5] Of, *i.e.* upon ; still the dialect of Yorkshire.

But in this are included a considerable part of Earl George's funeral expenses, together with his debts, which the fourth earl generously took upon himself. They did not, however, much exceed 700*l.*, for, when this nobleman's creditors grew importunate, he

Item, in plover, 3 doz. 5*s.*—Item, in stints, 5 doz. 9*s.*—Item, in sturgeon on goile, 5*s.*—Item, one seal, 13*s.* 4*d.*—Item, one purpose, 13*s.* 4*d.*——Sum total, 46*l.* 5*s.* 8*d.*

For Fridays and Saturdays.

First, leich *brayne*—Item, fromety to pottage—Item, whole ling and haberdine—Item, great guils of salt salmon—Item, great salt eels—Item, great salt sturgeon guils—Item, fresh ling—Item, fresh turbot—Item, great pike—Item, great guils fresh salmon—Item, great rudds—Item, baken turbuts—Item, tarts of 3 several meats.

Second Course.

First martens to pottage—Item, a great fresh sturgeon goil—Item, fresh eel roasted—Item, great brett—Item, salmon *chins* broiled—Item, roasted eels—Item, roasted lampreys—Item, roasted lamprons—Item, great burbuts—Item, salmon baken—Item, fresh eel baken—Item, fresh lampreys baken—Item, clear *gilley*—Item, gingebread.

Waiters at the said Marriage.

Storrers, carver ; Mr. Henry Nevill, sewer ; Mr. Thomas Drax, cupbearer ; Mr. George Paslew for the ewer-boarde's end : John Marys, John Mitchells, marshalls ; Robert Smallpage, for the cupboard ; William Page, for the cellar ; William Barker, for the ewer ; Robert Sycke the younger, John Hipperon, for the butterye.—Richard Thornton, Edmund North, Robert Syke, elder, William Longley, Robert Liel, William Cooke—to wait in the parlour.

Sir John Burton, Steward.

My brother Stapylton and servant ; my son Rockley and servant, to serve in the hall. Finis."

"The Charges of Sir JOHN NEVILL of Chevet, Knight, being Sheriff of Yorkshire, in the nineteenth year of the Reign of King Henry the Eighth, 1528.

Lent Assizes.

Imprimis, in wheat, 8 qrs. 8*l.*—Item, in malt, 11 qrs. 7*l.* 6*s.* 8*d.*—Item, in beans, 4 qrs. 3*l.* 4*s.*—Item, in hay, 6 loads, 1*l.* 5*s.*—Item, in litter, 2 loads, 4*s.*—Item, in part of the judges horses in the Inn, 13*s.* 4*d.*—Item, five hogsheads of wine, 3 claret, 1 white, 1 red, 10*l.* 16*s.* 4*d.*—Item, salt-fish, 76 couple, 3*l.* 16*s.*—Item, two barrells of herrings, 1*l.* 5*s.* 6*d.*—Item, two barrels of salmon, 3*l.* 1*s.*—Item, 12 seams of sea-fish, 6*l.* 4*s.*—Item, in great pike, and pickering, received of Rither, 6 score, 8*l.*—Item, 12 great pike from Ramsay, 2*l.*—Item, in pickerings from Holderness iiii CC. 3*l.*—Item, received of the said Rither 20 great breams, 1*l.*—Item, received of the said Rither, 12 great tenches, 16*s.*—Item, received of the said Rither 12 great eells and one hundred and six *jowling* eels, and 200 brewitt eels, and twenty great rudds, 2*l.*—Item, in great fresh salmon, 28 ; 3*l.* 16*s.* 8*d.*—Item, a barrell of sturgeon, 2*l.* 6*s.* 8*d.*—Item, a firkin of seal, 16*s.* 8*d.*—Item, a little barrell of sirope, 6*s.* 8*d.*—Item, two barrels of all manner of spices, 4*l.* 10*s.*—Item, one bag of ising-glass, 3*s.*—Item, a little barrell of aranges, 4*s.*—Item, 24 gallons of malmsey, 16*s.*—Item, two little barrells of green ginger and sucketts, 3*s.*—Item, three bretts, 12*s.*—Item, in vinegar 13 gallons 1 quart, 6*s.* 8*d.*—Item, eight large table-cloths, of 8 yards in length, 7 of them 12*d.* per yard, and one 16*d.* 3*l.* 6*s.* 8*d.*—Item, 6 doz. manchetts, 6*s.*—Item, 6 gallons of varges, 4*s.* 8*d.*—Item, in mayne bread, 1*s.* —Item, bread bought for marchpayne, 8*d.*—Item, for sugar and almonds bought besides the two barrells, 11*s.*—Item, for salt, 5*s.* 2*d.*—Item, for 5 gallons of mustard, 2*s.* 6*d.*—Item, a draught of fish, 2 great pikes, and 200 breams, 1*l.* 6*s.* 8*d.*— Item, three gallons of honey, 3*s.* 9*d.*—Item, six horse-loads of charcoal, 2*s.* 8*d.*—Item, 3 load of falwood and bavings, 3*s.* 4*d.* Item, for four streyners, 1*s.*—Item, for grains, 4*d.*—Item, for 20 doz. of cupps, 6*s.* 8*d.* - Item, for 6 flasketts and maund, 3*s.* 4*d.*—Item, for one doz. of earthen potts, 6*d.*—Item, for two staffe torches, 4*s.*—Item, for herbes five daies, 1*s.* 8*d.*—Item, for wafferens five daies, 1*s.* 8*d.*—Item, for onions, 1*s.*—Item, for 2 gallipots, 8*d.*—Item, for yeast, in five daies, 1*s.* 8*d.*—Item, for 20 doz. borrowed vessels, 5*s.* 1*d.*—Item, for carriage of wheat, malt, wine, and wood from the water-side, 15*s.*—Item, for Parker the cooke, and other cookes, and water-bearers, 4*l.* 10*s.*—Item, for 6 doz. trenchers, 4*d.*—Item, for making a cupboard, 1*s.* 4*d.*

The Charge of the said Sir JOHN NEVILL of Chevet, at Lammas Assizes, in the Twentieth Year of the Reign of King Henry the Eighth, as followeth :

Imprimis, in wheat, nine quarters, 12*l.*—Item, in malt, 12 qr. 10*l.*—Item, five oxen, 6*l.* 13*s.* 4*d.*—Item, 24 weathers, 3*l.* 4*s.*—Item, 6 calves, 1*l.*—Item, 60 capons of grease, 1*l.* 5*s.*—Item, other capons, 3*l.* 14*s.*—Item, 24 pigs, 14*s.*—Item, three hogsheads of wine, 8*l.* 11*s.* 8*d.*—Item, 22 swans, 5*l.* 10*s.*—Item, 12 cranes, 4*l.*—Item, 30 heronsews, 1*l.* 10*s.*—Item, 12 shovelards, 12*s.*—Item, 10 bytterns, 13*s.* 4*d.*—Item, 80 partridges, 1*l.* 6*s.* 8*d.*—Item, 12 ffeasants, 1*l.*—Item, 20 curlews, 1*l.* 6*s.* 8*d.*—Item, curlew knaves 32, 1*l.* 12*s.*—Item, 6 doz. plovers, 12*s.*—Item, 30 doz. pigeons, 7*s.* 6*d.*—Item, mallards, teale, and other small fowls, 2*l.* 2*s.*—Item, two basketts of all manner of spice, 5*l.*—Item, in malmsey, 24 gallons, 1*l.* 12*s.*—Item, in bucks, 10*l.*—Item, in staggs. . . . .

Friday and Saturday.

First, three couple of great ling, 12*s.*—Item, 70 couple of heberdines, 2*l.*—Item, salt salmon, 1*l.*—Item, fresh salmon and great, 3*l.* 6*s.* 8*d.*—Item, 6 great pikes, 12*s.*—Item, 80 pickerings, 4*l.*—Item, 300 great breams, 15*l.*—Item, 40 tenches, 1*l.* 6*s.* 8*d.*—Item, 80 jowling eels, and brevet eels, and 15 rudds, 1*l.* 12*s.*—Item, a firkin of sturgeon, 16*s.*—Item, in fresh

chose rather to sell than to borrow upon bond. His maxim seems to have been that of Persius—

> "—— *Nunc et de cespite vivo*
> *Frange aliquid.*"

In the following years, the family expenses are reduced to little more than 3,000*l.*, a sum still exceeding the income; to meet which there is a regular title under the receipts, "for lands sold." After all, their tradesmen's bills were ill paid; but the family, though imprudent, were conscientious, and generally allowed an interest of ten *per cent.* after the first year. It would be well if debtors of the same rank, at present, would allow their tradesmen half that sum.

seals, 13*s.* 4*d.*—Item, eight seam of fresh fish, 4*l.*—Item, 2 bretts, 8*s.*—Item, a barrell green ginger, and sucketts, 4*s.*—Item, 14 gallons of vinegar, 7*s.* 7*d*½.—Item, 6 horse-load of charcoal, 2*s.* 4*d.*—Item, for 40 load of cutwood and bavins, 2*l.* 13*s.* 4*d.* Item, for salt, 5*s.* 2*d.*— Item, for six dozen of manchetts, 6*s.*—Item, gingerbread for marchpayne, 8*d.*—Item, five gallon of mustard, 2*s.* 6*d.*—Item, for the loan of 6 dozen of vessels, 5*s.* 2*d.*—Item, three gallons of honey, 3*s.* 9*d.*—Item, for the costs of cooks and water-bearers, 4*l.*—Item, for the judges and clark of the assizes for their horsmeat in the Inn, and for their house-keeper's meat, and the clerk of the assize fee, 10*l.*—Item, for my livery coats, embroidered, 50*l.*—Item, for my horses provender, hay-litter, and grass at both the assizes, 6*l.* 13*s.* 4*d.*"

At these marriages, the bridegroom's dress—at least in the latter instance—was evidently a gown of velvet, richly trimmed with skins, together with a jacket and doublet of black satin. The lady was also clad in black satin, but had only *one chemise!* The marriage-dinner of Gervis Clifton would at least have sufficed for 2,000 people, but, comparing it with the provisions for the *week* at Mr. Rockley's marriage, I conclude that it must have been intended to last for the same time. In the two bills of fare, the first circumstance which strikes a modern eye is the astonishing cheapness of wine—scarcely sixpence a gallon, and not more than double the price of strong malt liquor in the same year. This is not accounted for by the absence of taxation, but by the perfection of the French vineyards, and the extreme imperfection of English husbandry at this time. Of wild-fowl the catalogue is curious. The crane ("There stalked the stately crane, as though he marched in war"—Drayton), the heron sewe, the bittern, the curlew, the curlew's knave, which I suppose to be the whimbrell, or lesser curlew), and the stint, or *Tringa cinclus.* Of tame fowl, beside the swan, of which five would have bought an ox, we have the peacock, and the capon of grease—that is, fat capon, as hart of grease is called *cervus de crassitudine.* The goose and tame duck are not mentioned; neither is the woodcock, though both marriages were in winter. The same is to be observed of the grouse, which, in the immense extent of the Yorkshire moors in 1530, must have abounded. The catalogue of fish is equally curious; for beside the kinds generally in use at modern tables, which *are* mentioned, and the trout, which is not, we have the royal sturgeon, then apparently very common, and breams in much larger numbers than could now be supplied. The silence of the bill of fare as to the carp favours the opinion that it was introduced into England rather later than this time. Then there appear heberdines, which were dried or pickled cod-fish from Aberdeen; the rudd—*i.e.*, the *Cyprinus orfus*, yet found in the pools of Holderness; and, above all, the seal and porpoise. Of the more common species, I do not understand the difference between "great eels," "*jowling* eels," and brevet eels. These were sometimes roasted— a mode of cookery prescribed long after by Isaac Walton. I have also to learn what were "martens to pottage," whether the bird or the quadruped; for those who could eat porpoises might have endured the sweet mart, if not its stinking relative the pole-cat. Tarts were plainly meat pies. What flampetts, leichbrayne, and stoke fritters may have been, I leave to the skilful in old cookery to discover. Mayne bread is the "Payne de Mayne" of Chaucer, a very fine sort, of which it is not determined by the critics whether it were so called as Panis Matutinus, or from the city of that name. "Marchpayne," which the fair Dowsabell was skilled in preparing, was a kind of biscuit (here it was made in part of gingerbread), much used in old deserts. "Save me a piece of Marchpane," says the servant ("Romeo and Juliet," act i. sc. v.) when the tables were taken away. At the marriage of Mr. Rockley, we see all the old pomp of sewers and senescalls, marshalls and carvers. A knight was steward, and the bridegroom himself, attended by a servant, waited in the hall. Their merriment was persevering enough to have subdued modern constitutions, for the dancing continued a whole week; on the wedding-night was first a play and next a mask; after which followed a "banket" of 110 dishes. This was in order. In the passage above referred to is a curious scene of bustle and confusion in clearing the hall after dinner for the maskers. "Away with the joint stools—remove the Court cupboard—look to the plate, Antony and Potpan!" And when the mask is over, Old Capulet says, "Nay, gentlemen, prepare not to be gone; we have a trifling foolish banket toward."

After such dinners as had preceded these entertainments, we may presume that the 110 dishes of the banket might be called, comparatively, trifling, and would somewhat resemble a modern table in lightness. Pike was the only fish served up with the flesh dinners. The arrangement of the first and second course with respect to fish, &c., seems to have been indiscriminate. Not a vegetable appears at either entertainment. Apples were introduced with the cheese, and stewed with sugar and sage. Confectioneries seem to have been good and plentiful. At the sheriff's feast, 8 long tables of 8 yards each will nearly give the number of guests—viz., about 24 at each table, or 192 in all—no extraordinary number for the grand jury, counsel, magistrates, and gentry of this great county, assembled on such an occasion.

The splendour of their establishment does not account for so much waste. The household of Skipton Castle consisted of about thirty-two servants, who, with economy, might then have been supported on much less than even 1,000*l. per annum.** But the great consumption of money was in wines, journeys, clothes, presents, and tobacco. With respect to the first, they drank such quantities of claret, sack, and muscadine, that I suppose the upper servants must have shared with them in the first at least. Spirituous liquors, so far as I remember, are never mentioned but once, where there is a small payment for aqua vitæ. Their journeys were very expensive, for they were never at rest in any one place—London, Newcastle, Scotland, Brougham, Grafton, kept the young lord perpetually in motion. A single pair of seal-skin gloves cost 20s. Sleeping-gloves of an inferior price are mentioned, probably to whiten the hands. The last heavy article of expense was tobacco, of which the finest sort cost 18s. per pound, and an inferior kind 12s. A single bill for this article amounted to 36l. 7s. 8d.

With respect to presents, the house was supplied with a profusion of fish,† wild fowl,‡

---

* I have since discovered that at this time there was a household at Londesborough of 90 persons.

† Notwithstanding what has been said on this subject under Malham, the earl, as chief lord of the Percy fee, had certainly a share, at least, in the fishery of Malham Water, in 1606; for in the Account Book of that year is this entry: "P'd to H. H. being at Mawater, watching the well-head for stealing the trouts coming unto this Ritt Time, 2s. 6d.," and in 1638 is a charge for a stone of *Pick* for the Tarn at Mawater. This must have been for pitching a boat. [Why not for pike to stock the Tarn?]

‡ Amongst these was black game, as well as grouse. In 1638, two roes were sent out of Cumberland by Sir Thomas Dacre, undoubtedly from Martindale Forest. This is the latest notice I have found of that species in South Britain. A fowling-piece for my lord cost 20s., but he certainly did not shoot flying. The coals consumed in the castle came from Colne; but they made use of much peat, and sometimes 1,600 loads of ling *per annum* pulled upon the neighbouring moors for heating the ovens. These were not like the diminutive ovens of the present day, but vaults of stone, capable of holding a flock of sheep before they baked them; and they were seldom unemployed. Baked meats were more in use two centuries ago than now; and when a part of the Clifford family resided at Grafton, in Northamptonshire, not only pasties of red deer venison were sent thither by express from Skipton, but carcases of stags, two, four, or more, at once, were baked whole, and despatched to the same place.

The following items will not only illustrate the foregoing remarks, but throw farther light on the manners and habits of the two last earls:

1606, "Paid for baking of horsebread, 4d." It seems probable that horses were sometimes fed with a coarse oaten bread, baked on purpose.

"Five hundred of oysters, 2s. 6d.," or 6d. *per* hundred.

"Sixteen bushels of malt, at 4s. 8d. the bushel.

"Halfe toone of wyne for my lord, 8l. 5s.

"Wyne bestowed upon the justices, and *sugar* for the same, viz. Sir Richard Tempest, Sir Stephen Tempest, Mr. Heber, 2s. 6d.

"For three bushels of wheat to bake two staggs, 18s." Wheat was then as dear as in cheap seasons at present.

"Whit wyne and *sugare* for Sir Stephen Tempest, 12d.

"Wyne and sugarr to my lords counsell, Sir Stephen, Mr. Lyster, &c." Sugar was then a great delicacy, and very dear. Sir Stephen Tempest seems to have had something of Falstaff's taste for sack and sugar; but I suppose they were generally drank together.

"White sugar hires the taste, the brains to drown."
Fletcher's "Purple Island," 1633.

"For troote and pickerells gotten at Mawater Tarne, 2s.

"To the fishers for 21 trootes and cheavones, being great ones, 3s. It. for cheavons, trootes, and roches, 1s. 4d. It. for 31 trootes, eles, and oomberes, 1s. 6d." (N.B.—The perch is never mentioned in these accounts.) "Paid to William Townley for 6 lb. and 1 oz. of pepper, for baking a stagg sent to Grafton; for another sent to Westm'land and Cumb'land for the assizes, and one bestowed by my lo. in the countrey upon divers, 18s. 8d. For ¼ lb. of sugar which Sir Stephen Tempest had in wyne, 5d.

"It. For currants and limons which they put in the stag pies." I am inclined to think that our cooks know much better how to season venison pasties at present.

From the quantity of flour used, these enormous structures must have been standing pies, a kind of pastry castles, of

&c., by the neighbouring gentry, for which the bearers frequently received as much as it was worth. Vails were also high; Lady Clifford visited at Denton, Bracewell, Broughton, and Stonyhurst, and bestowed liberally upon the servants—at Bracewell she gave 19s. To Sir Stephen Tempest, of Broughton, she sometimes lost 40s. at a time at billiards. To the king, in 1639, Earl Francis presented 20l. in gold, as a new year's gift. He also gave two exhibitions of 15l. each to scholars at the university; and when he went to Skipton Church a dole was distributed to the poor. This duty he did not omit when fourscore, and in the severest weather, though he had a chapel within the castle.

The public exercises of religion were then countenanced by the presence of the great. " Alas, how changed, how fallen " now!

ANNE BARONESS CLIFFORD, FOURTEENTH *LORD* OF THE HONOUR OF SKIPTON.

By the death of the last earl, the long contest for the barony of Skipton was finally closed,* and, after thirty-eight years of family discord, Anne Clifford, Countess Dowager of Dorset, and then Countess of Pembroke and Montgomery, entered upon the inheritance of her ancestors.

She was one of the most illustrious women of her own or of any age. By the blessing of a religious education, and the example of an excellent mother, she imbibed in childhood those principles which, in middle life, preserved her untainted from the profligacy of one husband and the fanaticism of another; and, after her deliverance from both, conducted her

---

which the walls were of the same material with the roof. I must add that the office of pasty baker was distinct from that of the cook or baker of the family. In the year 1606 one Atkinson, of Barden, was famous for this accomplishment, and in 1634 widow Bland was paid by instalments 3l. 4s. 2d. for baking pasties when my old lord kept house.

" It. Paid for 4 lb. of cotton weak lights which were used when the judges were here (at Skipton), 1s. 6d." Does it not follow from this article that on common occasions the family used rush-lights?

" 1633-4, To captayne Robinson by my lo. com'ds for writing letters of news to his l'p for a half year, 5l."

Before the introduction of printed newspapers, it appears that the great families had a sort of gazetteers in London who transmitted to them the news of the day in written letters; but the practice was continued by this family till the year 1687.

" 1634, Paid for a quayle pipe for poudring hair." Portraits, I think, afford no example of hair-powder worn so early. It appears to have been blown upon the head out of a tube. " It. 3 lb. of Damaske powder for lynen at 4s. *per* lb." What was the use of this?

" To Roger the piper, his reward for attending here in X'mas, 10s." A relic of the ancient minstrelsy.

" To ould Symon of Carlile for a cast of Merlins, 1l. 10s. 0d." The merlin was the most diminutive hawk used in falconry.

" It. To four yards of sattin for a doublet trimming for my lord, 7l. 8s. 6d. It. To a demicaster for my old lord."— A hat made half of beaver and half of wool.

" It. For 114 lbs. of malt delivered to the castle last year, 50l." Malt is greatly reduced in price since 1606.

" It. To 60 muttons, 10l.

" It. To Sir Ralph Assheton's man that brought my lady a basket of apricocks, 2s. 6d." This fruit would ripen much better in the climate of Whalley Abbey than of Skipton.

" 1638, To Sir William Lister's groom, when my lord dyned at the wedding there, for setting up the horses, 2s. 6d.

" To I. H. for his journey to Woodstock with a horse given by my lo. to the kinge, 2l.

" It. Paid for fourscore lb. of sugar for my lady, 4l." On the whole, the necessaries of life were at this time very cheap, the luxuries extremely dear. Animal food in particular bore a very low price; a fat wether would not have purchased two pounds of sugar. " When strange bottoms," saith Holinshed, " were suffered to come in, wee had sugar for IVd. the pound, which is now (1577) worthe half a crowne, raisons of Corinth for Id. a lb. nowe holden at VId." In the Compotus of Whalley Abbey, currants, which are here meant, are called " Raceme de Coran." Raisin is a corruption of "raceme," a bunch of grapes, and currant is the Italian Coranto, or Corinth. But clothing in general was very expensive; a single doublet of satin for my lord was equal to the price of forty fat sheep. The old earl sometimes wore plain suits of Spanish broad-cloth, which cost 20s. the yard.

* With the exception of Barden.

to the close of a long life in the uniform exercise of every virtue which became her sex, her rank, and her Christian profession.

She had all the courage and liberality of the other sex, united to all the devotion, order, and economy (perhaps not all the softness) of her own. She was the oldest but most independent courtier in the kingdom; had known and admired Queen Elizabeth; had refused what she deemed an iniquitous award of King James; rebuilt her dismantled castles in defiance of Cromwell, and repelled, with disdain, the interposition of a profligate Minister under Charles II.

In her second widowhood, and as soon as the iniquity of the times would permit, her genius began to expand itself. Her first husband was like all the Buckhursts, a man of sense and spirit, but of licentious morals; her second was the weak and illiterate tool of a party which she despised.* Accordingly, we find her complaining that the bowers of Knowle, in Kent, and of Wilton, in Wiltshire, had been to her no better than the painted abodes of sorrow. Yet, perhaps, if there were a failing point about her character, it was that she loved independence, and even authority, too well for a wife.†

But the time now came when every impediment was to be removed; and, with two rich jointures added to her paternal inheritance, she withdrew into the north, and set about her great work of " repairing the breach, and restoring the paths to dwell in." Six of the houses of her ancestors were in ruins; ‡ the church of Skipton, in consequence of the damage it had sustained during the siege of the castle, was in little better condition; but her unexpensive, though magnificent habits, the integrity and economy of her agents, and, above all, her own personal inspection, enabled her, in a short time, to remove every vestige of devastation which the civil wars had left. These great works she was not backward to

---

* What must have been her feelings, when she saw her lord employed by the Parliament, in expelling from the University of Oxford her own friends (and such friends as) Sheldon, Sanderson, Morley, and Fell! But he was precisely " the tool that knaves do work with."

[† " I must confess with inexpressible thankfulness, that, through the goodness of Almighty God, and the mercies of my Saviour Jesus Christ, Redeemer of the World, I was born a happy creature in mind, body, and fortune; and that those two lords of mine, to whom I was afterwards, by Divine Providence, married, were in their several kinds as worthy noblemen as any there were in this kingdom; yet it was my misfortune to have contradictions and crosses with them both. With my first lord, about the desire he had to make me sell my rights in the land of my ancient inheritance for a sum of money, which I never did, nor ever would consent unto, insomuch, that this matter was the cause of a long contention betwixt us; as also for his profusion in consuming his estate; and some other extravagancies of his; and with my second lord, because my youngest daughter, the Lady Isabella Sackville, would not be brought to marry one of his younger sons, and that I would not relinquish my interest I had in five thousand pounds, being part of her portion out of my lands in Craven. Nor did there want malicious ill-willers, to blow and foment the coals of dissension between us, so as in both their lifetimes, the marble pillars of Knowle, in Kent, and Wilton, in Wiltshire, were to me oftentimes but the gay arbours of anguish, insomuch as a wise man, that knew the insides of my fortune, would often say, that I lived in both these my lord's great families as the river Roan or Rhodanus runs through the Lake of Geneva without mingling any part of its streams with that lake; for I gave myself up wholly to retirement as much as I could in both those great families, and made good books and virtuous thoughts my companions, which can never discern affliction, nor be daunted when it unjustly happens; and by a happy genius I overcame all those troubles, the prayers of my blessed mother helping me therein."— " Memoirs of the Dowager Countess Ann," by herself, quoted by Lodge in his " Portraits of Illustrious Personages."]

‡ I fear she never forgave the man who bought the timber roof of Skipton Castle, for, in a letter to Thomas Earl of Thanet, from one of his age, I meet with the following passage:—

" Skipton, 6 Ap. 1711. May it please your lordship,

" I have made enquiry about William Watson's paying twenty pounds per annum to Mr. Sedgwick, and find several persons can remember it; and they say, that the reason of my lady Pembroke's anger against his father was, that he had bought timber of one Curror, that had been governor of Skipton castle, and carried it away from the castle, after it had been demolished, to Silsden More."

commemorate. Most of her erections bore, *mutatis mutandis*, the same inscription, and perhaps there is no English character so frequently and so copiously recorded in stone and marble as the Countess of Pembroke.

An early taste for poetry and history was instilled into her by her tutor Daniel,* who was eminent in both. These services she repaid by an epitaph, in which her own name, as usual, is not forgotten.† She erected the monument of Spenser ‡ in Westminster Abbey,§ and that of her father at Skipton (where she re-inscribed the tomb of the first and second Earl of Cumberland), together with a statue of her beloved mother at Appleby.

It is still more to her honour that she patronised the poets of her youth, and the distressed loyalists of her maturer age ; that she enabled her aged servants to end their days in ease and independence ; and, above all, that she educated and portioned the illegitimate children of her first husband, the Earl of Dorset. Removing from castle to castle, she diffused plenty and happiness around her, by consuming on the spot the produce of her vast domains in hospitality and charity. Equally remote from the undistinguishing profusion of ancient times, and the parsimonious elegance of modern habits, her house was a school for the young, and a retreat for the aged, an asylum for the persecuted, a college for the learned, and a pattern for all.

The favourite authors of her early days may be conjectured from the library depicted on her great family portrait. When her eyes began to fail, she employed a reader, who marked on every volume or pamphlet the day when he began and ended his task. Many books so noted yet remain in the Evidence Room at Skipton.

Ingenuous curiosity, and perhaps, too, the necessary investigation of her claims to the baronies of the family, led her to compile their history—an industrious and diffuse, not always an accurate work, in which more, perhaps, might have been expected from the assistance of Sir Matthew Hale, who, though a languid writer, was a man of great acuteness and comprehension.

Her life was extended, by the especial blessing of Providence, frequently bestowed on

---

* A MS. copy of " Part of the Civile Wars," by this poet, is among her evidences at Skipton.

[† The following is the inscription upon the monument erected in the church of Beckington, in Somersetshire, by Anne Countess Dowager of Pembroke and Montgomery, to the memory of her tutor :—

"HERE LIES EXPECTING THE SECOND COMING OF OUR LORD AND SAVIOUR JESUS CHRIST, THE DEAD BODY OF SAMUEL DANIEL ESQ. THAT EXCELLENT POET AND HISTORIAN, WHO WAS TUTOR TO THE LADY ANNE CLIFFORD IN HER YOUTH. SHE WAS DAUGHTER AND HEIR TO GEORGE, EARL OF CUMBERLAND, WHO IN GRATITUDE TO HIM ERECTED THIS MONUMENT TO HIS MEMORY A LONG TIME AFTER, WHEN SHE WAS COUNTESS DOWAGER OF PEMBROKE, DORSET, & MONTGOMERY. HE DIED IN OCTOBER. ANNO 1619.]

‡ See Stone, the "Statuaries Diary," published by Lord Orford. Spenser was patronised by her father, to whom the poet has inscribed not the best sonnet prefixed to the " Faery Queene."

[§ The inscription is—

HERE LIES
(EXPECTING THE COMINGE OF OUR SAVIOUR
JESUS CHRIST)
EDMONDE SPENCER
THE PRINCE OF POETS IN HIS TIME
WHOSE DIVINE SPIRIT
NEEDS NOE OTHER WITNESSE
THAN THE WORKS WHICHE HE LEFT BEHINDE HIM
HE WAS BORNE IN LONDON
IN THE YEARE 1510
AND DYED IN THE YEARE 1596.]

2 X

eminently virtuous characters, to a period beyond which she could no longer hope to enjoy herself, or be useful to others ; and she died March 22nd, 1675, aged 87.

Her person was tall and upright ; her dress, after she resided in the north, usually of black serge ; her features more expressive of firmness than benignity. The principles of physiognomy are certainly fallacious, for no one who ever saw the picture of Lady Pembroke, without knowing whom it represented, would suppose it to have been meant for a beneficent and amiable woman.*

Margaret Countess of Cumberland having died during the heat of the contest with Earl Francis, would probably have been refused interment at Skipton. At all events, she was buried at Appleby,† where her illustrious daughter, partly from affection to her, and partly, it may be, from aversion to her uncle and cousin, whose bodies, as hath been said, did not completely close the vault, chose to accompany her ; and a monument in that church, not unworthy of her name and virtues, commemorates, and, I hope, will long commemorate, ANNE Countess Dowager of Pembroke, Dorset, and Montgomery.‡

After this general account of Lady Anne Clifford, the following particulars relating to her, at different periods of her life, may, perhaps, not be unacceptable. And,

1st, Among the papers at Skipton Castle I met with an original book of accounts filled with memoranda relating to this lady's education, from 1600 to 1602.

In the beginning is the following prayer, intended, I suppose, to be used on entering the church—

"O Lord, increase o'r fayth, and make us evermore attentyve hearers, true conceivers, and diligent fulfillers, of thy heavenly will !"

_____

[* The following description of herself is from a manuscript apparently written by the countess's secretary, and preserved amongst the Skipton evidences—

"The Colour of her Eyes was black like her Father's, with a Peak of Hair on her forehead and a dimple in her chin like her father —full cheeks and round-fac'd like her Mother and an excellent shape of body resembling her Father—but then (when she begun to dictate her dyary) she said that time and age had ended all those beauties, which are compared to the Grasse of the Field. The hair of her head was brown and very thick, and so long that it reached to the calf of her leggs when she stood upright. And when she caused these Memorialls of herself to be written she had passed the year of 63 of her age ; she said the perfections of her minde were much above those of her body. She had a strong and copious memory, a sound Judgment & a discerning spirit, and so much of a strong imagination in her as that many times even her dreams and apprehensions before hand prov'd true."]

[† The Countess Dowager of Pembroke seems never to have missed an opportunity of setting up an inscription. Accordingly she caused to be erected a stone pillar in the parish of Brougham, on the road between Penrith and Appleby, to commemorate her last parting with her mother. The inscription is—

"This pillar was erected A.D. 1656 by the Right honourable Anne Countess Dowager of Pembroke, and sole heir of the Right honourable George Earl of Cumberland, for a memorial of her last parting with her good and pious mother, the Right honourable Margaret Countess Dowager of Cumberland, the 2d April 1616. In memory whereof she also left an annuity of 4l. to be distributed to the poor within this parish of Brougham every 2d day of April, for ever, upon the stone hereby. Laus Deo."

This rent-charge is paid out of an estate at Yanwath, in the parish of Barton, which is charged with the payment thereof, and is distributed about the 2nd April, by the minister and churchwardens, amongst two, three, or four families not receiving weekly relief, under the name of " Pillar Money."

The poet Rogers, in "The Pleasures of Memory," thus alludes to this memorial—

"Hast thou through Eden's wild wood vales pursued
Each mountain scene majestically rude ;
Nor there awhile with lifted eye revered
That modest stone which pious Pembroke reared ;
Which still records, beyond the pencil's power,
The silent sorrows of a parting hour ;
Still to the musing pilgrim points the place
Her sainted spirit most delights to trace ?"]

[‡ Her monument—one of a very handsome and unusual character—is placed against the north wall of the chancel, and consists of an altar-tomb covered with a plain slab of black marble, and a large upright slab, also of black marble, standing on the tomb, and fixed to the wall. Upon the last-mentioned slab is a complete table of the main descent of the Cliffords,

And after—

> " To wish and will it is my part,
> To yow, good lady, from my hart,
> The yeares of Nestor God yow send,
> W'th hapynes to your life's end ! "

These lines are, I think, in the handwriting of Samuel Daniel, her tutor ; and, when compared with the future history and long life of this young lady, then only eleven years old, it cannot be denied that their prayer was heard. She actually saw ninety years, wanting only three, and the " happiness " of the last thirty had no abatement to her " life's end."

She was now in London, under the direction of Mrs. Taylor, her governess, the whole receipts acknowledged by whom, from August, 1600, to August, 1602, amounted only to 38*l.* 12*s.* 1*d.*, and the whole sum expended, 35*l.* 13*s.* 3*d.* Of these receipts a large proportion consisted of presents, sometimes in gold, sometimes in groats, threepences, &c., in small silver barrels, sent by Lady Warwick, Mrs. Elmes, and her other friends.

The directions of the countess, her mother, with respect to her dress, expenses, &c., are very numerous and particular ; the earl is never mentioned, from beginning to end.

Out of a multitude of particulars, I will select such as have any tendency to illustrate the manners of the times.

> To my lady Awdley's man, w'ch brought my lady Anne XII litel glasses of Coodyneck,* 11*s.*
> Item, a reward for fynding her la'p's golden picture† lost, 11*s.*

---

commencing with Robert Veteripont, who married Idonea de Buley, and ending with Anne Lady Clifford, and her daughters Margaret and Isabella Sackville. The names of the husbands and wives are given, but no dates, and there are twenty-four shields of arms emblazoned in colours ; and as these are all described elsewhere in this work, it is useless to repeat them here.

Upon the front of the altar-tomb is the following inscription—

> HERE LYES EXPECTING Yᴱ SECOND COMING OF OVR LORD AND SAVIOUR JESUS CHRIST,
> Yᴱ DEAD BODY OF Yᴱ LADY ANNE CLIFFORD, DAUGHTER AND SOLE HEIR TO GEORGE CLIFFORD,
> 3ʀᴅ EARL OF CUMBERLAND BY HIS BLESSED WIFE MARGARET RUSSEL COUNTESS OF CUMBERLAND,
> Wᶜᴴ LADY ANNE WAS BORN IN SKIPTON CASTLE, IN CRAVEN, YE 30ᴛʜ OF JANUARY (BEING FRY
> DAY) IN Yᴱ YEARE 1590, AS Yᴱ YEAR BEGINS ON NEW YEARES-DAY ; & BY A LONG CONTINVED
> DESCENT FROM HER FATHER & HIS NOBLE AVCESTORS, SHE WAS BARONESSE OF CLIFFORD,
> WESTMERELAND, & VESCY ; HIGH SHERIFESSE OF Yᴱ COVNTY OF WESTMERELAND AND LADY OF Yᴱ HONOUR OF
> SKIPTON IN CRAVEN AFORESAID. SHE MARRIED FOR HER FIRST HUSBAND RICHARD SACKVILLE EARL
> OF DORSET, & FOR HER SECOND HUSBAND PHILIP HERBERTE EARL OF PEMBROKE &
> MONTGOMERY ; LEAVING BEHIND HER ONLY TWO DAVGHTERS THAT LIVED, Wᶜᴴ SHE HAD
> BY HER FIRSTE HUSBAND ; THE ELDER MARGARET COUNTESSE OF THANNETT ; AND
> THE YOUNGER, ISABEL COUNTESSE OF NORTHAMPTON.
> WHICH LADY ANNE CLIFFORD COUNTESSE DOWAGER OF PEMBROKE, DORSET, AND MOVNTGO
> MERY, DECEASED AT HER CASTLE OF BROVGHAM Yᴱ 22ɴᴅ DAY OF MARCH, IN THE YEAR OF OUR LORD 1675,
> CHRISTIANLY, WILLINGLY AND QVIETLY, HAVING BEFORE HER DEATH SEEN
> A PLENTIFUL ISSVE BY HER TWO DAUGHTERS OF THIRTEEN GRAND-CHILDREN : AND HER BODY LYES BVRIED IN THIS VAVLTE.]

* What is Coodyneck? Probably some sweetmeat ; for in Holinshed, vol. i. p. 95, I find " Jellies, Conserves, and Codinacs," mentioned together.

† Were there any miniatures at this time, or was this merely an ornament to wear about the neck ? [" Dr. Whitaker writes upon this article, ' Were there any miniatures at this time ?' Has he forgotten Portia's caskets ? Has he forgotten, or did he ever read, a play called ' Hamlet,' written near the time he is inquiring about ? If the pictures Hamlet shows to the queen were not miniatures, but full-length portraits, yet there is another passage which puts the question to rest at once—' It is not very strange, for my uncle is King of Denmark, and those who would have made mouths at him while my father lived give twenty, forty, fifty, and a hundred ducats a-piece for his *picture in little.*' The wearing of miniatures, richly set in gold, pearls, or diamonds, was a fashion in the courts of Elizabeth and the first Stuarts. Hiliard and the elder Oliver, the first Englishmen who could be called artists, were both miniature-painters, and both living in 1600. Another item in her ladyship's accounts is, ' An ivory box to put a picture in, XII*d.*' "—Hartley Coleridge's " Northern Worthies," ii. 53.

The following examples of brooches with pictures may also be quoted. They occur in the inventory of the jewels belonging to the Lady Mary, daughter to King Henry VIII., 1542-46—

It'm oon Broche of golde of the History of Moyses set with 11 Litle Damonde.
It'm a Broche of golde wᵗ oon Balace and of the History of Susanne.
It'm a Broche of golde enamyled blacke wᵗ an agate of the story of Abrahm wᵗ 1111 small Rocke Rubies.
It'm a Boke of golde with the Kings face and hir graces mothers.
It'm a Rounde Tablet blacke enameled wᵗ the Kings Picture and quene Janes.
It'm a grene Tablet garneshed wᵗ golde having the Picture of the trinite in it.
It'm a Broche of golde of thistory of Moyses striking water out of the Rok and a Balace set in the same.]

Item, for bringing her la'p her looking-glass* lost, VI*s*.

Item, to captain Davies' man when he came to my la. with Indyan clothes,† VI*d*.

Lady Darbie's man, that br't my lady a pair of writing tables, II*s*.

Item, for a boxe of ivery to putt a picture in, XII*d*.

Item, to a Frenche woman for a rabato weyer, VII*s*.

Item, b't at the sign of the holie lamb, at St. Martin's, a y'd and q'r of lawne.‡

Item, a payre of Jersey stockings, IIII*s*.

Item, two pair of shoes of Spanish lether, and one of calves lether, XIIII*d*.

Item, Holland, at II*s*. X*d*. per ell, for my la's smockes.

Item, an ell of Holland for my la's hand-chiefs, II*s*. X*d*.§

An hower glass,‖ IV*d*.

A maske for my la. II*s*.

A verdyngale and verdyngale wyre, V*s*. II*d*.

Musicyons for playinge at my la's chamber-doore, II*s*. VI*d*.

Item, to the same who played at my la. Anne's maske, X*s*.

Item, to a porter that br't my la. a brasse of faysants from Lilleford carryers, II*d*.

Item, 2 knotts of virginall wyre.

Item, at Cheynes, to a woman that made her lp's breakfast and washed her lynen, III*s*.

Item, to the growme at Cheynes, that made feyers and looked to the chamber, II*s*. VI*d*.

Item, geven to Stephens, that teacheth my la. to dawnce, for 1 monthe, XX*s*.¶

Item, p'd for sleave silk, XXXIII*s*.**

Item, p'd for litel silkworms, V*s*.

Item, p'd for mendyng the cross-bowe for arrowes,†† XII*d*.

Item, p'd for drawing your l'ipp in canvas, III*s*.‡‡

Item, for foore basket pendants of goulde and pearle, XII*s*.

Item, a wi't coyffe and forked cloth for my la. V*s*.

Item, for II bunches of glass fethers for her la'p, VI*d*.

Item, a p'r of grene worsted stockyngs for my la. IIII*s*. III*d*.

Item, two pap' bookes; 1 for accompte, the other to write her catachisme in.§§

Item, p'd for a ringe and jewell, IX*s*. III*d*.

Item, 2 dozen of glasse flowers, VII*s*.

With respect to the general habits of this young lady, so far as can be collected from her own account-book, it appears that she visited the Countesses of Northumberland, Derby, and Warwick, and Lady Scroope, in their own coaches; that she received from them, and her other friends, frequent presents of gold, trinkets, venison (once a whole stag at a time), fish, and fruit; that she was taught French, music, dancing; and, above all, that she was brought up in habits of early religion and charity. With an allowance so limited as frequently to reduce her to borrowing, almost one-fourth of the numerous articles in her expenditure consisted of acts of bounty. Thus wisely were laid the foundations of those habits which, in riper years, rendered her a blessing to whole provinces.

---

* Pocket looking-glasses were at that time probably in use.

† Perhaps some of the spoil of her father's voyages.

‡ All the shops at that time had signs, like modern inns.

§ Hence I conclude that the holland which Quickly bought for Falstaft's shirts was three shillings an ell, not eight. The numerals III might easily be mistaken for VIII in an ill-written MS. and by a careless compositor.

‖ Watches were not yet in general use even among persons of the highest rank, and Lady Anne is twice drawn with an hour-glass beside her.

¶ The least useful accomplishment in which she was instructed was the most expensive. This is often the case.

** This brings to mind Bishop Rainbow's expression in his funeral sermon for this lady, "that she could discourse well on all subjects, from predestination to slea-silk."

†† Undoubtedly for my lady's use.

‡‡ This is probably the original from which the copy of the young portrait of Lady Anne Clifford, at Skipton, was taken. On this occasion it is not to be supposed that an inferior artist would be employed. How low then must portrait-painting have been in the reign of Elizabeth!

§§ I wish it were a part of modern education in the same rank to require young ladies either to write or read their "Catachisme." But modern education takes a different course, and therefore produces no such characters as Lady Anne Clifford. Instead of principle, we now hear of nothing but sentiment; and fine feelings have taken the place of Christian charity.

During the time of either marriage,* or in her first widowhood, I find no memorial of this lady in the family papers. At the decease of the Earl of Pembroke, she was probably at Skipton, where I met with the following imperfect letter from Caldecott, his chaplain, of whose name Butler has made no very decent use in his account of this nobleman's death-bed. These are scenes which the vices of the dying often render terrible; but which their follies should never convert into subjects of ridicule.

" MADAM,
" The honour y———
duty of perform......wards my lord, deceased, brings mee to acquaint your hon'r that I am newly come hither from the last office I could do him, his interment, where I met your hon'rs letter, most pretious to his memory, which I doe keep as a significant favour from y'r hon'r; nor can I possibly returne my sence sufficiently. But if ever I enjoy the happiness to kisse your hon'rs hand, it will be to testify the great rejoyceinge I have in beeinge
" Yo'r hon'rs most humble and faithful servant,
" *Cock-pit,* 23 *Feb.* 1649." " R. CALDECOTT.

Next follow two letters from herself to Mr. Brogden, reader of Bethmesley Hospital, which are now deposited in the chest of that house. They contain nothing very interesting, but serve to show the authoritative manner in which she issued her injunctions; and that, however beneficent, she had none of that weakness which suffers tenants to incur arrears to their own injury.

" GOOD JOHN BROGDEN,
" I have received yo'r letter, and in itt one from L. C. to the mother and sisters of Beamsley, desyringe their forbearance of ye rent due to them for some season, w'ch moc'on of his I doe utterlye dislyke, and will by noe meanes give my assent to; for if I or they shold hearken to such moc'ons, they shold soon be in a very sadd condic'on. Therfore I charge you, and give you attorety under my one hande, forthewithe to distraine for the sayad rentte; and iff itt bee nott theruppon payed, I will usse the strictest course I cann to turne him outt of the farme. And I praye you shew him thees lines of mine, to witness this my purpose and intention. And so, committing you to the Almighty, I rest
" Your assured frinde,
" *Appellby Castelle, this* 29 *of May,* 1655." " ANNE PEMBROOKE.

" MR. BROGDEN,
" I have received yo'r letter by this bearer, and ye enclosed petic'on of D. G. widdow, w'th my refference thereunto, dated at Brougham Castle, 2nd Feb. 1664–1665. And by the letter of yo'rs I perceive there is now a vacant place in my Almeshouse at Beamesley, by the late death of E. B.
" I have nowe, here inclosed, sent you a warrant under my hand, for the placing therein, in her stead, D. G. aforesayd.
" Which warrant I desire may be communicated by you to the mother and sisters, that shee may be settled therein accordingly. And so, committing you to ye Divine Protecc'on, I rest,
" *Pendragon Castell, this* 12*th day of June,* 1666. " ANNE PEMBROOKE.
" Provided that this widow Gill goe to church, and to heare com'on prayer in ye almeshouse, or otherwise itt will bring the house out of order."

[* The following letter from the Countess Anne, addressed to her uncle Edward, Earl of Bedford, shows the state of happiness in which she lived with the Earl of Pembroke :—
" MY LORD,
" Yesterday by Mr. Marshe I received your Lordship's letter, by which I perceived how much you were troubled at the report of my being sick, for which I humbly thank your Lordship. I was so ill that I did make full account to die; but now I thank God I am something better. And now, my Lord, give me leave to desire that favour from your Lordship as to speak earnestly to my Lord for my coming up to the town this term, either to Bainarde's Castle, or the Cock-pitt; and I protest I will be ready to return back hither again whensoever my Lord appoints it. I have to this purpose written now to my Lord, and put it enclosed in a letter of mine to my Lady of Carnarvon, as desiring her to deliver it to her father, which I know she will do with all the advantage she can, to further this business; and if your Lordship will join with her in it, you shall afford a charitable and a most acceptable favour to your Lordship's cousin, and humble friend to command
" ANNE PEMBROKE.
" *Ramossbury this* 14*th of January* 1638.
" If my Lord should deny my coming, then I desire your Lordship I may understand it as soon as may be, that so I may order my poor business as well as I can without any one coming to town; for I dare not venture to come up without his leave, lest he should take that occasion to turn me out of his house, as he did out of Whitehall, and then I shall not know where to put my head. I desire not to stay in the town above ten days or a fortnight at the most."—Harl. MSS. . . . quoted in Lodge's "Portraits of Illustrious Personages."]

I regret my inability to lay before the reader any more interesting parts of her correspondence, much of which, I am persuaded, has been removed to Hothfield.*

In consequence of King James's grant of the reversion† to Earl Francis, Lady Pembroke was seised of the castle and honour of Skipton in fee; a right of which she availed herself by settling them on her grandsons, and their issue, in order of birth. But tradition reports that there was a contest between the two who stood first in the entail, and that the younger actually held Skipton Castle for some time against the elder; who presented himself at the gates, accompanied by such of the tenants who favoured his pretensions, and demanded admittance in vain.

But of this transaction the family papers afford no proof.‡

Nicholas, the third Earl of Thanet, however, dying without issue, November 24, 1679, was succeeded by the same Sir John Tufton, his brother, who survived him little more than five months, and died in Skipton Castle. In the parish register is the following entry relating to him :

"1680, April 27. The right h'ble John earle of Theanett died in Skipton Castell, and his corps was embalmed and carried away from thence to be buried at Reynham, in Kent, May 12th, in the valt their amongst his anchestors."

His successor in the honour of Skipton was Richard, his younger brother, who died unmarried, March 8, 1683, leaving his estates and honours to the next child of that fruitful bed, Thomas the sixth earl, who was born August 30th, 1644, and died July 30th, 1729, after having held the honour of Skipton longer, and applied the revenues of it better, than any of his ancestors, with the exception of Anne Clifford, whose spirit seemed to revive in him. He was a nobleman of the old school, a true son of the Church of England; virtuous, devout, and charitable. Such characters, in his rank of life, were then far from being uncommon. His munificence was not so splendid§ as that of the Countess of Pembroke; but it was large and useful. His letters to his agent at Skipton abound with directions for the distribution of clothing to the poor, with many of whom he was personally acquainted. In the same letters he sends many messages of exhortation and reproof to the curates and schoolmasters in the neighbourhood ; warning them to expect no further favours from him unless they did their duty. His only public work of beneficence in Craven was endowing the chapel of Silsden ; but his whole influence was applied to salutary purposes.

He was resident in Skipton Castle the year before the Revolution ; and there are still

* Among the evidences of Skipton are several memoranda of large parcels of papers sent away by order of Thomas Earl of Thanet.

† Vide p. 358. Still there is a cloud resting on this part of the family history, which I am unable to dispel. On the demise of Earl Henry, without male issue, this reversion ought to have vested in the Countess of Cork, his daughter. And why, at the same time and for the same reason, did not Lady Pembroke succeed to Bolton, and the other *unentailed* lands in Craven, agreeably to the will of Earl George? Perhaps she was barred by some fine levied by Earl Francis and Henry his son, which I have not met with. Of the time and manner in which Barden was separated from the honour of Skipton, an account is given in its proper place.

‡ I am obliged to a respectable correspondent, the Rev. Dr. Swire, rector of Melsonby, for the following anecdote, relating to this transaction. Nicholas Earl of Thanet gave to John Coates, of Kildwick Grange, a set of silver beakers, with his arms engraven thereon ; and another set, plain, to Roger Coates, of Royd House, who were both attorneys, and had particularly assisted him in recovering his estates in Craven, which were forcibly held by his brother Sir John Tufton ; and especially by prevailing upon the tenants of Selsden to attorn to Nicholas.—The first set are still in the possession of the Swire family.

§ Thoresby says that he appropriated fifteen hundred pounds per annum to acts of charity !

extant in the Evidence Room a multitude of written despatches, without a name, which were sent to him from London. Though little less circumstantial than modern newspapers, they scarcely contain anything more than is already known of the transactions of that critical time.*

What remains on this subject may be despatched in few words, without injury to any one.

Earl Thomas was succeeded by Sackville, son of Sackville Tufton, his youngest brother, who died December 4th, 1753, leaving Sackville the eighth earl, who died April 10th, 1786, and was succeeded by Sackville, ninth Earl of Thanet, and present lord of the honour of Skipton.†

[Before dismissing the history of the Clifford family, a few notes upon the heraldry will be useful.

The original coat of the Cliffords was checky or and azure a fess gules. In the thirteenth century Roger Clifford married Isabel, daughter and co-heiress of Robert de Veteripont or Vipont, and so acquired the coat, gules, six annulets or. At some time (but the time and occasion is not known), an augmentation was granted to the Cliffords, which Guillim calls "three murthering chain shots." ‡ In the fifteenth century John Lord Clifford married Margaret, daughter and heiress of Henry Bromflete, Baron de Vescy, and acquired the additional coats of *Bromflete*, sable a bend fleur-de-lisé or; *Vescy*, or a cross sable; *Atton*, Barry of six or and azure on a canton gules, a cross patonce or; and *St. John*, argent on a chief, indented gules, an annulet between two mullets or. There was also a coat, which is shown over the outer entrance gateway, the inner entrance, and over the doorway at the east end of the Conduit Court of Skipton Castle, vert three flint stones argent, assigned by Guillim to the name of *Flint*,§ but why quartered by the Cliffords I cannot ascertain. In a very unaccountable way this coat has been changed on a brass on the tomb of Francis Lord Clifford in Skipton Church to three roses, and this has been followed by the restorer of the brasses on the tomb of Henry, first Earl of Cumberland.

---

* Among the pictures removed to Appleby, when Skipton Castle was shut up to save the window-tax, was one of this earl, and another of his countess. The first inscribed "Thomas Earl of Thanet, who succeeded to the estate and titles of Baron Clifford, Westmoreland, and Vescy, and lord of the honour of Skipton, in right of his mother, who was grandchild and sole heir to George earl of Cumberland, 1687. Lambert fecit."

The second, Catharine Cavendish, the daughter to Henry Duke of Newcastle, wife to the Earl of Thanet, 1687. Lambert fecit.

This painter was John Lambert, of Calton, Esq., son of Major-General Lambert. One of the daughters of this marriage, Lady Margaret Tufton, inherited the baronies, and with them the sense, the spirit, and somewhat of the piety, of her ancestors. She married Thomas Coke, Earl of Leicester, whom she long survived, and, in my memory, lived with princely magnificence at Holkham, in Norfolk. When young, her beauty and descent together entitled her to the name of the second Rosamond.

[† The successors to the barony of Clifford are shown on the genealogical table of the descent of the barony from its origin to the present time.]

[‡ "The field is saphire three murthering chain shots Topaz. This Coat armour was borne by the Right Honourable the Earl of Cumberland next to his paternal Coat and it is thought to be an augmentation. Some have taken these to be the heads of clubs called Holy Water Sprinkles, others suppose them to be Balls of Wildfire; I rather think them to be some murthering chain shot."—Guillim, edit. 1724, p. 230.]

[§ "He beareth vert three Flint Stones Argent by the name of FLINT. This Coat is quartered by the Right Honourable the Earl of Cumberland."—Guillim, p. 110.]

The quarterings ordinarily used by the Earls of Cumberland are as shown upon the following engraving.

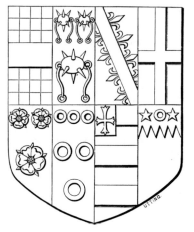

Shield of Arms from brass plate upon tomb of Francis Clifford in Skipton Church, and arranged :—

1. Clifford.   2. Augmentation coat.   3. Bromflete.   4. Vescy.   5. Flint (or its substitute).   6. Vipont.   7. Atton. 8. St. John.

There are, however, variations, as :—

Constable's roll, in "Tonge's Visitation" (Surtees Society), p. ii., gives for Henry Clifford, Earl of Cumberland, 1558 :— Quarterly—1. Chequy, or and az. a fess gu., *Clifford.*   2. Sa. a bend counterflory or, *Bromflete.*   3. Or a plain cross sa., *Vesci.* 4. Quarterly 1 and 4, gu. 6 annulets or, 3, 2, 1, *Vipont.*   2 and 3, vert 3 flint-stones arg., *Flynt.*

Arms of George Clifford, Earl of Cumberland, in stained glass in Serjeants' Inn, Chancery Lane, in 1664 :—

Quarterly of 9—3, 3 and 3.   1. Clifford.   2. Vipont.   3. Augmentation.   4. Flint.   5. Bromflete.   6. Atton.   7. Vescy. 8. Barry of 6 or and az. a bend gu.   9. St. John.   Supporters : Dexter a wyvern gu. ; sinister, a leopard arg. spotted and collared and chained or.   Motto : "Desormais."—Dugdale's "Origines Juridiciales," p. 335.

A work-book of Thomas Penson, herald painter, gives :—

Clifford, quarterly of 9—3, 3, and 3.   1. Clifford.   2. A fess betw. 3 estoiles.   3. Vipont.   4. Clare, 3 chevs. and a label of 3.   5. Bromflete.   6. St. John.   7. Atton.   8. Vesci.   9. Flint, vt. 3 flint-stones arg.   The whole impaling Russell, with 8 quartering.   Crest : A wyvern sejant.   Supporters : Dexter a wyvern gu. ; sinister a goat.   The augmentation of 3 chain-shot is not quartered, but placed within a garter outside of the shield.

And for "Francis Clifford Earl of Cumberland, Baron Clifford, Lord Bromflete, Westmerland, Vipont, Atton, Vescy, and Fyson : "—

Quarterly—1 and 4. Clifford.   2. Vipont.   3. Vescy, or a cross sa.   4. Clifford.   Supporters—Dexter a wyvern gu.; sinister, an ape ppr. with band round the loins or lined.   Crest : A wyvern sejant.   Motto : "Des Hormayes.   There is a note under the sinister supporter—"Sometymes they beare a tyger on this syde arg. and or parted per pale collared and chened or."—From Penson's "Work-book," MS. in the possession of the Editor.

And Edmondson in his "Baronage," plate 363, shows the following as the coats proper to be borne by Margaret, daughter of Thomas Tufton, sixth Earl of Thanet, who married Thomas Coke, Earl of Leicester, and who was in 1734, Baroness of Clifford in her own right.

The Names of all the Quarterings belonging to the Right Honourable Margaret Countess of Leicester, in her own right Baroness Clifford :—

1. Tufton—Sa. an eagle displ. erm. in a bordure arg.
2. Hever—Gu. a cross arg. a label of 3 points az.
3. Brown—Gu. a chev. arg. betw. 3 lions gambs erased or, all within a bordure arg.
4. Charlton—Az. a chev. betw. 3 swans close arg.
5. Francis—Per bend or and sa. a lion ramp. counterchanged.
6. Sackville—Quarterly or and gu. over all a bend vair.
7. Den—Arg. fretty gu.
8. Aquillon—Gu. a fleur-de-lis arg.
9. Dallingruge—Arg. a cross engr. gu.
10. Nevile—Lozengy or and gu. on a canton arg. 6 billets sa.
11. Courcy—Arg. 3 eagles displ. gu. crowned.
12. Clifford—Chequy or and az. a fess gu.
13. Augmentation—Az. 3 ? chain shots or.
14. Cundy—Arg. 2 lions passant guard. in pale az. crowned.
15. Ewias—Arg. a fess qu. betw. 3 pierced mullets of 6 points sa.
16. Vipont—Gu. 6 annulets or, 3, 2, and 1.
17. Fitz-John—Quarterly or and gu. a bordure vair.
18. Clare—Or 3 chevs. qu. in chief a label of 5 points az.
19. Gloucester—Gu. 3 clarions (or rests) or.
20. Consul—Gu. a lion pass. guard. or.
21. Fitz-Hamon—Az. a lion ramp. guard. or.
22. Marshal—Per pale or and vert. a lion ramp. gu.
23. Marshal—Gu. a bend fusilly or.
24. Strongbow—Or 6 chev. gu.
25. McMurrough—Sa. 3 garbs or.
26. Fitz-Gerald—Arg. a saltire gu.
27. Bromflete—Sa. a bend fleur-de-lisé or.
28. Vescy—Or a cross sa.
29. Flint—Vert 3 flint-stones arg.
30. Atton—Barry of 6 or and az. on a canton gu. a cross patonce or.
31. St. John—Arg. on a chief indented gu. an annulet betw. 2 mullets or.
32. Cavendish—Sa. 3 bucks' heads cabossed arg.
33. Smith—Arg. a chev. qu. betw. 3 crosses crosslet sa.
34. Hardwick—Arg. a saltire engr. az. on a chief of the last 3 roses of the field.
35. Scudamore—Gu. 3 stirrups leathered or.
36. Ogle—Arg. a fess betw. 3 crescents gu.
37. Heppel—Arg. an escu. within a bordure engr. gu.
38. Chartney—Per chev. arg. and gu. 3 crosses crosslet counterchanged.
39. Gobion—Bendy of 6 or and az. a lion pass. guard...... on a chief gu. 3 saltires arg.
40. Heyton—Vert. a lion ramp. arg.
41. Atton—Or a bat displ. vert.
42. Bertram—Or an orle az.
43. Kirkby—Arg. 2 bars gu. on a canton of the last a cross patonce or.
44. Carnaby—Arg. 2 bars az. in chief 3 hurts.
45. Hatton—Per pale gu. and az. a lion ramp. guard. or.
46. Bassett of Blore—Or 3 piles in point gu. on a canton arg. a griffin segreant sa.
47. Buke—Gu. a cross erm.
48. De la Ward—Vairy arg. and sa.
49. Byron—Arg. 3 bendlets enhanced sa.

Edmonson's "Baronage," Plate 363.

Finally, the Standard of the Lord Clifford, *temp.* Hen. VIII., was, per fess white and gold semy on both parts of annulets or. The device, a wyvern, wings expanded gules. Motto: "Desormais."—"Collectanea Topographica et Genealogica," vol. iii., from Harl. MS. 4632.]

Before we take leave of the Cliffords, it will be proper to throw together a number of articles, extracted from their Household Book, either not reducible to any of the former heads, or not discovered when they were printed off, but strongly illustrative of the habits of the family. And first for their minstrelsy—

1521. Payd to the French Wheyn * Mynstrell iiis. ivd. Mynstrell of Newer Daye vis. viiid.
1595. To Lord Willowby's men playing at this hows twice, xxxs.

* The "Wheyn (Quean) Minstrell" of 1521, and the "roguish players" of the next century, were equally intended to express the writer's opinion of their calling, as of loose and idle vagabonds. There is no proof to be drawn from their papers that the Cliffords maintained a company of minstrels or players as a part of their establishment. Yet, why they did not, as well as Lord Willoughby, Lord Wharton, and Lord Vaux, all their inferiors, it would not be easy to discover. Of the dramatic powers of these vagrants, who strolled about the country from one nobleman's house to another, and were rewarded for each entertainment with a few shillings, it is impossible to form any high idea. They were probably of no higher rank, or greater talents, than those who are now content to amuse a country village in a barn. Dramatic *composition* was at its height before dramatic *representation* had emerged far above barbarism. That elegant but too often licentious amusement will never attain to any very high degree of excellence, till a wealthy and luxurious age has made the rewards of it a national object, which again will often not take place till the powers of dramatic composition, which usually reaches its acmè a little before that period of society, are on the decline. It follows, that the highest gratification in this walk will be obtained by a judicious combination of the dramas of one period with the performance of another; from the want of which Jonson, Beaumont, Fletcher, and Shakespeare, it is more than probable, never conceived the full force of some of their own greatest characters. Meanwhile, the rant or the buffoonery of strollers would pass for fine acting in the halls of Londesborough and Skipton; and intellectual gratification, though very imperfect, might contribute to suspend the orgies of intemperance, to awaken the latent sparks of feeling or sentiment, and to soften the general ferocity of manners. These objects might, however, have been attained by better means, and without that mixture of evil which always adheres to dramatic performances. Of the writers of "The Knight of the Burning Pestle," the moral pravity is extreme.

2 Y

1609. Payd to the musitioners which were appointed to play at Londesbr. at the play the 12 Marche, Sir ——— Hutton and divers others being there, IIII*s*.

Ditto, 27 April. Given to the waites of Halifaxe who plaied in the Court, Sir Step. Tempest being there, II*s*.

Given to a company of players, my Lord Vawses men, in reward not playing, because it was Lent, and therefore not fitting, X*s*.

1614. Given to my Lord Wharton, his players, who played one playe before my Lord and the Ladies at Hazlewood. . . . . .

1619. Given to 15 men that were players, who belonged to the late Queene, but did not play, XIII*s*. IV*d*.

Sept. 28. Given to a companie of players, being Prince Charles's servants, who came to Londesbro' and played a play, XI*s*.

1624. Gave to a set of players, going by the name of y*e* King's players, who played 3 times, III*l*.

1633. To certain players itinerants, I*l*.

July 26. To certain French musicians and a singer, which were at my Lord Dungarvan's marriage, VI*l*.

Same day, to the music of Stamford, for their reward and service at my Lady Dungarvan's marriage, 9 weeks, XV*l*.

For tuning the organ, and mending other instruments, I*l*.

1635. To a certeyne company of *roguish* players, who represented " A New Way to pay Old Debts," I*l*.

To Adam Gerdler, whom my Lord sent for from York to act a part in " The Knight of the Burning Pestell," V*s*.

To the music of York, when my Lord Digby was here at Skipton, V*l*.

Next, for their amusements of a more boisterous kind. In the earlier part of the reign of James I. the following fees were paid to foresters and park-keepers within Craven :—

1609. To Lister Symonson, in p't for kepyng his lo'p's deere* at Birks,† XXV*s*.

Rob. Smith of Gressington, in p'te for his kep'shipp there, X*s*.

Kep'shipp at Old Parke, X*s*.

Kep'shipp at the Hawe, in p't, XV*s*.

Kep'shipp at Threshfield, XXX*s*.

Kep'shipp at Brodshawe and the Liberties thereof, L*s*.

Walking of Craco Fell, and p't of Wm. Atkinson's office, due this Pentecost, XVI*s*.

Sir Rich. Musgrave, knt. his half yeres annuities,‡ XXV*l*.

Kepyng Carlton Park, IIII*l*.

Kep'shipp at Barden, XXX*s*.

Kepyng his l'p's deer in Longstrothe, XL*s*.

Kep'shipp of the great new P'ke here at Skipton al. P'ke George, VIII*l*.

Looking to my lo. deare on Thorpe Fell, XX*s*.

John Taylor of Littondale, for his kep'shipp there, XL*s*.

P'd for going to the Birks with a letter for bringing six red deer hither picked out of Lister Simonson's herd, XII*d*.

——— For going to Londesbro. with the great buck of Threshfield, IX*s*.

Gave to Mr. Michael Lister's man and maide, who brought 2 hyndes calves and a cowe from their master (the cowe he gave unto my lo.) XII*d*.

John Wardman, for the charge of himself and two men carrying 13 kyne and 25 hynde calves to my lady Suffolke at Saffron Walden, on whom my lo. did bestowe them, VIII*l*.

Given to the keepers of Wighil-park, Mr. Hen. Stapleton's men, my lo. having killed two buckes in his parke, XX*s*.

To the keeper of Allerton Mallw'r p'ke, where my lo. killed a buck, XIII*s*. IV*d*.

1609. For getting 33 pearch and troot from Mawater for my lo. and judge, II*s*. VI*d*.

March 27. For 10 burden of rishes against the judge coming, XX*d*.

August 27. For later parcels provided for my lo. and his companie being here at Skipton between 17 July last and 25 of the same, at which tyme he should have layne at Bolton, XLVIII*s*. ; and for this later tyme, my lo. being here, my lo. Rutland, my lo. Clyfford, Sir Geo. Manners, Sir Is. Savile, Sir Wm. Inglebie, Sir Thomas Metcalfe, Sir Stephen Tempest, and a great companie of about 140 persons daylie, between 8th of Aug. and 20th of the same, XI*l*. III*s*. VI*d*.

1622. April 14. Four men that brought the wild beastes from Craven. . . . . .

---

* Thirteen keepers prove how large a portion of Craven was then ranged by deer. It seems also to have been the practice, whenever a nobleman killed a buck in the park of one of his friends, to make a liberal present to the keeper. The expectations of these officers on the delivery of venison were then, as at present, considerable; so that when Earl Francis sent half a stag to Dr. Lister at York, and the bearer received only IS. for his pains, the doctor's parsimony is left upon record in the Household Book. The items of the cows and hynde calves are curious. The earl had engaged to supply the Countess of Suffolk with red deer (which seem to have been rare in the South) in order to stock the park at Audley End, and for that purpose seems to have had several hynde calves taught to suck cows, by which means the difficulty of conveyance was obviated, as the young creatures would spontaneously follow their foster-dams. The great buck of Threshfield was, no doubt, a stately animal, and famous in his generation. Fancy, surveying what once was park and forest in Are and Wharfdale, will still look back to these feudal times with regret.

† Now Birk House, near Buckden.

‡ Qu. Whether as Master Forester?

The following Items are purely miscellaneous.

1595. P'd for VI cabishes, and some caret rootts bought at Hull, IIs.

Ditto, Given to ———— for bringing II ropes of onyons from Hull, VId.

1609, 23 March. P'd for fishing in Mawater tarne for the judge at this assize here, Xs.

1610, 21 July. P'd to Xtopher Beckewith, yₑ old man, for going about my lo. catle and shepe in everie place here in Craven, to kepe them, with God's helpe, from the murryn, or any other sickness, Vs.

1614. By my lordes appointm't, to my lord Clifford, my la. Clifford, my la. Marg't, and my la. Frances, to each of them in gold X twenty shilling peices, as new year's guift, XLIIIl.

Ditto, A reward to one that brought a book to my lord about planting wood, VIs.

Ditto, P'd Sir W'm Paddie for his opinion in prescribing my lo. a course for taking of phisicke, IIIl. VIs.—Dr. Lister in golde, for the like, XLIIIs. ; Vl. IOs.

A lease of hawkes, XVIl.

To D. Trusler, for taking LX doz. of pigeons for hawksmeat, XXs.

1618. P'd for a pair of carnation silk stockings, and a pair of asshe-coloured taffata garters and roses, edged with silver lace, given by my lo. to Mrs. Douglas Shiefeld, she drawing my lo. for her valentyne, IIIl. Xs.

1619. To my lord Clifford for his journey to Normanbie, to be the king's deputy at the cristening of my lo. Sheffield his son, Xl.

———— Given to my lo. to play at Tables in the Great Chamber, Vs.

———— P'd to his lo. losses at shovelboard, Xs.

1640. His Maj'ies new yeares gift this year, presented in gold, XXl.

———— Rec'd for my lorde new years guifts from his maj'te for plate, w'ch was allowed in money for two yeares, XVIl.

———— Wages of R. Wiggen, keeper of Mawater Tarne, for one yeare, Il. XIIIs.

Disbursed in my lady's journey from London to Londesbro', being eleven days, with 32 horses, LXVIIIl. XVIIIs. IXd.

1642, May 9. Delivered to his lordship for his journey from London to the court at York, Ll.

1651. Riding charges of her* honours journey and the whole family from Bolton to Londesbro' with the remove of the goods, VIl. VIIIs. VId.

1652. For a *Chutions*, wheron is their honors armes graven and quartered for the wearing of there hon'rs Swanherd on the carrs in Holderness, XXIIIs. Xd.

———— Given to T. Preston Bayliffe of Long Preston, a reward for discovery of gold found there, two trees, value Xs.†

Having thus brought down our account of the house of Clifford, in its connection with Craven, to the present time, it remains that we take a survey of the

CASTLE OF SKIPTON, THEIR RESIDENCE.

That the basis of this pile was the work of Robert de Romillè, probably in the end of the Conqueror's, or the beginning of his son's reign, there can be little doubt, as it is affirmed by Camden, who, though he quotes no authority, seldom asserts at random. Of the original building, however, little, I think, besides the western doorway of the inner castle now remains. But as that consists of a treble semicircular arch, supported upon square piers, it can scarcely be assigned to a later period. The rest of Romillè's work, besides a

---

* Lady Cork.

† From these accounts it is evident that the commonest garden vegetables were in 1595 brought from Holland. In 1609, the floors of Skipton Castle were strewed with rushes for the judges and other guests. In 1610, a charm appears to have been employed (with God's help) to preserve the earl's cattle from the murrain. In 1614, inoculation of trees was beginning to be practised, and my lord, at least, thought and read about planting. Nearly at the same time, I find a person sent for out of Nottinghamshire to teach the people of Craven to lay and pleach hedges. Hawking was very expensive. A leash of these birds cost 16l. and their voracity in eating up sixty dozen of pigeons is very revolting to modern economy. Physicians' fees were liberal. Lady Clifford travelled with thirty-two horses, and was eleven days on her way from Londesborough to London. On their way the family rested one night at Buckden with the Bishop of Lincoln, and *watchers* were paid who waked with the horses. On the way from Londesborough to Skipton, they usually spent their first night at Bishopthorp. From Skipton into Westmoreland, I find that they pursued the direct way by Settle, Kirkby Lonsdale, Kendale, &c., direct to Brougham. In 1652, is a late instance of a swanherd, with his coat and badge. Antiquarian curiosity is strongly excited by the hint of this golden treasure-trove at Long Preston. Pity that we are not told whether it was consisted of coins, vessels, or ornaments in that metal. A keeper was regularly maintained by the family upon Malham Tarn. Cater parcels, often mentioned in the Household Book, seem to have consisted of miscellaneous articles of food ; and it is remarkable, that twelve days' provisions for 140 persons cost no more than 11l. 3s. 6d. But the parks and forests, while they supplied amusement and stimulated appetite, would furnish the principal luxury of the table—and wine is otherwise accounted for.

bailey and lodgings about it, must have consisted, according to the uniform * style of castles in that period, of a square tower, with perpendicular buttresses of little projection at the angles, and of single, round-headed lights in the walls.   Every vestige, however, of such an edifice has perished, with the single exception mentioned above [unless the dungeon and northern tower of the gateway are included]; and the oldest part of Skipton Castle now remaining consists of seven round towers,† partly in the sides and partly in the angles of the building, connected by rectilinear apartments, which form an irregular quadrangular court within.‡   The walls are from twelve to nine feet thick; yet, when the castle was slighted by ordinance of Parliament, in the last century, they were demolished in some places, as appears, half way, and in others almost wholly to the foundation.   This part was the work of Robert de Clifford, in the beginning of Edward II.'s time; for, according to his descendant Lady Pembroke, " he was the chief builder of the most strong parts of Skipton Castle, which had been out of repair and ruinous from the Albemarles' time."§   But the eastern part, a single range of building, at least sixty yards long, terminated by an octagon tower, is known to have been built by the first Earl of Cumberland, in the short period of four or five months, for the reception of "the Lady Eleanor Brandon's grace," who married his son, in the twenty-seventh of that reign [1535–6].   This part, which was meant for state rather than defence, was not slighted with the "main part of the castle,"‖ and remains nearly in its pristine condition, as the wainscot, carved with fluted, or, as they are sometimes styled, canework panels, and even some of the original furniture, serve to prove.   The upper windows only were altered by the Countess of Pembroke.   The Lady Eleanor's grace appears to have been received by the family—who, no doubt, were proud of such an alliance—with the honours of royalty; and a long gallery was then considered as a necessary appendage to every princely residence.

Another apartment, equally necessary to such a mansion in those days, though of a

* Such was the part of the Tower of London built by Rufus; the castle of Norwich; that of Castle Rising in the county of Norfolk; and that of Lancaster.   Upon a smaller scale, Gundulph's Tower at Rochester; the Keeps of Conisboro' and Richmond, Yorkshire, and Clitheroe in Lancashire; which last would probably most resemble in size the castle of Robert de Romillè at Skipton.

† Round towers became fashionable in England during the reign of Edward I., who, in the graceful cylinders of Conway Castle, left behind him a monument worthy of his genius and splendour.   That of Harlech, his workmanship also, and in the same style, is every way inferior to the former.

[‡ See the plan.]

[§ The arms and quarterings of the Cliffords, with their supporters, the two wyverns, appear over the door on the east side of the Conduit Court, whilst those of Bromflete, the mother of the " Shepherd Lord," are carved over the doorway to the staircase on the south side.   The style of architecture, I think, points to this period.

The castle was now better fitted for the residence of a noble family, but at the same time left available for defence, the external portions remaining unaltered, there being only loop-holes in the outer walls, whilst the rooms were lighted by large windows opening into the court-yard, except in the large kitchen and drawing-room, where windows could be placed without much danger, as they overlooked the cliff.   The " Conduit Court" is so called from the conduit which conveyed water from Skipton Rocks, about three-fourths of a mile from the castle, terminating in this court.   At this period the castle would have the form of the portion shown black upon the plan, and the towers would have been higher than they now are, furnished with battlements, and having flat roofs covered with lead, with platforms for cannon.   On the 1st and 2nd of October, 1323, King Edward II. was at Skipton, as is known by several mandates to John de Fienles, Robert de Fienles, John de Stonor, John de Bousser, and Ranulph de Dacre, printed in Rymer's " Fœdera," edit. 1818, ii. 536-7, each ending, " Teste Rege apud Skipton in Craven."   " Per ipsum Regem."]

‖ Which gallery and tower, so suddenly built, was the chief mansion to the Countess of Pembroke, and the tower her lodging-room, the castle itself being totally demolished in December, 1649, and the month following, by reason of the great rebellion, having been made a garrison on both sides.—MS. Memoirs at Appleby Castle.

character as different from the former as that of the oppressed from the oppressor, was a dungeon, by which is here meant the prison, not the keep. This, at Skipton, was a dismal vaulted room down a flight of steps on the left of the entrance into the inner court. From a memorandum among the family papers, I find that as early as the reign of King John, prisoners for offences within the fee of Albemarle were committed to this castle, and afterwards removed for trial to York.

In the latter end of Henry VIII.'s reign, the first Earl of Cumberland held several persons in custody within Skipton Castle, particularly one West, of Grassington, a notorious deer-stealer, and two persons committed for non-payment of fines imposed upon them at the Leet. West was discharged, after entering into recognisances " to be of good abearing to the deere." The earl and his stewards do not appear to have been very exact in point of law, as sureties for the abearing must have reference to the *person*, not the property of the complainant ; and as to a commitment in execution, which appears to have been the nature of the other case, if the steward of a court-leet were to venture upon such a step at present an English jury would teach him not to repeat the experiment. Such, however, in all likelihood, was every castle of our ancient barons, contrived at once for the purposes of security, magnificence, and oppression ; a mixture of palace, gaol, and garrison.

As a place of defence, however, this castle has always laboured under one great inconvenience, in having neither spring nor well within the walls. *Magna utilitas est*, saith Vegetius, *cum perennes fontes murus includet, quod si natura non præstat cujuslibet altitudinis effodiendi sunt putei.* (De re mil. l. iv. c. 10.) In defect of both these advantages, the garrison of Skipton trusted to pipes laid from without the works ; and when these were cut off (as there would seldom want a traitor to reveal their course), they were left to the chance of rain in this dripping climate, and half an acre of leaden roofs to collect it.

Of the progressive improvements made in this castle, I can only find one memorial in the evidences of the family. It is contained in the Compotus of 1437.

Pro le Batyllyng turris super Cameram generosarum. { In sol. pro domate turris super Cam^m generosarum infra Castrum de Skipton hoc anno de novo fabricat' facte & cooperte. In sol. W. Pacok & socio suo sarrantibus boscum ad grossum meremium pro dict. domate quasi unius hominis XVIII^{dies} pro victu & stip. per d. vd.

Pro car. VI plaustr. merem. a, Caldre qual^t. plaustr. VIId.

In lucratione petrarum liberalium (free-stone) pro le batyllyng dicte turris de novo batillate.

Et in sol. pro Carr. $_v^{xx}$XII plaust. a Staynrig usq. dict. Cast. qual. plaust. VId.

Et in vadiis . . . Bellerby capitalis latumi operant. sup. le batilling dict. turris per XXII sept^s. capiente. pro qualibet sept. ultra victum XXd. plus in toto VIIId.

Et in vadiis Rob. & Tho. Hawmond latumis operant. in oper^{bus} p'dict. quasi unius hominis per XLVI sept^s and II dies, pro qual sept. XVIIId. ultra victum.

Et in sol. uxori W. Clerke pro mensa dict. trium latomorum per temp. p'dict. cum diebus festival. IVl. IIs. IVd.

Et in vadiis R. Plummer cum servis operant^s, tam super liquationem antiqui plumbi, nuper super dict. domale tecti, quam super novam retecturam plumbi, quasi per XXId. pro die XIId. cum Xs. Xd. in mensa earund. &c. cum Vicario XXXs. Xd.

Laborata.—In victu & stip. laborantium in volutatione petrarum apud le Ferue usque ad altitudinem dict. turris, carriag. luti, sabuli, &c. quasi unius hominis $_v^{xx}$X capient. per diem pro vict. & stip. IVd. cum. XIId. solut. pro carriag. dict. Ferue a Bolton.

Et in XI quarteriis calcis empt. de Priore de Bolton pro op. p'dict. qualibet quart. cum carriag. XVIIId. cum Xd. in IIII busellis calcis empt. apud Adyngham cum car. XVIIs. IIIId.

In these ancient records of economy and manners, nothing is more striking than the disproportion between the prices of different commodities then, and at present. Thus, in the year 1437, undoubtedly a season of uncommon plenty, a quarter of lime at Skipton (evidently consisting of only eight bushels, as appears from the next article) cost one-third more than the same measure of oats.*

In the next place, it is equally singular, that the lord of Skipton Castle, which stands upon a limestone rock, should be compelled to fetch his lime from Bolton, and even from Addingham.

Hence, I think it is evident, that lime was little in use at that time, even for cement, excepting in buildings of a superior order, and not at all for the improvement of land. Otherwise, there must have been kilns within less than six miles of Skipton.

And what was the Ferue borrowed at Bolton Abbey for the elevation of stonets to the top of the tower above the gentlewomen's chamber ? It can only have been a crane : but the word is unknown to all our etymologists ; and, so far as I know, to all our old writers. Ferue, indeed, is old French, but it signifies only measure, or proportion. Our word, I think, is plainly Saxon, from ꝼeꞃıan to carry. Ferry, which nearly resembles it, is allowed by etymologists to be derived from the same source.

The workmen's wages, from 4*d.* to 5*d. per diem* (according to the same scale, the price of grain) were ample, as an inferior labourer would earn two quarters of oats weekly. It is remarkable that several of them boarded with the vicar of Skipton.

No accounts remain of the disbursements in erecting the gallery, nor any other memorial of the place, during a period of 130 years : but the following Inventory of Apparel, Household Furniture, and Farming Stock, together with Artillery and Armour, belonging to Skipton Castle, which was taken in 1572,† after the death of the second earl, will afford, perhaps, the completest specimen of the habits and general economy of a great nobleman's family, in the 16th century, which has yet been made public. It is transcribed from an original roll among the papers at Bolton Abbey.

"The furniture of oure houses excelleth, and is growne in maner even to passing delicacie.—Certes, in noblemen's houses it is not rare to see rich hangings of tapestrie, silver vessels, and soe much other plate as maie furnish sundrie cubbords to yᵉ sume ofttimes of M*l.* or MM*l.* wherebye the value of this and yᵉ rest of their stuff doth growe to bee inestimable." ‡

SKIPTON CASTELL.

WARDROPP.

My Lord's App'ell.§

Impr. A black velvet gown, laide w'th black laice, furred with squyrels, and faced with jenets furr something decayed, x*l.*

Item, One single gown of black sattan, garded with velvet, very olde, xx*s.*

Item, Another blacke sattan gowne, garded with velvet, layed with silke lace, and lyned with buckram, something in decay, XLVI*s.* VIII*d.*

---

* See Silsden.

[† In this inventory the following rooms are mentioned in the castle, but we cannot now identify many of them :—The stranger's chamber, the corner chamber in the high lodgings, the great well chamber, the Conyers chamber, the little well chamber, Mr. Clifford's chamber, the helmet chamber, Mr. Eltoft's chamber, the nursery, the receiver's chamber, chamber over porter's lodge, Lady Bellyngham's chamber, the great chamber in the high lodging, the old wardrobe, kitchen, west larder, pantry, buttery, eurie, the hall, the cellar, the middle chamber in the gallery, and low tower at the gallery end.]

‡ Holinshed, vol. i. p. 85.

§ The ordinary habit of a nobleman, at that time, consisted of a doublet and hose, a cloak, or sometimes a long, sometimes a short gown with sleeves. It must be remembered, that the gown was originally a common, not a professional habit only ; but that, as state and gravity yielded to convenience in ordinary dress, it was exchanged for a short cloak, which, about the reign of Charles the Second, gave way in its turn to the coat, as that is nothing more than the ancient sleeved doublet prolonged. In the meantime, ecclesiastics and other members of the learned professions, whose habits, varying little at first from the common dress of the times, had those little distinctions fixed by canons and statutes, persevered in the use of their old costume ; in consequence of which they retain the gown, under various modifications, to the present day. The same observation may be made with respect to the hood, which, however ill adapted to common use, was the ancient covering for the head in

(For Mr. F. C.*) Item, A clooke of tawney checquered velvet, laid with II pome laices of gold furred with swirrels, XLs.

Item, A black velvett jacket, imbrothered with silver, faced with luserdes, and furred thorowly with whyte lambe, something decayed, XLs.

Item, One black sattan jackett, stocked, garded with black velvett, layed with silver laice, buttons of black silke and syle, XXXIIIs. IVd.

Item, One black velvett jackett, chyen stitched, and layed with frynge laice, and furred with squyrrels, XXXs. IVd.

Summa, XXl. XIIIs. IVd.

Adhuc my Lord's app'ell and oth' things.

Item, A blacke velvett iyrkine, withe gold lace, havyng XVI buttons, enameled blacke, lyned with sarcenet, verey olde, Xs.

Item, A blacke sattan ierkyne, faced with whit hayre, and furred with lambe, something decayed, XXXs.

Item, One kyrtle† of cremesyn velvett, lyned with whyte sarsenet, and a hode for knyght of Garter to weare at Seynt George feast, VIl.

Item, One robe ‡ of blewe velvet, lyned with sarcenet, the Garter imbrothered thereon, and a yarde of blewe silke and golde tyed at sholders, for the seide S. George's feast, VIl.

Item, One hole horse-harness for a trapper, sett w'th whit and blew, and enameled, and one covering of black vellvett, with a garde of gold, and enameled whyt and blewe, sutable for the same, XIIIs. IVd.

Item, One oth' harnesse of red vellvett, cont'g VI peices ; and one other harnesse of black velvett, imbrothered with silver gilted, cont'g VII peice, XIIIs. IVd. §

Item, IIII peice of clothe of tussaye, for covering of a courser at a tryumphe, edged with a frynge of red sylke and gold, LIIIs. IVd.

Some trifling articles omitted.

Summa, XXIIl. Vs. IVd.

Adhuc my Lord's app'ell, &c.

Item, III paynes of clothe of golde, and II of tawney velvett, w'th a redd dragon lokyng furthe of a whit castell, ‖ mad of sylver tyssay, Vs.

Item, III rydynge hatts : one of cremysyn velvett with a golde bande, and another of tawney velvett with a golde band, and the III laiced with silver laice, XXs.

Mr. Francis Clifford, dunn hatt, Mr. Eltofts, a tawny hatt.

Item, One murreon ¶ cov'd w'th cremesyn vellvett and laid w'th lacce of golde, Xs.

ordinary clothing. The different orders of monks, the different degrees in the universities, only varied the cut or the material of the hood for distinction's sake. But, for common use, the hood was supplanted by the round citizen's cap, yet retained by the Yeomen of the Guard, such as is seen, though much contracted, and of meaner materials, in the engravings to the old editions of Foxe's " Martyrs." This was succeeded by the hat, which, I think, first became general in Queen Elizabeth's time, nearly of the shape of the modern round hat, though turned up on one side.

It will be remarked, that in a nobleman's wardrobe at that time everything was showy and costly : velvet, satin, sarcenet, gold lace, and fur. At the same time, it is curious to observe how many articles are described as old and far worn. A wardrobe at that time lasted for life, or more ; for I am persuaded that many articles here enumerated had belonged to the first earl. How much more rational is a plain broad-cloth suit, frequently renewed, and accompanied with daily changes of very fine linen, &c., in which alone a nobleman now differs from a tradesman. The subject of lusardes', squirrels', and jennets' furs, will best be explained by Minshew's Commentary on the statute of the 24th of Hen. VIII. " Of furre we find strange kinds in st. an. 24 Hen. VIII. c. 13, as of sables, which is a riche furre, black and browne, being the skin of a beaste called a sable, and of fashion like a polecat, bred in Russia, but most and best in Tartaria. Lucerns, which is the skinne of a beast so called, being near the bignesse of a wolfe, something mayled like a cat, and mingled with blacke spots, bred in Muscovie and Russia, and is a very rich furre. Genets, the skin of a beast so called, of bigness between a cat and a wesell, mayled like a cat, bred in Spayne. Foynes is a fashion like the sable, bred in Fraunce for the moste parte, the top of the furre blacke, and the ground whitish. Martern is a beast very like the sable. Miniver is nothing but the bellies of squirrels, as some doe say. Others say it is a vermine like unto a wesel, milk white, and cometh from Muscovie. Fitch is that which we otherwise call the polecat heare in England. Shankes be the skin of the shanke or legge of a kind of kidde, which beareth the furre that we call Budge. Calaber is a little beaste about the bignesse of a squirrel, of colour gray, and bred especially in High Germanie." (Minshew, *in voce* Furre.)

* Francis Clifford, who long afterwards succeeded to the titles and estates of the family.

† The kirtle was the surcoat of the Knights of the Garter. This word, though in the language of the later times generally appropriated to female habits, at the institution of this order signified a man's close upper vestment. Thus Chaucer's parish clerk :

" Yclad he was full smal and properly,
All in a kirtel of a light waget."

‡ These were certainly the Garter robes of the first earl. The parliamentary robes of an earl, mentioned in the former inventory, being hereditary, are not included in this inventory.

§ These articles lay hold on the imagination, and carry back to the scenes

" Where throngs of knights and barons bold
In weeds of peace high triumphs hold."

It is remarkable that in the inventory the word triumph is used in the same sense as by Milton. See Mr. Warton's note on this passage. Perhaps these trappings had formed part of the magnificence of the Champ de Drap d'Or.

‖ The crest of the Clifford family.

¶ The morion is supposed to have been a sort of helmet originally worn by the Moors. As it is not classed with the " munition " of the castle, it was probably a light iron scull-cap used for the defence of the head in hunting, as leathern caps are now. Spenser has given a morion to Spring :

" And on his head, as fit for warlike stoures,
A gilt engraven morion he did weare."—" Faery Queen," b. vii. c. 7.

Item, a caice for the Garter of cremesyn velvett,* VIs. VIIId.

Item, I short cremesyn sattan gowne, garded with cremesyn vellvett, and laide with fayre lacce of golde, Cs.

Item, I shorte gowne of purple vellvett, with IIs. pomell lacce of silver, XLVIs. VIIId.

Item, A black damaske gowne, with II yardes of vellvett not lyned, and having XVII paire of anglets of gold, Cs.

Item, One sleveless jackett of clothe of golde, edged with p'chment lacce of gold enamelled blewe, XLVIs. VIIId.

Item, An ancel † of redd and white sarsynett, with a redd rose and a dragon.

Sum, with omissions, XXVII. XVs.

Adhuc my lord's app'ell, and other things.

Item, One dublet of cremesyn velvett, embrothered with golde, and lyned with lynnynge cloth, w'th a p'r hosen of crem' vellvett of the same, embrothered, LXs.

Item, One dublett of whit sattan, embr'd with sylv' and lyned with verey fine lynnyne, and a p'r of hose of whit velvet suitable to the same, XLVIs. VIIId.

Item, A swerd girdle of redd vellvett, with gilted buckles, IIIs. IVd.

Item, A p'r of gilted spurs, and one oth'r p'r ungilted, being graven, Vs.

Item, One old cote of tawney vellvett, laide with rounde silv' lacce, XXs.

Item, One foteclothe of black vellvett, XLs.

Summa, with several trifling articles omitted, XIXl. VIIIs. IIIId.

Item, One other foteclothe of black vellvett, frynged with blacke silke and gold, XXs.

Item, One trussing bedd for the field,‡ in two trounks of rede cloth, w'th my L. armes on, frynged with rede silke, and lyned with rede sarcynet, LXVIs. VIIId.

Item, One bedd of downe, and a bolster therto belongynge, XLs.

Item, One matteress there, IIIIs.

Item, One old quyssyn of estait, w'th catt' of mount'n on the same, XIIIs. IIIId.

Summa as before, Xl. Xs. VIIId.

Item, In the wardroppe, one teister of whit and blewe satten of Bridges,§ w'th curteins of yellow and sarcenett, XXs.

Beddinge, and oth' Household Stuffe.

La. Strange' Chamb'r.‖

Impr' One bedd of downe, w'th a bolster to the same, Cs.

Item, A p'r of futcheon blanketts to the same bedd, XIIIs. IVd.

Item, a counterpoynt y'to belongyng, LIIIs. IVd.

Item, III olde federbedds, II bolsters, and I pillow, XXXs.

Item, One teaster to the said bedd, of tynsell and blake vellvett, with armes, havynge curtains of sylke, w'th frynges, XXl.

Item, II old quyssings of estait, w'th armes and hawthorne off thone, and alsoe armes of thother with Ɖ and C, XXXIIIs. IVd.

Item, I bedstede, and a cobbord and stole, Vs.

Corner Chamb'r, in theigh Lodginge.

One teaster of blacke velvett and tynsell, with curtaynes of silke, and frynges of sylke and gold.

Item, One other old teaster of velvett, pynked with golde and tawney satten.

Rest nearly the same as above.

Summa, LXl. XIs.

Great Well Chamber.

A teaster of grene tawney vellvett and tynsell, w'th armes on y', and also curtaines of grene and yalowe sarcenett, and frynges of sylke.

The rest nearly as before.

La. Conyers Chamber.

One old teaster of purple velvett and blewe sattyn, w'th droppes and II cortens of sarcenett, and frynges of sylke, &c.

Little Well Chamb'r.

Nothing remarkable.

---

* The Garter itself had been returned to the Sovereign after the death of the first earl.

† An Ancel. Among all the etymologists I can only catch a glimpse of this word in Du Cange, *voce* "Pannus ancellatus," who quotes the following passage from an ancient will, "Item legamus—pannum ancellatum album deauratum nostris armis circumquaque signatum." Du Cange conjectures the word to have been derived from "anca," the same with "anca, anser femina," with which armorial bearing the first of these had been blazoned. "From the red rose and dragon," I believe this to have been a kind of armorial achievement belonging to the Lady Eleanor Brandon.

‡ This equipage, of which the accommodation is sufficiently luxurious, was probably meant, not only for war, but for hunting-parties; as it might be used either in a tent, or in any ordinary house where it might be necessary to spend the night, and where every convenience might be wanting. After a hard day's chase in Longstrothdale, for instance, it would be too much for a wearied train of men and horses to return to Skipton. In this case, my lord would betake himself to his trussing bed, and his servants to the hay-mow.

§ That is, Bruges. On the contrary, Bridges, the surname of the Chandos family, about this time was frequently spelt Bruges.

‖ This is the state bed-chamber, and not inferior in magnificence, as far as its accommodations went, to the same apartment in a modern nobleman's house. The beds were of down, the tester of tinsell and black velvet, the curtains of silk with fringe. The "cobbord" answered, I suppose, partly to a wardrobe, and partly to a toilet. There was only one stool besides. Not a glass, a carpet, or even a chair, appears in any of the bed-rooms. I do not exactly know what was meant by cushions of estate.

Mr. Clifford's Chamb'r.

One olde teaster of tynsell and blacke sattyn, with dragon and the anlet.*

Helmett Chamb'r.

One old teaster of tawney vellvett and whit sattyn, with frynge of sylke.

Summa, XXV*l.* VIII*d.*

Rec'avor's Chamb'r.
Chamb'r above Porter Lodge.
In Lady Bellyngham Chamb'r. } Nothing remarkable.
In the Law Ewry.
In thold Wardropp.

II verey olde hangyngs, with this word, **Jhus**, V*s.*

Item, To household serv'ts, VIII mattrasses, VIII bolsters, IIII coverleds.

Hangings and Carpetts.†

1st, A VI peice of hanginge of ladies Femynye,‡ XXX*s.*

Item, A VI piece hangynge of Distruc'con of Troye, XX*s.*

Item, A tenth peice of the Storie of David, XXVI*l.* XIII*s.* IV*d.*

Item, An VIII peice hangynge of the conduyt worke, some of the same in great decaye, XII*l.*

Item, A XVI peice hangynge for thalle (the hall) of redd, olde and sore decayed, with racke and the anlett wrought in the same,§ IX*l.* VI*s.* VIII*d.*

Item, A XIV peice hangynge of huntinge and hawkinge, XXI*l.* VI*s.* VIII*d.*

Item, A V piece hangynge of red, whit, and other colers, with armes, XXXIII*s.* IIII*d.*

Item, One piece hangynge of Adam and Eve, LIII*s.* IV*d.*

Item, One cowcher, or carpett, for a longe table, LVI*s.* VIII*d.*

Item, II olde carpetts of carpett work for long tables, LIII*s.* IV*d.*

Item, IV longe carpetts for tables of oversee‖ work, XX*s.*

Item, V carpetts for cubbords, of carpett worke, wherof III in decaye, XL*s.*

Item, Fyve other carpetts for cubbords and short tables, in decaye, XX*s.*

Summa, CXLIIII*l.* XIII*s.* IV*d.*

In the Kytchine, West Larder, Paintree, Butteree, Law Ewrie, Backhouse, and Bruhouse.

(Nothing remarkable. The apparatus of the kitchen scarcely differs in any respect from modern utensils for the same purpose.)

In Thall. ¶

V bourds furnished with formes and one cubbord to remain, XXXIII*s.* IV*d.*

Seller.

One bagginge ** of wyne, red claret and whit, in sev'all hogsheads, remainge aft' burial, XXXVI*s.* VIII*d.*

(It is to be noted, that there was fyve hoggsheads of red, whyt, and claret wyne, expend' at my lords buryall.)

---

* This was probably a cognizance.

Only ten bed-chambers appear in this account ; so that, whatever may have been the hospitality of the table, few guests can have passed the night in Skipton Castle. It is remarkable too, that, for a train of thirty-five servants at least, here are only eight mattresses and bolsters. I think it may be inferred, from this circumstance, that the inferior servants still continued to sleep on straw, and probably the grooms over the stables.

† In our ancient castles, the inner surface of the walls was nothing more than naked masonry. But the apartments, when in actual use, were hung with suits of movable arras, which would give them a rich and showy appearance. Carpets were not used to cover floors, but tables and cupboards—a situation in which they are often seen in old pictures.

‡ Ladies of Femynye. This is the language of Chaucer and Gower :—

" So fer forth that Penthisile,
Whiche was the Quene of Femine."—" Confess. Amantis," l. 4, fol. 75, Ed. Berthelet.

" He conquer'd all the regne of Feminie
That whileom was ycleped Scythia."—Chaucer's " Knight's Tale."

Ladies of Femynye, therefore, are the Amazons. Nymphs, in the language of this age, were ladies ; as

" The Lady of the Lake "

in the " Princely Pleasures of Killingworth."

Perhaps Milton is the last who used the word in this sense :

" And Ladies of the Hesperides."

§ Racke and Anlett. I am far from being certain as to the meaning of these words. There is a piece of tapestry yet remaining in Skipton Castle certainly older than this time, as appears by the old English character of the inscriptions, which represents several modes of torture ; but it is not on a red ground. The Anlet, or Annulet, may possibly be some ancient instrument for the same purpose.

‖ " Oversee," foreign.

¶ The hall, which I have no doubt was in the same situation with the present one, had five long tables—*i.e.*, a high table across the upper end, and two down each side, together with a cupboard or sideboard. See the Inventory after the death of the last earl.

** I do not know what bagginge is. One skin could not be distributed into several hogsheads. The second earl died at Brougham, but his funeral, we see, was celebrated (and according to the profusion of the age upon such occasions) at Skipton, where he was interred.

Almost every part of the furniture at Skipton Castle being represented as old and decayed, must be referred to a much higher period than 1572 ; and, on the whole, this inventory may fairly be allowed to represent the interior of a great baronial castle in the reign of Henry VIII., and, in some respects, much earlier. There were, not improbably, figures in their arras which had frowned on Richard III., and even on Black-faced Clifford, two tyrants themselves as savage as ever grinned in old tapestry.

App'ell in a cheist, in great Chamber in thigh Lodginge.[*]

1st, A frenge gowne, with a longe trayne of blacke satten, edged with black velvet, Cs.

Item, One gown of black damask, garded with black velvet, IIII*l*.

Item, A purple satten gowne, playted w'th fyve p'c of gold aglets garded with velvett, faced with grayn coloured sarcenet, Cs.

Item, One gown of black velvett, layd w'th powmet laice, VI*l*.

Item, A kirtle[†] of cremesyn damask, w'th one overbodie of satten of bridges, and welted with cremyson velvett, LIII*s*. IV*d*.

Item, One olde kirtle of cloth of tyssay purple, coloured with overbodie of satten of bridges, XX*s*.

Item, A hinderp'te of one kirtle of clothe of golde, standing w'th red color, with overbodie of yalow damaske, XL*s*.

Item, one other kirtle of cloth of golde, somthinge decayed, IIII*l*.

Item, One gowne of cloth of tynsell, garded with blacke velvet, XIII*l*. VI*s*. VIII*d*.

Item, One kirtle of cloth of gold, overbodied with black sattin, and lined with redd cloth, Cs.

Item, One pair of sleves of black velvett, of the Frenche fac'on, XX*s*.

Item, One pair of lowse sleeves of cloth of golde, of the Frenche fac'on, XL*s*.

Item, II cremysyn peices off clothe of golde for a girtle, XXXIII*s*. IV*d*.

Item, I black damask nurcis[‡] gowne, w'th IIII burgullion gardes, &c. &c. XX*s*.

Item, II parre of velvett shoys, grene, redd, and whit, III*s*. IV*d*.

Item, A border of clothe of golde, w'th images of pictures, VI*s*. VIII*d*.

Playt §, weighed w'th Troye Weight.

Skipton.

In the Seller.

1st, One nest of bowles,[||] duble gilt, embost with imag' or antic' weighing $^{XX}_{VI}$XII ounces, prized at V*s*. IIII*d*. onze with I cover, XXXV*l*. VI*s*. VIII*d*.

Item, I nest of bowles, double gilt, graven w'th branches, at V*s*. II*d*. XXVI*l*. XXII*d*.

Item, I standing cupp, w'th a cover, broken, duble gilt, graven, and in the top of the cover an imag lyk a boy with a shield, at V*s*. II*d*. VIII*l*. II*d*.

Item, One standyng cup, with a lyk image of a boy standing upon III eagles, at V*s*. II*d*. X*l*. XI*s*. X*d*.

In the Seller.

Item, Foure olde playtts of sylv', wherof two with lybards, and th'other two with dragons, &c. &c. VII*l*. XIII*s*. VIII*d*.

In the Paintree.

1st, Two great salts, w'th one cov'r, havynge knoppes, duble gilt, with purcullions and the rose graven, LVI oz. at V*s*. XIII*l*. II*s*. VI*d*.

Item, Two other salts, duble gilt, with a cov'r, having purcullus and rose graven, VIII*l*. X*s*.

&c. &c.

Item, XX sylv' playtes, whereof II with dragons, and XVIII with lybard heads, and stampted after IV*s*. VIII*d*. the oz. XXXVI*l*. XI*s*.

&c. &c.

In the Ewrie.[¶]

1st, III sylv' troughs, w'th rickets, IX*l*. IX*s*.

---

[*] I think there can be little doubt that this was the wardrobe of Lady Eleanor Brandon. The great chamber in the high lodging was probably the upper chamber at the end of the long gallery, which was built for her reception. It was not agreeable to the economy of those times, when dress was hereditary, to bestow the clothes of a deceased lady upon her maid ; and the second wife of this earl, a plain domestic woman, might forbear, from delicacy, to wear the habiliments of a princess of the blood.

[†] In all these instances, the word kirtle evidently means a female habit.

[‡] A nurse's gown, made to open at the breasts, so as to admit the mouth of the infant to the teat. This lady bore, and undoubtedly nursed, one daughter, afterwards Countess of Derby.

[§] The quantity of plate was not considerable. I have selected the most remarkable particulars ; several of which, from the crests and cognizances, seem to have been part of the portion of Lady Eleanor Brandon.

[||] I believe wine was, at this time, generally drunk out of bowls ; though it appears, from Falstaff's advice to Quickly, that glasses were in use about thirty years after.

"*Hostess.* I must be fain to pawn my plate.

Fal. Glasses, glasses is the only drinking."—2nd Part of " Henry IV."

(Entered at Stationers' Hall in 1600.)

The use of the silver troughs, with pricketts, I am unable to explain. The table-service of silver consisted of twenty-four plates only : the dishes were of pewter. If I understand the use of the basyn and ewer, they answered the end of water-glasses, excepting that they were handed round with napkins to the guests before dinner. Our ancestors were not profuse of light : three silver candlesticks in the hall, or great gallery at Skipton, must have spread " darkness visible."

Plate, it must be observed, was still extremely dear ; five shillings, the price of an ounce, being equivalent to twenty at present ; but the mines of Peru had as yet very partially spread their " precious bane " over the remoter parts of Europe.

[¶] [Ewry. The office of the royal household in which the ewers or basons, &c., for washing the hands before and after meals were kept. A full account of this office, which still exists (1830), and of the duty of the persons attached to it, will be found in the " Liber Niger Domus Regis," Edward IV., p. 83, printed by the Society of Antiquaries, in the " Collection of Ordinances and Regulations for the Government of the Royal Household."]

Item, III round sylv. candlesticks, weighing XXV oz. CXIs. VIIId.
Item, I basyn and ewer, with a blew flower upon either, XVIIIl. XIIIIs. VIId.

Corne and Grayn.

In the Garners at Skipton.

Ist, LX quart' of havermalte,* at VIIIs. the quarter XXIIIl.
Item, IX quart' of barley malte, at XIIIs. IVd. ; VIl.
Item, XII quarters of wheat, at IIs. VIIId. bus. XIIl. XVIs.

Cattel and Sheepe.

Demaynes of Bolton.

Ist, XX oxen, at XLs. peice, XLl.
Item, XIII oxen, XVIIl. VIs. VIIId.
Item, XXVI stotts, XXXIIIs. IVd. peice, XXVIl. XIIIs. IVd.
&c. &c.
Item, $^{XX}_V$XII wedders, IIIIl. XIIIs. IVd. score, XXVIl. IIs. VIIId.
Item, CCII wedders, at LIIIs. IVd. score, CXLIVl. VIIs. IVd.
Item, C$^{XX}_{IIII}$XIIII mo' wedders and twints, at LIIIs. IVd. score, XXVIIIl. Xs. VIIId.
Item, $^{XX}_V$X yowes, at XLVIs. VIIId. score, XIIl. XVIs. VIIId.
Item, IX tupps, at IIs. piece, XVIIIs.
Item, C$^{XX}_{IIII}$ hoggs and rigalds, at XXXVIs. VIIId. score, XVIIIl. VIs. VIIId.
Summa, CCXXVIl. Vs. IVd

Horses and Geldings, XXXVI.

Of which, Great Marcantony, stoned, prized to XXl.
Young Marcantony, stoned, XVIl.
Grey Clyfford, XIl.
Whyte Dacre, Xl.
Sorrell Tempest, IVl.
Whit Tempest, Vl.
Baye Tempest, Vl.
Baye Myddleton, XXs.

Mayres and ther followers, XI.
Carthorses, X.

Wolle in the Woolhouses, at Vs. IIIId. ev'y stone, XLVl. IIIIs.
Salt in the Garners at Skipton, XLs.

On the stock of cattle, I have few observations to make. The deer in the parks were not appraised, because they belonged by law to the heir ; and in the forests, both for the same reason, and because it would have been impossible to count them.

Tupps are rams ; which I should not have thought it necessary to observe, had not Shakespeare's commentators stumbled at an indelicate passage in " Othello," where the word is used as a verb. A sensible north-country farmer would often explain our old poets better than their learned editors.

It will be observed, that the rams bore a lower price than ewes ; a proof that no attention was paid to the breed, in proportion to which the value of the male always rises.

A stone of wool was worth two ewes ; twice as much as at present, even in the smaller breeds.

Riggalds are defective male sheep ; so called qu. " Rig-holds, quia alter testiculus infra dorsum (the Rig) retinetur, neque in scrotum descendit."

With respect to the earl's stud of horses, there was something much more noble in naming these fine animals from his own family, or that of the friends from whom he had

---

* Havermalte. This is the latest instance I have met with of malt made in any considerable quantity from oats. The inferiority of price shows its quality. I suppose it to have been so called as being the fodder of the *averia*, or beasts of burden.

Wheat at one pound one shilling and fourpence the quarter was, comparatively, much dearer than at present ; two quarters would have done more than purchase the best ox—a proof that husbandry was little attended to.

purchased them—as, *e.g.*, Grey Clifford, White Dacre, Sorell Tempest, Bay Midelton—than the contemptible and nonsensical manner of denominating race-horses at present. It brings to the recollection, " Saddle White Surrey for the field to-morrow."*

† Ord'nance and Munyc'ons at Skipton, with other Furniture for the warrs.‡

In the Port'ward.

Imp. I iron peice cassen, called a diculveron, with a stocke.

Item, a great chambre for the yron slyngge.

Item, II greet yron peice with chambres lying betwixt the gatts.

At Seller Door.

One facon of brasse with a stock.

Item, I brasse peice with a chambre.

In Mrs. Conyers and Mr. Eltoft's Chambres.§

III lytel brasses with III chambres.

In the Nurs'ye.

I yron peice w'th II chambres, and II mo' other chambres and I brass peice w'th a chambre.

In the Seller.

I yron peice w'th a chambre.

In the Ewrie.

I yron peice casson, called a diculveron.

On the leads.

Item, I facon of brass.

Item, I slynge of yron, with a chambre.

Item, I yron peice casson, called a facon.

Item, II harquebusses of crocke.‖

In the Larder.

I harquebuss of crocke.

In the Porter's Lodge.

I harquebuss of crocke and I oth' lytel harquebuss.

Adhuc Ordnance and Munyc'ons.

In the Midle Chambre in the Galarye.

Item, XXVI corsletts furnyshed,¶ havyng but LII capps and XLV gorghetts, XXVI*l.*

Item, XII di launces, whyt, havyng but X pare off graves and XI p'r of gantletts, XII*l.*

Item, V di launces, black, lacking V graves, C*s.*

Item, XII black corsletts, furnished, XII*l.*

Item, LX almon revetts, furnished, LX*l.*

Item, II brygantynes covered with black vellvett,** and one capp covered, the one whyt nayles and a murrion, IV*l.*

Item, XXVII harquebusses, longe and short, prized to V*s.* a peice, VI*l.* XV*s.*

Item, VII daggs with caices, XXXV*s.*

---

* Shakespeare, " Richard III."

† " As for the armories of sundrie of the nobilitie, they are soe well furnished within some one Baron's Castle, that I have seen III score corslets at once, beside culverynes, handgunnes, bowes, & sheaves of arrowes, the verie sight whereof appalled my corage."—Holinshed, vol. i. p. 85, Ed. 1577.

‡ This is undoubtedly the ordnance with which the first earl repulsed the attacks of the Pilgrimage of Grace. But it is very extraordinary that one of the old slings should be found in use so long after the introduction of cannon. These awkward and clumsy instruments, copied from the Roman Balistæ, were in use through the whole of the Middle Ages, and may be found in contemporary writers under the names of Mangona, Mangonella, Petraria, Fundibula, &c.

" Interea grossos, Petraria mittit ab intus,
Assidui lapides Mangonellusque minores."

Will. Brotto, as quoted by Du Cange, *in voce* Mangonellus.

A wooden engraving of one of them may be seen in an edition of Vegetius, printed at Paris, A.D. 1532, where are represented many military engines not used by the ancients, and some too absurd to be used at any time.

§ A modern fine lady would think cannon in her chamber something like Slender's bears, which, as he said, " women could not abide, for they were very ill-favoured rough things " (" Merry Wives of Windsor ").

‖ Arquebusses were heavy muskets with rests. Crock is pot-metal ; that is, cast iron : a very brittle and dangerous material for slender guns. At the siege of Leith, the English had many " Arquebusiers of Crocke " (Holinshed).

¶ I am not able to discriminate these different sorts of armour with accuracy ; neither do I understand why twenty-six corslets should be considered as defective because they had only fifty-two caps and forty-five gorgets. Perhaps there is some error in the numbers.

Most of these, probably, had borne the brunt

" Of York and Lancaster's old warrs."

** The two brigantines covered with black velvet seem to have been for the use of the lords themselves ; and how frequent with the old writers of romance, is the figure of a black knight traversing a forest, and how completely must it have been realised by the Cliffords within their own domains !

Item, I basse pece of yron, XL*s*.
Item, XII paire of yron moulds.
Item, harnesses for poudre, XI*d*.
Item, XLIIII lead mawles.*
Item, XXXII battell axes made of yron.*
    In the Low Tower at Galary End.
Item, LX almon revitts, furnished, lacking 26 capps.
Item, XXX old backs, and XXX breasts, unsutable harnesse.
Item, I great brandreth,† w'th a bolte, and a lesse brandreth, and I yron pintle for a great gowne.
Item, I yron cuvell.
Item, a closs carte, and other hustlement of household.
    In the Newe Wark.
Item, II brasse peices, I a diculveron, and thother a facon ; they bothe havynge my lordes armes on them.
Item, I longe slynge w'th a chambre.
Item, III of the seven susters.

It is highly probable that these were part of the spoil of Flodden Field which had fallen to the share of Henry Lord Clifford ; for, saith Holinshed in his account of that battle, " Also in like manner all the Scottish ensigns were taken, and a two and twentie peices of great ordinaunce, among the which were seaven culverines of a large assize, and very faire peices. King James named them, for that they were in making one verie like to another, the ' Seaven Sisters.' " ‡

    In the Gallarye.
Item, XL Flanders corsletts compleat, lacking VI p'r of pulsons, and also lacking VIII p'r of canons or vomebraces.
Item, XLV speirs.
    Netts in the Gallarye.
Item, Ther is in the gallary netts, *viz.* a great sene and less sene,§ as draught netts.
Item, a long threde nett with rings.
Item, a tregles nett with two staves.
Item, an olde nette, with IIII tramel netts.
    In the Storehouse.
1st, I tent and a haile (or harle).
Item, III tubbs with saltpeter and a pann ; and a pann with saltpeter in the said tubbs.‖
    Item, in Cross Bowes at Skipton.
Sir W. Ingleby had II, and II racks.¶
Edm. Eltoftes, Esquyer, I, and I racke.
William Farrande, I, and II racks.
Remaining in Skipton Castle II, and . . . rack.

In or about the year 1591 is another inventory of the furniture of this castle, which, as the old finery of the two first earls was mostly swept away, may be presumed to

---

  * Battle-axes, as we all know, were in use during the wars between the Houses. Lead mallets were formidable weapons for beating in slender helmets, and by that means fracturing the skull. The following passages will prove that they were used at Flodden Field, where Henry Lord Clifford, the Shepherd, was engaged :—

        " The morrish pikes, and mells of lead
        Did deal there many a dreadful twack."

And again—

        " Who manfully met with their foes
        With leaden mells and lances long."

  That neither bows nor arrows are mentioned in this catalogue is, I think, to be accounted for from the long interval of peace and security which had taken place from 1537, the era of the Pilgrimage of Grace, to 1572, during which these weapons had gradually disappeared at Skipton, in consequence of their portable and perishable nature.

  [† An iron tripod on which a pot or kettle is placed over a fire.—Wright.]

  ‡ Holinshed, vol. ii. p. 1493.

  § Sene is undoubtedly from Sagena, though I do not find the word in any etymologist. Some of these nets were probably for fish, and others for grouse and partridges.

  ‖ Hence it appears that the family or garrison manufactured their own gunpowder.

  ¶ I conclude from these expressions that the racks for stringing cross-bows at that time were separate instruments. This appears to be the case from specimens lately engraved by Mr. Johnes for his translation of Froissart.

have been in the newest style of fashion. I shall select only a few of the most curious particulars :—

"Drawing Chamber. Three hangings of arris worke bought of Mr. Yorke. One hanging or counterpoint of forest worke, wth Clifford armes. Two table-cloths of grene clothe, fringed abo't with grene silke fringe. Two cheares of estate of clothe of silver ; three long quisheons suited to the same ; one low stoole suitable. Two cupboard clothes, grene clothe w'th grene fringe. One litel cheare of estate covered w'th blewe velvet embroidered w'th silver twiste a tussheay ? One low cheare cov'd w'th velvet a tusshaye ? Five buffetts covered with crimson velvet, and five with grene velvet. One buffet cov'd with clothe of gold. One lowe stand of needle-worke. Three square qwisheons of Turkie worke. One p'r of great copper andirons.* One sconce of wickers. One chimney clothe set in frayme of wod. One long table, 2 tressels, and two square cupboards."

"The Chamb' of Estate. One qwilt of purpl' satten brodered with gowld and silver twine, w'th Clifford & Bedford armes. One sparver, bordered w'th greapes and clothe of gowld ; one cheare, w'th two stools suitable to the same sparver. Large carpet for fote clothe. Two traversers of purple taffatie. Three hangings of Isaac & Rebeckey. One gret glass gilt, w'th litel curtain of sarcanet for same. 1 perfuming-pan. Frayme for sparver."

"Hangings of Dornix" are mentioned in several apartments. What the "sparver" was, I know not : "Dornix" is conjectured by Mr. Chalmers † to have been (linen) damask ; which is pretty nearly refuted by his own quotation, where we find a "smok of Dornix." Perfuming-pans are found in all the principal bed-rooms, as well as another utensil, to the effects of which they seem to have been opposed.

In the last interval of twenty years, paintings had found their way to Skipton; for in the "Wardropp" were XIII of Harculas pictures, and XXIII "Vislereus." What were these last?

In the "Heigh Closset" was the *Library* of the Cliffords, contained in the following brief inventory :—"1 bowke of Bocas. 1 greatt owld bowck. 1 great bowke or grele for singing. 1 trunk of wickers covert with letter w'th bowcks & scrowles in."

"In the low Drawing Chamber, fower pece of hanging of the Amannets" (*i.e.* Ammonites). These are still remaining.

The Buttry and Pantry were very sparingly furnished. "Sylv. spoones VI. Knives II case, and IV glasses, II gilt, w'th one cover. Trenchers IV doz."

The Ewery contained some accommodations for guests, which *we* should not be willing to borrow :—"1 combe-case, p'cel gilt. 3 ivory combes. 1 pare sheasers (probably scissors). Damaske worke. V towth pyckes & eare pyckes of silv'r. Bassins 7. Ewers 7."

The northern wall of Skipton Castle stands on the brink of a perpendicular rock, washed by a torrent, to the bed of which from the battlements is a depth of 200 feet. In the glen beneath *was* the pleasure-ground of the Cliffords, consisting of fish-ponds, walks, and "topiary" works, such as appear to have been introduced in the reign of Henry VIII. Forty years ago a little improvement would have rendered this a very beautiful spot, as the depth of the glen gives a consequence to the castle, which it assumes from no other point, and the rest of the scene would have been proportionably solemn and exclusive. But now ! . . . . .‡

In the Bailey stood, till of late years, a majestic tree, sprung from an acorn of the royal oak of Boscobel, and planted, no doubt, by Lady Pembroke, as a symbol of the ancient loyalty of the family. However, the sign and the thing signified have, very consistently, disappeared together. In the centre of the inner [or Conduit] court, within a basement of masonry adorned with blank shields, stands a flourishing yew-tree, which, as it is directly opposite to the great breach, must have been planted by the same lady to replace

* Copper andirons. Accurate as well as important conclusions may often be drawn from premises seemingly trifling. The Cliffords were not equal in magnificence to the Stanleys ; for at this very time, when Ferdinando Earl of Derby was poisoned, he had *silver* andirons in his bed-chamber.

† "Caledonia," vol. ii.

[‡ In 1773 the Right Hon. Sackville, Earl of Thanet, obtained an Act of Parliament to make the canal at the foot of the cliff "from a place called the Spring, lying near Skipton Castle, co. York, to join and communicate with the navigable canal from Leeds to Liverpool, in a close called Hebble End Close, in the township of Skipton, in the said co. of York."]

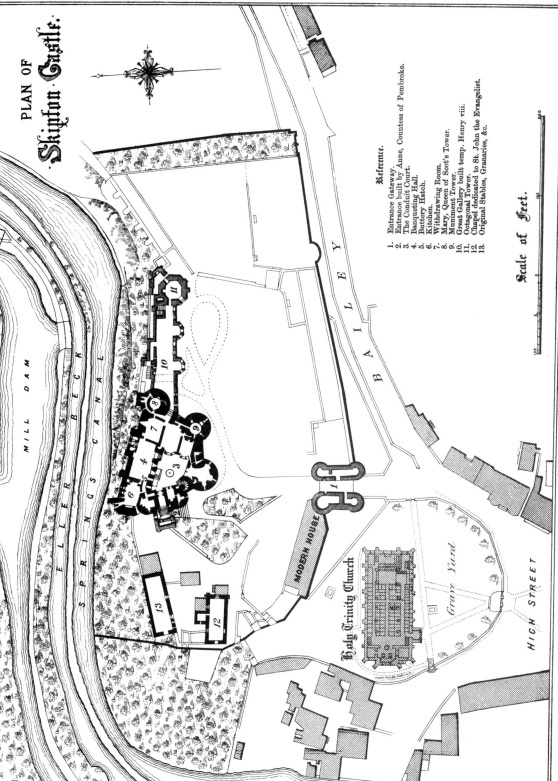

PLAN OF Skipton Castle.

MILL DAM

ELLER BECK

SPRINGS CANAL

MODERN HOUSE

Holy Trinity Church

Grave Yard

HIGH STREET

B A I L E Y

Reference.

1. Entrance Gateway.
2. Entrance built by Anne, Countess of Pembroke.
3. The Conduit Court.
4. Banqueting Hall.
5. Buttery Hatch.
6. Kitchen.
7. Withdrawing Room.
8. Mary, Queen of Scot's Tower.
9. Muniment Tower.
10. Great Gallery built temp. Henry viii.
11. Octagonal Tower.
12. Chapel dedicated to St. John the Evangelist.
13. Original Stables, Granaries, &c.

Scale of Feet.

JOSEPH DODSON, PUBLISHER, LEEDS.

one of much higher antiquity destroyed during the siege. On such standards, planted in the atria of ancient houses, and sacred to the household gods, a dissertation might be written. But the household gods of this castle are fled, and therefore—

"——— Quid te, quæ mediis servata penatibus arbor,
Tecta per et postes liquidas emergis in auras,
Quo *nunc* sub Domino duras passura bipennes?"*

The present entrance to the castle, concealing the original Norman doorway, was added by Lady Pembroke; and it is remarkable that this is the only part which threatens to fall, as

THE CONDUIT COURT, SKIPTON CASTLE.

the old rounders, constructed of imperishable stone and cement, which last even hardens with time, contain in themselves no more principle of decay than the rock on which they stand; nor does the additional building of Henry VIII.'s time bear any external mark of the precipitance with which it is said to have been erected. The decay of masonry in England is almost inversely as its age—a truth which, as it ought to be a warning to modern innovators not to tamper with better workmanship than their own, affords at the same time one consolation, that *their* substitutions will not long offend the eyes of mankind.

Within, however, all is desolation and decay—the new roof, laid by the Countess of

* Statii Sylvæ, lib. i. 3, 60.

Pembroke on the old part, to the shame of her agents and workmen, who had the woods of Barden at their command, is extremely slight; and as there is no hope that any future attention will be paid to the building, a century more may leave it without a roof at all.* Or, long before that time, some agent may suggest the value of the lead, and complete at once that ruin which time is effecting more slowly, but with equal certainty. A worse fate than either of these might be predicted, were it not that such a prophecy, unless expressed with a due degree of obscurity, would possibly lead to its own accomplishment.

In the second great rounder from the entrance is the muniment room of the Cliffords; a place of impenetrable security from everything but mice and damp, which, as it has not been opened more than twice in the last forty years, have been carrying on their depredations during all that time with uninterrupted perseverance. In one drawer had been deposited the ancient charters of the Romillès, Albemarles, Percys, and earlier Cliffords, of which nine parts out of ten I found in 1802 gnawed to fritters; of the remainder I have not failed to avail myself in this work. The compotuses, house-books, &c., of the later Cliffords, being principally written upon paper, are in somewhat better preservation.†

The apartments formed about fifty years since out of the gallery, contain several portraits in a perishing state; particularly the great historical picture, of which an account has already been given. [This picture was sent to the Leeds Exhibition in 1868, and has since been removed from Skipton Castle to Hothfield.] Of the first or second‡ earls there are no paintings. A head of Sir Ingram Clifford remains, on board. And another, called Fair Rosamond, has probably been intended for Lady Margaret Percy; but, for anything now remaining of the features, it may have represented either beauty or deformity, majesty or meanness. An accidental circumstance lately brought to light here a half-length picture on board, evidently of Henry VIII.'s time, which I am persuaded was meant for Lady Eleanor Brandon. A sketch of the face, with that of Sir Ingram Clifford, is annexed. [In the miscellaneous plate.] The person is remarkably tall and large, the face oval and handsome, the hair and eyes dark brown, and the whole figure such as might be expected in a daughter of the houses of Brandon and Tudor.

[* I believe that the roofs have been renewed since that time, as in the view taken for Dr. Whitaker, and given in this work, they are shown more pointed than they are at present, and from tufts of grass on the parapets they would seem to have been in a neglected state.]

† This apartment was, I suppose, the Treasure-house mentioned in the will of the second Earl of Cumberland in 1569; where he leaves "to his brother-in-law Leander Dacre, Esq., the custodie of his evidences, writings, and muniments, and the keys of his Treasure House, which Treasure House hath three lockes and two keys."

‡ There is at Appleby Castle a portrait of a slender and delicate man upon board, inscribed A.D. 1567, æt. 51. This accords with the age of the second earl; but on his left hand is a lion rampant gules, which agrees neither with the coat of Percy nor Brandon; the lion rampant of the one being azure, and of the other sable. On the whole I am inclined to think that there is a mistake in the colour, and that the picture really belongs to this nobleman, who certainly was tall, thin, and of a hectic constitution. At Londesborough is a portrait of Earl Francis, and at Holkham, in Norfolk, a head, said to be that of a Lord Clifford, in the dress of Charles I.'s time, which I believe to belong to the last Earl Henry. It strikes me as resembling Earl George, his uncle, in the features, though not in the sullen ferocity which invariably marks the countenance of the latter, whose face a painter would copy for a leader of banditti, rather than a gallant and chivalrous peer.

Drawn & J. Griffith del.

S. Allom, fect.

Nixton Castle.

Over the modern entrance to the castle is the following inscription :—

> This Skipton Castle was repayred
> by the Lady Anne Clifford,* Countess
> Dowager of Pembrookee, Dorsett, and
> Montgomerie, Baronesse Clifford, West
> merland, and Veseie, Ladye of the honour
> of Skipton in Craven, and High Sheriff
> esse by Inheritance of the Countie
> of Westmoreland, in the yeares 1657
> and 1658, after this maine part of itt had
> layne rvinovs ever since December 16
> 48, and the Janvary followinge, when
> itt was then pulled downe and demol
> isht, almost to the foundacon, by the
> command of the Parliament, then
> sitting at Westminster, because
> itt had bin a garrison in the then
> civill warres in England.
> Isa. chap. 58, ver. 12.   God's Name be praised.

By the words "maine part," in this inscription, we are to understand the old castle only, as distinct from the gallery.† Mr. Gray inferred too much from this inscription when he informed his correspondent, "that this was one of our good countess's buildings, but upon old foundations."

After all, may we not be allowed to suspect that the good lady expressed herself too strongly with respect to the total demolition even of this part of the castle, in order to magnify her own achievement in restoring it? However this may be, I will endeavour to state the fact with accuracy, partly from appearances, and partly from her own MS. Memoirs.‡

First then, the west end, and that only, had been demolished nearly to the foundations ; for here the great breach was made by a battery planted on a neighbouring eminence.§

[* Born at Skipton Castle 30ᵗʰ Jan. 15⁸⁹⁄₉₀. Married 26 Feb. 1609 to Richd. Sackville, then Lord Buckhurst, afterwards Earl of Dorset; he died 28 March 1624. Married 2ⁿᵈˡʸ 3ᵈ June 1630 to Philip Herbert, Earl of Pembroke and Montgomery. On 18ᵗʰ July 1649 she arrived at Skipton Castle, which had been demolished about 6 months before. She remained at Skipton until the 7ᵗʰ Aug. On 13 Feb. 1650 she again came to Skipton, and spent twelve months in repairing the Castle and causing her boundaries to be ridden and her Courts kept. On 18 Feb. 1651 she went to Appleby Castle. On 24 Feb. 1652 she returned to Skipton. About the beginning of Oct. 1665, being at Skipton Castle, she begun to get the rubbish to be carry'd out of the Old Castle there which had lain in it since it was demolish'd in December 1648. On 25ᵗʰ May 1656 she began to repair Skipton Castle, and about Michaelmas following there were thirteen Rooms finished, seven whereof were Upper Rooms, in one of which she was born and her uncle Thomas Earl of Cumberland dy'd, and the Conduit Court was cleared of the Rubbish and the Rooms were covered with slate and the Gutters with lead. But she was not suffered to cover the Rooms with lead.—MS. amongst Skipton Evidences, written by Anne Countess of Pembroke.]

† Mr. Gray's Letters, p. 377.

[‡ This wonderful woman, the Countess Anne of Pembroke, who was much given to self-laudation and to the setting up of inscriptions, in this instance evidently makes too much of the damage done by the Roundheads, for it is easy to see that only the upper part of the rounders were destroyed, except the southern tower of the entrance and the tower adjoining, which seem to have been nearly demolished; and as the castle was not allowed to be made capable of being fortified again, the walls were pulled down to a level line and then rebuilt, the masonry being thinner above this line, as is well seen in the southern tower. The old flat roofs were no doubt destroyed, and the countess replaced them with sloping roofs, which would not admit of cannon being placed upon them. She also diverted the roadway which formerly led to the entrance, and built the new entrance in a civil style of architecture, with a chamber over it and a bold flight of steps leading up to the gateway. The coat of arms carved over the entrance doorway is seemingly out of place; for it consists of the arms of Clifford, with quarterings, impaling Percy with quarterings, and relates to the marriage of Henry Lord Clifford, first Earl of Cumberland, with Margaret, daughter of Henry Percy, Earl of Northumberland.]

§ The platform of the battery is still visible near the division of the roads to Gargrave and Rilston.

3 A

Next (with respect to the demolition by order of Parliament) ; the whole of this part of the castle was unroofed, the lead and wood sold, and the upper part of the walls pulled down, in some places, about one third of their height, when the workmen evidently desisted from weariness. This may be proved by examining the rounders within (for without it is difficult to discover the line which separates the old and new masonry. Here the upper part of the wall is little more than half the original thickness ; and some of the apartments within the rounders have a sort of platform, occasioned by the separation, about half-way, between the floor and roof. Lady Pembroke informs us, that she came to Skipton July 18,

THE OUTER ENTRANCE, SKIPTON CASTLE.

1649 (*i.e.* a few months after * the slighting of the castle); stayed ten days in the town; and on the 28th, removed to Barden. On the 13th of February following she came to Skipton again, where she remained for the greater part of twelve months holding courts, causing boundaries to be ridden, and making repairs. During this time she inhabited the gallery and adjoining apartments, which had never been slighted. The great Octagon Room was her bed-chamber.

But the "old castle" itself lay in ruins till about October, 1655, when she set about removing the rubbish, which had lain there ever since 1648. The 25th of March following she began to repair the building; and, by Michaelmas, thirteen apartments were finished ; seven of them upper rooms, in one of which herself was born, and her uncle, Earl Francis,

* From Newcastle, Oct. 16, 1648. " The committee at York have ordered the slighting of Skipton, &c."—Rushworth.

died. Had the demolition been complete, this could not have been said with propriety. The walls, at least, of the room must in part have remained to identify it.

August 4, 1659, she came again to Skipton, where she found the walls still damp, and was incommoded by a garrison, which the jealousy of the governing powers, though in a time of profound peace, thought proper to continue in the castle. With these rude companions, however, she took up her abode till December 9, when she removed to Barden Tower.

It was owing to the same cause that she was obliged to slate the roof of the gallery, as well as the dismantled parts of the castle, in order to take away the possibility of mounting cannon upon the battlements any more.*

In the Bailey wall, on the south, are the remains of a large rounder; and the gateway itself which opens into the town, near the east end of the church, has four strong and bulky round towers, which appear to have been beaten down about half-way to the foundation in the seventeenth century, and repaired by the good countess. Over the arch, however, are the arms of Henry† Lord Clifford, with the cypher H. C. and date 1629 beneath.‡ The pierced battlement has on one side in large characters.§

GEORGII MERITUM MARMORE PERENNIUS.

And on the other the ancient motto of the family,

DESORMAIS.

On the two remaining sides,

NON AQVILO IMPOTENS—POSSIT DIRVERE. ‖

[* The severity with which Skipton Castle was dismantled, or, as the phrase was, *slighted* by the Rump Parliament, is to be ascribed to the difficulty of maintaining it as a place of defence, owing to its being commanded by two heights, while it afforded a temptation and temporary shelter to the loose marauding parties of Cavaliers. It was not till after its seizure by, and recovery from, the Royalists of Duke Hamilton's expedition, that it was thus hardly dealt with.—Hartley Coleridge's Life of Lady Anne Clifford, in "Northern Worthies," ii. p. 74.]

[† This Henry would appear, from the initials H. C. over the shield of arms in front of the outer entrance, to have altered this gateway, but the date given by Whitaker as 1629 would be during his brother Francis' life; the last two figures are very indistinct. The shield contains the full Clifford quarterings, and is supported by a wyvern and a dog. Round the hollow of the moulding of the parapet is an inscription in Latin, stating that the work was erected as a monument to the memory of his father, George.]

‡ Over the several doors in the inner quadrangle of the castle are the arms and quarterings of the family excellently cut in white stone. Among them is one which the Heralds seem unable to appropriate: *viz.*, Vert, three flint-stones argent; I suspect this to belong to Fitz-Peirs, in allusion to the name. See Gwillim's "Heraldry," edit. 1, p. 136. [This is not the case; Gwillim states that they are those of the family of Flint.]

[§ The central chamber of the Gate House has been raised by the Countess Anne, and on the parapet extending round in a hollow moulding is the following inscription :—

GEORGII. MERITVM. MARM. PERENNIVS	*South.*
REGALIQVE. SITV. PYRAMIDVM. ALTIVS QVOD. NON. IMBER. EDAR. . .	*East.*
NON. AQVILO. IMPOTENS. POSSIT. DIRVERE	*North.*
AVT INNVMERABILIS ANNORVM SERIES ET FVGA TEMPORVM	*West.*

The above is an adaptation of the commencement of the last ode of the 3rd Book of Horace, commencing " Exegi monumentum Aere," and the meaning of the inscription is : " The merit of George is more enduring than marble, and loftier than the regal structure of the Pyramids, which neither the devouring rain, nor the powerless north wind, or innumerable series of years and lapse of time, can destroy." In this entrance is a room on the right-hand side, called the " Shell Room," so called from being quaintly decorated with sea-shells, said to have been brought over and placed here by George Clifford, the third Earl, but upon what authority I cannot say. The open parapet bears the family motto— " DESORMAIS." On comparing the outer and the inner arch of the Gate House it will be seen that the latter has been altered.]

‖ A refinement upon the pierced battlements of the reign of Henry VIII. was introduced about the end of Elizabeth, and continued to the reign of Charles I.—namely, the practice of forming the parapets of great houses into inscriptions,

Skipton Castle, from its own importance, and the military character of the families to which it successively belonged, has undergone several sieges. If it be meant by the Munitiuncula of Richard of Hexham, it must have been destroyed by the Scots in the reign of Stephen. In 1318, the descendants of those plunderers burnt the town; but were probably in no force to attack the castle. In the civil wars of York and Lancaster, in which the Cliffords took a part so fatal to themselves, their residence appears to have been spared. But here the Pilgrimage of Grace, a fanatical rabble of priests and peasants, headed by some men of military skill, besieged the first Earl of Cumberland, who sent to assure his master, Henry the Eighth,* that though five hundred gentlemen, retained at his cost, had deserted him, he would defend his castle of Skipton against them all.

From this assurance it has been inferred by our historians, that the rebels were baffled in their attempt; but, in an abstract † of a letter from that earl to the king, which I have lately met with, he complains that the insurgents had entered his house, torn his evidences in pieces, and rifled his treasures wherewith he should have assisted the King's Highness. In fact, as Skipton Castle is commanded by two adjoining heights, it could not long be tenable against battering cannon, and I have never been able to conceive how, in this instance, it should have held out against a force which had taken York and Pontefract Castle, or how in the next century it could stand a siege of three years, conducted by such officers as Lambert, Poyntz, and Rossiter. But, excepting two or three brisk assaults, the last was probably a languid blockade.

Of this siege ‡ I have collected the following memorials. It appears that the Earl of Cumberland attempted to execute the commission of array, as Lord Lieutenant of the West Riding, in June 1642, but was resisted by Sir Thomas Fairfax. On this occasion, undoubtedly, he would garrison his own castle. The governor who defended it, was John Mallory, of Studley,§ an old and faithful friend of the family. At what precise time the

---

sometimes consisting of texts of Scripture, and sometimes of the family name and titles, or both. A specimen of this custom is given by Dr. Plot, in his engraving of the old house of the Levesons at Trentham, in Staffordshire. Another I remember at Temple Newsom, near Leeds, which was rebuilt by Sir Arthur Ingram after the old house was burnt, 1635.

　* See Lord Herbert's "Life of Henry VIII." p. 483, and the king's curious letter to the Commons of Craven, Dent, Sedbergh, &c., whom, with more truth perhaps than courtesy, he calls "Brutes and inexpert Folk;" the swinish multitude of the day. Amidst the general defection of the neighbouring religious houses, the canons of Bolton seem to have been kept within the line of duty on this occasion, by the influence of their patron.

　† Barden Case, in Bolton MSS. referring to an Old Book, 27 Henry VIII.

　‡ "Nov. 11, 1643. P'd George Dent, armour-dresser, in p't of his bill for dressing of arms and guns at Skipton Castle, xv*l*.—To more work done at Skypton, iv*l*. xiii*s*. iv*d*.—1642-3, Feb. 18. P'd W'm Wrighte for a paire of new gates for Appleby Castle, and for iron for dressing the old guns, and iron for the iron grates, xxiii*l*. v*s*. v*d*.—1640,'8 Oct. P'd George Dent, whitesmith, for dressing my l'ds carbines and petterals, and other works at Appleby Castle, xiii*s*.—P'd D° for dressing up the old armour there, vii*l*. x*s*."

　Notwithstanding these preparations, no attempt seems to have been made to defend any of the other castles of the family, which, it may therefore be presumed, were untenable.

　§ He has a monument and epitaph in the [south transept of the] collegiate church of Ripon, where this circumstance, the most honourable of his life, is unnoticed.

　[Here lyeth Sɪʀ Jᴏʜɴ Mᴀʟʟᴏʀɪᴇ of great Studley als Studley Royall in y^e in County of Yᴏʀᴋᴇ K^t a Loyall Subject to his Prince, who marryed Mᴀʀʏ one of ye daughters and Coheires of Jᴏʜɴ Mᴏsᴇʟᴇʏ of ye Citty of Yᴏʀᴋᴇ, Esq and upon ye 23 of January 1655 and in ye 45th yeare of his age departed this life, he had seven Children six daughters and one son Wɪʟʟɪᴀᴍ Mᴀʟʟᴏʀɪᴇ whoe dyed ye 9th of February 1666 And in ye 20th yeare of his Age and was buryed neare this monument which ye Lᴀᴅʏ Mᴀʟʟᴏʀɪᴇ in ye yeare 1678 in Memory of her husband and son Caused to be erected.

　　　　Above is a shield, or a lion ramp. gu. impaling az. a fess betw. 3 trefoils slipped or.

　There is a portrait of Sir John Mallory, Kt., a full-length, with his wife and child, in the possession of Earl de Grey

siege commenced I do not know. In the Parish Register the first entry of a soldier slain is Dec. 23, 1642.* The castle held out till December 22, † 1645, when it was surrendered upon articles. I suspect, however, that, about the time of Duke Hamilton's unfortunate expedition, it was seized and possessed once more for the king; from whose party it seems to have been re-taken in May, 1648; for, in the Parish Register, many are said to have been slain on the 16th of that month.

The confusion of the times occasioned a chasm in that record, from April, 1645, to March, 1648; otherwise more particulars would have appeared to throw light on that interesting period. Before this cessation, there are only two material entries which appear to have any reference to the civil war :—" Feb. 19, 1644, buried, Major John Hughes,‡ a most valiant soldier;" and July 5th, in the same year, " buried, Sir Nicholas Fortescue, Knight of Malta." It is not improbable that the last had received a mortal wound at Marston Moor, three days before, and had reached Skipton with a flying party of the Royalists, to die and find a grave there.

During the siege of this castle the following warrant was granted by the king to Sir John Mallory, empowering him to collect the rents due to the late Earl of Cumberland for Bolton and the Norton's Lands, towards the maintenance of the garrison. §

"CHARLES R.

" Our will and pleasure is, that for us, and in our names, you demand and receive all such rents and arrears as are or shall be due to us before or upon the feast of St. Michael the Archangel next, from Henry late Earle of Cumberland and his heirs: and that you dispose the same for the maintenance of our garrison of Skipton, as may most conduce to our service ; for which this shall be your warrant and their discharge, upon acknowledgment of the receipt thereof to our Receiver General.

" Given under our signet, at our court at Oxford, the 30th day of March, in the 21st yeare of our reigne. [1646.]

" To our trusty and well-beloved Sir John Mallory, knight, collonell and governor of our garrison at Skipton."

The last Earl of Cumberland died, as the reader has been already informed, in the early part of this siege ; and the inventory of his effects in Skipton Castle at that time, which is here abstracted, may not only be compared with the former inventories, taken at

and Ripon. He was born at Studley, and was M.P. for Ripon in 1640. He was Royalist Governor of Skipton Castle, and held it for three years against the Parliamentarian forces, but was compelled to surrender it to Colonel Richard Thornton, 21st December, 1645. He died in 1655.]

[* The siege appears to have commenced about December, 1642. There is very little information about it to be found, except that Sir John Mallory was in command of the garrison, and on 17th February, 1644, a party of about 150 of his men from Skipton Castle beat up Colonel Brandling's quarters at Keighley, surprised the guards, came into the town, and took about 100 prisoners, sixty horses, and other booty ; but as they returned Colonel Lambert's men fell upon them, rescued their friends and the booty, took Captain Hughes who commanded the King's party, killed his lieutenant and about fifteen of his men, and took about twenty prisoners, and pursued the remainder to Skipton. Samer, one of Lambert's captains, and about eight of his men, were killed, and on the 11th August, 1645, Major-General Pointz took the church and outworks of the castle of Skipton, divers of their horse and men, and their conduit water.—"Whitelock's Memorials."

On the 21st December, 1645, the castle, having become untenable, was surrendered by Sir John Mallory to Colonel Richard Thornton, the Commander-in-Chief of the Parliamentarian forces before Skipton. Mr. Hailstone in his valuable collection of Yorkshire books, &c., has a rare tract, entitled, " Articles of Agreement between Col. Richard Thornton. Commander-in-Chief of the forces before Skipton Castle of the one party, and Sir John Mallory, Knight, Colonel and Governor of Skipton Castle, on the other Party, about the surrender and delivery of the said Castle, 21 Dec. 1645."]

† Leycester's " Civile Warres of England," p. 110. The day is not mentioned by Whitelock, who only notices the arrival of the news, December 26. In Rushworth I find no mention made of it.

‡ He was Lieutenant-Governor.

§ Bolton MSS. See more on this subject under Rilston.

the decease of his grandfather, and in the lifetime of his uncle, but will throw some light upon the state and provisions of the garrison.

Jan. 23d, 1643.

In the Great Hall.

Imprimis, 7 large peices of hangings, w'th the earle's armes at large in every one of them, and poudered with the severall coates of the house.

3 long great tables on standard frames, 6 long forms, 1 short one, 1 court cupbard, 1 fayre brass lantern, 1 iron cradle w'th wheeles for charcoale, 1 almes tubb, 1 great auncyent clock, with the bell, weights, &c. 20 long pikes, 1 great Church Bible, 1 booke of Common Prayer, 2 laced cloth cushons for the steward.

This holds up a very complete and vivid representation; so that a good painter, with some help from fancy, might give an interior view of the old hall at Skipton. But let us examine the particulars. The court cupboard,* I am persuaded, is the same which has been already noticed, as ordered to remain in the great hall, in 1572. The "fayre brass lantern" was probably suspended at the upper end, to give light to the high table. The iron cradle for charcoal proves that this hall had no fireplace; but was warmed like some college halls at present, by a central fire in a movable grate, the vapour of which escaped through a cupola above. The "almes tubb" was probably in or near the screen below, where the poor received a stated dole of oatmeal—a primitive and laudable practice, continued in some old families within my recollection. The great "auncient clock" with the bell was probably over the screen, where the hall-bells of colleges are generally found at present. It is remarkable that few other arms are mentioned in the whole inventory than the twenty pikes.

The Bible and Book of Common Prayer might probably be removed out of the chapel, which was much exposed to the enemy's fire, that the garrison might at least perform their devotions without danger.

With respect to the "laced cushons" for the steward, the great hall seems to have been the place where he presided on court-days, and where I suppose he was seated, like Mr. Vellum, when he held his courts, in the largest elbow-chair in the house.†

The outline of the old hall was the same with the present, and something less than sixty feet long.

In the Parler.

3 peices of aunceyent French hangings, and two peices of another suite of the story in my lord's chamber, 1 oval table, 1 side-boarde, 1 cupboarde, &c. &c. 1 payre of organs, 1 harpsicon.

The parlour, I think, was the large room immediately beyond the hall, where the family,

---

* One of this description yet remains. It is about five feet high, rather more than four in width and two in depth. The sides are fluted panels of Henry VIII.'s time. In front are three doors and two drawers; on one of the uppermost doors are the arms and supporters of the family, on the other the Garter: between them a beautiful Gothic tabernacle. On one of the drawers below was remaining till lately, the word ℳ𝔢𝔯𝔠𝔶𝔢: on the other, encircled with rich Gothic carving, is the cypher 𝕴𝕳𝕾. It was evidently made in the interval between 1527, when the first earl was installed Knight of the Garter, and 1542, when he died. Court cupboards, the side-boards of our ancient nobility, were constant appendages to the high table in the hall. See Shakespeare's "Romeo and Juliet," act i. scene v. :—"Away with the joint stools, remove the court cupboard." Capulet's hall was on this occasion to be converted into a ball-room, and the court cupboard stood in the way. I cannot trace the use of court cupboards lower than the installation feast of Charles II. in St. George's Hall at Windsor Castle, of which an engraving by Hollar is given in Ashmole's "Order of the Garter"—a magnificent work, which owes more to the engraver than the author, and which the rage of modern innovation has rendered doubly valuable.

† See Addison's "Drummer," act v. scene i.

in later days, ate in private.   The last countess, as appears from the account-books, was very musical.   Lutes and theorboes are mentioned in other apartments.

In the Kitching, &c. &c. &c.

One great brewing fatt, with powdered beef, 35 great large beefe flicks, 50 small beef flicks and more, besides peices. In all 33½ carcasses of beef. (This enormous quantity of dried beef was evidently laid in for the use of the garrison, and not the family.)

In the Buttery.

1 silver tumbler. (No other silver vessel mentioned. The family plate had evidently been removed to York, where the Countess of Cork, the earl's sole heiress, complains, in another paper, that, at the surrender of the city, she had effects taken from her to the amount of 1,500*l.* contrary to the articles.)

In the Byllyard Chamber and Terrayse.

1 byllard-board. The picture of our Saviour and Virgin Mary.   12 pictures in black and whyte, 3 landskippes in frames, 16 mappes of cities and shires.

In the Great Chamber.

5 peices of aunceyant rich French * aras hangings, w'th the story of Charlemane, &c. ; 12 high chayres of green damaske ; two low chayres ; 1 great chayre with armes, &c.   Item, 2 tables ; 1 cubberd-bed ; 2 grene carpetts ; 1 sett-worke carpett ; 2 large window curteynes of grene ; 8 pictures.

Item, 1 Turkey-worke foote carpet, a large one.

This was what would now be called the drawing-room ; yet so imperfect was the discrimination of apartments at that time, that, like the dining-rooms in some parts of Scotland, or the parlours of indifferent English inns, it had a closet-bed.   Here, for the first time, I meet with a floor carpet ; the rest are all covers for tables.

In my Lord's Chamber.

4 hanging of rich tapestry, 6 pole-axes, 1 buckler, 4 pictures, 1 crossbooe, &c., 1 livery-cubbord.

Livery cupboards were ancient wardrobes, shaped like small four-post beds, with curtains, within which all sorts of wearing apparell were kept from dust.

(My Lady's and Lady Frances's Chambers contain nothing remarkable.)

In the Closet.

My lady Frances gettorne and 2 trowlemadams † or pigeon-holes.

In the Music Roome.

1 great picture of the countess of Cumberlande.

1 statue of her grandfather Burleigh, in stone.‡

These, and all other relics § of the two last earls, and their families, appear to have been removed by Lady Pembroke, with a degree of prejudice not very commendable, on her accession to the estate.   For the same reason, not a vestige of them appears at

---

* The books of the Northumberland family, however, relating to the Percy fee, afford the following proof, that arras, in 1502, was manufactured by the nobility in their own houses.

" P'd for two lod of wood to the arres-makers in Wresyll Castell, 1x*d.*"

This is a curious fact, of which I do not know that there is any other evidence.

† See Shakespeare's " Winter's Tale," act i. scene ii., and Mr. Steevens's note on this word, where he says, the old English name of this game was pigeon-holes.

‡ Would not this statue be in marble ? and may we not read, instead of "in stone," "by Stone," the great statuary of that time ?

§ But from an inventory taken May 7, 1645, after the siege, it appears that little of the furniture had been damaged. The Hall, in particular, was nearly in the same state in which it had been described two years before.   In the Evidence Room were " One box of writings, v great pictures, both suits of my l'ds *guilt* armour, & *the* statue." This paper is indorsed by Lady Cork : " Inventory of goods left in Skipton after the surrender, wh'ch of right belonged to me, & not to the C. of Pembroke." Doubtless, for whatever might be the case with respect to fixtures, her father's personal property was hers. I trust, however, that Lady P. was too conscientious to retain what she had no right to. At all events, however, that was not the greatest loss to which the loyalty of Lady Cork exposed her, for on "April 4, 1646, all the lands of the late earl of Cumberland in the Wapp' of Staincliff & Ewecross (excluding, however, the *barony* of Skipton, of which Lady Pembroke had now undisputed possession) were demised by the standing committee of the West Riding, for one year, to a man of the name of Thompson, at the rent of 500*l.*, reserving to the Countess of Cork her fifths out of the same.

Appleby. Their portraits may probably be found at Londesborough,* which I have never seen. But, in lieu of these, Lady Pembroke has introduced into her own apartment portraits of her two daughters and their husbands, Lord Tufton and Lord Compton ; with a fifth, representing a plain pug-nosed female, who has the crown of England beside her. This is undoubtedly Queen Anne of Denmark, her great patroness. But the piety and gratitude of " our good countess " are more to be commended than her taste ; for even in the great historical portrait of her father and his family, at a time when the pencil of Mytens or Vandyke might have been commanded, she contented herself with a very inferior artist.

In the foregoing inventory are enumerated fifty-seven apartments, great and small, and forty-two bedsteads, sufficient for a train of sixty servants, which appears from the account-books to have been Earl Francis's establishment in his later days. The hangings of the principal rooms were arras ; of a few, gilt leather : the better beds were hung with silk or velvet ; one counterpane was made of leopards' skins. There was only a single looking-glass in the house, and that not in my lady's chamber, but my lord's. In the kitchen was a great iron peele for venison pasties. I have already called these structures "castles in pastry," and the peele, which was a frame or mould to confine them in baking, actually signifies a small castle.

A curious scene of family jealousy, which took place after the surrender of Skipton Castle, is disclosed in the following letter :—

" For the Right Ho'ble the Countesse of Corke these,.at Lonsbrough pr'sent.

" MADAM,
        "This morneinge by 5 in the morneinge I sent yo'r letter to Mr. Fairfax, whoe this day had formerly appointed to viewe the writeings, he retorneing me answer, that he could not protract any further, came to Skipton, to the intent that the Earle and Countess of Pembrooke had appointed him by their war'nt w'th Mr. Dodsworth.† And according to your Hono'rs desire & authoritie I obteyned my cousin Vavasour to come w'th me to Skipton (haveinge nott tyme to p'cure either Mr. Radcliffe or Mr. Sunderland,‡ whoe I heare is an antiquary). Upon o'r way, both Mr. Fairfax and Mr. Dodsworth (whome we overtooke) p'ceivinge to what purpose our journey was, expressed their unwillingness to p'mitt o'r entervewe, for that they had noe authoriety to admitt the same. Notwithstandinge wee came on to the Castle, desireing to joyne w'th them, as yo'r Hono'r authorized. Their intencons declared by the way, they then absolutely manifested, denyeing to lett us soe much as to stand by them whilst they p'used the writeings, althoe I gave them to understand what yo'r hono'r had writt to the Earle of Salisbury. I told them upon what condition the Castle was rendered in that that concerned yo'r Hon'r & the Countesse of Pembrooke, and many other reasons, sheweinge them alsoe yo'r authority, and soe much of yo'r letters as toucht yo'r *ordresse* to the Earl & Countesse of Pembrooke ; yett nothinge would pr'vaile, theyre chefest inference beinge that there was no reason for us to vewe with them, because yo'r Hon'r had seene them formerly w'th'out knowledge to the Countesse of Pembrooke. Then I addressed myself to the Commander in chiefe of the Castle, and to lieften'nt Coll. Currer, intymateinge to him to what purpose wee came, desireinge to execute o'r authority w'th Mr. Fairfax & Mr. Dodsworth. Answer was given without by some from them, he could not assent to o'r requests, yett very civilly alsoe I must confesse. Mr. Fairfax gave yo'r Hon'r much respect, & seemed willinge to condissend to doe yo'r Hon'r right, but th'other resolutely unwillinge to satisfie us in any guise, tellinge us that he would take noe notice of the artickles of rendition. Many other passages to longe here to relate, & in conclusion, after o'r being an houre in the chamber next the evidences, capitulateing w'th them, yett with all respects due to all persons mencioned in o'r discourse, haveinge received an absolute denyal to o'r request, wee s'p'r'ted. This in hast I send to yo' Hon'r, that y'r discretion by the next post may be used. This all for the pr'sent can come from yo'r

" faithfull servant

" *Skipton, this 4th Febr.* 1645."   " HEN. TH.

It only remains for me to throw together a few memorials with respect to the ancient officers of this castle :—

---

        * See note ‡, p. 408.   † The celebrated antiquary.   ‡ Curate of Bolton Abbey.

Reginald de Fleming, Senescallus de Skipton, by deed s. d., but from circumstances probably as old as the reign of Stephen.

Wilhelmus Anglicus Baillivus de Skipton, s. d.

The following constables have occurred to me; but, as none of the charters in which their names occur have dates, it is impossible to arrange them chronologically; but it may be presumed that none are later than the reign of Edward I. :—

D's Radulphus de Normanvile, Constabularius de Skepton.
Thomas de Leathley.
Wilhelmus de Hebdene.
D's Martinus de Campoflore.
Henricus de Chesterhunt.
Johan de Cotterhow.

The Compotus of Bolton adds—

Baldwin Tyas, A.D. 1316.[*]

The office of porter to this castle was hereditary in the family of Ferrant (a Norman name), who probably accompanied the Earls of Albemarle into England, and merited, by long fidelity, to have their trust rendered perpetual. This appears from the following curious instrument :—

" Sciant, &c. quod ego Will'us de Fortibus, comes Albemarle, dedi, &c. Hugoni Ferando et her. suis, custodiam januæ castelli de Scypton, cum omn. pert.—tenend' et habend &c. Hiis testibus, D'o Gaufrido de Chaund, Emerico de Claris Vallibus, Fulco de Oyri, Vassallo de Affoulcis, Petro Gyllot, Will'mo Maloleporario, Petro de Marton, Rob. le Vavassour, et multis aliis."

In the time of the grandson of this grantee, when the castle and honour of Skipton had devolved upon the Crown, the foregoing charter was contested by the bailiffs of the Queen Dowager Eleanor, then in possession of the castle; on which occasion Edward I. directed the following writ of inquiry to Richard Oysel, his escheator north of Trent :—

"Edwardus, &c. monstravit nobis per peticionem suam coram nobis et consilio n'ro exhibitam supplicando Hugo Ferrant de Skipton, in Craven, quod cum Wil'mus de Fortibus, quondam comes Albemarlie, per cart. suam ded. et conc. Hugoni Ferraunt, avo præfati Hugonis, custodiam januæ castelli de Skipton, habend. sibi et her. suis, et præfatus Hugo avus totâ vitâ suâ post confectionem cartæ prædictæ, et post ejus decessum Henricus filius suus et hæres et pater prædicti Hugonis nunc petentis tenuerint custodiam antedictam, cum omnibus ad eam spectant'; quousque castrum præd. quod ad manus n'ras per mortem Isabellæ de Fortibus quondam comitissæ Albemarliæ devenit, bonæ memoriæ Alianoræ quondam reginæ Angliæ, matri n'ræ carissimæ,[†] cujus Baillivi Castri p'dict' præfatum Henricum à dict. cust. amoverunt. Duximus assignandum sibi super hoc remedium congruum, et vos certiorari velimus, si præfati Hugo et Henr. fil. et pater p'dict. Hugonis nunc petentis, seiziti fuerint de cust. p'dict per factum p'dict' com. nec ne et si sic tunc per quem,[‡] &c."

The following document will prove that Ferrant was reinstated in his office, and that it long continued in his descendants :—

" To the Right Hon'ble George Earl of Shrewsbury, Marshall of England.

" MY VERY GOOD LORD,

" Forasmuch as in respect of your office, being Erle Marshall of England (your l'p) is reputed to be, as it were, the prince's eye, to see and take knowledge of well-desearving persons, and accordingly remunerate the same, by exempting them from the vulgar sort of people : I am willingly become petitioner unto your l'p for William Farrand, one that my lord

---

[* Roger de Clifford ch'r pro Nich'o de Grayndorge. Skipton in Craven offic' constabularii castri de Skipton & magistri forestarie.—Inq. *post mortem*, 47th Edward III., 1373-4.]

† The words " concessum est," or something to the same effect, are wanting here.

‡ Glover, Coll. B. fol. 48, in Coll. Arm.

3 B

my bro'r seteth no little store by, both for the fidelity and good service of himself and all his auncesters to our house ever since our possession of Skipton Castle for this three hundred yeres contynuin, and more also for his owne virtues, which mak him worthie of better place, and yᵉ uttermost of such favours as y'r l'p, by virtue of y'r said office, shall be pleased to bestow upon him, which I desire should be by interposynge of y'r l'p's authoritie with the herauld and officer of armes of these Northe partes, that he may be exempt from the state plebeiall, and be admitted into the Societie and Fellowship of the Gentrie, and allowed to bear armes ; whereunto both by abilitie, education, and otherwise, he is sufficiently enabled. Your lordship's favour extended in this sort shall not only be rightlie bestowed upon such a one as will prove a verie benefyciall member of this commonwelthe : but my lord my bro'r, I am right well assured, wyll acknowledge hymselfe no less beholden then I shall account myselfe even depely boundyn unto y'r good l'p for him, whome, for his virtues and good partes, we bothe love and greatly esteeme.　Thus, &c.

"FR. CLIFFORD." *

In consequence of this request, a coat of arms was granted to Ferrand, March 20, 1586, which nearly fixes the date of the letter. It is scarcely necessary to add, that it was written by Sir Francis Clifford, afterwards the fourth Earl of Cumberland. It is extant in the Heralds' College, among the MSS. of Robert Glover, Somerset.

At the west end of the Bailey stands the castle chapel [dedicated to St. John the Evangelist]; a well-proportioned oblong building, of which the original shell is entire ; and the shape of the buttresses, together with a lancet-window yet remaining in the sacristy, which is a small projecting building on the north side, confirms the account that this was a foundation of Alice de Romillè.† [The original door and windows can easily be traced, and the piscina remains. The date is probably Edward II.]

The first mention of this chapel is copied into an inspeximus of Henry Lord Clifford, the Shepherd, dated May 2, 1512, in which the endowment is referred by mistake to an Earl of Albemarle. The same error is committed in Archbishop Holgate's " Return of Chantries."

"Henry lord Clifford, Westmoreland, and Vesey.

"Knowe ye me to have seen cert'n evidences belonging to my free chappell of Joh. Evang. within yᵉ castell of yᵉ fondacyon of yᵉ erle of Albemarle, presentlie belonging unto me, in which are conteigned cert'n libtyes and dutyes to yᵉ P'son, or Chaplayne, and his successors ; and also one copie of certain of yᵉ same evidenses are written in two mess bookes, one newe, the oth' oulde ; in one of which the said erle graunteth that the seide chaplaine shal have meate and drinke sufficent w'thin yᵉ hall of yᵉ lord of yᵉ castell, for hym and one garcon w'th hym. And yf the lord be ab't,‡ and noe house kept, yᵉⁿ he and his successors shal have for ev'ry 10 weeks one q'r of whete, or vis. viiid. and ivs. in moneye, and one robe or gowne yerely, at yᵉ Nativitie of o'r Lorde, or xiiis. ivd. in monie.

"Wherefore bee yt knowen, that I Henrie lord Clifford, in honoure of God, our blessed Ladye, and St. John yᵉ Evang. and for yᵉ helthe of mye sowle, ratifye for mee and my heires all such lib'ties, lands, ten'ts, rents, poss'ns, tythes, and duties, as yᵉ seid p'son and his p'decessors enjoyed."

To this account of the endowment of the castle chapel the following inquisition, dated 36 Edward III. [1362-3], adds some interesting particulars :—

"Inv't juratores quod pro singulis x septimanis capellanus p'dict' habet i quarteriam frumenti, et iv solidos argenti, et i robam clericalem in Natale D'ni, et i cameram fenestratam (a chamber with a window seems to have been a luxury in that age), et pasturam in Crokeris, et Elso pro viii bobus, iv vaccis, et ii equis, et sufficiens maeremium pro dom's et cameris suis reparand' et siccum boscum pro focali."

---

* Armorial bearings had their value when such recommendations were required in order to obtain them. The progressive change of manners and ideas ought always to be recorded. I have seen a letter from a nobleman, even in the beginning of the present reign, severely reproving a herald for presuming to confer a coat of arms resembling his own upon a person of inferior rank, but of the same name. In an interval of forty years, such has been the progress of commercial wealth, and its companion, indifference to ancient distinctions, that if a *manufacturer* of the present day should think proper to quarter upon his *coach* the bearings of Percy and Clifford, it would excite no other emotion than a smile. But where is the wonder when, by an unnatural alacrity in sinking, even noblemen are become democratical?

† See " Mon. Angl." I. 986.

‡ Absent.

To the same effect was the following warrant :—

" Hen. lord Clifford, &c. To my auditor or auditors, receyvor or receyvors, gretyng. And I wyll y^t ye allow from hensforth yerely at my audyt at St. Lukemas unto Sir Will. Stubbes, p'son of my castell of Skypton, in full payment of such dewes as belong to his p'sonage, for ev'y yere y^t I lye not at my seid castell, XXVI*s.* VIII*d.* for IV quarters of whete, and thretene sh. and four *d.* for a gowne ; and for ye space y^t Y lie at my seid castell at eny tyme within ye seid yere or yeres ye to abate as muche of ye seid allowance, accordyng to ye olde and auncyent custome.

"Yeven at my lodge in Berden XXVII of Sept. in ye VIII yere of King Henry VIII." [1516.]

The next document relating to this foundation is the presentation of a chaplain by the second Earl of Cumberland, probably after the death of Stubbs.

"Henry erle of Cumbreland, lord of ye honor of Skypton and of ye Percy Fee :* for ye s'vice done by my chaplane Sir W'm Thyrkeylde unto my lord my father (of whose sowle God have mercie †) and to me, have given unto hym the Free Chappell wythin ye Castell, of w'ch I the said erle ys‡ ye undoubted patron. To have, hould, &c. with a comodities, &c. as it dothe appeare in an oulde mess booke remaynyng in ye chapel, or in ould precedent, or estryment in wryteing on parchment, soe that he shal singe and min'r in ye chappele, according to the ould custom, or at ye pleasure and commandment of ye said Erle.

" *Dat.* 20 *Jun.* 1542, 34 Hen. VIII."

During the incumbency of Threlkeld, who was probably related to Sir Lancelot, the second husband of old Lady Clifford, the chantries and free chapels were dissolved. On that occasion the following return was made of this chapel :—

" Skipton Castle. { W'm Thurkeld incumbent, 48 years of age, serveth the cure himself, having houselinge § people nine score, or thereabouts, w'th the lorde of Cumb'land his household servants. The necessitie therof is to serve the said erle, and his houshold in the castel. Goods and plate belonginge to the said service, as appeireth, goods II*l.* plate II*l.* The yearly value of frehould landes to ye said s'vice belongyng, as apeireth by ye rental, CVIII*s.* II*d.* Copyhould II*l.* wherof resolutes and deductions II*l.* Remayneth cleare to the kinge's majestie, CVIII*s.* II*d.*"

Next to this return follows a grant of C*s.* to Thurkeld for life, dated 1 September, 2 Edward VI. [1548].

But, after all, a doubt arose whether the chapel of Skipton Castle were a free chapel or a parsonage, and for some time the latter opinion appeared to prevail, so that Threlkeld was actually reinstated by the following order from the Augmentation Office, bearing date 5 November, 6 Edward VI [1552].

" In the matter betweene the kinge's highnesse and the p'son of Skipton Castell. Forasmuche as no matter or cawse is proved on the kinge's behalfe that ye p'sonage w'thin the castell of Skipton shoulde be a free chapel, but that it is a p'sonage ; ordered, that the said p'son shal continue in the quiet possession of the said parsonage until better matter be shewed for ye king."

But this seems to have been in consequence of a petition from Threlkeld to Sir Richard Sackville for an augmentation of his pension, when the court thought it better to let him receive the whole income belonging to the foundation.

When this incumbent died, or what became of him, I do not know ; but upon his demise or removal, a scheme seems to have been formed by the Clifford family to present no more rectors or chaplains, and to suffer the endowment gradually to sink into oblivion ; for in the 15th of Elizabeth [1572–3] a commission was granted to Richard Assheton and

---

* This is the first instance in which a Clifford is styled Lord of the Percy Fee ; to which this earl, then Lord Clifford, had succeeded, after the decease of his uncle Henry, Earl of Northumberland, four years before.

† The first earl had not been dead quite two months at the date of this instrument.

‡ Several vestiges of the Craven dialect, as distinct from old English, appear in these instruments—I is, *e.g.*, for I am—and mak for make.

§ *I.e.* Communicants ; from Þurel, Sacrificium. The word is used as a verb by Chaucer, " to ben houseled."

John Braddyll, the purchasers of Whalley Abbey, to institute an inquiry "de terris concelatis capellæ de Skipton;" in consequence of which the old endowment once more came to light, and the chapel, with its appurtenances, was sold to one Francis Proctor and Thomas Browne. The year following these parties assigned the premises once more to a John Proctor, who, in the 18th Elizabeth, conveyed the whole to George Earl of Cumberland. Whether the family neglected, in the first instance, to buy in so inconvenient a rent-charge upon their demesne, or the Crown, offended with the concealment, refused to deal with them, I cannot tell.

Long after this time, however, and even as late as the year 1612, the endowment of this chapel, and duties of the chaplain, are set forth in a memorial remaining in Skipton Castle. July 5, 1635, Richard Lord Dungarvan was married within it to Elizabeth Clifford, daughter and sole heiress of Henry Lord Clifford, afterwards the fifth Earl of Cumberland.

This sacred edifice is now a stable. In whose time, or by whose order, it was perverted to that indecent and disgraceful use I do not know ; but it may be affirmed without risk, though without evidence, that it retained its original destination till after the death of Thomas, the good Earl of Thanet.

Before I take leave of this great family at Skipton, I must be permitted to trace them to their northern principality in Westmoreland.

From Skipton to Brougham the distance is nearly seventy miles, the whole of which extensive district, excepting an interval of ten miles between the top of Longstroth Dale and Hell Gill, after the acquisition of the Percy fee, belonged to the Cliffords. In Westmoreland they had the castles of Pendragon, Brough, Appleby, and Brougham, on the architecture of which, as it has not even been hinted at by Dr. Burn, I will make a few remarks.

I suspect them all to have been the work of Ranulph de Meschines, in the reign of the Conqueror. Brough must have been chosen in order to fortify the pass of Stainmore ; Pendragon, that of Mallerstang ; Appleby, for its central as well as strong and beautiful situation in the barony ; and Brougham to guard its northern boundary.

Of this last the remains are very magnificent. It stands without any advantage of situation, excepting what is derived from the ramparts of the Roman Brovonacum (probably very strong at its first erection) within which it was placed. The donjon, unquestionably of the era of Ranulph de Meschines, is a vast square Norman tower, four storeys high, of which the lowest was vaulted with rib-work, and the next appears to have been the great hall. The different apartments, many of which have round-headed lights, were approached by staircases and galleries in the thickness of the walls. A small chamber at the top of the south-east angle has been richly groined. The gateway and apartments adjoining, which bore the inscription, " 𝕿𝖍𝖎𝖘 𝖒𝖆𝖉𝖊 𝕽𝖔𝖌𝖊𝖗 "—apparently an imitation of "𝕿𝖍𝖎𝖘 𝖒𝖆𝖉𝖊 𝖂𝖆𝖑𝖙𝖍𝖆𝖒 "—may with greater probability be ascribed to Roger Lord Clifford, in the reign of Richard II., than to his ancestor of the same name. The chapel and adjoining suite of apartments on the south appear to be of the same age, and are probably the work of the same hand. The inner gateway can scarcely be older than Henry VIII. Brougham appears not to have been much frequented by the two last Earls of Cumberland, after the king's visit there in 1617 ; and at the decease of Earl Henry in 1643 was probably in a state of dilapidation, as it certainly was without furniture. Appleby alone, of all the castles of the family in Westmoreland, may be proved by the inventories* taken at that time to have been partially furnished.

The public has been frequently informed of late that Sir Philip Sydney's "Arcadia" was principally written at Brougham Castle, then the residence of Anne Countess of Pembroke, to whom the work is inscribed. Had this story been repeated by twenty ordinary tourists, I should have suffered them to enjoy their "Arcadia" in peace; but as it has been adopted by Mrs. Ratcliff, a writer of another class and order, I hold it due to *her* to correct the mistake. The truth is that Sir Philip Sydney was killed three years before Anne Clifford was born, and the lady to whom he really inscribed that work was his sister Mary, daughter of Sir Henry Sydney, Knight of the Garter, and second wife of Henry Herbert, Earl of Pembroke, who died in 1601—

"Sydney's sister, Pembroke's mother."

Surely a fatality hangs over this part of the history of the Cliffords, when touched by modern hands; for, among some posthumous Dialogues lately published, the work of that respectable writer and worthy man, Mr. Gilpin, the interlocutors of one, Lord Burleigh and Sir Philip Sydney, are gravely introduced, bewailing the premature fate of that young nobleman George Earl of Cumberland, who, notwithstanding, survived them both. Neither do I know where Mr. Gilpin learned that this peer had any taste for the charms of nature.

Brougham is first mentioned in an inquisition taken after the majority of Robert de Vipont, in the time of Henry III. However this may be, it continued, with the interval mentioned above, to be the stated residence of the Cliffords in Westmoreland from the time of the first Earl of Cumberland to the death of the Countess of Pembroke, who, as well as her mother, expired at Brougham. Here, likewise, Earl George was born, and here his father died.

At Appleby is a fine Norman tower [now called Cæsar's Tower], with perpendicular buttresses, evidently the work of Ralph de Meschines, who expressly mentions the castellum de Apleby in one of his charters. In the Countess of Pembroke's MS. Memoirs this " castel " is said to have been ruined in the insurrection of the Earls of Northumberland and Westmoreland, A.D. 1569; but Leland speaks of it as dilapidated in his time [c. 1540]. It does not appear to have been much frequented by the Cliffords, excepting at the assizes, or on some public occasions, though it was not a ruin at the death of the last earl; but, by a contrary fate to that of its neighbours, Appleby Castle was restored by Thomas Earl of Thanet, who destroyed all the other seats of the family in Westmoreland, and fitted up with a suite of good modern apartments.

The great tower of Brough is evidently Norman, like that of Appleby. This castle was burnt down (*i.e.*, the roof and floors were consumed) after a noble Christmas kept there by Henry Lord Clifford, the Shepherd, in his later days; and remained a ruin till the Countess of Pembroke's time, when it was repaired only to be demolished once more by her grandson.

Pendragon, equally romantic in name and situation, though manifestly of the same age,

---

* Londesborough Papers.

is of a different form from all the rest.   It has been one of those low square Norman castles, which, having had no bailey, enclosed a small area, and had many diminutive apartments in their massy walls opening inward.

With respect to the name, which, among authentic records, first appears in an inquisition of the 8th of Edward II. [1314–5], I shall only observe that, as this place was certainly included in the limits of the Strath-Cluyd Britons, a fortress might really have been erected on the spot by Uther.   It is easy to defer too little as well as too much to remote traditions.

The following passage from " Mort Arthur," whatever it may add to the credibility of the tradition, will at least throw over this rude and sequestered scene the wild colouring of romance :—

" how Sir Lancelot made La Cote male Taile lord of the castle of Pendragon." " As Sir Lancelot came by the castle of Pendragon, there he put Sir Brian de les Isles from his lands, and all that castle of Pendragon and all the lands thereof he gave unto Sir Cote male Taile.   And then Sir Lancelot sent for Sir Neroveus, and he made him to have all the rule of that castle and of the country under La Cote male Taile."

"Mort Arthur," C. L.

At this castle, in 1337, Edward Baliol was honourably received, on his expulsion out of Scotland by Roger de Clifford, and entertained with magnificent huntings in the adjoining forest of Mallerstang.*   It was unroofed in 1541,† but the shell of the building, of which the walls were four yards thick, continued entire, and in this state it remained without farther change till Lady Pembroke restored it, in 1661, with no better auspices than Brough.

To mortify the vanity of human expectations, the final ruin of three of these castles within ten years after the death of their restorer, may be compared with her prophetical motto, " Thou shalt build up *the foundations of many generations ;* and thou shalt be called the repairer of the breach, the restorer of paths to dwell in."

PARISH CHURCH OF SKIPTON.

I shall hereafter assign my reasons for supposing that the original church belonging to the fee of Earl Edwin was at Bolton.   With respect to the church of Skipton, it seems to have been founded at the same time with the castle, to which it immediately adjoins, by Robert de Romillè ; at least, it is never heard of before, and it appears immediately after.   The first notice of it is a donation to the priory of Huntingdon from William de Meschines " ecclesiæ S'ti Trinitatis de Scipeton cum pert."‡   How that grant was retracted or avoided does not appear ; yet, in the year 1120, this church, with the chapel of Carlton and village of Embsay, formed the original endowment of the priory of Embsay, by the same William de Meschines

---

* Lady Pembroke's MS.   This wild tract was, I suppose, so called, qu. Mallard-stank, the pool of the Mallard, referring to some early expansion of the Eden, which has long since burst its mounds.

† Lady Pembroke's inscription over the entrance.   Dr. Burn says, but I know not on what authority, that it was burnt by the Scots in the 15th Edward III. [1341–2].   It does not appear that they made any incursion that year.

‡ See the confirmation of Henry I., " Mon. Ang." vol. ii. p. 24.

and Cecilia his wife. The priory of Huntingdon, however, not only persisted in their claim to this church, but even attempted, in consequence of it, to subject the priory of Bolton itself to their jurisdiction.

Yet it was not long before it was appropriated, with all its fruits, to Reginald the prior, and the canons of Embsay. But no vicarage was yet endowed, and in this state the cure must have been served, for a season, by the canons themselves. Nothing further appears on the subject till the year 1326, at least two centuries from the appropriation, when a vicarage was endowed by Archbishop Melton. But, as in this instrument [which is dated 16th September, 1326] the former endowment of the vicarage is expressly referred to as insufficient, and as an institution of a vicar occurs in 1267, it is certain that a former endowment must have taken place in that interval, though it is now lost.

The particulars of this endowment, which is very long and circumstantial, are as follows : viz., That the said vicarage shall consist in

"A manse, in the town of Skipton, with its appurtenances, which the vicars have been accustomed to inhabit, mortuaries, living and dead, of Skipton, Thoralby, Stretton, Holm, Skybden, Draghton, Berewick, Bethmesley, Ryehill, Langberg, Holme, and Notelshagh. In white tithes, and those of calves, poultry, young pigs, and goats, in the said places, and in Halton, Dearstanes, Hesselwood, Rucrofts, and Storithes. Likewise in all oblations, quadragesimals, tithe of flax, gardens, curtelages, geese, hens, eggs. In purifications, espousals, and other small tithes, in all the above places, and in the vills of Emmesay and Esteby. Likewise in tithe of lamb within Skipton, Thoralby, Stretton, Holme, Skybeden, Draghton, Berewics, Emmesay, Esteby, and Halton. And in the tithes of the mills of Bethmesley and Draghton. In tithe hay of Skipton, Skybedon, and Draghton ; and in espousals of the forest, and of the Sacristaria,* excepting mortuaries of the lords of Skipton Castle, and of all the tenants of the Religious of Boulton on this side of Kexbeck. Likewise in the tithe of the park of Skipton, and the Forest, and in oblations, purifications, espousals, tithes, and mortuaries, of Sir William Mauliverer and his heirs. Likewise in all oblations made in the churches of Boulton and Emmesay. [And all tithes, purifications, and oblations of all the tenants of the Sacristaria, and all manner of tithes of the mansions, granges, cattle byres, and sheep folds † of the said Religious in whosesoever hands they may be, which and all others not above set forth as belonging to the Church of Skipton, shall remain with the Convent of Bolton and their successors wholly and for ever. The Vicar to bear the ordinary and accustomed burdens except the rebuilding and reparation of the Chancels, which the said Religious shall do when necessary, but extraordinary expenses shall be defrayed by the Religious and the Vicar for the time being according to their portions."—Extended from an attested copy in Latin in the hands of the Rev. C. Bellairs, Rector of Bolton Abbey.]

[At the Dissolution it was given to the dean and canons of Christ Church, Oxford, who are the present impropriators.]

Vicarii de Skipton.

Temp. Inst.	Vicarii.	Patroni.	Vacat.
8 id. Maii, 1267.	D's *N. de Fangefosse,* Cap.	{ Prior et Conv. de *Bolton,* sed A'pus pro hac vice per laps.	
Kal. 1275.	D's *W. de Lunecroft.*	Iidem.	
	D's *Hen. de Erdeslaw.*	Iidem.	per mort.
5 id. Maii, 1334.	D's *W. de Draghton,* Cap.	Iidem.	per resig.
7 kal. Apr. 1342.	Fr. *Tho. de Manygham,* Can. de Bolton.	Iidem.	per resig.
29 Jul. 1354.	Fr. *Laur de Wath,* Can.	Iidem.	per resig.

* I once thought this word, which Dr. Burton mis-read *Pacraria,* meant the chapelry belonging to the Sacristy, or chapel in the castle. But I have since discovered that the office of Sacrist in the religious houses had often a separate endowment in lands. These lands, therefore, were the *Sacristaria* of Bolton Abbey. Du Cange has the word with various spellings and various meanings ; among the rest *Sacristaria,* which he defines, Sacristæ munus monachicum cum reditu ac prædiis annexis. Et ex chartâ dat. 1240. A.B. recognovit se vendidisse Sacristæ B.M. ad opus Sacristariæ quoddam tenementum.

[† Mansorum, grangiarum, vaccariarum et bercariarum.]

Temp. Inst		Vicarii.	Patroni.	Vacat.
25 Apr.	1369.	Fr. *T. de Kydale*, Can. de B.	Prior et Conv. de *Bolton*.	
30 Jan.	1402.	Fr. *Tho. Ferror*, Can. de B.	Iidem.	per mort.
10 Feb.	1415.	Fr. *Joh. de Farnehill*.	Iidem.	{ per electionem in prioratum de Bolton.
7 Mar.	1430.	Fr. *Rob. Lupton*, Pr. C. ibm.	Iidem.	
		Fr. *Tho. Skipton*, Can.	Iidem.	per mort.
22 Mar.	1460.	Fr. *Tho. Botson*, nuper Prior de Bolton.	Iidem.	per mort.
11 Mar.	1477.	Fr. *Rob. Law*, Can. ibm.	Iidem.	per mort.
18 Sept.	1479.	Fr. *Tho. Pillesworth*, Can.	Iidem.	per mort.
24 Sept.	1490.	Fr. *Gilb. Mayrden*, Can.	A'pus per laps.	per mort.
22 Jan.	1512.	Fr. *Jac. Thorneburgh*, Can.	Prior et Conv.	per resig.
12 Aug.	1514.	D's *X'topher Baran*.	Iidem.	
24 Maii,	1521.	Fr. *W'm Blackburn*, Can. de Bolton.*		
		Thomas Jollie,† Cl.		
30 Aug.	1587.	*Ric. Gibson*, Cl.	Dec. et Cap. Ec. X'ti Oxon.	per resig.
11 Aug.	1591.	*Edw. Horseman*, Cl. A.M.	Iidem.	per mort.
27 Aug.	1604.	*Barth. Wylde*, Cl.	Iidem.	per mort.
22 Oct.	1621.	*Rob. Sutton*,‡ Cl. A.M.	Iidem.	per mort.
13 Feb.	1665.	*Tho. Sutton*.§ Cl. A.M., ob. 1683.	Iidem.	per mort.
21 Nov.	1683.	*Timothy Ferrand*, ob. Nov. 1685.	Iidem.	per mort.
13 March,	1686.	*George Holroyd*, A.M., occurs in 1704.	Iidem.	per resig.
25 Apr.	1705.	*Roger Mitton*, A.M., ob. June, 1740.	Iidem.	per mort.
25 Sept.	1740.	*Jeremiah Harrison*, A.M.	Iidem.	per resig.
4 Nov.	1748.	*Walter Priest*, A.M., ob. Dec. 1768.	Iidem.	per mort.
23 Mar.	1769.	*Daniel Poate*, A.M.	Iidem.	per mort.
19 Dec.	1771.	*John Parry*, A.M., ob. Feb. 1778.	Iidem.	per mort.
8 Aug.	1778.	*Ric. Hinde*, D.D., ob. Feb. 1790.	Iidem.	per mort.
12 June,	1790.	*Thomas Marsden*, A.M.	Iidem.	per mort.
12 May,	1806.	*John Pering*, A.M.	Iidem.	per mort.
11 Aug.	1843.	*Philip Chabert Kidd.*	Iidem.	

[The register books commence in 1592. No entries of burials from 1644 to 1648.]

* The following dispensation from Archbishop Cranmer, dated 25 Hen. VIII. [1533–4], to this vicar, one of the earliest acts of the Legatine power after it was transferred by statute to the see of Canterbury, is not a little curious, as it exhibits the first Protestant primate extolling the merits of the monastic life. But, perhaps, this was only the customary language of the office—

"Thomas, &c. dilecto nobis in X'to Wil'mo Blackburne, vicario perp. eccl. de Skipton, presb. regularem vitam professo, sal. Meritis devotionis tue inducimur ut te special' favoribus prosequamur ; hinc te, quod, ut asseris, regularem observantiam juxta divi Augustini regulam in domo Prioratus de Boulton professus eras, necnon capellanus nobilis viri d'ni Henr. com. Cumbr. existis, a quibusdam censuris eccl. harum serie absolvendum fore censuimus, et una cum dictâ vicariâ unum et sine illâ duo alia curata retinere, vel ex causâ permutationis dimittere dispensamus."—MSS. in Off. Arm., Skipton Box.

† His name only occurs in the foundation-deed of the school, 2 Edw. VI. [1548–9].

‡ 1664, Feb. 24, Rob. Sutton, A.M., formerly chaplain of Christ Church, and vicar of Skipton, departed this life, aged 80 years and upwards, 43 of which he was vicar of the said place. His funeral sermon was preached by his only son, Thomas Sutton.

§ In 1683, Mr. Thomas Sutton, vicar of Skipton and Carlton, the best of preachers, and a very peaceable, good man, buried September 25th.—The following miscellaneous entries in the parish register of Skipton, relating partly to the slaughter of the civil wars, and partly to instances of longevity, may not improperly find a place here. "Buried, 1640, Feb. 12, three soldiers. March 13, three soldiers. 1642, Dec. 23, a man slayne ; Dec. 28, a man slayn by the rebels at Tharnton. 1643, 9 (month omitted), three souldiers belonging to captain Prideaux, slain at Carelton. 1644, Dec. 31, major John Hughes, a most valiant soldier. 1648, April 22, burials, May 16 ; ditto, many slayne at this time. 1665, July 22, William Wade, who lived at London, coming to see his father, died at Rumell's moor, as it was supposed, of the plague, therefore buried there. Feb. 8, widow Allenby, of Thorelby, been one hundred and eleven years and upwards. 1671, Jan. 26, Robert Mountgummery, a Scotchman, he lived many years at Skipton, aged six score and six, *ut dicunt*." These qualifying words in the original register deserve to be attended to : for in the Philosophical Transactions, and in every other account from that time to the present, of English longevity, this man is *positively* said to have lived 126 years. Evidence is very apt to strengthen in the direction in which it ought to grow weaker.

Baptized, 1664, Nov. 27, William, son of William Gudgeon, of Skipton, who was the seventh son that gave boote for the King's Evil. I never heard before that the medical powers of a seventh son encroached on the prerogative of "the true prince." Boote, in old English, is benefit, the opposite of bale.

Baptisms at Skipton.						Burials.
1600	... 40	.	.	.	.	. 43
1700	... 40	.	.	.	.	. 68
1800	... 77	.	.	.	.	. 74

[On the 27th April, 1719, a faculty was granted to new pew the church; on the 7th Dec. 1786, one to erect the west gallery; on the 26th Nov. 1802, one to erect an organ and gallery; and on 28th July, 1835, another to erect an additional gallery on the north side. In 1855 the south gallery was erected.]

[The church is dedicated to the Holy Trinity, and is large and spacious, being about 110 feet by 55 feet inside, exclusive of the tower, and now consists of nave and chancel, with clerestory, north and south aisles, continuous for the whole length, with seven bays of arches, and no chancel arch. The piers of the four westernmost bays, and the respond adjoining the tower, are in plan a square set diagonally, with four three-quarter circular shafts springing from the angles. Those of the three eastern bays and the respond are octagonal. The western part of the church is probably of the end of the 13th or commencement of the 14th century, as are the sedilia now built into the wall of south aisle, which is possibly not their original position. The aisle buttresses terminate in pinnacles. The lower portion of the tower, which is at the west end, is of the same date as the western part of the church. The aisles have been carried partly at the sides of the tower, and there are arches between them and the tower, and also the usual tower arch. The western ends of the aisles are now divided from the church by walls filling up the arches, the northern chamber being used as the vestry, and the southern as a choristers' vestry and Petyt's Library. The screen mentioned by Dr. Whitaker has been restored, and is now fixed across the church at the second pier from the east end. The inscription has entirely disappeared. The south porch is modern. It has this inscription : "This porch was erected to the memory of Susan, the wife of John Robinson, of Ravenshaw, who died at Croft House July 1, 1850, and was interred near the east end of this church."

In the tower is a peal of six bells, cast by Lester and Pack in 1759.

The roof is that constructed in the time of Richard III., and is of oak, well moulded, and very flat. After the church was struck by lightning on the 19th June, 1853, it was repaired under the direction of Mr. John A. Cory, architect, of Carlisle. He found it in a dangerous condition. The ends of all the main beams were decayed, as were those of the common rafters. He had them taken down, pieced, and wall-pieces and brackets introduced to give them security. He thus obtained a good bearing, and preserved the roof. The cornice was also inserted to carry the rafters and admit ventilation.

During the alterations an original altar-slab was found, and is now placed in the north aisle of the chancel. It measures 9 feet in length, 2 feet 7 inches in width, and is 7 inches in thickness.

There is a beautiful carved stone reredos designed by Sir Gilbert Scott, representing Our Lord in majesty surrounded by the emblems of the four evangelists. On either side are three niches containing statuettes of St. Peter, St. Paul, the Blessed Virgin, St. Stephen, St. Mary Magdalen, and a male figure with archiepiscopal crozier and a sword. It was erected in memory of Henry Alcock, Esq., of Aireville.]

[Upon a brass plate—

Here lieth the Body of
Robert Benson Esqr.
of *Halton*
Who departed this Life
the 15th Day of November
1818
Aged 49 Years.

Cut in the stone of the north-east pier of the tower is the following inscription—

Pridie Kalendarum mensis July Anno Domini Millessimo Sexcentessimo nonagessimo sexto, corpus *Willelmi Johannes Jackman* de Skipton Generosi natu minoris filii cum annum vicessimum sextum ab ortu primo vix compluerat huic tumulus est impositum flevit uterque parens flerunt cum fratre sorores extinctum madidas imbre regante genas vixit enim constant et maxima cura parentum vixit honos cecidit luctas amorque domus quando ætas puerum rerum fandique peritum ingenium et mores edoque re virum cum virtute potens certavit gratia linguoq doctior an melior viserit ille polum.

3 C

On a brass in the south aisle—

Arms—Gu. a fess erm. between three cocks' heads erased arg.

In this aisle rest interred the Remains óf Ann Alcock, sister of John Alcock, of this town, Attorney at Law, died 26th March, 1761, aged 54.

Matthew Alcock, brother of the said John, died 9th March, 1762, aged 35. Mary, daughter of the above John Alcock, died 18 March, 1764, aged 15. Mary, the wife of the said John Alcock, died 8 Sept. 1765, aged 49. Grace, daughter of the said John and Mary Alcock, died 18 March, 1770, aged 29. John, son of the above, died 25 April, 1770, aged 26. The above John Alcock died 1 March, 1783, aged 71. Peter, son of William Alcock, and Elizabeth his wife, and grandson of the last-named John, died Sept. 30, 1795, aged 3. Sarah Alcock, daughter of the last-named John, died 23 March, 1803, aged 53.

Elizabeth, the wife of the said William Alcock, and daughter of the late J. Nicholson, Esqr., of Appleby, died May 1, 1803, aged 45.

Richard Chamberlain died 21 May, 1787, aged 46. Elizabeth his wife died Feb. 20, 1792, aged 40. Also Thomas and Frances, father and mother of the above Richard. He died March 17, 1789, aged 81 ; she died April 9, 1768, aged 53.

Arms—Gules an escutcheon or within an orle of mullets argent.

Mary Chamberlain died 14 Jan. 1737, aged 47. Also William Chamberlain, son of George and Mary Chamberlain, died 4 Feb. 1716.

Elizabeth Dynley died January 13, 1772, aged 25.

On a brass in the north aisle—

Crest—A lion's head erased collared.

In this aisle are interred the remains of Henry Currer, of Skipton, Gent., who died the 25th June, 1750, in the 67th year of his age.

Also Jane Currer, wife to the above-named Henry Currer, who died the 8th Feb. 1757, aged 63 years. Also Alice Currer, daughter of the above-named Henry and Jane Currer. She died the 4th March, 1803, aged 82 years. Also Jane Currer, daughter of the above Henry and Jane, who died Feb. 25, 1807, aged 88 years. Also the remains of Sarah, the last surviving daughter of the above Henry and Jane Currer, who died 25 May, 1811, aged 85.

Arms—Sable three otters passant in pale argent ; impaling, sable three dolphins embowed in pale argent. *Crest*—A dolphin embowed.

John Birtwhistle, Esq., died Decr. 1, 1786, aged 75. Janet, his wife, died 28 Aug. 1761, aged 38. Their sons Thomas, William, John, Alexander, Richard, Charles, and Robert. Also Elizabeth Swan Guy, wife of Thomas, and to Mary Purdie, wife of Alexander. Erected by John, son of Alexander.

Sacred to the Memory of Matthew Tillotson, of Skipton, Esqr., younger son of Mr. Hugh Tillotson and Dorothy his wife, who was 2nd daughter of Matthew Wilson, of Eshton Hall, and of Ann his wife, the daughter of Francis Blackburn, Esqr., of Morrich Abbey, in this county. He was born May 22nd, 1743 ; died unmarried 8 March, 1815, aged 71.

Arms—Azure two bends sinister (in error) between two garbs all or. *Crest*—A garb or.

In the north aisle is a stained glass window to the memory of John Birtwhistle, of Dundrich and Barharrow, died at Cheltenham Dec. 4, 1869.

Arms—Birtwhistle impaling Birtwhistle. *Crest*—A dolphin embowed. *Motto*—" Serenus in arduis."

The east window of the south aisle is filled with stained glass to the memory of William Marsden, who died on St. Luke's Eve, 1868.

There is a stained glass window in the north aisle to the memory of Martha Maria, relict of the late John Birtwhistle, of Dundrich and Barharrow, died at Cheltenham 14 May, 1872.

Arms—Sable a chevron ermine between three others ; impaling the same.

There are also the following monumental inscriptions :—

Hic Jacet
Gul : Banks A.M.
Qui Scholæ Grammaticalis
de Skipton Magister
Obiit
Die Decembris 11mo
Anno Domini 1730mo
Ætatis suæ 31mo.

———

Near this Place are interred
William Moorhouse M.D. late of Skipton
Who died June 25 A.D. 1813, aged 81 years.
Also
Margaret his wife
Daughter of Henry Currer, Gent. of Skipton
who died Feb. 10, A.D. 1799, aged 68 years
This Monument was erected
by their affectionate Daughter and only surviving child
Jane Backhouse.

———

Captain William Aird Birtwhistle, of the 33nd or Cornwall Regiment of Light Infantry, who died at Kussowlie, in India, 14 Oct. 1856. This tablet was erected by his brother-officers. He was 2nd son of John and Martha Maria Birtwhistle.

———

To Alexander Charles Birtwhistle, Lieut. R.N. of H.M.S. St. George, died 1 June, 1855, eldest son of John Birtwhistle, Esq., D.P. of the Stewardry of Kircudbright, and Martha Maria his wife. He served with distinction throughout the Chinese War and in various parts of the world, and received a medal from the Royal Humane Society for his gallantry in saving the lives of seamen.

———

Christopher Netherwood, Esqr., of Skipton, died 19 April, 1834, aged 75.
Also Ann his wife, daughter of William Baynes, Esqr. She died 18 Dec. 1819, aged 63.
Also their son, John Baynes Netherwood, Esqr., who died 12 Nov. 1830, aged 31.
Arms—...three bars...on a canton a demi savage holding a club, impaling Baynes. *Crest*—A tree in full leaf. *Motto* —" Frappez fort."

———

William Netherwood, of this Town,
Died 9th Dec. 1787, aged 61.

———

Rev. Richard Oglesby,
Curate of this church,
Died 18 Feb. 1840, aged 41 years.

———

Lieut. Joseph Tindal, of the East India Company's Bengal Engineers, 3rd son of William and Ann Tindal, of this place, who after a short but not undistinguished career met the death of a soldier at the memorable siege of Bhurtpore, on the 1st Jan. 1826, in the 23^{d} year of his age.
Near the spot where he fell a monument erected by his brother officers marks his grave.

———

Oglethorpe Wainman, M.D.
Died April 25, 1800, aged 49.
Elizabeth Wainman died 7 Jan. 1820, aged 60.
Eleanor Wainman died 27 Dec. 1825, aged 77.

———

Mr. John Wainman, Surgeon, died Sept. 20, 1794, aged 72.
Elizabeth his wife died Feb. 15, 1794, aged 74
Their son John Wainman, M.D., died at Spalding, co. Lincoln, Dec. 17, 1788, aged 32.
Also their daughters Anne and Mary. The first died an infant ; the latter 3 April, 1793, aged 36.

On a tablet on the south wall of the south chancel aisle—

Arms—Sable on a chevron between three stags' heads erased or, three 5-foils.   On an escutcheon of pretence or six eagles displayed 3, 2, and 1, sa.   *Crest*—A stag's head erased...

In Memory of
Margaret, wife of Robinson Chippendale
of Skipton, Esqr., and only child of the late
William Baxter of Kendal Esqr.
Obiit 2nd April 1817, Æt. 45.

In Memory of George Kendall
of Halton in this Parish.   Died 16 June
1786, aged 68.

William Alcock of Skipton
17 Nov. 1819, aged 72.
Elizabeth his wife died 1 May 1803
aged 45.

Arms—Two shin-bones in cross.   *Crest*—A hand grasping a jaw-bone.

John Baynes died 3 Jan. 1820, aged 64, the only son of William Baynes, Esq., of Steeton Hall, who was eldest son of Ralph Baynes, Esq., of Mewith Head Hall in this county.   This monument was erected by his nephew, William Nettlewood, Esq., who died 2 April, 1868, aged 77.

Mr. John Swire died 20 Nov. 1760, aged 48.

Arms—Or a fess sable in chief three mullets...Impaling.   Per chevron or and sable three mullets counterchanged.   *Crest* —A boar's head.

The Rev^d. Samuel Plomer, A.M., late Fellow of Lincoln College, Oxford, and Master of the Grammar Schools in this town.

Margaret his wife, widow of Edward Dyneley, of Westhall, Esq.   She died 6 Dec. 1779, aged 63.   He died 17 Oct. 1780, aged 58.

Also Robert Dyneley, of Halton, in this parish, son of the said Edward and Margaret Dyneley, who died 3 Aug. 1788, aged 44.

There is a hatchment—

Gu. a fess erm. between three cock's heads erased arg. wattled or, *Alcock* Impaling ; gu. on a chief arg. two mullets sa. *Bacon.   Crest*—A cock.   *Motto*—" Vigilans audax."]

The present church of Skipton is a spacious and respectable building, though of very different periods.   Perhaps no part of the original structure remains ; but four stone seats, with pointed arches and cylindrical columns, now in the south wall of the nave, may perhaps be referred to the earlier part of the thirteenth century.   These, if they have not been removed (of which there is neither tradition nor appearance), will prove, first, that the former church consisted of one, or at most of two, aisles only ; secondly, that the whole choir of three aisles has been added to the original building eastward ; and the appearances of the masonry confirm this supposition.

From the general appearance of this latter work, together with a document which will next be adduced, I am inclined to refer it to the time of Richard III.   For whether it were that this church, in the rage of party zeal against the Cliffords, had felt the vengeance of the Yorkists, or that Richard, after his accession to the throne, retained some affection for the place of his occasional residence in an inferior station, there is extant, among the MSS. of the Heralds' Office, a warrant, under the privy seal of this king, dated Oct. 15, A.R. 2do, directing the payment of 20*l.* to the wardens of the parish of Skipton, for the repair of their parish church.

Yet the roof can scarcely be older than Henry VIII.'s time : it is extremely handsome ;

flat, but with light flying springers, like that of the castle of Hurst Monceaux in Sussex, engraved by Mr. Grose. At the east end are the arms of the priory of Bolton.

The screen, which supported a very ornamental rood-loft, now displaced for the organ-gallery, is inscribed,

Anno D'ni milessimo quingentissimo tricessimo tertio et año regni Regis Henrici octavi UJJJ, vicessimo quinto.*

[The letters were painted white upon a black ground, but when the screen was repaired they were destroyed, and are now covered by new carving inserted in the hollow. The Rev. Canon Boyd some years ago carefully examined the inscription, and found two inaccuracies in Dr. Whitaker's reading, which are here corrected.]

The steeple was nearly beaten down by random balls in battering the castle during the long siege; but Lady Pembroke, who would not " dwell in ceiled houses, and let the House of God lie waste," rebuilt it as it stands at present, and left this inscription on the [north] east pinnacle, "THIS CHURCH & STEEPLE WAS REPAIRED BY YE LADY ANNE CLIFFORD, COUNTESSE DOWAGER OF PEMBROOKE, AN°· DNI. 1655." The windows of the church seem to have been entirely broken at the same time with the destruction of the steeple, and to have been restored by the same benefactress; for the cypher A. P. in a square of painted glass remains in almost every window.†

Beneath the altar, unusually elevated on that account [the chancel floor rises by two steps from the nave, and the altar is six steps higher], is the vault of the Cliffords, the place of their interment from the dissolution of Bolton Priory to the death of the last Earl of Cumberland; which, after having been closed many years, I obtained permission to examine, March 29, 1803. The original vault, intended only for the first earl and his second lady, had undergone two enlargements; and the bodies having been deposited in chronological order, first, and immediately under his tomb, lay Henry the first earl, whose lead coffin was much corroded, and exhibited the skeleton of a short and very stout man, with a long head of flaxen hair gathered in a knot behind the skull. The coffin had been closely fitted to the body, and proved him to have been very corpulent as well as muscular. Next lay the remains of Margaret Percy, his second countess, whose coffin was still entire. She must have been a slender and diminutive woman. The third was "the Lady Ellenor's Grace," whose coffin was much decayed, and exhibited the skeleton (as might be expected in a daughter of Charles Brandon and the sister of Henry VIII.) of a tall and large-limbed female. At her right hand was Henry, the second earl, a very tall and slender man, whose thin envelope of lead really resembled a winding sheet, and folded, like coarse

---

* The decorations of Popery had attained to their greatest height but a little time before their fall. Almost all the rich and gilded rood-lofts with which I am acquainted were of this period. They are generally known by carved work, consisting of fantastic bodies of animals, and a running pattern of vines laden with grapes. In the year 1520 was erected in Great St. Mary's Church, Cambridge, a gorgeous rood-loft, with a profusion of gilding, which was styled "Theatrum imaginis Crucifixi."—Strype's " Life of Archbishop Parker," p. 5.

[† " In the summer 1655, whilst there she was at Appleby Castle at her own charge, she caus'd the steeple of Skipton Church to be built up again, which was pulled down in the time of the late warrs, and leaded it over, and then repaired some part of the church, and now glaz'd the windows, in every of which window she put quaries stain'd with a yellow colour, these two letters, viz., ◈ ◈, and under them the year 1655, most of which quaries still remains. Besides she raised up a noble tomb of Black Marble in memory of her warlike Father."—MS. Life of Anne Countess of Pembroke, written by herself, now in Skipton Evidences.]

drapery, over the limbs.   The head was beaten to the left side ; something of the shape of the face might be distinguished, and a long prominent nose was very conspicuous.   Next lay Francis Lord Clifford, a boy.   At his right hand was his father, George, the third earl, whose lead coffin precisely resembled the outer case of an Egyptian mummy, with a rude face, and something like female mammæ cast upon it ; as were also the figures and letters G. C. 1605.   The body was closely wrapped in ten folds of coarse cerecloth, which being removed, exhibited the face so entire (only turned to copper colour) as plainly to resemble his portraits.   All his painters, however, had the complaisance to omit three large warts upon the left cheek.   The coffin of Earl Francis, who lay next to his brother, was of the modern shape, and alone had had an outer shell of wood, which was covered with leather ; the soldering had decayed, and nothing appeared but the ordinary skeleton of a tall man. This earl had never been embalmed.*   Over him lay another coffin, much decayed, which, I suspect, had contained the Lady Anne Dacre, his mother.   Last lay Henry, the fifth earl, in a coffin † of the same form with that of his father.   Lead not allowing of absorption, or a narrow vault of much evaporation, a good deal of moisture remained in the coffin, and some hair about the skull.   Both these coffins had been cut open.

Room might have been found for another slender body ; but the Countess of Pembroke chose to be buried at Appleby ; partly, perhaps, because her beloved mother was interred there, and partly that she might not mingle her ashes with rivals and enemies.

It is curious to contrast with these humiliating relics of departed greatness the pomp of heraldry, and the pride of genealogy, which are displayed above.   First, and immediately over their remains, is a grey marble tomb of Henry, the first earl, and Margaret Percy, his wife   On the slab are grooves for two figures ; from the outline of which I suspect the figure of the earl to have been in the Garter robes.   There are also inlets for four shields of arms within the Garter.   All these brasses were stolen in the civil wars [they have all been restored by the Duke of Devonshire ; the state of the tomb is as described upon the next page] ; but the epitaphs had been transcribed in the year 1619, and were afterwards copied by Dugdale into his " Visitation Book " for the year 1665.‡

Skipton in Craven ⎱   In Ecclesiâ de Skipton in Craven,
  9 Aprilis, 1619. ⎰   circa tumulum marmoreum ibidem :

Margret hic dormit Perceiis edita, conjux
Henrici Comitis Cumbria clara, tui,
Quo Domino Clesey, quo Westmarlandia gaudet
Cui Skipton decus et Garthricus ordo ferunt ;
Praeripit hunc sponso tumulum, sed corpus ut unum
Idem sic lectus, sic locus unus habet.
Die mensis Novembris XXC A. Christi §
Millessimo quingentissimo quadragessimo.

* Countess of Pembroke's Memoirs, MS.

† I suspect that these two coffins had not been placed in order of time ; for the last earl is known to have been a tall man.

‡ MS. entitled Yorkshire Arms, by William Dugdale, Norroy, fol. 57, &c.

§ The priory of Bolton was surrendered January 29, this year.   The comparison of the two dates will show how immediately the choir of Bolton, where the old vault of the Cliffords was, had been desecrated after the surrender.   The interval was not quite ten months.

The Tomb of George third Earl of Cumberland, at Skipton.

The Tomb of Henry first Earl of Cumberland, at Skipton.

To this Dugdale has added the following note :—

" Inter cancellum et alam borealem extat tumulus marmoreus, super quem figuræ Henrici primi comitis Cumbriæ ac uxoris suæ, cum quatuor scutis insignium Garteriatis, ac etiam epitaphium ejus in laminis æreis affixæ erant : sæviente vero fanaticorum rabie nuperrimâ, extortæ et ablatæ. In memoriam eorum nobilissima domina Anna modo Comitissa Pembrochiæ hanc inscriptionem ad pedes ejusdem tumuli in marmore nigro apponi curavit."

HERE LYES, EXPECTING ẙ SECOND CO'MING OF OUR LORD & SAVIOUR JESUS CHRIST, ẙ
BODY OF HENRY CLIFFORD, FIRST EARLE OF CUMBERLAND OF YT FAMILY, & KT OF ẙ MOST
NOBLE ORDER OF ẙ GARTER : WHO, BY RIGHT OF INHERITANCE FROM A LONGE CONTINWED
DESCENT OF AVNCESTORS, WAS LORD VETERIPONT, BARON CLIFFORD, WESTMORELAND, & VESCY,
LORD OF Y HONOUR OF SKIPTON IN CRAVEN, & HEREDITARY HIGH SHIREFFE OF THE COUNTY OF WESTMORLAND.
HE HAD BY HIS SECOND WIFE LADY MARGARETT PERCY, DAUGHT'R TO ẙ EARLE OF NOR-
THUMBERLAND, TWO SONNES & THREE DAUGHTERS : HIS ELDEST SONNE SUCCEEDED HIM
IN ẙ EARLDOME ; & HIS ELDEST DAUGHTER WAS FIRST MARRYED TO JOHN LORD
SCROOPE, & SECONDLY TO SR RICHARD CHOLMELEY, FROM WHOM SIR HUGH & SIR
HENRY CHOLMELEY, NOW LIVING, ARE DESCENDED.[*]
THIS NOBLE EARLE DYED IN SKIPTON CASTLE THE 22TH DAY OF APRILL, 1542.[†]
AND HERE LYES ALSOE INTERRED IN THIS VAULT THIS EARLES ELDEST SONNE HENRY
CLIFFORD,[‡] SECOND EARLE OF CUMBERLAND, & HIS FIRST WIFE THE LADY
ELEANOR BRANDON'S GRACE,[§] BY WHOM HE HAD ONE ONELY DAUGHTER THAT
LIVED, ẙ LADY MARGARET CLIFFORD, AFTERWARDS COUNTESSE OF DARBY ;
AND BY HIS SECOND WIFE ANNE DACRES (WHO ALSO LYES HERE IN-
TERRED),‖ HE HAD HIS 2 SONNES, GEORGE & FRANCIS, SUCCESSIVE
EARLES OF CUMBERLAND AFTER HIM ; & LADY FRANCES CLIFFORD, WIFE
TO PHILIP LORD WHARTON, & GRANDMOTHER TO PHILIP LORD WHARTON, NOW LIVING.
HE WAS ALSO BY DESCENT LORD VETERIPONT, BARON CLIFFORD, WESTMORLAND AND VESCY,
LORD OF ẙ HONOR OF SKIPTON IN CRAVEN, AND HÆREDITARY HIGH SHEREFFE
OF ẙ COUNTY OF WESTMORLAND, & DIED IN BROUGHAM CASTLE, IN THAT
COUNTY, ẙ 8TH DAY OF JANUARY, IN ẙ YEARE OF OUR LORD GOD 1570.

On the north side of the chancel is the tomb of Henry Clifford, first Earl of Cumberland, and his wife—a slab of black marble, supported by a high tomb of Purbeck marble, richly panelled and ornamented with brass shields of arms, each within the Garter.

Inscription round the edge of the slab—

𝔒f pour charite pray for the soule of 𝔖ir henry 𝔠lifford 𝕶npght of the most noble order of the 𝔊arter 𝔢arle of 𝔠umberland sumtyme 𝔊ouernor of the town and castle of 𝔠arlisle and 𝔓resident of the 𝕶ing's 𝔠ouncil in the 𝔑orth also of 𝔣argaret his wyfe daughter of 𝔖ir henry 𝔓ercy 𝕶npght 𝔢arle of 𝔑orthumberland whyche 𝔖ir henry departed thys lyfe the rrii dape of 𝔄pril in the pere of our lorde 𝔊od 𝔐𝔠𝔠𝔠𝔠𝔠𝕃𝔍𝔍 on whose soules 𝔍esu haue mercy 𝔄men.

---

* Why was Lady Elizabeth, wife of Sir Christopher Metcalf of Nappy, omitted ?

† He was interred May 2.—Londesborough Papers.

‡ By his last will, dated May 8, 1569, Henry Earl of Cumberland, then not healthful in bodye, gives his soul to Almighty God and our Ladie St. Marie and all the heavenlie companye, and his body to be buried on the north side of the church of Skipton in one place ther prepared for the same.

Are we to conclude from his mention of the Virgin Mary, &c. that he was a Catholic ? I think not.

§ She was buried Nov. 27, 1547.—Londsborough Papers.

‖ July 3, 1581, died at Skipton Castle, the Lady Anne (mother to G.) Countesse of Cumberland, and was buried at the church of Skipton the 1st day of August.—*Ibid.*

The second son was Sir Ingram Clifford, who, marrying the heiress of Rocliffe (not Ratcliffe, as Dugdale calls him), was interred in the church of Cowthorp, com. Ebor. with this Sternholdian epitaph :—

Since growsome[1] grave of force must have	You Gentiles all, no more let fall
Sir Ingram Clifford, knight ;	Your tears from blubbered eye,
And age by kind were[2] out of mind	But praye the Lord, with one accord,
Each worthy living wight ;	That rules above the skye :
And since man must return to dust	For Christ hath wrought, and dearly bought,
By course of his creation,	The price of his redemption ;
As doctors sage in every age	And therefore we, no doubt, shall see
To us have made relation :	His joyful resurrection.

---

[1] *Growsome*, which I have nowhere else met with, probably signifies frightful, from the old Scotch word *grue*, to thrill.

[2] *Were, i.e.,* wear.

Upon the slab are the effigies in brass of the earl and his wife.   He is clad in armour, having cuirass, skirt of mail and tuiles, pauldrons, vambraces and rerebraces, but the hands are bare ; his legs are encased in plate armour, and he wears broad-toed sabatons.   Round his left leg is the Garter ; his head is bare, and rests upon a tilting helmet, having his crest a wyvern sejant.   He is armed with a sword and dagger, and his feet rest upon a greyhound. Round his neck is a chain, from which is suspended a cross.

The Countess reposes with her head upon a handsome pillow.   She wears a gown, and over it a mantle charged with the arms of Clifford, Percy and Lucy quarterly, Bromflete, Old Percy, Vesci and Poynings.   The mantle is fastened at the neck by a long cord passed through a ball at the waist, and terminating in two tassels near the feet, which rest upon a dog.   She wears a flat head-dress and a coronet.

Over the head of Sir Henry is a shield with the arms of Clifford ; over his wife's head the arms of Old Percy— azure 5 fusils in fess or ; beneath his feet Clifford impaling Old Percy, and beneath her feet Clifford only.   The shields are all within the Garter.   Round the sides of the tomb are the following shields, beginning at the north-east corner :—1. Quarterly of eight, four and four, 1, Clifford ; 2, Augmentation ; 3, Bromflete ; 4, Vesci ; 5, az. 3 roses ; 6, Vipont ; 7, Atton ; and 8, St. John of Bletsoe.   Next follows a roundle with 𝕴𝖍𝕮.   2. Clifford impaling Old Percy ; then a roundle with 𝕸'𝕮𝖄.   3. Same as 1.   4. At west end, Clifford quartering Augmentation, &c., as shield 1 ; and impaling Percy quartering Lucy, Old Percy, Poynings, Strange, and Bryan.   On the south side, 5 same as 1. 6. Clifford impaling Old Percy : and 7, same as 1.   The two roundles as above described also occur on either side of number 6.

Upon a stone standing vertically upon the slab, and at the head of it, are brasses of 3 sons kneeling in tabards, two of them charged with the arms of Clifford differenced with an annulet and the third having the arms of Clifford impaling Dacre.   Over their heads is a scroll inscribed—

𝕾'𝖈𝖙𝖆 𝖙𝖗𝖎𝖓𝖎𝖙𝖆𝖘 𝖚𝖓̃ 𝕯𝖊𝖚𝖘 𝖒𝖎𝖘𝖊𝖗𝖊𝖗𝖊 𝖓𝖔𝖇̃.

To the right are four daughters also kneeling ; two are in mantles, the first charged with Clifford impaling Dacre, the second with Clifford only ; the two others are in plain gowns.   All wear head-dresses, such as Mary Queen of Scots is usually represented in.

Over their heads is a scroll—

𝕻𝖆𝖙𝖊𝖗 𝖉𝖊 𝖈𝖊𝖑𝖎𝖘 𝖉𝖊' 𝖒𝖎𝖘𝖊𝖗𝖊𝖗𝖊 𝖓𝖔𝖇̃.

Above the figures in the centre of the slab is a representation of the Trinity, and at the corners are the emblems of the Evangelists.

Beneath the figures is this inscription—

𝕳𝖊𝖗𝖊 𝖑𝖎𝖊𝖙𝖍 𝕾𝖎𝖗 𝕳𝖊𝖓𝖗𝖞 𝕮𝖑𝖎𝖋𝖋𝖔𝖗𝖉 𝕶𝖓𝖞𝖌𝖍𝖙 𝕰𝖆𝖗𝖑𝖊 𝖔𝖋 𝕮𝖚𝖒𝖇𝖊𝖗𝖑𝖆𝖓𝖉 𝖆𝖓𝖉 𝕬𝖓𝖓𝖊 𝖍𝖞𝖘 𝖜𝖞𝖋𝖋𝖊 𝖉𝖆𝖚𝖌𝖍𝖙𝖊𝖗 𝖔𝖋 𝖂𝖎𝖑𝖑𝖎𝖆𝖒 𝕷𝖔𝖗𝖉 𝕯𝖆𝖈𝖗𝖊 𝖔𝖋 𝕲𝖎𝖑𝖑𝖊𝖘𝖑𝖆𝖓𝖉 𝖜𝖍𝖎𝖈𝖍 𝕾𝖎𝖗 𝕳𝖊𝖓𝖗𝖞 𝖉𝖊𝖕𝖆𝖗𝖙𝖊𝖉 𝖙𝖍𝖎𝖘 𝖑𝖎𝖋𝖊 𝖙𝖍𝖊 𝖊𝖎𝖌𝖍𝖙𝖍 𝖉𝖆𝖞𝖊 𝖔𝖋 𝕵𝖆𝖓𝖚𝖆𝖗𝖎𝖊 𝖎𝖓 𝖙𝖍𝖊 𝖞𝖊𝖗𝖊 𝖔𝖋 𝖔𝖚𝖗 𝖑𝖔𝖗𝖉 𝕲𝖔𝖉 𝕸𝕮𝕮𝕮𝕮𝕮𝕷𝖄𝖄.

Formerly this slab was concealed by the tablet containing the inscription now fixed in the east wall of the chancel, but in 1844 it fell down, and exposed the original slab with the matrices of the brasses above described. The figure of the Trinity and that of the youngest son were afterwards found in pulling down an old farm-house at Thorlby, near Skipton, and are replaced ; the other pieces are modern restorations.

At the head of the last is a small altar tomb, originally inscribed thus :—

3 D

Here lyeth the body of Francis late lord Clifford, eldest son of the most puissant lord George earle of Cumberland, lord of the honour of Skipton in Craven, lord Clifford, lord Westmerland and Vesey; which child departed from this life the viiith of December, 1588, being of the age of six yeares and eight months. An infant of most rare towardnesse in all thappearances that might promise wisdome and magnanimity.

Qui veniet fructus flos foliumque notant
Stemmate nobilior,
Henrici mentis nituit dum candor in isto *
Vivida quo potuit scandere virtus erat,
Hunc raptim e terris fata invidiosa tulere,
Anglia, spondentem magnaque fausta tibi.
Dicite mortales quae sit spes carnis et inde
Reddere, quod dignum est, optima quaeque Deo.

This also having been stolen away, was replaced by the following inscription [on a brass plate], now remaining :—

HERE LYES, (EXPECTING ✝ SECOND COMEING OF OUR LORD AND SAVIOUR JESUS CHRIST), THE DEAD BODY OF FRANCIS LORD CLIFFORD, FIRST CHILD TO GEORGE CLIFFORD THIRD EARLE OF CUMBERLAND, BY HIS BLESSED WIFE MARGARET RUSSELL COUNTESSE OF CUMBERLAND; WHICH FRANCIS LORD CLIFFORD DIED (WHERE HE WAS BORNE) IN SKIPTON CASTLE ✝ IN CRAVEN, ABOUT THE ELEAVENTH OF DECEMBER, IN 1589, BEING OF ✝ AGE OF 5 YEARES AND 8 MONTHES. ‡

MORS. LUCRUM.
BEATI QUI MORIUNTUR IN DNO.

[Upon the small high tomb, at the head of that of Henry Clifford, first Earl of Cumberland, is a slab, with a plain plate of brass, probably for an inscription to George Clifford, third Earl of Cumberland, and his wife Lady Margaret Russell, the father and mother of Francis Lord Clifford); above it are two shields.—1. Quarterly of eight, Clifford with an annulet for difference, Augmentation, Bromflete, Vesci,......3 roses......, Vipont, Atton, and St. John. 2. Quarterly of eight, Russell, De la Tour, barry of eight......Heringham, Froxmore, Wyse, Sapcote, and......on a cross five mullets. Beneath this plate is a shield of the arms of Clifford, with quartering as numbered. The shields 1 and 2 were found in pulling down an old house at Thorlby, near Skipton.]

At the south side of the communion-table is another stately tomb of black marble, enclosed with iron rails [now removed], and erected by the good countess to the memory of her father. At the feet, upon a perpendicular slab, affixed to the wall [now fixed to the east wall near the reredos], is this inscription :—

HERE LYES, EXPECTING THE SECOND COMMING OF OUR LORD AND SAVIOUR JESUS
CHRIST, THE BODY OF GEORGE CLIFFORD, THIRD EARLE OF CUMBERLAND, OF THAT
FAMILY, AND KNIGHT OF THE MOST NOBLE ORDER OF THE GARTER, WHO, BY RIGHT OF
INHERITANCE FROM A LONG CONTINUED DESCENT OF ANCESTORS, WAS LORD VETERIPONT,
BARON CLIFFORD, WESTMERLAND AND VESCIE, LORD OF THE HONOUR OF SKIPTON IN
CRAVEN, & HEREDITARY HIGH SHIREFFE OF WESTMERLAND, AND WAS THE LAST HEIRE
MALE OF THE CLIFFORDS THAT RIGHTFULLY ENJOYED THOSE ANCIENT LANDS OF
INHERITANCE IN WESTMERLAND AND IN CRAVEN, WITH THE BARONIES
AND HONOURS APPERTAININGE TO THEM ;
FOR HE LEFTE BUT ONE LEGITIMATE CHILDE BEHINDE HIM, HIS DAUGHTER & SOLE HEYRE,
THE LADY ANNE CLIFFORD, NOW COUNTESSE DOWAGER OF PEMBROKE, DORSETT, AND
MONTGOMERYE, WHO, IN MEMORY OF HER FATHER, ERECTED THIS MONUMENT IN 1654.
THIS NOBLE GEORGE EARLE OF CUMBERLANDE WAS BORNE IN BROUGHAM CASTLE, IN
WESTMERLAND, THE EIGHTH DAY OF AUGUST, IN THE YEARE 1558; AND DIED
PENITENTLY, IN THE DUTCHY HOUSE BY THE SAVOY, ATT LONDON, THE 30TH DAY OF

---

* Alluding to the amiable character of the second earl.
† He died at Carlton Lodge, or Newbiggin.—Londesborough Papers.
‡ On the authority of the elder epitaph, *six* years.

OCTOBER, 1605, & WAS BURYED IN THE VAULT HERE THE 13TH DAY OF MARCH FOLLOWING.*
HEE WAS THE 17TH OF HIS BLOOD HEREDITARY HIGH SHIRIFFE OF WESTMERLAND, AND
13TH OF HIS BLOOD THAT WAS LORD OF THE HONOR OF SKIPTON IN CRAVEN, AND WAS
ONE OF THE NOBLEST PERSONAGES OF ENGLAND IN HIS TYME, HAVINGE UNDERTAKEN
MANY SEA VOYAGES AT HIS OWN CHARGE, FOR YE GOOD & HONOR OF HIS COUNTREY.
HE MARRYED THE BLESSED AND VIRTUOUS LADY THE LADY MARGARET RUSSELL,
YOUNGEST DAUGHTER TO FRANCIS RUSSELL, SECOND EARLE OF BEDFORD OF THAT
NAME, BY WHOME HE HAD TWO SONNES THAT DYED YOUNGE IN HIS LIFE-TYME, & ONE ONELY DAUGHTER, ABOVE
NAMED, THAT LIVED TO BEE HIS HEIRE;
WHICH LADY MARGARETT HIS WIFE (THEN COUNTESSE DOWAGER OF CUMBERLAND), DYED IN
BROUGHAM CASTLE, THE 24TH DAY OF MAY, 1616, AND LYES BURYED IN APPLEBY CHURCH.

Round the sides of this tomb are the following shields :—1. Clifford and Russell within the Garter, an earl's coronet above. 2. Clifford between Brandon and Dacre. 3. Clifford and Percy within the Garter, a coronet above. 4. Veteripont and Buly. 5. Veteripont and Ferrers. 6. Veteripont and FitzPeirs. 7. Clifford and Veteripont. 8. Clifford and Clare. 9. Quarterly, Clifford and Veteripont. 10. Clifford and Beauchamp. 11. Clifford and Roos. 12. Clifford and Percy, within the Garter. 13. Clifford and Dacre. 14. Clifford and Bromflet (de Vesci). 15. Clifford and St. John of Bletsho. 16. Clifford and Berkley. 17. Clifford and Nevill.†

I much doubt whether such an assemblage of noble bearings can be found on the tomb of any other Englishman.

The last epitaph belonging to this great family is conceived in much fewer words and better taste than any of the foregoing [it is on a tablet fixed to the north wall of the nave] :—

---

* It appears from the parish register that his obsequies were indeed celebrated on that day, but that the body had been interred some time before.

" 1605. Oct. the 29th, departed this lyf George earle of Cumbreland, lord Clifford, Vipounte, and Vessie, lord of the honor of Skipton in Craven, knyghte of the most noble order of the Garter, and one of his highnesses privie councell, lord warden of the citie of Carlell and the West Marches; and was honorably buried at Skipton, the XXIXth of December, and his funeral was solemnized the XIIIth day of March then next following."

[† These shields are as follow :—

On the slab at foot of the tomb :—In the centre, surmounted by an earl's coronet, Clifford quartering Vipont; on the dexter, barry of ten, arg. and gu., a lion ramp. or, crowned per pale, of the first and second; on the sinister, gu. three escallops arg. For Henry Clifford, second Earl of Cumberland, who died in 1570, and his wives—Eleanor, daughter of Charles Brandon, Duke of Suffolk, and Anne, daughter of William Lord Dacre, of Gillesland.

On the left, surmounted by an earl's coronet, and placed within the Garter :—Clifford quartering Vipont, and impaling, quarterly 1 and 4, or a lion ramp. az., Percy; 2 and 3, gu., three lucies arg., Lucy. For Henry Clifford, first Earl of Cumberland, and Margaret Percy, his second wife.

On the right, also surmounted by an earl's coronet, and placed within the Garter :—Clifford quartering Vipont, and impaling or a lion ramp. gu., on a chief sa. three escallops arg. For George Clifford, third Earl of Cumberland, and his wife, Margaret Russell, daughter of Francis, second Earl of Bedford.

On the sides of the tomb, beginning at the north-east corner, are :—1. Gu. six annulets or, Vipont, impaling gu. a cinquefoil or, Busly. (This is in error; the arms should be gu. a besant.) 2. Vipont impaling arg. six horseshoes sa., Ferrers. 3. Vipont impaling quarterly or and gu. a bordure vair, Fitz-John. 4. Chequy or and az. a fess gu., Clifford impaling Vipont. 5. Clifford quartering Vipont, and impaling or three chevrons gu., a crescent for diff., Clare. 6. Clifford quartering Vipont.

At the west end :— 1. Clifford quartering Vipont, and impaling gu. a chevron between ten crosses patty arg., Berkeley. 2. Clifford quartering Vipont, and impaling gu. a saltire arg., Neville.

On the south side :—1. Clifford quartering Vipont, and impaling gu. a fess between six crosses crosslet or, Beauchamp. 2. Clifford quartering Vipont, and impaling gu. three water bougets arg., Ros. 3. Within the Garter, Clifford quartering Vipont, and impaling Percy and Lucy. 4. Clifford quartering Vipont, and impaling gu. three escallops arg., Dacre. 5. Clifford quartering Vipont, and impaling or a cross sa., Vescy. 6. Clifford quartering Vipont, and impaling arg. a bend gu., on a chief dancetty of the second, two mullets or, St. John. (The bend is an error.)]

IMMENSI DOLORIS MONUMENTUM ANGUSTUM HENRICUS PATER

DEFLET

FRANCISCUM,

CAROLUM &

HENRICUM,

A. D. MDCXXXI.*

CIƆ : IƆCXXXI.

These were the sons of the last earl, all of whom died in their infancy.　By cutting off five heirs male in the compass of two generations, Providence seems to have decreed the extinction of the name of Clifford.

In a ground room at the west end of the church is a library, the history of which, and of its worthy founder, is thus related in an inscription over the door :—

"Sylvester Petyt, Gentleman, who was born at Storithes, in this Parish, was some time Principal of Barnard's Inn in London, and still a worthy Member of ye said Society, and a Munificent Founder of this valuable Library.　This Monument is in token of humble gratitude, 1719." †

---

* "Charles Clifforde, sonne of the Right Hon'ble Henry Lord Clifforde, died at Londesborough, 19th Feb. 1621, and was interred in the tombe at Skipton one and twentieth of the same.

"Henric, the sonne of the Right Hon'ble Henry lord Clifford, dyed at Londesborough, 30, and was interred in the tomb at Skipton 31st　1622."—Reg. Par. Skipton.

Why or how the bodies of these two children, especially the last, should be conveyed sixty miles for interment in so short a time it is not easy to conceive.　Their coffins are still in the vault.　Francis does not appear to have been interred at Skipton.

"1620, Aug. 10.　Baptised Charles, the sonne of the Right Hon. Henrie lord Clifford, of Skipton Castle."—Reg. *ibid.*

The baptism of Elizabeth, afterwards Countess of Cork, and heiress of this branch of the family, is thus ignorantly recorded :—

"1612, Oct. 7th.　Elizabethe Clifford, d'r to the Rt. Hon. Henrie lorde Clifforde, was born in Skipton Castle, the 18th day of Sept. 1613, the seaventh day of October ; the lord Thomas Haworth, erle of Sussex, being godfather, the Lord Philip Wharton his deputie ; the countess of Darbie and the ladie Wotton godmothers, their deputies the ladie Marg't Wentworth and her sister the ladie Frances Clifforde."

[† Sylvester Petyt also left the munificent legacy of 24,048*l.* South Sea Annuities, the surplus of which, after paying 20*l.* a year to Christ College, Cambridge, small salaries to a schoolmaster and librarian at Skipton, and the expense of apprenticing fourteen poor children of the county of York, was directed to be appropriated to the relief of objects requiring immediate assistance, wherever resident.　His brother, William Petyt, Esq., gave 200*l.* for the support of two poor scholars at Christ Church, Cambridge.

This brother, William Petyt, of the Inner Temple, was Keeper of the Records in the Tower.　Stow (in his "Survey of London," book i. p. 115, ed. 1720) states, "He was a strong asserter of the Liberties of England, and how well he acquitted himself therein his Books printed against Dr. Brady do shew."　He died at Chelsea, and left a large library of manuscripts and books to the Inner Temple ; and his brother Sylvester set up a monument to his memory in the Temple Church, where he is buried.

The inscription is—

Heic juxta sita sunt Reliquiæ.

WILHELMI PETYT . Armig.　Qui olim Medii Alumnus fuit, nuper Interioris Templi Socius, & Thesaurarius Rotulorum ac Archivorum, in Turri Londinensi remanentium, Custos fidelissimus, quamplurimis tam Genere quam Doctrina viris insiquibus benè notus & in magna æstimatione habitus.　Omnia sua cum amicis habuit communia.　Neq; sane cuiquam Literarum veterum Studioso, vel operam suam vel consilium unquam negabat; quod in pluribus Euruditorum Scriptis apparet.

Municipalis Patris jura, Historica & Antiquitates, Monumenta Actaq. ; Parliamentaria optime callebat : Antiquæ Constitutionis, Legum ac Libertatum Angliæ strenuissimus assertor erat.　Et ne operam & oleum perderet, & evanescerent Labores, mundo valedicturus omnia sua MSS. (quæ varia implent Volumina) una cum libris impressis, Juridicis, Historicis, atq.　Antiquitatum & Processuum Parliamentorum Monumentis (quæ magno labore, studio & sumptibus sibi comparavit) amicis quibusdam melioris Notæ, in fidei commisso ad servanda integra & illibita, ultimo suo Testamento publicæ Utilitatis gratia, legavit.　Qua propter locum certum, qui illis visus fuerit maximè accommodatus, eos eligere voluit.　Et centum & quinquaginta libras Bibliothecæ ædificandæ destinavit.

In *Storithes* prope Abbatiam de *Bolton*, non eta longe a vico de *Skipton* in *Craven* in Comitat. *Eborum*, natus fuit.　Ad plures abiit apud *Chelseam*, in Agro *Middlesex* 3º die *Octobris*.　Anno Domini MDCCVII. ætat suæ LXXII.

Neq; dum vixit ipsius *Chelsæ* immemor fuit, sed erigebat ibi Œdificium, quod eidem Parochiæ alacri & libera manu dedit.　In se complectens (quod dicitus) Vestiarium, in usum Parochianovum, Gymnacium ad pueros erudiendos, & Cameras Præceptori Satis Commodas.

Monumentum hoc *Sylvester Petyt*, de Hospitio *Bernardiensi*, Gen. & ejusdem olim Principalis ad memoriam charissimi sui Fratris, posuit.

William Petyt published the following works :—"The Ancient Right of the Commons of England asserted," 8vo,

[In the vestry is his portrait, with shield of arms (arg. a lion ramp. gu., on a canton ...... a pheon ......, a crescent for diff.), and an inscription giving the date of his death— 1 October, 1712.]

[A new church (Christchurch) was built and consecrated on the 25th of September, 1839, and a district parish was assigned to it by Order of Council dated July, 1840. It is a vicarage, in the patronage of the Rector of Skipton. The incumbents have been—

23 June, 1840.	*Richard Ward.*
11 Apr. 1846.	*John Blau*, M.A.
26 Nov. 1849.	*Wright Willett.*
24 June, 1862.	*William Henry Clarke.*]

TOWN OF SKIPTON.

SKIPTON has long enjoyed the benefit of a well-endowed grammar school, founded in the second year of Edward VI. [1548] by William Ermestead, Canon Residentiary of St. Paul's [London, and Chaplain to Queen Mary], who vested for this purpose in Sir Ingram Clifford, Knight, William Tankard, Stephen Tempest, Esquires, Tristram Bolling, Lancelot Marton, Thomas Lister of Westby, Gentlemen, and others, divers lands in Addingham, Skipton, and Eastby; the whole rental of which then amounted to no more than 9*l.* 15*s.* 4*d.*, the average rate per oxgang being 6*s.* The extended value at present is understood to be 400*l. per annum* [now (1877) more than 800*l. per annum;* new buildings, costing about 12,000*l.*, are in course of erection].

By the charter of foundation, the appointment of a master is vested in the vicar and churchwardens of Skipton for the time being; and if within one calendar month from the avoidance these electors neglect to appoint *unum habilem et idoneum capellanum*, the right

London, 1680; "Miscellanea Parliamentaria," 8vo, London, 1681; "Jus Parliamentarium; or, the Ancient Power, Jurisdiction, Rights, and Liberties of the Most High Court of Parliament revived and asserted," folio, London, 1739.

"He beareth *argent* a lyon rampant *gules* in the dexter chief a Pheon *sable*, by the Name of *Petyt.* This is the Coat Armour of *Petyt* of *Cornwall*, as also of *Yorkshire*, from whom is descended *William Petyt* of the Middle Temple, Esq., whose ancestor was William Petyt, Esq., Lord of the Mannor of *Sharlesteane*, and diverse other Lands in *Oteley* near *Whearf* in *Yorkshire*, who, in the 13th Year of Henry the Sixth (with *J. Cardinal* and Archbishop of *York, Richard* Duke of *York* and others) was *Justiciarius Regis ad pacem in partibus de Westrithingo in Com. Ebor. &c.* and younger son of *Sir John Petyt*, Lord *Ardover* in *Cornwall;* which Sir *John* married *Margaret* daughter and coheir of *Thomas Carnino*, Grandson to Sir *Oliver Carnino*, Kt., Chamberlain to King *Edward* the Second, who married *Elizabeth* sister to *Thomas Holland* Earl of *Kent* and Duke of *Surry*, who dy'd the 10th Year of Henry the Sixth, descended from an ancient Family of *Petyts*, Lords of *Ardover* in the time of *Henry* the First. Of which Family there have been six Knights, all which appears by the Descent and Pedigree of that Family; and by several inquisitions *post mortem.*"—Guillim's "Display of Heraldry," ed. 1724, p. 334.

George Holmes, a very learned antiquary, was born at Skipton. He republished the first seventeen volumes of Rymer's "Fœdera" in 1727–28.

At Skipton was also born Nathaniel Simpson, Scholar and Fellow of Trinity College, Oxford. He was a good mathematician, and compiled for the use of the Juniors of his College a book called "Arithmeticæ Compendium;" this he afterwards enlarged. It was printed in 1622. He died the same day that Edge Hill fight happened, in Oct. 1642, and was buried in Trinity College Chapel.—Cox's "Magna Britannia," p. 422.

Some instances of persons living to a very advanced age have occurred in Skipton. In 1670 a man named Robert Montgomery was living here, but born in Scotland; he declared to Dr. Lister that he was 126 years old: which to confirm the doctor inquired of his neighbours, and found that the oldest man in Skipton never knew him any other than an old man. He went up and down at that time a begging. Mary Allison, of Thorlby, died in 1668, aged 108. She spun a web of linen-cloth a year or two before she died.—Cox's "Magna Britannia," p. 423.]

of nomination devolves upon the Rector and Fellows of Lincoln College, Oxford (the rector mentioned is Dr. Weston, well known for the odious part he bore in the deaths of Cranmer, Ridley, and Latimer); and in case of a similar neglect for the same space of time on their part, the right next devolves on the Dean and Chapter of St. Paul's, London; and lastly, if, after notice given of such omission on the part of Lincoln College, the said dean and chapter shall also defer to nominate for one calendar month, the power of appointing, after this long tour, completes the circle, and returns to the vicar and churchwardens.

With respect to the master's duty, he is required to explain to the scholars Virgil, Terence, Ovid, and the other Latin poets (without any mention of historians and orators in that language, or any authors in Greek); and to teach them to compose epistles, orations, and verses.

The devotions of the school, as might be expected from the state of religion at that time, are a mixture of Popery and Protestantism. In the morning is appointed to be said the Psalm, *Miserere mei Deus,* with a prayer for the King and the Archbishop, and the Collect, *O Deus, Protector, in te sperantium;* and in the evening, *Antiphona Beatæ Mariæ Virginis.*

The master is further required to attend in the choir of the parish church on all Sundays and festivals, and when service is performed by Pricksong, unless hindered by some reasonable cause, to celebrate, before seven in the morning, on such days, and three other days in the week. Likewise, that the said chaplain shall be vested in a surplice, to sing or read, as shall seem meet to the vicar.

This instrument bears date Sept. 1, 1548, or 2 Edw. VI.; and it accords exactly with the state of the national worship at that time. Images had then been removed out of churches, and the new Communion Book * introduced; but, with this exception, the rest of the Popish service was sung as usual in the choir. The first Liturgy of Edward VI. was not published till the 16th of June following.

Skipton, the capital and mart of Craven, had anciently, and by prescription, the following fairs and markets—viz., a market *die Sabbati, i.e.,* every Saturday; and two fairs, one on the feast of St. Martin, the other of St. John in winter. Also on the eve of Palm Sunday, on Monday in Whitsun-week, and on St. Luke's Day.

But, besides these, a charter was obtained by George Earl of Cumberland, a° 38 Elizabeth, for a fair to be held every second Wednesday from Easter to Christmas, of which the following is an abstract :—

" Elizabeth, D. G. Cum dilecti subditi nostri inhabitantes burgi de Skipton in Craven, nobis humiliter supplicaverunt quatenus unam feriam in Burgo de Skipton in die Martis qualibet secundâ septimanâ inter festum Pasche et festum natalis D'ni concedere dignaremur : Cumque informamur ex relatione reverendissimi patris Matthæi arch. Ebor. quod dicte ferie nullo modo prejudiciales erunt aliis vicinis feriis, sed valdè utiles commorantibus infra XL M. P. prope burgum pred' pro empc'o'e, vend', et expos' equorum, vaccarum, juvencorum, ovium, &c. Sciatis igitur quod nos licentiam dedimus dilecto et fideli consanguineo n'ro Georgio com. Cumbr. quod habeant, teneant, &c. fer' p'dict. Dat. XXIV d'e Maii, A. R. XXXVIII."

At Skipton was an ancient hospital, of which I find only a single notice, in the person of one Robert, styling himself Capellanum Hospitalis de Skipton, 24 Edw. III. [1350–1].

* Burnet's " History of the Reformation," vol. ii. p. 64.

The great collection of Memorials, Petitions, &c., relating to the estates of the Cliffords, now at Bolton Abbey, affords some amusing particulars with respect to the ancient state of husbandry at Skipton.

In the year 1577 an old dispute between the "husbands" (occupiers of lands) and cottagers of Skipton broke out afresh, and was referred to the Earl of Cumberland's council. The cottagers, it seems, claimed a right of turning their cattle upon the open fields, to eat up the stubble edish, along with those of the husbandmen, as soon as the corn was housed. This the latter resisted; but the cottagers proved, by the evidence of aged persons, one almost ninety years old, that this had been an ancient custom; at which however, the husbands had always murmured; and, about forty years before, brought the dispute before the first Earl of Cumberland and Henry Lord Clifford his son, who, after a very deliberate hearing, determined that the cottagers had no right to turn their cattle into the Ings; and that, with respect to the stubble edish, the husbandmen should turn in their cattle for *over-hushing*,* a day or two, for an hour in a day, or thereabouts, after which the goods of both should run in common till winter; and, to prevent trespass upon the new-sown wheat, the husbands should, at their own expense, hedge in a certain part of the common field for that purpose.

This dispute, perhaps, occasioned the enclosure of the common fields of Skipton, which had certainly taken place before the survey of 1612.

It appears from the following entry in the Compotus of Thomas Lord Clifford, 14th Henry VI., that there was at that time a pool in the township of Skipton called Alanwath Tarn : "Pro arcis anguillarum de Alanwath Tarne, vs." This seems to have been on one of the spongy flats now drained and enclosed on the road leading to Rilston. From the mention of Arcæ, I should conjecture that the eels were caught in a kind of trunks, or boxes.† The produce was considerable, equivalent in that year to the price of five quarters of oats. If I am right in my conjecture as to the place, it must have been a muddy shallow pool, well adapted to the habits of these fish, with which it seems to have swarmed. In Saxton's excellent Map of Yorkshire, there is a pool precisely in this situation, and only entitled " The Tarne."

Winterwell Hall, in Skipton, so called, probably, from a well never frozen in winter, which is now swallowed up in the canal, was more than half destroyed when that was cut. Part of it, however, remains on the right hand of the canal-bridge, on entering the town from Broughton. This was, about the middle of Henry VIII.'s reign, the residence of the Lamberts. And it seems not to have been without a degree of magnificence; for, in an old rental of John Lambert, son of the lawyer, I find it described as containing the following apartments—viz., " the tower, the grete parlor and chamb' ov' it, the study chamber and parlour or study under it." This, which was inhabited by the widow of John Lambert the first, was comparatively new, and had probably been his father's work before he

---

* *I.e.* I suppose, scouring or purging the cattle.

† If I understand Linnæus, it was the practice in Sweden to enclose eels in the hollow trunks of birch-trees.—" Anguilla coercetur trunco albo Betulæ." ("Systema Nat." i. 426.) It is curious to trace such affinities in the minuter habits of nations, originally the same.

removed to Calton; for, at the same time, one John, son of Christopher Lambert, held "veteres structuras capitalis messuagii p'dicti." In the same inventory John Lambert the son mentions a burgage held by "Alina Midilbroke vidua, quæ fuit nutrix mea à cunabulis;" notwithstanding which he did not forget to make her pay 4*s. per annum* for the said burgage.

The parish of Skipton may be considered in three divisions. 1st, The demesnes of the castle, as Skipton, Stirton, Holme, Thoralby, Skybeden. 2ndly, The manors which only belong to the Clifford fee, namely, Berwick with Draughton. 3rdly, The demesnes and dependencies of the priory of Bolton. The first of these has been sufficiently attended to. The second will give little trouble. To the last I hasten with the anxiety of a fond admirer.

On the skirts of Romell's Moor lie the two villages and manors of Berwick and Draughton, which constitute one township, as it appears that they were anciently one manor.

In the 9th Edw. II. [1315–6] Adam de Midelton and Henry le Vavasour were lords of Draughton.*

In the year 1603, William Midelton of Stockeld, Esq., granted a moiety of the said manor to William Newby. This moiety is the present manor of Berwick; for, in 1757, Rowland Newby, I suppose a descendant of the first purchaser of the moiety of Draughton, conveyed this estate to one William Marsden, who, in the year following, sold it to Mr. Coulthurst, of Gargrave, in consequence of which John Coulthurst, Esq., is now lord of the manor.

With respect to Draughton, the freeholders are now esteemed joint lords.

THE SAXON CURE.

THE estates of Bolton Priory stretched above four miles from that place on the way to Skipton. The most distant of these is Embsay,† where the priory itself was originally planted. Embsay is derived by Thoresby from ymb, *circa;* and ea, *aqua;* but, as it is spelt in the earliest charter extant Ambseia, I am rather inclined to deduce it from Ame, or Eme,‡ a Saxon personal name, with the sign of the genitive case and ea. At Embsay a church was continued long after the translation of the priory, and from many notices in the accounts

---

[* DRAYTHON ET BEREWIC.—In eadem villa (Skipton) sunt IIII^or car. terræ quæ tenentur de rege et domino castri, et quælibet car. redd. per ann. ad finem prædictum III*d.* ob. q.; unde summa est XIIII*d.*—Kirkby's "Inquest," A.D. 1284.

The two farms of East and West Berwick are about a mile from the village of Draughton.]

[† William de Meschines and Cecily his wife gave the town of Embsay to the priory, and Alice de Rumeli confirmed the gift, the boundaries were from those of Skipton and Skibedone to those of Rilston and Barden, in length; and from the demesne hedges (Haya) of Crookside to Routandbeck in breadth; and the canons had rent out of the mill here, with the tolls.—Burt. "Mon." 116.]

‡ Eme in Saxon is also *avunculus.* This etymology is not improbable: for thus we have Brotherwater in Cumberland.

of Bolton Priory it appears never to have been permitted to dilapidate till after the dissolution of the house.

Embsay Kirk, during thirty years the site of the priory, is now the property of William Baynes, Esq.,* who has erected an excellent house upon the spot; in digging the foundations for which, many relics of ancient interments, &c., were discovered. It seems to stand in the middle of the cloister-court; for when the late occupier, who finished the grounds, began to level a few yards north from the house, the foundations of the priory church were discovered; and, had any skilful or attentive person been at hand, a ground-plan of the whole might have been retrieved. A few years ago a complete Saxon doorway of the original fabric was remaining in one of the outhouses, but has been destroyed in the late alterations.

I cannot discover when Embsay was finally desecrated. In the year 1318, there is a charge in the Compotus, " Pro petrâ in quâ stat Beatus Cudbertus apud Embsay tallianda." In the year 1320 the churchyard was repaired. The wardrobe, from the mention of which apartment I conclude that the canons still maintained a cell there, was rebuilt shortly after. A spring behind the house still bears the name of St. Cuthbert's Well.

In an imperfect Compotus for the 4th year of Henry V. [1416–17] is the following account of Embsay :—

" Prior de Boulton tenet manerium de Emsay et totam villam integram in dominico, ut glabam Eccl. de Skypton et liberam, puram, et perpetuam eleemosynam, de quibus Robertus de Grene nuper Prior tenet capitale messuagium, quod extenditur ad LIIIs. IVd. et tenent' in bondagio resid. de villa vid. XXXIII toft. XXXV bov. ter. et VIII acr. de Forland."

Prior Grene, therefore, had retired to Embsay after his resignation. The last notice from which the existence of the old priory church here can be inferred, is in an inventory of the furniture of Skipton Castle, about 1591 : " Clock-house, one litel bell, which came from Embsay."

I cannot take leave of Embsay† without a tribute of respect to the memory of John Baynes, Esq., son of the former, and Fellow of Trinity College, Cambridge, who, after receiving the highest honours in the University, and aspiring, with the fairest expectations, to those of the Bar, was cut off by a premature death, at the age of 28. The following epitaph, by the classical hand of Dr. Parr, is the more interesting, because it has never been inscribed; and I have only to add to this short account, that had the subject of it survived a few years longer, the public would have seen a very different " History of Craven " from

[* Mr. Preston, of Skipton, married a daughter of Mr. Baynes and inherited this property. The property was sold in 1877.]

[† EMBSAY-CUM-EASTBY.—The church consists of nave, north aisle, chancel, and tower with one bell. It is in the Early English style of Gothic, and was consecrated 17th May, 1853; the dedication is Saint Mary the Virgin. It was made into a district chapelry by Order of Council, 21st May, 1855. The living is a vicarage, constituted 5th April, 1866, and is in the gift of the Vicar of Skipton.

The east window is filled with stained glass by Capronnier of Brussels, the subject is the Ascension; it was placed as a memorial to the Rev. Henry Cooper.

INCUMBENTS.

7th Aug. 1855.   *Henry Cooper*, Perpetual Curate.
26th Oct. 1865.   *Charles Leonard Hardman*, B.A.]

3 E

that which is now submitted to their candour.　　But his collections were merely begun at the time of his decease.

☧

IOANNI · BAYNES · A.M.
COLLEGII · S. TRINITATIS · APVD · CANTABRIGIENSES · SOCIO
IVVENI · DISERTO · ET · SINE · MALEDICTIS · FACETO
VI · INGENII · AD · EXCOGITANDVM · ACVTA
ET · FIRMA · AD · MEMORIAM · MIRIFICE · PRAEDITO
GRAECIS · ET · LATINIS · LITERIS · PENITVS · IMBVTO
LEGVM · ANGLICARUM · INTERIORI
ET · RECONDITA · DISCIPLINA · ERVDITO
LIBERTATIS · CONSERVANDAE · PERSTVDIOSO
PATRIAE · BONORVMQUE · CIVIVM · AMANTISSIMO
SIMPLICI · IVSTO · ET · PROPOSITI
ANIMOSE · ET · FORTITER · TENACI
QVI · VIXIT · ANN · XXVIII · MENS · III · DIEB · XXVIII
DECESSIT · LONDINI · PRIDIE · NON · AVGVST
ANNO · SACRO
M.DCC.LXXX.VII.
GVLIELMVS · BAYNES
CONTRA · VOTUM · SUPERSTES
FILIO · BENE · MERENTI
H. M. P.

Embsay,* Eastby, and part of Halton, were included in the purchase of the estates of Bolton Priory, by the first Earl of Cumberland, and parcelled out in various grants by his two last successors, with a reservation of the manorial rights in the titles.† Under one of these titles a principal estate at Halton is held by —— Dineley, Esq., of the ancient family of Bramhope. Another has long been in possession of the Bensons, from whom the first Benson Lord Bingley is, with great probability, supposed to have descended. The ancient tenure of Halton is expressed in the Compotus of 4th Henry V. as follows : " Prior de Boulton tenet manerium de Halton et totam villam integram tam in dominico quam in servicio pro XXX toft. et VI car. terre. De quibus III car. tenent' de Dominis Castri Skypton, faciend' forinsec. servic. et sect. curie et fin. wapent. omag. duntaxat excepto, quantum pert. ad III car. unde XIIII car. faciunt feod. I mil. Et II car. tenent' de Joh. Essheton et her. suis in pura eleemosyna et I car. de domino Ric. de Kyghtley et her. suis, ut patet per cartam.

Another very ancient member of the Saxon Cure is Bethmesley, of which the hall and all the demesne west of Kexbeck is within the parish of Skipton. Bethmesley is the Field of Bethm, probably the same word with the German Boehm, as it is pronounced Beamsley. This manor, with Hawkswick, part of Malham, &c., was given by Robert de Romillè to

---

[* A bronze torque was found near Embsay, and is in possession of R. H. Sedgwick, Esq., of Skipton.]

† From a perambulation of Earl Francis's time, I find that the boundaries of Embsay were certain ancient stones marked with the *trunk* and *anlets*, probably the fess of Clifford, and annulets of Vipont. At the same time there was standing a tower called Clifford's Tower on the confines of Embsay and Crookris. Another boundary was called the Queen of Fairies' Chair.—Bolton MSS. Near the same place a cleft betwixt two moor-stones, just wide enough to suspend a stag by the horns, is called the Deer Gallows.

Helte or Helto Mauliverer and Billiholt* his wife, names† unknown in the common pedigrees of the family, as is that of their descendant Helto, who gave Hawkswick to the monks of Fountains, A.D. 1175.

The manors of Allerton and Bethmesley continued in the direct line of this family till William Mauliverer, who had three sons, Ralph, Henry, and William, gave the latter to his third son, from whom descended in succession William, Giles, and William, which last had Sir William Mauliverer, Knight, father of Sir Peter Mauliverer, who lived in the reign of Edward III., and left two daughters and co-heiresses, Alice, married to Sir John Middleton, of Stockeld, and Thomasine to William de la Moore, of Otterburne, by whom he had Elizabeth, his only daughter and heiress, who, marrying Thomas Clapham, brought the manor of Bethmesley into that family.

The oldest son of this match was John Clapham, a "famous esquire" in the wars between the houses of York and Lancaster, who is said to have beheaded with his own hands the Earl of Pembroke, in the church porch of Banbury. He was a vehement partisan of the house of Lancaster, in whom the spirit of his chieftains, the Cliffords, seemed to survive. But, as the pedigree of the Claphams‡ is given by Thoresby, under Cottingly near Leeds, where they occasionally resided, I shall not repeat it. All that I know further with respect to Bethmesley is, that Sheffield Clapham, Esq., was resident here in the year 1665 [at this time Sir Christopher Clapham, Kt., was the head of the house, and residing at Beamsley], and that in the year 1703 the estate had been sold to the Morleys, whose descendant now enjoys it. The little which remains of the house is very conspicuously elevated on a knoll above the Wharf; but, from the foundations, which may be traced eastward in an adjoining field, the old mansion, with its offices, seems to have covered a very large extent of ground.

This family sprung from Clapham, or Clapdale Castle, on the skirts of Ingleborough, of which the following account is given by Dodsworth :—" John Clapham, ye last of Clapdale, past ytt to W'm Clapham, of Beamesley, father of George, that sold it to Ingleby *circa* 40 *annis elapsis*. Clapdale Castle hath been very large and strong, and standeth on the skirt of the high hill, Ingleborrow, w'ch shooteth tow'ds Clapham, and was the desmayne of y⁰ Claphams in later times, but I think itt was builded by Adam de Staveley, or o'e of his ancestors, who sold the chace of Ingleborrow to Roger Mowbray, temp. Joh'is." This is good sense and solid information.

What follows will prove, if this work have not sufficiently proved already, into what absurdities family vanity will lead men who abandon themselves to the inventions of venal heralds or flattering dependants.

In one of the windows of Hollen Hall, near Bethmesley, but unquestionably brought from the latter, when the old house was pulled down, are these inscriptions :—

---

* See Malham.

† Though omitted by Thoresby, they were known to Dodsworth, and stand thus: Helto Malolep.—Gul. fil. Helt.— Gul. f. & h. Gul. an. 21 Hen. II.—(Vol. iii. fol. 18.) The second William seems to have been father of the second Helt.

[‡ Their pedigree is also given in Glover's "Visitation of Yorkshire," 1584-5, and in Dugdale's "Visitation," in 1665. The arms proved were, argent on a bend azure, six fleurs-de-lis or 2, 2, and 2 ; with five quarterings, and the crest, a lion rampant sable, holding a sword argent, hilt and pomel or.]

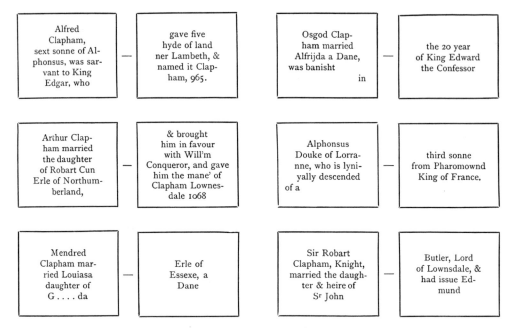

Alfred Clapham, sext sonne of Alphonsus, was sarvant to King Edgar, who	gave five hyde of land ner Lambeth, & named it Clapham, 965.	Osgod Clapham married Alfrijda a Dane, was banisht in	the 20 year of King Edward the Confessor
Arthur Clapham married the daughter of Robart Cun Erle of Northumberland,	& brought him in favour with Will'm Conqueror, and gave him the mane' of Clapham Lownesdale 1068	Alphonsus Douke of Lorranne, who is lynially descended of a	third sonne from Pharomownd King of France.
Mendred Clapham married Louiasa daughter of G . . . . da	Erle of Essexe, a Dane	Sir Robart Clapham, Knight, married the daughter & heire of Sr John	Butler, Lord of Lownsdale, & had issue Edmund

This out-Lamberts Lambert!

At the east end of the north aisle of Bolton Priory Church is a chantry belonging to Bethmesley Hall, and a vault, where, according to tradition, the Claphams were interred upright. I have looked into it through an aperture in the pavement, but could discover no remains of coffins, excepting one of the Morley family. Perhaps this unnatural position of the bodies had caused them and their coffins to collapse, in consequence of which they may have been removed.*

The canons must have felt themselves cramped by the demesne of Bethmesley, which, on the opposite side of the river, extended almost up to the offices of the house. I have little doubt that in a calm day, and at low water, when Verbeia condescended to be silent, the Mauliverers and Claphams, standing on their own ground, might have enjoyed the swell of the organ within the choir of Bolton.†

In the 35th of Elizabeth [1592–3], Margaret Countess of Cumberland founded a hospital for a mother and twelve sisters at Bethmesley, for which she obtained letters patent from the queen. A part of the preamble deserves to be recited.

"Cum predilecta consanguinea n'ra Margareta comitissa Cumbrie sæpissimè nobis dedit intelligi, quod in partibus borealibus, et præcipuè juxta Skipton in Craven, sunt quamplurime mulieres decrepite et summo senio confecte, que cibo

---

* By will, dated Die Martis prox. ante fest. Sci Bart. 1399, and proved March 8, following, Catherine and Marg't, daughters of Sir Peter Mauleverer, leave their bodies to be buried in the Abbey of Bolton. I have never met with another instance of a joint will. But it is probable from the early probate, that both the testratrices were dangerously ill at the time. And, Jan. 1, 1400, John Clapham made his last will, proved 12 Jan. 1402, bequeathing his body as above.

[† In a cottage near the south-west angle of Bolton Bridge is preserved an ancient oak beam inscribed, "𝕿𝖍𝖔𝖜 𝖕𝖆𝖙 𝖕𝖆𝖘𝖘𝖞𝖘 𝖇𝖞 𝖞𝖎𝖘 𝖜𝖆𝖞 𝖔𝖓𝖊 𝖆𝖇𝖊 𝖒𝖆𝖗𝖎𝖆 𝖍𝖊𝖗𝖊 𝖞𝖔𝖚 𝖘𝖆𝖞."]

mendicato pascuntur, et sine ullo receptaculo vel relevamine* vitam inopem et vagam degunt; predictaque comitissa commiseratione mota nobis diu et humiliter supplicaverit, ut in villâ de Beamesley in Craven unum hospitale ad melius relevamen et uberiorem sustentationem tredecim hujusmodi pauperum et decrepitarum mulierum, que propter summam senectutem et magnam corporum debilitatem victum et vestitum laborando acquirere non possunt, erigere, fundare, et stabilire dignaremus : Sciatis, &c."

By this foundation the first mother and sisters were to be appointed by George Earl of Cumberland and Margaret his countess, or either of them, or their heirs; after which every vacancy, by death or *amotion*,† was to be filled by the remaining sisters. The said earl and countess, and their heirs, were invested with the power of holding an annual visitation, to audit accounts, inquire into offences, expel the criminous and disobedient, and approve and instate others into the places† of the sisters so removed, according to their discretion. Also the said earl and countess, and their heirs, with the advice and consent of the Lord Chancellor or Keeper, or the Archbishop of York for the time being, were empowered to make fitting and wholesome statutes for the government of the said hospital. A valuable estate at Harwood was added to the original foundation by Lady Pembroke.

The original building of this hospital (for a second has been added to it) is very singular, and surely very inconvenient. It is circular, and so contrived that the apartments of the mother and sisters can only be approached through the central room, which is the chapel.‡

* This patent is dated eight years before the statute of the 43rd of Elizabeth for the parochial relief of the poor ; and the representation contained in the preamble places in a very strong light the necessity of that act.

† There is an apparent inconsistency between these two provisions ; to remove which, it must be understood that the right vested in the visitors by the latter clause, " approbandi et allocandi," is merely that of confirming and instating the person previously elected—something like the right of institution in the ordinary.

[‡ It is situated at the side of the road leading from Knaresborough to Skipton. Sir H. J. Tufton, Bart., is now the heir or representative of the Earl and Countess of Cumberland, and has the management of the estates and revenues of the hospital. According to the Report of the Charity Commissioners, the revenue is about 360*l. per annum.*

The hospital or almshouses consist of a circular building about thirty feet in diameter, with a chapel in the centre fifteen feet in diameter, with a passage leading to it, and seven rooms radiating round it, five opening with doors direct into the chapel and two into the entrance-passage. Adjoining the road there are six cottages, thus making accommodation for a mother and twelve sisters.

Over the entrance archway next the road are two shields, *Clifford* impaling *Vipont*, and *Clifford* impaling *Russell*, and over it an earl's coronet.

The inscription has been re-cut, and is as follows (the original stone with inscription is built into the side wall of pathway leading to the hospital, and is in quaint Roman capitals, like all the inscriptions set up by the Countess Anne)—

" THIS ALMES-HOUSE WAS FOUNDED BY THAT EXCELLENT LADY MARGARET RUSSELL COUNTESSE OF CUMBERLAND, WIFE OF GEORGE CLIFFORD THIRD EARL OF CUMBERLAND, 1593, AND WAS MORE PERFECTLY FINISHED BY HER ONLY CHILD THE LADY ANNE CLIFFORD, COUNTESSE DOWAGER OF PEMBROKE DORSETT AND MONTGOMERY. GOD'S NAME BE PRAISED."

At present (November, 1877) each inmate or sister receives 18*l.* 12*s. per annum,* paid monthly, and the mother 1*l.* 16*s. per annum* extra.]

𝔅𝔒𝔏𝔗𝔒𝔘𝔑𝔈 ℭ𝔥𝔞𝔫𝔬𝔲𝔫𝔰.

A S I have already proved that Botleton, or Bolton, was the seat of Earl Edwin's barony before and for some years after the Conquest, it seems probable, notwithstanding the silence of Domesday, that here was a church in the Saxon times. This opinion is confirmed by several circumstances; as, 1st, that the parochial chapelry of Bolton is to this day called the Saxon Cure; 2ndly, that the priory of Embsay, when translated hither, appears to have been engrafted on an old parochial foundation, as the oblations made at the altar were reserved to the church of Skipton.

However this may have been, in the year 1121 William de Meschines and Cecilia his wife founded at Embsay a priory for Canons Regular, which was dedicated to St. Mary and St. Cuthbert, and continued there about thirty-three years, when it is said by tradition to have been translated to Bolton, on the following account :—

The founders of Embsay were now dead, and had left a daughter, who adopted her mother's name, Romillè, and was married to William FitzDuncan,* with whom the reader is already but too well acquainted. They had issue a son, commonly called the Boy of Egremond (one of his grandfather's baronies, where he was probably born), who, surviving an elder brother, became the last hope of the family.

In the deep solitude of the woods betwixt Bolton and Barden, the Wharf† suddenly contracts itself to a rocky channel little more than four feet wide, and pours through the tremendous fissure with a rapidity proportioned to its confinement. This place was then, as it is yet, called the Strid, from a feat often exercised by persons of more agility than prudence, who stride from brink to brink, regardless of the destruction which awaits a faltering step. Such, according to tradition, was the fate of young Romillè, who inconsiderately bounding over the chasm with a greyhound in his leash, the animal hung back, and drew his unfortunate master into the torrent. The forester who accompanied Romillè, and beheld his fate, returned to the Lady Aaliza, and, with despair in his countenance, inquired, "What is good for a bootless Bene?" To which the mother, apprehending that some great calamity had befallen her son, instantly replied, "Endless sorrow."

The language of this question, almost unintelligible at present, proves the antiquity of the story, which nearly amounts to proving its truth. But "bootless Bene" is unavailing

---

* See the Introduction, p. 14.

† First mentioned after the Roman Verbeia in the deed of Translation by Aaliz de Romillè.

prayer; and the meaning, though imperfectly expressed, seems to have been, "What remains when prayer is useless?"*

This misfortune is said to have occasioned the translation of the priory from Embsay to Bolton, which was the nearest eligible site to the place where it happened. The lady was now in a proper situation of mind to take any impression from her spiritual comforters; but the views of the two parties were different. They spoke, no doubt, and she thought, of proximity to the scene of her son's death; but it was the fields and woods of Bolton for which they secretly languished. †

Thus far I have copied, and even reasoned upon, the vulgar tradition, in which Dodsworth, Dr. Johnston, and Dr. Burton have successively acquiesced, without reflecting that this drowned son of the second foundress is himself a party and witness to the charter of translation. ‡ Yet I have little doubt that the story is true in the main; but

[* Wordsworth has introduced this legend in his beautiful poem, the "Force of Prayer:"—

"𝕎𝕙𝕒𝕥 𝕚𝕤 𝕘𝕠𝕠𝕕 for a 𝕓𝕠𝕠𝕥𝕝𝕖𝕤𝕤 𝕓𝕖𝕟𝕖?"
  With these dark words begins my tale;
And their meaning is, "Whence can comfort spring,
  When prayer is of no avail?"

"𝕎𝕙𝕒𝕥 𝕚𝕤 𝕘𝕠𝕠𝕕 for a 𝕓𝕠𝕠𝕥𝕝𝕖𝕤𝕤 𝕓𝕖𝕟𝕖?"
  The falconer to the lady said;
And she made answer, "Endless sorrow!"
  For she knew that her son was dead.

She knew it by the falconer's words,
  And from the look of the falconer's eye,
And from the love which was in her soul
  For her youthful Romilly.

Young Romilly through Barden Woods
  Is ranging high and low;
And holds a greyhound in a leash,
  To let slip upon buck or doe.

And the pair have reached that fearful chasm,
  How tempting to bestride!
For lordly Wharf is there pent in
  With rocks on either side.

This striding-place is call'd "The Strid,"
  A name which it took of yore:
A thousand years hath it borne that name,
  And shall a thousand more.

And hither is young Romilly come,
  And what may now forbid

That he, perhaps for the hundredth time,
  Shall bound across "The Strid?"

He sprang in glee, for what cared he?
  And the river was strong, and the rocks were steep!
But the greyhound in the leash hung back,
  And check'd him in his leap.

The boy is in the arms of Wharf,
  And strangled by a merciless force;
For never more was young Romilly seen
  Till he rose a lifeless corse.
    *   *   *   *
Long, long in darkness did she sit,
  And her first words were, "Let there be
In Bolton, on the field of Wharf,
  A stately priory!"

The stately priory was rear'd,
  And Wharf, as he moved along,
To matins joined a mournful voice,
  Nor fail'd at evensong.

And the lady pray'd in heaviness
  That look'd not for relief;
But slowly did her succour come,
  And a patience to her grief.

Oh! there is never sorrow of heart
  That shall lack a timely end,
If but to God we turn, and ask
  Of Him to be our friend!]

† For the particulars of the endowment of this house, and everything else hitherto known concerning it, I refer the reader to the "Monasticon Anglicanum," and to Burton's "Monasticon Eboracense."

‡ See "Mon. Ang." vol. ii. p. 102. [The legend cannot, however, be implicitly received; for, when Alice gave the canons her manor of Bolton in exchange for their manors of Skibdun and Stretton, her son William (and in a pedigree, exhibited to Parliament in 1315, he is set down as her only son) appears in the charter[1] as a consenting party to the transaction; but may it not be better reconciled with this stubborn piece of evidence by supposing that the manor of Bolton has been exchanged, for the convenience of Alice, before the accident; and that, subsequently, the canons were glad to find

[1 "Mon. Ang." vol. ii. p. 101.]

that it refers to one of the sons of Cecilia de Romillè, the first foundress, both of whom are known to have died young.

From the Compotus of Bolton, a folio of a thousand pages, very fairly written, Dr. Burton has printed the accounts of one year, with many inaccuracies, and without a single note or reflection. On this account I choose to exhibit the accounts of the first year at large, and afterwards to extract a few particulars only from each year, subjoining at the same time explanatory observations. The original contractions, which I have everywhere preserved, will afford a pleasant exercise to the sagacity of antiquaries, while the annotations will render the general sense of each extract intelligible to ordinary readers. The language of this volume is a kind of patois, consisting of Byzantine Greek, Italian, old French, and Latinised English ; in short, it is precisely the jargon which has been illustrated with such a wonderful compass of learning by Du Cange, in his " Glossarium Mediæ et Infimæ Latinitatis."

The Compotus of Bolton begins in 1290, and ends in 1325.

Comp' Monasterii be' Mar' de Boulton in Craven a festo s'c'i Martini in hieme anno D'ni M⁰. CC⁰. nonages' octavo usque ad idem festu' anno D'ni M⁰ CC⁰. nonagesimo nono, per unum annum integrum.

Arrerag' recept'.

De arrerag' de Wyntewurth anni p'teriti XLs.	De Geyreg've XIId.
De fr'e Joh'e conv'so IIIIs.	De fr'e Petro de Miton' IIIs. IIId.
De Will'o Gylemyn Vs. Vd. qu.	De Ad' p̅p̅. de Emmesey XVd.
De fr'e Ad' converso XId.	

S'm' LVs. Xd. qu.

Firme t'raru'.

De firmis de Malghum p' annu' LIs. VId.	De Burghley, IIs.
De Scosthorp XXIIs. IId.	De Wytheton & Westskoiht, £IIII. VIIs.
De Calton LIIIIs. Xd.	De Harewode, XXXIs. VId.
De Crakehow, XXXVIIs. IIIId.	De villa de Roudon, XLIIs.
De Apeltrewick, XIXs.	De Lofthous', IIIIs. IIIId.
De Arneclyf, XIId.	De Bramdon, XXIs. VId.
De Newseom, VId.	De Wyntewurth, £IX. VIs. VIIId.
De Skypton, VIs.	De Manerio de Quynnefeld, VIs. VIIId.
De Esteby, CIIs. VIIId. ob.	De Gildusflat, VIs.
De Storthes, £IIII. Vs. VIId. ob.	De Ayrton, XXVIIs.
De Farnhil, XXIIs.	De Marton, XLs.
De Cockeholm, Vs.	De Thorp, XVs.
De Bradeley, IIId.	De Geyreg've, XIs.
De Kildewik, LXXIIs. XId. qu.	De Thresfeld, XIId.

a pretext, in her disconsolate lamentations, for descending from the bleak and cheerless heights of Embsay to the warm and sheltered seclusion of their newly-acquired possession. This is the more probable, because neither in this deed of exchange, nor in its confirmation by King Henry II.,[1] is there any allusion or reference to the future disposition of their donation ; and, in another charter, made apparently soon after, whereby she confirmed the grants of her parents and herself, she states that the translation was made "by here wish, assent, and ordination." It is in the latter part of this second chapter only, that it is recited that she " gave to the church of Bolton that place, and the whole vill of Bolton to found there a church of Canons Regular ; " and added the donation of "the place called Stede, and the land between Poseford and Spectbek, and the river Wharfe and Walksburn." It is remarkable, that after the first grant of the manor of Bolton her son is never again mentioned in these records, and that her husband was not joined with her in her donation ; though it is said that he was living, and was established by the King of Scotland in his possessions in Craven in 1152. It is also regular that she confirmed Bolton without any pious prelude, or any expression of sorrow and regret, and merely declared the confirmation of Hildwick, which was made subsequent to the translation of the house, to have been for the health of her soul and that of her parents and ancestors.]

[1 " Mon. Ang." vol. ii. p. 101.]

Grant by Cecily de Romille to the Canons of Embsay of the Mill at Silsden.

Kuŋo dŋo ꝯ pað̃ suo. C. Archiepo eboꝛac ꝯ oïbȝ xp̃i fidelibȝ p̃ſenꞇibȝ ꝯ fuꞇꝰ. Cecilia De ꝛumelio
ſalꞇ ꝑn dŋo. Sciaꞇꝭ me dediſſe ꝯ ꝗceſſiſſe ꝯ p̃ſenꞇi cꝛꞇ̃a ꝗfirmaſſe Deo ꝯ Beaꞇe mꝑarie ꝯ ſc̃o Chuꝛbꞇo
emeſaẏ ꝯ canonꝭ ꝑbidẽ do ſeꝛuieꞇibȝ molendinũ de ſigheleſdeẏ cu oĩ molꞇa eẏde ſꝑille. ꝯ oꝑe
molendiꝛẏ ꝗ n̄ debebaꞇuꝛ. ꝯ c̃ oïbȝ libꝛꞇaꞇȝ ꝯ libꞇꝭ ꝗueꞇudinibȝ ꝗꝗ ego habuẏ ꝑredicꞇo
molendino ꝗn Aliꝗ Beꞇenenꞇo ꝑ libaꝛẏ puꝛa̅ ꝯ ꝑꝑeꞇuꝺ helemoſiẏa. iꞇa ſciꞇ ꝗꝺ Aliuꞇ
molendiꝛũ ab Aliꝗ homꝛẏu gñ uoluꝛꞇaꞇe ꝯ ꝗſenſu canonicoꝛ In eadeꝛꝭ uilla ꝯ fiaꞇ.
Hec ꝯ ꝛaꝛꝛꝭ mola habeaꞇ. Siꝗȝ Auꞇ de ꝑdicꞇa Villa ſeꝛueꝛiꞇ ueꝛꝛe Ad ꝑdicꞇẏ
molenꝺꝛꝛũ Ego ꝯ heꝛedeſ ꝛꝛeẏ coꝑelleꝛꝭ euꝭ illꝺ ſeꝗꝭ. iꞇa ꝗꝺ ſi ſeꝑꞇꝰ fuꝛꞇ ueꝛꝛeꝛꝭ ab Alio
molenꝺꝛno ſaccuſ ꝯ Blaꝺꝭ eꝛꞇ canonꝛcoꝛũ ꝯ eꝗꝰ ꝯ foꝛꝭſacꞇẏ eꝛꞇ ꝛꝛeꝺ ꝯ heꝛeꝺũ
ꝛꝛeoꝛ. hiꝭ ꞇeſꞇibȝ. Raꝛꝛeꝛo dapꝭ Iboꝛe ꝗꞇabuꞇ. Huꝗ̃. Capꞇꞇ. Waꞇꞇ. picoꞇ. Wꝛꞇꞇo
uꞇꝺꝛꝺ. Regꝛaldo ꝛeꝛel.

Grant to the Canons of Embsay of the Vill of Childewic.

W. duneꞇani filiuſ. Oïb, h̃oꝛb, de craua ꝼranal ꝯ angliſ ſaꞇ
Sciaꞇꝭ me ꝗceſſiſſe dno d̃o ꝯ ſc̃e marꞇe ꝯ ſc̃o cudberꞇo de ameſeꝭa
ꝯ canonicaſ eꝺ̃ loci ꞇoꞇa uilla de childeuꝛic ꞇu molino ꝯ c̃ ſocꝭa
molꝛꝛi ꝯ q̊c̊d ad ꝑdicꞇa uilla ꝑꞇꝛeꞇ ꝑ boſco ꝑ plano ꝑ aꝗſ ꝯ paſcuꝭ
in elemolꝛꝛa. libe ab oꝭ ſeculaꝛi ſeruicio. ꝯabſoluꞇe. ꝑ ſaluꞇe aꝭe
meꝭ ꝯ paꞇꝛiſ ꝯ maꞇꝛ̃ meꝭ ꝯ uxoꝛꝭ meꝭ ꝯ anꞇeceſſoꝛ ꝛꝛoꝛ c̃ adã ſua
in filio. ꝯ ꝛamulfo de lindelia. ꝯ Walꞇo de maneꝛl ꝯ roꝺꞇo engerra
filio. ꝯ durando. ꝯ Wꝛꞇꞇo de archiſ. ꝯ helꞇone malleuꝛeꝛ. ꝯ ricardo
elſulꞇ filio. ꝯ roꝗo ꞇepeꞇꞇe. ꝯ ſimone golpaꞇꞇ filio. ꝯ ꝛoꝗo fafꞇꞇon.
ꝯ aldredo ulſi filio ꝯ raneꝛo fꝛe ſuo. ꝯ Wꝛꞇꞇo de riſleꞇꞇona ꝯ drogo
ne breu facꞇoꝛe. F 8

J.ᵉ Basire sc.

De Stretton, VIII*s*. IIII*d*.
De Emmesey, £XI. VII*d*.
De Halton, £IIII. XI*s*. IX*d*.
De Conedley, £IIII. X*s*. VII*d*. ob'.
De Styveto' & Estburn', XXIII*s*.
De Gloseburne, XII*d*.
De Newbiggin', XII*s*. IIII*d*.
De Stubhum & Scalewra, IX*s*. I*d*.

De Hurrocstanes, III*s*. IIII*d*.
De Wirdeley, VIII*s*. VIII*d*.
De d'nicis de Roudon, LXII*s*. VII*d*.
De Ihedon, X*s*.
De Wygedon, XXV*s*. IX*d*.
De Ebor', XXIX*s*.
De Drayhtton, VI*d*.

S'm' £LXXVII. XIX*s*. ob'. qu.

Adhuc firme t'rar'.

De G'ngia de Kildewik £X. XIII*s*. IIII*d*.

De Sabina de Scosthorp' XXIIII*s*. V*d*.

S'm' £XI. XVII*s*. IX*d*.

Firm' molend'.

De molendino de Ayrton, XL*s*.
De molend' de Helghfeld, XII*d*.
De molend' de Raveneswaht, X*s*.
De molend' de Harewode, £X.
De molend' de Aldwaldeley, V*s*.
De molend' de Roudon, XIII*s*.

De molend' de Marton, LX*s*.
De molend' de Ayrdale, £XII. XIII*s*. IIII*d*.
De molend' de Casteley, X*s*.
De molend' de Wigedon, XXX*s*. IIII*d*.
De molend' de Kesewik, XIII*s*. IIII*d*.

S'm' £XXXI. XVI*s*.

Op'a relaxata & tolnet'.

De op'ibus de Emmesey relaxat', LXXVII*s*.

De tolnet' nundinar' de Emmesey, £VIII. XIIII*s*. VIII*d*.

S'm' £XII. XI*s*. VIII*d*.

Pensiones recept'.

De eccl'ia de Kygheley, XIII*s*. IIII*d*.
De Preston p' tribus annis, VI*s*.

De Ketelwell, XX*s*.
Et sic est quiet' de anno p'esequente.

S'm' XXXIX*s*. IIII*d*.

Debita recept'.

De Will'o fil' Cecil' de Skipton, VI*s*. VIII*d*.
De W. de pinc'na p' H. crocbain, XL*s*.
De Rectore de Preston in s'bsid' v. Scotiam, XXXIII*s*.
IIII*d*.
De Rectore de Ilkeley p' eod', XXVI*s*. VIII*d*.

De Thom' de Weston, £XIII. VII*s*. VIII*d*.
De Ric'o le Peutrer, XV*s*.
De executor' Raym' del gile, XII*d*.
De Joh' fil' Bateman p' Unkethorp, X*s*.

S'm' £XIX. XIX*s*. IIII*d*.

Vendicio lane.

De Joh' Resceuont & sociis suis de debito remanente
super compot', £XX.

De eisdem p' XXIX saccis lane, £CCLX.
De lokett' et lana de refus, £IX. IIII*s*.

S'm'—CC.$\overset{XX}{\underset{IIII}{}}$.IX. IIII*s*.

Vendicio stauri.

De II equis vend' ap'd Rypon, £IX. XIII*s*. IIII*d*.
De I eq' de mortuar' G. de Hamelton, V*s*.
De sex bovett' vend', LIX*s*.
De I vacc' ap'd Malghum, X*s*. VI*d*.

De I vacc' p' Ad' Instaurariu', XII*s*.
De XXII ovibus vend', XXXVI*s*.
De agnis de dec' de Ayrdale, LXXVIII*s*.

S'm' £XIX. XIII*s*. X*d*.

De vend' bosci n'l hoc anno.

Vendic'o bladi.

De IIII qr. V b'. frum' VI b'. di. fab' in p'och de Skypton vend' p' Ad' $\overline{ppm}$, XXIIII*s*. VIII*d*.
De VIII qr. avene de Broyhtton. VII qr. di. avene ap'd Carleton, XXXI*s*.
De I qr. VI b'. avene ap'd Skybdon, III*s*. VI*d*.
De X qr. VI b'. avene de decim' de Airdale vend', XIIII*s*. X*d*.
De III b'. siliginis. VI qr. di. avene de Conedley, XII*s*. VI*d*.
De II b'. ordei. II qr. avene de Malghum, V*s*.
De VI b'. frum' XII qr. II b'. avene vend' ap'd How Stede Riddyngg' et Storthes, XX*s*. VI*d*. ob. q'.
De IIII b'. fab'. V qr. VI b'. avene vend' apud Unkethorp, XIIII*s*. II*d*.

S'm' £VI. VI*s*. ob. qu.

3 F

Vendicio p'ti.

> De p'to in herba vend' apud Thonnocker, IIIIs. IIIId.
>
> > S'm' IIIIs. IIIId.

Alteragiu'.

> De alteragio de Kildewik hoc anno, £IIII. IXs. VIIId.
>
> > S'm' £IIII. IXs. VIIId.

Perquisita & fines.

> De p'quisitis Prioris et Celerarii, XLVIIIs. IIIId.   De fin' Wapn ap'd Harewod, IIs. VIIId.
>
> > S'm' LIs.

Corrod' vend'.

> De Isabella de Haukeswik p' corrod' in p'te, £VII. VIs. VIIId.
>
> > S'm' £VII. VIs. VIIId.

Minuta recepta.

> De fimis vend' ap'd Conedley, VIs. VId.
> De arrura ibid. IIs.
> De lacte uni' vacce apud Unkethorp, XIIIId.
>
> > S'm' IXs. VIIId.

Sartrina.*

> De Sartrina hoc anno, £XVI.
>
> > S'm' £XVI.

Recept' ex mutuo de mercatorib'.

> De Joh'e Resceuont' et sociis suis post recepc'o'm lane,   De eodem per man' mag'ri Nich'i de Tyngewik ap'd
> £LX.   Lond', £XXVI.
> De eodem in Nundinis s'c'i Botulph', £XXII. IIIs. IIIId.   De eodem p' man' Coppe cotenne, £XLVII.
> De eodem per manus Sacriste, £IIII.   De Bernard' Manifred, £CC.
>
> > S'm' £CCCLIX. IIIs. IIIId.

Minut. recept' ex mutuo.

> De Eva de Landa ex mutuo, XXs.   De Gilian' de Ebor', XXs.
>
> > S'm' XLs.
> > S'm' total' toci' Recept' £DCCCLXV. XVIIs. VId. ob. qu.

Expens' denarior'.

Decas' & condonacio firme.

> In decasu† firme de p'to de Aldyhtmyre q; in manu   In condonac' firme Steph'i fil' Nelle in Emmesey p' eod'
> Prioris, IIIs. VId.   t'mino, XVIIId.
> In decasu uni' tofti in Esteby p' t'mino s'c'i Martini, XIId.   In decasu firme Ruccroft' apud Storthes, IIs.
> In condonac'o'e firme Th' de Askelhale p' eodem termino,   In decasu firme molendini de Alwaldeley, Vs.
> XXXs. VId.   In decasu firme molendini de Kesewik, XIIIs. IIIId.
>
> > S'm' LVIs. Xd.

Firme solute.

> Castro de Skipton p' Lobwyht p' ann', VIs. VIIId.   D'no Hug' fil' Henr' p' t'ra in Ayrton p' ann', VIs.
> Domui de Kirkestal p' t'io Pent' anno p'cedente,   Domui de fontibus p' t'ra in Malghum p' ann', VId.
> XVIs. VIIId.   Canonicis de Kirkeby p. dec' feni in Malghum, XVIℓ.
> Eidem domui p' t'io s'c'i Martini anno p'sente,   D'ne Margar' de Nevyll p' terra in Geyreg've, Xs.
> XVIs. VIIId.   D'no Joh'i Giliott' p' terra in Swynewaht, Id. ob.
> Domui s'c'i Leonardi p' t'io s'c'i Martini hoc anno,   Castro de Skipton p' g'ngia de Siglesdene, XIId.
> VIs. VIIId.   Et apud Drayhtton' p' Lynlandes, IId.
> Momalibus de Munketon p' duob' terminis hoc anno, XXs.
>
> > S'm' £IIII. Vs. IXd. ob.

Pensiones solute.

> In pensione soluta domui de Huntyngdon, CVIs. VIIId.   Et Ric'o de Vescy, LXs.
> Et eccl'ie de Ilkeley p' pensione, Xs.   Et Joh'i Gunwall' p' corrodio suo in p'te, XLs.
> Et p' p'curac'o'e mag'ri Gilfrid p' q'tuor annos, XXVIIIs.   Et Will'o Spirhard p' salario suo, Ls.
>
> > S'm' £XIIII. XIIIIs. VIIId.

[* Officina sartoris vel locus in monasteriis ubi sarciuntur vel reponuntur vestes—the tailor's workshop in a monastery. — "Lexicon Manuale ad Scriptores Mediæ et Infimæ Latinitatis," by W. H. Maigne D'Arnis.]

[† Decasus, waste or loss of rent.]

Debita soluta.

Mag'ro Thome de Arneclyf, £XI.
Thom' de Hornby p' fact'a dom' in Ebor', XXXIIIIs.
Joh'i Resceuont' in allocac'o'e f'c'a eid', £CXXXIX. VIs. VIIId.
Refectorario, Xs.
Et eid' ex convenc'o'e p' Cyrog'ph', £XIII. VIs. VIIId.
Cuidam mulieri de Rypon, Vs.
Et W. de Hamelton p' J. Rescevont', £LXVI. XIIIs. IIIId.

Et eidem, CVIs. VIIId.
Gregorio de Thornton p' uno eq' in p'te, XLs.
Arnoldo Wenge, XXd.
D'no J. de M'kyngfeld p' blado anni p'teriti, £VI. Xs.
Will'o de Pyncerna, XLs.
Executorib' W. de Langefeld, £VI. XIIIs. IIIId.
Et D'no W. de Hamelton, £XX.

S'm' £CCLXXV. VIIIs.

C'tus circa pl'ita & amerciamenta.

Cirog'phario Reg' p' fine de Rither, IIIs.
Ballio de Barston p' seysina ej'dem, IIs. IId.
Pro br'ib' impet'tis p' div'sos ho'i'es, XIs. Xd.
Pro t'ib' am'ciam'tis in viridi cera, XXs. VId.
Duodene de Craven p' pl'ito de Neubigg', VIIIs.
Mag'ro Ade Tong p' instrument', Xs. VIIId.

Cuidam de banco p' auxilio, IIIs. IIIId.
Mich'i de Kendale p'curatori Ebor', VIs. VIIId.
Ap'd Skipton p' defectu R. de Nevill, IIIIs.
Advocatis p' defensione co' p'visiones, XXs.
Pro cartis Reg' de domib' Gil. de Craven, XXXIIIIs. Vd.

S'm' £VI. Vs. Id.

Empcio bladi.

Pro fructib' eccl'ie de Broyhton anno p'terito, LIIIIs. IIIId.
Pro fructib' ej'dem p' anno p'sente & fut'o, £XXVI. XIIIs. IIIId.
Pro blado empto ap'd Geyreg've anno p'terito, XIs.
Pro XXX qr. frum' ibid. £VII. XIIIs. IIIId.
Pro VI qr. frum' empt' ibid. XXXs.

Pro III qr. frum' ap'd Broyhto', XIIIIs.
Pro XL qr. frum' apud Eyston, £X. VIs. VIIId.
Pro VIII qr. de Ric'o Favvel, XLs.
Pro LX qr. apud Holm, £XVI.
Pro v b'. ap'd Riddingg', IIIs. IXd.
Pro X qr. avene de Celerario, XXs.

S'm' £LXIX. Vs. Vd.

Empcio stauri.

Pro uno eq'o de H. de Kygheley, £IIII.
Pro uno equo de Ad' p'fet, XLs.
Pro uno eq'o de J. de Midleton, XLVIs. VIIId.
Pro uno eq'o de Eva de Landa, XLIs. Vd.

Pro uno eq'o de Alan' de Unkethorp', IIIIs. VIIId.
Pro uno equo de Sart'na, Ls.
Pro capris apud Otteley, XXVIIIs. VIIId.
Pro capris ap'd Conedley, XXVIs. VIIId.

S'm' £XV. XVIIIs. Id.

Empcio lane.

Pro XXVIII saccis III petr' di' lane empt' £CᴵᴵᴵᴵˣˣXV. IIIIs. IIId.

S'm' patet.

Expens' coq'ne.

In porcis emptis de Goydcher anno p'terito, XVIs. VIIId.
In carn' salsata empt' ap'd Clithop' in p'te, £XI. VIs. Id.
In bob' vacc' vitul' et porc' empt' p' parcellas, LXIIIs. XId.
In aucis gallinis et capriolis empt' p' vices, XIXs. IId.
In Warnestura piscis empt' ap'd Apelton', £IIII. XIIIs. IIIId.

In Warnestura piscis ap'd s'm Botulph'm, £IIII. VIIIs. IIIId.
In pisce et allece p' parcell' emp't, £VIII. XIIIs. XId. ob.
In ovis empt' p' parcellas, XXIs. IId.
In companag' div'sor' infra Cur' et ext', XXVIIs. IId.
In Warnestura* cont' annu' futurum, £X.

S'm' £XLVI. IXs. IXd. ob.

Empcio salis.

In XVIII qr. salis emptis, XLIIs.

S'm' XLIIs.

P'videncia co' assumpc'o'm.

In p'videncia cont' festum assumpc' anno p'terito, in p'te, LXXVIs.
In pip'e croco amigdal' & aliis spe'ib' eodem anno, Vs.

In p'videnc' cont' idem festum hoc anno, £IX. IXs. VIId.
In pip'e croco amigdal' & aliis sp'ieb' eodem anno, XIXs. Id.
In trib' dolcis vini emptis cu' cariac'o'e eor'd', £VII. XVs. IId.

S'm' £XXII. IIIIs. Xd.

Custus forgie.

In ferro empto anno p'terito, IIIs.
In ferro empto hoc anno, XXXIIIs. IId.

In carbonibus ardendis, XVIIIs. IId.
In ferris equor' cu' clavis, IIIs. IXd.

[* See note under the year A.D. 1298.]

In una falce apud g'ngias, xiid.
In una falce ap'd Conedley, xid. ob.
In acero empto, iiis. iiid.
In pice & sufflatoriis rep'and', xixd.
In secur' scruris & cultell' p' coq'na, iis. vd.
In ferro ferrura affror' & in stip'n' fabri ap'd Conedley, iis. iid.

In ferr' pedalib' vom'ib' et in stip'nd' fab' ap'd Kildewik, viiis. iiid.
In i falce & iii falcill' ibid. xiiiid.
In ferr' & stip'n' fab' ap'd Unkethorp', iiiis. vid.
In p'vis falcillis ibid. viid.
In ferr' carucar' ap'd Malghum, xiid.

S'm' £iiii. vs. ob.

Emend'c'o domor'.

In nava domo faciend' ap'd Ebor' in p'te anno p'terito, iiiis. vid. ob. qu.
In emendac'o'e veteris bercar' ap'd Malghum, xiiiis.
In m'emio empto in Thursdene cum cariac'o'e ejusd', vs.
In m'emio* empto ad stagnum de Harewode, xiis. iiiid.
In m'emio sarrando apud Rither, xxxs. xd.
In sparstan sclatstan et aliis ad camara' de Rither, £vi. iiis. xd.
In sarrac'o'e m'emii & bord' faciend' in foresta & alibi, lviis. iid.
In stip'n' Ric'i de Baildon & W. de Dysford' p' carpentaria p' ann', xxxvis.
In g'ngiis de Boulton rep'and' & cum pet' cop'end' in p'te, cixs. viiid.
Pro eccl'ia & domib' rep'and' infra Cur', ixs.

Cuidam carpentario in arris p' factura Camare de Wygedon, xxvs. iiiid.
Pro molis cariand' ad molendinu' de Marton, iiis. iiiid.
Pro mille bordis ad bercariam de Malghum, xxxs.
Pro g'ngia de Siglesdene rep'and' & cum pet' cop'end', £iiii. xvis. ixd.
Pro rep'ac'o'e p've dom' ibidem, iis. iiiid.
Pro factura uni' p've dom' ap'd Carleton, xiis. iid.
Pro factura dom' Gilb'ti Racche in Halton, xxd.
Pro domib' rep'and' apud G'ngiam de Kildewik, iiis. vid.
Pro g'ngiis in p'och' de Skipton rep'and', vs. iiiid.
In rep'ac'o'e domor' ap'd Conedley Geyreg've & Unkethorp, xiis. iiiid.
In rep'ac' domor' de How Stede Riddingg' Som'scal' & Bradescahe, viis. viid.

S'm' £xxx. iis. viiid. ob. qu.

Fact'a caruc' & plaustror'.

In rep'ac'o'e carucaru' ap'd Unkethorp, vd. ob.
In fact'a caruc' & plaustror' ap'd Conedley, xixd.
In caruc' & plaustris apud Kildewick, iiis. vid.

S'm' vis. vid. ob.

Fossura et haya.†

In fossura & haya ap'd le Stede How & Lobwiht cu' assarcac'o'e p'ti ibid. viiis. id. ob.
In fossura apud Kildewik juxta boscum, xviiis. xid.
In fossur' ap'd Unkethorp, iiiid.
In clausura circa Westybank, iis.

S'm' xxixs. iiiid. ob.

Custus oviu'.

In oleo sepo & pinguedine empto ad oves unguend', £iiii xs. viid. ob.
In vivo argento & viridi colore empt' ap'd Ebor', xxiis. ixd.
In xxiiii li. virid' coloris & xii li. vivi argenti ap'd S'm Botulph'm, xxxiis.
In feno ap'd Unkethorp empto, ixs. vid.
In lacte ad agnos, xixs. id. ob.
In locione tonsione barmeclathes & mulierib' lactantib' oves, xvs. iid. ob.

S'm' £ix. ixs. iiiid. ob.

Custos equor'.

In oleo & pinguedine cum stipend' uni' Marescalli ap'd Ebor', iiiis. id. ob.
Henr' fab'o de Apeltrewik p' labore suo, iiis.
Duob' equatorib', iiis. vid.

S'm' xs. viid. ob.

Expens' Prioris.

In expens' Prioris in omnib' intin'ib' suis c'ca negocia dom' p' ann', £viii. xvd. qu.

S'm' £viii xvd. qu.

Necc'ia Prioris.

In necc'ariis Prioris & stabuli sui empt' ap'd Ebor' & domi, lxviiis. iiid.
In sp'ieb' sargiis & uno Mazer empt' ad eund' ap'd S'c'm Botulph'm, xlvs. xd. ob.

S'm' cxiiiis. id. ob.

[* Meremium, timber.]   [† In ditching and hedging.]

Dona & elemosina Prioris.

 In div'sis donis & exenniis* f'tis Magnatib' p' utilitate dom' cu' elemosina, £XIII. IIIIs. IIIId. ob.

    S'm £XIII. IIIIs. IIIId. ob.

Expens' & necc'ia Celerarii.

 In expens' & necc'iis Celerarii, XXXIXs. IIId. ob.

    S'm' XXXIXs. IIId. ob.

Expens' nuncior'.

 In expens' nuncior' p' annu', XXXVs. VId. ob.

    S'm' XXXVs. VId. ob.

P'videnc' ap'd Sc'm Botulph'm.

 In panno & furruris empt' ap'd Ebor' anno p'terito, £XII. IIIIs. IIIId. ob

 In panno & furruris empt' ap'd S'c'm Botulph'm, £XV. IIIIs. VIIId.

 In di. cent' carentinill' & XXVI ulnis linee tele, XXVIs. VIIId. ob. qu.

 In croco pip'e galenga kanel' amigdal. Rys & Zucuricio, LVs. VId.

 In cordis ciliciis brocagiis paccatorib' & portatorib', XIIs. Id. ob.

 In expens fr'is Ric'i de Ebor' c'ca eandem p'videnc' fac', XXIs. Vd. ob.

    S'm' £XXXIIII. IIIIs. Xd. qu.

Minuta.

 In sepo ad Celarium & vaccarias, albo coreo & p'camen', XIIIIs. VIIId.

 In politridiis crebris & untensilib. coq'ne b'cine carpenterie & vaccariar', XIIIs. VId.

 In cannabo cyngul' capistris retib. tela factis & factura hernasii, XVIs. IId. ob.

 In emendac'o'e uni' Mazer de Camera & in ciphis cont' f'm Assumpc', IIIs. Xd.

 Pro uno eq' st'ngulato cum canib. dom' & deterione I eqi de Adyngh'm, IIIIs. IXd.

 In cirotecis bovarior' & sotular' garc'onum Prioris, XIIs. IXd.

 In expens' hercianc' de p'car' & portac'o'e straminis, IIIs. IId.

 Et Ric'o le Peutrer p' labore suo de div'sis utensilib. XVIs. VIIId.

    S'm' £IIII. XIs. VIIId.

T'turac'o & vent'.

 In blad' triturand' apud Boulton, XLIs. IIIId.

 In blad' t'turand' & metend' apud Otteley, XXXVs. Id.

 In dec' de Ayrdale t'turand' & vent', XLVIIs. XId.

 In t'turac' & vent' ap'd Conedley, VIIIs. Xd. ob.

 In t'turac' & vent' ap'd Riddingg, Stede, How, Berewik, & Storthes, XVs. ob. qu.

 In t'tur' & vent' ap'd Carleton, Broyhton, & in p'och' de Skipton, LIIIs. XId. ob. qu.

    S'm' £X. IIs. IId. ob. qu.

Stipend' infra Cur'.

Ade Pog p' pent' anno p'cedente, IIIs. IIIId.	Cuidam hocario p' pent', XIId.
Eidem Ade hoc anno, VIIs. IIIId.	Cuidam in aula hospitu', IIs.
Will'o giglyngg' p' ann', Vs.	Joylenedy p' uno t'mino, IIs. VId.
Rob'to pistori, Vs.	Jurd' pagio carectarii, IIs. VId.
Elie braciatori, Vs.	Rob'to Quyrle, IIs. VId.
Rog'o Smalpas, IIIs. VId.	Dudde p' pent', XIId.
Rob'to fabro, VIIIs.	Cuidam i' infirmar' conv'sor', XVIIId.
Will'o carpentario, Xs.	Petro le Moker Ric'o hercsar', ⎫ IIIIs.
Rog'o molendinario, IIIs. VId.	Elie longo & Hull', p' pent', ⎭
Ric'o carpn̄ p' t'io S'c'i Martini, Vs.	Nich'o dyerhs & byrs, IIs. VIIId.
Joh'i de Roudon, VIIIs.	Alano Pynnyng p' pent', IIs. VId.
Duob. hocariis, VIs.	

    S'm' £IIII XIs. Xd.

Stipend' ext' Cur'.

 In stipend' Simon Paunche, VIIs. VIIId.

 Jurd' ad g'ngians p' pent', IIs. VId.

 Ric'o beche novem bovar' & duob. pastorib. bou' ap'd le Hynehous, LXVIIIs.

 Duob. apud g'ngias & cuidam siccatrici ibid. VIIs.

 Rado le q'ereur, fagotario, hercsar' & seminatori, XIIIs. VIIId.

 Forestariis de Speyhttehow, Berden, & How, VIs.

 Eq'ciario, garc'o'i instaurarii & plaustrario ejusdem, IXs. VIIId.

 Bovariis de Riddingg, Stede, & How, XXs.

    [* Exennium, a present.]

Bovariis de Broyhton, Unkethorp, & Conedley, & Kildewik, XXXVIIs.
Bovar' de Malghum, cuidam Dayce & uni pastori bou' ibid. Xs. VIIId.
Q'tuor vaccariis & IIII pastorib. steriliu' animaliu', XXs.
Cuidam messori & Alex' garc'o'i Celerarii, Vs. VId.
Cuidam forman & q'tuor bercariis ap'd bercariam, XIs. VId.

S'm' £X. XVIIIs. VIId.

Empcio p'ti et agistamenta.

In p'to empto ap'd Holm anno p'terito, XXVIIIs.
Pro p'to ap'd Snaghal' eod' anno, XVIs. VIIId.
Pro p'to ibidem hoc anno, XXVs. VIIId.
Pro le Cotcheng' apud Skypton, XVIIIs.
Pro le calvefal de Crofton, IIs.
Pro II acr' p'ti ap'd Rither captis ad t'minu' XII annor' de domo S'c'i Nich'i de Ebor', XIs.

S'm' £VI. Xs. IVd.

Falcacio p'ti.*

In p'tis falcand' ap'd Boulton, XVIIIs. VId.
In falcac' & sp'sione de Snaghal, VIs. VIIId.
In feno levand' ibid. IIIIs. Xd.
In falc' apud Esteby, IIIs. Xd.
In fac' & levac' ap'd Kildewik, XVIIs. IIId.
In falc' ap' Malghum, Vs. IIIId.
In falc' ap'd Som'scales, Vs. IIId.
In falc' ap'd Riddingg', IIIs. IIId.
In falc' ap'd Ryther, VIs. VIIId.

In falcac' & sp'sione ap'd Holm, Vs. IIId.
In falcac' del Cotcheng, IIs. IXd.
In falc' de Lythebank, IIIIs. IIIId. ob.
In falc' ap'd Conedley, XIId.
In fen' levand' ap'd Unkethorp, XIId.
In falc' ap'd Bradescagh, Vs.
In falc' ap'd How, IIIIs.
In falc' ap'd Broyhtton, VIs. VIIId.

S'm' CIs. VIId. ob.

Sarclac'o bladi.†

In blad' sarcland' ap'd Kildewik, XVIIId.

In blad' apud Unkethorp sarcland', XIIId.

S'm' IIs. VIId.

Messio bladi.‡

In bladis metend' ap'd Boulton, Angru', How, Stede, et Riddingg, £XIV. IXs. IId. ob.
Et ap'd Broyhtton, XXXIIIs. IIIId.
Et ap'd Conedley, XIXs. VId.
Et ap'd Unkethorp, XXIIIs. Vd.

Et ap'd Malghum, VIIs.
Et ap'd Kildewik, XXXIXs. VId.

S'm' £XX. XIs. XId. ob.

Collecc' decim'.

In decimis colligend' in Ayrdale, LVs. IIIId.
Et ap'd Broyhtton, Vs. IIId. ob.

Et ap'd Skipton & Carleton anno p'terito, XXIIIs. VId.
Et ibidem hoc anno, XVIIIs.

S'm' CIIs. Id. ob.

Cariag' decim'.

In decim' cariand' in p'och' de Skypton, XVs.

In dec' cariand' in Ayrdale, XLIs.

S'm' LVIs.

Cariagia forinseca.

In car' bladi de Carleton usq. Boulton, XIIIs. IIIId.
Pro blad' de Ayrdale car', XXXVIIs. XId.

In car' bladi usq. Ebor', VIIs. Xd.
Pro ferro de Kertmel car', XIIIId.

S'm' LXs. IIId.

Deportac'o Canonicor.

D'no Supp'ori, IIIs.
D'no H. de Landa v' Oxon', XIIIs. IIIId.

Fr'i Joh'i de Bradeford, IIIs.
Et eid' p' Celerarium, XVId.

S'm' XXs. VIIId.

Vestura fr'um.

In vestura fr'is Simon' de Otteley, Xs.
Ade instaurario, XXs.

Waltero de Marton, J. conv'so, ⎫
　　　& Walt'o Arkyl,　　　　 ⎬ XVd. ob.
　　　　　　　　　　　　　　 ⎭

S'm' XXXIs. IIId. ob.

S'm' total' toci' expens' £DCCCXLI. XVIIIs. Xd. ob.
Et sic sunt in arreragiis, £XXIII. XVIIIs. VIIId. qu.
De quibus d'n's Roger' rector eccl'ie de Preston debet p' panno & sp'ieb', CIIs. IId.

[* Mowing meadows.]　　　　　　[† Weeding grain.]　　　　　　[‡ Harvesting grain.]

Idem debet p' den' mutuatis eid' ap'd Ebor' ad Warnesturam emend', XIIs.

D'n's Petr' du Lound ex mutuo, XXXIIIs. IIIId.
Cleric' d'ni W. de Hamelton, IIIs.
Walterus de Midleton, XLs.
Mag'r J. de Ilkley p' agnis, XXIIIs. VIIId.
Ric's le Peutrer, XXVIs. Xd.
De arr' J. de Feysergh hoc anno, Vs. VId.
De fr'e J. converso, VId.
De Thorp, VId.
De p͞p de Emmese', IIs. IXd. ob.
De Thounoker, IIIIs. IIIId.
De Drayhtton, VId.
De Neusum, VId.
De Stubhum & Scalewra, IIId.
De Wirdeley, VIIIs. VIIId.·
De molend' de Casteley, Vs.
De man'io de Quynnefel', VIs. VIIId.

Reyner' de Knol, LIIIs. IIIId.
Jacobus de Eyston, LIIIs. IIIId.
Abbas Furnesie, Xs.
Henr' de Otteley, XXs.
De Gildusflat, IIIs. VId.
De Geyrg've, VId.
De Apeltrewik, VId.
De Storthes, IIIs. IXd. ob.
De Conedley, IIIId.
De Ayrdale, IIIs. IXd. qu.
De Burghley, IIs.
De Hurrocstanes, XXd.
De Wyntewurth, XLs.
De molend' de Helgfeld, XIId.
Et fr' S. de Otteley d. VIIIs. IXd.

S'm' debitor' de arreragiis £XXIII. XVIIIs. VIIId. qu. ; et eq.

Debita que debent' Domui.

D'n's Rog' rector eccl'ie de Preston d. p' uno doleo vini, car' ej'd' & I carcas' bovis LXIIIIs. VId.
Idem Roger' debet £LXVI. XIIIs. IIIId.
Simon de Stutewill, £XXVI. XIIIs. IIIId.
S'm' £$_{IIII}^{XX}$X. XIs. IId.
S'm' toci' debiti q'd debetur domui £CXX. IXs. Xd. qu.

Debita que Dom' debet.

Joh'i Resceunt' & sociis suis, £CLIX. IIIs. IIIId.
D'no W. de Hamelton, LXXIXs. VIIId.
Mag'ro Th' de Arneclyf, £XIII. VIs. VIIId.
P' lard' ap'd Clethop' in p'te, £IIII.
Will'o de Haverbergh, XXXIIIs. IIIId.

Bernardo Manifred, £CC.
Joh'i de Croxley, £XXXIII. VIs. VIIId.
Ade de Midleton, £X.
P' p'to ap'd Holm, XXXIIIIs. VIIId.

S'm' toci' debiti quod Dom' debet, £CCCCXXVII. IIIIs. IIIId.

Comp' g'ngiaru' in p'och' de Kildewik, Skipton, Carleton, et Broyhtton.

Frument'. Parochia de Kildewik respondit hoc anno de IX qr. VI b' frument'.
Siligo. Et de XIIII qr. I b' siliginis.
Ord'. Et de XXII qr. VII b' ordei.
Avena. Et de DLI qr. I b' avene.
S'm' duri bladi in Ayrdale XLVI qr. VI b'.—S'm' toci' avene DLI qr. I b'.

Frument'. Parochia de Skipton respondit hoc anno de $_{IIII}^{XX}$XV qr. di. frumenti.
Siligo. Et de VII qr. II b' siliginis.
Fab'.* Et de IV qr. VI b' di. fab'.
Ord'. Et de IX qr. VI b' ordei.
Avena. Et de DXVI qr. VI b' avene.
S'm' duri bladi in p'och' de Skipton $_V^{XX}$XVII qr. II b' di.—S'm' avene DXVI qr. VI b'.

Carleton respondit hoc anno de XVII qr. I b' di. frum', III qr. di. siliginis, VI qr. ord', & III qr. III b' fab'.
Eadem g'ngia respondit hoc anno de CV qr. avene.
S'm' duri bladi apud Carleton XXX qr. di. b'.—S'm' avene CV qr.

Broyhton respondit hoc anno de LXII qr. frum'ti, II qr. di. fab', et VII qr. ordei.
Et eadem g'ngia respondit hoc anno de CXI qr. VI b'.
S'm' duri bladi LXXI qr. di.—S'm' avene CXI qr. VI b'.

De frumento g'ngie de Boulton non fit hic mencio, q. non trituratur hoc anno.
Set g'ngia de Boulton respondit hoc anno de LXV qr. siliginis, XXVII qr. di. fab', & XXXII qr. ordei.
Et eadem g'ngia respondit hoc anno DLXIX qr. avene.
S'm' duri bladi CIIII qr. di. S'm' avene DLXIX qr.
S'm' summaru' toci' suprad'c'i duri bladi, CCCXXX qr. I b'.
S'm' summaru' toci' avene, MDCCCXXXIII qr. V b'.

Memorand' q'd expend' fuer't hoc anno infra dom' de Boulton ex certo, C$_{IIII}^{XX}$VIII qr. frumenti.
Et ibidem p' ann' extra certum infra Cur', XLI qr. V b'.

[* Fabera, beans.]

Et in pane ap'd Malghum, Kildewik, Emmesey, Skirgile, & con' f'm Assumpcionis, XVIII qr.
Et Nigillo de Nescefeld p' corrodio suo p' ann', IIII qr. II b' di.
Et in pane p' carpentariis et cariantib' m'emii in div'sis locis, I qr. IIII b' di.
Et in semine apud Boulton, Angrum, How, & Riddingg', XXXV qr. V b'.

S'm' expens' frum' CCLXIX qr. I b'.

Memorand' q'd expend' fuer't hoc anno de silig' fab' ord' & farina in elemosina, XXXII qr. di.
Et in pane ad Celariu' hoc anno, CI qr. VI b'.
Et in lib' pagior' ap'd g'ngias, porcarii & in pane ad trituratores, XII qr. IIII b' di.
Et in pane ad op' sarclanciu', potagio messor' & colligenciu' decim', VIII qr. di.
Et in putura * porcor. p'cellor. aucaru', & in pane ad equos & aliis minutis, XIIII qr. VI b'.
Et in semine apud Boulton IX qr. III b'. di. silig', V qr. V b'. di. fab', & VII qr. ordei.

S'm' expens' silig' fab' ord' & farine, C^{xx}_{iiii}XII qr. I b'. di.

Memorand' q'd in braseo f'c'o expend' fuerunt hoc anno, DCCCXLVIII qr. avene.
Et in semine apud Boulton, C^{xx}_{v}V qr. di.
Et in p'bn' equor' infra Cur' & extra, CCCXXXIIII qr. V b'.
Et in farina f'c'a ad potagium in coquina, $^{xx}_{iiii}$IIII qr.
Et in furfure canum hoc anno, LV qr.
Et in putura boum, pullanor' & agnor', cum Spitelcorn p' estimac'o'm in garbis, LIX qr.
Et in putura porcor', aucarum & caponu', XXII qr. di.
Et in p'bn' apud Skirgile cont' adventu' d'ni W. de Hamelton, V qr.
Et Joh'i G'unwall ex convenc'o'e p' annu' III qr.
Et in diversis lib' infra Cur' & extra & in aliis minutis ut in Comp' g'natarii CCXXVI qr. II b'.

S'm' expens' toci' avene MDCCCXLII qr. VII b'.

Clarum de Maneriis.

Halton.
    Manerium de Halton R. hoc anno de L qr. frumenti p' estimac'o'm in garbis, p' qr. V*s*.
S'm' de claro £XII. X*s*.

    Et rem' ibidem—
Riddyngg'.
    Mansura de Riddingg' R. hoc anno de claro de XVII qr. frumenti, p' qr. V*s*.
    Et de XXXVI qr. avene, p' qr. XX*d*.
S'm' £VII. V*s*.

    De quibus subtrahunt' VI*s*. VIII*d*. quos receptor solvit p' stipend' bovarior' ibid.
    Et sic respondit de claro de £VI. XVIII*s*. IIII*d*.
    Et rem' ibidem XII boves.

Stede.
    Mansura del Stede R. hoc anno de I qr. II b' silig', p' qr. IIII*s*.
    Et de LXXI qr. avene, p' qr. XVIII*d*.
S'm' CXI*s*. VI*d*.

    De quibus subtrahunt' VI*s*. VIII*d*. quos bursari' solvit p' stipend' bovarior' ibid.
    Et sic respondit de claro hoc anno de CIIII*s*. X*d*.
    Et rem' ibidem XIII boves.

How.
    Mansura del How R. hoc anno de I qr. di. frum', p' qr. V*s*.
    Et de VII qr. II b' siliginis, p' qr. IIII*s*.
    Et de XLIII qr. avene, p' qr. XVIII*d*.
S'm' CI*s*.

    De quibus subt'hunt' VI*s*. VIII*d*. quos bursari' solvit p' stipend' bovarior' ibid.
    Et sic respondit de claro hoc anno de £IIII. XIIII*s*. IIII*d*.
    Et rem' ibidem XII boves.

Malghum.
    Mansura de Malghum R. hoc anno de X qr. mixtilionis frum' & ordei, p' qr. IIII*s*. & de XXIII*d*. in potu carianc' m'emiu'.
    Et de XXXIIII qr. VII b' avene, p' qr. II*s*.
S'm' CIX*s*. XI*d*.

    De quibus subtrahunt' VI*s*. VIII*d*. quos bursari' solvit p' stipend' bovarior' ibid. Et VII*s*. quos idem bursari' solvit p' blad metend' ibid'.

[* Putura. Id omne quod in cibum homini vel animalibus tribuitur unde translata exinde hæc vox ad designandum *jus gisti* seu *procurationis* quo dominus a vassallis hospitio et conviviis excipitur : *ce qui sert à la nourriture de l'homme et du cheval*, et par l'extension : *droit de gîte ou de procuration.*—" Lexicon Mediæ et Infimæ Latinitatis."]

Et sic R. de claro de £IIII. XVI*s.* III*d.*

Et rem' ibidem—XVI boves. I vacca. I juvenca in t'cio anno. I jumentum. I pullan'* in tercio anno, & I pullan' in s'c'do anno.

Conedley.

Mansura de Conedly R. hoc anno de I qr. V b' siliginis, p' qr. IIII*s.*

Et de I qr. VI b' ordei, p' qr. XL*d.*

Et de LXVIII qr. avene, p' qr. XX*d.*

S'm' £VI. V*s.* VIII*d.*

De quibus subtrahunt XXI*s.* VIII*d.* q's bursari' solvit p' stipend' bovarior' & expens' autumpni ibid.

Et sic R. de claro de CIIII*s.*

Et nullum instauru' ibid. rem.

Kildewick.

De claro de Kildewik non fit mencio hoc anno q. non fuit in manu Prioris.

Set rem' ibidem—I jumentu' affr' cum pull'. III affri masculi. Item I jumentu' de Conedley. I pult' in tercio anno. I pull' q'tuor annor'. I pull' t'um annor'. I pull' in tercio anno. It'm XXX boves. II bovett' in tercio anno. II bovetti in s'c'do anno. XI vacce. It'm I vacc' & I bovett' in q'rto anno. recept' apud Conedley.

Unkethorp.

Unkethorp n'l R. hoc anno.

Et rem' ibidem—I jumentu' cu' I pull' huj' anni. I pultra in q'rto anno. XX boves. IIII vacc'. VI vitul' de exitu huj' anni, quor' duo sunt masculi.

Hinehous.

Apud le Hynehous rem' $^{XX}_{V}$IX boves.

Vaccarie.

In Vaccar' rem'—IIII tauri. C$^{XX}_{V}$VI vacce. XXXIX juvence in s'c'do anno. XLIII juvenc' in tercio anno. I bovett' in q'nto anno. L bovett' in q'rto anno. XXXIIII bovett' in tercio anno, et XLVII bovett' in s'c'do anno. Pret' hec rem' II bovett' rec' de Ric'o de Ebor' et S. de Otteley.

Equiciu'.

In equicio rem'—I staloun. XXVII jumenta. VI pultr' in tercio anno. IIII pultre in s'c'do anno. II pull' in q'rto anno VI pull' in tercio anno. IIII pull' in s'c'do anno.

Oves.

It'm rem'—DCXXVII multon'. DC oves matrices. CCCC$^{XX}_{V}$ hogg' ut'usq' sex'.

Item in plaustro instaurarii rem' IX boves.

Vaccaria del How.

Memorand' q'd ad Invenc'o'm S'c'e Crucis anno D'ni M$_o$. CC^o. nonagesimo nono Adam de Eleshow cepit vaccaria del How cum XXVI vaccis, ten' ad respond' p' qualib' vacca de IIII petr' casei et II petr' butiri. S'm' petr' casei ^{XX}IIII S'm' butiri LII petr'.—De quib' solvit ad Celarium LXXV petr' casei et XXXIX petr' butiri et CCC$^{XX}_{V}$X lagen' lactis, p'ciu' lagene ob. ; quod quidem lac allocat' eidem p' XXIX petr' casei & p' XIII petr' butiri preter II*d.* et sic debet unam petr' casei et II*d.*

Vaccar' de Riddingg'.

Die & anno sup'd'c'is Ad. Parcour cepit vaccaria' de Riddingg' cum XXI vacc', ten' ad R. p' qualib' vaccade IIII petr casei & II petr' butiri. S'm' casei $^{XX}_{IIII}$IIII petr' et butiri XLII petr'.—De quib' solvit ad Celariu' $^{XX}_{IIII}$ petr' casei et XXXV. petr' butiri et $^{XX}_{V}$ lagenas lactis, p'c' ut su. ; quod quidem lac allocat' eidem p' VI petr' butiri preter II*d.* et sic deb' III petras casei et II*d.*

Somerscales.

Die & anno sup'd'c'is Henr' vaccari' cepit vaccaria' de Som'scales cum XVIII vacc', ten' ad R. p' qualibet vacca de III petr' di. casei et I petr' di. butiri. S'm' casei LXIII petr', et s'm' butiri XXVII petr'.—De quibus solvit ad Celariu' LIII petr' casei et XXVII petr' butiri et $^{XX}_{V}$ lagen' lact' que allocant' p' X petris casei, et sic eque.

Vaccar' del Stede.

Die et anno sup'd'c'is Rob's de Som'scales cepit vaccaria' del Stede cum XVII vacc', ten' ad R. p' qualib' vacca de IIII petr' casei et de II petr' butiri. S'm' casei LXVIII petr'. S'm' butiri XXXIIII petr'.—De quib' solvit LXVI petr' casei et XXVIII petr' butiri et $^{XX}_{IIII}$XIII lagen' lactis, que allocant' eidem p' V petr' di. butiri, et sic debet II petr' casei et di. petram butiri.

S'm' toci' casei CCLXXIX petr'.—S'm' toci' butiri CXXXV petr'.

———

A^o MCCXCIV. Deb. soluta.

Mercator. de societate Frescobaldi,† CCXIII*l.* VI*s.* VIII*d.*

[* Pullanus, a foal.]

† The Lombard merchants, with the Jews, were, in the 13th century, the bankers of Europe. The Frescobaldi were Florentines, and subsisted in that capacity at least two centuries after this time.

3 G

In Carbon' marin. ad forgiam, X*s.*

Ad fabricam* ecc'e, XLVI*s.* VI*d.* ob.

    S'm' exp' in hoc ann. DCVIII*l.* X*s.* V*d.* et sic exp. exc. recept. XLIIII*l.* XII*s.* q.

    S'm' tot. debitor' CCC$^{xx}_{IIII}$VIII*l.* XII*s.* VI*d.*

MCCXCVI.

Pro fenest' vitreis ad bord', meremio, &c. ad fabricam eccl. CXVI*s.* III*d.*

MCCXCVII.

Exp. avene.

In farina† facta ad potagium in coquina $^{xx}_{v}$VIII qr.

It. in furfure canum† XXIII qu. di.

MCCXCVIII.

In exp. coquine, pro warnestura‡ et alio pisce.

In carb. marin. ad calcem ardend', XVII*s.*

In sapo et cotoun§ ad candelam, XVII*s.* I*d.*

Pro auro et coloribus‖ ad picturam, et pro uno missali luminand' et ligand', XVI*s.*

Adam de Elshow capit vaccariam del Howe cum XIX vaccis ; ten'r ad respond' p' qualibet vacca de IIII petr. casei et II petr. butyri, pro petra casei V*d.* pro petra butyri VIII*d.*—De quibus solvit XLVII di. petr. cas. et XXXVII di. petr. butyri et CCCXL lagenas lactis pro lagena ob. que quidem lagene allocant. pro XL petr. casei.¶

MCCXCIX. Rec.

De Sartrina ** hoc anno XVI*l.*

In div'sis donis et exenniis †† factis magnatibus pr. util. Ds. cum eleemos. XIII*l.* IIII*s.* III*d.* ob.

In Politridiis. ‡‡

Prov. ap'd S'ctum Botulphum. §§   In Panno et furruris empt' ap'd Ebor. XIII*l.* III*s.* IV*d.*

Cuidam hocario.‖‖   Cuidam in infirmario c'versorum.   Cuidam in Aula hospitum D'no Subpriori.   In vestura Fr. Adam de Ottely, X*s.*¶¶

      Summa exp' frum' hoc an. CCLXIX. qr. I bu.

      Summa exp' totius avene MDCCCXLII qr. VII bu.***

A° MCCC.

De XLI saccis lani ††† vend. CCLXXIII*l.* VI*s.* VIII*d.*   Pro tribus vaccis vend. XXII*s.*

---

   * The fabric of the priory church had long been finished ; but I suspect these two articles to refer to the ramified windows of the choir, which were broken out about this time, instead of the narrow single lights of the original church. Meremium, or building-timber, might be wanted for some repairs of the roof.

   † A hundred and eight quarters of oatmeal were consumed this year in the single article of pottage, and twenty-three and a half upon the hounds, of which I think the prior always kept a pack. Furfur is not bran, but what is called groundmeat, with which pigs are frequently fatted.

   ‡ Warnestura—Guarnastura—Garnestura. This word often occurs, and is always coupled with fish. In the monkish writers it usually signifies provisions in general : "Sustentamenta quæ Garnesturas appellant." (Matth. Paris. Vide Du Cange, in voce.)

   § Cotoun [cotton]. This substance, of which the manufactory is become so extensive and so pernicious, was then imported in small quantities from the Levant.

   ‖ For gold and colours, and for illuminating and binding a missal, 16*s.* From the high price paid, I conclude this to have been an elaborate and curious work. Sixteen shillings was one-third more than the yearly clothing of a canon cost.

   ¶ I have extracted this article in order to direct the reader's attention to a very ancient mode of letting a farm. The tenant had it in his choice to pay either a proportion of the produce, or by commutation in money. But the consideration, four stones of cheese and two of butter for each milch cow, was extremely easy.

   ** The sartrina in the religious houses was the tailor's office : "Vestiarius sartrinum habere debet extra officinas claustri interiores." (Lib. Ord. St. Victor. Paris, as quoted by Du Cange.) But how the canons of Bolton should make a profit of this amounting to 16*l.* unless their tailors wrought for all the country around them, or even then, I do not understand.

   †† Exennia were presents given to great persons, who were their guests : ξενια, from which the Latin word is formed by prefixing the letter *e.*

   ‡‡ Politridiis. I insert this word to correct my own mistake with respect to it in "History of Whalley," p. 95. It means a sieve, from "pollen trudere," and is sometimes spelt Pollentrudium. From this substantive the writers of the Middle Ages formed a verb still more awkward and inharmonious, Pollentrudinizare.

   §§ Providentia apud S'ctum Botulphum. It must be observed, that in these times there were few or no shops ; private families, therefore, as well as the religious, constantly attended the great annual fairs, where the necessaries of life not produced within their own domains were purchased. In every year of this Compotus there is an account of wine, cloth, groceries, &c., bought apud S'ctum Botulphum. Distant as Boston (Botulph's Town) in Lincolnshire was, our canons certainly resorted to the great annual fair held at that place, from whence the necessaries purchased by them might easily be conveyed by water as far as York.

   ‖‖ A man working *hoco,* with a hook or bill.

   ¶¶ The lay brethren had an infirmary of their own. The guests had a hall for their own entertainment. The Subprior was styled My Lord. Ten shillings was above the average expense of clothing a canon.

   *** 1,842 quarters of oats—what a prodigious consumption !

   ††† Wool was always dear in ancient times. This commodity sold for more than 6*l.* a sack ; while the price of a cow was 7*s.* 4*d.* The legal sack consisted of 26 stones of 14 lb. each,—*i.e.,* nearly 5*s.* each stone. This was a very unusual price, and for the time it lasted would have the singular effect of rendering the wild moors and sheep-walks belonging to the canons equally valuable with their richest pastures. It also taught them the advantage of abstaining, in a great measure, from mutton. The sarpler was half a sack. See "Fleta," b. ii. c. 12, and Spelman in voce Saccus. The wool now produced on the same commons scarcely fetches twenty shillings.

De II qr. VII bu. frum. vend. XVIIs. IIId.

Pro uno equo empto XIIIl. VIs. VIIId. *

Venditio bosci.   De coponibus † reman. de merem. in Crokerys, VIs.

Jacobo de Eyston ‡ pro maner. de Apeltrewyk in p'te, XIVl. XVId.

Pro cartis D'ni Regis pro eod. manerio, XXXIIs. VIIId.

Pro auro regine,‡ VIl. XIIIs. IVd.

Pro fine facto D'no Hen. de Hertlinton pro eod. maner', VIl. XIIIs. IVd.

Armigero Regis § venienti pro plaustris habend. in Scociam, VIIs. VId.

Bovariis fugantibus eadem plaustra in Scociam, IIIs. VIIId.

In Banastris et Durnes.‖   In panno empto ad opus Cobb. pagii prioris, IIIIs.

In exp. prioris in Angl. et in curiam Romanam,¶ XXXIVl. XIIIs. ob.

Dona prioris D'no archiepiscopo Ebor. ad tronizacion. suam,** VIl. XIIIs. IVd.

   This year there were twenty-four servants *infra curiam* (that is, domestics within the close), who received in wages IIIIl. XVIs. VIId.; and eighty servants in husbandry, shepherds, and herdsmen, &c., at Bolton, and upon the different granges, who received XIIl. XXd.

      Sum. tot. exp. hoc an. DCXXXIIl. IXs. VIId.

         Et sic exp. excedunt recepta XIIIl. VIs. IId. ob. qu.

         Debita quæ debet domus, CCCCXLVl. XIs. IVd.

A° MCCCI.

   Canonicis de Kirkby †† pro dec fen. in Malghum Mercatoribus de societate Bernardi, pro expens. Prioris circa Appeltrewick, VIl. VIs. VIIId.

   Eisdem pro exp. prioris in Cur. Rom. XIIl.

   Jacobo de Eston in p'te pro Apeltrewic, XIIl.

   Nicholao de Warwyk pro auxilio contra domum de Marton, XIIIs. IVd.

Custos minere—‡‡

   In expens. op'antiu' in minera plumbi, CVIs. VIIId.

   In exp. prioris in cur. Rom. XIIl. Vs. IVd.

   Debita quæ domus debet. Mercatoribus de circulo nigro Vannino et Banco mercatoribus,§§ &c. Jacobo de Eston, XXIl. VIs. VIIId.

The stock of the house this year at Bolton and the Granges was 713 horned cattle, of which 252 were oxen; 2,193 sheep; 95 pigs; and 91 goats. The number of horses is not mentioned.

In uncto, sepo et vindigrec. ad oves unguend. Xl. IIs.‖‖‖   In diversis herensiis et utensilibus.¶¶

   * 13l. 6s. 8d. a very high price for a horse.

   † Coponibus. These were boughs or loppings from large trees, which, it appears, were then growing in Crokerys. Hence " Coppice wood, Sylva cædua—Willaume de Forest disoit a avoir en sa terre de forest le coppuis." (Vet. Cart. ap. Du Cange.)

   ‡ This year the prior and canons purchased the manor of Appletrewic from James de Eshton. Here is a curious instance of Queen Gold, which is defined by Blackstone to be a revenue belonging to every Queen Consort from all persons who have made a fine to the King of ten marks or upward for any grant or privilege. (" Com." vol. i. p. 219.)

   § Their wains, drawn by oxen, were pressed for the conveyance of the king's baggage into Scotland.

   ‖ Panniers, or wicker baskets and water-pots.

   ¶ The Prior was obliged to undertake a journey to Rome in order to obtain a bull for Appletrewick.

   ** Ten marks were a pretty high consideration for his seat at the enthronisation feast of Archbishop Corbridge. But there was at this time something like an Oriental liberality to the great.

   †† It appears from this expression that there was a cell at Kirkby Malghdale ; otherwise the canons would have been called de Dereham.

   ‡‡ It appears that they were now working a lead-mine, though it is not said on what part of their estates.

   §§ These, and the Societas Bernardi, mentioned above, were all Lombard merchants, who purchased their wool, and often advanced them money.

   ‖‖ The canons of Bolton had two great bercaries—one at Malham, the other at Nussay on the borders of Knaresborough Forest. I shall take the present opportunity of explaining this part of their economy. The bercaries were lodges in the neighbourhood of the moors, where the shepherds belonging to the religious houses resided. Here they had folds, pens, washpits, and every other necessary apparatus of a great sheep-farm. The word " bercaria " was first contracted from " berbecaria," as that was formed by a change of two labials from " vervecaria ;" and all from " vervex," a wether sheep. It appears that they smeared their sheep with tar, verdigris, and quicksilver. Tar and butter only are now used for the purpose ; though it is very doubtful whether anything more than the collected perspiration of the animal within the fleece is necessary to protect it from cold. The wool is certainly injured by any unction. Quicksilver must have been intended merely to kill their vermin. Barmeclathes were the sheepshearer's aprons, from Saxon, Bapme, *sinus*. The leaders of the flock had bells. Sarpillaria were packsheets for the wool. See Rymer's " Fœdera," tom. xii. p. 714. " Idem paccator super omnes serplerias cognomen suum scribet." And again, tom. xiii. p. 138, in anno 1566, " Easdem lanas ex serpelleriis et saccis extrahere." A sarpler of wool was a package less than a sack. From the compotus of another year it appears that the bercary of Malham was covered with shingles. That of Nussay seems to have been thatched with ling (bruera) and feuger, which is supposed to have been fern. The word is mentioned by the author of " Fleta," and perhaps by him alone of all our old English lawyers or historians. It was unknown to Spelman. The Compan. and Curial. Bercariorum were treats and presents made to the shepherds at their washings and shearings—scenes of innocent and rustic festivity yet maintained, in their primitive simplicity, though upon a smaller scale, among the Dalesmen.

   ¶¶ Hence the modern " harness."

In tela pro caseo, barmeclathes, et tintinabilibus, IIIs. XId.

In companagio et curialitate bercariorum, IIIs.

In filo ad sarpilaria, IXd.

Pro $\frac{XX}{IIII}$ ulnis carentuilt.*

In XXVI ulnis ad sarpilar', IXs. IId.

Pro furruris, XXIs.

MCCCII.

In dolio vini empti, LXVIs. VIIId.

In CCC Dogdraves† et CC duris piscibus.

MCCCIII et IV.

In vivo argento, verdigrees, et bitumine, ad oves‡ unguend'.

Hayne Janitori§ Regis, pro liberatione plaustorum in Scotiâ, VIs. VIIId.

In expensis D'ni W. de Hamelton post Nathale, et venatorum suorum in Autumpno capientium venationem in Longstrothe'.||

Clerici arch'i pro cartâ appropr' eccl' de Preston scribendâ, XXs.¶

Clericis capit. Ebor. scribentibus eand. cart. et confirm. eccl' de Carlton, XLs.¶

Pro carucâ plumbi Tho. de Dibb,** XXXs.

In pane pro D'no W. de Hamelton, quando fuit in partibus istis, pro venatoribus suis circa Chaceam de Longstrothe',†† XXII dim. qr't' frum'.

D'no Regi pro ingressu eccl' de Preston, XLVs.—Cs. condonabantur.¶

Et pro auro Regine pro eodem ingressu, Cs.¶

Thesaurario Regis pro auxil. in diversis negotiis, LXXIIIs. IVd.¶

Cancellario Regis pro favore h'nd' XIIs. IId.¶

Prov' S'ci Botulphi.

In pelurâ‡‡ empt. ad opus D'ni Rogeri, XXXVIs.

In C carentuil' et I Fentro§§ ad paccand.

MCCCIV.

In facturâ Cancelle de Skipton in p'te, LXVs. VId.

This year VIIIl. Xs. XId. are paid to 53 servants *infra curiam*, and VIIIl. XVs. VIIId. to 59 *extra curiam;* besides XIIs. magistro Johanni Janitori.

S'm tot. exp. DCCXIVl. Xs. VIIId.

Et sic exp. excedunt recepta, CCCVIl. XIXs.

MCCCV.

Pro cartâ ferie de Emmesay |||| renovatâ et confirm' in Cancellariâ, IVl. Vs.

Prov' S'ci Botulphi.

Pro pannis sericis et pall' ad vest'ment' et mattis ad hosp. IVl. XVs. Id.

In constructione pontis de Kyldwyk,¶¶ in p'te, XXIl. XIIs. IXd.

Exp. Prioris, XVl. XVIIs. ob. qu.

Pro quodam Libro Sententiarum empt. *** XXXs.

Deb. mercatoribus de societate P'uch,††† CCl.

In pane pro triphyrdes‡‡‡ sarculant' metent'.

In stauro hoc anno oves ᴄᴏM.CXIII. Boves omn. æt. CCCCXLI. Equi LVI.

---

* This word, which, from every passage where it occurs, evidently means a kind of coarse sheeting for packing wool, is unknown to all the etymologists. The two first syllables seem to be derived from Carena, or Lent, as it might be worn for mortification at that season ; and, with respect to the last, some textures of cloth are said to be twilled at present.

† Dogdraves, in the compotus of other years, is sometimes spelt Dogdragh. This being opposed to Duri Pisces, or Stockfish, must have been some sort of pickled fish ; may it not have been the rank and disgusting dogfish, which, under the name of gobbock, is so great a favourite with the common people in the Isle of Man ?

[‡ See note |||| on p. 459.]

§ It seems that they had to bribe the king's porter to allow their wains to return out of Scotland.

|| I should little have expected to meet with an account of a hunting party in Longstrothdale 500 years ago. I know nothing, however, of this ancient hunter, and have only to remark that he was probably a friend of the Percies, and that he, his huntsman and hounds, must have been long and liberally entertained at Bolton, where they consumed twenty-two quarters of wheat. The canons were noble housekeepers !

¶ The church of Long Preston was appropriated this year. I have put down several items of the expenses attending this acquisition, to show how dearly these concessions and confirmations were purchased both from the diocesan and the crown. The great officers of state, beside their regular fees, evidently accepted presents on these occasions *pro favore habend'*.

** Dibb is a very romantic little valley near Coniston.

†† See note || above.

‡‡ A note will be bestowed on the Pelluræ hereafter.

§§ Carentuil, or Carentuilt, I suppose to have been a rough, coarse sort of linen cloth for package. Carentilla, in monkish Latin, is a curry-comb ; and the word might be transferred to this stuff from its roughness. The reader may take his choice between this and my former conjecture as to this word. The word "fentrum," unknown to all the etymologists, is, I think, partly retained in the modern "fent," a remnant.

|||| Embsay Fair is frequently mentioned ; and, from the sum paid for the renewal of the charter, the tolls must have been considerable.

¶¶ The building (qu. whether rebuilding ?) of Kildwick Bridge was an expensive work, which lasted several years.

*** The "Book of Sentences," by Peter Lombard, one of the most fashionable books of school divinity in the Middle Age. The price of this volume was nearly that of two good oxen. How expensive must it then have been to furnish a library with MSS ! But the canons of Bolton did not exhaust themselves in this way. I can only discover that they purchased three books in forty years !

††† Another society of Lombard merchants ; elsewhere in this volume called Peruch', and well known in the general histories of the age by the name of Peruchi.

‡‡‡ The triphyrds were goatherds, whose station probably was at Malham.

Lardar'.

M. quod mactat' fuer't ad Lardar. hoc anno XXXVIII boves et IX bov. impingu. contr' Pasch' ; et in æstate XL vaccæ et duæ juvencæ ; et de porcis LI. et de porcellis XXVI. et de bident. XXIII. et sept. carcoys empt. ap. Ebor. ; præter capreolos, aucas, &c.

Braseum.

DCCIV q'ria brasei provenient' de DCC$^{XX}_V$XII q'r's avene.

MCCCVI.

Dona recepta de Everardo Favvel,* ad fenestram vitream cancelli de Skypton, VI*s*. VIII*d*.
De quodam lecto plumal' dato et vendito, II*s*. VI*d*.
In camerâ D'ni Prioris in parte, XXXIV*s*. VI*d*.
In facturâ cori de Skypton,* LXIV*s*. VIII*d*.
Nuncio principis Walliæ.†
Pro una campanâ pro priore emptâ, VI*s*. VIII*d*.
Pro Constitutionibus ‡ scribendis.
Cuidam qui occidit lupum.§ Retibus ad piscem, et cum ducturâ hñdâ cum quadrigâ, usq. ad Scotiam, XXIII*l*. III*s*.
Pro Barmquers et q'syns ∥ ad cameram prioris.

Custos ovium.

Pro lacte empt' ad capreolos.—Hurtardi ¶ Multones.

Compotus Dayr'.

De butyro de ovibus de Malgham, IX petr.**

Compotus Granatoris.

In piis Pastelles et Newelles,†† IV qrt. 7 bush.

MCCCVII.

De telon. ferie de Embsay, VIII*l*. X*s*.
Pro subsidio Terre Sancte D'no Regi conc. XXVI*l*. XVIII*s*. XI*d*.

Prov' S'ti Botulphi.

Pro panno ad capam prioris, VIII*s*. ob.
Pro II furruris empt' ad caputium prioris, II*s*. VIII*d*.
Et pro furr' emp' ad opus d'ni Rogeri, XXI*s*. qu.
Pro VIII furr' ad opus armigerorum, XV*s*. IV*d*. ob.

In speciebus.

XII lb. cytonalent,‡‡ VII*s*.
VIII lb. zuker, VIII*d*.
C lb. rys, IV*s*.
Pro arcubus ad opus garcionum, VIII*d*.
Carpentariis, cæmentariis, &c. ad cameram §§ d'ni Prioris XXXII*l*. XII*s*. V*d*.
Cuidam qui occidit lupum.∥∥
Pro jocalibus ¶¶ empt' per fr. Pet. de Myton, LXXVIII*s*. XI*d*.
In turbis *** lucrand' et fodiend' apud Malghum.
In pane furnito gratis d'no de Percy et J. de Mowbray, II qr. frum.
Pro salm. pisc. allec. &c. ad sepulturam d'ni Rob. de Stiveton,††† XL*s*. IV*d*.
In pane furnito pro sepulturâ ejusdem, I qr. dim.

---

* From these articles it may fairly be inferred, that the old Norman church of Skipton was now receiving a considerable enlargement. I believe the stone seats now remaining in the south wall, though not of the original building, are yet older than this. Yet I think the whole of the present choir has been extended eastward and entirely rebuilt since this time. Everard Favvel, who contributed to the east window, was of a family often occurring in Craven charters.

† These are notices of the last expedition of Edward I. into Scotland. He died on the western border, and his march by Skipton or Bolton was evidently in that direction. A following article furnishes a very curious fact. It is well known that Edward, on his death-bed, bequeathed 32,000*l*. for the purpose of carrying his heart to the Holy Land. This was never performed ; but we here see that young Edward levied sums of money upon the religious houses on that pretence.

‡ The constitutions of their order.

§ Wolves, therefore, though rare, were not extinct in Craven in the beginning of the 14th century. This is an important circumstance in natural history.

∥ These, I think, are different sorts of napkins for the prior's table.

¶ The Hurtardi were rams, from the Italian " urtare," to push.

** Nine stones of butter were made this year at Malham, from sheep's milk.

†† Newelles—Nebulæ, or Neullæ. These were extremely thin cakes baked upon flat iron pans (Buccellæ quæ fiunt super ferrum, ut Nebulæ). In some churches it was the custom, during the celebration of high mass on Whitsunday, at the Gloria in Excelsis, to turn loose into the church a number of little birds, with these newles tied to their feet. Hence, I suppose, they were called nebulæ. But they were sometimes served at table on the festivals. (Du Cange, in Nebulæ.)

‡‡ They had all the common spices now in use from the East, as pepper, cinnamon, mace, &c., but I do not know what is cytonalent. Rice was about a halfpenny a pound.

§§ By the camera prioris, which was now building, we are not to understand a single apartment, but an entire and large house, with hall, chapel, kitchen, &c., distinct from those of the priory.

∥∥ See note § above.

¶¶ Joculare, jewel, was not a single precious stone, but an ornament of jeweller's work. This was probably for the altar.

*** Turbis, turf. This homely fuel, during the Middle Ages, was generally used, not only in England, but in France and Flanders. It is perhaps first mentioned by Pliny as a wretched substitute for wood, used in cookery by the Cauchi (Nat. Hist. L. XVI. C. 1). And from the Chronicle of Andres I find that it was not more agreeable to the fine ladies of those days than of our own : " Quod uxor ejus focum glebarum vel turbarum exosum habebat."

††† This article furnishes the precise date of the death of Sir Robert de Stiveton, whose tomb remains in Kildwick church, see p. 211. Funerals in those days were celebrated with excessive profusion in meat and drink ; and as they admitted of little time for preparation, and the religious houses had always great store of provisions beforehand, it seems to have been usual in the gentlemen's families to have recourse, on these occasions, to the nearest abbey. The funeral of Sir Adam de Midelton will furnish another instance.

Pro Cam. Prioris hoc ann. IX*l.* XII*s.* IV*d.*

Pro laticiis * ad corum de Skypton, III*s.* IV*d.*

Cust. ovium.

Pro lineâ telâ ad Naperouns.†

St. Botulph.

Pro furrurâ empt. ad opus d'ni Ad. de Midelton et matris prioris, XIV*s.* II*d.*

Pro furrurâ ad opus d'ni Rogeri et arm. XLIII*s.* VI*d.*

I q'rt de vermylon ‡, vlb. alb. plumb. IIlb. rub. plumb.

Diversis operant' ‡ circ' cam. prioris et capellam ejusd. in parte.

Pro bercariâ de Malghum reparand' et cooperiend' cum bordis in p'te, LX*s.*

Et pro DCC bordis emptis ad eandem, XXII*s.* VI*d.*

Cuidam medico in infirmitate prioris, XL*s.* §

Pro pellibus agninis ad furr' conficiend.

MCCCX. }
A fest. Mich. }   Pro p'dicibus et I heyron, et al' volatil' contra D'nam de Clifford ‖ per vices, X*s.* VIIII*d.*

Wil'mo pictori pro cam'a prioris in p'te, VIII*s.* VII*d.*

Pro serraturâ planchur' ¶ ad torale de Boulton, II*s.* VI*d.*

In quodam exhennio** Com'i Cornub. facto, XIX*s.* I*d.*

Pro uno libro qui vocatur V'itates Theologie,†† VI*s.*

Hogastri utriusque sexûs DCLXX.   Ex confessione Joh le Lambehirde. ‡‡

Rem. in off. cellar. de caseo ovium CXLVII petr. §§

In pane ad opus d'ni R. de Clifford, I qrt.

In prebendâ dextrariorum Com. Cornub.‖‖ XIX. qr.

MCCCXI.

Pro VI uln pan. ad capam prior. VIII. uln. de wurstede, III. uln. de fustyan, una pellic. I furr. de ventr. lepor' III furr. capic'on et III pann. de fenter' pro priore, XXXIII*s.* VI*d.*

Pro IV rison. ad opus rector' de Broughton, III*s.* VI*d.*

In III lb. cetonal.

Operant' apud Boulton circ' cap. prioris, VII*l.* VI*s.* VI*d.*

Pro plumbo empt. circ. eand' cap. in parte XLIII*s.* VI*d.*

Pro vitro ad eand. XX*s.*

Pro cap. talliand'¶¶ ad fen. ecc. de Kildwic, cum tabulis lap. ibm. XXVII*s.* V*d.*

Pro II aundirne ad cam. prioris, XVI*s.*

Pro carbon' marin' fodiend' et cariand.

---

* The new choir of Skipton church was therefore finished this year.   Lattices for the windows would be the last part of the expense attending it.

† This word occupies the place of barmcloths in the accounts of the foregoing years, and evidently points at the etymology of the word Apron. Napery is defined by Skinner, " Linteamenta domestica ; " and the word apron had plainly lost a letter, probably from a mistake in dividing it from the prefix, a naperoun, or an apron.

‡ The prior's lodgings and chapel were a long and expensive work.   I am rather at a loss to determine for what purpose red and white lead, as well as vermilion, were used at this early period.   The wood roof of the church of Bolton is painted with broad lines of red lead, but this work is two centuries later than the Compotus.

§ Forty shillings must have been the fee for several journeys of the physician, who probably came from York.   He, or Nature, however, prevailed over the disease, for Prior de Land lived many years after this time.

‖ This is the first appearance of the House of Clifford, on which account the present articles are extremely interesting.   Several entertainments were evidently made by the canons for their new patroness, who, besides partridges and other wild fowl, was treated with a delicacy deserving to be specified, namely, a single heron.   Contra means against the coming of.

¶ Sawing planks for a new floor for the kiln.   Plancher is, I think, still used in Norfolk for a boarded floor ; but wooden floors were then composed of strong planks.

** This year Peirs de Gavestone, for it is he who is intended by Comes Cornubiæ, took leave of his short-lived possession of the honour of Skipton, and this exhennium was probably a generous and disinterested tribute to departing greatness.

†† V'itates Theologiæ—in the beginning of the 14th century I can scarcely suppose that there was a book with so profane or so bold a title as Vanitates Theologiæ ; and, therefore, I understand this contraction to mean either veritates or utilitates.

‡‡ Lambherde, as shepherd, cowherd, calfherd, or calvert, &c.   This was now the name of an office, but, like many others, afterwards became hereditary ; and I think it highly probable that these lambherds, by occupation, gave origin to the family of Lambert, first of Skipton, and last of Calton.

§§ There were this year consumed at Bolton 147 stones of cheese made from ewes' milk.   I have tasted this preparation, and found it extremely disgusting.   But the canons probably left it to their husbandmen and garciones to eat sheep's cheese and drink oaten beer.

‖‖ The Dextrarii of the Earl of Cornwall, mentioned above, are the French Destrer, by which name Chaucer distinguishes the steed of Sir Thopas ; " And by him fed his Destrer."   They were, properly, war horses led by grooms till they were mounted by the knights for battle.   The Byzantine historians call them Δεξιοι.

¶¶ The Latinity of the Middle Ages was mingled in very large proportions with old French and Italian, and even Greek.   Indeed it abounds in hybrid words, compounded of Greek and Latin.   Talliandis is from the Italian, tagliare, " to cut."

Exhênnia Prioris.
 Pro jocalibus empt. et dat. D'ne de Clyfford * et fam. sue, CXVIIIs. VIIId.
 Pro camino † rect. de Gayrgrave faciendo, et dato eidem, IXs.
 In vesturâ XV canon', X*l.*
 In vest' II conv. XIIIs. IIIId.
 In prebendâ equor' prior' ap' Boulton, $\overset{xx}{\text{IIII}}$VIIII qr.
 (N.B. The provender of a colt V qu. VII bu.)

MCCCXII.
 Operant. ad capel' prior' in parte, VIIIs. VIIId.
 Pro div'sis coloribus ad pictur. ejusd. in p'te, XIIIs. IIId.
 Will. Pictori pro stip' suo in p'te, Vs.
 Exhênnia D'no Clifford et D'ne et fam. sue. in div'sis
   donis et jocalibus, XV*l.* Xs.

 Et in I candelâ datâ d'ce D'ne ad purif' suam,
   XVs. IIId.
 De coriis in morinâ.‡
 In pane ad Tippelhyrdes. §

MCCCXIII.
 Pro I apro empto ad braune, VIIs.
 Pro X lamprys‖ de Naunt, contra d'nam de Clyfford,
   IXs. VId.
 Pro XXX pikerel empt' ad instaurand' vivarium apud
   Ryther, XXd.
 W. de Calv'lay pro altare et sconces in eâdem, VIs.

 Pro quodam vestimento parand, ap'd Ebor' pro capell'
   prioris, XVs.
 Pro XXXV lb. cere ad cam'm ejusd. XIs. XId.
 Pro mappis et sannenapýs ¶ emp. ap' London.
 Pro II cygnis** emptis et missis comiti Lanc. XVIs. IId.
 Ministrallis, &c. LXXIVs.
 Pro chroniclis †† apud Ebor. scribendis, IIs.

MCCCXIV.
 Recept' de Evâ de Land ‡‡ pro ponte de Boulton de nov. faciend', VI*l.* XIIIs. IVd.

---

 * Much court was paid to Lady Clifford. She was feasted with the greatest delicacies, presented with expensive jewels, and, on the day of her purification, with one candle value fifteen shillings and three pence. For the reasons of this ceremony, such as they are, see Durand. Ration. l. 7, "De Purif. Mul."

 † Chimneys were at that time extremely rare, and none, probably, but the masons employed about the abbeys knew how to construct them. Before the introduction of these funnels our ancestors in winter had to balance between the choice of the cold and suffocation ; notwithstanding which, "Now," says Harrison, about 1570, "have we manye chimnyes, and yet our tenderlings complayn of rheums, catarrhs, and poses ; then had we nothing but rere-dofses, and yet our heads did never ache. For as the smoke in those days was supposed to be a sufficient hardening for the timber of the house, so it was reputed a farre better medicine to keepe the good man and his family from the quacke, or pose, wherewith, as then, very fewe were acquainted."—"Descr. of Britaine," b. II. To such idle complaints, the murmurs of ignorance and prejudice against reasonable innovation, the best answer is, that human life has not been shortened by the progress of improvement.
   The following quotation from King's "Vale Royal" will show how very lately chimneys were introduced into farm-houses in Cheshire :—"In building and furniture of their houses, till of late years, they used the old manner of the Saxons : for they had their fire in the midst of the house, against a hob of clay, and their oxen under the same roof ; but within these forty years they have builded chimnies." King's work was published in 1656. It is a curious fact, that the last farm-house of this most ancient construction was remaining in the township of Tong with Hough, near Bolton, in Lancashire, within the last twenty years.
   ‡ Morina is the murrain. The following quotation from "Fleta" will show the antiquity of those legal precautions, which are still used in this species of pestilence :—"Cum aliquis (ovis) pro mortuâ fuerit præsentata, et visa fuerit quod "mortua sit per morinam." But the word sometimes signified the skin or felt of an animal which had died of that complaint ; "Venire faciat baillivus coram se pelles ovium occisarum, necnon et morinas mortuarum."—"Fleta," l. ii. c. 79.
   § I am quite at a loss as to the meaning of Tippelhyrdes.
   ‖ Lampreys de Naunt are probably a more delicate species of lampreys, brought from Nantz. At Rither the canons had a house, and as it appears, a chapel. The prior frequently retired to this place.
   ¶ Sannenapys, cloths probably for the table ; of silk. Sannina is the same word with samita. *Vide* Du Cange in voce Exametum, which he defines to be "Vestis holo sericus."
   ** A pair of these noble birds was an elegant and well-judged present to a great nobleman. In a MS. of Swan Heraldry in the Bodleian Library, containing the cognisances of most of the old nobility and the principal religious houses, I have searched in vain for the swan-mark of Bolton Priory. The turbulence of Wharf is ill adapted to the tranquil and dignified movement of the swan. The reader will recollect that this was Thomas of Lancaster, then residing at Pontefract Castle.
   †† To the care and curiosity of the religious houses it is principally owing that the old chronicles of our country were preserved till the invention of printing.
   ‡‡ Eva de Land was, I believe, the prior's mother. Bolton Bridge was now rebuilding, probably at the expense of the canons, with such benefactions as they were able to collect. The depth or rapidity of the Wharf in this part of its course are such that there must have been a bridge here from the earliest period of population.
   Eva de Land was very munificent in the article of bridges, as appears by the following curious convention made in the foregoing year betwixt herself and the canons : "Prior & conventus tenentur eidem, per suum scriptum obligatorium, quod quidem scriptum illa liberabat eisdem sub hâc forma, quod in die sepulture sue in distribut' pauper' & in exhenniis faciend' & expensis supervenient' ad sepulturam suam expendent XII M. Item ordinavit de eisdem denariis ad pontem de Brigwath V M. Item ad pontem de Kyldwick V M. Et ut istam ordinationem plene & integre habeat, dictos religiosos in conscientiis suis & in periculo animarum ut coram Altissimo vellent respondere obligavit." A very solemn obligation, which the parties bound would, I doubt not, esteem of greater force than any penalty in money. Brigwath is in Cononley, whence it may probably be inferred, that Eva de Land, and, therefore, her son, the prior, was of that place or neighbourhood.

Pro panno de kamelyn ad opus d'ni de Midelton.*
Pro robâ ad opus vicarii de Carlton, XIIIIIIS.
Pro fururâ de bugetto ad opus d'ni prioris, IVS.
Pro II paribus botarum ad opus ejusdem, XVS.
Pro IIII cignis† missis com. Lancast. XXIVS. Id.
Calciatura garcionum prioris—
Pro calciaturâ garcionum ejusdem, XVS.
Pagio stabuli ejusdem, XIIS.

MCCCXV.

Ad cameram prioris, VIIIS. IId.
Pro II par. caligar', et fururâ pro sotular' ejusd. IVS.
Œx hominibus metentibus apud Boulton per unum diem, cuivis per diem IId., IXl. XVIIIS. IIIId. ¶
CCCVIII bonis metentibus per consuet. cuilibet pro cibo ob'.
Pro lampade in eccl'â de Kirkby sustentand', XIId.

MCCCXVI.¶¶

MCCCXVII.

Venatori, IIS.
Quatuor hom' eunt' apud Scotiam cum plaustris D'ni Reg. XVIS. IVd. ‡
Pro fœno § tassand'.
Cementar. pro sarcofagis faciend. in ecclesiâ, XIS. Xd. ‡
Executoribus D'ni R. de Clyfford, for CC trave forag. XXS.
Mattraces ad aulam hospitum. ||

Pro eccl'â de Embsay.** reparandâ, VIl.
De VI quart. brasei vend. Pet. de Mydelton†† pro sepulturâ D'ni Ad. de Mydelton, XLVIIIS.
Magistro de Kirkeby‡‡ pro decimis fœni in Malgham.
In exenniis sororibus episcopi Eliensis§§, XIIIS. IVd.
Pro II cofr' et I godshous ad h'nas. ||||
Pro I pr. de costrel et I pr. de bustes. ||||

In isto anno erant bona spi'tualia et temp'alia de novo taxata p'ter invasionem Scotorum in locis ubi Scoti erant.¶¶
Recept' de D'nâ de Percy*** ad celebrand. pro a'i'a Ric. de Arundel, VIl.
De dono Conv. ad exp. Prioris ad Parliamentum, XXVIS. VIIId.

---

* Kamelyn, Camelin, or Camelot, was originally cloth made of camels' hair. I know not whether it had yet acquired its present meaning. The following lines, quoted by Du Cange from an old MS., show that it was principally manufactured at Cambray :—

" De Vert de Gand ne de Douay,
Ne de Camelin de Cambray."

This distich brings to mind Kendal Green and "Coyntree" blue.

† See Note ** page 463.

‡ These successive articles are curious and affecting. Edward II., at the date of the first, was moving from Skipton towards Scotland, before the fatal battle of Bannockburn, where Robert de Clifford was killed. We know that his body was given up to the king. I presume, therefore, that he was brought to Bolton, and that the sarcophagi, or stone coffins, in the second article, were for him and some of his principal attendants who met the same fate. In the third the canons are settling accounts with his executors.

§ Tassare. Tassare is here to cock hay ; for tassa is in general a heap, and more particularly a haycock.

" To ransake in the taas of bodies dead."—CHAUCER'S "Knight's Tale."

|| Matteraces. These were not what we call mattrasses ; but mats, which were generally woven by the more ancient monks : " Lectum de mattâ Matteras Gallicè." (Vetus scriptor apud Du Cange in voce.)

It seems that these were spread in the guests' hall, as the only accommodation for their repose.

¶ This is so expressed, that I once inclined to believe that they assembled above a thousand men, and reaped all their corn in one day—what a busy and animated scene ! But, besides these, were three hundred and eight boon reapers, who had each a halfpenny a day allowed in lieu of meat.

** The old conventual church of Embsay was still kept up.

†† This fixes the date of the death of Sir Adam de Midelton, whose tomb and statue remain at Ilkley. See the note on Sir Robert de Stiveton, ††† p. 461 [and see also p. 281 where his effigy is described.]

‡‡ We have already proved that there was a small cell of canons from West Dereham settled at Kirkby Malghdale. This magister seems to be their superior.

§§ The compotus of 1315 extends from Martinmas in that year to the Martinmas following. July 20, 1316, John de Hotham, prebendary of York, and rector of Cottingham, was confirmed Bishop of Ely. It is probable that these exhennia were complimentary presents to the sisters of that prelate, who was descended of a very ancient Yorkshire family, on their brother's advancement.

|||| Among these ancient articles of furniture (Hernass) what the "Godshous" was, if it were not some small shrine in the shape of a church, I cannot conjecture. Costrells were drinking vessels, but of what materials I know not.

" And withal a Costrell taketh he tho',
And sayd, hereof a draught or two
Yeve him drink."—CHAUCER, "Leg. Women."

¶¶ After the fatal battle of Bannockburn, the Scots overran the north of England, partly for plunder, and partly out of contempt. Craven, which abounded in sheep and cattle, had long been the prey of these Abigei. In the year 1316, and three or four following ones, they seem to have repeated their unwelcome visits again and again ; and I will endeavour to throw together the several particulars of their devastations which affected the Priory of Bolton. At their first irruption the prior fled into Blackburnshire ; several of the canons took refuge in Skipton Castle, where part of their cattle were preserved ; the granges of Embsay, Carlton, Halton, and Stede were destroyed, and all their cattle driven away from Halton, where the corn-lands lay nearly untilled the next year. In 1320, another irruption so completely ruined the house, that the prior and canons dispersed ; the first retiring to Rither and York, the latter to St. Oswald of Nostel, to Worksop, Kirkham, &c. Five, however, remained upon a sort of board-wages at Bolton. Next year these marauders paid a third visit, when the movables of the priory were conveyed to Skipton Castle. In consequence of these losses, all the benefices in Craven, and the temporal and spiritual possessions of the religious houses, were taxed at a lower rate, according to which the poor canons were compelled to pay a tenth to the king for abandoning his subjects to destruction. Neither was this all : the rents of their tenants were in a great measure remitted ; yet amidst all these distresses, it must be remembered to the honour of the canons, that they had a pittance to spare for the relief of their ruined friends.

*** Eleanor, daughter of Richard Fitz-Alan, Earl of Arundel.

Condonatio tenent. de Emsay, Estby, et Preston, p'pter invasion' Scotorum——
Pro decimâ D'no Regi concessâ s'c'dum nov. taxationem p'pter invasion' Scotorum, C*l.* XII*s.*
Pro XV mubiel.* v*s.* VI*d.*
In exp's Prioris cum fuit ad tronization. D'ni Æp. Ebor.† XLIII*s.* VIII*d.*
In exp's ejusd. in Blackburnshire in adventu Scotorum, XX*s.* I*d.* ob.
In fururâ de Buget ‡ empt. ad opus ejusdem, v*s.*
In II cignis missis Cancellario Angl. X*s.*
Baldewin Tyays, Constabul. Castri de Skipton, pro bonis salvand. à Scotis, XIII*s.* VI*d.*
In vestura XIIII Canonicorum, IX*l.* VI*s.* VIII*d.*
Pro XIII novis lanceis emptis, XV*s.* VI*d.*
Recept. avene de Halton, LVIII qrt. et non plus, propter adventum Scotorum, et remotionem servientium ib'm.
Pro VI Gaddys aster.§
Pro Geldherds.‖
Pro Tripherds.¶

MCCCXVIII.

De Dextario qu. fuit mortuar.
D'ne de Nevill,** XIII*l.* VI*s.* VIII*d.*
Et de Palefrid. †† qu. fuit mortuar. ejusd. CVI*s.* VIII*d.*

De coriis de lard venditis sarcaris,‡‡ X*l.* XX*d.*
De vino vendito ho'ibus de Skipton in adventu Scotorum, XXVI*s.* VIII*d.* ††

---

* Mulvellus is the ancient name of the haddock. See Spelman, *in voce.*

† Archbishop William de Melton. At this installation either the prior could afford no present, or the Metropolitan would accept of none.

‡ In fururâ de Buget. In the Middle Ages fur of different species formed an elegant and comfortable appendage, not only to professional habits, but to the ordinary dress of both sexes, from the sovereign to the private gentleman. Beneath the latter rank, none but the coarsest kinds were ever in use.[1] The different sorts enumerated in the compotus are, the buget, or budge, gris, de ventre leporino, the white fur of the hare's belly, and de pellibus agninis, or lambs' skins. The last of these, which still forms the lining of the hoods of the Bachelors of Arts at Cambridge, was anciently worn both by bishops and noblemen. For the first, see Mr. Warton's note upon "Comus," edit. 1, p. 146, and the inventory of the wardrobe of the second Earl of Cumberland, in this volume. With respect to budge or buget, it is understood by Mr. Warton (note on "Comus," line 709) to be fur in general ; but this interpretation is negatived by the terms of the present article, furrura de buget. Whatever budge may have been, it is unknown to Du Cange, who has, with immense labour and erudition, collected everything known on the subject in the Middle Ages. It was certainly scarce and expensive, being used for the lining of the prior's hood alone. After all, I suspect it to have been the skin of the Lithuanian Weasel.[2] Even as late as Dr. Caius's time the hoods of the Regent Masters of Arts at Cambridge were lined "pelle arminâ seu Lituanâ[3] candida." If I am right in my conjecture therefore, budge so nearly resembled ermine that either skin might be used indifferently as a badge of the same academical rank. And this accounts for Milton's epithet budge, as applied to doctors, whose congregation robes at Cambridge are still faced with ermine. Gris, I think, was the skin of the grey or badger. The sleeves of Chaucer's monk, a "fayre prelate," who was gaily and expensively habited, were purfiled with gris ; and in the head of a bishop, in painted glass, I have a fine specimen of this fur, in the form of a tippet about the neck.

It seems that in the Middle Ages ecclesiastics were apt to luxuriate in the use of beautiful and costly furs : Ovium itaque et agnorum despiciuntur exuviæ ; Ermelini, Gibelini (sables) martores exquiruntur et vulpes." This vanity was checked by an English sumptuary law : "Statutum est ne quis escarleto, in Anglorum Gente, sabelino, vario, vel griseo utereter." Bromptone A° 1188. Again, in two MSS. quoted by Du Cange, to whom I am also indebted for the foregoing passage, the expensive furs are enumerated thus :—

"Vairs & Gris, & Ermines, & Sables de Rosie."

And again : "Sables, Ermines, & Vair, & Gris."

Vair was the skin of the Mus Ponticus, a kind of weasel, the same animal with the ermine, but in a different state, *i.e.,* killed in the summer, when the belly was white, and the back brown, whence it obtained the name of varia. The ancient "miniveere" was Minuta Varia, or fur composed of these diminutive skins ; and Drayton was learned and accurate when he gave his well-dressed shepherd "mittons of Bauson's skin," that is, of Gris, and a hood of miniveere. With respect to sables, I have only to add, that from their grave and sober elegance they were retained as tippets in the habits of bishops and other dignitaries in England to the time of Queen Elizabeth, when they gave place to a similar ornament of silk, the origin of the present scarf, which continued to be called a tippet till the reign of Charles II. See Baxter's Life, where we find that Puritan, when sworn in King's Chaplain, refusing to wear the tippet.

§ Which I read, Gaddys asteriatis. Oxgoads, therefore, at that time had rowels.

‖ Geldherds are elsewhere called the Pastores sterilium animalium. Hence the modern surname Geldert.

¶ Trip is a herd of goats, and, like Geldert, &c., has given origin to a surname yet remaining in Lancashire—Tripyer.

** Margaret de Neville, who died this year, was lady of the Neville or Colling fee, and seems to have resided partly at Cononley (where it appears from this Compotus that she had a domestic chapel), and partly at Neville Hall, in Gargrave. The mortuaries, however, must have belonged to the parish of Kildwick. The canons furnished no less than twenty-four quarters of malt, besides other necessaries, amounting to more than thirteen pounds sterling, for the funeral. The body must have been kept a considerable time for the brewing, working, &c., of all this malt liquor, which, at sixty gallons per quarter, and one gallon for every person who attended, would suffice for a company of 1,440 persons.

†† See note ¶¶ in p. 464.

‡‡ It appears from this article that they skinned their bacon hogs, and sold the hides to tanners.

---

[1] Which *they* certainly were ; for Chaucer, who intended to clothe his personification of Avarice in the garb of poverty, allows her, notwithstanding, "a burnette cote, furred with no meniveere, but with a furre rough of heere of lambe skynnes, hevy and black." ("Rom. Ros.")

[2] I have since discovered that budge is the same with "shanks," one of the many kinds of fur enumerated in the statute of the 24th of Henry VIII.—that is, a very delicate white skin stripped from the legs of a fine-haired kid, and almost equal in value as well as in appearance to ermine. It is not impossible that the name may have been derived from the verb "budge," as the legs are the instruments of locomotion. See Minshewe *in voce* Furre.

[3] Lituan is sometimes used by the old writers on heraldry as synonymous with ermine.

3 H

De sellâ * qu. fuit D'ne Marg't de Nevill, Cs.

De diversis provident. venditis ex'or's D'ne M. de Nevill, ad sepulturam d'c'e D'ne, XIII*l.* X*s.* IV*d.*†

Pro grangiâ de Halton de novo constructâ et per Scotos destructâ in p'te, VII*l.* XVI*s.* IX*d.* †

Pro grangiâ de Carlton de nov. constr. †

In grangiâ de Stede de nov. constr.†

In exp. Prioris ad II. Parliam. apud Ebor. III Convocat. et alias vices, XIX*l.* IV*s.* VI*d.*

Pro I capâ ‡ pluviali ad opus ejusd. X*s.*

Pro I amuc' de Bryga ‡ ad opus ejusd. XIIII*d.*

Pro II paribus caligar.§ empt. ad op. ejusd. II*s.* II*d.*

Will'o Allutar' pro calceament. ejusd. VII*s.* IV*d.*

Eleemos. ⎰ Wil'o de Farnel, destructo per Scotos, VI*s.* X*d.*
Prioris. ‖ ⎱ Ad' p'pe de ¶ Neuton, destructo per Scotos, III*s.* IV*d.*

In expens. canon. commorant. in castro de Skipton in adventu Scotor. et alibi, V*s.* II*d.*

Coronatori ** facto visu sup' quodam mortuo corpore, pro feodo IV*s.*

Eunti cum plaustro dato D'no Com. Lanc. usq. Scot.†† cum expensis usq. Pontefr. IV*s.* VI*d.*

Pro I Stirket lib. de man. balliv. apud Setyll post recessum Scotor. V*d.*

Braseum ‖——

In destructione per Scotos, XXX qrt.

In sepulturâ D'ne de Nevill, XXIV qrt.

Boves. ‖　Apud Halton nulli, quia omnes effugabantur per Scotos.

MCCCXIX.

No Compotus this year, propter adv. Scotorum. ‖

MCCCXX.

Pro novâ dom. fac. apud Embsay,‖ IV*l.* XV*d.*

Pro garderob. ib'm prosternenda, XII*d.*

Pro eadem de novo reficienda, XXVI*s.* V*d.*

In reparatione aule ib'm, XIIII*d.*

In exp. Prioris et alior. ‖ cariant. vestimenta, &c. ap' Ebor. XIII*l.* VI*s.*

In exp. ejusd. et conv. ‖ per duos adventus apud Boulton, XV*l.* VI*s.*

In exhennio misso D'no de Clyfford et Sagitt. eid. dat. XIII*l.* II*s.*

In exp. Canon. ‡‡ in eund. et redeund. de locis ubi morantur per vices, XLVII*s.* X*d.*

In exp. Prioris ‡‡ apud Ryther, VI*l.* VII*d.*

In exp. v. Canonicor. et Julianæ de Craven ‡‡ commorant. domi, XX*l.* XII*s.* VI*d.*

Pro XVIII rod. di. mur. lapid. fact' circa cœmeterium de Emesay, XII*s.* IV*d.*

Cariantib. pisces de stagn. de Skypton et de Ridlesden usq. ad stagnum de Boulton, IV*s.* III*d.*

Pro pictatione Beati Cudberti §§ apud Ebor. X*s.*

Pro informatione unius pulli ad ambulandum, ‖‖‖ II*s.* VI*d.*

In fundratione à festo S. Mich. ad festum St. Andree dum conv. extitit domi ᵢᵢᵢᵢ̽XVI qrt.

MCCCXXI.

Cuidam portanti virgam ¶¶ coram D'no Hug. le Despenser, III*s.* IV*d.*

---

* The caparisons of horses, not only of knights but ladies, were extremely rich. The saddle and trappings of Lady M. Nevile must have been worth in our money 70*l.*

† See note ¶¶ in p. 464.

‡ The capa pluvialis was a riding-cloak, or roquilaure. The amice, almutium, amucium or amicium, was a large hood worn by canons, sometimes lined with fur and sometimes not. The amice of the Prior of Bolton was of cloth of Bruges, a manufactory mentioned by Chaucer :—

"Of Brugges were his hosen broun."—*R. Sir Thopas.*

The head-piece of this hood was so contrived as to form, when put on, a quadrangular covering for the head, while the lower part fell down over the shoulders. "Unde," says Du Cange *in voce*, "ejusmodi pileorum quos vulgo bonnett quarrez appellamus usus fluxerit." Hence the square academical cap.

§ The caligæ of the Middle Ages, very unlike the Roman military shoe so denominated, were light boots, which bishops and abbots wore during the celebration of divine offices, before they put on the sandals.—Durand, Rat. l. III. c. 8. These are the sort of boots of which remains are sometimes found in the graves of ancient dignitaries. Botæ was the name of common boots for journeys. Calceamenta, ordinary shoes for the daytime ; and sotulares, a sort of clog, which were sometimes worn over the caligæ, and sometimes as slippers for the night—but the word is often used for shoes in general. Allutarius, for a shoemaker, is unknown to Du Cange and Spelman. Aluta means a tanned hide. Thus much for the calciatura.

‖ See note ¶¶ in p. 464.

¶ Adamo prophetæ.

** The useful institution of coroner's inquests is of great antiquity in England. We have here the fee of that officer *temp.* Edward II.—viz., 4*s.*

†† This was in one of those mock expeditions which Saint Thomas of Lancaster undertook against the Scots whilst he was secretly in league with them against his own sovereign.

‡‡ See note ¶¶ in page 464.

§§ We are not told whether this picture of their patron, St. Cuthbert, was on glass or wood. It must be remembered that by the canons a picture of the patron saint was required to be placed not only in every conventual, but every parish church. Imaginem principalem in cancello. Vide Const. Abp. Winchelsey, apud Lindwood, L. 3, T. 27.

‖‖‖ I have transcribed this article merely on account of the odd formality of the expression : it is for teaching a colt to amble. Breaking a horse then cost half-a-crown.

¶¶ This is a fee paid to the verger or mace-bearer of Hugh le Despencer. I do not know in what capacity he was thus attended : certainly not as Chancellor.

In exp. D'ni Æp. et fam. sue Prioris et Conven. et servient. temp. Visitationis,* XXIII*l.* XIX*s.* V*d.*

In exp. Prioris apud Kildwick et Emesey, eod. tempore, XLV*s.*

In exp. Prior et Can. venient' et redeuntium apud Boulton, Registro pro literis transcribend' pro canon. dispersione, &c. &c.

Domibus de S'c'o Oswaldo, Wyrksop, et Schelford,† pro sust. III Can. per an. X*l.*

Domino de Kyrkham, pro sust. I Can.† LVI*s.* VIII*d.*

Conventus commorant. domi pro sust. XXX*l.* XVII*s.* II*d.*

In quodam muro juxta coquinam et aquæ ductu' inter coquinam et garde robam prioris de nov. faciend. VI*s.* VIII*d.*

In exp. canon. commorant. in Castro de Skypton † hom. cariantium bona ad dict. castr. et custod. ea ib'm, et vigilant. una cum curial. facta Janitori in adventu Scotorum,‡ VII*s.* I*d.*

Cariant. I dolium vini de Ebor. usq. Skypton ad opus D'ni Clyfford, XII*d.*

In XLIII bident. furatis et liberatis de man' balliorum apud Covreham, X*s.* I*d.*

Staur. hoc anno. Equi LXXVI. Boves CLXII. Oves MDLXXIX. Porci XXXVII.

MCCCXXIIII.

In Fœno empto ad bidentes in hieme in tempestate, VIII*s.* X*d.*§

De Rob. fi. Joh. de Emsay pro manumissione suâ, IV*l.* ||

In exp. Prior. Convent. Hospitum, et operar. per tempus quo D'n's Rex commorabatur in patriâ, ¶ &c., X*l.* IX*s.* VII*d.*

In quodam exhennio misso D'no Regi, et div'sis donis factis hominibus ejusd. XXXI*s.* II*d.*

Filio Walteri de Scotton, filiolo prioris, in I annulo et argento, IX*s.* VI*d.*

Thomæ Cartario D'ni Regis commorantis apud castrum de Skipton, V*s.* X*d.*

Pro VII nappis mensis ** pro refector. et XXX ulnis tele pro sannenapeo et manuterg. ad lavator.

Thomæ cleric. cast. de Skipton II q'rt. aven.

In exp. domus per II adventus prioris apud Boulton, &c.

MCCCXXV.

Liberat. Priori apud Ryther, VII*l.* XVII*s.* II*d.*

Pro I Tabard empt. pro W. Barbator, III*s.*

Since the first edition of this work, I have met with another Compotus of Bolton, from which the following particulars are extracted :—

Dona Prioris.

Cuidam venienti de D'no de Clyfford cum auro, III*s.* IV*d.*

D'ne Eliz. uxori Tho. Clyfford, XIII*s.* IV*d.*

Joh. Spofforth, ministral. XVIII*d.*

Cuidam venient. de Magistro de Sallay cum quodam exen. ad Prior. VI*d.*

Will'o Myotts, ministral. XVIII*d.*

Mag'r' Ric. de Rybstane venient. ad Prior. temp. infirmitatis sue, XIII*s.* IV*d.*

Will'o de Malgham in die jubilat. sue ad vinum, VI*s.* VIII*d.*

Minstral. Baron. de Graystock, III*s.* IIII*d.*

* This year Archbishop Melton visited in person at Bolton, Kildwick, and Embsay. The expenses of his reception lay very heavy on the impoverished canons. His attendants must have been very numerous ; for the sum charged to this article would have been sufficient for two hundred men and horses : twenty times as many as a very stately prelate would now deem necessary. This conjecture will not be thought extravagant, when it is understood that in 1216 an archdeacon of Richmond visited with a train of ninety-seven horses. See " Hist. Whalley," p. 171. Another article relating to this visitation is extremely curious, " In prebendâ et furfure equorum et Canum D'ni A'ep'i xv qr. aven." This prelate certainly hunted with a pack of hounds in his progress from parish to parish !

† See note ¶¶ on p. 464.

‡ In the margin of the Coucher Book is this memorandum : " Le Prior & sez Homes *fled* ae Castle de Skipton per *Feare* dez *Scottes.*" Are we to suppose that the canons spoke this piebald dialect ?

§ I have inserted this article merely to show how ancient is the use of the word *storm* in the Northern sense—*i.e.*, of a long-continued frost and snow.

|| Four pounds, therefore, in this instance, were the consideration for manumitting a neife of the house. A good horse, at the same time, sold for more than thrice the sum. Are we then to conclude, that this was the comparative price of the two animals, or that the canons were favourable to the emancipation of their slaves ? I hope and believe the latter.

¶ Thomas of Lancaster was executed in 1321, and Andrew de Hercla, Earl of Carlisle, in 1322. Some time after the latter event, I find, from the " Fruyt of Tyme," printed by Wynkyn de Worde, 1528, that the king was then at 𝕮𝖗𝖆𝖛𝖊𝖓 𝖆𝖙 𝕾𝖈𝖎𝖕𝖙𝖔𝖓, 𝖇𝖊𝖈𝖆𝖚𝖘𝖊 𝖍𝖊 𝖘𝖍𝖔𝖚𝖑𝖉 𝖚𝖓𝖉𝖔 𝖙𝖍𝖊 𝖕𝖎𝖑𝖌𝖗𝖎𝖒𝖆𝖌𝖊𝖘 𝖒𝖆𝖉𝖊 𝖆𝖙 𝖙𝖍𝖊 𝖙𝖔𝖒𝖇 𝖔𝖋 𝖙𝖍𝖊 𝖋𝖔𝖗𝖒𝖊𝖗, which threatened to end in an insurrection. From these articles it seems that Edward II. was at Skipton in 1324.

** Hence it appears that the canons were beginning to re-furnish their house in order to return from their dispersion. It was now three years from the last incursion of the Scots ; a period nearly sufficient to restore their stock of cattle. One fruitful year would repair their losses in corn.

Expens. Canon.
In exp. Subprior' visitant. amicos, VIS. VIIId.
In exp. Rad. de Ledes, dᵒ, IIS. VId.
In exp. Celer. usque Ebor. cum tribus equis V dies ad convocat. Cleri ad tractand' cum Ric. Hamerton, VIIIS. XId.
     Vest. Can'm.
In vestura XVIII Can'm, XXIV*l.*
In vestura IIII Convers'm, XL*s.*
     Carucat.
Joh'i fil. W' Chapman carucant' apud Bolton, in die, I*d.*
     Vend. Lane.
In X Sacc. lan. p'parat. et vend. LX*l.*
In nigra lan. vend. ut pat. per prior. C*s.*
In I pet. nigr. lan. vend. per eund. V*s.*
     Custos forgie.
In Carbonibus empt. apud Colne et liberatis forgie, IIIS. IV*d.*
In Carbonibus lucratis per Jo. Jolyman, XXXS. IV*d.*

The prior here mentioned I suppose to have been Robert de Ottelay, who seems, from the physician's fee, to have had a dangerous sickness this year, and died not long after. There were eighteen canons and four conversi. One of the brethren, William de Malgham, celebrated his Jubilee (the fiftieth year of his profession) with no small festivity. The minstrels were liberally rewarded. In this statement nothing is more unaccountable or disproportionate than the high price of wool. The sack consisted of 26 stones, each weighing 14 lb. (see Spelman *in voce*), and every sack sold for 6*l.* Black wool, always more valuable than white, fetched 5*s.* the stone. At the same time, a labourer received only 1*d.* per day, and an ox was worth about 13*s.* 4*d.* ; whence it follows that at this time two stones and a half of wool would purchase an ox, and whereas a labourer will now earn the price of a stone of wool grown on the same commons in little more than a week, it would require at that time sixty days for the same purpose. From this representation another very singular fact may be inferred—namely, that at this time the high and wild sheep-walks belonging to the canons were equally profitable with their rich arable and grazing lands on the banks of the Wharf. I have transcribed the last article to prove what I did not know before—that coals were got in Blackburnshire as early as the latter end of Edward III.'s reign. But they were brought from that distance, as they are at present, only for the forge, the ordinary fuel of the canons being wrought out of the poor and meagre beds on the adjoining fells.

After these miscellaneous remarks on the habits and expenses of the canons of Bolton, I will endeavour to give a short and summary view of the whole subject.

Their establishment consisted, first, of the prior, who had lodgings, with a hall and chapel, stables, &c., distinct from those of the house. There were, on an average, fifteen canons and two conversi ;* besides whom were the armigeri,† or gentlemen dependent on the house, who had clothing, board, and lodging ; ‡ the liberi servientes, within and without ;

---

* The lay brethren were such as either from bodily deformity or mental dulness were incapable of holy orders. Many of the former were, no doubt, by the compensating bounty of Providence, blessed with fine understandings, and would be employed in delicate and ingenious works. One of these earned upwards of 7*l.*—equal nearly to 100*l.* at present—in one year ; it is not said by what means. Another had secreted 100 shillings of his savings, contrary to the rule of his order. These were found in his box after his decease. The latter often became excellent masons, carpenters, wheel-wrights, &c. I find one of the conversi of Whalley Abbey described in the "Liber Loci Benedicti" as "fortem et so Iertem Rotarium."

† See one of the patents from an abbot of Battel to one of his armigeri, in Spelman, *voce* "Armiger."

‡ The Armiger had also a Garcio to wait upon him, as appears from a passage in Ingulphus, relating to the abbey of Croyland : "Modo et mensura quibus ministratur garcioni unius Armigeri in abbatis aula." Du Cange in "Armiger."

and, lastly, the garciones, who were villeins in gross, or mere domestic slaves. Of the free servants *intra curiam* there were about thirty, among whom may be distinguished the master carpenter, the master and inferior cook, brewer, and baker, the master smith, the hokarius, the fagotarius, and the ductors accorum. These received wages from 10 to 3s. each *per annum*. The servants *extra curiam*, or those employed in husbandry upon the farms and granges, were from 70 to 108, of whom John de Lambhird is styled magister bercariæ.

If any antiquary should think fit to write a dissertation on the antiquity of nicknames in England, he may meet with ample materials in the Compotus of Bolton; for in this catalogue are found Adam Blunder, Simon Paunche, Richard Drunken, Tom Noght,[*] Botchcollock † the Cowper, and Whirle the Carter—the last, I suppose, by an antiphrasis, from the slowness of his rotatory motion.

The precise number of the garciones,‡ as they received no wages, it is impossible to discover, but it may be guessed at from the expense of their clothing, and the general consumption of provisions in the house. They wore the coarsest cloth, but the quantity purchased on their account was generally more than for the free servants. The prior alone must have had more than twenty, as their *calciatura* amounted to more than 20s. *per annum*. The cellarer had another class, employed probably about the kitchen and hall, and even the conversi seem to have had each a garcio to themselves.

Among those of the prior are enumerated the huntsman and page of the stable; but the garciones in general were furnished with bows and arrows, undoubtedly for the use of the chase, and certainly assisted in netting for game and fish, the implements of which amusements are distinctly mentioned. In other respects undoubtedly they performed the lowest offices of drudgery about the house.

On the whole, I cannot but persuade myself that the whole establishment at Bolton consisted of more than two hundred persons; an opinion which, with every reasonable allowance for hospitality to strangers, will be fortified by the following accurate statement of one year's provisions :—Wheat flour used in conventual or gruel (coarse) bread, 319 quarters; barley-meal for the same, 112 quarters; oatmeal for pottage, 80 quarters; ditto for dogs, 39 quarters; provender for the horses, 411 quarters; oats malted for ale, 636 quarters; barley, or mixtilio (to be explained hereafter), 80 quarters. They generally brewed 12 quarters at each pandoxation, as it was termed, and that once every week, and sometimes oftener.

Thus much for their bread, beer, and pottage. With respect to animal food, besides venison, fish, poultry, &c., they slaughtered, in one year, 64 oxen, 35 cows, one steer, 140 sheep,§ and 69 pigs. To lubricate this immense quantity of shambles-meat, and for every

---

* The southern reader may require to be told that "noght" is the same with the Latin "nequam," good for "nothing," in the positive sense of the expression.

† "Collock" is properly translated by Junius *haustellum*, a small wooden vessel to draw water. The word is still used in Lancashire.

‡ The word is plainly the French "garçon" and the Irish "gossoon," which last the readers of that lively and original picture of Hibernian manners, "Castle Rackrent," will instantly recollect.

§ Mutton in the compotus is always called "caro mutilina." *Mutilo*, of which the derivation and reason are obvious, was a wether. The word was afterwards corrupted into *multo*, and hence the English "mutton."

other domestic purpose, they consumed, in the same year, only 113 stones of butter; and yet four quarters of fine flour were used in pies and pasties.

Of a garden or orchard, or the productions of either, there is no mention, any more than of honey, though mead was very fashionable in those times, and the " Bestocks de Berden " are annually accounted for in the compotuses of Henry Lord Clifford the Shepherd two centuries after.

Their spiceries, though expensive, were used with no sparing hand; *e.g.*, in one year, " almonds 200 lb. 33*s.*　Rys (rice) 72 lb. 9*s.*　Pepper, 19 lb. 21*s.* 7*d.*　Saffron, 4 lb. 23*s.*　Cummin, 25 lb. 2*s.* 8*d.*　One quartern of Maces.　One rase of figs and reysins," &c. &c.*

Most of these were bought for the great festival of the Assumption, which was celebrated as the foundation-day of the priory; and, for the same occasion, the canons purchased three salmons, 24 lampreys de Naunt,† an esturgeon, 200 and a quarter of lamprons, and 300 eels.

The reader has now pretty nearly the bill of fare for a festival-dinner at Bolton five centuries ago.

But the canons held, that a good dinner required a certain proportion of wine; and accordingly I find, that in one year they paid for one dolium of wine, at Hulle, 50*s.* for two dolia 6*l.*, for three dolia 7*l.* 10*s.*, for one dolium 56*s.* 8*d.*　The dolium was a tun of 252 gallons, and the average price about 3*d.* a gallon; so that the consumption of one year (at least the stock laid in), was nearly 1,800 gallons, or at least 8,000 bottles, at, or about, ob. qu. a bottle; not a fortieth part of the present value.‡

In these entertainments, the ear was gratified as well as the palate; for I find, at every festival, the minstrels very liberally rewarded.

On the subject of clothing I have little to add to the notes.　The habits of the canons were fine cloth, of 3*s.* a yard (much dearer than the finest broad-cloth at present); the novices wore " frizons," the servants and garciones were clothed in a manufacture of their own refuse wool; and, as nothing is ever mentioned under this head but shoes and coarse cloth, I conclude that they had doublets, trousers, and a kind of stockings of the same. Nay, the coverings for their heads must have been hoods of the same material, as no caps were ever purchased for their use.　The word robe did not then convey an idea of dignity; for " roba garcionis " was the dress of a slave.

One practice of the canons was good-natured and accommodating: resorting annually to St. Botolph's Fair,§ they purchased articles of dress of a superior quality, such as could not be had at home, for the gentlemen, and even the ladies of Craven; which prove how

---

* In the Providentia Domûs of another year are several articles, which I should be glad to see explained: *e.g.*, Pro 1 lb. de quibib. pro 5 lb. de galeng. pro 3lb. cetonalent. pro 16lb. fenicli. pro 4lb. de pioigne.　Alexandrian sugar seems to have been immoderately dear: pro 13 lb. de zuker Alexandri, 20*s.* 10*d.*　But perhaps a cypher has been omitted.

† These, I think, were the Petromyzon Marinus, as the Lampron, still called by that name in Cumberland, was the Petr. Fluviatilis.　The former were bought "cum furnatione," ready dressed and highly seasoned.　In this state they were probably sent from Nantz.　Epicurism is not peculiar to modern times.　We learn from Dugdale, that the Neviles sent fish ready cooked from Warwick to Middleham.

‡ This may seem very low; but see Fleetwood's " Chronicon Preciosum," p. 59.

§ Which I am now certain was the great Fair of Boston.

expensively they were clothed : " Half a piece of cloth, with fur, for the lady of Stiveton, 71*s.* 4*d.* One robe for Ralph de Otterburn, 19*s.* 4*d.* Furs bought for Sir Adam de Midelton, for two years' wear, 19*s.*"

These articles are extracted at random from the " Providentia S'ci Botulphi, for 1313."

Multiply 19*s.* 4*d.* by 15, and it will leave 14*l.* 10*s.* as the price of a single suit for a country gentleman.

It may also be observed, that ladies, at least of ordinary rank, wore woollen cloth faced with fur, like the gowns of gentlemen, and probably not greatly differing from them in shape. In this they consulted their own comfort and the nature of the climate.

The physician's fee for visiting a canon, I suppose from York, was 6*s.* 1*d.* ; a Ric. Apotecarius made up the medicines ; but his practice in the house must have been a bad one ; for all the articles that I meet with are, " Lectuar' ad opus fr. W. de Donyngton et 1 lb. of Lenitif. Laxatif."

In their husbandry there is little peculiar. They fallowed for wheat, a process which they termed sarculation. Their implements were the same as at present, excepting that their ploughs seem to have had no coulters ;* at least the Custos Forgie is silent about them, though ploughshares, and even the minutest articles of ironwork about them, are perpetually mentioned. After a flood there is one entry " pro fœno in orreo triturando," for thrashing hay in the barn.

The bounty of the canons was divided into three classes :—Exennia, or presents to great men ; Curialitates, or acts of courtesy to persons of inferior rank ; and, thirdly, the Distributio Pauperum ; which last, except the sacred oblations, consisted principally in grain. Under the second head was one curious article ; they presented their haymakers, tithe-gatherers, herdsmen, &c., with a pair of gloves each.† On others they bestowed silk purses.

They consumed vast quantities of oatmeal pottage ; but made no oat bread, excepting for horses ; a practice continued in Craven three centuries after, as it is mentioned in the accounts of Francis Earl of Cumberland as late as the reign of James I.

But, in lieu of oat bread, they had an odd composition, which they called mixtilio, consisting of the following proportions—*viz.,* 49 bushels of wheat-flour, 16 of rye, 70 of barley, 73 of oats, and sometimes a small proportion of bean-meal. This was subdivided into two kinds ; the finer called convent bread ; the coarser, panis gruellus. They even malted and brewed this mixture.

Their wool, though occasionally much dearer, sold, on an average, at 2*s.* 6*d.* a stone : the produce of 2,000 sheep came to about 70*l.* A sheep sold for a shilling ; so that the wool was worth two-thirds of the animal.

---

* Pliny alone, among the ancients, mentions the coulter as part of a plough ; but this was not added to the plough-share, but a kind of share itself fixed in a distinct frame, and employed to scarify the surface, and mark out the line of the furrows in stiff lands, before they were cut by the ordinary instrument. See " Nat. Hist." L. 17, c. 18.

† I find a hint of this practice in a Constitution of Simon Mepham, Abp. Cant. apud Lindwood, L. iii. T. 16. "Alii etiam, nisi prius Chirothecæ seu quicquam aliud eis dentur Decimas asportant et consumunt." I have lately been told, that in Suffolk it is still customary to present reapers with gloves, which are used to prevent their cutting their fingers. The reapers of Yorkshire at present are more hardy or more cautious than their forefathers.

Their best cloth was purchased at St. Botolph's Fair. Sometimes the cloth thus purchased was shorn the first time, and sometimes a second time, at home.

The average wages of a man-servant, with meat and clothing, were from three to five shillings only *per annum;* yet they paid their reapers 2*d.* a day; 260 stones and a half of lead cost 4*l.* 9*s.* 5*d.,* or nearly 2*l.* 5*s.* a ton. Thirty quarters of fossil coal were bought for 17*s.* 6*d.*

In order to reduce these sums to the present standard, we must first multiply by three, as the weight of every penny in silver was thrice as much as at present; we may then multiply once more by five, or thereabouts. By this rule the receipts and expenditure of the canons of Bolton would amount to about 10,000*l. per annum* of our money.

One circumstance in their economy I find it difficult to account for: they were generally about a year's income in debt, and were borrowing and paying every year.

Their principal creditors were the Lombard merchants, who bought their wool, and often advanced them large sums, *ex arrhâ,* in earnest, as they expressed it, for the next two or three years' stock.

In these accounts I cannot discover a vestige of usury, which, no doubt, the canons professed to be unlawful; and therefore prudently, or scrupulously, abstained from any intercourse with the Jews. But men whose money was profitably employed in trade would scarcely part with it two or three years beforehand without any consideration. It seems most probable, therefore, that a proportionate abatement was made in the price of the wool when delivered; and what is this but usury without the name?[*]

Prior de Land was an active man, and lived in an eventful period. He built the prior's lodgings and chapel; attended at Skipton or Bolton two sovereigns, Edward I. and II.; saw the extinction of the Albemarles; the escheat of Skipton Castle to the Crown; the rise and ruin of Peirs Gavestone in Craven, with the introduction of the Cliffords into his place; entertained two metropolitans, Greenfield and Melton; took two journeys to Rome; attended many convocations, most of the general chapters of his order, and three Parliaments.[†] His old age was clouded with misfortune; he was driven from his house, and saw the dispersion of his convent by the ravages of the Scots; but he survived the last of these calamities several years, and, though he had resigned his dignity, died, as he deserved, in honour.[‡]

---

[*] Since this was written I think I have discovered the nature of these transactions:—"Mercatoribus de Peruch' ex curialitate IIII sac. lane." Four sacks of wool were worth twenty-four pounds; but the monks and the merchants understood each other—they were a present!

I insert, though rather out of place, one more article from the compotus. "Custod. ovium pro telâ de Keselyp." What was this? Cheselop (the same word) in old English was the calf's stomach, or earning bag, employed to lop, or *lopper—i.e.,* to coagulate milk for cheese. See Skinner, the only etymologist who has preserved the word. Here, however, it means the ewe's milk itself when coagulated, and the "tela de Keselyp" was linen cloth, used to collect and receive it before it was put into the vat to be pressed.

[†] It is well known that before the reign of Edward III. the number of abbots and priors summoned to Parliament was quite indefinite. The name of the Prior of Bolton is not found on any Parliament rolls now extant; but the evidence of the compotus is decisive; and Mr. Selden remarks that many omissions appear to have been made in those rolls by the clerks—"Titles of Honour," Works, vol. v. p. 745. Our priors did not hold *per Baroniam;* and therefore, when summoned to Parliament, were spiritual barons by writ; an order which does not exist at present.

[‡] It may be proper to inform the reader that every particular in this general view of the subject is verified by a distinct article in the compotus.

After relating the domestic habits of the canons of Bolton in the thirteenth and fourteenth centuries, I will subjoin a few specimens of their literature at a later period. The reader would smile were I to call them poets, chemists, or astronomers; but I shall prove at least that they made verses, practised alchemy, and observed the stars. How prosaic were their strains, how rude or fanciful their science, was of little moment; the vainest or the most unsuccessful of these pursuits was better than mental inactivity; it preserved them from idleness, and consequently from vice.

This subject was glanced at in my account of Henry Lord Clifford the Shepherd; but since that was printed off the discovery of another MS. at Bolton enables me to be more particular.

The English language underwent no very considerable change from the reign of Edward III. to that of Edward IV. The style of Gower is not materially different from that of Lydgate, nor that of Lydgate from that of the rhymers who followed him at the distance of half a century. Of Langland and Chaucer I say nothing. The great poet wrote the language of no age;[*] the rude satirist, if he belonged indeed to the former reign, that of an age long prior to his own. After these observations I confess myself at a loss whereabouts in that interval of a century to place the following lines, in which Mercury is the speaker, exhorting a poor man to the pursuit of alchemy[†]:—

I. H. S. Maria.

Why artt thow soo poure man, and I ame soo ryche?
   Habundans off tressowr þ'u maste in me fynde,
In Natur' I ame : : : to þee soo lykke
   I am propinquiss' nextt off thy kynde :
The ryche men of þe poure now have no petye,
   In me þ'rfore þ'u have thy confidens ;
Itt ys oftene seyne in towne & cyte
   Ill at es he ys þ't hathe no crafte nor scyans.
The ryche off þe powr now hathe despytt,
   That they be ther conyng ony goods scholde wyne,
To gyffe þe powre almos þe have noo delytt,
   Lyttyll ys the cheryte þt ys them w'tine
And exemple of Dives þe ryche us sc'ptor dos telle,
   The pover Lazarus for defawtt dyede at hys gatt,
Hade he gyffene hyme allmes hee had nott gone to hell ;
   And now to repente hyme ytt ys vere laatt.
Thow hast noo good, mane, bott God dos þe ytt send,
   Part w't yt, Broyþer, as God yᵉ comandys :

* This may be said of Chaucer with more truth, perhaps, than it was long after observed of Spenser, by Johnson. Skinner's remark on the elder bard is well known : " Integra verborum plaustra invexit."

† Such oracles, it seems, were about this era not unfrequently delivered in rhyme : witness the strains of our countryman Sir George Ripley, who taught this pretended science in a jargon and metre resembling that of the canons of Bolton about the year 1470. Of *his* work the following may serve as a short specimen :—

"For as of one mass was made all thing,
   Right so must it in our practice be ;
All our secrets of one image must spring:
   In Philosophers' book, therefore who lust to see,
Our Stone is called the less world one and three,
   Proportionate by nature most perfectly."

But the orthography has been unwarrantably modernised by Elias Ashmole, who published some of Ripley's works in the " Theatrum Chemicum." As Ripley was in his later days an anchoret at Boston, may not the canons of Bolton, who annually resorted thither, have, among other commodities of greater value, imported their alchemy from that place ?

3 I

Thy lyffe ytt wylle the bett' the' amende,
    Deythe wythe þᵉ maks bott a sodyne chans ;
All the worldly gooddes þ'u schaltt forsake,
    And gyffe ev'y beest ageyne thatt att hys deew : *

Then shall þe bodye both trymble and quake.
    Deth þⁿ of þᵉ wyll nothygne rewe.
Why so fare, mane, & I so ner
    Hast þᵘ noo G'ce, mane, wythe me for to mette,
Soo ofte as I to þᵉ apeyr
    And zytt off me thou taks no keppe.
          .   .   .

The comyne M'cury is nothynge good,
    For ytt bryngs a mane in sorow & caar ;
Itt maks hys her grow thorow hys hudde,†
    And hys purs full thyne and baar.
I am he þᵗ wysemen seeke :
    Mercury, þᵉ wyche ys most off myght
Hott & moyst, lyght & wett.
          .   .   .

Look þᵗ zow keppe þis booke secretly,
    If þᵗ ony man off zow ytt wolde crave,
I made ytt nott for ev'y mane.
    Look þᵗ he be wyse þᵗ þᵉ copye schold have.
For it ys not for them þᵗ nothynge care,
    Boot for me and for mye Breþʳ.
          .   .   .

Now God, in whome all goodnes ys,
    And gyffs ev'y mane aftur hys wyll,
Hee grant hus grace þᵗ wee dow nott mysse,
    And after þˢ lyffe to cu' hyme tylle,
Soo þᵗ by hys grace we may obteyne,
    And the p'fect'ones þᵗ wee maye see,
That ffor us one þᵉ crosse was scleyne.
    Amene, Jesus, ffor charyte.

Not only the place where this MS. was discovered, and the mention of the writer's brethren, but the dialect and orthography, which are those of Craven, fix it upon the canons of Bolton. Thus, late is spelt laat ; bare, baar ; make, mak ; made, maade ; and water, wattur ; us, hus ; come, cum. In the prose part, which follows, the lecturer always addresses his hearers by the style of, Faþ'rs, or Woorshipful Faþ'rs.

I shall now employ these MSS. as a commentary on some parts of the " Chanones Yeman's Tale," in order to show with what exactness Chaucer copied while he derided the jargon of that pretended science.

    " I woll you tell, as was me taught also,
    The foure spirites and the bodies sevene,
    By ordere, as oft I herde my Lord hem nevene.
    The first spirit Quicksilver cleped is ;
    The second, Orpiment ; the thridde, y wis,
    Sal Armoniack ; and the fourth, Brimstone.

---

* Perhaps the meaning is this : Many of the particles of which human bodies consist, have belonged to grazing animals. After the dissolution of the body in the earth, these particles may be sucked up by the roots of plants, and of consequence be eaten once more by sheep and oxen, so that every beast may have his due again.

† Poverty makes a man's hair grow through his hood : that is, it forces him to wear his hood till it is full of holes. No bad image ; but it was an appearance oftener produced by the *practice* than the *neglect* of alchemy.

The bodies sevene eke lo hem here anon :
Sol, Gold is ; and Luna, Silver we threpe ;
Mars, Iren ; Mercurie, Quicksilver we clepe ;
Saturnus, Led ; and Jupiter is Tin ;
And Venus, Copper, by my Fader Kin."

Let us now turn to the Bolton MS.

"*Here begynethe a Tretyce that tretythe of a Scyence for to turne all Metalls to Silv' and Golde.* First, y$_u$ shall well wyt y^t y^r ar VII Bodyes ; y^t ys furst for to saye, Silv', Golde, Brasse, Yren, Cop', Tyne, Lede, and thes VII bodis and y^s tretice is eft'—the VII Planets. Now the Sprytes ar thes, Qwykke Silv', Arsenek, Sal-Armonak, Sulphur vyve : thes er IIII Sprites y^t gyvethe color to all metalls, and turnethe theme p'fitely to golde or to sylv' ; bot y'u shall well wytte y^t the spirites behoves to have mekill working and clensing."

Again :

"Why besie me to tellen you the names ;
As Orpiment, brent bones, iron squames,
And of the esie Fire and smert also
Which that was made, and of the care and woe
That we had in our matteres subliming,
And in amalgaming, and calcening
Of Quicksilver, ycleped Mercurie crude,
Our Orpiment and sublimed Mercurie,
Our grounden Literge eke on the Porphurie.
What nedeth for to rehers them all,
Waters rubyfying and bolles galle,
Arseneke, Sal Ammoniak, and Brinstone.
Our Furnese eke of calcinatioun,
And of Waters Albificatioune,
Unslekked Lyme, Chalk, and glerre of an Ey,
And combust materes and coagulat.
Rosalgar and other materes embibing,
And eke of our materes encorporing,
And of our Silver Citrination,
Our cementing and fermentation, &c.
Yet forgat I to maken rehersail
Of waters corrosif and of limaile,
And of bodies mollification,
And also of her induration.
Oils, Ablutions, Metal fusible, &c."

For to mayke the XII. Watters.

The first is the rede watter.

The secounde watter is persaunde.

The III watter ys watter y^t softenes and inters metalls.

Tayke a p'te of byrk ashes and II p'tes of qwykke lyme and a p'te of sal alkalye, so y^t there be als mekill of salt as of lyme, and than putt to theyme XII tymes y^s to thare weght of watter, and then sett all togyder in a hatte oven, and late it stand XIIII days, and styre all togyd' ylk a day ; then aft VII days lat all stand styll for to keill oþer VII dayes or mayre, for y^t is all the bett' and the more sustenand metalls y^t is slokened y'in.

The IIIIth watter ys called Watt'r of Weght, or Watt'r of Grete Name.

Tayke grene ar'ment, and putt in a vessall well closed with lutu' sapiencie all a day and all a nyght, to the tyme thy vessall wax rede ; than loke y^t you have good vinag. thryse dystilled, and then tayke þis red arnement w't the pomed', and put in y^t the vinagr' in the vessal of glass, and latt it stande soo VII days, ylke daye III or IIII tymes sterand it toged'. Aft'warde putt all to dystill, and then thou shall have rede watt'r, and is of this virtue y^t it will light candell, and make lightnes in houses.

The Vth watter ys called Watt' of the Fyere, and ys mayde in y^s man'r.

Tayke a part of sall armonyake and a parte of sulphur vyf and III p'ts of leterger and of whyte wyne XV p'ts, and all this put togyd' in a styllatorye well closyd, and dystyll ye matters w'th soft fyers.

The VI watter is called Watt' of Sulphur.

Tayke a p'te of sal vitr' and a p'te of sulphur sitrine, and stampe theyme well to small poud', and then putt ye poud' in a violl of glasse, and close it well, and late it stande a day and a nyght, and then tayke uppe the poud' eft', and than tayke an unce of that poud', and put to III unce of hote welland watt', and late yᵗ stande a litell whyle covered, and thou shall have rede watt'.

    The VII watter is Watter of Askes.

    Take III p'ts of askes and as mekil of rosalgar and as mekill of qwykke lyme, and put all thes well menged in a strong vessall, and putt to them III so mykill watt', and lat theyme wel togyd'r.

    The VIII watt'r is called the Watt' of Gold.

    Tayke yolk of egges hard soden and stampe theyme well till they be thykke as growell, and herof fyrst dystill watt', and then aft'warde the whyte of eggs row, and turne all theyme well to they be thyne as water, and then tayke yᵉ . . . so that thei be coverde w'th the whites, and than set all this on a soft fyre for to dystill : and than shalt thou have a man' of oyll. Than tayke the oyll and the wat' yᵗ was dystilled and meng all togyd', and put all yˢ in for to sublyme, and than shall you find a man'r of thing lyke to a man'r of gume ; the whilke gume is of this effecte, that putt it on a peny of silv' and it shall seme gold.

    The IX watt' is Watt' Citrine.

    Tayke clene yalow marcasite, and putt it in a vessall of glasse, and putt y'rto good strong vynag', and than dystill it : yt is of this effecte : paynt w'th yˢ watt' a swerd well burnished, or a merow well polyst, and sone aft' it shall wax blacke, and than wype it w'th a lyne cloth, and it shal seme gold begyldyd.

    The Xth wat' is Wat' White.

    Tayke sal gem almiladre and rede arsenike and alum de plume, and then tayke vertgrece and wad askes of ylk ane elyke mĕkyll ; put yᵐ in a vessal yᵗ is strang, than putt to theym vinag'r and clene urine elyke mekill ; eft put theym all in a stillatorye and continue yᵉ distillacionals long als any moystour will cu'. Tayke this : and cast on molten copper, and it gives a fayre blaunchour. The watter also is of this kynde, yᵗ tayke coper clensed, and melt it, and sloken it III tymes y'in, and it shall be p'fet and blaunched.

    The XI wat' ys Congelatine.

    Wat' to mayke metalls soft and ducible.

    Then follows a receipt, beginning, " B'n'dicite D'no in nom' P'ris et Filii et Spiritûs S'ci. Amen."

    Tayke an unce of m'cury, a q'teron of sal armoniac, &c. and grind all othes well togyd' on a m'bylle stone ; but this wil have grete travyle, and it behoves be done on a m'bill stone, &c.

    B'n'dicite D'no for yᵉ long rede work. Amen.

    Tayke of lymale of gold, &c.

    Thus much for the alchemy of the canons of Bolton.

    But they were occasionally employed in a much more solid and respectable pursuit, for the second part of the same MS. consists of a treatise on astronomy, in two books, expressed in very perspicuous Latin. What they knew of the subject may, in some measure, be collected from the rubrics of the several chapters. In addition to which I shall give a passage or two at length, in order to enable the reader to form a better judgment of the state of this science in the religious houses.

    In the MS. now before me, the first book is defective in the beginning, and the second in the end ; but the entire chapters are thus entitled :—

    " Quid sint planetaru' dracones.—Quid sit solis et lune declinatio.—Quid sit solis et lune conjunctio.—Quid sit solis et lune oppositio.—Quid lune defectus qui g'ce (Græce) eclipsis dicitur.—Quid sit solis defectus.—Quid sit arcus, quid chorda, quid sagitta.—Quid sint signorum ascensiones, et cur in div'sis regionibus div'se inveniantur.—Quid sint XII domorum equationes.—Quid sit motus pla'rum diurnu', horari', et momentarius."

    " Explicit liber primus. Incipit prologus libri secundi.

    " Incipiunt Capitula.—De r'one inceptionis et compos'n's canonum.

    " Qualiter opifex astronom', ad huj' artis effect' per tabulas omn' canonum ingrediatur.

    " Qualiter longitudo inveniatur. De medio cursu solis et cæterorum planetarum inveniendo. De solis coequatione—De coeq'tione capit. Draconis. De Sat'ni, Jovis, et Martis coequatione—De coequa'nibus Ven'is et M'curii. De latitudine lunæ inveniendâ. De latit. reliquor' pla'ru' inveniend'. De solis declinatione. De progressione, et statione, et retrogradatione pla'ru'."

    I will now endeavour to decipher (for it is exceedingly contracted and obscure), a part of the chapter " De solis defectu." Where I do not understand it, I will leave the contractions to exercise the sagacity of better critics.

" Defectus autem solaris, qui Græcè eclipsis dicitur, ejus luminis est totalis seu partialis. privatio, cum videlicet absque lune latitudine in uno eodemque aliquo loco solis ac lune reperitur unita conjunctio. Cum enim luna, quamvis sole minor sit, terre tamen feratur vicinior, quotiens absque latitudine collateralis seu linealis soli subjecta extiterit, aut ejus luminis paɪte aliqua, objectu sui corporis, necesse est illam obumbrare. Collateralis etenim (qu ? etiam) soli absque latitudine luna erit quotiens ejus orbis radiatio ad corpus solis extenditur. Orbis autem lune radiatio geg XII in suo circulo circumquaque concluditur. Et quum de radiatione orbis lune mentionem fecimus, de radiatione orbis solis etiam mentionem faciamus. In ₒᶜcu'z (forte quocunque) gradu signi cinglibus gradus solis inventus fuerit ejus orbis radiatio gradus XV ccu'q'z (circumquaque?) obtinebit. Ut verbi gratiâ, si sol in XV gradu signi Arietis extiterit, ejus orbis radiationes ad primum gradum signi Arietis atque primum gradum signi Tauri extendit (sic). Cum igʳr orbis lune radiatio quæ XII est graduum collateraliter corpus solis tetigerit, necesse est lunam infra solis radiationem quæ XV gradibus extenditur tum quadam quantitate v'sari. Et cum finierit, necesse est solis radiationes tum quadam quantitate in ea parte eclipsari."

To this quotation I will subjoin two lines copied *literatim* from the original, that readers who are unacquainted with MSS. may be enabled to form some conception of the difficulties under which first transcribers and editors labour; difficulties which, if men had not been found patient enough to encounter, the world had wanted better things than the astronomy of the canons of Bolton :—

> g'dibz extendit tu' q'dem q'n'tate w'sari in ea p'te
> metu' l'nis luna t'c nequ'at eclipsari hor g'i dim.

I shall, in the last place, present the reader with a specimen of their knowledge in the economy of the human body. A modern anatomist will probably be amused with their account of the fœtus in utero* :—

" The previte and the lyffe of ev'y thynge ys wattur ; wattur ys that that in whett is flowr ; and in the olyffe the oylle ; and in the tres the gume ; and in bestys the fatnes ; and in all trees the frutt ; and also the begynynge off generacyone off mane is of wattur ; for when . . . . VII days unto that ytt be congelyde, and ytt ys maade fleyshe, and ytt cums apone the boons, and ytt ys maade boons, and yt cums apone her' and synnews, and ytt ys maade lyke unto them, and thene yt ys congelyde in X days, and ytt ys maade as cheese, and thene yt waxis redde in XVI days and his collowr ys maade lyke the collowr off fleche, and then in the XXth daye ytt begyns to be dessev'yde, and to have membres lyke unto heers, and in the XXX daye ytt ys formyde in the forme of mane, and in ye XL ytt apeyrs as that theyre sume lyffe in ytt, and froo the XL daye ytt begyns to be norycheyde w't' the bloode of the moþr by hys cowrs att the navylle, and thene ytt waxys lyttyll and lyttyle, and streyns.—And understunde zee well, yᵗ the elementt of wattur keeps ytt in the moþy's wome the III fyrste monthes, and the aeyr the oþ'r three monthes, and then the fyre the oþr III monthes sethys hym, and p'formys hyme ; and whene that neyne monthes are fullfyllde, the blowde wherwythe that hee was norycheyde dep'ts, and assends uppe to the brests of the wooman, and ys theyre, as ytt wer, a thyke kreeme, and after hys byrthe hee ys norycheyde w't mylke off his moþ'r."

It would have given me pleasure to discover what attention the canons of Bolton had paid to mineralogy and botany in a situation so favourable to those pursuits; but my researches have not been attended with success. On these subjects they probably thought practical knowledge enough; with respect to the first, they pursued, though perhaps with little skill, the veins of lead, iron, and coal, in their estates; and for the second, though without any botanical arrangement in their heads, they knew, as well as Linnæus could have taught them, what species of plants would make bread, fatten an ox, roof a church, or blaze upon a hearth.

Yet they must have had some rude nomenclature of their own indigenous herbs, and would apply them in some fanciful and superstitious way to medical uses.

On the whole, their information, though far short of real science, was equally remote

---

* Taken from a third MS. in the same hand with the Metrical Treatise on Alchemy, quoted above.

from total ignorance; a dawn which indicated approaching light, " quale est quod ex obscuro specu emergentibus paullatim se ostendit inter lucem tenebrasque medium."[*]

But the habits of this order were favourable to literature. Chaucer's Alchemist was a Canon Regular.   The Augustinians were gentlemen ; and though the laxity of their rule, especially as interpreted in later times, might be too favourable to habits of dissipation, it left their faculties, at least, unchained by those benumbing fetters which cramped every movement of intellect in the poorer or the severer orders. A comparison of the state of literature in our own universities at present, and in times when they were filled with mendicant scholars, under a narrow and illiberal discipline, will prove that a certain degree both of freedom and elegance is equally, perhaps more, conducive to improvement in science.

I have now to state a few miscellaneous notices prior to the dissolution.

Among the Harl. MSS. 604, f. 106 a, is one entitled, " P'gressus D'ni Suffraganei," which is a collection of memoranda by some suffragan of the Archbishop of York, in his progress through this part of the diocese. I conjecture it to be about the time of Henry VI., though it resembles the piebald Anglo-Latin style of Leland. But the Saxon þ was not, I think, continued after the reign of Edward IV. " It. revertendo ad Chrystallum & from þens to Boltonne in Chanouns,[†] of þe order of Seynt Austeyn, of þe furst fu'dacon' off þe Lord Meschynne & Lady Cysley Romiley ys wyeff & ther heyrrys, in þe zeer of our Lord a MˡᵒCᵒXX. in the second yeer of Kyng Henry þe furst, & 2ᵒ anno Thrustini epi. Now lord Clyfford ys ther fu'dar xii mylys fro' Chrystall."

Letter of demolishing Bolton.—Dodsworth's MSS., vol. xxvi. f. 15.

" EBOR.   " A l're to   CRUMWELL, 15 Dec. 1537.

" Ower most noble singuler good lord, ower bounden dewty lowly premisede, pleass itt your honourable lordeshyppe to be advertisede, we have lately received your l'res contcyninge the kynge's majesties pleasure anenst the order of leed and belles appertayninge to such houses of religion contayned in the kynges graces letters com'ission to us addressed, whereof we have already com'ytte the salve custodye to substantial honest p'sons hable to answere therefore, and have not sold ne intended to sell, any parcell therof. We have quyetly taken the surrenders, and dissolved the Monasteries of Wyrkesope, Monkbretton, Sante Andrewes in York, Byland, Ryvalle, Kirkham, and Ellerton, the Freyers at Tykell and Doncastere, Pontefract, and the citie of York, where we p'ceyved no murmure or griefe in any behalf ; but were thankefully receyved, as we shall within six dayes more plainely certifye your lordshipp. And where itt hath pleased yo'r lordshipp too wryte fore reservynge of led and belles att Bolton in Chanouns, there is ass yet no such com'yssion cummyne to our handes, as Jesus knowethe ; who preserve youre lordeshippe in helth and honor.

" Your lordshippes humble bounden orators,
" GEORGE LAWSON,
" RICHARD BELASSES,
" WILL'AM BLITHMAN.

" Att Yorke, the 15th day of December."

This letter seems to prove that there was an intention of including Bolton in the number of smaller houses. But this turned out to be a mistake, and it stood somewhat more than two years longer.

---

[*] Grotius.

[†] Bolton *in* Chanouns. It was first styled Bolton Canonicorum, which being translated, and the word spelt Boltonne, some person, I suppose, mistook the two letters *ne* for the preposition *in*, which is nonsense. The place does not seem to have acquired the addition of Canonicorum very early. The first instance in which I have seen it so called, is in a charter relating to the manor of Flasceby, executed " apud Bolton Canonicorum," A.D. 1429.

Harl. MSS. 604, fo. 92.

" Com. Ebor.

" A brefe certificate made upon the dissolutions of div'se Monasteres and Priores ther surrendred, in the moneths of December, Januar', and Februar. in the xxxth year of the regne of oure sov'ane Lord Kyng Henri theght as insuyth.

The namez of the howsez, with the keepers of them :

Bolton Canonn. in Craven, Rob. Riche, Esquier.

The Clere Valers of the Possessiouns, ov' and above the annual Reprisez,

£cc$^{xxx}_{iiii}$xviii. xvs. id. ob.

The Nombre of the Priors and Brethren, with ther Pencions,

Prior, £xl. and xiv Confr. £lxxvi. vis. viiid.

The cleare Monay remanynge of the yerely Possessiouns, £c$^{xx}_{iiii}$iv. viiis. ivd. ob. qu.

The Stock, Store, and Domestical Stuff, old, with dettys receyvyed, £ccvii. xiiiis. viid.

Rewards, with portions paid unto the Prior, &c.

Confr. et P'ori, £lxviii. iiis. ivd. S'vient. . . . . £x. xis. iiiid.

The Remaynes of the price of Goodds and Catalls sold, £cxxviii. xixs. xid.

Lead and bells remanyng, Lead, xiii ff.—Bells iii.

Woods and underwoods, c Acr'.

Playt and Jewells, cccxxix. Unc.

Detts owyne unto the Howssez, &c. £cclxxi. viis. id.

Detts owyng by the Howsez, £ii."*

The surrender of this house, by Richard Moone the prior, and fourteen canons, bears date Jan. 29, 1540,† and is literally as follows :—

" Om'ibus Christi fidelibus ad quos presens scriptum p'venerit, Richardus Moone, prior Monasterij sive Prioratûs de Bolton Cano'icor', al's dict' Bolton in Craven, ordinis Sancti Augustini, Eboracen' Dioc', et ejusdem loci Conventus Sal't'm in D'no sempiternam et fidem indubiam presentibus adhibere. Noveritis nos prefatos Priorem et Conventu, unanimi assensu et consensu n'ris, animisque delib'atis, ac certa sc'a et mero motu n'ris, ex quibusdam ca'is justis et rationabilibus a'i'as et conscientias n'ras sp'ial'r moventib', ultro et sponte dedisse concessisse ac p' p'ntes dare et concedere, reddere delib'are, et confirmare illustrissimo in Xpo Principi et D'no n'ro Henrico Octavo Dei gr'a Anglie et Francie Regi' fidei defensori, D'no Hib'nie, et in terr' supremo Eccl'ie Anglicane sub Chr'o capiti, Totu' dict' Prioratu' nostr' de Bolton predict', ac totu' scitu', fundu', circuitu' et precinctu' ejusd', necno' o'i'a et singula maneria, d'nia, mesuagia, gardina, curtilagia, toft', terr', et ten'ta n'ra, prata pasc', past', boscos, subboscos, rev'siones, redditus, s'vicia, mollendina, passagia, feoda militu', ward' maritag', nativos villanos cu' eor' sequelis, co'i'as, libertates, ffranchesias, jurisdictiones, officia, cur' let', hundred', vis' franc' pleg', feria, m'cata, p'cas, waren'ia, vivaria, aquas, pisc', vias, chyminia, vacua, fundos, advocat'o'es, no'iat'o'es, presentac'o'es, et donac'o'es eccl'iar', vicariar', cant', capellar', hospitaliu', et alior' beneficior' eccl'iasticor quoru'cu'que, rectorias, vicarias, cant', pensiones, porciones, annuitates, decimas, oblaciones, ac o'i'a et sing'la emolumenta, proficua, possessiones, hereditamenta, ac jura n'ra sp'ualia et temporalia quecu'q ; tam infra com' Ebor' q'm infra com' . . . . [*so left blank in record*] . . . . et alibi infra regnu' Anglie ubicu'q ; eidem Mon^{rio} n'ro de Bolton predict' quoquo modo p'tin', spectan', appenden', sive incu'bentia, ac om'imod' cartas, evidentias, scripta, et munimenta dicto Mon' n'ro, maneriis, terr' et ten'tis ejusd' ac ceteris p'miss' cu' p'tinen', sive alicujus inde p'celle, quoquo modo spectan' sive conc'nen' : Habend', tenend' gaudend', et lib'e p'cipiend' dict' prioratu', scitum, fundu', circuitu' et precinctu' ejusd', necno' o'i'a et singula p'dict' maneria, d'nia, mesuag', gardina, terr', ten'ta, et cetera p'missa, cu' om'ibus et singulis suis p'tin', p'fato invictissimo principi et d'no n'ro Regi, hered' et assign' suis, imp'petuu' ; cui in hac parte ad om'em juris effectum qui exinde sequi poterit aut potest nos et p'oratu' n'r'm p'dict' ac o'i'a jura nobis qualitercu'q ; acquisita (ut decet) subicim' et submittim', dantes et concedentes eidem regie majestati om'em et o'imod' plenam et lib'am facultatem auc'tem et p'tatem nos et p'oratu' n'r'm de Boltone p'dict' unacu' o'ibus et singulis man'iis, terris, ten't', redd', rev'sionib', s'viciis ac singulis p'missis cu' suis juribus et p'tin' univ's', disponend', ac p' sue lib'e volu'tat' regie libito ad quoscu'q ; usus majestati sue placentes alienand', dona'd' convertend' et transferrend', h'm'di disposic'o'es, alienac'o'es, donac'o'es, et convers'o'es, p' dict' majestatem suam regiam quovismodo fiend' ex nu'c ratificantes, ratasq ; et gratas ac p'petuo firmas nos h'itur' p'mittim' p' p'ntes. Et ut premissa o'i'a et sing'la suu' debitu' sortiri valeant effectu' electionib' insup' nobis et successor' n'ris, necno' om'ib' querelis, p'vocationib', appellacionib', actionib', litibus, et instan', aliisq ; quibuscunq ; juris et facti remedijs ac beneficijs, nobis forsan

---

* There was, it seems, at Bolton an altar of St. Nicholas ; for in the accounts of the Clifford family for the year 1521 is this entry : " To Seynt Nicholas Clarks of Bolton, iiis. ivd."—" Item, p'd the Prior of Bolton & the convent for my auld Lady Obbeyt, xviiis." In the same accounts are " The Names of those that are admit in all my Lord's Beyd Rolls," amounting nearly to 300 tenants and dependants on the estates of the family. In the same year are paid for a Buke calyd Claudii Tholomeii, xiiis. ivd.—For Buke of Yngling French and Duch, id.—Item, for Ynglis Bukis iis. iid.—Item, to the Prior of Bolton for all man'r of Deuties in discharge of my Lord's conscience, xiiis. ivd.

† Of this instrument, which remains in the Augmentation Office, I have, since the first edition of this work, obtained a transcript from the gentleman who has the charge of it. My readers will be pleased to accept an apology for my having omitted the surrender of Kirkstall in its proper place.

et successorib' n'ris in ea p'te p'textu disposic'o'is, alienac'o'is, donac'o'is, et conv'sionis p'dict' et ceteroru' p'missoru qual'rcu'q; competen' et competitur', om'ibus doli, metus, erroris, ignorantie, vel alterius materie sive disposic'o'is, exceptionib', objectionib', et allegacionib', prorsus semotis et depo'it', pala' pure et exp'sse ex certa sc' ia n'ra a'isq; n'ris spontaneis renu'ciavim' et cessim', p'ut p' p'ntes renu'ciamus et cedimus ac ab eisdem recedimus in hiis scriptis. Et nos p'dict Prior et Conventus et successores n'ri dict' p'orat' n'r'm, precinctu', scitu', mansione', et eccl'iam n'ram de Bolton p'dict' ac o'i'a et sing'la man'ia, d'nia, mesuag', gardina, curtilag', toft', p'ta, pasc', past', boscos, subboscos, terr', ten'ta, ac o'i'a et sing'la cetera p'missa cu' suis juribus et p'tin' univ's', prefato d'no n'ro Regi, hered' et assign' suis, contra o'es gentes warantizabim' imp'petuu' p' p'sentes. In quor' testi'o^m nos p'fati P'or et Convent' sigillu' n'r'm co'e p'ntibus apponi fecim'. Dat' in domo n'ra capit'lari XXIX° die mens' Januarii anno regni Regis Henrici Octavi tricesimo.

p' me RYCHARD, p'ore'.	p' me EDWARDU' HYLL, p'b'r'm.
p' me CHRISTOFERU' LEDS, p'sbiteru'.	p' me JOHANEM BOLTON, p'sbiteru'.
p' me THOMA' CASTELL' p'b'r'm.	p' me ROB'TU' KNARESBURGH, p'sbiteru'.
p' me GEORGIU' RICHMUND', p'b'r'm.	p' me JOHA' HALIFAX, p'sbiteru'.
p' me JHO'M CRUMOKE, p'b'r'm.	p' me LAURENCIU' PLINTON, p'sbiteru'.
p' me WILL'M WYLKS, p'sbiteru'.	p' me THOMA' FONTANS, p'b'r'm.
p' me WILL'M MALLHOME, p'b'r'm.	p' me ROBERTU' BURDUS, subdiaconu'."
p' me THOMA' PYKERYNG, p'b'r'm.	

Of the subscribers to this instrument, Leeds and Castley continued in 1553 to receive annuities of 6*l*. 13*s*. 4*d*. each; Wilkes 6*l*. Pickering, Malholme, Cromoke, Hill, Bolton, Richmond, and Knaresborough 5*l*. 6*s*. 8*d*. each, and Bowrdeux (so spelt) 4*l*. The three other canons were either dead or otherwise provided for. The seal is nearly destroyed.*

After this Bolton remained in the king's hands till April 3, 1542,† when the site and demesnes, together with many other estates, enumerated below, ‡ were sold to Henry Earl of Cumberland, for the sum of £2,490.

Whether the habitable parts of the house were demolished immediately after the Dissolution, or not till this alienation, does not appear.

The following particulars, extracted from an inventory of effects belonging to the second Earl of Cumberland, at Skipton Castle, in 1572, exhibit, I think, the Ecclesiastical Vestments of Bolton.

For this opinion I have the following reasons :—

First, They are by far too numerous to have belonged to any private church or chapel.

Secondly, The number of vestments, copes, &c., is nearly the same with the number of the canons of Bolton at the Dissolution.

Thirdly, The house of Bolton being purchased by the first Earl of Cumberland almost immediately after the Dissolution, it is highly probable that the remaining vestments would be removed to Skipton, when the vestry where they were kept was pulled down.

---

* See Browne Willis's " Mitred Abbeys," vol. ii. page 269.

† Only nineteen days before the earl's death.

‡ Besides the site of the priory, with the lordships of Bolton, Storithes, and Hesselwood, there were included under this purchase, the manors of Wigton, Brandon, Embsay, Eastby, Cononley, Rawdon, and Yeadon, with certain lands and tenements in Berwick and Draughton, Skipton, Long Preston, Gargrave, Steeton, Marton, Crakehou, Thresfield, and Barden ; together with the advowsons of the rectories of Kighley and Marton. Bolton MSS. These were all the estates of the priory, excepting Malham and Appletrewick, both which had been previously granted out. The consideration was less than ten years' purchase, upon the low rental of that time. If two ciphers were added to this sum, it would scarcely repurchase these premises now. Much, however, must be allowed for enc'osures and improvements.

P me Rychard ford

P me Cristoferus clerk psbiter

P me ß thoma ryskell pbr

P me Georgius ß richardus pbr

P me John

P me Willm wyth þrumoko pbr psbidm

P me Willm Mathome pbr

P me thoma rykbyng pbr

P me Edwardw hyll pbr

P me Johanem bolton psbiter

P us Robt' krayskurgh psbiter

P me John kahfax psbiter

P me lanzanow phistow psbiter

P me thomd sfontanis pbr

P me Roberd burdus
subdiaconus

The East end of Bolton Abbey.

"Churche Garments in the Wardropp of Skipton.

First, VI copes of fustian,* with roses and branches.

Item, a vestment of whyt and p'ple fustian and russells,† w'th the pycture and image, upon the back, of Chryst hanging upon the crosse.

Item, a cope of whyte and tawney damaske imbrodered w'th flower-de-luce and branches of clothe of gold and sylke, and twoo other vestments, for deacon and subdeacon, of whyt damaske and tawney velvett imbrodered w'th flowers of sylke and gold, all lyned w'th blew buckram.

Item, twoo ould copes, wherof thone of sylk and myngled w'th golde, with branches imbrodered ; and of thother verey lyke, w'th pycktures also imbrodered.

Item, a vestment of changeable colours of sylke, with grene and blewe.

Item, twoo old vestments of sylk frynged with the armes before and behynd, inwrought.

Item, another old vestment of sylk with cheaquers of gold and sylk upon the back, and lykwyse cheaquers before with some armes.‡

Item, an old vestment of blew saye and tawny chamlett, with an image upon the back, with branches alsoe.

Item, a verey old vestment of blewe sattan and redd, crost upon the back, with branches of flowers.

Item, a vestment of whyt damask and redd velvett, with one pyckture upon the back and branches embrodered.

Item, an old vestment of changeable sarsenett, lyned with blewe lynyn.

Item, a vestment of whyt damaske and cremysyn velvett, with half moone and tyretts, and a pycture of Chryst upon the back.

Item, twoo vestments of clothe of golde and cremysyn velvett, frynged with grene, redd, and whytt sylk, with branches behynd and before, and XVth peace of clothe of golde, app'teyning to the same, lapped with a vale.

Item, a canabye of changeable sarsenett, frynged with whyt, yallow, grene, and tawney sylyke.

Item, twoo lytell peace of redd and changeable sylk, having twoo camells of them.

Item, twoo lytell old peace of blew russells, w'meaten, with thre Jesus', for vestments, sewed together.

Item, twoo lytel peace of whyt damaske to sett upon an albe.

Item, V corpus caces, with IV lynen clothes.

Item, IV albes with ther furnytur for the head of lynyn clothe.

I have now to describe the situation of this priory, and its remains, in their present state.

Bolton Priory stands upon a beautiful curvature of the Wharf, on a level sufficiently elevated to protect it from inundations, and low enough for every purpose of picturesque effect.

In the latter respect it has no equal among the northern houses, perhaps not in the kingdom. Fountains, as a building, is more entire, more spacious, and magnificent ; but the valley of the Skell is insignificant, and without features. Furness, which is more dilapidated, ranks still lower in point of situation. Kirkstall, as a mere ruin, is superior to Bolton ; but, though deficient neither in water nor wood, it wants the seclusion of a deep valley, and the termination of a bold rocky background. Tintern, which, perhaps, most resembles it, has rock, wood, and water in perfection, but no foreground whatever.

Opposite to the east window of the priory church the river washes the foot of a rock nearly perpendicular, and of the richest purple, where several of the mineral beds—which break out, instead of maintaining their usual inclination to the horizon—are twisted, by some inconceivable process, into undulating and spiral lines. To the south, all is soft and delicious ; the eye reposes upon a few rich pastures, a moderate reach of the river,

---

* Fustian, pannus fustaneus, was a very ancient material for ecclesiastical vestments. See "Mon. Angl." vol. i. p. 700 ; where the early Cistercians, then reforming on the splendour and luxury of the Benedictines, bound themselves to use no chesibles, *nisi de fustaneo.*

† I cannot find out the meaning of this word. [" Russell, a kind of satin."—Wright.]

‡ These vestments were probably used at the obits of the Clifford family, or perhaps in their private chantry in the priory church. Had they belonged to the chapel in the castle, they would have been reposited in the sacristy there, which was still in repair.

3 J

sufficiently tranquil to form a mirror to the sun, and the bounding fells beyond, neither too near nor too lofty to exclude, even in winter, any considerable portion of his rays.

But, after all, the glories of Bolton are on the north ; for there, whatever the most fastidious taste could require to constitute a perfect landscape is not only found, but in its proper place.   In front, and immediately under the eye, lies a smooth expanse of park-like inclosure, spotted with native elm, ash, &c., of the finest growth ; on the right, an oak wood, with jutting points of grey rock ; on the left, a rising copse.   Still forward are seen the aged groves of Bolton Park, the growth of centuries ; and farther yet, the barren and rocky distances of Simon Seat and Barden Fell, contrasted to the warmth, fertility, and luxuriant foliage of the valley below.

About half a mile above Bolton the valley closes, and on either side the Wharf is overhung by deep and solemn woods, from which huge perpendicular masses of gritstone jut out at intervals.

This sequestered scene was almost inaccessible till of late, that ridings have been cut on both sides of the river, and the most interesting points laid open, by judicious thinnings in the woods.   These have been well rewarded, for here a tributary stream rushes from a waterfall, and bursts through a woody glen to mingle its waters with the Wharf.   There the Wharf itself is nearly lost in a deep cleft of the rock, and next becomes an "horned flood," inclosing a woody island.   Sometimes it appears to repose for a moment, and then resumes its native character—lively, irregular, and impetuous.

The cleft mentioned above is the tremendous Strid.[*]   This chasm, being incapable of receiving the winter floods, has formed on either side a broad strand of naked gritstone, full of rock-basins, or "pots of the lin,"[†] which bear witness to the restless impetuosity of so many northern torrents.   But, if Wharf is here lost to the eye, it amply repays another sense by its deep and solemn roar, like the voice "of the angry spirit of the waters,"[‡] heard far above and beneath, amidst the silence of the surrounding woods.

The terminating object of the landscape are the remains of Barden Tower, interesting from their form and situation, but still more so from the recollections which they excite.[§]

On the whole, this is one of the few and privileged spots where, within the compass of a walk, and almost of a single glance, the admiring visitor may exclaim, with a true painter and poet—

> "———— Some Lancastrian baron bold,
> To awe his vassals, or to stem his foes,
> *Yon* massy bulwark built ; on *yonder* pile,
> In ruin beauteous, I distinctly mark
> The ruthless traces of stern Henry's hand."
>
> Mason's " English Garden," b. v. p. 385, &c.

The noble owner, too, may deem himself happy in the possession of a domain which verifies, in every feature, the same poet's idea of a perfect English landscape—

---

[*] See p. 446.
[†] See the " Minstrelsy of the Borders," vol. ii. p. 48.
[‡] "Douglas."
[§] See the account of Henry Lord Clifford ; his residence at Barden, and his intercourse with the canons of Bolton.

The Rev.d J. Griffith del.

S. Alken. Fecit.

A view of Bolton Abbey.

"—— —— Where nature and where time
Have work'd congénial ; where a scatter'd host
Of antique oaks darken thy sidelong hills ;
While, rushing through their branches, rifted cliffs
Dart their white heads, and glitter through the gloom :
More happy still, if one superior rock
Bear on its brow the shiver'd fragment huge
Of some old Norman fortress ; happier far—
Ah ! then most happy—if thy vale below
Wash with the crystal coolness of its rills
Some mouldering abbey's ivy-vested wall."

To these lines, descriptive as they are of Bolton, may be opposed, both in point of beauty and accuracy of representation, the following passage from a Latin poet, who, though he lived under the decline of taste for composition, had an eye and a feeling for the charms of nature little inferior to Virgil.

" Ingenium, quàm mite solo !   Quæ forma beatis
Arte manûs concessa locis !   Non largius usquam
Indulsit natura sibi.   Nemora alta citatis
Incubuere vadis ; fallax responsat imago
Frondibus, et longas eadem fugit umbra per undas.
Ipse Anien (miranda fides) infraque superque
Saxeus, hic tumidam rabiem spumosaque ponit
Murmura——
Huc oculis, huc mente trahor : venerabile dicam
Lucorum senium ?   Te quæ vada fluminis infra
Cernis ?   An ad silvas quæ respicis aula tacentes ? " *

Let the reader only substitute the Wharf for the Anio, and he will find in these lines a portrait of Bolton.   The aspect of the mansion up and down the vale, the alternate inquietude and repose of the stream, the age and bulk of the forest trees ;† the hanging shade and continuity of the underwoods, and, lastly, the works of art which they embrace, may all be transferred to this chosen spot from the villa of Manlius Vopiscus.

But it is time to return ; for such are the enchantments of this place, that designing only a walk about the ruins of Bolton, I have been insensibly carried to the extent of its demesnes.

Of Bolton Priory, the whole cloister quadrangle has been destroyed.   In the centre of it is remembered the stump of a vast yew-tree (such as were usually planted in that situation ; not merely for shade and ornament, but probably with a religious allusion).   Yew was, in northern countries, employed as a substitute for the palm in processions ; and the frequency with which the remains of this long-lived tree are seen in the courts of religious houses, may be accounted for from Psalm xcii. 12, 13.   " The righteous shall flourish like a palm-tree : those that be planted in the house of the Lord shall flourish in the courts of our

---

* Statii Sylvæ, L. 1.

† Mr. Mason thought, no doubt, that he had called in a high antiquity to the aid of imagination when he supposed his oaks to have heard " A Sydney's, nay, perhaps a Surrey's reed ; " but this might have been the privilege of mere saplings in comparison of many gigantic trunks scattered about the woods of Bolton, of which it is not too much to believe that they may have heard the minstrelsy of Saxon bards.   A mere shell, more than thirty feet in circumference, was lately discovered in pushing a new walk through the depth of a solitude heretofore unexplored.

God." But I confess that this idea is my own, having vainly sought for it in the "Rationale" of Durand, the ingenious and fanciful collector of such analogies.

The shell of the church is nearly entire. The nave, having been reserved at the Dissolution for the use of the Saxon Cure, is still a parochial chapel,* and, by the attention and good taste of the present exemplary minister, has been restored from a state of dilapidation to that of complete repair, and is now as well kept as the neatest English cathedral. This may serve as an example to some wealthy parishes, who are allowing the magnificent conventual churches reserved for parochial use at the Dissolution, to moulder in unregarded decay, till they are ready to fall upon their heads.

The cemetery at Bolton † is on the north side of the church; and, as it has one tomb at least prior to the Dissolution, I am confirmed in my opinion, that, during the existence of the priory, the parishioners of the Saxon Cure had the right of burial at the priory church, as they certainly made their oblations at the altar.

The architecture of the church is of two distinct styles. The translation took place in 1154, and, from many decisive marks in the stonework, as well as the necessity of the case, the canons must have begun with the choir, which they finished at one effort, and, most probably, before their removal from Embsay. This is proved by the Saxon capitals, which extend westward to the transept. The fine ramified east window, and the spacious apertures on the north and south sides of the choir, afford no objection to this statement; as the first has evidently been inserted in the place of the three round-headed lights which must originally have occupied the east end, while the latter are enlargements of single lights of the same shape. Marks of insertion are evident in the masonry as well as the buttresses, which last have been plainly added to the perpendicular Norman projections in the original wall.

The nave exactly resembles the priory church of Lanercost in Cumberland, belonging to the same Order,‡ which was finished and consecrated A.D. 1165. In both a south aisle is wanting: the columns of each are alternately cylindrical and angular, and the hatched ornament of the capitals and windows is common to both. This church, indeed, as belonging to a much more wealthy house, is greatly superior on the whole; yet, what antiquary, and what man of taste, can forbear to regret that the tombs of the Cliffords do not yet remain at Bolton, like those of the Dacres at Lanercost, which are scattered in the most beautiful disorder about the ruined choir, while elder, and other funereal plants, spire up among coronets and garters!

The original west front of Bolton, though unhappily darkened, is extremely rich. It is broken into a great variety of surfaces, by small pointed arches, with single shaft columns,

---

* Here are a silver chalice and cover, which appear to have been given by the first grantee immediately after the priory fell into his hands, as the former has, beneath an earl's coronet, the arms and quarterings of the family down only to his mother, a St. John; [the arms upon it are those shown by the woodcut upon p. 392; and there is also a silver paten inscribed, " *This Communion Plate Given To Boulton Chapple by Elizabeth Morley*, 1703."]

† This was the case at Stratfleur Abbey, in Cardiganshire, of which it is observed by Leland : "The cemiteri wherein the cunteri about doth buri, is veri large, and meanly waullid with stoone. In it be XXXIX great hui trees." "Itin." vol. iii. p. 77. A forest of sepulchral gloom !

‡ This circumstance is not unimportant ; for, independently of the general characteristics of the age, I have observed in the religious houses of the same Order a peculiarity of style and manner more easy to be discerned than described.

T.Taylor

West Front of the Priory Church at Bolton.

and originally gave light to the west end of the church by three tall and graceful lancet-windows.

Over the transept was a tower. This is proved, not only from the mention of bells at the Dissolution, when they could have had no other place, but from the pointed roof of the choir, which must have terminated westward, in some building of superior height to the ridge.

The want of this feature at present is the only defect of Bolton as an object. An abbey without a tower is like a face without a nose. But instead of this appears a very singular and misplaced work at the west end—I mean the base of another tower, of exquisite workmanship, with the annexed inscription on a kind of frieze,

✣✣✣ In the zer of olbr lozd ❀ucxxb u

bc gaon thcs ſonda coon on quebo cobſ

ꝺoꝺ haur marcc amcn

begun by the last prior; which partly hides, and partly darkens, the beautiful west front of the church. To compensate, however, for this injury, it is built of the finest masonry, and adorned with shields,* statues, and one window of exquisite tracery. Amongst other ornaments on this part of the work, is the statue of a pilgrim with a staff in one hand, and a broad flat round hat in the other, facing the south ; and on the west two sitting figures of dogs resembling stout greyhounds, by which it may be doubted whether Prior Moone did not mean to commemorate his uncanonical office of Master Forester to his patron.

The design of this front shows great taste and originality of invention. The tabernacles in particular, instead of terminating, according to the style of the age, in an obtusely

[* The shields which are over the west door are two in number, one charged with the arms of Clifford, the other with the cross patonce vair of the Earls of Albemarle.
Tonge, Norroy King of Arms, in his visitation of the northern counties in 1530 says of BOLTON ABBEY :
Arms.—Gu. a cross patonce vaire.

BE YT NOTID that the Monastery of Bolton in Cravyn of Blak Chanons, was furst founded by MESSIENES, who maried the daughter and heyre of the COUNT ABEMARLE, and the said monastery was founded of the landes of the said Abemarle, and founded after him was our Soverain lord the Kyng. And now founder ys the ryght honorable Lord th' Erle of Cumberland, and Lord Clyfford, by exchange with the Kyng.—Tonge's Visitation, p. 88.

Second shield. Quarterly. 1. Clifford, 2 & 3. Bromflete quartering Vesci, & 4. Vipont.

THIS YS THE ARMES of the ryght honorable lord THE ERLE OF COMBERLAND and founder of the Monastery of Bolton in Cravyn.—Tonge's Visitation, p. 88.

In the inscription upon the tower the unusual manner in which the date 1520 is expressed should be remarked : it is shown ꝳꝺꝶ, and might easily be mistaken for 1620.]

pointed arch, expand above the springers into diminutive castles of two towers each, with battlements and embrasures, carved with all the delicacy of statuary in mezzo relievo.

I have only to add one or two particulars with respect to the church. The dimensions are these :—

	Feet.	Inches.
Total length, on the outside, from west to east . . .	261	7
Inside length	233	11
Inside length of the nave (the present church) . .	88	6•
Inside length of the transept	121	5
Total width of the choir	40	4
Inside width of ditto	30	9
Width of the nave within	31	3
Diameter of the columns	4	8
North aisle of the nave	11	7

The roof of the nave appears to have been relaid by Prior Moone about the time when he began the new tower. It is of flat oakwork, covered with lead ; and has been painted, like most of the roofs in Craven about that time, with broad lines of minium. The springers of the beams are adorned with rude figures of angels. On the south side is a triforium running the whole length of the nave. North of the high altar is the rich canopy of a tomb within a recess of the wall, beneath which a skeleton was lately found, and part of a filleting of brass with the Longobardic letters NЄVI. ; from which it seems to belong to Lady Margaret Nevile, whose funeral I have mentioned in the compotus. †

Bolton was the burial-place of such of the Cliffords as died in Yorkshire ; for those who ended their days in Westmoreland would probably be interred at Shap. But of this martial family from the time of Robert de Clifford, the original grantee of Skipton, to the first Earl of Cumberland, in whose time the priory was dissolved, four died in the bed of honour and one upon the scaffold, and the place of interment of all these is unknown. But

[* The nave has been restored and reseated by the Duke of Devonshire, and the windows on the south side filled with stained glass executed at Munich at a cost of £3,000. The history of our Lord, beginning with the Annunciation and ending with the Ascension, is depicted in a series of thirty-six groups. The western window of the aisle has stained glass, by Clayton and Bell, representing the stoning of Stephen, the burning of St. Polycarp, and the martyrdom of St. Ignatius. In 1877 a stone screen was erected to complete the east end of the church.]

[† In the floor of the Mauleverer Chapel are three small brass plates, with inscriptions to—

Josias Morley of Scale House, died 6 Oct. 1731, aged 80 years and 8 months.
Mrs. Ann Morley, his relict, died 21 Nov. 1746, aged 61 years.
Elizabeth Morley, 1st wife of Josias Morley, died 13 March, 1715, aged 77 years and 3 months.

Upon tablets in the north aisle are inscriptions to—

John Lee, of the Abbey of Knaresborough, born 1766, died 1847.
Henry Thomas Lee, died 25 July, 1816, aged 9.
Emma Maria, died June 21, 1834, aged 24.
John Lee, died 1838, aged 42.
Maria, wife of John Lee, died 6 May, 1839, aged 69.
John Ward of Gowflat, died 1826, aged 49.

In the churchyard are these noteworthy inscriptions—

GVLIELMVS : CARR : P'B'R : HVIVS : LOCI : PER :
ANNOS : LIIII : SACELLANVS : OBIIT :
OCTOGENARIVS : ANNO : XRI . MDCCCXLIII :

John Carr, 18 June, 1852.
Rev John Umpleby, died 16 Apr. 1863, aged 81, in the 57th year of his ministry of this place.
Stephen Brigg, died 28 Jan. 1782, æt. 105.
Major Brigg of Barmbowers, his son, died 7 July, 1803, æt. 90.
John Headache, ob. March 31, 1842, æt. 104.]

as there is now remaining part of a slab of grey marble, in the wall of an outhouse at Bolton, with a groove for the Garter; and as John Lord Clifford, slain at Meaux 10th Henry V., was the only one of his family who had that honour before the first earl, I conclude that his body was brought home for interment.* However this may be, there are on the south side of the choir the remains of a chantry opening into it by a rich ornamented arch beneath, which appears to have been a tomb, with a doorway, as usual, at the head. Under this is the mouth of a vault, now almost choked with rubbish; and here, most probably, was the resting-place of the lords of Skipton and patrons of Bolton.

It is difficult to say what became of their remains at the Dissolution. The Earl of Cumberland would certainly be able to protect them from exposure and insult. Yet the vault at Bolton was empty when explored about thirty years ago; and they were certainly not removed into that at Skipton. On the whole I am inclined to believe that the vault was left closed at the Dissolution; but that, in the progress of subsequent decay, part of the arch may have fallen in, which would leave the lead a prey to sacrilegious hands, in consequence of which the bodies so exposed would gradually disappear.

In the windows of the north aisle of the nave are several heads of a king [one is of a woman], of no majestic presence, wearing the antique crown without bendlets, and surrounded with red and blue roses [*i.e.*, fragments of a ruby border, with cinquefoils and fleurs-de-lis, a red quatrefoil enclosing a mascle, some red roses, and white quarries, ornamented with oak-leaves and acorns]—a compliment, no doubt, to the unhappy monarch for whom two of the Cliffords successively fought and died.

In the year 1670 this church was rich in trophies of ancient heraldry, which have since perished. It was then visited by Dr. Johnston of Pontefract, physician, and an antiquary; but he neither observed nor reported very distinctly, and we are left to conjecture whether the shields of arms which he mentions in the nave were in wood or glass. Had they been in stone, as that part of the church has been protected, they must have remained. I will take what he saw upon his credit, and endeavour to assign, as far as I am able, the several bearings to their owners.

On the north side of the nave were—1. Arg. three greyhounds cursant S. collared of the first, *Mauleverer*. 2. Arg. five fusils in fess or, charged with as many roses, *Old Percy* [Query, intended for *Plumpton*]. 3. *England.* 4. Gu. a fess between two greyhounds currant arg. [MALEVERER]. On the south side—1. *England.* 2. Arg. a saltire gu., *Nevile.* 3. Gu. a cross formée and varry, arg. and az., *Albemarle.* 4. Arg. a lion rampant gu. crowned or, in a bordure az. bezantee, *Richard* Earl of *Cornwall.* 5. *Old Percy.* 6. A plain shield. 7. *Nevile.*

Next, on the south side of the choir and near the high altar, are the mutilated remains of five stone seats for the officiating priests, carved with a delicacy little inferior to statuary, and all, except the bases, of the stone used at York, where the work was undoubtedly executed. The whole was in that light and rich style which prevailed in works of little

* I have now ascertained this fact from the following passage in the "Chronicon de Kirkstall," Cotton Library, A. 16.— "Circa cujus urbis (Mews) obsidionem occisus est inclitus D'nus Joh. de Clyfford, cujus corpus delatum est in Angliam, & sepultum apud Canonicos de BOLTON in Craven."

magnitude about the reign of Edward I., and of which specimens remain in Queen Eleanor's crosses, the tomb of John of Eltham at Westminster, and several others. On various escutcheons about this work were, as appears, the following shields :—1. A cross formee [should be flory] between four martlets, beneath the crown of England—a coat assigned to *Edward the Confessor* soon after the origin of heraldry. On one side a lion rampant and a bordure of fleurs-de-lys, *John of Eltham;* and opposite, a lion rampant holding a battle-axe ? Next, a fess between two chevrons, *Del Isle?* 2. On two [Query, three ?] piles in chief as many cross crosslets fitchee ? [*Totbury.*] 3. Six annulets, 3, 2, and 1, *Vipont.* 4. A fret of four pieces (the *Harrington* knot). 5. Five fusils in fess, *Old Percy.* 6. A bend and file of three points surmounted, *Scroop* [*of Masham*]. 7. Barrè of eight, and upon it three chaplets ? [*Fitzwilliam* or *Greystock.*] Next, three lions passant. 2. The same in a bordure of fleurs-de-lys. 3. A lion passant and bend *surmontee.* 4. A fess between three rocks [*Rooke* or *Swanton*], *Fitzpiers ?* 5. Seme of fleurs-de-lys and a lion rampant, quartered by *Holland* Earl of Kent. 5. On a fess three escallops between five fleurs-de-lys, two in chief, three in base. 6. Three luces in pale, *Lucy.* Next, a plain cross, *St. George;* then *England;* and on a little pillar a lion rampant, *Percy.* Again, the cross formee [flory] and four martlets, *Edward the Confessor.* On the other side a horse trapped, meant, perhaps, for the kingdom of *Kent.* On the next arch three crowns, for King *Oswy* or *Edwin.* Next, three legs meeting, on each heel a spur within a bordure engrailed, *Man.* On the other side, a cross crosslet between two small crosslets. Lastly, *Castile* and *Leon.* The last shield proves, I think, this work to be as late as the reign of Edward I., and the omission of the arms of Clifford affords a very strong presumption that it was erected before that family took possession of the barony of Skipton in the reign of his son. Supposing this date to be correct, the work before us affords, perhaps, the earliest instance in which armorial bearings were ascribed to the Saxon kings or kingdoms.

On the whole, as several of the great persons whose arms appear on this highly-adorned work, had no immediate connection with Bolton, nor held any lands in the neighbourhood, what conjecture can be more probable than that it was a common offering of them, and others more nearly interested, and who are equally recorded with them, when they had experienced the hospitality of the house on their way to or from an expedition into Scotland ?

The entire outline of the close at Bolton cannot now be traced, but it certainly extended from the great gateway north and south, and touched upon the Wharf behind the churchyard at one point, and near Prior's Pool at another. Part of the wall, however, by the wayside yet remains, strong, and well constructed of ashlar. Within this inclosure, as usual, were all the apartments and offices of the house.

The cloister-court, containing the chapter-house, refectory, kitchen, dormitory, &c., with the exception of a few fragments, is destroyed. The chapter-house was an octagon, and perhaps the only specimen of a chapter-house of that form, which was not placed northward from the choir. All these apartments appear to have been coeval with the translation of the house, and to have been vaulted and groined with excellent masonry, of which some of the grotesque carved key-stones remain. To the south-east, but connected with these, stood the prior's lodgings, of which the outline is distinctly traceable by the foundations. On the site of the kitchens stands the schoolmaster's house, a foundation of the incomparable Robert Boyle, where the old school has been modernised by the taste of the present inhabitant into a light and pleasant dining-room. The present school was one of the offices of the priory, as old as the foundation.*

At a small distance from this stands a most picturesque timber building, in which tradition reports that the last prior ended his days. In the parlour has been a long oblique perforation, through the wall, turned towards the kitchens, through which the inhabitants whoever they were, might receive their commons.

All the modern additions in the inside of this building having lately been removed, an entire hall appeared in the centre open to the roof, and in the middle was the base of an ancient reredos, resembling a millstone, much smoked and burnt. Here the fire had evidently been kindled, and the smoke had found its way out at some aperture in the roof. Stone chimneys had been added to the building at some later period. On the whole, from the situation of this building near the gateway, and still nearer to the kitchens of the house, I am inclined to believe that it was the Aula Hospitum.

Near this, and unconnected with any building, was the priory oven, of such extent that the tenant of the demesne, missing sixty sheep, after some research found them sheltered under that ample arch. It was, in fact, a hemisphere eighteen feet in diameter.

In the general wreck of the offices at Bolton, the gateway alone escaped.† Probably

---

[* Over the porch of the rectory-house is a shield with the arms of Boyle—per bend embattled arg. and gu. a martlet for diff.; and upon a stone underneath is the following inscription :—

Schole Boyliana Robertus Boyle arm sumptus et stipendia huic scholæ fundandæ perpetuande que legavit Carolus comes Burlington et Corke fundum lignum lapides et alia desiderata ad ædes erigendas munifice donavit.

AD MDCC

This building was formerly a school-house, called Boyle's School, and its history appears to be as follows :—

The Hon. Robert Boyle (a younger son of the first Earl of Cork, and well known as the philosopher) left a portion of his estate (in trust) to his nephew the Earl of Burlington for charitable purposes, without any strict definition.

Lord Burlington applied to Chancery for directions, and it was ordered that he should build either an almshouse or a school at Bolton Abbey and purchase lands for the endowment thereof. He chose the latter, and conveyed the site on which the present rectory stands to trustees for the purpose, A.D. 1700. On this site (being part of the base court of the abbey) the trustees either erected an entirely new house, or more probably adapted a portion of the old monastic buildings for the purpose, and it was formed into a grammar school, with statutes, and endowed with land, &c., to the value of about 100l. a year. This residence was assigned to the head master, who was appointed by the Earls of Burlington and their successors, the Dukes of Devonshire. They always appointed the "sacellanus," chaplain of the abbey, to be head master; and so it continued to be the residence of the chaplain and head master, *combined in one*, until the resignation of Canon Robinson in 1874, when the Charity Commissioners consented that *this* house should be sold to the Duke of Devonshire, and that the present new school and house at Beamsley should be built with the proceeds, which has been done, and this house has been assigned by the duke as a rectory.

The endowment of the Hon. Robert Boyle's school consists of 52 acres of land at East Halton, and a rent-charge of 20l. per acre on Scale Park, near Kettlewell.]

[† The entrance-gateway has been preserved, and converted into an entrance-hall, and buildings have been added right and left of it, forming a residence called Bolton Hall, which the Dukes of Devonshire sometimes occupy during the shooting season. There are in the building some interesting pictures :—Lord Charles Clifford, eldest brother of the second Earl of Burlington; he died young in 1675, and is represented full length as a hunter, with two dogs, and is known as the "Boy of Egremont"—said to be by Lely; Henry Clifford, in armour, the fifth and last Earl of Cumberland; Anne, the Countess Dowager of Dorset, Pembroke, and Montgomery, dated 1672; a half-length of Richard Earl of Burlington; George Calvert, Lord Baltimore; and a very curious picture on canvas, attributed to Lucas de Heere, representing William Brooke, Lord Cobham, who died in 1596; his second wife, Frances Newton, with Johanna her sister, standing behind a table, around which six children are seated; and walking about amongst the dishes of fruit are a parrot and a little dog.]

3 K

the Earl of Cumberland thought it might be of use as a temporary retreat for himself, or a residence for his bailiffs.   Here, too, the records of the priory were kept ; and in the same repository* many of the evidences of the Cliffords which enrich the present work have been discovered.   It is a strong square castellated building, of late Gothic architecture, of which the outer and inner arch having been walled up, a handsome groined and vaulted apartment has been obtained within.

[Mr. J. T. Micklethwaite, F.S.A., architect, of London, who has specially studied monastic buildings, has supplied the following description of the abbey :—

The church of a house of canons has peculiarities which differ altogether from those which we find in the churches of any of the monastic orders.   One of the commonest, and at first sight most unaccountable, of these is that the nave has only one aisle, as we find it here and at Easby, at Kirkham, at Brinkbourn, at Lanercost, at Hexham, at Dorchester, at Boxgrove, and at many other places.   Most of these churches are buildings of considerable architectural pretension, in which the absence of south aisle—for it is generally the south that is wanting—appears as a great defect, and people generally put it down as an exhibition of that caprice which is supposed to have animated the mediæval builders.   Now, as I am one of those who hold that mediæval English builders were not, as a rule, capricious, I wish to show that this one-aisled plan came perfectly naturally, and was the legitimate consequence of the conditions under which the work was executed.

The monastic and collegiate church plans, though in late times they often became very much alike, have distinct origins.   The ordinary monastic church from the earliest time was a large cruciform building, with aisles, and this so far satisfied later ideas of magnificence that we often find, that throughout all subsequent rebuildings the Norman plan was retained unaltered, except by the addition of a few chapels about the east end.   Westminster, Gloucester, and Winchester are examples.   Whilst even in churches such as Canterbury, which have been considerably enlarged, the change has taken the form of extension rather than alteration of the original plan.   The secular cathedrals seem early to have imitated the abbeys.   But many other foundations of canons, whether regular or secular, are built on a quite different model—namely, the parish church.   In fact, most canons' churches actually were parish churches, either before they were made collegiate or from their foundation, if they were absolutely new.

Now the original parish church plan differed from the monastic in that it was entirely without aisles.   Our parish churches as first built were sometimes cruciform, and sometimes without transepts, but in either case aisleless ; and if there was a tower it was in the centre of the building over the chancel, the sanctuary forming the eastern arm, and the transepts, if there were any, the north and south.   The canons took the cruciform, which was the finer type of parish church before them, and glorified it by making it larger—so much so sometimes as to make it vie with the cathedrals in scale, but still keeping its characteristic want of aisles.   Here at Bolton, for example, if we look for the remains of the original twelfth-century work, we shall find none in any part which cannot have belonged to an aisleless church, with chapels east of the transepts ; we find that as usual the work has begun with the choir, and worked gradually westward.   The earliest part is the lower part of the side walls of the choir, which, though it was afterwards lengthened, and almost wholly rebuilt, kept its aisleless form to the last.   The early work here must date from about the time of the foundation.   The great piers of the crossing show remains a little more advanced in style, and in the lower part of the south wall of the nave, which is all that remains there of the original work, we find the pointed arch and other characteristics of the Transitional period.

The church had not been long finished before the alterations began, as they did in nearly every other church of the same sort.   The canons felt that their churches were inferior to those of the monks, and, notwithstanding their length, they were cramped for want of breadth.   They craved for the addition of aisles, which were now becoming common, even in parish churches.   But here the regular canons, and some of the seculars also, were met with a difficulty.   Along one wall of the nave ran the cloister, and important buildings abutted against it towards its west end.   To add an aisle on that side would have been expensive and very inconvenient ; so they were content with one on the other side only, where the ground was free.   Where there was no cloister, as at Ripon, two aisles were added ; and the alteration was so general that Bayham, in Sussex, and Lilleshall, in Shropshire, are

---

* The evidence rooms of colleges at present, as of monasteries in former times, are generally over the principal gateway ; a situation in which, by means of the stone vaulting beneath, their contents are protected both from fire and damp.

the only churches of any size which I remember to have kept their aisleless naves up to the time of the general suppression. At Bristol it had just been pulled down with the intention, as it appears, of rebuilding with one aisle, which rebuilding has only now been carried out, with the addition of a second aisle obtained by taking a slip off the cloister. In Scotland and Ireland, where money was scarce, examples of the unaltered plan are not uncommon.

The aisle at Bolton was added, as the west front shows, early in the thirteenth century—very few years after the church was finished. It has been somewhat altered in parts since, but in plan it remains the same. To compensate for the want of aisle on the south side, the wall was taken down as far as the roof of the cloister, and the existing range of five fine windows set up in its place. These windows were only carried for the length of the cloister, because further west a lofty range of building abutted upon the church. That part of the wall was therefore not taken down, and on the inside we can trace the difference between its masonry and that of the newer work.

In the fourteenth century the choir and transepts were magnificently rebuilt almost from the foundations, and at the same time somewhat extended. The choir, even in its present condition, is one of the most beautiful architectural compositions in England.

The latest work at this church is especially interesting, because it shows us arrested half way, a process which has been applied to half the parish churches in England, and which has entirely altered their external character. I said just now that when a church had a tower at its first building it was always in the centre. Whence comes it, then, that nine out of ten, as we now see them, are at the west end? The reason is that such towers are always additions. The greater number of parish churches were without towers at first. We may take the little church of Adel as an unaltered and typical example of what most others have grown from. But in later times, and chiefly in the fourteenth and fifteenth centuries, towers became fashionable, and it was a very poor parish which was without one in the sixteenth. These towers were built very slowly—sometimes, I believe, they were going on for the greater part of a century—and it was important to avoid disturbing the church and interfering with its continued use, as would have been done by breaking into it, especially in the middle. The new towers were therefore built on fresh ground outside the church, generally at the west end; and then, when the work was done, the west end of the nave was taken down and the building joined on to the tower. The same was also often done in churches which, like this one, had at first central towers, for, if for any reason the tower had to be rebuilt, it was easier to do it outside than inside the church. And this was the common case, for twelfth-century towers were much given to tumbling down, and the earlier ones had very heavy piers, which took up a great deal of room, and were likely to be condemned as obstructions during the progress of later improvements. Thus it has come about that in spite of the central position being the normal one in a parish church, it has been almost wholly superseded by the western.

What became of the original central tower at Bolton is, I think, not known. Perhaps its fall may have caused the general rebuilding of choir and transepts in the fourteenth century; perhaps it may have been taken down at that time and not rebuilt; or perhaps it may have stood till the end, and only fallen when the whole eastern part of the church was allowed to go to ruin. I do not think the last is very likely; but, however it may have been, it was thought fit in the sixteenth century to build another tower at the west end, and as the inscription tells us, it was begun in 1520. At the suppression, twenty years later, the work had only reached the height of the nave, and in that state it has come down to us. The thirteenth century west front is still standing, and close to it is the large arch of the tower, which, if the work had been allowed to go on a few years longer, would have opened into the nave.

The process, which is here so clearly displayed to us, may be traced in nearly every church with a western tower, except that in a few the nave itself has been rebuilt, either together with, or after the tower.

Before leaving the church we must say a few words about its ancient furniture, although unfortunately scarcely anything remains of it now. The canons, although, as we have seen, they took the general form of their church from that of a parish church, arranged it entirely in their own way. A parish church is all one, the nave and chancel being only different divisions of the same apartment. But the canons made it two. They wanted the choir for their own services, and so they fenced it off in a way which takes from it all ritual resemblance to the parish chancel. The choir was cut off from the nave by two solid screens, one in the eastern and one in the western arch of the central tower. The eastern screen, called in Latin *pulpitum*, and at Ripon, if not elsewhere, in English *purpille*, had a broad gallery above it from which parts of the service were sung, and where the organ generally stood, as it continued to do in most of our cathedrals till quite lately. The western screen was the rood screen— not a light wooden screen such as we are accustomed to associate with that name in parish churches, but a solid wall with an altar in the middle, and a pair of little doors, one at each end. This arrangement was also found in the monastic churches. The only instances I remember where the rood screen of this form still exists are at St. Albans and at Boxgrave. I think it is also at Wymondham, but I am not sure; and I have a strong suspicion that *both* screens remained at Howden till the alteration some years ago, by which the tower was opened to the church.

This altar, which, from its position, generally had the name of the *Jesus Altar*, or the *Altar of St. Cross*, was for the use of the public, and when a church was partly parochial, this was the parish altar. Here at Bolton it stood exactly where the parish altar still stands, and in the south wall of the nave is the piscina which belonged to it; and near is also a plain stone bench which served for what we now call the *sedilia*. The presence of this altar, and the public use of it, has saved the naves of several fine churches when the choirs have gone to ruin. In Yorkshire we have besides Bolton, Howden and Bridlington.

The screen at the west end of the nave contains some old fragments which no doubt at one time formed part of the enclosure of some of the chapels. There is a story that the screen at Skipton comes from here, but it is very unlikely. There is no place here that it would suit, and it looks very much as if it had been made for the church it is now in. In the south transept are the remains of two altars, and lying in the tower is the slab of another which was removed from the floor of the chapel at the east end of the aisle of the nave, when the new pavement was laid down lately. This last has a rectangular sinking in the middle, which has been taken for the " sepulchre" or place for the reception of relics which were enclosed there under the small stone called the " seal " of the altar. But it is much too shallow for that use, and is probably no more than the matrix of a brass plate, which has been let into the stone at some time when it has been re-used to cover a grave. Sealed altar-stones are exceedingly rare. I only know of six in England. Also lying in the tower is a dished stone, such as are sometimes found (as at Jervaulx) in the floor at the south side of altars. These are generally confounded with the piscina, but their use is quite different, and is connected with the preparation of the chalice before the offertory. They are often found where there is the usual piscina in the wall, though, perhaps, sometimes they may have served its purpose as well as their own.

The three panels over the Early English west door have been painted. The subject appears to have been our Lord seated, and with angels on either side. These are the only external mediæval pictures I have seen in England, but there are traces of decorative painting outside the Lady Chapel at Ely.

Of the domestic buildings of the priory little remains except foundations. Those surrounding the cloister are easily identified, because there is one arrangement of them, which is at least as old as the ninth century, and was followed by nearly all the Orders. Mr. Sharpe has talked so often about the Cistercian plan that some are, I think, rather apt to regard it as peculiarly Cistercian, whereas the Cistercians did but follow with such slight modifications as suited their circumstances a plan which had been used centuries before their time.

The cloister here was small. It had the usual doors into the nave, and close to the eastern one is another into the south transept, which may serve to remind us how complete was the separation between the nave and the part of the church which the canons reserved for their own use. Next the end of the south transept is a passage leading to the chapter-house, which was a small octagonal building. The Dorter or dormitory ran south from the transept above the passage to the chapter-house and some other apartments, the most important of which was the common-house. This, as well as the Dorter, was, I think, reached from the cloister by the door in the south-east corner. The Frater or hall took up the whole south side of the cloister. It was raised upon a basement, part of which formed passages, and the rest was no doubt a cellar for stores. Near the south-west corner of the cloister is a mass of masonry, which, I think, marks the foot of the stairs to the Frater. On the west side was a large building, the height of which may be seen by the marks which remain where it joined the south wall of the church. This building was appropriated to the cellarer, who had charge of the general stores and of the lay-servants of the house and the greater number of the guests, for which purposes he required a great deal of space both for warehouse and lodging-room. This is the building which Mr. Sharpe called the *domus conversorum* in his Cistercian plan, and, laying aside the controversy about the name, he was right to a certain extent. But it was a good deal more than the house of the *conversi*, and where it remains in a reasonable state of preservation it is generally easy to trace the divisions.

There have been buildings running southwards from the end of the Dorter, some of which remain, and there is good reason for believing that here was the prior's lodge. It seems to have formed part of a second quadrangle which existed south of the cloister. The present rectory appears to mark the south side of this quadrangle, and is probably built upon old foundations.

The foundations which run eastwards from the end of the Dorter mark the site of the Reredorter; and still further east, near the river, is a good deal of broken ground which tells of buildings there. They may not

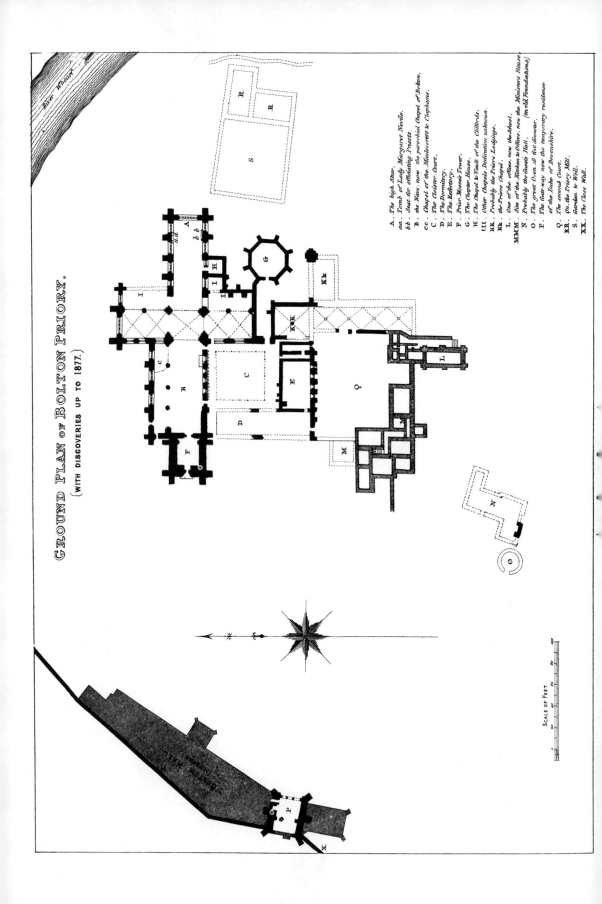

GROUND PLAN of BOLTON PRIORY.

(WITH DISCOVERIES UP TO 1877.)

A. The high Altar.
aa. Tomb of Lady Margaret Nevile.
bb. Seats for officiating Priests.
cc. the Nave, now the parochial Chapel or Bolton.
C. Chapel of the Mauleverers & Claphams.
C. The Cloister Court.
D. The Dormitory.
E. The Refectory.
F. Prior Moone's Tower.
G. The Chapter-House.
H. The Chapel & Vault of the Cliffords.
III. Other Chapels Dedication unknown.
KK. Probably the Priors Lodgings.
Kk. the Priors Chapel.
L. One of the offices, now the School.
MMM. Size of the Kitchen & Offices, now the Ministers House.
N. Probably the Guests Hall. (in old Foundations.)
O. The great Oven at first dinner.
P. The Gateway now the temporary residence of the Duke of Devonshire.
Q. The second Court.
RR. On the Priory Mill.
S. Garden & Well.
XX. The Close Wall.

SCALE of FEET

River Wheaf.

BOLTON HILL (Pasture.)

The Revd J. Griffith delt.

S. Alken fecit.

A View of Bolton Abbey.

improbably have been the infirmary; but nothing short of excavation of the whole site can enable us to speak with any confidence of the domestic buildings beyond the cloister. A good deal of the precinct-wall remains, and the gate-house is worked up into the present Hall.

A short distance above the abbey are remains of a river-wall on the left bank. It is of squared stone, built upon oak beams, and pinned to the earth with "tail-piles."]

Having now told what Bolton has been and what it is, I shall in the next place hint, with due reverence, at what it may become.

No man is a more determined enemy than the author of this work to the rash and innovating spirit by which our finest churches have lately been mutilated and deformed. But here the object is to restore, and not to innovate.

The removal of the central tower has already been lamented and while the long, unbroken line of wall and roof is continued from end to end, every judicious eye will be dissatisfied. But the restoration only of a few yards of masonry, properly broken and ragged, and the fragment of a window rifted in the midst, without any appearance of corbel or parapet to indicate the original height, though a hazardous undertaking, ought to be attempted, and in good hands would almost certainly be successful.

To this it will be objected that no instance occurs of a modern addition to genuine Gothic architecture in which a skilful eye does not discover the imposture, and, above all, that it would require a century to soften down the glare of modern masonry, so as to harmonise with the mellow tints of antiquity. These are real objections, but surely not insuperable; for, with respect to the former, I have, in this instance, a right to suppose taste and skill united with great diffidence; and, for the second, there are upon the spot useless and unornamental masses of old wall, which would serve as quarries of stone, already grey with age.

Neither is everything quite as it should be on the surface.

Yet I must again protest against that miserable taste which can level the floor of a conventual church to a bowling-green, or dress up the area which surrounds it with the spruceness of a modern pleasure-ground. A certain appearance of neglect, an attention to preserve rugged fragments of ruin in their proper places, and a due encouragement of many plants which would be rejected from the shrubbery, are here indispensable.

But the object of an improver working upon such materials is to remove, and not to add; to lay open, and not to embellish. For this purpose, and with a view to the perfection of Bolton as an object, the long walls which form a lane to the church, the stable and cottages which shoulder it beyond, and, in short, every impediment, excepting the fragments of genuine ruin between the gateway and the margin of the river, should be removed. Above all, the principal approach ought to be through the gateway, as of old. No part of this plan would affect the churchyard; the trifling violation of private property would easily be compensated; Bolton Priory would then be as perfect without as the church is already within.*

* Since the first edition of this work was published, I have had the unspeakable satisfaction of seeing the plan here proposed carried into execution, almost in every part. The former account has been retained, in order to be contrasted with the present appearance of the place.

The discoveries of old foundations which have been made in the progress of this work will be represented by surfaces faintly traced on the annexed ground-plan, for which I am indebted to Mr. Potter, a respectable land-surveyor. [The plan has been corrected to show all that is known in October, 1877.]

A Catalogue of the Priors of Bolton.

			Vac. by
A.D. 1120.	1	*Reginald.*	Cess.
Circ. 1180.	2	*Johannes.**	
1186.	3	*Walter,*† Prior de Boeltonâ.	
1222.	4	*Robert* occurs.	
[1267.	5	*William de Danfield,* 4 kal. May.]	
1274.	6	*Richard de Burlington ;* ‡ cess. ab officio 19 kal. Feb.	Cess.
1274.	7	*William* dictus *Hog.*	Amot.
3 Nov. 1275.	8	*John de Land ;* [Lund (Dugdale)] 3 Jan. 1330, cessavit.	Cess.
1330.	9	*Thomas de Copeley.*	Mort.
16 kal. Nov. 1340.	10	*Robert de Halton* [*Harton*]	Mort.
Oct. 2, 1369.	11	*Robert de Otteley,*§ Subprior.	
[12		*Robert de Grene* occurs in 1398.]	
	13	*John Farnhill.*	Res.
Ult. Mart. 1416.	14	*Robert Harton* [Catton (Dugdale)].	Mort.
6 Mart. 1430.	15	*John Farnhill,* Canon, ibid.	
	16	*Thomas Botson.*	Res.
20 Nov. 1456.	17	*William Man,* Subprior, ibid.	Res.
14 Nov. 1471.	18	*Christopher Lofthouse,* Canon.	
	19	*Gilbert Marsden* [suspended by the Archbishop for his dilapidations and irregularities of life, 10 April, 1482; he after resigned.]	Res.
10 Jul. 1483.	20	*Christopher Wood.*	Res.
27 Oct. 1495.	21	*Thomas Ottelay.*	Mort.
4 April, 1513.	22	*Richard Moyne,* or *Moone,* Canon.	

The ministers of this church, since the commencement of the Register, have been—

——— Idson, 1603.

[Mr. Brown, c. 1660.

Timothy Ferrand, 1680 ; afterwards Vicar of Skipton.]

James Snowden, who occurs in 1697, and died in 1722.

[11 Oct. 1726.] James Carr, A.B., of Christ College, Cambridge, Rector of Addingham, who, dying in 1745, was succeeded by his son,

[24 Sept. 1747.] Thomas Carr, A.M., of University College, Oxford, Vicar of Bugthorp ; while resident at Bolton, the faithful instructor of many respectable pupils yet alive, and afterwards master of Skipton School ; on his appointment to which, he resigned Bolton in favour of his son,

Thomas Carr, of University College, Oxford, who died 1789, and was succeeded by his brother,

[26 Aug. 1789.] William Carr, B.D., late Fellow of Magdalen College, Oxford, now rector of Aston Torald and Tubney, Berks ; to whose indefatigable attention the public are indebted for so many of the charms of Bolton which heretofore lay concealed and almost inaccessible. As minister of Bolton

---

* Harl. MSS. No. 1394, p. 51.

† Townley MSS. G. 18, ann. 1186.

‡ Elected Nov. 3, 1268, Reg. Abp. Giffard. These are the only additions which I have been able to make to Dr. Burton's Catalogue.

[§ Mentioned as a canon of Bolton in Archbishop Melton's ordination of Long Preston church in 1322.]

Abbey, his people are indebted to him for better things: but the example of Mr. Gilpin has already shown that the pursuits of taste are by no means incompatible with the active exertions of a good parish priest. [He died in 1843, aged 80. See p. 486.]

[Since then the incumbents have been—

Date of Institution.	Incumbents.	Patrons.	How Vacated.
20 Aug. 1843.	*John Umpleby,* ob. 1863, aged 80.	The Duke of Devonshire.	Per Mort.
	Rectors.*		
8 Sept. 1863.	*Hugh George Robinson.*	„ „	Per Resig.
15 Jan. 1875.	*Charles Bellairs.*	„ „	

The register-books commence in 1689.]

Before I take leave of Bolton, which it is impossible to do without regret, it will be proper to throw together a few miscellaneous particulars relating to it.

Approaching this priory from the south, a traveller, before he descries the other beauties of the place, will be struck with that sudden expanse of fertility and verdure which Shenstone saw with the eye of a poet and a painter, as marking the environs of a great religious house:—

> "While through the land the musing pilgrim sees
> A tract of brighter green, and in the midst
> Appears a mouldering wall with ivy crown'd,
> Or Gothic turret, pride of ancient days."

After this hint, few *pilgrims*, it may be presumed, who travel in this direction will fail to "*muse*" upon each of the latter features, as they successively present themselves at Bolton in the order of these exquisite lines.

Bolton Bridge had anciently a chapel,† like many others, for the benefit of travellers, of which the incumbent was undoubtedly maintained by the prior and canons. The town field, a plain of inexhaustible fertility, stretched from the bridge to the priory wall; and on this, though waving with corn almost ready ‡ for the sickle, Prince Rupert is said by tradition to have encamped on his way to Marston Moor, in the last week of July, 1644. The elm under which he dined is remembered by persons now alive. At a small distance, above the great gateway, stood the Prior's Oak, which was felled about the year 1720, and sold for 70*l.* According to the price of wood at that time, it could scarcely have contained less than 1,400 feet of timber.

The lead pipes of the priory, many of which have been taken up, consist of plates beaten about cylinders of wood, and soldered longitudinally. It is well known that the

---

[* Previous to this time the living had been only a chapelry, but in 1864 it was constituted a separate parish, and the great tithes were purchased of Christ Church, Oxford, and made over, and thus it became a rectory. The endowment of the rectory consists of the great and small tithes of the parish and a farm of 126 acres at Kettlewell. There is also an ancient payment of £35 per annum from the patron to the rector as chaplain of the abbey.]

† Skipton MSS.

‡ In the family accounts for 1645, an allowance of 20*l.* is made to the tenant of Hameldon, an adjoining field, which had been *foiled* by Prince Rupert's horses. Such have ever been the unfeeling ravages of war. "Quod maturi erat circa demessum et convectum est, viride, ne hostes mox haberent, protritum et corruptum."—Livy, xxxv. 26.

invention of casting cylindrical pipes without seams is of no earlier date than 1533, only seven years before the dissolution of the greater houses.

In the thickest part of the woods, above Bolton, are two lime-trees, at a distance from each other, and many miles from any plantation of that tree, which have therefore every appearance of being indigenous.

In Agill (Akeȝill, or the "Gully of Oaks"), within Gamelswath, is a rocking-stone, about four yards long, one yard and three-quarters high, and one yard and a half broad, which appears to have acquired that property from the accidental wearing away of its lower part, by the gradual operations of time and weather.

The same perhaps may be said of another "roggan stone," so called from the old Saxon participle of the verb *rogg*, to shake, which is used by Chaucer :—

"And him shee roggeth and awaketh soft."—*Legend of Good Women.*

Some violence has been used to destroy the equilibrium of this stone, but without effect.

The domains of Bolton anciently stretched to the Washburn, within which this roggan stone is situated; but, through a degree of negligence of which the canons of Bolton would not have been guilty, some thousand acres of common have been lost to the estate by being allowed to be included in the survey of Knaresborough Forest,* previous to the inclosure of that extensive and yet unproductive tract.

But the township of Bolton, properly so called, which was given to the canons of Embsay in exchange for Skibeden and Stretton, by Alice du Rumelle, stretched from Lumgill to Barden Beck, along the Wharf, which it nowhere passed; the Locus de Stede, extending from Posford Beck † to Spectebeck, and from Wharf to the Washburn, was another and distinct donation of the same benefactress.‡

From the purchase of Bolton by the first Earl of Cumberland after the Dissolution, to the death of the last earl, it appears, from the original accounts, to have been occupied by the family.

In consequence of his delinquency, and that of the Earl of Corke, his son-in-law, it was sequestered in the great rebellion, and valued, on that occasion, at 570*l. per annum.*

---

* But the following extract will prove that this dispute is of very ancient date: " Inq. capt. per manus Com. Cornubie in Curia de Knaresbro' anno XXII regni regis Edwardi fil. regis Henrici. Prior & Canonici de Boulton & ten⁵ eorum in villenagio in Bethmesley consueverunt commeare ubique in moris & pasturis apud Walkesburne Head, quousque ejecti fuerunt per Senescallum Alman. patris Dom. Com. Cornubie qui nunc temp. regis Henrici."—Bolton MSS.

Part of the lands which gave the prior and canons this right of common was a bovate, formerly held by Leuwine, and given with his body by W. Mauliverer.—*Ibid.* Leland says that the forest extended "to verie Boltonne in Cravene."

† A rapid and often an outrageous torrent, the deep and woody dingle of which, forking off from the principal valley, forms one of the most striking features of the scenery of Bolton. Above, and within the park, it forms a beautiful waterfall. The character of this brook is well expressed in the name. To "poss," in old English, is to toss :

" Thus betwixen twaine,
I possed am, and alle forcaste in paine."—Chaucer.

‡ See "Mon. Ang." vol. ii. p. 102. But it was rather *confirmed* by Alice de Romillè, as chief lady of the fee, having been already given to the canons of Bolton by Helte Mauliverer.—Bolton MSS.

The descent of the family from that nobleman to the present owner, His Grace the Duke of Devonshire, is here subjoined :—

Richard, second earl of Corke, created Lord Clifford of=Lady Elizabeth Clifford, daughter and heiress Londsborough and earl of Burlington, born 1612 ; of Henry last earl of Cumberland, born Sept. ob. Jan. 15, 1698, æt. 86.* 17, 1613 ; ob. Jan. 6, 1690.*

Charles, Lord Clifford, of=Lady Jane, daughter and co-heiress of Londsborough, ob. 1694. William duke of Somerset, ob. 1679.

Charles, second earl of Burlington and third earl=Juliana, daughter and heiress of Henry Noel, second son of of Corke, ob. Feb. 9, 1703-4, æt. 37. Henry viscount Campden ; died Oct. 17, 1750, æt. 78.*

† Richard earl of Burlington, K.G., born April=March 21, 1720-21, Dorothy, eldest daughter and co-heiress of William 25, 1695 ; ob. Dec. 3, 1753, æt. 60.* Savile, Marquis of Halifax, ob. Sept. 21, 1758, æt. 58.*

Dorothy, *s. p.*   Juliana, *s. p.*   Charlotte, born 1731 ; ob. 1751=William duke of Devonshire.

William duke of Devonshire, K.G., &c., died July 29, 1811, æt. 62.=

William Spencer, now [1812] duke of Devonshire, the present owner of Bolton, Barden, the Percy Fee, &c., and representative of the last earl of Cumberland.

* These dates are copied from the inscriptions on the coffins of the family in the vault at Londesborough.

† " Who plants like Bathurst, or who builds like Boyle?"

POPE.

Such, in seventy years, has been the improvement in one of these arts, and such, perhaps, the declension in the other, that if the poet's question were to be answered with respect to the present day, the reply would be, that a hundred plant like the first, while none builds like the second.

The dawn of this nobleman's taste for the fine arts may be traced in a volume of accounts now at Barden Tower, which were kept by an old steward during his lordship's tour in Italy, A.D. 1714, when he was only nineteen years old. The age of hawks and hounds, and bugle-horns and sheafs of arrows, which, in the memoirs of the Cliffords, have occupied so much of our attention, was now past ; and the following particulars from that volume, while they mark the progress of manners in the same family to the verge of modern refinement, will not be unamusing to connoisseurs.

The writer, it must be observed, was a true Englishman, and I shall give his Italian orthography as I find it.

For four chears to carry us all down *Mount Sinai* (*i.e.*, Mount Cenis ; but it may fairly be doubted whether the good man did not suppose himself to have reached the Arabian mount).

Rome. Paid Mr. Bendetto Mesquita for a picture of Artecture by Vivito, 24 crowns.

Paid Mr. Vintlema for the picture of St. Anthony, 300 crowns.

Paid Mr. Pietro Bianche for a Madonna, by Carlo Marat, 210 crowns.

Paid Mr. Jacomo Pacollo for three Porphry Jarrs, 140 crowns.

To Prince Burgess' (Borghese) gardener, for seeds, &c.

Paid Mr. Francis Rossett for a Madona, by Pascolina, 75 crowns.

Paid to Mr. Giovenale, Superior of the Convent of St. Amarea the Victorea, for a Madona, by Dominicina, 1,500 crowns.

Paid Mr. Antonio Bovion for three pictures ; one of Noah, one of the Nativity, one of Viviano, with figures and a Porphyry plate, 502 crowns.

To the Antiquary (the Byers, probably, or Jenkins at that time), 6 crowns.

6 Jul. Paid Mr. Francesco Guodole for a marble table, 80 crowns.

Four marble tables, 200 crowns.

To Benedetto Mesquaite for drawings, 39 crowns.

Paid to —— Naretal, Esq., for a Madona by Peter de Cortono (Pietro de Cortona), 150 crowns.

Paid Mr. Francesco Guidetto, in part, for two Porphyry Vases, 530 crowns.

3 L

PARISH OF BURNSAL.*

THIS is an extensive parish, nearly surrounding that of Linton. It consists of the townships of Burnsall, Thorp, Appletrewic, Hartlington, Rillston, Hetton, Bordley, Cracow, and Coniston with Kilnsey. [The area, according to the Ordnance Survey, is 30,615 a. o r. 37 p. The population in 1871, 1,262 persons, living in 242 houses.]

With respect to the etymology of the word there can be little doubt. It is spelt indifferently in charters : Brynsale, Brinsale, Brunsale, and Burnsall.†

Bꝛin, Bꝛun, and Buꝛn, are merely dialectical varieties of the same word ; derived from a verb, which, among all the branches of the Teutonic stock, is now found only in the Islandic bꝛinna, *adaquare ;* sal is *aula :* Brinsal, therefore, or Burnsal, is the " Hall upon the Stream ;" and the situation of the place is immediately upon the western bank of the Wharf.

In Domesday, the greater part of these townships were thus surveyed, under

TERRA TAINORV REGIS.‡

IN CRAVE.

Ⓜ
7 ᴮIn *BRINSHALE* 7 Torp. Hardul . III car 7 dim͞ ad gld.
    Hardulf hͭ idem de rege.

Ⓜ In *APLETREVVIC* . I . car̄ tre 7 dim͞ ad gld . Dolfin hͭ.

Ⓜ In *APLETREVVIC* . Chetel . II . car̄ 7 dim͞ ad gld . Orme hͭ.

[* Inclosure Acts were passed 11th George III. (Hetton) : 27th George III. (Cracoe) : 28th George III. (Grassington): 29th George III. (Thorpe): 45th George III. (Burnsall), and 55th George III. (Appletreewick).]

[† The Abbot of Fountains owned in this parish a tenement and lands called North Cote, part of the manor of Kilnsey, with a sheep-gate upon a close called Wyne Bank, Kilnsey Moor, two water-mills, one corn, the other a fulling-mill. Nether Bordley Manor, or Bordley Barony, and Over Bordley, Scarth Cote, Chapelhouse, Knolbank, Langerhouse, Cogilcote.]

[‡ Land of the King's Thanes. In Craven. Manor and Berewick.—In Brinshale (Burnsall) and Torp (Thorp), Hardulf had three carucates and a half to be taxed. Hardulf has the same of the king. Manor—In Apletrewic (Appletreewick), one carucate and a half to be taxed ; Dolfin has it. Manor—In Apletrewic, Chetel had two carucates and a half to be taxed ; Orme has it. Manor—In Herlintone (Harlington) Almunt had one carucate of land to be taxed ; Dolfin has it. Manor—In Herlintvn (Harlington), Norman had three carucates of land to be taxed; the same has it. Manor—In Rilistune (Rilstone), Ravenchil had one carucate and a half to be taxed ; the same has it. Manor—In Rilestun Almunt had four carucates to be taxed ; Dolfin has it. Manor—In Chileseie (Kilnsey), Gamel had six carucates of land to be taxed ; Ulf has it. Manor—In Cunestune (Conistone), Archil had three carucates to be taxed ; Chetel has it.]

Ⓜ In *HERLINTONE* . Almunt . ɪ car̄ t̄re ad gld. Dolfin h̄t.

Ⓜ In *HERLINTVN* . Norman . ɪɪɪ . car̄ f̄re ad gt̄d . Idē h̄t.

Ⓜ In *RILISTVNE* . Rauenchil . ɪ . car̄ 7 dīm ad gld . Idē h̄t.

Ⓜ In *RILESTVN* . Almunt . ɪɪɪɪ . car̄ t̄re ad ḡld. Dolfin h̄t.

Ⓜ In *CHILESEIE* . Gamel . vɪ . car̄ træ ad gld. Vlf h̄t.

Ⓜ In *CVNESTVNE* . Archil . ɪɪɪ . car̄ ad gld. Chetel h̄t.

But beside these the following estates are included under the Terra Osberni de Arches.*

.Ⓜ.
7 Ḃ In *HEBEDENE* . 7 Torp h̄b Dringel . ɪɪɪɪ . car̄ træ
7 ɪɪ . boù ad gt̄d.

Ⓜ.
7 Ḃ In *BRINESHALE* 7 Drebelaie h̄b Dringhel . ɪɪ . car̄
7 ɪɪ . bov̄ ad gt̄d.

Hetton and Bordley are surveyed under the head of Terra Rogeri Pictaviensis.†

Ⓜ In Borlaie . Suartcol . ɪɪ . car̄ ad gld.

Ⓜ In Hetune . Suartcol . ɪɪɪɪ . car̄ ad gld.

Cracow, which is not mentioned, was probably included under Rillstone.

Township of Hebden.

The reader must be apprised that this township is within the adjoining parish of Linton; but its ancient superiority over Burnsall, from the time of Domesday to Queen Elizabeth, and the opportunity which this arrangement affords of connecting a very curious chain of evidence, induce me to consider it here.

Hebden is the " High Valley;" a name‡ accurately expressive of the nature of the place, which consists of a deep gully, running up from the bed of Wharf to the summit of the lofty ridge which separates Craven from Netherdale.

We have already seen that at the time of Domesday the superior lord was Osbern de Arches; the mesne proprietor, Dringel; and that the manor or Berewic extended over part of Burnsal, Thorp, and Drebley.

[* Land of Osbern de Arches. Manor and Berewick.—In Hebedene and Torp (Hebden and Thorp), Dringel has four carucates of land and two oxgangs to be taxed. Manor and Berewick.—In Brineshale and Drebelaie (Burnsal and Dreblay), Dringhel has two carucates and two oxgangs to be taxed; Osbern de Arches has these lands, but they are all waste.]

[† Land of Roger of Poictou. Manor—In Borlaie (Bordley), Suartcol had two carucates to be taxed. Manor—In Hetune (Hetton), Suartcol had four carucates to be taxed.‡

Brinsall cum Thorp.—In eadem villa sunt ɪɪɪ car. terræ quarum duæ tenentur de rege et domino castri, et uno de Priore de Boulton ; et quælibet car. redd. per ann. ad finem prædictum ɪɪɪ*d.* ob. q. ; unde summa est xɪ*d.* q.—Kirkby's " Inquest," A.D. 1284. William de Hebbeden and Peter Giliot were Lords of the Manor 9th Edward II.]

‡ It is sometimes spelt Upeden ; of which family, I suppose, was John Upeden, Sheriff of Yorkshire 16th [1392-3] and 22nd [1398-9] of Richard II.

The superiority of Osbern seems to have been purchased very early by the Mowbrays; in consequence of which this manor became a member of the Mowbray fee, where XXVIII car. constituted a knight's fee.

The next transaction, which may be dated from circumstances about the year 1120, is explained by the following charter :—

" Rogerus de Mowbray, hominibus suis Francis et Anglis, &c.   Sc. quod ego d. et c. &c.   Uctredo filio Dolphin et her' suis totum manerium de Hebbedene cum pert. per divisas seq. : scil. ab Eskedensike, usque ad Loutandstan et Stanwath, et Brokeshougill, et inde usque ad Braddenford in Gatehopbec prope Holmekeld, et inde prout divise extendunt inter Apletrewic et Hebbedene, inde usque ad Samleseng, et Gathophou, et prout Swargil se extendit in Grisdale, inde usque ad Stanrayse prope Magare, et ultra Traneber Mire et Hissendene, quæ extendit usque in Werf—hab. et ten. cum omn. . . . . . ad manerium meum de . . . . . . (Kirkby Malessart ?) concessum mihi per Dominum Regem."

It appears from another charter that this grantee was son of a Gospatric de Rigton, in Knaresborough Forest, and father of Simon de Hebden, father of William.

In the year 1271, this estate was in the hands of William of York, chantor of that cathedral, Provost of Beverley, and one of the King's Justices Itinerant.   He was son of a Sir Nicholas de York, who must, I think, have been a younger son of Hebden.   This William purchased the manor of Eske, in Holderness, which he seems to have devised to his collateral relatives; for, in the 9th of Edward II. [1280–1] a charter of free warren in the manors of Hebden, Coniston, Brynsall, and Esk, was granted to another William de Hebden. John Hebden, Domicellus,[*] presents to a mediety of the living of Burnsal in 1431.   The last of this ancient name was Sir Nicholas Hebden, probably son or brother of John.   He married the heiress of the ancient family of Rie, and left two daughters and coheirs; one whose name is not recorded, who married to Sir Peirs Tempest, of Bracewell, and died 31 Hen. VI. [1452–3]; and Elizabeth, who married Sir Thomas Dymoke, of Scrivelby, in Lincoln-shire.   These coheiresses divided the estates.   The moiety of the Dymokes seems to have descended to the Augevyns; for, by inq. it appears that William Augevyn, Gent., died Dec. 10, 1499, seised of a moiety of the manor of Hebden, and lands in Thorp, Coniston, and Burnsall.   Charles Augevyn, son and heir, aged 16 years.   The arms of Hebden, though they principally held under Mowbray, were arms of affection for the Percies—viz., ermine, five fusils in fess gules.[†]

In the Tempest family their moiety remained till the beginning of Queen Elizabeth's reign, when it appears to have been parcelled out, either by Sir John Tempest, of Bracewell, or Richard Tempest, Esq., his nephew and successor in the estate.

The freeholders now account themselves joint lords.

The old manor-house is totally destroyed; but it is said, by tradition, to have stood near the lowest house in the village on the western side of the town, and nearly opposite to Thruskell.   This, besides being one of the most copious springs in Craven, is remarkable

---

[*] This word, or, more properly, Domnicellus, is a diminutive from Dom'nus ; as Baroncellus, from Baro, in the Latinity of the Middle Ages.   In the Saxon times it was synonymous with Atheling, or the heir of the kingdom.   But the Normans applied it, in a far inferior sense, to denote the heir apparent of any person who had the style of Dominus.   And, as knights were thus entitled, there is no doubt that the last of the Hebdens was styled Domicellus in this sense.   See Spelman and Du Cange in voce.

[†] MSS. J. C. Brooke, Arm. in Coll. Arm.

for having retained its original dedication through many centuries, from the days of Saxon Paganism ; for Thruskell is the " Fountain of Thor."

The worship of fountains was forbidden in the constitution of Canute, " de Gentilium superstitionibus abolendis," as a relic of paganism : ꝺ þe ꝼonbeaꝺaþ ꝥ man þeoꝛꝛize ꝼȳꝛe oþþe ꝼloꝺpæꬲeꝛ, pȳllaꝛ oþþe ꝛꬲanas oþþe æniȝaꝛ cynneꝛ puꝺu ꬲꝛeoꝛa.* Within little more than a century, the same practice was forbidden by Archbishop Anselm, as a *Christian* superstition. This shows how inveterate that principle is in the human heart ; and that, when deprived of one channel, it will seek another. Remnants of well-worship subsisted in Craven within half a century of the present time. St. Helen's Well, at Eshton, and Routand Well (*i.e.*, hꝛuꬲanꝺ, or the " Brawling Well"), betwixt Rilston and Hetton, were frequented by the young people on Sunday evenings, in summer, and their waters drank mingled with sugar. At the latter the inhabitants of each township punctiliously kept on their own side of the fountain. These harmless and pleasing observances are now lost, and nothing better, I fear, has been introduced in their place. It is, perhaps, as innocent at such hours of relaxation to drink water, even from a *consecrated* spring, as to swallow the poison of British distilleries at a public-house.

With respect to the parish of Burnsall itself, it appears that all the townships and manors belonging to the king's thanes were acquired by the Romillès, within little more than half a century of the date of Domesday, and became part of what I have called the second Skipton fee. And as these townships are much dispersed, and several of them much nearer the church of Linton than that of Burnsall, nothing can account for their having been united into one and the same parish, but to suppose that the latter was erected and endowed by the Romillès for the common benefit of their estates in Wharfdale,† as the contiguous parishes of Arncliffe and Kettlewell, with the remainder of Linton, belonged to another fee.

The following satisfactory charter, which may be placed about the year 1140, will throw considerable light upon the subject : " Sciant, &c. quod ego Aaliz. de Romile dedi, &c. Galfrido de Nevile et Emme ux. ejus servitium Rob. de Bulmer cum toto tenemento suo, vid. ii. Car. tr'e in Brynsale,‡ cum integrâ advocatione ecclesie de Brynsale, et iii Car. t're in Cunistane, et vi. Car. in Crakehou, et i Car. in Ayrtone, pro feodo i mil. et totam medietatem feodi mei in Epletrewic, vid. x bovatas, et reditum ii sol. in eadem villa."

This Emma was daughter of Bertram de Bulmer ; and she, together with Geoffrey de Nevile her husband, seems to have re-conveyed these lands, with the advowson, to Robert de Bulmer ; for, in the next place, appears another charter, to the following effect :—

Rob. de Bulmer, omn. pr. et fut. Sciatis quod ego d. et c. &c. Uctredo filio Dolphyn (founder of the family of Hebden) i car. t're in Brunisale, cum omnibus servitiis, faciendo servitium xii partis feodi mil. et advocationem medietatis ecclesie de. Brunishale ; et præterea concessi et confirmavi eodem Uctredo dim. car. in Thorp.

---

* A similar prohibition is generally understood by historians to be contained in the laws of Edgar, where, however, no such thing is to be found.

† Dreblay, however, though originally part of Burnsall, was excepted out of this endowment, on account of its vicinity to Barden ; in consequence of which it became a member of the demesnes of Skipton Castle and of the Castle parish.

[‡ In the 31st Edward I. Johannes Gylliot and Willelmus de Hebden each held from Radulphus de Neville one carucate in Brunsall.—" Knights' Fees."]

Uctred had, by Mowbray's grant of Hebden, already acquired the superiority over Dringel's lands in Burnsal; and though a moiety only of Bulmer's estate was conveyed by this grant, and only a mediety of the benefice, the Hebdens claimed, henceforward, the whole manor, and obtained a charter of free warren in Burnsal and Thorp, A. 9 Edward III. [1335–6], along with Hebden and Coniston.

These estates passed, as we have already seen, to the Tempests of Bracewell, with whom they continued till the 8th of Elizabeth [1565–6], when Richard Tempest, Esq., conveyed the manors of Burnsal * and Thorp to Thomas and John Proctor, of Cowpercoats, who sold them the year following to Henry Tempest of Broughton, Esq., from whom they have lineally descended to Stephen Tempest, Esq., the present lord.

The division of manors occasioned the splitting of benefices, a practice abhorred by the Canon Law, though for reasons more fanciful than solid.

" Exigit namque ars nostra Catholica, ut unicus in unâ ecclesiâ sit sacerdos ; sed non uni tantum datur una ecclesia, sed pluribus, prætextu plurium patronorum, ut sint plura capita in uno capite, quasi monstrum. †

" Unius enim ecclesiæ unus debet esse presbyter seu rector. ‡

" Sicut enim vestimentum domini non scissum est, sed de eo sortiti sunt, ita nec ecclesia scindi debet, quœ in unitate consistit." §

Setting aside these whimsical analogies, which are entirely in the spirit of the canonists, the practice of dividing livings may be either beneficial or the contrary, according to circumstances. Some inconvenience, indeed, may arise in all from the partition of tithes ; but, in small parishes and poor livings, like those of Wharfdale, where the whole duty may easily be discharged by one incumbent, and the whole income is no more than adequate to the decent support of one, medieties are an evil. In very populous parishes two portionists would often be of use ; in very wealthy ones they would easily be supported.

It may be observed that the true origin of medieties is here assigned by Cardinal Otho. It was " prætextu plurium patronorum," whose claims, after all, might have been compromised as well by alternate nominations.

It is remarkable that three adjoining livings in this valley, Burnsal, Linton, and Kettlewell, were all divided into portions, and all from the cause assigned above.

But to return :

We have seen that Robert de Bulmer divided this benefice, and conferred one mediety on Uctred, the son of Dolphyn ; but he retained the other mediety, which remained in the male line of his descendants till the marriage of Eve, daughter of Sir John Bulmer, with Henry Lord Fitzhugh. How long it continued in the latter family, and through what changes it has since passed, the following catalogue of patrons and incumbents will show.

But it may be proper to observe that the Fitzhughs presented twelve turns successively; for Sir Henry Willoughby, being nearly related to the family, was probably no more than an assign ; but Richard Lord Fitzhugh dying without male issue, 4th Henry VIII. [1512–3], his estates were divided among his heirs general ; and the manor of Areton, together with

* This proves, beyond a doubt, that these *manors* did not descend to the Tempests of Broughton through the Gilliotts from Crake, Thorp, &c.

† Const. Othonis. Ne eccl. una dividatur in plures.

‡ Extravagant. Joh. xxii. de Elect. dud.

§ Ibid. 16. Q. 7. Sicut. &c.

the mediety, which was considered as regardant to it, was purchased by John Lambert, Esq., the first of Calton, in whose descendants it was vested till the death of John Lambert, Esq., last of the name, in 1706. It was then purchased by the Alcock family.[*]

With respect to the mediety of Uctred, son of Dolphyn, it will be observed that the second patron in the following catalogue is Sir Elias de Rillestone, and the third William de Ebor. The latter, as I have already shown, was a Hebden, with the common addition of an ecclesiastical name. But the following charter will not only prove the accuracy of the ancient registers of the see of York at that early period, but how the moiety of this manor, and the regardant portion of the benefice, passed, in one instance, from the Hebdens to the Rillestones, and was by them re-granted to the former family :—

"Sciant, &c. quod ego Eustatius fil. Eliæ de Rillestone dedi, &c. Will'mo de Hebbedene et her' totam illam car. t're in Brynsale et Thorpe quam Huchtred avus p'd' Will'mi dedit Alicie fil. in maritagium cum Eliâ de Rillestone avo meo, cum omn. hominibus qui remanere debent [†] in terrâ p'dictâ, cum totâ sequela, vid. Will'mo Sartore, Sim. de Cringleker, Sinnet ux. Sim. de Brynsale, Ad. fil. Sim. de Ponte, &c. &c. Waltero Molendinario, &c., cum omn. aisiamentis et lib'tat. intra villam et extra præterquam Threpland, &c.

"Sciendum autem quod p'dict' Will'mus de Hebbedene pro hac donatione quietum clamavit mihi xxx marcas argenti, quas debeo Isaaco Judeo Northamton, et Aaron. fil. ejus."

Thirty marks, therefore, were the consideration paid for half the manor of Burnsal, about the year 1260.[‡]

Uctred's mediety of the benefice passed, with its own moiety of the manor, to the Tempests of Bracewell, and was afterwards purchased by the Craven family, anxious at that time to extend their property and influence in the parish which gave them birth. But I have not learned the time or conditions of this transaction.

The parish of Burnsall, most of which continues to pay a modus for corn-tithe to the rectors of Linton, is said by tradition to have been originally a member of the latter parish ; and it seems highly probable, especially from the dispersed situation of its different parts, all which are of the Skipton fee, that the church was endowed by Alice de Romillè, for the benefit of her dependents in that quarter. This conjecture is strengthened by some remains of the original structure at the east end, where the buttresses are precisely of that form which

---

[*] In the 8th of Elizabeth [1565-6] this mediety of Burnsal was settled in part of jointure upon Elizabeth Clifford, natural daughter of the second Earl of Cumberland, on her marriage with Benjamin, son of John Lambert, Esq., of Calton. From an original paper, written by the father, in which these articles are abstracted, it appears that he was disappointed in this match. He complains that he had received only sixty pounds for the lady's fortune, though one of the earl's council prevailed upon him to sign a release for one hundred pounds, saying it would be for my lord's honour (dishonour he should have said ; but I sincerely hope that the earl knew nothing of this pitiful trick).

Mr. Lambert then proceeds in the following strain :—

"Indede I was put in hope that Therle wolde be my gode L. and my sonnes, to myne availl and p'fit, and specially to my sonne ;

"And we sholde have manie gay things ;
But ther cometh neyther bags, belt, nor rynges.
So that I may truly conclude, to my grete coste,
My sonne hath a good wief, but my hope is loste."

And so on, much in the style of the humble Petition of Elizabeth Harris.

[†] That is, all the villans regardant to the manor. I must observe that at this time, about 1260, there were at Burnsal a bridge and a mill. From the curious grant of Silsden Mill, about 120 years before, and already engraved under Bolton [see p. 448], it appears that there was then a struggle between the ancient domestic querns and water-mills, which were beginning to be introduced. "Nec in manu mola habeatur."

[‡] For many particulars in this chain of evidence I am indebted to abstracts of the charters of the Hebden family, obligingly communicated to me by Mr. Swale, of Settle. But I have been compelled, for the sake of uniformity, to re-translate them into the original Latin.

prevailed in the reigns of Henry I. and Stephen, that is—with more projection than the true Saxon buttress, yet finishing in a slope beneath the roof. But the rest of the present church, excepting a part of the south choir, appears to be of the earlier part of Henry VIII.'s reign, when so many of the Craven churches were restored. It is handsomely and uniformly built of moor-stone, with a nave, choir, side-aisles, and tower. In Dodsworth's time this fragment of an inscription was remaining in the north window of the choir :—

Orate pro a'i'a Jacobi Metcalfe armigeri qui hanc fenestram * . . . .

Now it appears, from the records at Skipton, that this Metcalf was possessed of Hartlinton in 1520, and, as I have proved, that the present remains of painted glass in the Craven churches are generally contemporary with the restoration of the buildings, the date of the present edifice at Burnsall, excepting as above, may be fixed about that time. The flat roof of the choir is very handsome and strong, precisely like that of Linton, which I mention because the latter is now hid by a coat of plaster. At the entrance of the choir each rector has his own stall and pulpit, which look like the opposite Ambones in the primitive churches, or the respondent's and opponent's boxes in the schools. From these stalls alternately the service is performed, by a kind of early compromise between Popery and Protestantism— that is, within the choir, as of old, but with the minister's face turned to the congregation instead of the altar.

The situation of this church, and indeed of the village, is very pleasing, on a gentle declivity, falling eastward, to the bank of the Wharf, between which and the churchyard stand the two parsonage-houses, now much neglected ; the shells of which, I think, are not later than the reign of Henry VIII.

In the wall of that belonging to the first mediety is a shield charged with the chevronels of Fitzhugh.

[The church, which is, for this district, unusually fine, was well and completely restored in 1858–9, under the direction of Mr. John Varley, of Skipton. It comprises nave, with two aisles, each of three bays, clerestory, chancel with two bays. The base of the octagonal pier on south side is curious, having four grotesque faces at the angles of the square plinth. All the roofs are open-timbered. There is a chancel arch and arches across the aisles. In the south wall of the chancel is a singular recess, the use of which will probably puzzle future antiquaries ; but the architect for the restoration-works, being happily still alive, explains that he made it to preserve the corbel now within it, which, from an alteration in the outer wall at this point, would have been otherwise concealed. There is a western tower, with lofty tower-arch, and three-light west window. A new doorway has been formed in the west wall of the tower, to afford access to the belfry, in which are six bells, each inscribed "DALTON OF YORK FECIT, 1790." There were previously three old bells, which were broken up and used in the present peal. There is also a south porch, with stone seats.

In the churchyard is the original lich-gate, with the gate swinging on a centre post. During the restoration, several remains of crosses, of probably Saxon date, were found, and are preserved in the church, and there are indications of thirteenth century work at east end of the south aisle. The font is circular, and carved with grotesque animals and fishes. It is very possibly Saxon.

During the restorations, a beautiful carving in alabaster, representing the Adoration of the Magi, was found under the floor of the north chancel aisle. It is in fine preservation. It is preserved in the vestry in a carved oak frame, and protected by a glass. When first found, the colours and gilding were tolerably perfect, but peeled off when exposed to the atmosphere.

---

* He was afterwards knighted, and is mentioned by Leland as follows: "Sir James Metcalf hath a very goodly howse, caullid Nappe, in Wensedale."—"Itin." vol. iii. p. 112.

In 1858–9 Mr. Varley discovered the following texts, concealed by many coats of whitewash, upon the wall of the south aisle, near the east end. The writing was in old English :—

𝔈𝔵𝔬𝔡𝔲𝔰 𝔯𝔯𝔦𝔦 𝔈𝔥𝔞𝔭 [𝔍𝔣 𝔱𝔥𝔬𝔲 𝔩𝔢𝔫𝔡 𝔪𝔬𝔫𝔢𝔶 𝔱𝔬] 𝔞𝔫𝔶 𝔬𝔣 𝔪𝔶 𝔭𝔢𝔬𝔭𝔩𝔢 𝔟𝔶 𝔱𝔥𝔢, 𝔱𝔥𝔬𝔲 𝔰𝔥𝔞𝔩𝔱 𝔫𝔬𝔱 𝔟𝔢 𝔞𝔰 𝔞 𝔱𝔦𝔯𝔞𝔫𝔱 𝔲𝔫𝔱𝔬 𝔥𝔶𝔪 𝔫𝔢𝔭𝔱𝔥𝔢𝔯 𝔰𝔥𝔞𝔩𝔱 𝔱𝔥𝔬𝔲 𝔬𝔭𝔭𝔯𝔢𝔰𝔱𝔢 𝔥𝔶𝔪 𝔴𝔦𝔱𝔥 𝔲𝔰𝔲𝔯𝔶.

𝔯𝔯𝔦𝔦𝔦 [𝔗𝔥𝔬𝔲] 𝔰𝔥𝔞𝔩𝔱 𝔫𝔬𝔱 𝔞𝔠𝔠𝔢𝔭𝔱 𝔞 [𝔳𝔞𝔶𝔫𝔢] 𝔱𝔞𝔭𝔩𝔢 : 𝔫𝔢𝔭𝔱𝔥𝔢𝔯 𝔰𝔥𝔞𝔩𝔱 𝔭𝔲𝔱 𝔱𝔥𝔶𝔫𝔢 𝔥𝔞𝔫𝔡𝔢 𝔴𝔦𝔱𝔥 𝔱𝔥𝔢 𝔴𝔦𝔠𝔨𝔢𝔡 𝔱𝔬 𝔟𝔢 𝔞𝔫 𝔲𝔫𝔯𝔶𝔤𝔥𝔱𝔢𝔬𝔲𝔰 𝔴𝔦𝔱𝔫𝔢𝔰𝔰𝔢 : 𝔱𝔥𝔬𝔲 𝔰𝔥𝔞𝔩𝔱 𝔫𝔬𝔱 𝔣𝔬𝔩𝔩𝔬𝔴𝔢 𝔞 𝔪𝔲𝔩𝔱𝔦𝔱𝔲𝔡𝔢 𝔱𝔬 𝔡𝔬 𝔢𝔳𝔢𝔩, 𝔫𝔢𝔭𝔱𝔥𝔢𝔯 𝔞𝔫𝔰𝔴𝔢𝔯 𝔦𝔫 𝔞 𝔪𝔞𝔱𝔱𝔢𝔯 𝔬𝔣 𝔭𝔩𝔢𝔢 𝔱𝔥𝔞𝔱 𝔱𝔥𝔬𝔲 𝔴𝔬𝔲𝔩𝔡𝔢𝔰𝔱 𝔱𝔬 𝔣𝔬𝔩𝔩𝔬𝔴𝔢 𝔪𝔞𝔫𝔶 𝔱𝔶𝔯𝔫𝔢 𝔞𝔰𝔦𝔡𝔢 𝔣𝔯𝔬𝔪 𝔱𝔥𝔢 𝔱𝔯𝔲𝔱𝔥𝔢 𝔫𝔢𝔭𝔱𝔥𝔢𝔯 𝔰𝔥𝔞𝔩𝔱 𝔱𝔥𝔬𝔲 𝔭𝔞𝔦𝔫𝔱𝔢 𝔞 𝔭𝔬𝔬𝔯𝔢 𝔪𝔞𝔫𝔫𝔢𝔰 𝔠𝔞𝔲𝔰𝔢.

The above wording is found in the folio Bibles of 1540 and 1551.

On a brass in the north wall—

Cui dust Sepulchrale Marmor Effatur
Æs
Quod e terra erat sub pedibus jacet
Robti Heye, A.M.
Cujus si non Calentem temperas Favillam lacry^{mã}
leviter tamen Cippum premas
Qui Natus huc in Vicinia Scolam ad Ecclesiæ
Cæmeterium per duodemium rexit
Quam Spartam eque Adornavit
Cura ac doctrina non Statas Ejusdem
horas sed impendendo Aliarum succisivas
Suorum dum excoluit ingenia
Mores Quoad
Verus Dei & Ecclesiæ cultor Rect^{i} custos virtutis
Satelles suis Egregie chorus cæteris perhumantis
Obiit decimo nono die Januarii. Ætatis suæ 36
Annoq. Dom. 1694
Cujus Memoriæ hoc insigne paternæ dilectionis
lubens devovet tristis Superstesq. :
John Heye de Skierholme.

3 M

On a black marble slab—

Hic jacet Gulielmus Carr
Rect^r de Burnsall qui in alt^a medt^e
patri successit obiitq. mortem
An°. Domⁱ. 1754.
Ætatis 57.

There are tablets to—

Margaret Stackhouse, of Burnsall, died 28th Feb. 1814, aged 87 years and 2 months.
Margaret Tennant, of Burnsall, died 14th May, 1820, in the 76th year of her age.
Christopher Fountain, Gent., died 17 Oct. 1786, æt. 67.
Thomas Waddilove, of Thorpe Mason, died 29th July, 1802, aged 60.
Ann Waddilove, wife of John Waddilove, son of the above, died in London 17 Jan. 1805, aged 24.

Shield: Sa. a chev. betw. three goats passant arg. on a chief or, a demy savage holding a club, betw. two cinquefoils gu., Batty. Impaling gu. a fess betw. three cocks' heads erased arg., Alcock?

William Batty, Esq., of Thorp, died 4 Aug. 1759, aged 71 years.
Elizabeth his wife, died 24 Sept. 1726, aged 28.
John Batty, Esq., of Thorp, died 26 June, 1792, aged 69.
Ellen his wife, died July 30, 1762, aged 26.
Mary, daughter of William Batty, Esqr., of Thorp, died 23 June, 1798, aged 74.

There are stained glass windows to the memories of—

William Stockdale, died 27 Nov. 1838, aged 71 years.
Sarah his wife, died 11 Oct. 1848, aged 80 years.
Robert Bland, of Woodhouse, born 1746, died July 20th, 1819.
Mary, his wife, born 1759, died 16th April, 1817.
Hannah, wife of the Rev. A. C. Bland, died 6 June, 1858.

Tablet to Jonathan Hebden, died 24 Aug. 1843, aged 75.
Mary his wife, died 24th March, 1831, aged 48.]

The glebe of this benefice, now subdivided, was exactly a tenth part of the township of Burnsall; and it has evidently been half * a carucate, as the measurement of each portion proves it to have consisted of two oxgangs.

On the rocky and romantic margin of the Wharf, northward from the church, burst out three springs, one of which is called Parson's Well; the others are respectively dedicated to St. Margaret and St. Helen.

In this facility of choice it is extraordinary that St. Wilfrid, the patron, should have been overlooked; but it must be observed, that in the Popish superstition few springs and

---

* Half a carucate was the most frequent allotment of glebe in the endowment of the Craven churches.

In the Escheat Roll of the 31st of Edward I. [1302–3] seven churches within the Percy fee are mentioned; and of these two had glebes, consisting of a carucate each; one of two oxgangs only; and the remaining four of the half carucate or four oxgangs. They are enumerated thus:

De Rectore Eccl. de Boulton pro di. car. in Boulton.
De Persona de Giselburne pro unâ car. in eadem.
De Rectore de Thorneton pro IIII bov. in Thorneton.
De Rect. Eccl. de Giggleswic pro di. car. in ead.
Dos Eccl. de Abb. de Dereham pro II bov. in Kirkbie.
Dos Eccl. de Rect. de Carlton pro di. car. in ead.
Dos. Eccl. de Rect. de Preston pro unâ car. in ead.

fountains were dedicated to male saints; a proof of the affinity of that and the Pagan ritual, in which the nymphs exclusively enjoyed the same honour.

At Linton, also, the Saints' Well was consecrated to our Lady, not to St. Michael the patron; and thus St. Mary, St. Margaret, and St. Helena were the νυμφαι ενυδροι λειμωνιαδες * of Craven.

RECTORES DE BURNSAL.

Henr. & *Adam* Personæ de Brinshale, s. d.†

Temp. Inst.		Rectores Primæ Medietatis.	Patroni.	Vac.
4 kal. Mart.	1294.	D's *Adam de Herwerton*, Subd.	D's *Hugo Fitz Henry*, mil.	
23 Mai.	1309.	D's *Wm. de Bullmer*, Cl.	Hen. D's *Fitzhugh*.	per mort.
7 id. Jan.	1322.	D's *Joh. de Bowes*, Pres.	Idem.	per mort.
13 Mar.	1369.	D's *Adam de Carlton in Lindrike*, Presb.	} D's *Hen. Fitzhugh*.	
		D's *Joh. de Laton*.		{ per assumpt. alterius benef.
26 Apr.	1392.	D's *Tho. de Hude*, Presb.	Attorn. D'ni *Hen. Fitzhugh*.	per resig.
19 Apr.	1411.	D's *Wm. Appilton*, Presb.	Hen. D's *Fitzhugh*.	per resig.
16 Oct.	1425.	D's *Wm. Gregges*.		per resig.
2 Maii,	1426.	D's *Hen. Craven*.	*Will.* D's *Fitzhugh*.	per resig.
22 Jul.	1438.	D's *Tho. Kirkham*, Cap.	Idem.	per mort.
2 Maii,	1454.	D's *Rob. Coke*, Presb.	Hen. D's *Fitzhugh*.	per mort.
14 Maii,	1469.	Mr. *Tho. Sutton*.	Idem.	per resig.
9 Jan.	1471.	D's *Edw. Pudsay*, Cap.	Idem.	per mort.
5 Jul.	1505.	D's *Tho. Swyft*, Presb.	D's *Hen. Willoughby*, mil.	
		D's *Will. Helghfeld*.		per mort.
Ult. Jul.	1539.	D's *Ant. Holgate*, Cap.	*Joh. Lambert de Calton.*	per depriv.
10 Sept.	1554.	D's *Ric. Summerscales*, Cl.	Idem.	per mort.
6 Nov.	1562.	*Benj. Holgate*, Cl.	Idem.	per mort.
24 Maii,	1570.	*Hump. Dogeson*, Cl.	Idem.	per resig.
		John Topham, ob. 1618-19.		
6 Mar.	1618.	*Tho. Topham*, Cl. M.A.	*Tho. Topham*, sen.	
		Tho. Topham, ob. 1653.		
29 Jul.	1696.	*Tho. Topham*, Cl.	*Joh. Lambert*, arm.	per mort.
		Peter Lancaster, Cl.		per mort.
10 July,	1707.	*Thomas Clapham*.	*John Alcock*.	per resig.
20 Sept.	1708.	*Peter Alcock*, Cl.	*Joh. Alcock*, Gen.	per mort.
6 Dec.	1738.	*John Alcock*, A.M.	*Ellen Alcock* (widow).	per resig.

* Sophocl. Philoct. sub fin.

[In 1861, Mr. J. G. Uppleby, cloth merchant, of Leeds, died, and bequeathed large sums of money to various charities. Amongst these he left £50 to each of the poor schools of Burnsall, Coniston, and Rylston, to be disposed of by the incumbent of Burnsall.

In 1865 it was agreed between the Rev. William Bury, rector of Burnsall, William Stead, master of the Grammar School, and the Feoffees of the Burnsall Grammar School, that in consideration of the said £50 being expended in improvements in the school and house, the master and his successors, on account of the extra convenience, should for ever after teach, free of charge, at the school in the same manner, and at the same times as the other scholars, in all the branches of a sound English education, including grammar, writing, arithmetic, and geography, two children, male or female, of poor parents in the village or neighbourhood of Burnsall, such children to be called the "Uppleby Scholars," to wear a red girdle round their caps, and to be elected by the rector and churchwardens of Burnsall for the time being.]

† Coucher Book of Fountains. [Institution of Wm. de Reddemere, clerk, to the Church of Brunnestal, at the presentation of Wm. de Hebbeden.—*Register of Archbishop Gray, Reg. Otinton, 2 non Julii* xiii. 1228.]

Temp. Inst.	Rectores Primæ Medietatis.	Patroni.	Vac.
18 June, 1783.	*John Alcock*, A.B. ob. 1810.	*Rebecca* and *Dorothy Heber*, of *Marton*.	
	Richard Withenall, Cl. 1826.		per mort.
3 March, 1832.	*John Baines Graham.*	Rev. *John Graham*, of *York*.	per resig.
16 Feb. 1838.	*Gregory Rhodes*	Idem.	per resig.
14 Feb. 1839.	*William Bury.*	Idem.	per mort.

RECTORES DE BURNSAL.

Temp. Inst.	Rectores alterius Medietatis.	Patroni.	Vacat.
Id. Dec. 1230.	D's *Ric. de Burstall*, Cl.	*Joh. de Tilly.*	
3 kal. Maii, 1269.	D's *Joh. Sampson.*	D's *Elias de Rilliston.*	
16 kal. Jan. 1294.	D's *Adam de Lyncoln*, Subd.	*Wm. de Ebor.*	per mort.
12 Apr. 1348.	D's *Hugo Howell*, Cap.	D's *Ric. de Hebden*, mil.	per mort.
28 Aug. 1367.	D's *Wm. de Hebden*, Cl.	Idem.	per mort.
13 Jan. 1369.	D's *Wm. Amote*, Presb.	Idem.	
	D's *Wm. de Beckingham.*	Idem.	{ per res. pro vic. de *Edenstow*.
27 Feb. 1370.	D's *Wm. de Kirksall*, Presb.	Idem.	
	D's *Joh. de Suthwell.*		per mort.
9 Jan. 1389.	D's *Tho. Newsome*, Cl.	*Wm. de Newsome*, Arm.	
	D's *Joh. Grynton.*		per mort.
10 Dec. 1431.	D's *Wm. Vavasour*, Presb.	*Joh. Hebden*, Domicellus.	per mort.
5 Jul. 1472.	D's *Rad. Radclyff*, Cl.	{ D's *Rog. Clifford*, mil. et *Tho. Tempest*, arm.	
	D's *Rob. Talbot*,* Presb.		per mort.
13 Jan. 1545.	D's *Nic. Paver*, A.M.	Assig. *Ric. Tempest*, mil.	per mort.
25 Sept. 1551.	*Geo. Ellyson*, S.T.B.	Idem.	per mort.
21 Jun. 1552.	D's *Henri. Elso*, Cl.	D's *Joh. Tempest*, mil.	per mort.
12 Jul. 1569.	*Tho. Brockden*, Cl.		per resig.
5 Mai. 1579.	*Wm. Brockden*, Cl.	Assign. *Wm. Brockden.*	per mort.
Ult. Aug. 1618.	*Ric. Tennant*, Cl. A.M.	*Hen. Tennant.*	
	Jac. sive *Ric. Tennant.*		per mort.
	Rob. Topham.		
2 Feb. 1686.	*Ric. Carr*, Cl.	D's *Wm. Craven*, mil.	per mort.
28 Aug. 1734.	{ *William Carr*, Cl. fil. ejus, ob. 1754.	D's *Wm. Craven.*	per mort.
11 Nov. 1754.	{ *Wm. Matthew Knolles*, A.M. ob. 1776.	*Fulwar* Lord *Craven.*	per mort.
26 Jun. 1777.	*Joseph Atwel Small*, D.D.	*William* Lord *Craven.*	per cess.
22 Apr. 1797.	*Geo. Hickes*, A.M.	Idem.	per resig.
16 Apr. 1839.	*William Bury.*	Rev. *J. Graham* and Earl of *Craven*.	per mort.
13 Jul. 1875.	*Charles Henry Carlisle.*	*George Grimston*, Earl of *Craven*.	

The two medieties were consolidated by Order of Council, 21 July, 1876.

The principal testamentary burials in this church are the following :—

Henry Hertlinton, Esq. by will, dated Sept. 9, 1466.
William Hertlinton, Esq. April 8, 1473.
John Talbot, brother of Edmund Talbot of Bashall, Esq. leaves his body to be interred "in Ecclesia S'c'i Wilfrid de Burnsall," Jan. 20, 1475.
Lastly, Sir Henry Elso, Parson of the one mediety, Oct. 12, 1563.

---

* He was living 11th Hen. VIII. [1519-20], when his brother, Edmund Talbot of Bashal, Esq., bequeathed him an annuity of XXVI*s*. VIII*d*. for life, by the name of Sir Robert Talbot, Parson of Burnsal.—Townley MSS.

[The registers commence in 1560.]

Over the door of the church is this inscription, cut in mouldering stone, to record one of the many charities of a man who deserves a more durable monument :—

> THIS CHURCH WAS REPAIRED
> AND BUTIFIED AT THONLIE COSTES
> AND CHARGES OF SIR WILLM
> CRAVEN KNIGHT AND ALDERM
> OF THE CITIE OF LONDON
> AND LATE LORD MAYRE
> OF THE SAME. ANNO DM. 1612.*

They were formerly commemorated on the walls of the choir, in the following lamentable strain :—

> This Church of Beauty most repaired thus so bright
> Two hundred Pounds did coste Sir William Craven Knighte
> Many other Workes of Chartie whereof noe mention here
> True Tokens of his Bountie in this Parish did appeare
> The Place of his Nativitie in Appletrewick is seene
> And late of London Citie Lord Mayor hee hath beene
> The Care of this Worke soe beautiful and faire
> Was put to John Topham Clerke by the late Lord Mayor
> Of that most famous Citie of London so brighte
> By Sir William Craven that bountiful Knighte
> Borne in this Parish at Appletrewick Towne
> Who regarded noe Coste soe the Work was well done.

I grievously fear that John Topham Clerk was poet as well as master of the works on this occasion.

William Craven was born at Appletrewick, in this parish, of poor parents, who are said to have consigned him to a common carrier for his conveyance to London, where he entered into the service of a mercer or draper. In that situation nothing more is known of his history, till, by diligence and frugality, the old virtues of a citizen, he had raised himself to wealth and honour. In 1607, he is described by Camden as "equestri dignitate, et senator Londinensis." In 1611, he was chosen Lord Mayor. Of the time of his death I am not informed. In him the commercial spirit of the family ended as it had begun. William Craven, his eldest son, having been trained in the armies of Gustavus Adolphus and William Prince of Orange, became one of the most distinguished soldiers of his time. He was in the number of those gallant Englishmen who served the unfortunate King of Bohemia from a spirit of romantic attachment to his beautiful consort; and his services are generally supposed to have been privately rewarded with the hand of that princess after her return in widowhood to her native country.†

[* In 1812 the lead was sold from the church roofs, and blue slate substituted, the old roofs removed, and one with flat plaster ceiling erected.]

[† Lodge, in his "Portraits of Illustrious Personages," has engraved his portrait from one by Honthorst, in the collection of the Earl of Craven at Combe Abbey. As the earl's life was most interesting, and he took his title from the deanery, a short sketch of his career, we think, should be acceptable. Lodge states, that before young Craven became of age he saw active service in Germany and in the Netherlands under Henry Prince of Orange. He returned to England in the spring of 1626, was knighted on the 4th March, and on the 12th March in the same year created Lord Craven of Hamsted Marshall, in Berkshire. For a few years he remained in England in courtly and rural occupations, and when in 1631 the king despatched troops to the aid of Gustavus Adolphus—who had attacked the Emperor of Germany in his

Thus the son of a Wharfdale peasant matched with the sister of Charles I.: a remarkable instance of that Providence which "raiseth the poor out of the dust, and setteth him among princes, even the princes of his people."*

He was created Baron of Hamstead Marshall, 2 Charles I. [12 May, 1626] and Earl Craven, 16 Charles II. [16 March, 1665.]

But to return to Sir William Craven and his benefactions.†

country with a view to reinstate the Elector Palatine, nominal King of Bohemia, in his hereditary dominions—Lord Craven joined the expedition, and his conduct in the field, where he distinguished himself by a valour almost romantic, particularly at the siege of the strong fortress of Creutznach, so pleased the heroic Swede, that, brave as he was, he could not help telling him that "he gave his younger brother too many chances for his estate."

Soon after this the King of Sweden fell at Lutzen, and the King of Bohemia died. Craven now attached himself to the cause of that prince's son, until 1637, when the Emperor finally defeated him, and the Elector with difficulty saved himself by flight, his brother Rupert and Lord Craven being taken prisoners. He afterwards devoted himself to Elizabeth, the mother of the unfortunate princes, whose exquisitely amiable qualities, joined to no inconsiderable share of personal beauty, had justly obtained for her the title of the "Queen of Hearts." When she took refuge in Holland, where she intended to settle for the remainder of her life, he followed her and entered into the service of the House of Nassau. They became inseparable; he aided her impoverished purse, regulated her household, and superintended all her affairs. Reports naturally arose that they were secretly married, and there is abundant reason to believe that such was the fact.

He did not return to England until after the Restoration ; but no man contributed more largely to the necessities of the Crown, or suffered severer penalties for loyalty, than himself. The whole of his great revenue was devoted during the war to the king and to his sister the Queen of Bohemia, and afterwards to the court of the exiled Charles II. The Parliament at length marked him for a victim, and on the 16th March, 1650-1, resolved that "the Lord Craven was an offender within the meaning and intention of the declaration of the 24th August, 1649, that all persons who might adhere to or aid and assist Charles Stuart, son to the late king, should be deemed traitors and rebels ; that the estate of the said Lord Craven should be confiscated accordingly ; and that the Commissioners appointed for that purpose should seize and sequester all his estates, real and personal, and receive the rents and profits to the use of the Commonwealth." There was some hesitation in putting this sentence into execution, but on the 3rd August, 1653, a bill for the sale of all his property was passed by three votes, notwithstanding that the man Falconer who had informed and sworn against him had in the previous May been convicted of perjury in giving the very testimony which had furnished a pretext for the confiscation. His estates were then allotted.

Charles II. made some little compensation to him, as immediately after the Restoration (16th March, 1665) he created him Viscount Craven of Uffington, co. Berks, and Earl of Craven, co. York. He was also called to the Privy Council, and appointed Lord Lieutenant of the County of Middlesex, and Custos Rotulorum of Berks. He was afterwards made colonel of the Coldstream Guards ; also High Steward of the University of Cambridge ; and had a share in the proprietary of the province of Carolina, in North America. He was also Master of the Trinity House. Of the Earl of Craven it was said that "he was one of the most accomplished gentlemen in Europe ; a useful subject, charitable, abstemious as to himself, generous to others, familiar in his conversation, and universally beloved." He died in his house in Drury Lane, London, in the 89th year of his age, on the 9th April, 1697, and was buried at Binley, near Coventry. The ex-Queen of Bohemia settled in England in 1660, and died in London 13th February, 1662.]

* Psalm cxiii.

[† "The Deeds of Charitie done by Sir W^m. Craven, Kn^t., sometime Lord Mayor of London.

1. He founded a freeschole in Burnsall in com. Ebor. and endowed it with Land of xx^{li} per ann. to the Head Master and x^{li} per annum to the Usher.

2. He gave x^{li} per ann. lands for repairs of bridges and highwayes in the same parish.

3. He built three stone bridges—one over the river Barbon, another over the river Wherfe, and the third over the river Hogill, all in or near Burnsall, and paved the highwayes between Burnsall and Appletreewick.

4. He new-seated the church of Burnesall, repaired it well, and gave XLs. per ann. for the perpetuall repaire of it.

The Deedes of Charitie of Mary, wife of the aforesaid Sir William Craven, K^t.
She gave C^{li} for a stock for the poore of Burnesall Parish aforesaid.

The Deedes of Charitie done by John Ld Craven of Ryton, 2^d sonne of the aforesaid Sir William Craven, K^t.
1. He gave C^{li}, the one half for the putting of poore children apprentices of the parish of Burnesall, and the other half for a stock for the poore of that parish.
2. He gave CC^{li} to the poore of Skipton in Craven for a stock.
3. He gave CC^{li} to the poore of Rippon for a stock.
4. He gave CC^{li} to the poore of Ripley.
5. He gave CC^{li} to the poore of Knaresborough.
6. He gave CC^{li} to the poore of Burroughbrigg."—Dugdale's "Visitation," 1665.]

Besides repairing the parish church of Burnsall, and re-building the churchyard wall, at an expense, as is said, of 600*l.*, he erected and endowed a grammar-school in the same village ;* in addition to which he built four bridges in this neighbourhood, and among them that of Burnsall. †

APPLETREEWICK.‡

WE have already given the Domesday Survey of this township, and have recited the grant by Alice de Romillè of half her domain here—*viz.*, 1 car. and 2 oxgangs to Robert de Bulmer—Great part of what remained was granted by this lady in a charter, which I shall transcribe literally, as it was unknown before, and is the only original of the foundress of Bolton I have ever seen.

"Scia't ta' futuri q' p'sentes q'd ego Aalit' de Rumilli dedi et co'cessi Edulfo de Culnese§ et heredib' suis p'pt' homagiu' suu, et p'pt' pecunia' sua', scilic' dimidia' marca', VI bovatas t're i' Appelt'pic cu' oi'b' p'tine'ciis, salvo foresto meo, lib'e t'enend' de me et de meo herede in servicio militis q'tu' serviciu' p'tin' ad VI bovatas tre i'fra XIIII carucas. ‖ Et ut hec firma p'maneat, ha'c carta' et sigi'lli mei i'pressio'e co'firmavi, et hiis testib' ; Rog' tep' et Ric. fil. ej. Pet. de (Dart. Will. d' Rilest' Rog. Fasit. Pet. de Pigen, Sim. f. Rydulf, Acca de Thorelbi. Osmu'd capell. . . . Hug' Forestar', Stefan' Forestar."

But these lands, together with the remainder of the two car. et dim. which were the original fee of Aaliz de Romillè in this p'ace, were probably purchased either by Bulmer or his grandson Henry de Nevill, as they were altogether, excepting thirty acres, reserved for an intended donation to the priory of Munkton, conferred by this Henry on the priory of Marton, by the name of the manor of Woodhouse.

This grant was copied by Dodsworth, and is now in the " Mon. Angl." vol. ii. p. 103 ; but the original, with a fair seal, is now lying before me. The following confirmation, however, is new :—

"Omnibus, &c. Wil'mus de Fortibus, comes Almar. Sciatis nos confirmasse p' salute a'i'e n're antecessor' et successor', Man'm de Wodhuys, cum Domp'nio, &c. priori et canonicis de Marton ; q'i h'nt Wodhuys cu' Apletrewyk ex dono d'ni Henrici de Nevile, amici n'ri. Hiis test. d'no Godefr. de Altaripa, Joh. de Eston, Sim. de Marton, Ric. Te'pest, Wil'mo H'tlintun, H'nr. de Torp, et aliis."

The manor of Woodhouse was afterwards confounded with that of Appletrewick, at least in the apprehension of the priors of Marton ; but in the 19th of Henry VIII. [1527–8], the priors of Bolton and Marton referred the case of the superiority and royalty of Appletrewick to Sir J. Metcalfe, Sir J. Norton, Roger Cholmeley, and Anthonie Clifford, Esqs., by whose award it *seems* to have been determined that the prior and convent of Bolton should ever after be chief lords, and enjoy the royalty, paying to the prior and convent of Marton an annuity of xx*s.* The terms of this award might, very probably, mislead Sir John Yorke, in the next century ; for the superiority and paramount rights undoubtedly remained in the lords of the fee.

The manor of Woodhouse remained in the priory of Marton till the Dissolution, when it was granted, A.D. 1542, to Henry Earl of Cumberland.

The reader will be careful to distinguish between this manor and that of Appletrewick properly so called. This I suppose to have consisted of those three carucates which, at the time of Domesday, were held by Norman. It does not appear when they were acquired by the Romillès, or the Albemarles ; but, in the 5th of John [1203–4], Baldwine de Betune, Earl of Albemarle, had licence to afforest his lands at Appletrewick for two miles in length.

Nothing more is known with respect to this manor till the 6th of Edward I. [1277–8], when free warren was granted here to John de Eston. I have already stated the claim of this person upon the honour of Skipton and the earldom of Albemarle itself ; and as this was the very year in which he was bought off by Edward, it seems likely that the manor of Appletrewick was a part of the consideration.* In the next place, James de Eshton, brother of John, to whom it had been given 28 Edward I. [1299–1300] sold the manor of Appletrewick to the prior and canons of Bolton, † " una cum mineris Weyvis Telloniis et Stallagiis, &c." ‡

In the 4th of Edward II. [1310–1] a charter for a fair and free warren in Appletrewick was granted to the prior and canons aforesaid, at the instance of Peirs de Gavestone.

---

* John de Eston, in consideration of the manor of Appletrewick in Craven, released his claim to the estates of Aveline de Fortibus in England and Normandy. [See p. 298.] A copy of the acquittance is entered in the Liber Rubeum Feodorum of the Exchequer, fo. 249, b.

† Immediately after this purchase the old hall of Appletreewick was pulled down, and a new house built, and covered with slates.—Coucher Book of Bolton. I mention this as the earliest instance I have met with of a slated house in Craven. I omitted to mention, in its proper place, that at this time the choir of Long Preston Church was covered with shingles.

‡ Conf. Edward II. Pat. 5 Reg., " Mon. Ang." vol. ii. p. 102.

This house was surrendered Jan. 29th, 30th of Henry VIII. [1539] and, on the 28th of July following, the manor of Appletrewick was granted to Sir Christopher Hales, Knight, Master of the Rolls. By this means the Earl of Cumberland, whose grant of the site and other lands of Bolton did not take place till three years after, lost the chance of so desirable an addition to his estates, and left a door open to long and vexatious litigations, which took place about seventy years after.

In the year 1611, I find Sir John Yorke, of Gowthwaite, Lord of Appletrewick; but whether his family had purchased immediately from the Hales's, does not appear. However, in that year he laid claim to free chase and warren within this town, though it was not mentioned in the grant to Hales. This was resisted by Francis Earl of Cumberland, who contended, that Appletrewick was a member of the forest of Skipton; "that the inhabitants dwelling on the prior of Bolton's lands there did, both in the prior's time, and ever since, yearly pay Forster Oates to the Bowbearer, or the Forester, of the forest of Skipton; and also pay Forster Hens and Castle Hens, and do suit of court yearly at the Forest Court at Skipton. Also that the said earl and his ancestors have had their keepers at their wills, to range and view the deer within the townfields of Appletrewic; and have set courses, and made general huntings, on the commons, and through the fields and inclosures there.

"Also that Sir John Yorke, and his ancestors, never had any keepers there for deer; neither used to hunt there without leave of the earl and his ancestors, except by stealing * of them in the night-time, or of courtesie, when the said earl, and his ancestors, yearly bestowed deer on the said Sir John York, and his ancestors."†

I do not know how this litigation ended. Woodhouse was granted *salvo foresto*, and Appletrewick probably was the same. At all events there was a paramount right in the superior lord for the range of deer within the manor, as parcel of the forest; a right which might consist with free chase and warren in the mesne lord. But this is not the only instance in Wharfdale where these two claims have been confounded.

From the evidences at Skipton I find that this dispute came to blows; for some of Earl Francis's shepherds, resorting to Appletrewick fair, for the purpose of buying lean sheep to be fatted in the parks, and refusing to pay the accustomed tolls at the town's end, were fallen upon by Sir John Yorke's bailiff and servants, who seem to have beaten them soundly.

In another shape it came before the Star Chamber, which took cognisance at the time with severity enough of every instance of disrespect offered to a nobleman; for I learn, from the records of that court :—

"Hilar. 1 Car. Comes Cumbriæ versus York, Equ. &c. That the defendant Sir John York often gave directions to the defendants, Fenton and John York, to kill deer in Appletrewick Fields; and accordingly they, with others, 19 Jac. with a gun shot one of Plaintiff's staggs, and pursued him with a blood-hound, and John Hunt said they would hunt and kill the deer at their pleasure; and Fenton, at another time, in Sir John York's presence, shot with his gun at ten of the plaintiff's staggs in Appletrewick Fields, and Sir John, in a haughty manner, sent the plaintiff word he would kill and hunt deer there

---

* A very unhandsome insinuation with respect to a knight, or indeed a gentleman.
† Skipton MSS.

3 N

if he could ; and for this hunting and provoking speeches they were committed to the Fleet, and fined, Sir John 200*l.* Fenton 100*l.* and John York 50*l.* ; but with the title, touching the bounds of the plaintiff's chace of Skipton and Barden, and the defendant's manor of Appletrewick, the court would not meddle, but left it to the law." *

This may serve as a specimen of Star-Chamber justice. The title should, at all events, have been tried first ; for, till that was decided, no proof existed that the defendant was not hunting in his own free warren, and his threatenings might amount to no more than a declaration that he would maintain his own rights.

In a survey of the manors belonging to Robert de Clifford,......Edward II.,† mention is made of Gordale in Appletrewick. The name is now forgotten ; but the place, I am persuaded, is to be found in Troller's Gill, which forms the termination of a wild and solitary valley in this township.

It is a winding but nearly perpendicular fissure in the limestone rock, about half a mile in length, a very few yards in width, and, upon an average, about sixty feet high. The bottom forms the channel of a torrent often dry ; but when swollen by rains devolving huge masses of limestone, which interrupt and exasperate its course. On the whole, Troller's Gill wants the waterfall, the depth and majesty of the modern Gordale ; but its general resemblance to the other, its sudden contraction and perpendicular depression, give it an exclusive claim to be the ancient Gordale of Appletrewick.

A hamlet dependent upon the township of Burnsall is Thorp,‡ sometimes called Thorp subtus Montem, in a most retired situation, within a cavity so encircled by high grounds that it is difficult to conceive, at first sight, how the waters escape, and why it is not a lake.

In a pasture above this village is a cave, called Knave Knoll Hole, very difficult of access, and, from the narrowness of the entrance, equally difficult to be discovered. For these reasons it seems to have been a retreat of some ancient banditti. On descending into it several years ago, I discovered, besides many bones of sheep, &c., the remains of a human skeleton.

[In Appletrewick are three old mansions. Low Hall, formerly the property of the Prestons, who restored it in 1658. The initials of Thomas Preston are to be seen in the ornamental plaster-work of the south wing. The Prestons sold it to the Cavendish family, and it now belongs to John Procter, Esq., of Kirkby Malham, who bought the estate from Lord George Cavendish. The High Hall, in 1655 called the Elm Tree House, an Elizabethan mansion, with a large hall and gallery at one end of it, was once the residence of Sir William and Lord John Craven. It is now the property of the Earl of Craven. At Skyreholme is Percival Hall. Over the doorway are the initials CLCEP, 1671.]

---

* Rushworth, vol. iii. append. p. 3.

† Inter MSS. Ashmole, Oxf., for a copy of which I am indebted to the Rev. Thomas Heber, Esq., rector of Marton.

‡ Thorpe is, in the strictest sense, a hamlet, and thus precisely it is used by King Edgar—

Ic Æðgan ȝife mýnȝtre Ꝺeðehæmȝreðe
eale þa þoꝛꝑeꝛ þe peꝛto hn.

"Chron. Sax." ed. Gibson, p. 118.

[The manor of Thorpe belonged to the Tempests of Bracewell. Sir Stephen Tempest, who rebuilt Broughton Hall, leased out the manor in several estates, reserving the manorial rights.

The old hall is in ruins. In 1863 the roof was taken off, and removed to Copmanhow, on Malham Moor, and used to repair the farm-buildings. The Batty family had an estate and mansion in Thorpe, which descended to the Rev. Henry Wigglesworth, rector of Slaidburn, who married the heiress.

In the 29th George III. an Act was passed " for dividing and enclosing several open fields and stinted pastures within the township of Thorpe, in the parish of Burnsall, in the West Riding of the County of York.'

The award is dated 31st October, 1793.]

§ Bolton MSS.

HARTLINGTON.*

OPPOSITE to Burnsal is Hartlington, or the town of Hartil, a Saxon proper name, which occurs in Craven charters soon after the Conquest. The syllable " ing," in the composition of local names, is merely epenthetical, and arises from a vicious redundancy in pronunciation. Thus we find, in Domesday, Remitone instead of the modern Remington; Wadeton for Wadington; and, in the ballad of the "Tournament of Tottenham," Islington is called Hyssilton, as in St. Paul's Cathedral the prebend is styled "Prebenda de Issledon."

This village gave name and residence to a knightly family of high antiquity. Ketel de Hertlintuna must have been born in the latter end of the reign of the Conqueror, or the beginning of Rufus. He had a son Hugh, grantee of Arnforth, about 1140. William de Hartlinton died 8th Edward I. [1279-80], leaving a son and heir, William, æt. 30. He was seised of the manors of Hartlinton, Agenlith (Hanlith), and a carucate of land in Rillestone.

Dodsworth, vol. iii. fol. 99.

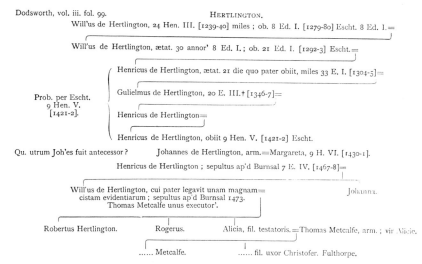

HERTLINGTON.

Will'us de Hertlington, 24 Hen. III. [1239-40] miles ; ob. 8 Ed. I. [1279-80] Escht. 8 Ed. I. =

Will'us de Hertlington, ætat. 30 annor' 8 Ed. I.; ob. 21 Ed. I. [1292-3] Escht. =

Henricus de Hertlington, ætat. 21 die quo pater obiit, miles 33 E. I. [1304-5] =

Prob. per Escht. 9 Hen. V. [1421-2].

Gulielmus de Hertlington, 20 E. III.† [1346-7] =

Henricus de Hertlington =

Henricus de Hertlington, obiit 9 Hen. V. [1421-2] Escht.

Qu. utrum Joh'es fuit antecessor ? Johannes de Hertlington, arm. = Margareta, 9 H. VI. [1430-1].

Henricus de Hertlington ; sepultus ap'd Burnsal 7 E. IV. [1467-8] =

Will'us de Hertlington, cui pater legavit unam magnam = cistam evidentiarum ; sepultus ap'd Burnsal 1473. Thomas Metcalfe unus executor'.

Johanna.

Robertus Hertlington. Rogerus. Alicia, fil. testatoris. = Thomas Metcalfe, arm. ; vir Alicie.

...... Metcalfe. ...... fil. uxor Christofer. Fulthorpe.

[Inquisition taken at Caterik 20 June, 9 Henry IV. (1408). The jurors say that Henry de Hertlington, chevalier, gave the Manor of Hertlyngton, in the County of York, to William de Hertlington, his son, and to the heirs of his body issuing, by virtue of which, the said William was seised in fee, in the time of Edward II., and from him it descended to his son Henry, son and heir, and after the death of the said William and his son Henry, to the aforesaid Henry that now is, and they say on oath that in the feast of St. Andrew the Apostle, 8 Edward II. (30th Nov. 1314), the aforesaid William de Hertlyngton was an adherent of Gilbert de Midelton, traitor of Edward II., and the said Gilbert and William were adherents of the Scotch enemies of the king, and that in the feast of St. Andrew, 8 Edward II., the aforesaid William de Hertlyngton was at the spoliation and robbery of the cardinals in the northern parts of England, by virtue of which the said Gilbert was condemned to death, and the said William withdrew. The jurors also say on oath that the said Manor was seised into the hands of the aforesaid late King Edward,‡ by virtue of an Inquisition before William de Reygate, late escheator of the said king, by which it was found that the said William de Hertlyngton, chevalier, was with the aforesaid Gilbert and Henry de Hertlyngton, chevalier, at the robbery of the cardinals, as by a certain Inquisition, before Thomas de Egmanton, escheator, 5 Aug., 8 Henry IV. (1407), taken at Tadcaster.—(Chancery, Inq. ad quod damnum, 9 Henry IV., No. 6.|

[Inquisition taken at Sherburne, in Elmet, before William de Raygate, escheator, on Thursday next after the feast of St. Michael the Archangel, 38 Edward III. (3 Oct. 1364). The jurors say that Henry de Hertlyngton died 8 Edw. III. (1334-5) and that the Manor of Hertlyngton descended to his son William. The said William holds other property in Brynsale, and Thorp near Brynsale, Rilleston, Haghenlith, Braham, Plumpton, Folefoit, Spotford, Norton near Nunwick, Nunwik near Ripon, &c. The writ is dated, 1 Nov., 10 Hen. IV. (1408).—(Chancery, Inq. ad quod damnum, 10 Henry IV., No. 34a.)]

[* HERTELINGTON.— In eadem villa sunt III car. terræ quæ tenentur de rege et domino castri (de Skypton) et quælibet car. redd. per ann. ad finem prædictum IIId. ob. q. ; unde summa est XId. q.—Kirkby's " Inquest," 13th Edward I.

In the 9th Edward II. Henry de Herlington was Lord of the Manor of Hertlington.—" Nomina Villarum."]

[† 33 Edward III. (1359-60) Willielmus de Herlyngton held the Manor of Hertlington and the vill of Haghenlych.—Inq. p.m.]

[‡ Edward III.; William de Reygate was Escheator, 37—41 Edw. III.]

The following is an abstract of the will of Henry Hartlington, Esq., who died in 1467. He was father of the last William :—

"In primis lego animam meam Deo omnip. b'te Marie matri ejus & omnibus sanctis, corpusq; meum sepeliend. in eccl'ia p'och' S'c'i Wilfridi de Burnsall.—It^m lego optimu' meum equ'm cum armatura p. corpore meo apt. ac lancia mea & gladio meo nomine mortuarii mei.—It^m lego rectoribus eccl. p'och' de Lynton VI*s.* VIII*d.* pro decimis meis oblitis.—It^m lego fabrice S'c'i Petri Ebor. X*s.*—It^m lego cuili't capellano Deo servient. pro sal. a'i'e mee die sepulture mee VIII*d.*—It^m lego cuili't clerico eodem die circa corpus meum Deo servient' pro sal. a'i'e mee IIII*d.*—It^m lego Will'mo filio meo unam magnam cistam cum cart. & evidenc^s meis.—It^m lego cuili't servient' meor' III*s.* IV*d.*—It^m lego Wil'mo Banke servienti meo XXVI*s.* VIII*d.*— It^m lego D^no Ric. Clerke capellano meo XII*l.* legalis mon. Angl. pro missis celebrand. in Eccl. p'och' de Burnsall pro sal' a'i'e mee p. tres annos p'x' post mortem meam.—It^m lego cuili't rectori & vicario Eccliar' de Burnsall, Lynton, Arnclyff, & Kirkby Malughdale III*s.* IV*d.* pro recomendacione a'i'e mee diebus d'nic' tempore rogacionis & predicacionis.—It^m lego Henrico Clyfford filio Johannis D^ni de Clyfford gladium meum & unum craterem stantem de argento.—It^m lego Marjorie Wesshengton servient' mee sex vaccas, viginti wethers, viginti berbicas,* & viginti agnos.

"*Dat.* 9° *Sept.* 1466."

"In codicillo: Imprimis leg^t Joh. Styring famule sue unam vaccam vel X solidos argenti.—It^m Marjorie famule sue optimum lectum suum cum curtino.—It^m summo altari S'c'e Marie de Burnsall unum nigrum vestimentum cum altercloth & towell, unam ymaginem beati Johannis & aliam ymaginem beate Marie Magdalene.—It^m D^no Henrico Burnsall capellano optimam suam togam penulatam.—It^m D^no Ric. Clerke Cap° secundam suam togam penulatam.—It^m Fr. W. Brerworth XX sol.—It^m cuilibet ordini fr'um infra civ. Ebor. VI*s.* VIII*d.*—It'm cuili't Domui leprosor' in suburbiis ejusdem civitatis III*s.* IV*d.* —It^m fraternitati S'c'i Xtopheri infra eandem civitatem X*s.*—It^m fr'ibus Richmond. VI*s.* VIII*d.*—It^m fraternitati S'c'i Roberti juxta Knarisburgh III*s.* IV*d.*—It^m Frat. S^ci Thome de Urbe Roma XX*d.*"

Henry Hartlington had been an officer† under the Cliffords above thirty years. What services the lance and sword here bequeathed had achieved in the hand of this trusty esquire of the family may easily be conjectured. He had fought by the side of Thomas and John Lord Clifford, and probably beheld the fall of both. His affection for the family was undiminished by their misfortunes, and through the dark cloud which then hung over them he seems to have beheld their restoration. A sword and standing goblet of silver were no legacies for a shepherd's boy. Indeed, a bequest to the heir of this attainted family by name, in a testament which must be publicly proved in the Ecclesiastical Court of York, leads to a suspicion that the concealment of Henry Clifford was not so entire, nor his situation so dangerous, as tradition has represented it. His person must have been neglected by his enemies, as was his education by his friends.

From the number of legacies to parsons, vicars, chaplains, and fraternities, the soldier in youth seems, as was usual at that time, to have become a devotee in age. The religion of the fifteenth century knew not how to appease the conscience by anything better than these poor substitutions.

His servants were sufficiently considered; but there is not a single item for the poor. The value of the different legacies may be computed by the circumstance of ten shillings being equivalent to a cow.

In the 6th of Edward VI. [1552–3] this manor, amongst others, is charged with a jointure of a hundred marks on the marriage of Sir Christopher Metcalf, Knight, with Lady Elizabeth Clifford, daughter of the first Earl of Cumberland.

In the 4th and 5th Philip and Mary [1557–8],‡ the same Sir Christopher Metcalf, for the consideration of 1,200*l.*, conveyed the manor of Hartlington, with the appurtenances in Burnsal, Appletrewick, and Calgarth, value 122*l. per annum,* to William Lyster, of Medehop, Esq., who in the same year conveys one undivided moiety of the said manor to Reginald Hayber, Gent., and the other to Gilbert Watson of Wigglesworth. And,

---

* Ewes.   † I find him bailiff of Kettlewelldale 15 Henry VI. [1436–7].   ‡ Bolton MSS.

In 21st Elizabeth [1578–9] is a deed of partition between the same Reginald Hayber and Anthony Watson, respecting Hartlington Hall and demesne lands, in which the manor-house is described as consisting of a centre and two wings.*

In consequence of this transaction one moiety is now, by descent, the property of Richard Heber, of Marton, Esq., and the other of Mr. Dawson.†

The manor-house is completely dilapidated and gone; but its site is just remembered by the name of Hall Garth, near which is Chapel Hill, where probably stood one of those ancient oratories so frequently attached to the manor-houses in the Saxon times, when parish churches were few, and therefore generally remote. ‡

These are the members of the parish of Burnsall, which immediately adjoin to that township. Those which follow are either wholly, or in part, divided from it by the parish of Linton.

RILSTON. §

IN the more northern aperture, between the hills which separate the valleys of Are and Wharf, is Rilston, or Rilliston, so called from the Danish Ryll, "rivus tacitè fluens," as it is situated among the forks of several inconsiderable brooks, all of which fall into the Are, excepting one, which finds its way eastward to the Wharf.

Rilston gave name and habitation to a family, perhaps of the first antiquity in Craven, as there is reason to suppose that William de Risletona, who occurs in the first charter of Cecilia de Romillè, was the William, son of Clarembald,‖ mentioned in the Black Book of the Exchequer, and undoubtedly a Saxon. The following singular monument of their devotion in the next century remains at Bolton Abbey:—

"Notum sit omnibus—hanc esse conventionem inter Monachos de Fontibus & Wil. de Rilestun, quod dict. Wil' dedit et confirmavit Monachis p'd. 1 dim. car. t're in Bordelay, scil. unam bovat. in initio hujus donationis et alias post discessum suum, vel ante si voluerit. Ecclesia autem de Fontibus recipiet ipsum quando voluerit in Monachum vel Conversum, si sic sanus fuerit, ut s'c'dum formam ord⁵ C'stertiensis possit recipi. Et uxorem suam nomine Efam in unâ domo sancti-monialium infra Eboraci Siriam¶ ut ipsa elegerit et conventum fuerit ponet in religionem. Unus vero filiorum ejus nomine Alan serviet in domo de Fontibus in habitu sæculari uno vel duobus annis; et si in conversum recipi voluerit, recipietur, vel si ante recesserit dabitur ei una marca, vel unus equus tanti pretii, et ad consulendum filium suum infirmum domus de Fontibus jam dedit p'd' Wil° xxxs. Helias fil. et heres confirmabit et in excambium recipiet dotem matris sue in Yeter

---

* Ex Chartis penes Ric. Heber arm.

[† The moiety of the manor remained in the family of Heber until 1841, when the estates were sold in lots, and the manorial rights bought by Sir Mathew Wilson of Eshton, Bart.; the other moiety descended to the Dawsons, and is now held by the Rev. Henry Dawson of Torquay, and Fred. Dawson, Esq., of Camberwell, London.]

‡ At Hartlington, according to tradition, lived a man of the name of Walters, who on a certain night was suddenly awoke out of his sleep by a voice calling to him, "Arise, Walters, and save life." He obeyed the call; took his bow and quiver, and, directed by a secret impulse, repaired to a remote part of Appletrewick pastures, where he found a young lady, a daughter of the family of Skipton Castle, struggling with ruffians. Walters, however, plied them so well with arrows that they soon dispersed, and left the lady uninjured. For this good service, it is added, that an estate was given to the deliverer, which his descendants long enjoyed. No other name, and no date, are mentioned in the story; for traditions generally despise such minutiæ. Some of my readers, perhaps, may commend this tale to the ingenious Mr. Aubrey; and others may compare it with Dr. Plot's thrilling story of the "Black Meer of Morridge," "Hist. Staffordshire," p. 291.

[§ RILSTON.—In eadem villa sunt v car. terræ quæ tenentur de rege et castro prædicto (Skipton) et quælibet car. redd. per ann. ad finem prædictum IIId. ob. q.; unde. Summa est XVIIId. ob.—Kirkby's "Inquest," A.D. 1284.

Dominus Henricus de Hertlington tenet in Rilleston I car. Hæres Eliæ de Rilleston qui est in custodia domini regis, tenet in capite de domino dicti castri (de Skipton) IIII car. et di. terræ in Rilleston et in Scothorp; et totum est in manu domini regis ratione custodiæ.—"Knights' Fees," 31st Edward I.

There was an Inclosure Act passed relative to the Stinted Pastures in the 11th George III.]

‖ Clarembald was the name of one of the Sempectæ of Croyland, mentioned by Ingulphus.

¶ *I.e.* Shire.

Rillestun. Si autem Wil⁵ sive Efa in sc'lo mortui fuerint, fiet pro eis tanquam pro monacho* fieri solet in domo de Fontibus.   Test. Symone presb. de Rillestun, Ranulph. Cap° de Kyrbi, Rad. f. Aldelmi, &c."†

As the party to this convention was undoubtedly William, father of the first Elias, it must be fixed about 1160, or 1170; and a chapel at Rilleston was extant at that time.

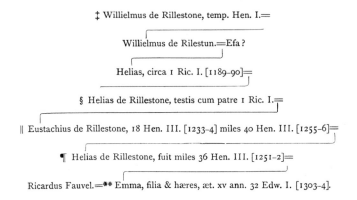

‡ Willielmus de Rillestone, temp. Hen. I.=

Willielmus de Rilestun.=Efa ?

Helias, circa 1 Ric. I. [1189–90]=

§ Helias de Rillestone, testis cum patre 1 Ric. I.=

‖ Eustachius de Rillestone, 18 Hen. III. [1233–4] miles 40 Hen. III. [1255–6]=

¶ Helias de Rillestone, fuit miles 36 Hen. III. [1251–2]=

Ricardus Fauvel.=** Emma, filia & hæres, æt. xv ann. 32 Edw. I. [1303–4].

Henry de Rillestone and Gilbert, his son, lived in the reign of Stephen; Gilbert married Matilda, daughter of Ralph Dean of Ketelwell.   About the same time a William de Rilleston attests one of the charters of Alice de Romillè.

In the 42nd of Henry III. [1257–8] free warren was granted to Eustace de Rillestone within his demesnes at that place.

By a return to a Quo Warranto, 21st Edward I. [1292–3], that a second Elias de Rillestone was son of this Eustace.

But in the 1st of Edward III. [1327–8] is an inspeximus and confirmation of the charter of free warren last mentioned, to Richard de Fauvel †† and Emma his wife, as next of kin to Eustace de Rilleston, deceased.   I suppose, therefore, the last Elias to have died s. p., and that Emma was his father's sister.   It seems probable that her descendants resumed the family name; for in the reign of Richard II. lived John de Rilston, the "cher compagnon" of Roger Lord Clifford.   Again, in the 29th of Henry VI. [1450–1] lived John de Rilleston and Joanna his wife.   Lastly, in the 34th year of the same reign lived William Rillestone, Esq., who must have died without issue, as the estates reverted to Isabella, daughter of John de Rilleston, probably the father of both, whose daughter and heir Isabel, about the year 1434, married Miles Radcliffe, son of Wilkin Radcliffe, of Threshfield, base son of William

---

   * Sic.
   † Bolton MSS.
   ‡ Dodsworth's MSS., vol. iii. p. 98.
   [§ In the 23rd Edward I., 1294–5, Elias Rilleston died possessed of the manor of Rilleston.—Inq. *post mortem*.]
   ‖ Cart. 42nd Henry III. [1257–8]—Rex concessit Eustachio de Rilleston lib. warr. in omnibus terris dom. suis de Rilleston.
   ¶ Elias de R. presentabat ad med'm ecclesiæ de Burnsall 53rd Henry III. [1268–9].
   ** Probatio ætat. Emmæ fil. & her. Elie de Rillestone uxoris Ric. Fauvell facta apud Skipton in Craven, in Vig. S'cti Gregorii Papæ, 32nd Edward I. [1303–4].   Fuit æt. xv an.
   [†† In the 9th Edw. II. (1315–16) Henry de Hertlington and Richard Fauvell were Lords of the Manor of Rilleston.— "Nomina Villarum."]

Radcliffe, Esq., of Todmorden and Merley, co. Lancaster, whom I have had frequent occasion to mention in the "History of Whalley." But the following petition from this person, or his son, to Cardinal Beaufort, which I had not discovered at the publication of that work, is too curious to be suppressed, and may therefore be indulged with a place here.

"To the full Rever'd Fader in God and right gracious Lord Bischope of Winchester, Cardinal of England.

"Besechen mekely y^r servitours William Radclyff ye younger and his cozen Worsley, of ye parish of Cliderowe, in the countie of Lancastre, y^t wheras Thomas the sonne of Sir Thomas Radcliff, of ye said countie, knight, be great ordeannance and forecasting against ye peace of o'r suveraine Lo. the Kinge, with ye numbre of XXIV harnaysed men, made a violent sawte upon your saaid besechers, and them greveosly maimed and wounded unto p'ill of dethe. In whiche debate ye said Thomas, atte defence of your saite besechers, was sleayne, as it is openly knowen to ye R't Honnorable Lordes ye Lorde of Duresme and ye Lorde of Salesbury ; and then, by ye ordinaunce of ye said Lorde of Salesbury, w'ch had al y^s matere hold in his rule, apoynted Thomas Harington, Esquyer, and Thomas Urswicke, Esquyer, as attrabutors to bee in meane and indifferent in ye seide metere we (were) through y^m apoynted demed and awarded, by scripture indented, under their seales, rehersing, that ye seide Thomas, in his seide assaute makyng, was sleyne, in ye defens of ye seide besechers ; and notwythstanding y^s, y^t ye seid besechers shal pay XI markes in moneye, ye w'ch y^s to greavose and importable charge of y^r seide besechers, w'thout they had, or myght have, ye graciouse almes of supportation and refreshing of Lordes. Wherefor pleas yt your noble Lords'p, of y'r gode grace, in consid'acion of ye p'misses, to refresh and releve y'r seide besechers w'th y'r moste graciose almes, after y'r gode plesure, atte reverence of God, and in waye of charitie." *

Here is a very late instance of the ancient Bloðpιƫe [Bloodveit or Bloodwit] or pecuniary compensation for homicide. The Ratcliffs were zealous retainers of the House of Lancaster, and this military prelate, it may be, felt no repugnance to assist a brave man of that party, though he came before him with hands dipped in blood.

But to return—

The descent of this branch of the Radcliffs is as follows :—

Jane, daughter of William Mansell, Esq.=Walkin, illegitimate son of William Radcliff, Esq.

Miles Radcliff ; living 1434.=Isabella, daughter and heiress of John † Rillestone, *alias* Fauvel, of Rillestone, Esq.

William Ratcliff, of Rillestone, Esq.=Jane, daughter of	John.	Ralph, a priest.	Eliza-=John beth. Proctor.	Roger of Linton.	Edward.	Several daughters.
eldest son and heir, born about 1450 ; Sir John Tempest, Knt. died about 14 Hen. VII. [1498–9].						

Anne Radcliff, sole heiress, born about 1478 ; living 37 Hen. VIII. [1545–6]=John Norton, Esq. ; living 37 Hen. VIII.

1. Susan, daugh-=Richard Norton, Esq., who was attainted for the part he bore in the insur-=2. Philippa, daughter
ter of Richard   rection of the Earls of Northumberland and Westmoreland, when his estates   of Thomas Trapps,
Lord Latimer.   were forfeited to the Crown, where they remained till the 2nd or 3rd of James.   of London, relict of
                      They were then granted to Francis Earl of Cumberland.   Sir George Gifford.

On this occasion a very accurate survey was made, from which I shall extract the most interesting particulars.

---

* Townley MSS. No. XXII.

† Ex cartis J. C. Brooke. But in an old compotus of John Lambert, Esq., the matter is stated thus : Ric. Norton, arm. p. m. John Norton, arm. patris sui, et Anne Norton, m'ris sui, defunct. filie et her. Willi Radcliff, arm. consanguinei et heredis Elie Rilleston.

NORTON LANDS.

Rilestone Manor.

Measure, 1,010 a. 10 p.
Old Rents received, £68 14*s.* 2*d.*
Clear Yearly Value, £139 17*s.* 8*d.*
Fee Simple at Fifteen Years' Purchase, £3,128 17*s.* 6*d.*

THE ancient manor-house was now in decay. *   Immediately adjoining lay a close called the Vivery; so called, undoubtedly, from the French *Vivier,* or modern Latin *Viverium ;*† for there are, near the house, large remains of a pleasure-ground, such as were introduced in the earlier part of Elizabeth's time, with topiary works, fish-ponds, an island, &c.   The demesne was something more than 400 acres.   The rest was divided into forty-three tenements; some of two oxgangs, others of one or less.   The oxgang averaged from twelve to thirteen acres.

In this survey the word homestead is constantly substituted to the old toft and croft.‡ There seems to have been a little inclosed meadowing about the houses; but the greater part, even of the hay ground, lay open in the town-field, which also contained all the arable land of the place.   There were two common pastures, the Fell and Langill, besides an unstinted common right upon the moors.

The whole township was ranged by 130 red deer, the property of the lord, which, together with the wood, had, after the attainder of Mr. Norton, been committed to Sir Stephen Tempest, of Broughton.   The latter, it seems, had been abandoned to depredation; for, upon a survey, there appeared the stumps of 86 oaks, 144 ashes, ellers § 217, hollies 99. Of these the oaks were valued at 1*s.* each; the ashes at 4*d.* ; the ellers and hollies at 1*d.* each.   Now, though we should be scarcely warranted in supposing these to have been the heaviest timber upon the estate, yet they must have been something more than walking-sticks; and if the valuation of 1603 be multiplied by ten, it will probably not equal the present value.   But the whole timber of the township was estimated in this survey at 300*l.,*

---

* On the site of the gardens still appear some dwarf and stunted flowers, which have survived the neglect of more than two centuries :

"And still where many a garden-flower grows wild"

affords a pleasing but melancholy image of continuance in the frailest part of the creation, compared with the life and fortunes of man.

Among these survivors at Rilston is a dwarf convallaria, or lily of the valley, said by botanists to be extremely scarce, but which has probably dwindled, from the absence of cultivation.

† Vide Du Cange in *Viverium.*

‡ The last instance I have met with of the old toft and croft is in the year 1579.   It had grown obsolete, therefore, in this interval of less than thirty years.   The most learned of our etymologists, Spelman, Bishop Kennet, and Du Cange, have fallen short of the precise meaning of toft.   Skinner alone has thrown a ray of light upon it, "locus arboribus minusculis consitus," a tuft of trees—Gall. *Touffe de Bois.*   But this gives only the literal, not the tralatitious sense of the word.   A toft was certainly a homestead in a village, so called from the small tufts of maple, elm, ash, and other wood, with which dwelling-houses were anciently overhung.   Hence the local surnames Mapletoft and Eltoft, qu. Elmtoft.

Even now it is impossible to enter a Craven village without being struck with the insulated homesteads, surrounded by their little garths, and overhung with tufts of trees.   These are the genuine tofts and crofts of our ancestors, with the substitution only of stone walls and slate to the wooden crocks and thatched roofs of antiquity.

[§ Alders.]

equal, according to the former ratio, to more than 3,000*l.* now, which, as it must have been confined, in a great measure, to the lower parts of the township, leaves the impression of a very forest-like and sylvan scene.

There was neither a freeholder nor cottager in the place ; the occupiers were, properly speaking, tenants at will, though the lord granted them verbal leases for life. The fines were entirely arbitrary ; but no heriots were paid. The tenement was usually granted, upon the demise of a tenant, to the eldest son, if there was one ; if not, to the eldest daughter. Among the old tenants is mentioned one " Richard Kitchen, butler to Mr. Norton, who rose in rebellion with his master, and was executed at Ripon."

This is the only notice which appears in the evidences at Bolton Abbey, relating to the insurrection of 1569, so fatal to the Norton family. Their ruin, in consequence of this unfortunate engagement, is generally understood from the old ballad entitled, " The Rising in the North," * where it is said,

> " Thee, Norton, wi' thine eight good sonnes,
>   They dom'd to dye, alas, for ruth !
> Thy reverend lockes thee could not save,
>   Nor them their faire and blooming youth." †

Camden, however, in his " Annals," mentions only three, viz.—Christopher, Marmaduke, and Thomas ; but, in the Townley MSS. G. 16, is a distinct enumeration of seventy-five persons, the ringleaders in this rebellion, who, having fled, were indicted, and many of them, probably, attainted in their absence. Among these appear the names of Richard Norton, of Norton,

[* The " Rising in the North " was caused by the persecution of the Catholics in England ; the leaders were Thomas Percy, the 7th Earl of Northumberland, the Earl of Westmoreland (whose wife was sister to the Duke of Norfolk), Egremont Ratcliffe, Leonard Dacre, the Tempests, Nortons, Markenfields, &c. They wished to re-establish the Catholic religion in England, and also to assist Mary Queen of Scots.

In October, 1569, the counties of York, Durham, and Northumberland, showed signs of insurrection, and on the 16th of November, the Earls of Northumberland and Westmoreland openly raised their banner of insurrection at Branspeth Castle. The common banner showed the cross and the five wounds of Christ, and was borne by Richard Norton. They proposed to march to Tutbury Castle to liberate Mary, and on their way, at Durham, they burnt the Bible and Book of Common Prayer, and celebrated mass in the cathedral. They marched as far as Clifford Moor, near Wetherby, when, finding themselves opposed in front by the royal army, under the Earl of Sussex, and in the rear by Sir George Bowes, they retreated to Raby Castle with 7,000 men. Sir George Bowes threw himself and forces into Barnard Castle. He was besieged by a portion of the insurgents, and was obliged to surrender in a few days. The remaining insurgents besieged and took the sea-port town of Hartlepool, where they waited, hoping to receive aid from the Spaniards in the Low Countries. During this time the royal army remained at York, and Queen Elizabeth, suspecting the loyalty of the Earl of Sussex, sent Sir Ralph Sadler to York, to endeavour to detect the reason. The Earl of Sussex, being joined by the Lord-Admiral, Lord Hunsden, and the Earl of Warwick, with 12,000 men, raised in the south, and undoubtedly Protestant and loyal, marched northward on the 13th December. The insurgents not having received any reinforcements, fled in all directions, but about 500 horse, accompanied by 300 Scottish horse, escaped into Liddlesdale.

The Earl of Westmoreland and his wife, Egremont Ratcliffe, Norton, Markenfield, Tempest, and others, were taken under the protection of the Humes, Scotts, Kers, and other border clans, but the Regent Moray bribed Hector Graham, of Harlow, and he betrayed the Earl of Northumberland, who was imprisoned in Lochleven Castle. The Earl and Countess of Westmoreland, Egremont Ratcliffe, and some others, escaped to the Spanish Netherlands.

The retainers and friends of the fugitives were, however, seized and persecuted. On the 4th and 5th of January, the Earl of Warwick and Sir George Bowes caused seventy-six persons to be executed in Durham alone, and then scoured the country between Newcastle and Wetherby, a district about sixty miles in length and forty miles in breadth, and Stow says, that, " finding many to be fautors in the said rebellion, he did see them executed in every market town and in every village."

For a very full and detailed account of the Rising in the North, Sir Cuthbert Sharp's work, " Memorials of the Rebellion of 1569 " (London : John Bowyer Nichols and Son, 1840), may be consulted.]

[† The earlier part of the poem, after describing how a "little foot-page" carried the letter from the Earl of

3 O

Esq.; Francis Norton, of Baldersby, Esq. ; Samuel Norton, of Wath, Gentleman ; Christopher Norton, of Norton, Gentleman ; Marmaduke Norton, of Norton, Gentleman; Thomas Norton, of Skyrningham, Gentleman.   But whether Francis Norton was the eldest son, whose aversion to engage in this desperate adventure is stigmatised in the ballad, and whether all the remaining four were sons, or one of them a collateral member of the family, it is now impossible to discover.   [The following table (see next page) shows the relationship of the Nortons at this period, and the actual fate of the various sons of Richard, by which it will be seen that the eight good sons were *not* doomed to die.]

The only Craven name besides in this catalogue is William Malham, of Elslack, Gentleman ; who seems not to have been attainted, as there is no evidence that his estates were forfeited.

I have already hinted at the bad neighbourhood which subsisted between the Nortons and their superior lords. *   Richard Norton in particular seems to have been a turbulent man, violently addicted to the old religion ; while the Cliffords were dutiful subjects, and favourers of the Reformation.   On this account it is probable that they beheld the ruin of their unquiet vassal with little compassion.

Northumberland to Richard Norton, and the letter being read aloud to the company, proceeds to state that Maister Norton spoke :—

"He sayd, Come hither, Christopher Norton,
    A gallant youth thou seemst to bee ;
What doest thou counsell me, my sonne,
    Now that good erle's in jeopardy ?

"Father, my counselle's fair and free,
    That Erle he is a noble Lord,
And whatsoever to him you hight,
    I wold not have you break your word.

"Gramercy, Christopher, my sonne,
    Thy counsell well it liketh mee,
And if we speed and scape with life,
    Well advanced thou shalt bee.

"Come you hither, my nine good sonnes ;
    Gallant men I trowe yeu bee.
How many of you, my children deare,
    Will stand by that good erle and mee ?

"Gramercy now, my children deare,
    You showe yourselves right bold and brave ;
And whethersoe'er I live or dye,
    A father's blessing you shall have.

"But what sayst thou, O Francis Norton,
    Thou art my eldest sonn and heir :
Somewhat lyes brooding in thy breast ;
    Whatever it bee, to mee declare.

"Father, you are an aged man,
    Your head is white, your beard is grey :
It were a shame at these your yeares
    For you to ryse in such a fray.

"Now fye upon the, coward Francis,
    Thou never learned this of mee ;
When thou wert yong and tender of age,
    Why did I make soe much of thee ?

"But, father, I will wend with you,
    Unarm'd and naked will I bee :
And he that strikes against the crowne,
    Ever an ill death may he dee.

"Then rose that reverend gentleman
    And with him came a goodlye band,
To join with the brave Erle Percy,
    And all the flower o' Northumberland.

"With them the noble Nevill came,
    The erle of Westmorland was hee :
At Wetherbye they mustred their host,
    Thirteen thousand faire to see.

"Lord Westmorland his ancyent raisde,
    The Dun Bull he rays'd on hye,
And three dogs with golden collars
    Were there sett out most royallye.

"Erle Percy there his ancyent spred,
    The Half-Moone shining all soe faire ;
The Nortons ancyent had the crosse,
    And the five wounds our Lord did beare."

        *   *   *   *   *   *

Percy's " Reliques of Ancient Poetry,"
        Edit. 1847, 290-293.]

* By a subpœna, directed out of the court at York to the first earl, it appears that this dispute commenced before the death of John Norton, the father ; for the suit is there styled, " a matt'r in trav'rs betwene you and John Nortone, Squier, concerning the liberties of youre foreste of Skyptone."   Without year, but probably about 1530.   Skipton MSS.

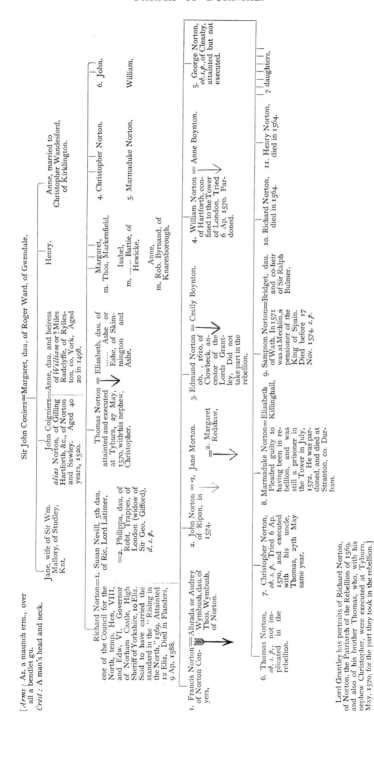

Lord Grantley has portraits of Richard Norton, of Norton, the Patriarch of the Rebellion of 1569, and also of his brother Thomas, who, with his nephew Christopher, were executed at Tyburn, May, 1570, for the part they took in the rebellion.]

Yet it was long before the Cliffords, with all their interest at court, could profit by this circumstance. The Nortons' lands, in the centre of their barony, and the object of long contentions, must have been a most desirable object; yet neither the merits and gallantry of Earl George, nor his just claims upon Queen Elizabeth, could ever obtain from her tenacious hand what the complaisance and assiduity of Earl Francis acquired from her easy successor.[*]

Rilston Fell yet exhibits a monument of the old warfare between the Nortons and Cliffords. On a point of very high ground, commanding an immense prospect, and protected by two deep ravines, are the remains of a square tower,[†] said by Dodsworth to have been built by Richard Norton. The walls are of strong groutwork, about four feet thick. It seems to have been three stories high. Breaches have been industriously made in all the sides, almost to the ground, to render it untenable.[‡]

We have already heard the complaints of the Earl of Cumberland's keepers against Norton for his contrivance to impound the deer; and it is curious enough that after almost three centuries, vestiges of this work should yet remain.

On the plain summit of the hill are the foundations of a strong wall, stretching from the S.W. to the N.E. corner of the tower, and to the edge of a very deep glen. From this glen a ditch, several hundred yards long, runs S. to another deep and rugged ravine. On the N. and W., where the banks are very steep, no wall or mound is discoverable, paling being the only fence which would stand on such ground. And this is the pound complained of.

From the "Minstrelsy of the Scottish Border"[§] it appears that such pounds for deer, sheep, &c., were far from being uncommon in the south of Scotland. The principle of them was something like that of a wire mouse-trap. On the declivity of a steep hill, the bottom and sides of which were fenced so as to be impassable, a wall was constructed nearly level with the surface on the outside, yet so high within that without wings it was impossible to escape in the opposite direction. Care was probably taken that these enclosures should contain better feed than the neighbouring parks or forests; and whoever is acquainted with the habits of these sequacious animals will easily conceive that, if the leader was once tempted to descend into the snare, a herd would follow; to recover which there were probably more frays than law-suits.

Among the Shrewsbury papers in the Heralds' College I have lately met with the

---

[*] I have heretofore supposed that they were granted to the third earl; but a paper entitled Barden Case, which I have lately met with in the Bolton papers, corrects, not only a mistake which I had made with respect to that place, but Rilston. This statement, with respect to Rilston, &c., is confirmed by the family rentals in which these estates are first mentioned, A.D. 1606.

[†] "Norton Lords of Rilston.—They say that Richard, last of the Nortons, builded a tower in the farthest part of his ordship of Rillestone, near Crookrise. He used to lie in summer always at his house at Rillestone, which his grandfather or great grandfather had by marriage of Radcliff's daughter and co-heir, which Radcliff's ancestor had formerly married Rillestone's daughter and heir."—Ex Apogr. J. C. Brooke, in Coll. Arm.

[‡ "On the opposite side of the deep ravine are visible the remains of an old building, containing two rooms about five yards square, called Newhall or Clifford's Tower, probably a hunting-box of the Cliffords. This building is an ancient boundary between the Manor of Embsay and Eastby, and that of Stirton and Thorlby; on the edge of Waterfall Gill. The next boundary, southward, is a large massive block of moor-stone, 40 feet long by 18 feet wide, and 12 or 14 feet in height, called the Fairies' Kist."—Note in the Rev. W. Carr's copy of the 1st edit.]

[§] Vol. i. p. 4.

following letter from the Privy Council in the latter end of Henry VIII.'s reign, on the subject of this dispute :—

"After commendations, &c.—Whereas complaynt hath lately byn made to the Quenes Highness (Catherine Parr) that my Lorde of Cumberlande, p'tending right of forest w'thin certayne grounds belonging to John Norton wher ye sayd Norton dothe clayme Free Warren, hathe now of late not onlie intruded ther, but causyd alsoe sundrie of his s'vants to cast downe ye hedges and dykes, &c.

"This shal bee to advertize yow that ye Quenes Graces pleasure is that yo' putting my s^d Lord of Cumb'rlande in rem'brance what unmet a tyme this is for th' attempting of such thinges, the Kinges Majestie beyng now owte of ye realme, yow shal wth good delyberation, as yow may, tak such ordre yn this matt^r, as to reason and good equitie shall ap'tayne : and if you shall not tak anie final ordre, yet staying yn such sorte as ye pece and good quyet of ye contre bee by neyth^r of you empeched. And thus we byd y^r good L'p most heartelee fare wel.

"*From Westm^r this* XIX *day of July* 1544.

"T. CANTUARIEN.   TH. WROTHESLEY, Canc.   E. HERTFORD.
            TH. WESTM.   W. PETRE.

"*To o^r very good Lord Therle of Shrewsburie, the Kinges Majesties Lieut'-general in ye Northe.*" *

In the days of high prerogative the Council took cognisance both of trespasses and riots ; and, in this dispute about deer and boundaries, Norton really adopted the means of redress which in a similar case Shallow threatened, and Falstaff treated with so much contempt : "' Knight, you have beaten my men, killed my deer, and broken open my lodge. . . . . The Council shall know this.' ' 'Twere better for you . . . . you'll be laughed at.' " † Yet Norton's complaint against a greater man than Falstaff, for pretty much the same behaviour, was not laughed at by the Council, but met with serious attention and redress.

After Rilston came into possession of the Cliffords, the same ground, with part of the fell above, was inclosed for a park, of which it still retains the name, and the name only.

At this time a white doe, say the aged people of the neighbourhood, long continued to make a weekly pilgrimage from hence over the fells to Bolton, and was constantly found in the abbey churchyard during divine service, after the close of which she returned home as regularly as the rest of the congregation.

This incident awakens the fancy. ‡ Shall we say that the soul of one of the Nortons had taken up its abode in that animal, and was condemned to do penance, for his transgressions against "the lords' deere," among their ashes ? But for such a spirit the wild stag would have been a fitter vehicle. Was it not, then, some fair and injured female, whose name and history are forgotten ? Had the milk-white doe performed her mysterious pilgrimage from Ettrick Forest to the precincts of Dryburgh or Melrose, the elegant and ingenious editor of the " Border Minstrelsy " would have wrought it into a beautiful story.

It is curious to observe in how many ways these picturesque animals have been employed by poetical or historical fiction. Under the milk-white hind Dryden personifies his own *immaculate* church. § Albert Dürer, the Ariosto of his art, has represented the conversion of St. Hubert in a forest by the miraculous appearance of a cross between the horns of a stag ; and Leland, from a nameless historian, assures us of Wlffade, Prince of Mercia, "quod cervum in silvis

* Shrewsbury Letters, v. p. 95.
[‡ See Wordsworth's poem, " The White Doe of Rylstone."]

† " Merry Wives of Windsor."
§ In his poem of " The Hind and the Panther."

persequens venit ad oratorium ubi fons erat quem recta petiit cervus (not because it was tired and thirsty), et baptizatus erat in fonte ad quem cervus confugerat."*

But, by Roos of Warwick,† this charitable stag, so instrumental in the conversion of Wlffade, is changed into a doe, who sustained St. Ceadda with her milk in his hermitage near Lichfield.

Norton Tower seems also to have been a sort of pleasure-house in summer, as there are adjoining to it several large mounds (two of them are pretty entire), of which no other account can be given than that they were butts for large companies of archers.

The place is savagely wild, and the situation admirably adapted to the use of a watch-tower.

We will now descend.

Adjoining to the manor-house is a chapel [dedicated to St. Peter] resembling a small parish church, with a tower, choir, and side aisles. The original structure has been at least as ancient as the reign of Stephen; for the buttresses at the east end of the middle choir exactly resemble those of Burnsall, and the font is cylindrical. It was probably a foundation of one of the earlier Rilstones. But the side aisles, with the tower, can claim no higher antiquity than the earlier part of Henry VIII.'s reign, and are probably the work of John Norton, who married the heiress of Radcliff. Of this there are two proofs : first, on one of the pillars of the south aisle is a shield, of which the dexter pale, undoubtedly charged with the arms of Norton, is hid behind the pulpit; the sinister is composed in a very singular manner of Radcliffe and Rilstone, as it consists of a bend engrailed sa. for Radcliff, between two saltires ; ‡ for Rilstone bore arg. a saltire sa. [this should be sa. a saltire arg., and is so shown by a drawing by Canon Boyd], which, out of much painted glass remaining within my memory in the chapel [that is, the south chapel], has alone escaped a late sweeping repair.§ The south chantry belongs to Rilston Hall, but has no memorials of the families interred within it. That on the north is appropriated to Bordley Hall.

Secondly, On one of the bells, which seems coeval with the building of the tower, is this cypher, 𝕵.𝕹., for John Norton, and the motto, "𝕲𝖔𝖉 𝖚𝖘 𝖆𝖞𝖉𝖊;" ‖ [on another, "𝕺𝖗𝖆 𝖕𝖗𝖔 𝖓𝖔𝖇𝖎𝖘 𝖘𝖈𝖊 𝕲𝖆𝖇𝖗𝖎𝖊𝖑;" and on another, "𝕲𝖑𝖔𝖗𝖎𝖆 𝖎𝖓 𝖊𝖝𝖈𝖊𝖑𝖘𝖎𝖘 𝕯𝖊𝖔, 1658."]

---

* Leland, "Coll." vol. i. p. 1.

† Plott's "Staffordshire," p. 407. If we may form a conjecture from the number of their parks and chases, some of St. Chad's successors would have preferred the haunch to the milk.

‡ This way of marshalling is censured by Gwillym. "But these," saith he, "may seem rather to be conceited formes than received grownds of marshalling, otherwise their use would have beene more frequent."—"Display of Heraldry," 2nd ed. p. 398.

[§ From drawings in the possession of the Rev. Canon Boyd, there was another shield, sa. a fess between three escallops arg. a canton of the last.]

‖ Wordsworth, in his poem, "The White Doe of Rylstone," has introduced in the seventh canto a verse suggested by this motto :—

"When the bells of Rylstone play'd
  Their Sabbath music—'𝕲𝖔𝖉 𝖚𝖘 𝖆𝖞𝖉𝖊!'
  That was the sound they seem'd to speak—
  Inscriptive legend which I ween
  May on these holy bells be seen,
  That legend and her grandsire's name ;
  And oftentimes the lady meek
  Had in her childhood read the same,

Words which she slighted at that day !
  But now, when such sad change was wrought,
  And of that lonely name she thought,
  The bells of Rylstone seem'd to say,
  Whilst she sat listening in the shade,
  With vocal music, '𝕲𝖔𝖉 𝖚𝖘 𝖆𝖞𝖉𝖊!'
  And all the hills were glad to bear
  Their part in this effectual prayer."

[The registers of baptisms and burials commence in 1539, and for marriages in 1803.]

[The church, from sketches in the possession of the Rev. Canon Boyd, of Arncliffe, appears in 1797 to have consisted of west tower, nave with clerestory, and two aisles, chancel with aisles, and south porch. In 1849 the clerestory had been removed, and the nave and chancel roofs were continuous.

The church has been recently entirely rebuilt, and now consists of west tower, with lofty arch; nave with clerestory, north and south aisles of four bays, chancel, and south porch. All the roofs are open-timbered. Not a vestige of the original structure remains, except the two carved stone shields mentioned by Dr. Whitaker.

These shields are:—1. A maunch, over all a bend for NORTON, impaling a bend engrailed between two saltires couped; and appear to be the arms of John Coigniers, *alias* Norton, who married Anne, daughter and sole heiress of William Radclyffe, of Rylstone. The licence to marry is dated 12 Jan. 1492. He died 10 Jan. 1556. She was living in 1541. 2. A falcon or query eagle displayed.

The living is now, with the Chapelry of Coniston, a rectory; the patrons are the Misses Graham.

On a brass tablet on the south wall of the chancel—

"This chancel is erected to the Glory of God and in memory of Richard Waddilove, Esqr., of Rylstone, who bequeathed the sum of one thousand pounds towards the rebuilding of this church. He died March 19th, 1850, aged 59."

There are inscriptions to—

Abraham Chamberlain, died 16 Oct. 1840, aged 57.

Elizabeth, daughter of Abraham and Sarah Chamberlain, died 8 Aug. 1824, aged 16.

Sarah Ffoster Butterton, daughter of Abraham and Sarah Chamberlain, and wife of the Rev. G. A. Butterton, D.D., died at Rhyl 23 Sept. 1866, aged 53.

Frances Mary Chamberlain, daughter of Abraham and Sarah Chamberlain, died 11 Jan. 1867, aged 51.

Sarah, widow of the above Abraham Chamberlain, died 17 July, 1869, aged 86.

Stephen Johnson, of Hetton, died Feb. 22, 1844, aged 68. Sarah, his wife, died 18 Jan. 1872, in her 91st year.

Sarah Yates, daughter of David and Susannah Yates, of Langer House, died 29 March, 1742.

There are stained glass windows in memory of the following persons :—

Sarah Chamberlain, died 17 July, 1869, aged 86.

Abraham Chamberlain, died 16 Oct. 1840, aged 57.

Erected by Ann Starkie, 6th Aug. 1870, to the memory of her parents, Abraham and Sarah Chamberlain, and of her sisters.

Sarah Ffoster Butterton, died 23 Sept. 1866, aged 53.

Frances Mary Chamberlain, died 11 Jan. 1867, aged 57.

John Thoroup, died 1 Aug. 1869, aged 80. Hannah, his wife, died 12 Jan. 1842, aged 37.

Anthony Hitching, died 13 March, 1831, aged 63. Mary, his wife, died 26 June, 1854, aged 87.

Henry Blake, J.P., died 17 Sept. 1869, aged 49.

William Blake, of Rylstone, died 26 Feb. 1844, aged 77.

William Blake, son of the above, died 25 Jan^y, 1824, aged 23.

William Maud, died 25 Sept. 1860, aged 79. Mary, his wife, died April 7, 1856, aged 81.

Thomas Wade, died 11 Oct. 1795, aged 82.

William Wade, died 28 Feb. 1831, aged 76.]

Here was an endowed chantry, certified by Archbishop Holgate to be of the foundation of Jeffray Proctor, and of the value of 4*l.* 4*s.** The Proctors were of Bordley, for which reason I suppose Our Lady's altar to have been in the north chantry.

The two chapels of Rilston and Coniston have no chaplains, or separate endowment; but are served in the primitive mode by the rectors of Burnsal. On this account they belong to a class unknown to the canon law. Both have cylindrical fonts of high antiquity, and therefore must always have had the Sacramentalia; but chapels, with these rights annexed, were always presentable, and served by chaplains, who took an oath of obedience to the rector, and were not removable at pleasure. Whereas mere chapels-of-ease, in the ancient sense, which were served by removable stipendiaries, or, as in the present instance, by the parish priests themselves, had not the rights of baptism and sepulture. These, therefore, constitute a new and curious link in the chain of ecclesiastical dependence.

CRAKEHOU,† qu. *CRAGEHOU,* or *The Craggy Hill,*

PRINCIPALLY belonged to Bolton Abbey, and was granted to the first Earl of Cumberland. I have seen a survey of this village made by order of the council of the third earl, from which it appears that every house and barn stood upon crocks, and was covered with thatch. Stone walls and slated roofs in Craven may generally be dated from the alienations of the Cliffords, and the origin of independent properties. The numerous dates over the doors of the houses of this rank in the reigns of James and Charles I. and Charles II. confirm this opinion.

Adjoining is

THREPLAND, *anciently* THERPOLE, *and at an intermediate period,* THERPOLELAND,

WHICH formerly paid to the Lords of Rilston 6*s.* 8*d.* for "overshot of beasts." This was a prescriptive payment for trespass, when the fields between township and township lay open.

Passing by Hetton ‡ and Bordley, which afford little worthy of observation, we turn the northern extremity of Linton parish, and descend once more into Wharfdale, at a point which, in that valley, has no superior, and no rival but in Bolton. This is the township of

---

[* In Archbishop Holgate's Survey the chantry of Our Lady, in the chapel of Rilleston, is said to be of the foundation of Jeffery Prockter, and of the yearly value of 4*l.* 0*s.* 4*d.* (Stevens' " Suppl. Mon. Ang." vol i. p. 71). In the " Valor. Eccl." vol. v. 144 : " Rilston cantar valet clare per ann., IIII*l.* XIX*s.*"]

[† CRACHOU.—In eadem villa sunt VI. car. terræ quæ tenentur de rege, et qualibet car. redd. per ann. ad finem prædictum IIII*d.* ob. q. ; unde summa est XXII*d.* ob.—Kirkby's " Inquest," 13 Edward I.

CRAKEHOWE.—Dominus Radulphus de Nevile tenet in capite de domino castri de Skypton XII car. terræ et faciunt feod. unius milit. quarum Prior de Marton tenet de ipso IIII*a* car. in Crakehowe ; Prior de Boulton tenet de eodem in eadem unum car. et di. ; Hæres de Rilleston tenet in eadem de eodem di. car. terræ.—" Knights' Fees," 31 Edward I.

Richard, Prior of Bolton, and the Prior of Marton, were lords of the manor of Crakehou in 9 Edw. II.—" Nomina Villarum."]

‡ Great part of this town belonged to the Nortons, and was granted, with the rest of their estates in Craven, to Francis Earl of Cumberland : but there is nothing interesting in the survey.

The Rev.ᵈ J. Griffith del.

S. Allen fecit.

Kilnsey Crag.

CONISTON *with* KILNSEY.*

WITH respect to the etymology of the latter word, if we adopt the spelling of Domesday, Chilesie, and derive the word from kÿle, *algor*, and ea, *aqua*, it will bring out a very elegant sense—the chilly stream : well suited to the cold and clear rivulet which passes through the village, or the still colder springs that burst from the foot of the rock beyond.

I have already noticed this astonishing mass of limestone, which stretches nearly half a mile along the valley, and, as a feature in a landscape, has greatly the advantage of Gordale itself.

By a perpendicular line, dropped from the highest point, its elevation was found to be 165 feet.

The annexed engraving will preclude the necessity of a verbal description.

But to return.

The spelling of this word a century after Domesday was Kulnesey ; which, if it be adopted, will compel us to derive it from kulne, *kilne*, and ea, *water* ; an etymology at least as probable as the other, though certainly less desirable.

Kilnsey, however acquired from the King's Thanes, who held it in the Conqueror's reign, soon became a member of the Skipton fee, and therefore of the parish of Burnsal. The early donations of lands here to the rising house of Fountains, and their confirmation by Alice de Romillè, may be seen in Dr. Burton's " Collection."

From the name of Chapel House it seems probable that the monks either had a small cell, or a grange, with a chapel annexed, in a picturesque and interesting situation, where an excellent house was built by the late John Tennant, Esq., whose ancestor, Jeffry Tennant, of Bordley, had purchased the estate from the Gresham family, the grantees of Fountains Abbey, in the 14th Elizabeth [1571–2].

It appears that the granges of the religious houses, when occupied by their owners, were exposed to the same oppressive claims of hospitality with the abbeys themselves. On this account the grange of Kilnsay, instead of yielding any profit to the monks of Fountains

---

[* " KILNESAY.—William, son of Dunkan, but nephew of the King of Scotland, and Adeliza di Rumeli, his wife, gave two carucates and a half in this town ; which Alexander, son of Geraldi, confirmed.

" Thurstinus de Arches gave all his land here lying between Kelnesay and Arnecliff. William, son of Fulco de Thresfeld, gave all his lands, from the head of the culture called Carlecroft, as specified in the boundaries, which were confirmed by Adam, son of William de Thresfeld.

" William de Forz, or de Fortibus, Earl of Albemarle, lord of the barony of Skipton, &c., confirmed the grant of this place to them, giving them free passage over his land ; and also gave them forty cart-loads of dead wood for their grange here : all these were confirmed by Baldwin de Betun, when Earl of Albemarle.

" Edolphus de Kylnesay, in A.D. 1174, gave half a carucate (*i.e.*, two oxgangs) of land here, which Simon, son of Edulf de Kylnsay, and all his brothers, confirmed ; which was likewise done by Alexander, son of Gerold, and by Aaliza de Rumellay, and by Gerard de Glanvers ; by John Malherbe and Matild, his wife, or fil. Ade, son of Suane ; by William de Novill, and Amabel his wife, another daughter of Adam, son of Suane ; by Roger de Munbegun ; and by Roger, son of Thomas de Appletrewyk ; by Simon de Monketon, son of Robert de Monketon, and by Aaliza de Rumelli, wife of G. (or T.) Pipard, daughter of the other Aaliza, ordering her corpse to be buried at Fountains.

" In A.D. 1156, 2 Henry II., Copside Redmet and Osbert, his son, gave one carucate of land here.

" All these were likewise confirmed by Pope Adrian IV., in A.D. 1156, in the first year of his Pontificate ; Alexander III., in A.D. 1162 ; Celestine III. ; by King Richard I., in A.D. 1198 ; by Pope Innocent III., in A.D. 1210 ; by Pope Alexander IV., in A.D. 1259 ; and by King Edward III., in A.D. 1366 ; and by King Richard II., in A.D. 1385.

" In A.D. 1292, 20 Edward I., the King granted them to have free warren here. There was a composition for the tithes of this place, made between the abbey of Fountains and the church of Brineshall, which Roger Archbishop of York confirmed."—Burt. " Mon." p. 174.]

3 P

in the reign of Edward III., on account of its situation in one of the great lines of march from the south of England to Scotland, and especially as forming the intermediate stage between Skipton and Middleham, was become a very inconvenient possession. To remedy so great an evil, the abbot and convent of Fountains were permitted to demise this part of their domains to a tenant by the following licence :—

"Coabbatti de Fontibus, Fr. Wil'mus Abbas Cistertiensis. Cum nuper accepimus quod vos aliquas terras apud Grangias vestras de Kilnesay, &c., super regiam viam habeatis jacentes, quæ per communem transitum magnatum & vulgi inter regna Anglie & Scocie ab annis pluribus inutiles extiterunt, in tantum quod sumptus quos apponitis valorem proficuorum quos inde præcipitis ad grave monasterii vestri dispendium plurimum excedunt : quas quidem terras si ad manus tenentium dimittere liceret, à sumptuum hujusmodi excessu, necnon & transeuntium rapinoso concursu, essent indempnes : Utilitati igitur Monasterii v'ri prospicere cupientes, definitione Capituli Gen. dimitti vobis concedimus.
"Factum apud Cistert. temp. Cap. Gen. A.D. 1336."*

Immediately before the battle of Blore Heath, I learn from Holinshed that the Earl of Salisbury marched from Middleham into Lancashire at the head of 4,000 men. Kilnsay, or Kettlewell, must have been his first stage.

I have already observed, that Kilnsey was the place to which the immense flocks of this abbey were driven from the surrounding hills for their annual sheep-shearing ; a scene of primitive festivity, to which the imagination delights on recurring.

The bleatings of the sheep, the echoes of the overhanging rocks, the picturesque habits of the monks, the uncouth dress, long beards, and cheerful countenances of the shepherds, the bustle of the morning, and the good cheer of the evening, would altogether form a picture and a concert to which nothing in modern appearances or living manners can be supposed to form any parallel. Yet even at present a large sheep-shearing is one of the most animating and cheerful scenes with which I am acquainted.

But with this operation, the last belonging to pastoral life, all poetical, and, indeed, all pleasing ideas on the subject terminate at once :—

"The wool-comber and the poet," says Dr. Johnson, "appear to me such discordant natures, that an attempt to bring them together is to couple the serpent with the fowl. When Dyer has done his utmost, the meanness naturally adhering, and the irreverence habitually annexed to trade and manufacture, sink him under insuperable oppression."†

At Kilnsey, too, as in the most accessible part of their domains, courts were kept for all the manors in Craven belonging to Fountains Abbey, excepting Litton and Longstrother, which last were holden at Litton. The walls of their court-house were remaining at Kilnsey in the 41st of Elizabeth [1598–9], when it was remembered that a pasture had been assigned for the horses of all the jurors and homagers in summer, and hay in winter, at the expense of the house. [Kilnsea Hall, formerly the residence of the Wade family, has been entirely dismantled, is now used for agricultural purposes, and is fast becoming a ruin. It appears to have been joined to the remains of a building of an earlier period, probably those of the court-house. Over one of the outer doors are the initials C. W., and the date 1648, and on the walls of one of the rooms are some good panels of ornamental plaster work, and a running pattern of leaves and flowers.]

* " Coucher Book " of Fountains.   † " Life of Dyer."

J.M.W Turner, R.A.P.P. del.

James Basire sculp.

South Transcept of Fountains Abbey Yorkshire

WEST CLOISTER of FOUNTAIN'S ABBEY.

J. Harris Sculp.t

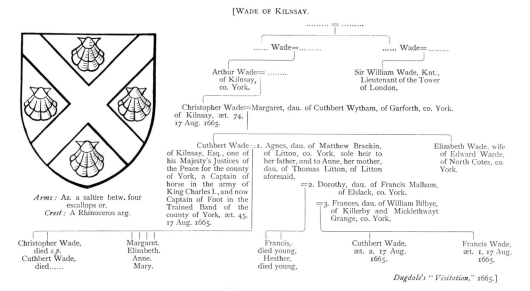

[WADE OF KILNSAY.

.... = ...

...... Wade=........   ...... Wade=........

Arthur Wade= ....   Sir William Wade, Knt.,
of Kilnsay,   Lieutenant of the Tower
co. York.   of London.

Christopher Wade=Margaret, dau. of Cuthbert Wytham, of Garforth, co. York.
of Kilnsay, æt. 74,
17 Aug. 1665.

Cuthbert Wade=1. Agnes, dau. of Matthew Brackin,   Elizabeth Wade, wife
of Kilnsay, Esq., one of | of Litton, co. York, sole heir to   of Edward Warde,
his Majesty's Justices of | her father, and to Anne, her mother,   of North Cotes, co.
the Peace for the county | dau. of Thomas Litton, of Litton   York.
of York, a Captain of | aforesaid.
horse in the army of
King Charles I., and now   =2. Dorothy, dau. of Francis Malham,
Captain of Foot in the   of Elslack, co. York.
Trained Band of the
county of York, æt. 45,   =3. Frances, dau. of William Bilbye,
17 Aug. 1665.   of Killerby and Micklethwayt
                                  Grange, co. York.

Arms : Az. a saltire betw. four
escallops or.
Crest : A Rhinoceros arg.

Christopher Wade,   Margaret.   Francis,-   Cuthbert Wade,   Francis Wade,
died *s.p.*   Elizabeth.   died young.   æt. 2, 17 Aug.   æt. 1, 17 Aug.
Cuthbert Wade,   Anne.   Hesther,   1665.   1665.
died......   Mary.   died young,

Dugdale's " Visitation," 1665.]

This, therefore, may be a proper place to introduce an account, abstracted from the original survey of the possessions of this great house in Craven, of the general grant of those possessions after the Dissolution, and of a great contest which took place in the last years of Queen Elizabeth between the representatives of the first grantee and George Earl of Cumberland, as lord of the Percy fee.

First, then, William Knight, archdeacon of Richmond, and others, by virtue of a commission, under the great seal of Henry VIII., return as follows :—

" Abbathia de Fontibus, Com. Ebor. Will'mus Abbas i'b'm.*

" Sit, Abbathiæ, cum gardinis, pomariis, clausis, parco, et mol. eid. annex. et in man. suis occupat. £XXVI. XIIIs. IVd. per annum."

Next follow many particulars unconnected with the subject of this work. Then

" CRAVEN. *

" Villa de Malham, £XVI. XVIIIs. Xd. Preston, XVIs. Xd. Holme Knottes, XLs. Arnefurth, £VIII. Wygelsworth, XXs. VIIId. West Side House, XLVIs. VIIId. Copmanhow, XLVIs. VIIId. Fernagill House, XLIIIs. IVd. Malwater House, LIIIs. IVd. Tranhous-hull, LIIIs. IVd. Midelsmore, XXs. Langerhouse, XLs. Grangia Nedderborlay cum p'tinen. £VIII. Knolbanks, XLs. Rugh Close, XXs. Cogilcote, LXVIs. VIIId. Vill de Ayrton, XXIVs. Newehouse, XXXs. Overborlay, £VI. VIs. Threshfield, LVIIIs. Xd. Linton, IXs. Brynsall, IIs. IVd. Conyston, XIIIIs. Hebden, VIIIs. Cogilhouse, XXVIs. VIIId. Kilnesay, £XIV. XVIIs. Id. Scarthcoite, XLIIs. Chappell House, £IV. IIIs. IVd. ob. Dernbroke, LXVIs. IXd. ob. Lytton, £VII. XIXs. Nether Hessylden, £VI. XIIIs. IVd. Ulcottes, IIIs. Overhessylden, £IV. XIIIs. IVd. Halton Gill, £XII. Foxope, £VIII. Greynfeld cote, LXs. Northcote, £IV. XIIIs. IVd. Arnecliffe cote, CIIIs. IVd. Horton, £IV. XVIs. IXd. Kettlewell, XXIs. Traynehouse, XXVIIs."
In all, £CLV. Xd.

These premises, independently of many scattered lands included in the rental, at Ayrton, Arneforth, Wigglesworth, Linton, Burnsal, Hebden, &c., contained in a ring fence, upon a very moderate computation, 100 square miles, or 64,000 acres. Much of this, however,

* From an office copy, dated 1680.

still lies, and more undoubtedly lay at that time, in common and sheep-walk ; but it is no exaggeration to say that some of the more fertile estates comprehended in this survey do, or would, bear an extended rent at present of fifty times the amount.

These extensive domains, and many more, together with the site of the abbey of Fountains itself, were granted, by letters patent, under the great seal of Henry VIII., dated October 1, A.R. 32, to Sir Richard Gresham, Knight, and his heirs for ever, subject to certain reserved rents payable to the crown, namely,

" Pro man'o de Malhome cum le Shepegate sup. moram XXXV*s*. III*d*. Newhouse, Roughclose, &c., X*s*. VIII*d*. Malwater House cum past. ovium, Trane House, &c. &c., Malham Water Terne, Tentis in Dernebroke, &c. &c., XLIIII*s*. Grenefeld Coshe, VI*s*. Harton Gill, XXIIII*s*. VI*d*. Foxhope, XVI*s*. Over and Nether Hesylden, XXII*s*. VIII*d*. Lytton, XV*s*. XI*d*. Stoderhall and Fountance Skayle, VI*s*. VIII*d*. Northcote, Conyston, and Kylnesey, LIX*s*. I*d*. Knolbanke, Langerhouse, and Cogylcote, Nether and Over Bordelay, XLIIII*s*."

I have seen the Compotus of Sir Richard Gresham for the 33rd of Henry VIII. [1541–2], from which it appears that the annual income of these estates had then been advanced very little above the former estimate, either because cheap purchases afford no excuse for racking of rents, or that, in the general discontent which prevailed in the north, on account of the Dissolution of religious houses, such a measure would have been impolitic and dangerous.

Nothing less than a perusal of the title-deeds to all the abbey-lands in Wharfdale, Littondale, and Longstrother, would enable me to pursue the successive alienations of these estates from the Greshams. The Licence of Alienation for the manor of Kilnsay bears date 6th Edward VI. ; but I do not find who was the purchaser.

The descents of the manor of Malham have, however, been traced, and I have before stated that Chapel House was sold to the Tennant family in the 14th of Elizabeth [1571–2] ; but one circumstance deserves to be remarked—namely, that to the dispersion of the abbey-lands in these valleys, in addition to the alienations of the Cliffords, which have been already mentioned, are owing those numerous independent properties, and, in general, that respectable condition of yeomanry which prevail throughout them ; a condition rapidly declining in England, and which nothing but the frugality and contented obscurity of this quiet people can preserve from the inroads of modern luxury, and the spirit of commercial gain.

In the 41st year of Queen Elizabeth [1598–9] an attempt was made, by the holders of these manors and estates, to resist the claim of George Earl of Cumberland to their attendance upon his court leet, as lord paramount of the Percy fee,* and to set up a new and independent fee, which they styled " The Liberty of St. Mary of Fountains." † Indeed, long before that time, and during the life of Henry, the second earl, several affrays had happened, in hunting, between his servants and those of the lords of Malham, Bordeley, &c., when the former hunted the deer upon those moors.

But to return.

* And with respect to Kilnsey, of the Clifford fee, to which it had belonged from the time of the Romillès.

† And which, for an obvious reason, in all the evidences relating to it in Skipton Castle, is called the " Pretended Liberty," as in truth it was.

In order to establish this claim, many aged persons were examined, who proved that courts had always been holden by the abbot and convent of Fountains for the manors in question; and that, so far as their memory extended, the tenants of the abbey had not been summoned to attend the leet by the Earls of Northumberland, or their agents.

Perhaps the monks were willing that this mark of ancient and rightful dependence upon their benefactors should be forgotten; and perhaps, too, the veneration in which they were held would prevent the stewards of the lords from being very frequent or importunate in their calls: but the whole dispute seems to have arisen from a confusion of ideas: the claimants of this exemption did not attend to the distinction between a court leet and court baron; the holding of which latter by the abbot and convent, as mesne lords, had alone been proved. But it is evident that, when the early Percies granted these extensive domains to the house of Fountains, they reserved the forest-rights, and with them what were called forensic services, and all others incident to the superior fee.

It is almost unnecessary to say that the claim was abandoned, as indeed it could not be sustained.

Opposite to Kilnsey is,

Coniston,* *anciently* Cunestone, *and originally* Conyȝrtun, *that is,* Kingston,†

Probably from no other relation to royalty than that of having been part of the demesnes of the Crown in the Saxon times.

This village, embosomed in beautiful ash-trees, has a chapel, served, like Rilston, by the rectors of Burnsal, and seated in a green and spacious yard. To one who has just escaped from populous towns, or dirty manufacturing villages, where the dead are heaped up in putrid masses to poison the living, such cemeteries as these, which are general in Wharfdale, will be reckoned among its beauties, no less than its accommodations.

The chapel itself may be considered, in part at least, as the oldest building now remaining in Craven. In general the oldest appearances about the churches in this deanery are of Henry I.'s time, which was certainly a great era of ecclesiastical architecture; but there is reason to suppose that many ‡ of the remote chapels existed prior to the foundation of the present parishes; some, perhaps, being converted at that time into churches, and rebuilt; while others were made dependent upon them.

At Coniston is a Norman doorway, with a plain double semicircular arch, together with the bases and capitals of two columns, now removed. These appearances are frequent in

---

[* An Inclosure Act was passed in 41st George III.]

[† Conyston in Kettelwelldale.—In eadem villa sunt VI car. terræ quæ tenentur de rege, et quælibet car. redd. per ann. ad finem prædictum IIIId. ob. q.: unde summa est, XXIId. ob.—Kirkby's "Inquest," 1284.

Conyngston—Willelmus de Hebden tenet in capite de domino dicti Castri (Skipton) VI car., unde, ut supra; quarum Abbas de Fontibus tenet in Conyngston VI bov.; Robertus Pychsall tenet de eodem in eadem, VI bov.; Willelmus de Ilketon tenet de eodem in eadem, II bov.; et IIII car. et II bov. sunt in manu sua propria. *Summa* VI car. terræ.—" Knights' Fees," 31 Edw. I.

Willelmus de Helbeden (or Hebden) was lord of the manor of Conigeston in Cotelwadale, in the 9th Edw. II.— " Nomina Villarum."]

‡ This opinion is countenanced by the following passage of a sensible antiquary—"There was anciently a multiplicity of chapels in this isle, which generally in all other places, as well as here, were the *originals* of *parish churches.*"—Chaloner's " Description of the Isle of Man," subjoined to King's " Vale Royal," 1656.

Craven; but between the nave and north aisle of this chapel are two semicircular arches, supported upon square cippi, each of the capitals of which is a simple abacus, and of the bases a plinth.   The oldest part of the nave at St. Albans is precisely in this style; but I know of few later specimens; and therefore refer these appearances, with little hesitation, to a period before the Conquest.*

[The chapel at Coniston, which is dedicated to St. Mary, until 1846 was in a thoroughly debased state, and the original Norman windows had been removed, and plain pointed windows inserted; at the west end was a small wooden bell-turret.   It does not appear that there ever was a chancel.

In 1846 Messrs. Sharpe and Paley of Lancaster, architects, were employed to restore the chapel, which they did in good Norman style.   The original arcade in the north wall, consisting of one square pier and two circular arches, and one octagonal pier with two pointed arches, the font, and a curious and rude double triangular window, now in the vestry, and perhaps the arch of the south doorway, are the only portions of the early building.   In the rebuilding, a chancel and porch have been added.

There are two bells, and an old oak alms-box.

The east windows are filled with stained glass by Winston, one to the memory of " a mother and ancestors here interred," given by J. R. Tennant, Esq. of Kildwick Hall, 1853; another to the memory of three infant children of the Rev. William Bury, 1853.

On a brass plate fixed to a pew—

Adjacent is interred the Body of
Mr. Thomas Wigglesworth of Con-
nistone who departed this life the
24th day of August in the 51st
year of his age and in
the year 1741.
Mourn not for me but silent keep
I am not dead but fallen asleep
Till the Archangel warning give
Then shall I rise Revive and live.

In the churchyard a tomb to the memory of the Rev. William Bury of Chapel House, and Rector of Burnsall, who died on the 10th February, 1875.

In the church, " A memorial of the Charitable Benefactions"—

Henry Motley left by will to the poor Persons of Conistone and Kilnsey, on St. Thomas Day, annually, £2 19s. 6d.

Left by will to be p^d out of Mr. Dawson's Estate in Conistone to the Poor as above annually, £9 5s. 0d.

The Registers commence in 1571, they are in Rolls until 1772.]

The botanist, as well as the man of taste, will be repaid for the trouble of visiting two rocky gullies in this township, Dib and Gurling Trough, both probably words of Danish origin, the first from DYB, deep; the second from GROLLEN, to murmur, a metathesis very common, as in *girn* and *grin*.   This may be added to the many names of northern torrents which are expressive of their noise and impetuosity.   But perhaps my version of the word is too gentle for the sense or the application; for Gurling Trough, according to the season, either produces no sound, or more than a murmur.   It is best expressed by the Latin *strepere.*

The origin of all property in the parish of Burnsal, excepting Rillston and its dependencies, may be traced to Alice de Romillè; and, amongst her donations, this lady

---

* They were in fact copied from the purest style of the Roman architects, who never turned arches upon columns. Some beautiful and perfectly correct engravings of this style have been given by Sir Richard Hoare, in his edition of Giraldus, from specimens existing in South Wales.

granted the manor of Coniston to Uctred, son of Dolphin, founder of the Hebden family, as follows :—

"Aaliz de Romille omnibus præs. et fut. notum facio quod dedi et conc. Uctredo filio Dolphin omnes terras ejus in Conyngstun, cum. sac. soc. tol. tem. &c. et cum omnibus libertatibus et juribus quanto melius et liberius de me tenet per servitium quod pertinet ad VI car. feodi militis, quod est XIIII car."

This was confirmed by Alex. Fitz Gerin, in the only charter which I have ever met with to which he is a party ; for which reason alone I recite it :—

"Alexander. fil. G. omnibus X'ti fidelibus notum facio quod ego d. c. &c. Uctredo filio Dolphin omnes terras suas, &c. in Conyngstun per serv. quod pertinet ad VI car. feodi mil. quod est XIIII car."

In the next place, free warren in Coniston was granted to William de Hebden in the 9th of Edward II. [1315–16].

In this family it seems to have continued till the earlier part of Queen Elizabeth's reign, when it was probably sold off in parcels to the freeholders, who now consider themselves as joint-lords, by Tempest and Angevin, in the general dispersion of the estates and manors of the Hebdens.

With the parish of Burnsal I take leave of the Clifford, or Skipton, fee ; where XIIII carucates constituted a knight's fee. The remaining parishes of Linton, Kettlewell, and Arncliff, with the exception of Hebden, are within the Percy fee.

PARISH OF LINTON.*

THE modern parish of this name, almost insulated by the different members of Burnsal, which appear to have been separated from it, consists of the townships of Linton, Threshfield with Skire † (*i.e.* Scar) Thorns, Grassington, and Hebden. At the time of the Domesday Survey these townships were enumerated as follows:—

TERRA REGIS.‡

IN CRAVE.   ⓜ In Ghersintone Gamebar . III . car ad gld

ⓜ In Freschefelt . Gamelbar IIII . car ad gld.

TERRA GISLEBERTI TISON.

IN CRAVE.

ⓜ In Ghersintone . In Lipton . In Freschefelt

TERRA OSBERNI DE ARCHES.

. ⓜ/7 . B In *HEBEDENE* . 7 Torp hb Dringel . IIII . car træ

7 II . boū ad gld.§

After this general statement I will begin with the township of Linton, which, according to the Coucher Book of Fountains, was of the Percy Fee, ‖ and reckoned twelve carucates to a knight's fee. But I know not by what means it was acquired by that family from the first Norman grantee, or when and how it was alienated to the mesne lords who appear below.

Small, however, as a manor consisting of two carucates only must have been, it was

---

[* The area, according to the Ordnance Survey, is 13,224 a. 2 r. 20 p. In 1871 the Census return showed a population of 1,557, living in 378 houses. An Inclosure Act was passed in the 30th George III.]

† This word is pure Danish, " Skier," *scopulus.*

[‡ Land of the king. In Craven. Manor.—In Ghersintone (Grassington) Gamelbar had three carucates to be taxed. Manor.—In Freschefelt (Threshfield) Gamelbar had four carucates to be taxed.

Land of Gislebert Tison. In Craven. Manors.—Gamelbar had in Ghersintone (Grassington) three carucates ; in Lipton (Linton) two carucates ; in Freschefelt (Threshfield) two carucates.

Land of Osbern de Arches. Manor and Berewick.—In Hebedene and Torp (Hebden and Thorp) Dringel had four carucates and two oxgangs to be taxed.]

§ I have endeavoured under Gisburne to account for the very inaccurate spelling of Domesday, of which in this short extract we have two instances, Freshfelt and Lipton—the latter probably occasioned by mistaking the old capital ᚠ for P.

[‖ Ric. and Wm. de Percy were found to have been possessed of the manors of Linton, Langstroche, Setell.—Inq. *post mortem*, 43 Henry III. (1258-9).]

subdivided into two portions from the earliest period of which, after Domesday, we have any account.

The first of these belonged to the Draycotes, then to the Grays of Rotherfield, then to the Earls of Westmoreland, together with the patronage of one mediety of the church ; the second to the Alemans, Le Grasses, Tempests, and Mallories, with the advowson of the other mediety. Of the Draycotes I know nothing more than that they presented twice in the latter end of the thirteenth century ; after which the Grays,* who certainly were lords of this moiety, held it till the extinction of the family in an heir general, when it was transferred to the Neviles, Earls of Westmoreland, who held it till the attainder of the last earl in 1569, on which it was forfeited to the Crown.†

The other moiety may be distinctly traced from about the year 1180, as follows—

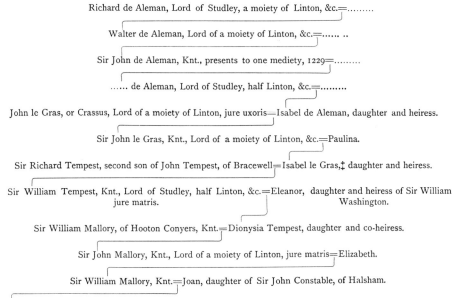

Richard de Aleman, Lord of Studley, a moiety of Linton, &c.=.........

Walter de Aleman, Lord of a moiety of Linton, &c.=...... ..

Sir John de Aleman, Knt., presents to one mediety, 1229=.........

...... de Aleman, Lord of Studley, half Linton, &c.=.........

John le Gras, or Crassus, Lord of a moiety of Linton, jure uxoris—Isabel de Aleman, daughter and heiress.

Sir John le Gras, Knt., Lord of a moiety of Linton, &c.=Paulina.

Sir Richard Tempest, second son of John Tempest, of Bracewell=Isabel le Gras,‡ daughter and heiress.

Sir William Tempest, Knt., Lord of Studley, half Linton, &c.=Eleanor, daughter and heiress of Sir William
jure matris.   Washington.

Sir William Mallory, of Hooton Conyers, Knt.=Dionysia Tempest, daughter and co-heiress.

Sir John Mallory, Knt., Lord of a moiety of Linton, jure matris=Elizabeth.

Sir William Mallory, Knt.=Joan, daughter of Sir John Constable, of Halsham.

Sir William Mallory, Knt., Lord of Studley, a moiety of Linton, &c., temp. Reg. Eliz. and patron of a mediety of the church of Linton. Sir John Mallory, his grandfather, was the last of his family who presented to the church—viz., in ˙540; and in 1570 I find that right exercised by the assigns of Richard Norton, of Rilston, Esq. Only three years before the forfeiture it had been exchanged, together with their portion of the manor, by the Mallories with the Nortons. Hence it came to pass, that in consequence of Norton's unfortunate engagement with the Earls of Northumberland and Westmoreland, this moiety of the manor, like the former, became forfeited to the Crown, and both were granted out again, along with the other estates of the Nortons, to Francis Earl of Cumberland, in consequence of which the whole manor is now vested in the Duke of Devonshire.

[Mallory of Studley bore for arms : Or a lion ramp. double queued gu. gorged with a ducal coronet arg. ; quartering (2) az. a maunch erm. for *Conyers* of Hoton Conyers ; (3) sa. an eagle disp. or for *Nunwick ;* (4) arg. a bend engr. between six martlets sa. *Tempest* of Studley ; (5) az. two bars and in chief three mullets pierced arg. for *Washington; Crest,* on a torce or and gu. a horse's head couped gu.—Visitation, 1584.]

* Though I do not find it enumerated among the manors of these great families, yet, as they continue to nominate to the mediety of the living till that time, I have no doubt of the fact, and am persuaded that they acquired it at the same time with Kettlewell. See Kettlewell.

† Vid. Dugdale's "Baronage," under "Gray of Rotherfield."

‡ The following passage in Dodsworth's MSS., vol. i. p. 23, compared with the actual descent of the manor and

In the Survey of Norton's Lands, in 1603, the whole manor, both portions being then vested by forfeiture in the Crown, was included under that title.

NORTON'S LANDS.

	A.	R.	P.	Old Rents. £ s. d.	Clear Value. £ s. d.	Fee Simple at 15 years' purchase. £ s. d.
Lintone.	579	2	10	12 15 1	98 8 9	1667 17 6

The ancient customs of the manor were, that the tenant paid, every tenth year, a year's rent by way of gressome, and, at the death of every tenant in possession, the best living or dead chattel of the deceased was taken as a heriot. During the time in which this manor was vested in the Crown these customs were gradually falling into disuse, on which account the tenants, in 1592, petitioned the Lord Treasurer Burleigh for a confirmation, when he commanded the auditors to make a rate of what each tenant ought to answer for, "and despatch the poor men away." But whether the rate was ever made, or the confirmation granted, I do not know.

At this time the town of Linton consisted of nineteen tenements, and was estimated at forty oxgangs; of which the glebe of the two rectories, one consisting of fifteen acres, and the other of eleven, was evidently the twentieth part, or only half the general endowment of the Craven churches.

A little meadow ground was inclosed, but the greater part lay in common, as well as the arable land.

The common pasture, measuring 240 acres, was stinted to 160 beasts' gaits, or four to every oxgang.

No account of wood at Linton was taken in this survey, excepting that the depredations are estimated at 2l. 16s. 10d. A proof that the township, which from its situation is naturally unfavourable to the growth of trees, was not much better clothed two centuries ago than at present.

The several tenements in Linton were sold off by Francis Earl of Cumberland, Henry Lord Clifford, his son, and the Earl and Countess of Cork. The first of these alienations bears date in 1608,* the last in 1651. A single estate is still the property of the Duke of Devonshire, who is also proprietor of the manor; for in all the conveyances of these lands the purchasers were discharged of heriots and boons, but suit of court and mill, free warren

---

advowson through this Isabel, induces me to believe not only that she had a sister who, though married, died *s. p.*, but that she herself had a former husband, who died childless also :—"17 Edw. III. Between Sir Thomas de Burn, knight, and Isabel his wife, plaintiffs : and William de la Pole, knight, and Katharine his wife, defendants ; of the manors of Stodelay and Linton, in Craven, &c. and of the advowson of a moiety of the church of the said manor of Linton, whereby the said Sir William and Katharine remised whatever right they had in said manors, &c. for the lives of the said Sir William and Katharine to the said Sir Thomas and Isabel, and to the heirs of the said Isabel for ever."

[LINTON.—In eadem villa sunt IIII car. terræ quas Johannes de Treycotes (Draycotes) et uxor sua tenent de Roberto le Grey, et idem Robertus de hæredibus de Percy, et iidem hæredes de rege in capite ; et reḍḍ. ad finem prædictum IIs.— Kirkby's " Inquest."

In the 9th Edward II. Johannes le Graas was Lord of the Manor of Linton.—" Nomina Villarum."

In the 22 Henry VI. (1443-4), William Tempest was found to have held the manor of Lynton in Craven.—Inq. *p. m.*]

* I think the old occupiers generally purchased their respective farms. Among these original purchasers appear the names of " Funtance " (Fountain), Deane, and Hewitt, whose ancestors in the condition of tenants may be traced by the light of old rentals up to the reign of Henry VIII.

and chase, with all the royalties and mines of copper, lead, coal, &c., were specially reserved to the lord.*

Out of the grant of the manor the two advowsons must have been excepted, as they have been presented to by the Crown from the time of the forfeiture to the present day.

The only testamentary burial which I have met with in this church is that of Wilkin Radcliff of Threshfield, A.D. 1450.

RECTORES UNIUS MEDIETATIS DE LINTON.

Temp. Inst.		Rectores unius Medietatis.	Patroni.	Vacat.
3 kal. Dec.	1279.	Dns. *Rob. de Swinlington*, Diaconus.	*Joh. de Draycotes* et *Isabella* Uxor.	
16 kal. Apr.	1289.	Dns. *Hugo de Symundeston.*	Dns. *Joh. de Draycote.*	
3 id. Dec.	1310.	Dns. *Nic. de Moreby*, Cl.	Dns. *Joh. De Gray*, mil.	per resig.
6 Maii,	1353.	Mr. *Ric.* (vel. *Rald.*) *Blaykeston*, Cap.	Idem.	per mort.
24 Oct.	1358.	Dns. *Joh. de Brikenhall*, Cap.	Idem.	per resig.
5 Aug.	1361.	Dns. *Rog. de Dalton*, Cl.	D'na *Amicia de Tanfeld.*	per resig.
24 Dec.	1380.	Dns. *Joh. Gamelyn*, Presb.	{ Dns. *Rob. Gray*, mil. { Dns. *de Rotherfeld.*	
11 Oct.	1409.	Dns. *Joh. Coke*, Presb.	*Alicia* D'na *Deincourt.*	per mort.
27 Julii,	1438.	Dns. *Rad. Hewyke*, Cl.	Dns. *Rad.* co. *Westmoreland.*	per resig. pro Eccl. de Slingsby.
27 Junii,	1457.	Dns. *Ric. Knott*, Presb.	Idem.	per resig.
17 Dec.	1462.	Dns. *Joh. Toller*, Presb.	Idem.	per mort.
19 Sept.	1483.	Dns. *Hen. Walton*, Cl.	*Franc.* Dns. *Lovell.*	per privat.
29 Ap.	1486.	Mr. *Rob. Este*, in Decr. Baccalaureus, ob. 1493.	} *Rad.* com. *Westmoreland.*	
		Dns. *Joh. Burgh.*		per mort.
4 Sept.	1508.	Dns. *Joh. Procter.*	*Tho.* Dns. *Darcy.*	per mort.
7 Maii,	1536.	Dns. *Tho. Stephenson*, Cap.	Assign. *Rad.* co. *Westmoreland.*	
		Dns. *Nic. Paver.*	Iidem.	per mort.
2 Sept.	1551.	Dns. *Hen. Dayne*, Cl.	Iidem.	per mort.
10 Jan.	1596.	*Gualt. Currer*, Cl. A.M.	*Elizabetha* Regina.	per mort.
1 Mart.	1602.	*Ric. Burton*, Cl. A.M. ob. 1615.	Eadem.	
25 Mart.	1615.	*Tho. Topham*, Cl. A.M. ob. 1651.	*Jac.* Rex.	per resig.
		Matthew Hewitt,† Cl. A.M. ob. 1674.	Idem.	per mort.
20 Maii,	1674.	*John Tennant*, Cl. A.M. ob. 1715.	*Car. II.*	per mort.
5 April,	1716.	*Thomas Gale*, ob. 1750.	*Geo. I.*	per mort.
		Tobias Croft, A.M. ob. 1767.	*Geo. II.*	per mort.
14 Dec.	1765.	*Thomas Welch*, A.M. ob. 1805.	*Geo. III.*	per mort.
18 Feb.	1806.	*Edward Unwin*, 1806.	Idem.	
		Charles Wray Haddlesey (non-resident).	Idem.	per mort.
19 June,	1833.	*Henry Crofts.*	*William IV.*	per mort.
20 July,	1855.	*Alexander Dawson Nowell.*		per mort.

[On the death of the Rev. Alexander Nowell, M.A., the two medieties of Linton were consolidated and made into one rectory by an Order of Council, 4th July, 1866.]

| | 1866. | *John Walker.* | *The Lord Chancellor.* | |

---

* Linton Inq. 16th Car. II. [1664–5]. Bolton MSS. [There was a grange here belonging to the priory of Old Malton.—Lawton's "Collections," p. 262.]

[† He founded the grammar-school in the parish of Linton, at Threshfield.]

Rectores alt. Medietatis de Linton.

Temp. Inst.	Rectores.	Patroni.	Vacat.
7 kal. Jan. 1229.	Dns. *Walter de Hedon.*	*Joh. le Aleman.*	
6 kal. Mar. 1251.	Dns. *Joh. le Gras*, Cl.	*Joh. le Gras.*	
5 kal. Sept. 1254.	Dns. *Ric. de la Turri*, Presb.	Dns. *Walter de Gray*, mil.	
... Nov. 1268.	Dns. *Joh. de Gray*, Cl.	{ *Rob. de Gray*, fil. et her. *Walteri*, militis.* }	} per resig.
16 kal. Jan. 1295.	Dns. *Wm. de Caumpeden*, Aco.	Idem *Rob.*	
14 kal. Oct. 1310.	Dns. *Symon de Graas*, Acoly.	Dns. *Joh. le Gras*, mil.	per resig.
3 id. Dec. 1310.	Dns. *Nic de Morby*, Cl.	Idem.	
5 id. Maii, 1316.	Dns. *Wil. de Gras*, Cl.	Idem.	per mort.
8 kal. Nov. 1337.	Dns. *Joh. de Skypton*, Cl.	Idem.	
	Dns. *Joh de Gillings.*		{ per resig. pro vic. de Alverton.
29 Jan. 1382.	Dns. *Joh. de Hayton*, Cap.	{ D'na *Isabella*, quondam ux. *Ric'i Tempest*, mil.	
	Dns. *Henric. Pollys.*		per mort.
30 Oct. 1409.	Dns. *Joh. Dene*, Cap.	Dns. *Wil. Tempest*, mil.	
	Dns. *Joh. Sherburne.*	Idem.	{ pro res. pro cant. mon. de Rypon.
3 Aug. 1436.	Mr. *Rob. Pyke*, Cap.	Idem.	per resig.
7 Mart. 1436.	Dns. *Tho. Gednay*, Cl.	Idem.	
13 Dec. 1438.	Dns. *Joh. Ingleby*, Cap.	Idem.	{ per resig. pro vic. de Beverley.
2 Feb. 1453.	Mr. *Wm. Lowe*, in Decr. Ba.	*Joh. Doreworth*, Arm.	per resig.
27 Apr. 1468.	Dns. *Petr. Toller*, Cap.	*W. Mallory*, ar. et ux. ejus.	per mort.
20 Jun. 1492.	Dns. *Petr. Toller*, Presb.	Dns. *W. de Mallory*, mil.	
	Dns. *Joh. Torne.*	Idem.	per mort.
20 Maii, 1498.	Mr. *Tho. Bakehouse*, Pr.	Idem.	per mort.
23 Sept. 1521.	Mr. *Humph. Gascoigne*, A.B.	Dns. *Joh. Mallory*, mil.	per mort.
3 Maii, 1540.	Dns. *Wm. Cumberland*, Cap.	Idem.	per mort.
8 Dec. 1570.	*Anthony Proctor*, Diac.	Assign. *Ric. Norton*, arm.	per resig.
30 Aug. 1607.	*Tho. Squire*, Cl. A.M.	*Jac.* Rex.	per resig.
11 Feb. 1607.	*Ric. Burton*,† Cl. A.M.	Idem.	per mort.
14 Apr. 1615.	*Henr. Hoyle*, Cl. A.M.	Idem.	
29 Aug. 1621.	*Joh. Akeroyd*, Cl. A.M. ob. 1653.	Idem.‡	per mort.
	Thomas Lancaster, ob. 1700.		per mort.
9 July, 1700.	*James Roberts*, ob. 1733.	*William III.* Rex.	per mort.
15 Jun. 1733.	*Benjamin Smith*, B.D. ob. 1776.	*Geo. II.* Rex.	per mort.
15 Jul. 1777.	{ *Christopher Naylor*, A.M. re-signed circ. 1780.	} *Geo. III.*	per resig.
8 Oct. 1780.	*John Preston*, A.M.	Idem.	per mort.
29 Sept. 1821.	*Edward Coulthurst.*		
26 June, 1850.	*John Walker.*		

[The two medieties were consolidated in May, 1866, by Order in Council, and since then the Rev. John Walker has been sole rector.]

---

　* From the names of the patrons I suspect these two incumbents to belong to the one mediety.

　† He was the only person that held both the medieties; for it is plain that this is the same person with the Ric. Burton mentioned in the former catalogue, as both the medieties were filled at the same time after his decease: for he died in March, 1615.

　‡ In Torre's MS. Akeroyd appears as rector of the one mediety; but in the list of West Riding Clergy, 4 Car., Nalson's MS. of Tenths and Subsidies, as of the other: and I think the latter account is right.

The following account of the Rev. Benjamin Smith, B.D., late rector of the other mediety of Linton, was communicated to the author by a respectable and learned friend, who was personally * acquainted with him :—

" Benjamin Smith was nephew by the half-blood, to Sir Isaac Newton. Robert Newton, of Colsterworth, father of that great man, died soon after the birth of his son ; Mrs. Newton then married the Rev. Benjamin Smith, rector of North Witham ; and one of her sons, by her second husband, was father to the subject of this narrative.

" He was born at or near Stamford, about the year 1700. When about eighteen years old his uncle sent for him, and at his house he chiefly resided till the death of Sir Isaac, in the year 1726.

" In many conversations with him on the subject, I could not learn much more than was known already with respect to Sir Isaac's habits, company, &c. ; but he generally confirmed what had been told by others.† He said that his uncle, when advanced in years, was rather corpulent, but not so much so as to diminish his activity ; that he was in general silent and reserved ; but when he gave his opinion on subjects of literature, it was peremptory and decisive. He confirmed the account that the Princess of Wales, afterwards Queen Caroline, when Sir Isaac, from his age and infirmities, could not wait upon her, frequently visited him : that Dr. Samuel Clarke, whom he called his chaplain, dined at his table very often ; and that of all his uncle's intimate friends he should say he (Sir Isaac) had the greatest regard for Dr. Clarke. Mr. Smith himself always mentioned Dr. Clarke's mild, accommodating manners and lively conversation, and particularly his condescending attentions to himself, with much respect and gratitude.

" He said that Dr. Bentley was, when in town, frequently at Sir Isaac's table, and that his behaviour was singularly haughty and inattentive to every one but Newton himself ; that he had heard his uncle mention Roger Cotes with much regret, and Dr. Halley with disapprobation, on account of his infidelity and licentious conduct.

" A little before his uncle's death, Mr. Smith was admitted Fellow Commoner at Pembroke Hall, Cambridge, and went to reside there for a short time.

" Sir Isaac left him about 500*l. per annum ;* consisting, so far as I understood him, of estates in Nottingham and Rutlandshire.

" Soon after the death of his great relative he left England, and resided at Paris about two years ; there he became acquainted with Mr. Philip Yorke, afterwards Earl of Hardwicke, and Lord Chancellor. He then went to Rome, where he stayed about three years more.

" About the year 1732 he returned to England, having greatly diminished his fortune, and sold whatever interest remained in his estates to Sir Robert Clifton, a Nottinghamshire baronet, for an annuity of 200*l. per annum* for their joint lives—a bargain which might have left him without bread to eat.

" As another resource to increase his scanty income, he took orders ; and having in his possession the MS. of Newton's Commentary on Daniel, he was advised by his friends to publish, and inscribe it to the Lord Chancellor, assured that the dedication of any work written by an author so illustrious would procure for him some good preferment in the Church.

" Soon after the publication, Lord King, the Chancellor, sent for him, and addressed him as follows : ' A mediety of the rectory of Linton, in Yorkshire, stated to me as worth £100 *per annum,* is now vacant : will you accept it ?' Mr. Smith remained silent some minutes. The Chancellor repeated exactly the same words in a stronger tone of voice. He now saw this was the only thing he should ever have offered, and that, from the look and tone of his patron, he had nothing farther to expect.

" He therefore accepted the living ; but always mentioned the interview and the offer as a cruel mockery, having fixed his own expectations upon £500 at least, and that in a situation more fitted to what he thought of his own taste and manners.

" In 1742,‡ compelled by necessity, he came to reside at Linton, and, after boarding in his own house three or four years, he took it into his own possession, and, fitting up a chamber for a study, with a bedroom adjoining, and a closet contiguous to it, for a man-servant, continued to live in it, with little variation, for the remainder of his life.

" He always kept an attendant, who could read to him Greek and Latin. When he could not sleep, he rang his bell ; his reader then arose, procured a light, and read to him two or three hours, till he found himself disposed to sleep. This was his custom five or six nights a week for many years.

" Circumstances now fell out, which drove him to the necessity of a long course of law to recover his annuity ; and during seven years of poverty and distress, he frequently applied to the Lord Chancellor, then Lord Hardwicke, for additional preferment ; but always met with a refusal. These repulses he never mentioned but with great asperity and indignation. §

* The Rev. William Sheepshanks, A.M., prebendary of Carlisle.

† Voltaire, in a small treatise on the character of Newton, ascribes his promotion in the Mint to an improper attachment of Lord Halifax to Mrs. Conduit. In order to investigate this point, I asked Mr. Smith what was the age of his cousin, Miss Smith, afterwards Mrs. Conduit. He answered, she was born in the same year with himself. He always declined to tell his age, but allowed me to conclude that he was born within two or three years of 1700 ; and, upon being told of Voltaire's calumny, said, that when his uncle was made Warden of the Mint by King William, Mrs. Conduit was not born ; and when he succeeded to the office of Master, she was only a child. S.

‡ In 1746 he took the degree of B.D. at Cambridge, under the statute " De his qui majores 24 annis, &c."

§ As Lord Hardwicke is known to have been an excellent patron, there is reason to believe that Mr. Smith over-stated the former intimacy with him, in his conversations on the subject with a person to whom he was desirous of magnifying his own importance.

"It seems probable that Lord Hardwicke disapproved of his conduct and character in early life. In no part of his life, so far as I know, had his conduct been so regular as that a patron who was acquainted with it could find any satisfaction in promoting him.

"His temper was very unamiable: he always considered his situation at Linton as a species of banishment. He despised his parishioners, and took no pains to conceal his contempt for them. Their habits, their general poverty, and, above all, their dialect, were the perpetual objects of his derision. He called them 'baptised brutes;' and they, in return, regarded him with dislike, and treated him with disrespect.*

"Among Mr. Smith's papers were several letters from Sir Isaac Newton. In these he addressed his nephew by the familiar name of Ben, and pressed him to choose a profession. There was some vulgar phraseology in them, which induced me to burn them, when I arranged his papers after his death."

He died in January, 1776, and was interred in the chancel of his own church. [His tombstone only bears his initials and the date, Jan. 1st, 1777.]

The church of Linton, dedicated to St. Michael, is a living in charge, of which the two medieties are valued in the King's Books at 16*l.* each; an estimate which, having been made when much more corn was grown in Craven than at present, has disappointed many successful candidates.

In the village are two parsonage-houses, nearly adjoining to each other.

The glebe has certainly been no more than one oxgang to each mediety; for, as the whole town consisted of forty oxgangs, and the gaits on the common pasture amounted to 160, each rector had an allotment of four. But the glebe belonging to the rector of the first mediety consists nearly of fifteen acres; and that of the second of eleven; which is to be accounted for by supposing that the first portionist stands in the place of the original incumbent of the benefice, and therefore that the berbage of the churchyard and the church-holme adjoining were permitted to remain with him. The tithes are equally divided.

The two incumbents discharge the duty alternately, week by week, and each performs it from his own stall, at the entrance of the choir; but the first portionist, for the reasons already assigned, has the right-hand stall. There is only one pulpit.

The church has been placed in a solitary situation, on the south bank of the Wharf, for the equal accommodation of the different townships which compose the parish. Nay, before the foundation of the parish of Burnsall, which is generally understood to have been taken out of it, the situation of Linton church was almost equally central. Of that fact, beside the tradition, there is very strong circumstantial evidence; for one-third of the corn-tithe in Burnsall and Thorpe is still paid to the rectors of Linton; a modus of 1*l.* 5*s.* out of Hartlington for corn and hay; of 6*s.* 8*d.* out of Appletrewick; of 13*s.* 4*d.* from the demesne of Rilston Hall; and 6*s.* 8*d.* for hay in Thorpe; besides that one house in Appletrewick is now in the parish of Linton, and pays Easter dues accordingly.†

---

* As a contrast to this, let the reader turn to my account of Father Tempest, under Bracewell.

† Baptisms at Linton.

	Baptisms	Burials.
1600.	18.	16.
1700.	24.	23.
1800.	32.	29.

An increase entirely confined to the town of Grassington, out of which, in 1700, were baptised 3, and buried 6; but in 1800, baptised 17, buried 12.

But to return.

The basis of the church of Linton has been a low Norman building, without tower or clerestory, with a nave, single choir, and north aisle only.

On the north side are two semicircular arches, supported by a short cylindrical column, and a demi-column of the same shape and proportion inserted in the square pier west of the choir.

The font is of the same shape and antiquity.

These are the remains of the primitive church.

In the reign of Henry VIII. this church, like most of its neighbours, underwent a thorough repair, and was greatly enlarged. The south aisle and clerestory of the nave were added; but no tower was ever built.

The choir is low, but spacious, with a flat roof, neatly moulded, and of the same date.

There are north and south chapels, with the original railing still entire.* [These screens are now removed, but a stone screen has been erected to enclose the north chapel and form a vestry.]

[The registers commence in 1562, but are defective to 1609.]

In the south wall of the nave are two arched recesses, and one in the north wall, for tombs; of which, however, there are no vestiges.

[The church, originally built *circa* 1150, consists of nave, with clerestory, and two aisles, with chancel arch and arches across aisles, a bell-turret of wood, for two bells, and a modern porch. The chancel has two bays of pointed arches on octagonal piers, all of decorated character. The chancel arch is plain and pointed, but upon Norman piers. In the north arcade the two eastern bays are Norman, *circa* 1150, with circular piers, one of which is built into the north respond of chancel arch. The two western arches are pointed, added when the church would seem to have been lengthened, in the fourteenth century, and part of the original nave taken into the chancel. The south arcade, built in the fourteenth century, has four arches, with three octagonal piers. The piers in the two arcades are not opposite to each other, which has a curious effect. The west window is of three lights, with flamboyant tracery. There is a sepulchral recess in the north wall, and another in the south, but no remains of any effigy or tomb.

In 1861 the church was restored by Mr. John Varley, of Skipton, architect; the porch was built, and all the roofs and seats renewed, the original Norman cylindrical font being retained.

In the south chancel aisle is a piscina, and during the alterations in 1861 an altar stone marked with the usual five crosses was discovered. This is now placed under the communion-table.

There is a bell, with the legend, "GLORIA IN ALTISSIMIS DEO, 1692."

There are some slabs in the floor, marked with initials and dates—**R. T. 1644**, and **A. L. 1665**.

A brass on the screen is inscribed—

Here lyeth the body of Mrs. Ann Hewitt
the wife of Mr. George Hewitt of Linton
buried the 11th of September 1678.

On another—

Here lyeth the body of Mrs. Elizabeth Redmayne of Linton
Who departed this life the tenth day of November in 1718 aged 77.

---

* Without the aid of the press, posterity, and no very late posterity, would be at a loss to know what parish churches once were. Alas, since the paragraph here referred to was written, all the lattice-work and railing of this church have been swept away by the rude hands of modern innovators. At the same time the handsome fluted oak roof of the choir has been covered by a ceiling of plaster!

On a brass plate under the east window of the south aisle is the following inscription :—

HERE LYETH THE BODIE OF
MR. THOMAS HAMMOND OF
THRESHFIELD HALL WHO DY
ED THE 24TH DAY OF MARCH
AN° DOMINI 1685. AND
WAS BURIED THE 27TH OF
THE SAID MARCH ANNO
DOMINI 1686.

.The above puzzling difference in the dates, would at first lead us to infer that his body remained unburied for a year and three days, when the time was really only three days. This is accounted for because in England, from the fourteenth century until the 1st Jan. 1752, the civil, ecclesiastical, and legal year commenced on the 25th of March. The Act for the reformation of the calendar is the 24th George II., c. 23.*

There are also inscriptions to—

Mr. William Fountaine, of Linton, who died the 2nd of May, 1733, in the 55th year of his age.

Richard Fountaine, Gent., died 3 Sept. 1779, æt. 78. With shield—a fess between three elephants' heads erased.

Anthony Fountaine, son of Richard Fountaine, Senr, of Linton, died 4th Jan. 1822, aged 72.

The Rev. George Fletcher, of Grassington, died 24th Aug. 1791, aged 50. Elizabeth, his wife, died Pridie Kalend Decembris (the 30th Nov^r), 1789, aged 40.

The Rev. Henry Crofts, for 20 years Rector of this Parish, died at Munich the 23^d April, 1857, aged 48 years.]

From Archbishop Holgate's " Surveys of Chantries" in this diocese, it appears that the ancestors of Sir John Tempest (the Hebdens, or their descendants in the female line) had left a yearly rent-charge of XIId. for the support of a lamp in the parish church of Linton. It seems most probable that the niches in the walls of the nave were intended for some persons of this family, the only ones of any great consideration who were ever interred there.

A church of this antiquity would no doubt have been rendered more interesting by cumbent statues of its ancient patrons, or rich brasses † of its incumbents; but, in the place

---

* See " The Chronology of History," by Sir Harris Nicolas, p. 41.

† One brass, however, though neither rich nor ancient, deserves to be copied, for the merits of the man whom it covers [It is now fixed against the vestry screen] :—

M. S.
Matthæi Hewitt, clerici,
Unius Medietatis hujus Parochiæ Rectoris,
Qui Novissimo suo Testamento
Ludū literariū instituit Atque ditavit,
Necnon Eleemosynā perpetuā annuati
Pauperibus distribuendam dedit ;
Atque etiam quatuor scholaribus Succedaneis
In collegio Divi Iohannis
Cantabrigiæ instituendis Exhibitiones
In perpetuum Solvendas Donavit.
Ejusdem ipse Collegii Quondam Alumnus
Ricūs Hewitt Nepos illius
Hunc lapidem
Amoris Ergo posuit
Ob. 4to die Maii,
A°. Salutis M DC LXXIIII.

In the churchyard, on a black marble slab, is the following inscription, which I am compelled to quote from memory,

of these durable and costly works of art, true taste will contemplate with equal pleasure a series of frail memorials inscribed to youth and innocence.

These are paper garlands, carried at the funerals of young unmarried women, inscribed with the name and age of the deceased, which are hung in this and most other churches of Wharfdale, upon the lattice-work of the choir. Short-lived as these records are, they have been substituted, as more durable, to the garlands of flowers which were anciently used on

and have forgotten the dates; though I well remember, and greatly esteemed, the subjects of it [The inscription, which is very erroneously given by Dr. Whitaker, is here corrected from the stone, which is now (1877) much broken]:--

> H. S. E.
> RICARDUS SHEEPSHANKS,
> Vici Linton Indigena,
> Et per Vitam perpetuus incola.
> Ibi obiit Decem. 22do 1779
> Etatis 69no.
> *Septem Filii Superstites*
> *In exiguum*
> *Tam patrii erga Se . . . as*
> *Quam Pietatis suo Tes . . . ium*
> H. M. P. C.
> *Ejusdem Jam Tumuli,*
> Ut et olim lecti particeps
> Hic Individum quoque condit
> SUSANNA Uxor Fidissima
> Fovendis, regendis, provehendis,
> Mater provida, sagax, strenua.
> *Harum memores virtutam*
> *Iidem filii,*
> *Pari in utrumque parentem observantiâ,*
> T. I. C.
> Obiit Jul 15to 1784
> Ætatis 63^{tio}.

[There are also in the churchyard the following :—

> Sacred
> to Memory in this
> Sepulchre lies interred the
> KS
> Body of RICHARD SHEEPSHAN
> late of Linton who departed
> this Life universally lamented
> the 11th Day of February 1780
> in the 72^{d} year of His Age
> leaving him a respectable
> Character among all his
> Neighbours Friends and
> Acquaintence (*sic*)
>
> A pale consumption gave the fatal blow
> The stroke was certain the effect was slow
> With wasting pain Death found me long opprest,
> Pity'd my sighs and kindly brought me rest.

> Here lieth
> The Remains of
> WILLIAM the son of
> JAMES SHEEPSHANKS
> of Linton who departed
> This Life June 15th 1808
> Aged 71 Years.

the same occasion, not only in the Middle Ages of Christianity, but among the Romans themselves :—

> "Sertisque sepulchrum
> Ornabit custos ad mea busta sedems." *

In the earlier times of Christianity this custom was indeed forbidden ; † but at a later period the specific practice of crowning the heads of virgins at their interment is mentioned by Cassalion : ‡ "Fuit quoque mos ad capita virginum apponendi florum coronas." These, too, were the "virgin crants" §—the maiden strewments allowed to Ophelia. ‖

From this circumstance, however, little can be inferred with respect to the transfusion of the rites of Paganism into those of the Christian Church.

Poets of every age and country have delighted to compare the frailty of human life to that of the flowers of the field ; the Christian Scriptures have not disdained to adopt the same idea ; and where is the wonder if, without traduction, without communication of any kind, successive religions should have been led to express their regret for those who are cut off in the *flower* of youth and beauty by emblems so natural and affecting ?

To enliven dry details of mere topography, the author has in this work uniformly mingled well-authenticated anecdotes of ancient manners in the district of which it treats : and in that view some new lights have been thrown on the habits of the religious houses

---

> In Memory
> of Anthony Fountaine
> Son of Richard Fountaine
> Senr of Linton who departed
> this Life Jany 4th 1822 aged
> 73 Years

> Shield of arms : a fess between three elephants' heads erased.
> S. M.
> RICHARDI FOUNTAINE Generofi
> Obiit Sep 5 1779.
> Æt. 78.]

* Propertius.

† As appears from a passage which I recommend at once to the classical and the Christian reader—to the one for its elegance, to the other for its solemnity : "Nec mortuos coronamus. Ego vero in hoc vos magis miror quemadmodum tribuatis aut sentienti facem, aut non sentienti coronam ; cum et beatus non egeat, et miser non gaudeat floribus. At enim nos exequias adornamus eadem tranquillitate quâ vivimus, nec adnectimus arescentem coronam, sed a Deo æternis floribus vividam sustinemus, quieti, modesti, Dei nostri liberalitate securi, spe futuræ felicitatis, fide præsentis ejus majestatis animamur.—Minucius Felix in Octavio, juxta Emend. Ouzelii—in Animadv. p. 211.

‡ Not to commit the paltry fraud of quoting from a book which I have never seen, I am bound to acknowledge that this passage is taken at second-hand from Burn's "Antiquities of the Common People," 1st edit. p. 57.

§ To confirm the reading of the old quarto editions, which had been displaced by Bishop Warburton, and was restored by Dr. Johnson, I must inform the reader that, in the Islandic, or old Danish, "krans" signifies a garland. The practice is alluded to in the "Bride's Burial :"—

> "A garland fresh and fair,
> Of lilies there was made,
> In sign of her virginitie,
> And on her coffin laid."
> Dr. Percy's "Old Songs," vol. iii. p. 150.

For the kindred practice of strewing graves with flowers, see Walton's "Life of Dr. Donne," ed. Zouch, p. 101, and "Cymbeline," act iv. sc. 5. There is something pathetically pleasing in this tribute of affection. It is still continued in the churches of North Wales ; and such, in some instances, is the fidelity of surviving grief, that I have seen it annually renewed on gravestones of forty years' standing.

‖ "Hamlet."

and of our old nobility. Another part of the subject yet remains in the antiquated modes of life which prevailed till within the last eighty years among the yeomanry of Wharfdale. These may be illustrated by the manners of Linton in particular, and may to some readers appear equally curious with either of the former.

I suspect them to be of high antiquity; for though the race of independent yeomanry, the happiest, and probably the most virtuous condition of life in the kingdom, arose in Wharfdale, partly from the dispersion of the estates of monasteries, and partly out of the vast alienations made by the Cliffords, yet, before either of those eras, the tenantry lived in so much plenty and security, the tenements descended so regularly from father to son, and the control exercised over them by their lords was of so mild a nature, that the transition from occupancy to property would not be marked by any violent change of manners and habits. But to be more particular.

There was a considerable quantity of hemp, and more anciently of line or flax, from which the place derives its name, grown within the township of Linton, which the inhabitants spun and prepared for themselves. Almost every woman could spin flax from the distaff, or rock, as it was called, and card and spin wool from the fleece. The women were principally dressed in their own homespun; they wore no ribbons, and the men no shoe-buckles. There were no poor's rates and no public-houses. In 1740 every house-keeper in the township, excepting one, kept a cow. The estates were small, and the number of little freeholders considerable in proportion; almost all of these farmed their own property, and lived upon the produce.

At this time tea was scarcely introduced; for I remember a very sensible man, who declared that when he first saw the schoolmaster drinking this beverage he could not conceive what refreshment he was taking.

Every landowner had a small flock of sheep, and fatted one or two hogs every winter. They all grew oats, which formed the principal article of their subsistence. The kiln, in which the grain was parched previously to its being ground, belonged to the township at large, and when in use was a sort of village coffee-house, where the politics of the place and the day were discussed.

Their bread, and most of their puddings, were made of oatmeal; and this, mixed with milk, or water when milk was scarce, supplied them with breakfast and supper. Each owner, too, grew his own barley, and manufactured his own malt. The large steeping-trough, which belonged to the village in general, remained within my recollection. Very little fresh meat was eaten excepting at their annual feasts, when cattle were slaughtered and sold by persons who never exercised the trade at any other time. Indeed, under such a system of manners there could scarcely be any tradesmen; every man exercised, however imperfectly, almost every trade for himself. The quantity of money in circulation must have been inconceivably small. One great advantage of these simple habits was, that superfluous wealth and abject poverty were equally excluded.

The number of openly profligate characters also bore a much smaller proportion to the general mass than at present.

But to return.

Almost everything was in common. There was a stone called the batting-stone, where the women of the place beat their linen with battledores after having rinsed it in the brook ; a necessary process, as it had been previously washed in a certain animal fluid,* a very disgusting substitute for soap and water. Their linen was rarely smoothed with heated irons.†

Their early hours rendered the consumption of candles, excepting in the depth of winter, very trifling, and those were merely rushes partly peeled and dipped in coarse fat.

Cheeses were almost universally made at home ; but as few kept a sufficient number of cows for this purpose, village partnerships were formed, and the milk of several farms thrown together in succession.

Few hired servants, male or female, were kept, but where this was done little distinction was kept up between the different members of the family ; they invariably ate and worked together, the only effectual method to insure diligence and prevent waste in dependants. The wages of labourers were very low, not exceeding twopence halfpenny a day with board. The facilities of learning were great. A grammar-school prepared many natives of the village for the University at no expense but of part of their time. The price of a day-school was two shillings per quarter, and an excellent writing-master attended for some weeks every year at the free school for sixpence a week per scholar. Young people of both sexes availed themselves of his instructions, and the time was considered as a sort of carnival.

But to proceed to the subject of amusements.

The Catholic religion was admirably calculated to lay hold on the imagination and senses of the vulgar. It was a religion of shows and festivities. Nor was its influence forgotten in Craven at the end of two centuries after the Reformation. The great holidays of the church, the feast of the patron saint, parochial perambulations, and religious epochs in private families, such as baptisms, thanksgivings after child-birth, marriages, and even burials, were all celebrated with carousings. To these may be added the masks, mummeries, and rude dramatic performances which evidently arose out of the mystery-plays anciently exhibited in parish churches by the ministers and clerks. And when we take into the account another class of feastings purely rustic, such as the sheep-shearing, hay-getting, and harvest-home, it cannot be denied that the life of a Craven peasant was sufficiently diversified and cheerful.

Many of these festivities, at least of the former kind, are well enumerated by an old poet in the dialect of the North of England :—

"At Ewle we wonten gambole, daunce, to carol and to sing,
To have gud spiced sewe and roste, and plum pies for a king ;
At Fastes Eve Pampuffes ; Gangtide Gates ‡ did alie Masses bring,

* From the word *lotium* 1 presume that this fluid was used for the same purpose by the lower order of people among the Romans.

† Heated irons for the purpose of giving a gloss to clean linen are rather a late invention. About the reign of Elizabeth and James I. large stones inscribed with texts of Scripture were used for that purpose. The late Sir Assheton Lever had one of these, and another was remaining in an old house in this neighbourhood when I was a boy.

‡ Gangtide Gates are perambulations. For "alie" I was once inclined to read "halie"—*i.e.*, holy ; but on such occasions, even when accompanied with some of the forms of religion, there is usually a greater abundance of ale than sanctity. The old reading, therefore, is not to be *solicited*.

At Paske begun oure Morris, and ere Pentecoste oure May,
Tho' Roben Hood, liell John, Frier Tucke and Marian deftly play,
And Lard and Ladie gang till Kirk with lads and lasses gay ;
Fra Masse and Een song sa gud cheere and glee on ery greene,
As, save oure wakes twixt Eames and Sibbes, like gam was never seene.
At Baptis day, with ale and cakes bout bonfires neighbors stood ;
At Martlemas wa turn'd a crabbe, thilke told of Roben Hood,
Till after long time Myrke when blest were windowes, dares, and lightes,
And pailes were fild, and harthes were swept, gainst Fairie elves and sprites ;
Rock* and Plow Monday gams sal gang with Saint feasts and Kirk sights."†

Many of these amusements, derived from the same source of Catholic superstition, were long after in use at Linton; while others, which were not connected with it, had a very pastoral and pleasing air.

The cows of the village being fed in a common pasture were placed under the care of a single herdsman, and driven morning and evening to the Green Loaning,‡ to be milked during the summer months.

Once every summer was "gud cheere and glee upon the greene;" vast syllabubs being mixed in pails at the place of milking; to which all the inhabitants contributed; and of which, if they thought proper, all partook. At the same time the young people danced upon the greensward, and the public intercourse of the two sexes promoted by these means was favourable to the morals of both :

"Quid nisi secretæ læserunt Phyllida sylvæ ?"

Among the seasons of periodical festivity was the rush-bearing, or the ceremony of conveying fresh rushes to strew the floor of the parish church. This method of covering floors was universal in houses while floors were of earth, but is now confined to places of worship. The bundles of the girls were adorned with wreaths of flowers, and the evening concluded with a dance.

Merry nights, as they were called, were often held in private houses, where young people were admitted without any particular invitation, and often danced in masks. The habits of the great always descend, and this was once a regal amusement. The maskers were very ludicrously dressed, and brought with them, as the *tessera* of admission, what was called a pass ;—*viz.*, a copy of verses, which they delivered in writing.

But the most popular of their amusements was the practice of acting old plays; continued, I have no doubt, from the old "Kirk Sights," and Clerk plays, though I can trace

---

* St. Rocke's day, as I learn from the Enchiridion of the church of Sarum, printed by Kerver in 1528, was August the 16th (equivalent to the 27th now), which, I suppose, was celebrated as a general harvest-home : " For," saith the Calendar of that work :

" The goodes of the erthe be gethered evermore
In August."

St. Rocke was also an *antiseptic* saint ; as it appears from a marginal note in a missal once belonging to Whitby Abbey, and now in my possession, that " whosoever will saye yˢ prayer following to God and St. Rock, shul not dye of yᵉ pestilence, by yᵉ grace of God." [St. Rock is shown in mediæval drawings as a pilgrim with a plague-spot on his thigh; an angel is talking to him and pointing to the spot. He is so represented upon the rood-screen at Stalham, in Norfolk, in Caxton's " Golden Legend," 1512, and in a primer of 1516.]

† Warner's "Albion's England," p. 121, ed. 1597.

‡ " Flowers of the Forest."

it in Craven no farther than 1606, when I find the following article in the accounts of Francis Earl of Cumberland :

"Item, paid to the yonge men of the town,* being his l'ps tenants and servants, to fit them for acting plays this Christmas, IIIIs."

In the interval of a century from this time it does not seem that they had much improved their stock of dramas; for, within the recollection of old persons with whom I have conversed, one of their favourite performances was " The Iron Age," by Heywood, a poet of the reign of James I., whose work, long since become scarce, and almost forgotten, had probably been handed down from father to son, through all that period. But, in every play, whether tragedy or comedy, the Vice constituted one of the *dramatis personæ*, and was armed, as of old, with a sword of lath, and habited in a loose parti-coloured dress, with a fur cap and fox's brush behind. In some parts of Craven these personages were called clowns, as in Shakespeare's time, and too often and too successfully attempted to excite a laugh by ribaldry and nonsense of their own; a practice which is very properly reprehended in " Hamlet."

In the " Destruction of Troy " this personage easily united with Thersites ; but he was often found in situations where his appearance was very incongruous.† These rustic actors had neither stage nor scenes, but performed in a large room, what is called the " house " of an ordinary dwelling.

Sometimes they fabricated a kind of rude drama for themselves ; in which case, as it is not likely that the plot would be very skilfully developed, the performers entered one by one, and each uttered a short metrical prologue, which they very properly chose to call a " forespeech." For why should these honest Englishmen be indebted to the Grecian stage for the word " prologue," when they were certainly beholden to it for nothing else ?

In these fabrications, I believe, the subjects were frequently taken from printed plays ; but the texture was of very inferior workmanship. For this I must beg my reader to give me credit ; though, if all readers had the same relish for what, in the language of dulness, is called low, with Dr. Farmer and Mr. Wharton, I could excite more than a smile by their travestie of the " Merchant of Venice." An old inhabitant of this place, whom I well knew, had the reputation of a dramatic manufacturer, though he had, in reality, no talents beyond those of an actor. But his fame drew upon him an awkward application, which, as the stated price of these services was three half-crowns, he parried very dexterously by demanding half-a-guinea. Thus much for the chapter of Amusements.

The great ornament of this village is an hospital founded by Richard Fountaine, Esq., a native of the place, who, having acquired a large fortune in London, by will dated July 15, 1721, ordered an estate to be purchased, out of which 26l. *per annum* should be equally divided among six poor men or women of this parish, to be appointed by his executors, and their representatives for ever.

---

* Skipton. The earlier notices on this subject which I have introduced into the present edition most probably refer to Londesborough.

† As, *e.g.*, in " George Barnwell."

He also left the sum of twenty pounds to the minister or ministers of the parish of Linton, provided they constantly reside in the parish, and read prayers twice every week to the poor persons in the hospital.

He farther directed the building to be erected on his estate at Linton, and the expenses to be defrayed out of his personal effects.

This was accordingly undertaken, and finished within a few years after the founder's decease. Though rather heavy, and in Sir John Vanbrugh's style, it is a handsome building, of red moor stone, with a centre, two wings, and a lofty cupola in the middle. Beneath is a small, well-proportioned chapel, now neglected and in decay. On each side are comfortable apartments for the poor people, with little gardens behind. It is said to have cost 1,500*l.*

Craven does not want a due proportion of eleemosynary foundations : it would be well, however, if the funds allotted to their support were always administered aright. But such is human nature, that the appointment of active and honest trustees seems to be attended with difficulties almost insuperable. It implies no ordinary measure of virtue to unite unrewarded attention to the concerns of others, more especially of the ignorant and unprotected, with fidelity and honour. The two last of these qualities may indeed be secured, or at least their opposites may be avoided, by the appointment of men of rank ; and the name of a duke, a chancellor, or an archbishop, while it soothes the vanity of a founder, will always sound well in the recital of a foundation-deed. But this is nearly all ; for it is not in the nature of things that persons in these exalted stations, the two last of which are also situations of continual engagement, should take a frequent or active part in trusts so numerous and unimportant.

On the other hand, *attention* in trustees may easily be obtained by nominating persons of small property upon the spot, rendered keen and vigilant by habits of minute investigation into their own concerns. But what will be the probable object of that attention ? Their own accommodation and emolument.

In this view, the worst of all trustees are the founder's kin ; who, generally conceiving themselves to be robbed by the foundation itself, have few scruples to restrain them from robbing the trust in return, to reimburse their own families.

Neither, as it will sometimes happen, ought trustees of any rank to be situated at too great a distance ; as, in that case, the administration of the charity will generally be committed to some inferior retainer of the law ; who, if inaccessible to a pecuniary bribe, may not be entirely free from the poet's imputation (very unjustly applied to the magistracy of the kingdom),—

"Wild fowl or venison, and his errand speeds." *

After all, amidst so many difficulties, the most eligible persons for the discharge of these trusts are gentlemen resident in the neighbourhood ; men who, to some sense of honour, unite habits of business ; who will neither take profitable leases of hospital estates to themselves ; nor, by their negligence, permit others to do so ; who will neither employ

* Cowper.

without wages the almsmen and women under their charge, nor connive at such a conduct in their agents. These hints will be *vocal* to the *intelligent*. [In 1812 new trustees were appointed by the Court of Chancery. The income arises from the rents of 280 acres of land.] Adjoining to Linton is

THRESHFIELD* *with* SKIRETHORNS,

ONE of the ancient manors of the Nortons ; which was surveyed, in 1603, as follows :—

	A. R. P.	Old Rent. £ s. d.	Clear Value. £ s. d.	Fee Simple at 15 years' purchase. £ s. d.
Threshfield,	872 2 30	33 7 6	112 12 1	2,188 18 5

The ancient customs of the manor were, that at every change of the lord one year's rent was paid by way of fine, and at every change of tenant an arbitrary fine, as lord and tenant could agree. Heriots were paid as at Linton. The tenement always descended to the eldest son, or, failing male issue, to the eldest daughter of the deceased.

Here was a town ing, or meadow, an arable town-field, a common-pasture, and common right on the moors.

In Threshfield, including Skirethorns, there were forty-two tenements. The oxgang averaged nearly sixteen acres.

The first lords of this town who are recorded, bore, as in most instances, the name of the place. The descents which have been collected are these :

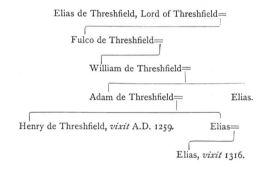

It is most probable that the estate passed into the Rilleston family by marriage with an heiress of the Threshfields. But of this I have no proof.

Here the Nortons had a park, noticed by Harrison in his " Description of Britain," where they kept their fallow-deer, of which, in 1603, the number was 120. The park measured eighty acres, and must have been filled with valuable wood, as it was estimated at no less than £400. While in the Crown, Sir Stephen Tempest was ranger. After it came into the possession of the Cliffords, it was still preserved.

* In 1634 I find a servant of Sir John Hotham † sent to kill deer in Threshfield Rise ‡ for his master; and, in 1639, £2 10*s.* were paid by the Earl of Cumberland's agents at Skipton for toils to catch the deer at Threshfield; and then it was, in all probability, that they were finally destroyed.

I have now done with the Norton lands, of which I have only to add, that they were alienated, partly in fee simple, and partly for long terms of years, by the two last Earls of Cumberland.

But, during the siege of Skipton Castle, I find that the old rents of these lands, payable to the Crown, were levied by Sir John Mallory,§ under the king's warrant, for the use of the garrison. After which the Parliament's Commissioners thought proper to demand them again. This produced the following petition:—

" To the Hon'ble Co'mittie for the Publicke Revene,
" The humble petition of us underwritten
" Sheweth,
" That your petitioners, being awed by ye power of Skipton garrison, paid their rents due for ye yeares 1643, 4, and 5, unto such officers as that garrison sent to collect them, which they durst not refuse, for feare of greater mischiefe.
" That y'r petic'ors suffered much by living under the power of that garrison, being plundered both by Scotch || and English of all sides, and paide double sessments a great space during the warre and two severall seeges of Skipton Castle; notwithstanding all which, your petic'ors are now threatened with a second leavy of those rents by order from this co'mitte, bearing date Feb. 8, 1650, [though they were paid, as aforesaid, by constraint, as will appear by an affidavit and acquittances hereunto annexed.]
" The pr'mises considered, y'r petic'ors humbly pray' y^t, in considerac'on of their great impoverishm't by the late warre, as also that though your petic'ors lived under the power of y^t garrison, yett they were alwaies well affected to the Parliam't, [this hono^ble comittee will be pleased to grant us particular order that may exempt us from the prejudice of the above said order of the 8th Feb^y· for the leavying of those rents, and y^r petic'ors shall ever pray].

" Signed by,	" EDW. RADCLIFFE,	GEO. HEWETT,	[JOHN SLINGER,	RICHARD LIGHTFOOT,
	" FRANCIS HEWETT,	THO. LUPTON,	RALPH PROCTER,	RICHARD COOK,
	from Threshfield.	JA. ATKINSON,	RALPH HARGRAVES,	THOMAS TOPHAM,
				from Linton."]

Much is not to be inferred from the latter clause of this petition with respect to the principles of the petitioners. It was now their interest to say that they had been always well affected to the Parliament, and therefore they chose to say so.

---

* From the family account-books.

† The following extract from the MS. memoirs of Sir Henry Slingsby, who suffered for his loyalty under the Usurpation, will prove the Earl of Cumberland's intimacy before the civil wars with the elder Hotham, as well as throw considerable light on the character of the latter:—
" I have often heard my Lord of Cumberland say, that he (Hotham) would be often talking to him many years before when we were happy in knowing nothing, and secure in believing never to find the effects of it here, that, if he had Hull, he would bring all Yorkshire into contribution. But it seems my lord of Newcastle knew how to work upon his distemper when he once found his pulse. But I rather think it was his son's journey, and disagreeing with my Lord Fairfax, that made him weary of being of one side, and more easily drawn to hearken to reason. He was one that was not easily drawn to believe as another doth, or hold an opinion for the author's sake, not out of judgment, but faction; for what he held was clearly his own, which made him but one half the Parliament's: he was mainly for the liberty of the subject and privilege of Parliament; but not at all for their new opinions in church government."

‡ Rise is properly a wood, from the Islandic hᵽuɼa. I take this opportunity of retracting my etymology of Crookrise, which I have now no doubt was so called, qu. the crooked or stunted wood. Chaucer used the word for a single bush:
" As white as is the blossome on the Rise."

§ See this warrant under Skipton [p. 413].

|| Perhaps by Leslie's army, in 1644, and Duke Hamilton's, in 1648.

3 S

The principal grantees of the Threshfield estate from the Cliffords seem to have been the Hammonds and Hewitts; of which latter family was Matthew Hewitt, Rector of the one mediety of Linton, who founded a grammar-school at Threshfield, endowing it with 20*l. per annum* for the master, and 10*l.* for the usher, and four exhibitions of 12*l.* each to scholars of St. John's College in Cambridge. But the great depreciation of money which has taken place in the last century proves the impolicy of such pensionary endowments; and the school has been so little distinguished, either for able masters or hopeful scholars, that it has not been unusual in St. John's College to apply to it the text, " Out of Galilee ariseth no prophet." In this opprobrium the author of the " History of Craven" must be content to partake. Yet a few exceptions might be mentioned. The late Bishop of Elphin, Dr. Dodgson, as well as the present learned and venerable master of St. John's College,* were among the number of Hewitt's exhibitioners; and, if delicacy would permit me to pay so public a tribute to private friendship, I could name a whole family of very superior attainments who owe their school education to this neglected seminary. But vigorous plants will thrive under every disadvantage of soil and exposure.

The propriety of this reserve is now in part removed by death.

William Sheepshanks was born in the village of Linton, on the 18th of March, 1740, of respectable parents. His father, who, having no trade or profession, lived upon and farmed his own estate, was a very sensible and intelligent man, so far superior to those among whom he lived, and so disinterested in the application of his talents, that he was highly popular and useful in his native village. His mother was a woman of very superior understanding.

He was educated at the grammar-school of the parish, and in 1761 was admitted of St. John's College, Cambridge.

His singular facility in the acquirement of philosophical knowledge quickly became so conspicuous in this situation, that, at a time when other undergraduates find sufficient employment in preparing for their own exercises and examinations, he had no less than six pupils.

At this time also he laid the foundation of a lasting friendship with two young men of great promise in the university, John Law and William Paley, both of Christ's College; the one afterwards Bishop of Elphin, the other wanting no addition, and above all titles. In St. John's he lived upon terms of almost equal intimacy with Mr. Arnald, the senior wrangler of his year, whose genius, always eccentric, after a short career of court ambition, sank in incurable lunacy. His academical exercises also connected him more or less with the late Lord Alvanley, the present Mr. Baron Graham, and the learned and pious Joseph Milner, afterwards of Hull; all of whom, as well as Law, took their first degrees at the same time with himself. Such a constellation of talent has scarcely been assembled in any single year from that time to the present.

In January, 1766, he took the degree of A.B.; and in 1767 was elected Fellow of

---

* Dr. William Craven, born at Gowthwaite Hall, in Netherdale.

his college, on the foundation of Mr. Platt. In 1769, he took the degree of A.M. In part of the years 1771 and 1772, he served the office of Moderator for the university with distinguished applause. During this period he numbered among his pupils several whom he lived to see advanced to high stations in their respective professions, particularly the present Bishop of Lincoln, and the Chief Justice of the King's Bench.

In 1773, he accepted from the university the rectory of Ovington in Norfolk; and, having married a highly respectable person, the object of his early attachment, settled at the village of Grassington, where he received into his house a limited number of pupils, among whom, in the years 1774 and 1775, was the writer of this article.

In the year 1777, he removed to Leeds; and in the same year, by the active friendship of Dr. John Law, then one of the Prebendaries of Carlisle, he was presented by that Chapter to the living of Sebergham in Cumberland.

In 1783 he was appointed to the valuable cure of St. John's Church, in Leeds.

In 1792 he was collated, by his former pupil Dr. Pretyman, Bishop of Lincoln, to a prebend in his cathedral, which, by the favour of the present Archbishop of York, he was enabled to exchange, in 1794 or 1795, for a much more valuable stall at Carlisle, vacated by the promotion of Dr. Paley to the Subdeanery of Lincoln. This was the last of his preferments, and probably the height of his wishes; for he was in his own nature very disinterested.

After having been afflicted for several years with calculous complaints, the scourges of indolent and literary men, he died at Leeds, July 26, 1810, and was interred in his own church.

In vigour and clearness of understanding Mr. Sheepshanks was excelled by few. His spirits were lively, and his conversation was inexhaustibly fertile in anecdote and reflection. His knowledge of common life, in all its modes, was that of an original and acute observer —his eyes were the most penetrating and expressive I ever beheld. In short, Nature had endowed him with faculties little, if at all, inferior to those of the two great men with whom he lived in habits of most intimate friendship. His conversation had much of the originality and humour which distinguished that of Dr. Paley; and, when he thought proper, it was equally profound and sagacious with that of Dr. Law. When he could be prevailed upon to write at all, he wrote with the clearness and force peculiar to *his School;* so that, if his industry had borne any proportion to his natural talents, and if these had been sedulously applied to elucidate and expand those branches of science in which he so much excelled, he would have wanted no other memorial. But a constitutional indolence robbed him of the fame which he might have attained; the privation, however, occasioned neither a struggle nor a pang; for his want of ambition was at least equal to his hatred of exertion; and, as far as could be gathered from a conversation in the highest degree open and undisguised, he was equally careless of living and of posthumous reputation. Had the same indifference extended to his surviving friends, this short account would not have been written.

NETHERSIDE HALL, THE SEAT OF THE REV. THOMAS WHITAKER NOWELL.

[A branch of the family of Radcliff was settled at Threshfield.]

Arms: Argent a bend
engrailed sable.

Anthony Radcliffe=
of Threshfield, in Craven,

Rafe Radcliffe=
of Threshfield,

"Was at the Assizes holden at the Castle of Yorke upon
Monday the third of August, in the 38th year of the
reigne of Queen Elizabeth, before John Clarcke and
Thomas Walmesley, then Justices of Assize, chosen
and nominated to be one of the High Constables in the
Wapentake of Staincliffe."

Charles Radcliffe=Dorothy, dau. of Mr. Spencer,
of Threshfield,   of Langtofte.
Clerk of the Peace in the West Riding, and Associate
before the Judges of Assize in the Northern Circuit.

Edward Radcliffe=Elizabeth,
of Threshfield.   dau. of Thos. Hesketh,
                  of Heslington, near
                  Yorke, Esq.

Francis=Elizabeth
Radcliffe dau. of Roger
had no   Nowell, of Read,
issue.   co. Lancaster, Esq.

Charles
Radcliffe,
Citizen of
London.

1. Anne Radcliffe, married Mr.
   Theophilus Braythwaite.
2. Mary Radcliffe, mar. to Major
   John Hughes, of Rilston,
   who did good service to his
   late sacred Ma'tye, and was
   slain in the wars.
3. Susan Radcliffe, married to
   Mr. Richard Baxter.

Jane Radcliffe,
dau. & heire.

From Harl. MS. 4,630, p. 481.

VIEW ON THE RIVER WHARFE, NETHERSIDE GLEN.

GRASSINGTON.*

WERE I to say that this word signifies the town of Grassy Ings,† almost every reader would acquiesce in the conjecture. But it has been variously written Garsington, Gersinton, or Girsington; and I have already shown the syllable "ing," in the composition of English local names, to be generally epenthetical. It is vulgarly pronounced Girston; which comes nearest to the truth. But the word is really Garston, the town of Garr or Garri, a personal Saxon name, from which Gargrave is also derived. The surname Gars is yet remaining in Craven.

Grassington is of the Percy fee; but the first mesne lords after the Conquest were the Plumptons. Of these the earliest on record was Nigel, who, from the known date of his grandson's death, must have been born about the year 1140. He had a brother Gilbert, who, in the 21st of Henry II. [1174–5] committed something like an Irish marriage with the heiress of Richard de Warelwast, and thereby incurred the displeasure of Ranulph de Glanville, Great Justiciary, who meant to have married her to a dependent of his own. Plumpton was, in consequence, indicted and convicted of a rape at Worcester; but at the very moment when the rope was fixed, and the executioner was drawing the culprit up to the gallows, Baldwin, Bishop of Worcester, running to the place, forbade the officers of justice, in the name of the Almighty, to proceed, and thus saved the criminal's life.§ An odd exertion of episcopal authority!

The grandson, either of Nigel or this Gilbert, was another Nigel, to whom R. de Stutevil granted leave to hunt in his forest of Knaresborough, reserving to himself *Cerfe et Bisse,*‖ *et Chevruil.* Nigel died 55 Henry III. [1250–1]. The roe was therefore extant on the borders of Craven at that time; and if so, probably in the forests of Craven itself. His son was Robert, who obtained a charter of free warren in Grassington, 9 Edward I. [1280–1] about which time I find there were many neifs in that town. A figure with yellow hair and in armour, marked with the letter R, and ascribed by the family to this person, was remaining in the windows of the chapel at Plumpton in 1613; but I suspect it to be of much later date. What I know further of him is, that he obtained licence to have a chapel in his manor-house of Nesfield, on condition of offering annually a pound of frankincense on the high altar of the parish church of Ilkley.

This Robert had William, who had another Robert, who being on board the king's fleet, 46 Edward III [1372–3], was licensed to return home, on account of bad health, with his esquire and two valets.

His son was another William, who suffered in the same cause with Archbishop Scroope, and was interred at Spofforth, with this epitaph :—

[* GERSINGTON.—In eadem villa sunt VI car. terræ ; de quibus Robertus de Plumton tenet V car. et di. de hæredibus de Percy, et iidem hæredes de rege in capite ; et Thomas Botte tenet di. car. de prædicto Roberto de Plumton, et idem Robertus de prædicto hæredibus de Percy.—Kirkby's " Inquest."

"Isabella quæ fuit uxor Roberti de Plumpton, et domina de Kyghley," were ladies of the manor of Gersington, *temp.* 9th Edward II.—" Nomina Villarum."

The township of Grassington contains 5,801*a.* 1*r.* 37*p.*]

† Still I hesitate about this etymology. Pasture grounds are called grassings, and Grassington may mean " The Town of Grassings." The character of the place is certainly favourable to this opinion.

§ This story is told by Roger Hoveden, Plumpton's countryman, in anno 21 Henry II. [1174–5].

‖ The Hind.

𝕸iles e𝔷am dudum 𝕻lompton 𝕲𝔦llim vocitatus,
𝕻raesulis atque nepos 𝕷e 𝕾croopi hic tumulatus.
𝕸ortis causa suae mihi causa fuit mo𝔷iendi,
𝕸ors capitis quippe nostri male praestat utrunque.
𝕬nno milleno quat' centum sit quoque quinto
𝕻entecostes me lu𝔵 crastina sumpsit ab o𝔷be.

Robert, son of this William, was killed in France, 9 Henry V. [1421–2], leaving a son, William, who, in the 27th of Henry VI. [1448–9], as saith the Chartulary, engaged and routed 300 men of the Cardinal of York, who were plundering the foresters of Knaresborough, on which occasion no less than 4,000 arrows were discharged. In the 39th of the same reign [1460–1] he was commissioned, along with Lord Clifford, to assemble as many men as possible, and fight the king's enemies. He died in 1480.

Sir Robert Plumpton, his son, seems to have been active in suppressing the Yorkshire insurrection, in which the fourth Earl of Northumberland lost his life at Cock Lodge; for to that event I suppose the following letter addressed to him by Henry VII. to refer :

"TRUSTIE AND WEL BELOVED, &c.

"Wher we understande by o'r squyer N. K. y'r true minde and faithful leegiance towards us, w'th y'r diligent acquittal for ye reducyng our people ther to o'r subjection and obediaunce, wee heartilee thanke yo' for ye same, assuring yo' y't by this y'r demeynng yo' have ministryd unto us cause as gaged to rememb'r yo' in anie thinge y't maie be for y'r p'ferment ; and as anie office in o'r gifte ther falles voide, wee shal reserve them unto suche tyme as wee maye bee informyd of suche men as maie be meet and able for ye same ; prayinge yo' y't if ther shal happen anie indisposition of o'r seid people, ye wyl, as ye have begon, endevor, from tyme to tyme, for ye spedie redressing therof

"Yeven under signett, at o'r man'r of Sheene, the xxx Oct." (no year).

This Sir Robert seems to have had two sons, William and Robert, the latter of whom lost the manor of Grassington ; for, after a long contest with three heirs female, one of whom was Margaret, wife of Sir John Rocliffe, Richard Fox, Bishop of Winchester, and others, chosen arbitrators between the parties, awarded the manor of Plumpton alone to Sir Robert, and eighteen other manors to the heirs general. Among these Grassington became the purparty of Margaret, wife of Rocliffe, whose daughter and heiress married Sir Ingram Clifford, younger son of the first Earl of Cumberland, and [Elizabeth] married to Henry Soothill, Esq.,* whose daughter Elizabeth, having married Sir William Drury, knight, sold her moiety to Henry second Earl of Cumberland.

Margaret and her sister were daughters of William, who appears to have been elder brother of Robert, the other party ; and the point at issue was, whether the manors in question were or were not entailed upon the male line.†

Lastly, Sir Ingram Clifford entailed ‡ the manors of Grassington and Steeton on the issue of his own body, remainder to Henry Earl of Cumberland, his brother, who, by will, dated May 8, 1569, devised the said remainder to George, afterwards the third earl, and his heirs.

This nobleman first mortgaged all the tenements in the township to the respective tenants, and afterwards sold the equity of redemption for the most part to the same persons. And this is the origin of all the titles to estates within Grassington.

[* Sir John Sothill, Knt. : "Visitation," 1585.]
† All these particulars are extracted from the Chartulary of Plumpton. Townley MSS. G. 24.
‡ It should have been only the moiety of Grassington.

The manor, however, was reserved, together with Grass Wood (the ancient Silva Gars of the Chartulary), the latter for the browse of deer,* to which I find, from the Skipton Papers, it continued to be applied in 1609.

I cannot discover from the Chartulary, or any other authority, at what time prædial slavery ceased in this manor. There were many neifs in the reign of Edward I. In 1579 it was wholly demised to tenants for life, each of whom paid a Gressom at the end of every five years.

Immediately before the alienation, two surveys of this manor were taken, from which I extract the following particulars.

The township then (A.D. 1603 and 1604) consisted of thirty-eight tenements. Many hemp-plots are mentioned; whence I conclude that plant to have been in general cultivation. The old crofts about the houses were called cagarths—that is, calf-garths † Cattle-gates were valued at 5s. each, and sheep-gates at 6d. Does not this prove the breed of cattle to have been large, and that of sheep small?

The number of oxgangs was sixty and a half, besides a pasture sold separately. The price of each oxgang, with three exceptions only, was 80l. The whole rental was 415l. 6s. 8d., of which twenty marks are deducted for grass-wood: and the other woodlands reserved for the browse of deer. The purchase-money for the whole township, with this single exception, amounted to 5,279l. 13s. 4d.

The rents appear to have been racked, as they are much above the average of the times.

The reservation of the manor was a fortunate circumstance. In 1638 the clear profit of the lord's portion to Francis Earl of Cumberland was 308l. 15s. 10d. In some years it may since have exceeded this in a fivefold proportion.

At what time lead-mines were first wrought in Craven I have no means of being informed. From a pig of that metal, discovered on Knaresborough Forest, the Romans appear to have carried on such works at no great distance; but they have left no vestiges of their industry in Wharfdale.‡ Neither is it probable that these treasures were disturbed during the uninquisitive era of the Saxons and Danes. But the Norman churches and chapels in this valley are uniformly covered with lead, which, for such humble foundations, would scarcely have been purchased at a dear rate, or conveyed from any great distance.

---

* As late as 1632 " Gressington P'ke, wherein is redd deer, in possession, was valued at x l."

† Ca, in the language of the Scottish ballads, is a calf :

"And sax poor cas stand in the sta."—*Border Minstrelsy*, vol. i. p. 100.

‡ The ancients were certainly unskilful miners. It has even been conjectured, from some appearances about their works in Derbyshire, and elsewhere, that they wrought only in open trench. But this is impossible, as not a hundredth part of the metals which they used could have been thus obtained. Besides, Pliny assures us, that the silver got in Spain was generally brought up *per puteos* (lib. xxxiii. 6). The same author mentions (ib.) a tunnel carried 1,500 paces into the side of a hill, and against the water, which they had no method of removing but casting it up with buckets. But the most extraordinary instance of their mismanagement is recorded in the attempt of Claudius to drain the Fucine Lake into the Garigliano, a distance of three miles. Here the workmen, instead of beginning in the bed of the river at the lowest point, and thus tapping the water as they proceeded, chose to work downward from the lake, which compelled them to raise the water by pumps " in verticem montis." The work was partly open trench, and partly tunnelling, " partim effosso, partim exciso," says Tacitus. In this undertaking, if the figures in Suetonius are right, that emperor employed 30,000 men for eleven years. Twenty English miners, by the help of gunpowder, which has given to the moderns a new empire over the mineral as well as animal world, would have accomplished it in a third part of the time. See Sueton. in Claudio, xxi., Tac. Ann. lib. xii., Plin. lib. xxxvi.—xv.

About the end of Edward I.'s reign we have seen that the canons of Bolton had lead-mines within their own estates. From the accounts of the Percy fee it appears that they were wrought in the upper parts of Wharfdale in the reign of Henry VII.

I can discover no vestiges of these works at Grassington before the reign of James I., when, from circumstances (one in particular, which I do not hold myself at liberty to disclose), I believe them to have been first undertaken, and principally, by miners from Derbyshire.

The first discoveries of this valuable metal consisted in great perpendicular trunks of ore called pipes, which sometimes appeared on the surface, and conducted the fortunate discoverer to sudden wealth without skill, and almost without effort.

When these were exhausted, the spirit of adventure, which they had excited, continued, as, indeed, it still continues, to the ruin of many families. For henceforward the veins of ore, irregular and capricious in their ramifications, gradually diminished, while the cost of pursuing them increased.

Expensive levels also became necessary, of which it is difficult to conceive how they were conducted before the application of gunpowder to the purposes of mining ; an improvement of infinite importance, which, though it had taken place in subterraneous works for military purposes at least two centuries before, was unknown among the miners in Staffordshire and Derbyshire as late as the reign of James II.* A reasonable inference is, that it was introduced into Craven still later.

From two letters of Charles Earl of Burlington to his agent at Bolton, dated in the years 1683 and 1685, I learn that the Marquis of Worcester, a great projector in those days, had taken a lease of some of the *rakes* of lead in this manor, the term of which he wished to extend to a hundred years.

The lead on Grassington Moor is extremely rich, a ton of ore sometimes yielding sixteen hundred pounds weight of metal. But it is poor in silver; for a very skilful mineralogist (Mr. Sheffield) lately employed by the Duke of Devonshire, after eighty different assays, found that the poorest specimens contained not more than half an ounce of silver per ton of lead, and the richest only four ounces and a half.†

I have only to add, that the miners who carry on these works—a collection from Derbyshire, Alston Moor, &c.—have contributed much more to the increase of population than to the improvement of order and good morals.

Excepting, what must always be excepted, the introduction of manufactories, I do not know a greater calamity which can befall a village than the discovery of a lead-mine in the neighbourhood.

A brass celt found some years ago on Grassington Moor was given to me by the late worthy and respectable Thomas Browne, Esq., of that place.

---

* See Dr. Plot's remarkable account of the rocks in Staffordshire, which the miners had no means of breaking but by kindling fires upon them. The art of blasting, therefore, must must have been unknown in 1686, when that work was published.—" History of Staffordshire," p. 134.

[† About 200 men are employed in these mines, and 700 tons of lead raised annually. One of the shafts is about 100 fathoms in depth, and the drainage is effected by an adit which was commenced in 1796, and completed in 1830, at a cost of 30,000*l.*]

PARISH OF KETTLEWELL.*

ETELWELL is the " Well of Ketel," a personal name often occurring in the earlier charters of this country.†

The survey of this manor in Domesday is as follows :—

Ⓜ In Chetelwell ħħ Ulf i . car' ad gℓđ Huburgeham . Stamphotone. ‡

It was then a part of the vast possessions of Roger de Poitou ; and soon after alienated to the Percies.   By them it was granted out at an uncertain, though undoubtedly an early period, to the family De Arches, who held it in the latter end of Henry I. or in the beginning of Stephen.   The witnesses to the Charter of Arnford,§ which is certainly of that period, are all inhabitants of Ketelwell and the neighbourhood ; and, as they are mostly Saxon, it is by no means improbable that some of them were born before the Conquest. Those who know the place in its present state, and who love to indulge their imaginations in views of distant antiquity, will not be displeased with the following catalogue of its principal inhabitants, and those of the neighbouring villages, at the date of that Charter ; Ralph the dean, and Ralph his chaplain, and Gregory the scribe, and Henry de Bukdene, and Pain de Ketelwell, and Horm de Littun and Ulph his brother, and Swane the prepositus (bailiff) of Ketelwell, and Harnold his brother, and Randulph, Berner, and Richard, sons of the dean, and Hornold son of Amfrid, and Fulcher.   These were the friends and principal dependents of the De Arches in this place more than seven hundred years ago.   I am unable to connect the later descents of this family with Osbern de Arches, one of the great proprietors of Craven at the Domesday survey.   The first who occurs afterwards was Peter, who certainly resided at Kettlewell, and was probably father of—

[* The parish includes the township of Starbottom, and contains, according to the Ordnance Survey, 8,412a. 3r.   In 1871 there were in the parish 498 inhabitants in 119 houses.   In the 41st and 56th George III. Inclosure Acts were passed for Starbottom and Buckden.]

[† KETELWELL CUM STAUERBOT.—In eisdem villis sunt VIII car. terræ ; de quibus Elyas de Knoll tenet II car. terræ de Roberto de Grey et Abbate de Coverham, et iidem Robertus et Abbas de Osberto de Archis, et hær' de Archis ten' de hæredibus de Percy ; et residuæ VI car. terræ, quarum Abbas de Coverham tenet III car. terræ, et Robertus de Grey alias III car. tenentur de hæredibus de Archis, et iidem hæredes de prædictis hæredibus de Percy ; et tota villa redd. ad finem prædictum IIIIs.—Kirkby's " Inquest."

The Lords of the manor of Kettlewell in the 9th Edward II. were the Abbot of Coverham, John de Gisburn, and John Lord Gray.   (John Lord Gray of Rotherfield died in 5th Edward II.   His heir was his son John.)—" Nomina Villarum."]

[‡ Manor.—In Chetelwell (Kettlewell), Ulf had I carucate to be taxed.   Huburgeham (Hubberholme), half a carucate. In Stamphotone (Starbottom), half a carucate.]

§ Vide Arnford, p. 155.

3 T

Arms : Gu. 3 arches arg.

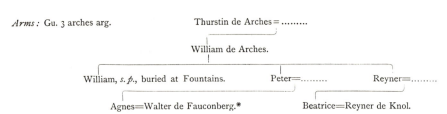

Thurstin de Arches = ...

William de Arches.

William, *s. p.*, buried at Fountains.   Peter=.........   Reyner=.........

Agnes=Walter de Fauconberg.*   Beatrice=Reyner de Knol.

Agnes de Arches had issue Walter and Peter. Walter gave to Peter half the manor, and a mediety of the advowson of Kettlewell. In the 21st Edward I. Robert de Gray held the said moiety of Sir Walter de Fauconberg,† for homage and service and one pair of gloves at Easter. John de Grey was heir, and of the age of 23 years.‡ At the time of Kirkby's Inquest, which must have been made before the death of Robert de Gray of Rotherfield, or 23rd Edward I. [actually in 13th Edward I.], it appears that there were eight carucates of land in Kettlewell (an eightfold increase in two centuries), of which Elias de Knol held two of Robert de Gray and the Abbot of Coverham, and they of Osbert de Arches, and he of the heirs of Percy, and they of the king *in capite :* and the Abbot of Coverham held three other carucates of Robert de Gray :§ and the remaining three carucates were held of the heirs of the Arches, who held them as before. Robert de Gray was grand nephew of Walter Gray, Archbishop of York, the founder of this branch of the family. By inquisition, after his death, it is found that he died seised of a moiety of the manor of Kettlewell ; and the monks of Coverham appear to have held the other ; but it nowhere appears how either the one or the other acquired their portions from the Arches. The remaining three carucates were held of this family by several inferior proprietors, who granted considerable portions of them to Fountains Abbey, which the Arches confirmed.

Free warren in Kettlewell was granted to the abbot and convent of Coverham, 55 Henry III. [1270-1] and long after—namely, 4 Edward III. [1330-1], to Sir John Gray of Rotherfield.§ Each of these, though referring only to its own moiety, is expressed as if it extended to the whole manor. After the extinction of the Grays of Rotherfield, by the death of the last heir male, 11 Richard II. [1387-8], leaving an infant daughter Joan, afterwards married to Sir John Deincourt, I find nothing more relating to this moiety of the manor till the reign of Henry IV., when it passed into the family of the Neviles, Earls of Westmoreland. No intermarriage took place between that family and the Deincourts which will account for this transfer ; but Sir John Deincourt above-mentioned was born at Middleham ; most probably a posthumous child, under the care of the Neviles ; his elder brother, who died *s. p.*, being only one year old at his father's death. I am inclined therefore to believe that this manor was obtained in the way of grant, or purchase, from this

---

* Coucher Book of Fountains.

[† Walter de Faukenbergh gave to the monks of Fountains his pasture in Kettlewell lying between Grasp and Dimlingdale.—Burt. "Mon." 174.]

‡ MSS. J. C. Brooke, in Off. Arm.

[§ John de Grey de Rotherfeld, and Margaret his wife, were found to have owned the manor and church of Ketelewell.—5th Edward II. (1311-12) Inq. *post mortem.*]

young man, by the Neviles ; for in the Patent Rolls of Henry IV., an. 6 and 7, and again, in the 11th year of the same reign [1409–10], are two successive licences granted to Ralph Earl of Westmoreland, of free warren in the vill of Kettelwell in Craven, together with a licence to inclose three hundred acres of land within the same for a park, and to build and kernel a lodge within it.

This is the origin of Skale Park, now divided into two large inclosures, and so called from a long and steep ascent within it from Craven into Coverdale.

If the reader will attend to the chronology of these two licences, he will find that John Deincourt was aged about 17 years at the date of the first, and 21 at that of the second. The Neviles, therefore, had just cause to doubt the validity of their former title, and to ratify it after the full age of Deincourt.

I have only to add, that this portion of the manor continued, without any other alienation, in the Westmoreland family till the attainder of the last unfortunate earl, A.D. 1569, when it became forfeited to the Crown, and has since been broken into many inconsiderable properties.*

The other moiety, belonging to the monks of Coverham, was already vested in the Crown ; and had, in all probability, been granted out already, as well as the estates in the parish belonging to Fountains. The manor is now claimed by the freeholders at large, and no considerable family has ever arisen in the parish to unite the dispersed members of it again.

In Kettlewell twelve carucates constituted a knight's fee.

Of the foundation of the church at Kettlewell there is no account. There can be little doubt that it was founded by the Arches in the time of Henry I., or perhaps a little before.†
The canons of Bolton had the advowson at a very early period, and continued long after to receive a pension out of it of 1*l. per annum.*

Among the attestations of some very ancient charters appears a Radulphus de Ketel-wella, and about half a century later an Adam Decanus de Ernecliff.

I had once conjectured that the word Decanus was improperly used in these places for Deacon, and was not displeased to find that the same idea had struck so able an antiquary as Mr. Brooke ; but am now convinced that we were both mistaken. For, first, in the original grant of Arnforth, which, from the names of the witnesses, was plainly made by Peter de Arches at Kettlewell, the first of the number is Radulphus Decanus, the second, Radulphus Capellanus Radulphi ; which proves the first to have been an ecclesiastic of consequence. Secondly, in the year 1186, I meet with an Adam Decanus de Craven, of whom there is the strongest reason to believe that he was the same with Adam Dean of

---

* It was sold off by Queen Elizabeth.—MSS. J. C. Brooke, Off. Arm.

† No account appears of their donation of this church to the priory of Bolton ; but among Mr. Brooke's papers is an abstract of a charter, by which Peter de Arches grants to that house 2 bovates which Seward held, and another bovate in his demesne, which he had given to Adam de Bukdene in marriage with his sister, and one essart of 16 acres, with a third part of the liberties and services which he held in Woods and Feedings in Ketelwell. With respect to the assignment of this advowson, there is the following entry in the Compotus of Christopher Lofthouse, Prior of Bolton, 12 Edward IV. :—

" Ketylwell.—Abbat de Coverh'm pr. Advocacio'e Eccl'ie de Ketylwell xxs. per an. pro qui' quidem xxs. idem Abbas obligavit villam de Wallerburne, &c. ad districtionem, &c. si in solucio'e dict. xxs. defecerit pro anno. D'ns Ric' Dux Gloucest' ten't libe' ib'm div. ten't ut patet in cartis D'ni Walt. Gray."

Arncliffe.　From these premises my conclusion is, that these two ecclesiastics were respectively rectors of Kettlewell and Arncliff, who, being also rural deans of Craven, were denominated not from the district over which they presided, but from the place of their residence.

At that early period the office of rural dean was of considerable use and authority. It has since been in a great measure superseded by the office of archdeacon.*

In the 6th of Henry III. [1221–2], six years before the first presentation of the Abbot of Coverham, is a fine between Con..... abbot of that house, and Robert prior of Bolton, his disturber, of a moiety of the advowson of Ketelwell, which the prior acknowledges to be the right of the said abbot; receiving in consideration of the same one oxgang in Kettlewell, and paying in return to the abbot one pound of pure incense. I suppose this was afterwards commuted into a rent-charge of 20s.

The next document, which also points to the era of married priests, I shall give in the words of the charter itself—

"Lecia quondam uxor Alex. clerici de Ketelwel, in purâ viduitate d. &c. Agneti filie Helie de Ketelwell unum toftum inter Domos Canonicorum de Coverham et Domum Randolph' Mutte, reddendo lumini Beate Marie in Ketelwel 1 den. in Natale Domini. Test. Rob. clerico avunculo meo." †

RECTORS OF KETTLEWELL.

Radulphus decanus de Ketelwella circ. A.D. 1140.
Ricardus persona de Ketelwell, S.D.

ABBOT'S MEDIETY.

Temp. Inst.		Rectores.	Patroni.	Vacat.
6 kal. Maii,	1229.	Tho. fil. Mathei, nepos.	Ab. et Conv. de Coverham.	
		Tho. titulo Se. Sabine, Presb. Cardinalis.‡	Æ'pus per lapsum.	
6 kal. Oct.	1280.	Dns. Joh. de Blunham, Subdiac.	Ab. et Conv. de Coverham.	
14 kal. Feb.	1283.	Dns. Rob. de Lydington, Diac.	Iidem.	
2 kal. Aug.	1306.	Dns. Joh. de Mirks, vel Monketon, Cl.	Iidem.	per resig.
	1307.	Dns. Wm. de Sherburne, Cap.	Iidem.	per resig.
8 id. Oct.	1310	Dns. Joh. de Sutton, Acoly.	Iidem.	
3 non. Oct.	1315.	Dns. Rog. de la More, Presb.	Iidem.	per resig.
2 kal. Aug.	1331.	Dns. Adam de Aynho, Presb.	Iidem.	{ per res. pro eccl. de Berningham.
	1333.	Dns. Hen. de Ascryks.	Iidem.	per resig.
	1348.	Fr. Tho. de Burton.	Iidem.	

GREY'S MEDIETY.

4 kal. Jul.	1300.	Dns. W. de Moreby, Presb.	Dns. Joh. Grey, miles, de Rotherfeld.	
3 id. Feb.	1301.	Dns. Baldwin de Stonore, Subd.	Idem.	

* See Bishop Kennet's learned and accurate Dissertation on Rural Deans, "Paroch. Ant." p. 685 & seq.

† Townley MSS.

‡ This obscure and diminutive parish is the only one in the Deanery which has been honoured with a Cardinal for its incumbent. The scarlet hat was little to be expected at Kettlewell.

[Collation of Thos., son of Matthew, nephew of Thos., cardinal-priest of S. Sabina, to the church of Kettlewell, which has come to us through a dispute about the patronage.—Archbishop Gray's Register, Sireburn, 6 kal. Martii, 1228.]

Temp. Inst.	Rectores.	Patroni.	Vacat.
2 id. Mart. 1308.	Dns. *Joh. Kent de Campedon,* Acolythus. }	Dns. *Joh. Grey.*	
	Dns. *Ric. de Wethby.*	Idem.	per resig.
9 kal. Sept. 1339.	Dns. *Joh. de Brygenhall,* Acolythus. }	Idem.	per mort.
29 Aug. 1349.	Dns. *Wm. de Wyntringham,* Cl.	Idem.	per resig.
26 Maii, 1362.	Dns. *Wm. Cayham,* Presb.	Idem.*	

Thus much for the rectory of Kettelwell, of which it is altogether uncertain when it was divided into two medieties; though the probability is that the separation took place when the two portions of the manor itself were severally alienated to the Greys of Rotherfield, and the abbey of Coverham by the family De Arches.

It is remarkable that no presentation on the part of the Greys appears to have taken place till more than seventy years after the first appointment by the monks; but this is far from proving that no mediety then existed, as the four nominations by the latter which took place in that interval refer to a mediety only. The difficulty may be solved by supposing that the anonymous institution in the former catalogue (anonymous with respect to the patron as well as the clerk), A.D. 1280, has been misplaced, and belonged to the portion of the Greys.

I must also remark another error in Torre's MS., whence the foregoing catalogue was extracted, as it appears from the register of Archbishop Zouch that Askrig was rector of Grey's mediety; and this observation brings me to the endowment of the vicarage; for, on the 4th of December, 1344, this mediety, which must have been previously bestowed upon the abbey of Coverham by the Greys, was appropriated to the said house after the cession or decease of Henry de Askrig, then rector of that portion, the archbishop ordaining that there should be in the church of Kettelwell a vicar, presentable by the said house for ever; and that the vicarage should consist in the mansion of the rectory and in seven marks sterling, payable out of the fruits of the said mediety. And, in the year 1388, the whole church was once more appropriated by the commissary of Archbishop Alexander Nevile, who ordained the vicarage to consist in the manse, as above, and in 5*l.* sterling, payable by the abbot and convent at Pentecost and Martinmas, in equal portions.

A third endowment, which is the present one, must have taken place; but I have not met with it.

The reduced taxation of this church in the year 1318, after the ravages of the Scots, is XII marks.

Vicars of Kettlewell.

Temp. Inst.	Vicarii.	Patroni.	Vacat.
10 Nov. 1348.	Fr. *Tho. de Bruton,* Canonicus Domûs de Coverham. }	Ab. et Conv. ejusd.	per resig.
24 Aug. 1367.	Dns. *Joh. de Ryply,* Can. ib'm.	Iidem.	per resig.
29 Maii, 1412.	Fr. *Rob. Monkton,* Can.	Iidem.	

* By this is only meant that all these presentations run in the same name; but, in the period of sixty-two years, it denoted the grandfather, father, and son.

Temp. Inst.		Vicarii.	Patroni.	Vacat.
		Fr. *Joh. Cartmell*, Can. ib'm.	Ab. et Conv. ejusd.	per mort.
5 Feb.	1476.	Fr. *Joh. York*, Confrater Mon. de Coverham.	Iidem.	per mort.
19 Junii,	1495.	Fr. *Tho. Wensley,** Can. Dns. de Coverham.	Iidem.	per mort.
30 Maii,	1511.	Fr. *Christopher Hilton*, Can.	Iidem.	
2 Maii,	1521.	Fr. *Joh. Gysburgh*, Can. mon. ib'm.	Iidem.	per mort.
26 Aug.	1521.	Fr. *Gerv. Marrick*, Can. ib'm.	Iidem.	
		Henr. Hill, Cl.		per mort.
7 Maii,	1585.	*John Lyndoe*, Cl. A.M.	A'ep'us per laps.	per mort.
4 Jan.	1593.	*Edm. Tatham*, Cl.	*Geo. Lister*, Gent.	per mort.
13 Mar.	1603.	*Hen. Motley*.	Idem.†	per mort.
7 Maii,	1632.	*Ric. Tennant*, Cl. A.M.	*Hen. Hoyle*, Cl. A.M.	
		Tho. Motley, Cl.		per resig.
27 Aug.	1670.	*Henry Motley*, Cl.	*Wil'mus Currer*, Gent.	per mort.
12 May,	1699.	*Henry Birch*.	*William Fawcett*, Gent.	
28 Jan.	1740.	*John Currer*, A.B.	Rex *Geo. II.* per laps.	per mort.
29 Sept.	1760.	*W'm Tennant*, Cl.	*Rich. Tennant* of *Hebden*, Gent.	per mort.
18 Dec.	1786.	*Joh. Norton*, A.B.	*Richard Tennant* of *Rothwell*.	per mort.
1 Nov.	1822.	*Jonathan Foster*.	*R. Foster*, Esq., of *Beggamans*.	per mort.
25 March,	1867.	*Dickens Haslewood*.	Miss *Bolland*.	

The only testamentary burial which I have met with in this church is of John Cartmell, vicar, by will dated 4th October, 1476.

In the last Compotus of Coverham Abbey the rectory of Kettlewell is valued at 8*l.* 10*s.*, of which 6*l.* arose out of the tithes of wool and lamb, and only 15*s.* from that of corn. This shows how small a proportion of land was then in cultivation, though more, perhaps, than at present.

The vicarage of Kettlewell is a discharged living, valued at 22*l.* 11*s.* 6*d.* clear.

The church, dedicated to St. Mary, is of high antiquity. The nave in particular, which has neither columns nor side-aisles, has narrow, round-headed windows, and cannot be later than the time of Henry I. The whole building is covered with lead, and has no tower. The Norman doorway and capitals of the two side columns remain. As no family of any considerable antiquity or wealth has ever been seated in the parish, here are no sepulchral memorials within the church or without which deserve to be recorded.

[A faculty was granted 21st August, 1819, and the church was entirely pulled down and rebuilt in 1820, in the worst style of even that period, and is now utterly uninteresting.] ‡

The font is extremely curious. It is cylindrical, like all others of the Saxon or Norman era, but with this peculiarity, that it has an aperture in the bottom for the purpose of drawing off the water when it grew foul. Beneath is another opening in the floor, by means of which the consecrated element might sink and be absorbed in holy ground; and, in order to keep this, too, open, the font itself is not placed, as usual, upon a solid base, but is mounted on four

---

* Al. Spensley.—Grose, vol. vi. p. 86.

† In the 4th of Charles I. [1628–9], Henry Kettlewell was vicar of this place.—Nelson's MS. Account of Tenths and Subsidies paid by the Clergy of the West Riding in that year. I do not know how the omission happened, or whether it were the fault of the registrar, of Mr. Torre, or of my transcriber.

[‡ There is a tombstone to the Rev. Jonathan Foster, forty-five years vicar of this parish, died 26th September, 1855, aged 82.]

square pedestals of stone, with large intervals between them. [This font is the only relic of the old church now remaining.]

This parish consists only of the townships of Kettlewell and Starbotom, anciently Stanerbotom, the latter of which has nothing remarkable about it but the stony course of a rapid mountain torrent, from which it derived its name ; for Staner, in the dialect of Craven, like Stannary in that of Lancashire, signifies the stony bed of a torrent.

[Solomon Swale built a school-house on the waste at Kettlewell, and gave five sheep-gates on Middles Moor for keeping the buildings in repair. An allotment of about two acres was given on the division of the moor (some years before 1826) in lieu of the sheep-gates.]

The old registers of this parish being lost,* I am unable to derive my account of a dreadful catastrophe which once befel these villages from any clearer source than the "Magna Britannia Antiqua et Nova," a compilation published about the year 1720, of which the following paragraph may serve as a specimen :—

" In 1686, by a tempest, with thunder, the inhabitants of this village and Starbotton were almost all drowned with a violent flood. These towns are situate under a great hill, from whence the rain descended with such violence for an hour and a half together, the hill on the side opening, and casting up water into the air to the height of an ordinary church-steeple, that it demolished several houses, and carried away the stones entirely ; " (after which it) "filled them with gravel to the chamber-windows, drove the inhabitants away" (they had almost all been drowned before), "filled the meadows with stones and gravel," &c. &c. †

The northern boundary of Skale Park, which is also that of Craven and the West Riding, has been a deep and broad trench, cut with infinite toil out of the limestone rock. ‡ It seems rather the work of an army than of common labourers, and to have been intended to defend this important pass between valley and valley. I do not know that it is distinguished by any name, or that there is any tradition with respect to its use or antiquity.

At the bottom of this park, and on the margin of the brook eastward from the entrance, is Dove Cove, the finest cavern in the district. Its proportions are those of a lofty vaulted Gothic chapel, and the stalactites which adorn the sides and roof prove, I think, beyond controversy from what source the later enrichments of that order were derived.

From a late attempt to ascertain the height of Whernside, above Kettlewell, by the

---

* For the same reason it is impossible to give a comparative table of baptisms and burials. [This is not so ; only a portion is missing ; the registers commence in 1698.]

† For the clearness and consistency of this story the writer seems to have been indebted to the old saw—
" It so fell out they all fell in ;
The rest they ran away."

[‡ This intrenchment is a long, irregular line, facing down the valley to the south-east, south, and south-west, and forming a barrier to any invader from the south.

It can hardly be called a broad trench, for though there is a trench, the scaur is the main noticeable feature. It would seem that, when there was no natural perpendicular face, one had been made artificially, so that the whole line is made to follow and utilise the natural escarpment of the rock to a height of from five feet to fifteen feet. At the base, all along the line, the trench or fosse has in many places been cut out of the solid rock, and above, on the top of the scaur, a rampart or vallum of stones and earth erected, of varying height, but even now from two to ten feet. The whole presented a somewhat formidable front, including the fosse, the scaur, and the vallum. The works commenced at the south-east end, on the very flank of Whernside, and were continued to the north-west for not less than about a mile and a half, to the Cam or top of the little Skale Park Gill. At the extreme south-east end of the intrenchment, towards Whernside, are about fifteen inclosures of rough stones, running at right angles to the vallum, and about twenty yards in length. They were probably inclosures for cattle.—From Notes by the Rev. Canon Boyd and Mr. R. Sidgwick.]

barometer, it appeared that the descent of the mercury from that village to the summit of the hill was only $1\frac{5}{10}$ inches, and consequently that the height of the mountain, from its immediate base, is only $1,305\frac{68}{100}$ feet.

From Bolton Abbey to Kettlewell the mercury fell $\frac{5}{10}$, which makes the ascent 255 feet. If, therefore, 150 feet be allowed for the elevation of Bolton above the sea, the whole height of Whernside above the universal level will not exceed 1,710 feet.[*]

It has often been matter of regret with me that I have been unable to retrieve any remains of traditionary poetry written by natives of Craven.[†] Their country was romantic, their manners pastoral, their dialect poetical,[‡] and their amusements not devoid of imagination.   But their efforts of invention seem to have been confined to the composition of rude dramatic performances such as have been already described.   To remedy this defect I shall transgress—if, indeed, it be to transgress—the limits of the present work ; for the parish of Kettlewell, since it fell into the hands of the Neviles, has often been considered as a member of the fee of Middleham, and therefore of the honour of Richmond.

This must be my excuse for introducing here an ancient poem, the author of which has told his story, such as it is, with great spirit, and in a vein of flowing and harmonious verse. The manners are strictly correct.   A mendicant friar would fight for a bacon-hog as eagerly as a knight would encounter a wild boar.   The ideas and terms of chivalry, too, are everywhere kept in view.   The circumstances of the poem do not enable me to fix its date.   It does not appear when Freer Theobald was warden ; and if it did, the poem may have been written long after the incident happened.   From the style, I should suppose it to be prior to the reign of Henry VII.   It is printed from a manuscript in my possession.

The Felon Sowe and the Freeres of Richmonde.

FITTE THE FIRSTE.

Ye men that wylle of auncestors wynne §
That late within this land hath bin
  Of on I can yow telle ;
Of a sowe that was sae strang,
Alas ! that ever shee lived sae lang
  For fell folke did she whell.

Shee was mare than other three,
The grizeliest beast that ever mote bee,
  Her hede was gret and gray :
Shee was bred in Rokebye Woode,
Ther were few that thither yoode
  That cam on live awaye.

Her walke was endlang Greta Syde,
Was no barne that colde her byde
  That was frae heven to helle,
Ne never man that had that myght
That ever durste com in her syght,
  Her force y^t was so felle.

Raphe of Rokebye wth full gode wyll
The freers of Richmonde yaf her tyll
  Full wele to gar thayme fare ;
Freer Myddeltone by name
Hee was sent to fetch her hame,
  Yt rewed hym syne ful sare.

[* For the heights of various parts of Craven above the level of the sea, see p. 277. Great Whernside is 2,310 feet, Kettlewell churchyard is about 700 feet, above the sea.

 † The poetry of the canons of Bolton, already given, is neither traditionary nor of a popular nature.

 ‡ At least, it is the dialect which has been made the vehicle of much delightful poetry in the Border Minstrelsy, and to which it certainly adds most of its graces.

 § I do not understand this expression. Probably kynne or kenne. Mr. Hamper.—It may mean, " profit by the recital of your ancestors' valour."

Wth hym tooke he wyght men two,
Peter of Dale was on of tho
  Tother was Bryan of Beare,
Y^t wele durst strike wth swerde and knife
And fyght ful manfully for theyr lyfe
  What tyme as musters wer.

Thes thre men wended at theyr wyll,
This Felon Sowe qwhyl they cam tyll
  Liggand under a tree,
Rugg'd and rustie was her here
Scho rase up wth a felon fere
  To fight again the thre.

Grizely was scho for to meete.
Scho rave the earthe up wth her feete,
  The barke cam fro' the tre :
When Freer Myddelton her saugh,
Wete yow wele he list not laugh,
  Ful earnsful luked he.

Thes men of auncestors were soe wight *
They bound thayme baudly for the fight
  And strake att her ful sore,
Until a kilne they garred her flee,
Wolde God sende thayme ye victorye
  They wolde ask him na meare.

The sowe was in y^t kiln hole down,
And they wer on the banke aboone
  For hurting of theyr feete ;
They were so sauted wth this sowe
That 'mang theym was a stalwarth stewe
  The kiln began to reeke :

Durste noe man nighe her wth his hande,
But put a rope downe wth a wande
  And heltered her ful meeke.
They hauled her furth agayne her wyll
Whyl they cam until a hill
  A little from ye Streete, †

And ther scho made y^m such a fray
As had they lived until Domesday
  They cold y^t nere forgete.
Scho brayded up on every syde
And ranne on thayme gapyng ful wyde,
  For nothing wolde scho lete.

Scho gaf such hard braydes at the bande
That Peter of Dale had in his hand
  Hee might not holde hys feete.
Scho chased thayme soe to and fro,
The wight men never wer soe woe,
  Ther mesure was not mete.

Scho bund her boldly for to bide
To Peter of Dale scho cam aside
  Wth many a hideous yell,
Scho gaped soe wide and cryed soe high
. . . .
  As if a fiend of hell.

(Desunt nonnulla.)

Thou art comed hider for sum trayne,
I conjure the to go agayne
  Wher thou art wont to dwell,
Hee signed hym wth crosse and creede,
Took furth a booke, began to reade
  Of saint Ihon hys gospell. ‡

The Sowe scho wold noe Latyn here,
But rudely rushed at ye Frere
  Th^t blinked al hys ble ;
And when scho shuld have taken holde
The Freer lapt as I. H. S. wolde
  And bealde hym wid a tre.

Scho was brim as anie boare,
And gave a griezly hideous roare,
  To thayme y^t was no bote ;
On tree and buske y^t by her stode
Scho venged her as scho were woode
  And rave y^m upp byth roote.

He sayde, Alas that I were Freer !
I shal be lugged asunder here,
  Hard ys my destinie !
Y wist my breder in this houre
That I was set in sike a stoure
  They wolde pray for mee.

This wicked beast y^t wrought y^s woe
Twan the rope from tother two,
  And then they fled al thre ;
They fledd away by Watling Strete,
They had noe succor bud ther fete,
  It was the more pittye.

FITTE SECOND.

When Freer Myddelton cam home,
His breder wer ful faine ilchone
  And thankt God for his lyfe ;
He tolde thayme al unto ye end
How he had foughten wth a fiend,
  And went through mickle strife.

And Peter of Dale wolde never blinn,
But as faste as he colde rinn
  Till he cam till his wyfe :
The Warden sayde I am ful woe,
That yow should bee tormented soe
  And had wee wth yow bene—

Had wee bene ther yowr brether al,
Wee wolde have garred the Carle fal,
  That wrought yow all this teene.
But Myddeltone he answered naye,
In faythe ye wolde have ren awaye
  When most mis-stirre had bin.
Yow can al speke wordes at home,
The fiend wold ding yow downe ilk one,
  An y^t bee as I wene.

* *I.e.* descended from fighting families.
† The great Roman road from Catterick to Bowes.
‡ Which was of approved efficacy on these occasions.

3 U

He luked soe grizely al y^t nyght,
The warden sayde yon man wol fight,
 If ye saye ought but gode :
The beast hath grieved hym soe sare,
Holde y^r tongues and speke nae meare,
 He lukes as he were woode.

The warden waged on the morne
Two boldest men that ev^r was borne
 I weyne or ere shal bee ;
Tone was Gilbert Griffin's sonne,
Full mickle worschip had he wonne
 Both by land and sea.

Tother a bastard sonne of Spayne,
Many a Sarasen had he slain
 His dint had garred * y^m flee.
Theis men ye battell undertoke
Against the sowe as seith ye boke
 And sealed securitye.

That they should boldly bide and fight,
And scomfit her in main and might,
 Or ther for shuld they dye.
The Warden sealed to y^m agayne,
And seid, yf ye in field be sleyne
 This condition make I.

Wee shall for you syng and reade
Untill Domesdaye wth heartye speed,
 With al oure progenie.
Than ye lettres were wel made,
The bondes were bounde wth seales brade
 As dedes of armes should bee †.

These men at armes were soe wyght,
And wth ther armour burnished bright,
 They went y^s sowe to see ;
Scho made at y^m sike a roare,
That for her they feared sore,
 And almost bounde to flee.

Scho cam runnyng them agayne
And sawe ye bastard son of Spayne,
 He brayded out his brand,
Full spiteously at her he strake,
Yet, for the fence that he colde make,
 Scho strake y^t fro his hande,
And rave asunder halfe his shielde,
And bare him backwarde in ye fielde
 He mought not her gainstande.

Scho wolde have riven . . . . .
But Gilbert wth his swerde of warre
 He strake at her ful sore ;

In her schulder he held the swerde,
Than was Gilberte sore afearde
 Whan the blade brak in twang.

And whan in hand he had her tane,
Scho took him by the schulder bane
 And held her hold full fast.
He strave soe stifly in that stowr
Scho bit through al his rich armour,
 Till bloud cam out at last.

Than Gilbert grieved was so sare,
That hee rave off the hyde of haire,
 The flesh cam fro the bane,
And wth force hee held her ther,
And wan her worthilie in warre,
 And band her him alane.

They hoisted her on a horse so hee
On two . . . . of tree,
 And to Richmond anon.
Whan they sawe the Felon come,
They sang merrilye Te Deum
 The Freers evrichone.

They thankyd God and Saynte Frauncis
That they had wonne ye beste of pris,
 And nere a man was sleyne ;
Ther nev^r didde man more manlye,
The Knyght Marous or Sir Guye,
 Nor Louis of Lothraine.

  . . . .

Yf ‡ yow wol any more of y^s,
Ith' Frees at Richmond written yt is
 In parchment gude and fyne ;
How Freer Myddeltone so hende
Att Greta Bridge conjured a fiende
 In lykenes of a swyne.

Yt is well knowen to manye a man
That Freer Theobald was warden than,
 And this fel in his tyme.
And Chryst them bles both ferre and nere
Al that for solas this doe here,
 And hym y^t made the ryme.

Raphe of Rokeby wid ful gode wyl
The Freers of Richmond gave her tyll
 This Sowe to mend ther fare :
Freer Myddeltone by name
He wold bring the Felon hame
 That rewed hym sine ful sare.§

---

* Giora, *facere*—Danish.
† Alluding to the old indentures of military service, which were executed with every legal formality.
‡ The Gray Friars, whose house is thus described by Leland : " At the bakke of the Frenchgate is the Grey Freres a litel withowte the waullis. —Ther house, meadow, orchard, and a litel wood is waullid yn. There ys a conduite of water at the Grey Freres, else there ys none in Richemont." —" Itin." vol. iii. p. 109.   Had Leland read " the parchment gude and fyne ? "
§ This tale, saith my MS., was known of old to a few families only, and by them held so precious that it was never intrusted to the memory of the son till the father was on his death-bed. But times are altered, for since the first edition of this work a certain bookseller has reprinted it verbatim, with little acknowledgment to the first editor. He might have recollected that, as " The Felon Sowe ", had been already reclaimed, *Property vested.*   However, as he is an ingenious and deserving man, this hint shall suffice.

PARISH OF ARNCLIFFE.*

AT the extremity of the parish of Burnsal the valley of Wharf forks off into two great branches, one of which retains the name of Wharfdale, to the source of the river; the other, usually called Littondale, but more anciently and properly Amerdale, is watered by the Skirfare. The whole of this latter valley, together with that part of Wharfdale, properly so called, which lies north from Kettlewell, constitutes the extensive parish of Arncliffe.† Amerdale is, unquestionably, so named from Amer, Almer, Aylmer, or Almeric (for in so many ways is the word spelt), which probably denominated its first planter in the Saxon times. All the local names of this district are strongly tinctured with that language, or the kindred Danish.‡ Arncliffe, anciently Erncleve,

[* ARNECLYFE.—In eadem villa sunt V car. terræ; quarum Abbas de Fontibus tenet I car. in puram et perpetuam elemosinam de Elia de Knoll, et idem Elias de hæredibus de Percy, et iidem hæredes de rege et nihil redd.; et ecclesia dotata est de II bov. terræ; et residuæ III car. terræ et VI bov. tenentur de Alicia de Buckeden, et eadem Alicia de Elia de Knoll, et idem Elias de hæredibus de Brakenberg, et iidem hæredes de hæredibus de Percy, et iidem hæredes de rege; et nullum inde fit servitium de quo fit mentio in inquisitionibus prædictis.—Kirkby's " Inquest."

In 9th Edward II. William de Haukeswyk was lord of the manor of Arnecliff.—"Nomina Villarum."

In the parish of Arncliffe the Abbot of Fountains owned the following places in the Manor of Litton: Greenefell Coshe Moor, Halton Gill Moor, Foxhop Moor, Hesselden Moor, and a tenement called Overhesselden, and another called Netherhesselden, Litton Moor.

Part of the possessions of the abbot and convent of Fountains was called the "Sleghts," and is thus described in the schedule made shortly after the Dissolution :—

THE SLEGHTS.

Parcell of the Manor of Malham, and is in the parishe of Arncliffe, and contenyth all the lands that the late Monastery hadd ther; and is parcell of this valewe.

Richard Faucet and Marmaduke Abbott holde by Indentor under Covent seale datyd VIImo die Junii anno regni Regis Henrici VIIIvi, XXXmo, for terme of XL annorum, one pasture, with the appurtenances, being in Litton in Craven, callyd the Sleghts, payinge therefore by the yere Cs.

Two of this man's ancestors, Richard and James Faucyd, had kept the abbot's cattle at this same place in 1456.

Richard Fawsied was a tenant of the abbot at Over-Hesiden, in the parish of Arncliffe, in 1455, as was James Fawcet in 1496.—Walbran's " Memorials of Fountains," p. 311.

In April, 1871, the population of the parish was found to be 681 persons, living in 144 houses.]

[† Containing, according to the Ordnance Survey, 34,078a. 2r. 6p., and comprising the townships of Arncliffe, Buckden, Halton Gill, Hawkswick, and Litton. Inclosure Acts have been passed 8th George III. (Litton), 6th George III. (Stinted Pastures), and 56th George III. (Hawkswick).]

‡ To have entered into a general investigation of a dialect like that of Craven would have been disgusting to many readers, and have afforded little satisfaction even to the lovers of etymological research; for many of its peculiarities may be dismissed as modern vulgarisms, a kind of *slang*, which humour and whim are perpetually introducing into the phraseology of the common people

In the following observations, therefore, I confine myself to words descriptive of local ideas, as being in their own nature more permanent than others.

The Northumbrian kingdom was almost depopulated by the Danes, who, with their colonies, introduced their own barbarous dialect. But, whatever may be the cause, the fact is certain, that throughout the lowlands of Scotland, the northern counties of England, and to the southern extremity of Craven, a similar language prevails, unlike that of any other province in the kingdom. The basis of this I consider as Dano-Saxon.

On the western side of England, the river Mersey was, properly speaking, the limit between the kingdoms of Northumberland and Mercia; but, northward from that river, and as far as the north-east boundary of Lancashire, another

which has given name to the parish, is evidently derived from Eaɲn, *aquila*, and clyᵽᵽ, *rupes*, the Eagle's Rock,* as it would afford many secure retreats for that bird in its long ridges of perpendicular limestone.† Skirfare is so called in contradistinction to the little collateral streams‡ which fall into it from the hills on either side, from Scyɲe, *penitus*, and ᵱaɲan, *permeare*, the stream which traverses the valley throughout.‡ Doukbottom Cove, a well-known cavern in the neighbourhood, is evidently from Doukan, *subire;* and coᵱa, *cavea.* Dernbrook, which runs along an obscure valley from the north-west, is as evidently derived from Deaɲnian, *occultare;*§ and Thorgill, one of the feeders of Dernbrook, carries its etymology along with it. Litton is from Lȳꞇ, *exiguus*, and ꞇun, *villa*, the little town, not from Liꞇꞇun, a churchyard, which it never had.

Dowkabottom Hole ‖ is about two miles north from Kilnsey Crag, high up in the hills, and surrounded by cliffs of limestone. The entrance is an oblong chasm in the surface, overhung with ivy and fern. At the south end is a narrow but lofty opening into

dialect prevails, which, in the neighbourhood of Colne, is imperceptibly shaded off into that of Craven. Of this the basis unquestionably, was the Mercno-Saxon, traces of which are distinctly perceivable, by a skilful ear, in Cheshire, Derbyshire, Staffordshire, and even as far as Warwickshire.

It is to be lamented that the Danish dialect, having been spoken by a people almost wholly illiterate, was seldom committed to writing ; but it may be very nearly identified with the Islandic, of which a learned and an accurate account has been given by Runolphus Jonas.

Assuming, therefore, my position of the general identity of those dialects as granted, I shall select, from substantives of place still for the most part found in Craven, a sufficient number to prove the point for which I contend, that, of all the branches from the Teutonic stock, the language of this district approaches most nearly to the Danish.

Barf, BERG, vel BIARG, *saxum.* This example will show how Craven has been obtained from CRAGEN, as Dwarf from DUERGAR. Beck, a rivulet, BECKUR. Dale, DALUR. Dub, a deep pool in a river, and Dib, a deep valley, ᴅɪɴꞰꞱ Mœs. Goth. et DYB. Isl. Cove, a cave, or hollow rock, COFA. Fors, a waterfall, FOSS. Fell, a mountain, FELL. Fleet, a flat bog, FLOOT. Gnipe, the rocky summit of a hill, GNYPA. Gill, gully, the narrow course of a torrent, GILL, *hiatus montium.* Groof, a hollow in the earth, GROOF. Haugh, a hillock, HAUGHUR, *tumulus.* Ing, a meadow, ING, *pratum*, Dan. Lin, a waterfall, LIND, *aqua scaturiens.* Rayse, a heap of stones, as Stanrayse, Dunmalrayse, REYSA, *erigere.* Lache, a boggy depression in the moors, LAAG, *vallis.* Moor and moss, a spongy piece of ground, MOOR, gen. MOOS. Stank, a boggy piece of ground, STAEN, idem. Scar, SKIER, *scopulus.* Scrogg, shrogg, a stunted wood, SKOOGUR, *sylva.* Tarn, a lake, TIORN, idem. Wath and with, often used in composition, as Langwith, Deerwath, &c. A ford, VAD.

Here I will just remark that fell is often used in composition, as HELGAFELL, the holy mountain, SNEEFIOLL, the snowy hills, and SKRATTAFELL, the mountain haunted by demons ; which last will show that the common people of the north are right in their pronunciation of the name of a certain being which their betters have perverted into " Scratch." After all the labours of antiquaries to trace the different migrations of Puck, it has not been observed that he is known in Iceland by the name of PUKE ; but he seems to have been familiar to all the Teutonic tribes.

To the local words above, deduced from the Danish or Islandic dialect, I will add a few others of an anomalous kind— as Hope, a narrow valley without an outlet at the top ; Swire, a surname only in Craven ; the ridge of a hill, Keld, very frequent in old perambulations, the *cold* summit of a hill ; and, lastly, Car, thus explained by Leland, who, I think, is the only writer that mentions it :—

" There is a pratty Car, or Pole, in Bishopsdale."— " Itin." v. p. 115.

If the Roman Verbeia had not fixed the British origin of Wharf beyond a doubt, this dialect would have afforded an excellent etymology, WIRFEN, *projicere*—to impel rapidly.

* As a trait of old ornithology, I must inform the reader that Craven had formerly two very different birds, long since extinct —the eagle and the nightingale. The existence of the first in Wharfdale is proved by the etymology of Arncleve, that of the latter in Ribblesdale by Nichtgale-riding, the name of a place in the parish of Bolton, mentioned in the Coucher Book of Sallay.

† Among which is Arnberg Scar, another instance of the same derivation.

‡ These were called in Islandic " *Thever aa* " amnes, qui vallem non per longitudinem secant qui e montibus ruentes eandem transversim interluunt.

§ This word is used as an adjective by Harrison, in his "Description of Britain," 1577 :—"Helbeck is so called because it riseth in the derne and elenge hills." But the language is two centuries older than his time. Elenge is used by Chaucer and Piers Plowman in the sense of dreary or comfortless.

[‖ This cave has been explored by Mr. Jackson, the discoverer of the Victoria Cave, and by Mr. Farrer and Mr. Denny. See *Proc. Geol. and Polytechnic Soc. of West Riding of Yorkshire*, 1859, p. 45, 1864-5, p. 114 *et seq.*]

a cavern of no great extent. The view downward from the north is tremendous. On this side it is very lofty, and extends to a considerable distance. The rocks at the top, and particularly near the entrance, hang down in the most picturesque shapes; and both these and the sides are covered with petrified moss, richly tinted. The bottom at first is rugged, but afterwards changes to a brown clay, which has been found to answer the end of fuller's earth, and is in some places petrified in masses as hard as marble, with a pellucid stream running over it, from which this deposit is formed.* A sudden turn to the left at once changes the scene; the cavern now becoming very spacious, and forming a set of magnificent Gothic arches, composed of petrified matter white as new-fallen snow. After gaining a rugged ascent, the incrustations on the sides continue, but the roof changes to a flat ceiling of dark-blue rock with white seams, from which depend stalactites of various hues, rugged all over, and sharp as the points of lances. Beyond, the rocky ascent leads to a narrower part of the cavern, where the water becomes too deep to admit of any farther progress. When Bishop Pococke had seen Dowkabottom, he exclaimed—"This is Antiparos in miniature; and except that cavern, I have never seen its equal."

The western side of this valley extends to Penigent, on the skirts of which mountain are many ancient places of interment, called Giants' Graves, which are probably Danish.

The bodies have been inclosed in a sort of rude Kist Vaens, consisting of limestones pitched on edge, within which they appear to have been artificially bedded in peat earth. But this substance, in consequence of lying dry, and in small quantities, has lost its well-known property of tanning animal substances, for all the remains which have been disinterred from these deposits are reduced to skeletons.

The upper part of Amerdale, stretching to the confines of Longstrothdale on the north and east, was a distinct manor under the Percy fee, as well as a forest. Though principally inclosed, it is for the most part a bleak and cold valley, with very little wood. The Skirfare in its course along a rocky bed in dry seasons alternately merges and re-appears.

The state of the whole forest with respect to wood, deer, &c., may be collected from the following inquisition, taken A.D. 1579, immediately after George, the third Earl of Cumberland, came of age, which I select for the antique and curious language in which it is expressed :—

"Wee finde (say the Jurors) that the Fleets and Mosses are nott to be estymatyd by Acre Tayle wth a saife conscience, bothe for wyllde Hidde † and closs Lynge, and for that alsoe as wee believe ther ys 1000 acres and more of Fleet, Mosses, and Cragg wch ys or maie bee convenient for the Game, and yett more hurtfull then proffitable to my L^{ds} Tennants.

"It^{m}, in Upper Hesseldene ther is a Skayling of Wood of Warranty and certain olde Skruddle Hessels. It^{m}, in another Gyll in Nether Hesseldene are certein yonge Esshe Spires and Thornes and scrubbie Hessels. It^{m}, A certain Thycke or Ryse of Thornes and Underwood and some smal scayling of Wood of Warrant. It^{m}, the gret Decaye of my Lordes Woods hathe bene p'tly by Forraners and p'tly by Warrants graunted for bylding and necessarie upholding of Houses now erected on my L^{ds} Lannd wch are manie—and as for ye Game ye same is sins my oild L^{d} deceasyd encresyd dooble ; nev'theless ther hathe bene divers misdemenors touching the same duryng the Minoritie of my Lorde, ye true Knowledge of wch maie bee understanden by p'sentments sence ye decease of myne oild Lord, whose Soule God blesse!"

[* A fragment of an armlet of bluish glass was discovered by Mr. Farrer in the Dowkerbottom Caves, in company with various remains of a Romano-British character, not unlike some found at Settle, an account of which will be found in Mr. Roach Smith's "Collectanea."—*Journal of the Archæological Institute*, XV. 160.]

† Dan. HEED, Heath.

Following the boundaries of the parish into Wharfdale, we first meet with Buckden, which is not mentioned in Domesday; Hubberholm is evidently from the Danish Hubba, or Hubber, as the word was differently pronounced. Raisgill from RAA, the roebuck, in the same language, proves the existence of that animal in Longstrothdale. Yoken-thwaite is the division or boundary of oaks, from Єac, pronounced as ẏak, thwaite; on which latter word, so general in the composition of local names in the north of England, as it has never been satisfactorily explained, I must be allowed to make a few observations. The word þꝑıtan, to divide, or cut, or cut off, is genuine Saxon: it is used by King Alfred in his version of Bede, "oꝼ þæꝑeẏlcan ꞅtẏþe ꞅþonaꞅ þþoton," *ex ipsâ destina assulas exciderunt;* by Chaucer, R.R. 933, "And it was peinted wel and thwittan;" and by the common people in Lancashire to this day. Thwaite, therefore, is a participial substantive formed from this verb, and signifies a division or separate district. Next is Deepdale, which, though pure English, is pure Saxon also; then Beckurmons, as it is properly spelt in charters, from the Danish BECKUR, a rivulet, and MUND, a mouth;* and still higher, and nearer to the source of Wharf, Outershaw,† from utteꞃ, *extremus,* and skua, *nemus,* the farthest or uttermost wood.‡ The last word, so common in the composition of English local names, runs through almost all the dialects of the Teutonic stock.

The name of this valley is Longstroth, or Longstrother, resembling in sound and origin the Scottish *Strothur*, which means a spongy flat in a valley, and probably gave birth

---

* Thus the outlet of Ulleswater, sometimes spelt the Eeman, and sometimes the Eamot, is rightly pronounced by the common people *Eamont—i.e.* the mouth of the water.

[† Oughtershaw is a hamlet of Buckden, in the chapelry of St. Michael, Hubberholme, in the parish of Arncliffe. It occupies the entire head and upper springs of the river Wharfe, but is distinguished as Langstrothdale, as far as Starbotton. It formed in ancient times a part of Langstrothdale Chase, and probably derives its name from its being the limit of the wooded part of the valley; as the village stands just where the ancient copse-wood ceases, and the open moor commences, although numerous stems of trees, mostly birch, are met with in the peat bogs, higher up the dale. The whole of the hamlet is more than 1,000 feet above the sea.

The climate is naturally cold and backward, yet though ordinary vegetables come forward about a month later than is usual, the commoner fruits ripen well. The rainfall averages about eighty-six inches per annum, in the bottom of the valley, and some fifteen to twenty inches less on the moor-tops, 1,000 feet higher. The total area of the hamlet is about 4,000 acres, mostly belonging to Charles H. L. Woodd, Esq., with the exception of some small allotments belonging to old proprietors. Until 1849, it was a stinted pasture, with limited rights of pasturage to the owners of old inclosures. On July 5th, 1849, it was allotted in proportion under the Act Vic. 8 & 9, chap. 118, retaining 13*a.* 1*r.* 4*p.* for peat-ground made over to the overseers.

The estate came into possession of the family of Woodd by purchases at sundry times during the last fifty years. It was bought from the owners, Lodge, Foster, Atkinson, and the family of Drake, by Basil George Woodd of Hillfield, Hampstead, Middlesex, and passed, at his death, to the present owner. In the year 1852, the inclosing and reclaiming, draining and liming was commenced, some 700 acres of which are now completed, and two excellent farms of over 1,000 acres each, have been formed upon the new allotments. Swarthghyll and Netherghyll, now yielding good meadow hay, where of old only coarse herbage and rough sheep-pasture existed. The Hall was commenced in 1850, on a site overlooking the river Wharfe, where it falls over its rocky bed, in a highly romantic ghyll or valley, clothed with flourishing plantations. There were remains of some ancient tenement, on the site, though nothing of importance. The Hall has of late been considerably enlarged by the present proprietor, under the architect, Ewan Christian, of London, in the prevailing style of the old manor-houses of the country, the late Tudor style, which has lingered on in the dales until the present time: the stone-mullioned windows giving a more than ordinary character to the humblest buildings. The old farm-houses mostly date from about 1640 to 1680. The deeds contain some of the original grants, signed by Francis Lord Clifford, in the reign of Charles II.

A school-house was erected in 1857, by the present proprietor, in memory of his first wife, who died at Pau. The inhabitants continue to retain many of the primitive manners and habits of the dalesmen, and are distinguished by hearty good feeling and honesty. They are a contented, hard-working, unsophisticated race, one so rarely to be met with in the present day.]

‡ Or possibly from Uctred.

to John de Longstrother, prior of St. John of Jerusalem,* so greatly distinguished in the wars between the two Houses.

But it is far more interesting to suggest, that from this remote and obscure place probably sprang the two northern scholars of Soleres Hall, whom Chaucer has made the subject of his " Reeve's Tale," and whose dialect, evidently not the language of the author, is precisely the modern dialect of Craven. Let the northern reader judge for himself from the following specimen ; after being told that—

> " Of a † town were they both that highte Strother
> Farre in the North can I nat tell where.
>
> Our Manciple I hope he will be dede
> Swa werkes aye the wanges in his hede,
> And therefore is I come and eke Alayn,
> We praye you spede us heme in that ye maye.
>
> — Right by the Hopper wol I stand,
> Qd John, and see how gates the corn goth in.
> Alayn answered, Johan, wilt thou sa
> I is as ill a miller as is ye—
>
> I is full swift as is a Raa,
> He shal nat skape us bathe,
> Why ne hadst thou put the Capel in the Lathe ? " ‡

I think the two scholars have by this time pretty clearly ascertained by their tongues the point which Chaucer was doubtful about—namely, where was Strother, the place of their birth : and it is material to the present purpose that no other place of the name occurs in the " Villare " of the Northern Counties. § From these circumstances I am inclined to believe the story a real one, or at least that Chaucer had heard the dialect of Alan and John spoken in Solere Hall.

In the reign of Edward III. it might not be incompatible with academical manners to represent two undergraduates laying a plan, in concert with the master of their college, to detect the frauds of a miller, or even undertaking to convey in person the college grain to and from Trumpington Mill on a pack-horse.

But even then, as there were different ranks, there would be different manners in the same society ; and perhaps in that age, gross as it was, decorum might require the poet to select for his purpose two scholars of the lowest order, coarse, untaught natives " of a Town fer in the North ; " but, from their early habits, adroit in detecting frauds.

But to return—

The several manors in the parishes of Arncliff and Kettlewell at the time of the Conqueror's Survey belonged to Roger of Poitou, but were soon alienated to the Percys, and became part of that great fee. Litton, however, was surveyed as a Berewick of the

---

[* John Longstrother, Prior of St. John's, in England, went with Edward Duke of Somerset and others, to Beaulieu Abbey, to welcome Queen Margaret, 10th Edward IV.—Hall, p. 298. The Battle of Tewkesbury fought. He with Edmd. Duke of Somerset, Sir Garnays Clyfton, and Sir Thos. Tresham and XII other knights and gentlemen, beheaded, 5th May, 1471.—Hall, p. 301.]

† A—*i.e.* one.

‡ Mr. Tyrwhitt, the sagacious editor of the " Canterbury Tales," has observed that this is not the language of Chaucer.

§ Yet a place of the name of Green Strother, in Northumberland, is mentioned in the " Monasticon Anglicanum."

manor of Giggleswick; and Hubberholm and Starbottom as portions of Kettlewell, consisting of half a carucate each.

      ⓜ In Arneclif . Thorfin ħɓ . IIII . car ad gld.

      ⓜ In Hocheswic . ħɓ . Gamel . III . car ad głđ.*

Under the Percys, however, a mesne lordship arose at Arncliff, of which the first owners upon record were the ancient family De Arches, in all probability founders of the church. The first person of the name whom I meet with here is Thurstin de Arches, who lived in the reign of King John, and gave four oxgangs of land in Arncliff to the monks of Fountains. He had a son William, who had Rayner de Arches, who by Sarah his wife had a daughter Beatrice, married to Reginald or Rayner de Knol lord of Helgefeld, and, as appears from circumstances, another daughter, Maud, married to John de Altaripa.

By Fine in the 33rd Edward I. [1304–5] between Reyner de Knol and Beatrix his wife, plaintiffs, and Rob. de Knol, deforcient, of the manors of Knol, Helgefeld, and Stanerbottom, with the advowson of the church of Arncliff, the said manors and advowson are limited to the said Reyner and Beatrice and their heirs, remainder to William de Knol and his heirs, remainder to Helias, brother of Reyner, as to Knol and Helgfeld, then to Helias, son of Ric. de Knol and his heirs; remainder as to the manor of Stanerbotom and advowson of Arnclive to Alan de Arches and his heirs. This Alan was probably uncle of Beatrix.

The next transaction † relating to this advowson will go far towards establishing my conjecture, that the De Arches were founders of the church of Arncliff; for by charter s. d. but evidently subsequent to the time of 33rd Edward I. [1304–5] Reyner de Knol grants to Sir Henry de Percy a moiety of the advowson of the church of Arncliff, which advowson the said Reyner and Sir Thomas de Altaripa held in parcenary of the inheritance of their ancestors. Again, Reiner de Knol, knight, enfeoffed Sir Henry de Percy in the advowson of Arnecliff, and lordship of the town, for which the said Henry paid 40 marks, dated at Helgfeld, 1 Ed. fil R. Ed. ‡ This is accompanied by a release from Elias, son of Elias de Knol, of all his right and claim in the said advowson. And lastly, Sir Thomas de Altaripa confirms to the said Sir Henry de Percy the advowson of this church, which Sir Roger (it should be Reyner) de Knol, and he the said Sir Thomas held in parcenary.§

Still it is possible that the Percies themselves may have been founders of the church before the manor was granted to De Arches. That they either acquired or recovered it by this step from the mesne lords is certain.

Helias de Knol was son of Reyner, the husband of Beatrix, and none of their ancestors had any claim upon this manor and advowson. I am therefore compelled to give the

---

[* Manor—In Arneclif, Thorfin had 4 carucates to be taxed. Manor—In Hocheswic (Hawkswick), Gamel had 3 carucates to be taxed.]

  † Dodsw. MSS. v. 83.

  ‡ Dodsw. v. 8. fol. 28.

[§ *Parcenary*, co-heirship; the holding or occupation of lands of inheritance by two or more persons. It differs from *joint-tenancy*, which is created by deed or devise; whereas *parcenary* or co-parcenary, is created by the descent of lands from an ancestor, to be held in common with another or others, as his daughters, sisters, aunts, cousins, or their representatives. In this case all the heirs inherit as parceners or co-heirs.]

following transaction as I find it, without being able to reconcile the chronology of it with the foregoing transactions.

In the 49th Henry III., or 1269 [1264–5], is a covenant between Elias, son of Elias de Knol and Hawise his wife, on one part, and John de Altaripa and Maud his wife on the other, concerning the inheritance which belonged to Reyner de Arches, by which all the estate of Stanerbotom and all that meadow which Reyner held in Longstroth, near the chapel,* with the homage and service of Arncleve, were limited to Helias and Hawise and their heirs; and all the estate of the said Reyner in Hapton,† and all that Reyner and Sarah his wife held in Rauthmel, was limited to John de Altaripa and Maud his wife and their heirs. And whereas certain disputes had been moved with respect to the advowson of Arncliff, it was farther agreed that Helias and Hawise should present at that time, the church being then vacant, next John and Maud, and so alternately for the future.‡

At all events, their representatives about the end of Edward I.'s reign conveyed it to Sir Henry Percy, lord of the fee. The advowson of Arncliff continued in this great family till the 21st Henry VI. [1442–3], when Henry, the second Earl of Northumberland, an engraving of whose seal is given in the miscellaneous plate, as his autograph has been already given, conferred the advowson, together with three acres of land adjoining, upon the master and scholars of University College, Oxford,§ for the support of three Fellows of that society, to which, though very inadequate at present, it was fully adequate at that time, as I find from the records of the society that a lease of this rectory had been granted in 1441 by Thomas Newton, rector, to William, Abbot of Sallay, for 46*l. per annum.*‖ The licence of appropriation from Cardinal Kemp bears date March 3rd, 1443. Newton died in 1451, having left five marks to the repairs of the chancel, which, I suppose, his conscience accused him of having neglected.

On his decease, possession was given to the college by the Archdeacon of York.¶

This church, like most others in the deanery, appears to have been nearly rebuilt, with the addition of a steeple, in the reign of Henry VIII. But a single cylindrical column of the original structure remained to bear witness to its foundation about the time of Henry I., the great era of church-building in Craven.

[The church was, with the exception of the tower, partially rebuilt in the year 1800, and, from sketches in the possession of the Rev. Canon Boyd, appears to have been designed in the wretched style of that period, with

---

* Undoubtedly Hubberholm.

† See "History of Whalley," under Hapton.

‡ Dodsw. MSS. v. 83.

§ It may be worth while to subjoin Wood's account of this benefaction, which is very distinct and satisfactory:—
"Henricus Percy Com. North. precibus instante Academiâ (quòd attenuatæ adeò jam essent Collegii opes ut Cancellarius redituum præfecti et sociorum partem præcipuam solvendo æri alieno ac edificiis recreandis addixerit), Patrocinium Rectoratûs de Arncliffe apud Cravenam com. Ebor. cum III fundi jugeribus ibidem jacentibus, donavit 22 Hen. VI. eâ verò rege, ut Collegii sociis Academici tres Artium vel Mag. vel Bac. è diœcecibus Dunelm. Carleol. et Ebor. assumerentur, qui Theologiæ operam darent. Post paulo rationibus id suis conducere advertens Collegium appropriandum sibi prædictum beneficium impetravit annuâ XX marc. summâ vicario in stipendium reservatâ, quâ de reservatione Epistolas binas, alteram nempe ad Joh. Kempe Archiepiscopum, ad decanum vero et capitulum Ebor. alteram, transmisit Academia."

‖ Even as late as Henry VIII.'s reign 6*l. per annum* were accepted by St. John's College, Cambridge, for the endowment of a fellowship.—Baker's History of the College, MS.

¶ The particulars are extracted from the archives of that respectable society, with the perusal of which I have been favoured.

3 V

windows with wooden frames, and a roof with flat ceiling.   In 1841 Anthony Salvin was employed to restore it.   As originally built, the church had consisted of a nave, north aisle, chancel, and west tower, but the piers and arches dividing the aisle from the nave at some distant period had been removed, and in the restoration were not rebuilt, so that at present there is only west tower, built about the end of the 14th century, nave with south porch, and chancel. The chancel, which was entirely rebuilt in 1843, is erected in its proper line, and upon the old foundation, and is therefore not in the centre of the church, which has an unusual appearance.   The roofs are open-timbered.   The stained glass windows in the chancel are by Wailes, of Newcastle.

In the tower are three bells, one ancient, with this inscription in Lombardic characters :—

✠ PETRE : POLI : CLAVIS : FAC : UT : INTREMUS : PRECE : QUA : VIS

The other two bells are modern.

There are the following monumental inscriptions :—
On a tablet on the chancel wall—

Hic jacet quod mortale est
Milonis Tennant hujus Ecclesiæ
Annos ferme 51 Vicarii—
In liberis Educundis
Authoritate usus est puteoria
Miro tamen et tenerrimo
In suos affectu temperatâ.
In sacris officiis obeundis
Dei gloriam, gregisque sui salu-
-tem unice ob oculos Lubuit.
Duas duxit uxores Margeriam
Filiam Josiæ Lambert clerici,
Et Juditham, filiam Laurentii
Et Dorotheæ Lodge de Starbot-
-ton : Dierum satur obiit Dec͏ʳ.
19. A.D 1732 : Ætat. 74.

H. J.
Henricus Tennant, A.M.
Parochiarum Arncliviensis et Carltonensis
Vicarius, Colleguque Universitatis Oxon
haud ita pridem socius—
obiit 23ᵗⁱᵒ die Junii A.D. M.DCCLXXIX.
Ætatis LXXVI.

There are also monuments to—
Thos. Foster, of Nether Hesleden, died March 17, 1778, aged 35.
Janet, his wife, died 17 March, 1810, aged 67.

On a brass—

Hic jacent cineres Saræ Dawson
uxoris Guillielmi Dawson
de Halton Gill
To whom she five sons and five daughters bore,
Was just and kind and merciful to the poor.
Obiit 6ᵗᵒ die Septⁱ
1696.

In a stained glass window are these arms :—Quarterly (1) az. on a bend engr. arg. three daws ppr., *Dawson;* (2) vert a chev. betw. three pierced mullets or, *Pudsey;* (3) gu. a chev. betw. three mullets arg. in dexter and sinister chief a birdbolt head downwards or, *Boulton;* (4) arg. a fess betw. six crosses crosslet fitchy sa., *Layton.* An escutcheon of pretence of the first quar. a ◡ or for diff. for *Dawson* of Halton Gill. Dawson of Langcliffe and Hornby Castle. For Pudsey-Dawson; and Jane Constantine Dawson, daughter and co-heiress of Rev. Ric. Dawson, of Halton Gill.

The Rev. Canon Boyd has in his possession a silver coin of Vigmund, Archbishop of York, A.D. 836. It was found in the vicarage grounds.]

I have already had repeated opportunities of showing that the painted glass in the old churches of this district is universally coeval with their restoration ; and the following arms, remaining till within the last eight years, are certainly of Henry VIII.'s time, and after the 26th of that reign, when the Percy fee was settled upon the Clifford family :—

(1) *Clifford;* (2) *Percy;* (3) or, a cross sable, *Vescy;* (4) gu. a saltire arg., *Nevill;* (5) or, a fess between 2 chevrons gu., *Fitzwalter;* (6) gu. a cinquefoil surrounded by seven small ones or.

RECTORES DE ARNCLIFFE.

Adam Decanus sive Persona de Erneclif circ. 1180.
Roger Rector de Arncliff * 1230.

Temp. Inst.		Rectores.	Patroni.	Vacat.
10 kal. Oct.	1302.	Dns. *Adam de Mydelton*, acolythus.	Dns. *Tho. de Altaripa*, miles.	
9 kal. Maii,	1317.	Dns. *Joh. de Arundel*, Subdiac.	Dns. *Alianora de Percy.*†	per mort.
16 kal. Junii,	1331.	Dns. *Wm. de Barton*, Cl.	Dns. *Hen. de Percy*, mil.	per mort.
25 Mart.	1345.	Dns. *Wm. de Severby de Barton*, Subd.	Idem.	per mort.
11 Junii,	1349.	Dns. *Wm. de Newport*, acolythus.‡	Idem.	
17 Mart.	1356.	Dns. *Pet. de Richmond*, Cl.	Idem.	per mort.
1 Nov.	1362.	Dns. *Joh. Jordan*, Cap.	Idem.	
20 Jan.	1394.	{ Dns. *Joh. de Wyndhill*,§ Cler. ob. 1433, et sepult. est in Mon. de Alnwick. }	Dns. *Henr. Percy*, Comes North'land.	
		Dns. *Tho. de Neuton.*		

VICARII DE ARNCLIFFE.

			Patroni	
7 Oct.	1451.	Dns. *Wm. Dixon*, Presb.	{ Mag. et Scholares Coll. Univ. Oxon. }	per mort.
11 Feb.	1471.	Dns. *Rad. Thompson*, Cap.	Iidem.	per resig.
3 Aug.	1472.	Dns. *Ric. Fawcett*, Cap.	Iidem.	per mort.
9 Nov.	1500.	Mr. *Edm. Crofton.*	Iidem.	per resig.
9 Dec.	1506.	Mr. *Joh. Lethome*, pbr.	Iidem.	per mort.
19 Mart.	1508.	Mr. *Edw. Colyer*, M.A.	Iidem.	per resig.
9 Junii,	1517.	Dns. *Xtoph. Elyson*, Presb. ‖	Iidem.	per mort.

* Burton, "Mon. Ebor.," under Fountains.

[† Beatrice, wife of Reyner de Knolle was found to have died possessed of the Advowson of the Church of Arnecliffe.—Inq. *post mortem*, 19 Edw. II. 1325–6.]

‡ Afterwards Rector of Spofforth.

[§ His will dated 16th Sept. 1431, and proved 15 Jan. 1433, is printed in the "Testamenta Eboracensia," vol. ii., published by the Surtees Society, and is very interesting.]

‖ By will dated June 9th, 1552, he bequeathed his body to be buried in the parish church of Arncliff. Qu. was he father of George Ellyson his successor ?

Temp. Inst.	Rectores.	Patroni.	Vacat.
19 Oct. 1552.	*Geo. Ellyson,** A.M.	{ Assignati Mag'ri et Coll'i Dunelm.† &c.	
	Dns. *Anthonius Tophane.* ‡	Iidem Assignat.	per resig.
27 Oct. 1585.	*Hen. Tophane,* Cl. A.M.	Iidem.	per mort.
5 Jul. 1608.	*Arthur Coldwell,§* Cl. A.M.	Iidem.	
	Marmaduke Lambert.	{ Mag. et Scol. Coll. Univers. Oxon. }	per resig.
13 Aug. 1661.	*Iosiah Lambert,* Cl. sep. Oct. ult. 1681.	Iidem.	per mort.
13 Mar. 1681.	*Milo Tennant,* A.M. sep. Dec. 24, 1732.	Iidem.	per mort.
11 May, 1733.	*Thomas Kay,* A.M.	Iidem.	per resig.
1737.	*Joh. T. Chapman,* A.M. sep. Nov. 8, 1764.	Iidem.	per mort.
30 Apr. 1765.	*Henr. Tennant,* A.M. sep. Jun. 26, 1779.	Iidem.	per mort.
11 Dec. 1779.	*George Croft,* D.D.	Iidem.	per mort.
1809.	*Eardley Norton,* A.M. Instituted a second time 19 March, 1817.		per mort.
19 June, 1835.	*William Boyd,* M.A.		

Baptisms at Arncliffe including Hubberholm.　　　　　Burials at Do.

1680, 13,	In 1669, as the register is defective	.	.	5.
1700, 17,	.	.	.	13.
1800, 16,	.	.	.	10.

[The Register Books commence in 1669.]

Arncliffe is a discharged living, dedicated to St. Oswald, and returned as of the clear value of 39*l.* 12*s.* The shell of a handsome vicarage house was erected by the last incumbent; and the church itself growing ruinous was lately taken down, excepting the tower, and rebuilt with all the attention to economy and all the neglect both of modern elegance and ancient form, which characterises the religious edifices of the present day.

If the disposition of our ancient churches cannot be adhered to, if modern art can no longer imitate the solemn effect produced by clustered columns and pointed arches, by the dignified separation of family chantries, the long perspective of a choir, and the rich tracery of its ramified window; surely the genius of an establishment calls for something in its most frugal erections more imposing than bare walls and unbroken surfaces, something at least which may inform a stranger at his entrance that he is not putting his head into a conventicle. Even the rubric requires that chancels shall remain as they have done in times past.

It would be well if all plans for the erecting of new churches, or the rebuilding of old ones, were subject to the immediate cognisance of the ordinary or the archdeacon. At present the business is usually transacted between a selfish vestry and a *junto* of ignorant masons, while the faculty is granted as a matter of course by those who have no object but their fees.

---

* A George Ellison, A.M., was then master of the college.—Wood, "Hist. and Ant. Ox." L. 2, p. 60.
† The great benefactor and in reality the founder of this college was William Archdeacon of Durham; whence, saith Wood, this William, by whose money an adjoining hall was purchased, *cognomen ei nonnunquam impertierit.*—Wood, L. 2, p. 57.
‡ An Anthony Tophan, parson of Marton, bequeaths his body to be buried in the church of Arncliff, Dec. 25, 1590.
§ Otherwise Coldcal.

The following passage in an old historian, while it confirms my conjecture as to the foundation of most of the Craven churches in the reign of Henry I., tempts me to extend my observations on the different eras of church-building in this and the neighbouring districts, beyond the hints already given in the introduction to this work :—

" Narrationi nostræ perhibent evidens testimonium novæ basilicæ et multa oratoria nuper condita per vicos Angliæ et operosa claustra cœnobiorum, cum aliis officinis monachorum quæ constructa sunt Henrici regis tempore. Omnis enim ordo religiosorum pace fruens et prosperitate in omnibus quæ ad cultum Deitatis pertinent intus et exterius suam diligentiam sategit exhibere. Unde templa domosque fervens fidelium devotio præsumit prosternere, eademque meliorando et renovando iterare. Prisca ergo ædificia quæ sub Edgaro, vel Edvardo, aliisque Christianis regibus, constructa sunt, dejiciuntur ut amplitudine, vel operis elegantiâ, ad laudem Creatoris competenter emendentur."[*]

To apply this passage to the subject of the present work :—

The Craven churches which are known to have existed before the Conquest were, Ilkley, Long-Preston, Kirby Malghdale, Kildwick, and Bernoldswick ; to which may probably be added Bolton in Wharfdale. I am now inclined to defer more to the authority of Domesday than heretofore ; and am disposed to consider the silence of that record with respect to the existence of any other churches within the district as decisive. If, in the next place, there were no more churches, neither were there any other parishes. But how, it may be asked, were the several claims of patrons, incumbents, &c., compromised, in order to allow of so many new and independent foundations ? This difficulty will be removed by reflecting, that shortly after the Conquest this whole district became united into two or three great fees, the paramount lords of which might assume to themselves, upon every avoidance at least, a right of parcelling out the primitive parishes at pleasure. And when this work coincided with the fashion of the age, was considered as meritorious, and supported by the ordinary, there can be little doubt but that they would actually exercise this right either in person or by permitting the mesne lords to erect and endow churches for themselves. We know, that at this very time Bracewell and Marton, and perhaps Thornton, were taken out of Bernoldswick. Gisburne too was founded within the Percy fee ; and there is no difficulty in supposing that the other parishes within it (most of which may be traced up nearly to the time of Henry I.) as Gargrave, Giggleswick, Bolton juxta Bowland, nay, perhaps Arncliff and Kettlewell, were parts of those two primitive parishes, and severed from them upon the same principle.

Another and opposite reason of the subdivision of the primitive parishes was, that their members consisted of two fees ; an idea which has been illustrated in the case of Linton and Burnsall.

With respect to the fee of Earl Edwin, out of the Saxon cure of Bolton, pretty certainly arose the parishes of Skipton with Carlton [†] (long since separated), and that of Addingham ; the first of the foundation of the lords paramount, the latter of the mesne lords, and all in this very reign of Henry I., as appears either from written or architectural evidence.

Of the original and properly Saxon structures of these churches, it is needless to say

[*] Orderici Vitalis Angligenæ cœnobii Uticensis Monachi, Eccl. Hist. l. 10.

[†] Carlton was within the Percy fee, and probably separated from the mother church of Skipton the earlier on that account.

that not a vestige remains. They were probably levelled to make way for those more spacious and elegant buildings of which Ordericus speaks as having been so universally substituted to the others in the reign of Henry I.

On this authority therefore, as well as the many striking appearances of their architecture, I assign the interval between 1100 and 1135, as the first great era of church-building in Craven.

Still further to illustrate the historian, I shall show that the fashion was equally prevalent at the same time in the adjoining districts.

There is the strongest evidence that in this reign the parish of Halifax was severed from the ancient Saxon parish of Dewsbury. And if the parish of Blackburn were endowed a little earlier, and that of Alvetham a few years later, Rochdale is almost certainly to be referred to the reign of Henry I. In point of architecture, the churches of Whalley and Rochdale, as well as the chapels of Clitheroe and Colne, contain indubitable marks of the same period. The fact seems to have been this, that in addition to Ordericus's reason— namely, the general tranquillity of the age—property was now consolidated, the wounds left by the Conquest were healed, and the Norman lords, feeling themselves at home, began to indulge their piety and their taste without control or apprehension.

In this state our churches continued at least four centuries ; when, either from increase of population or change of fashion, a general enlargement in their structures took place. At the same time many new chapels were founded and endowed. Of these, in the parish of Whalley four were certainly, and two others probably, erected during the reign of Henry VIII. ; besides that, six were enlarged and altered according to the new model. Of the twelve chapels in the parish of Halifax six were founded in the same reign.

From that time to the beginning of the present reign, a period of about 250 years, little farther change took place ; but within the last forty years eight chapels have decayed, and been rebuilt, in the parish of Whalley; four in that of Halifax ; and three in Rochdale. Nearly uniform in their style, as well as contemporary in their foundations, all these might seem to have been set by their builders, like so many time-pieces, to go and to run down together.

The present reign, therefore, may be considered as the third great era of church-building amongst us.

Of the style and marks belonging to the two former periods enough has already been said. Of the last, what can be said, but that, excepting weakness and deformity, it has no character at all ? A plain, oblong, ill-constructed building, without aisles, choir, columns, battlements, or buttresses ; the roof and wainscoting of deal ; the covering of slate, and the walls running down with wet. To the builders of such edifices the scoff of Tobiah the Ammonite may justly be applied : " That which they do build, if a fox go up, he shall even break down." *

It is but lately that this spirit has shown itself in Craven ; and, indeed, the church of Arncliff is as yet the only perfect specimen of it. In the shape of repairs, it has made no small devastation.

* Nehem. iv. 3.

But how, it may be asked, are our dilapidating churches to be rebuilt, or how restored? Certainly not with a puerile affectation of what is called Gothicism, while it really consists in nothing more than piked sash-windows, which every other feature of the place belies. This, as it costs little, and makes one step to meet ancient prejudice, is perpetually attempted in the most frugal ecclesiastical works.

But I am no advocate for what is called modern Gothic of a more expensive and elaborate kind. The cloven foot *will* appear; for modern architects have an incurable propensity to mix their own absurd and unauthorised fancies with the genuine models of antiquity. They want alike taste to invent, and modesty to copy. Neither am I so superstitiously addicted to what however I extremely venerate, the *forms* of our ancient churches, as to maintain that they ought not in any case to be abandoned. No modern, even though a good Catholic, perhaps, would go all the lengths of Durand, who can discover a spiritual sense in nave, side-aisles, choir, columns, and arches; nay, who can find types in mullions, and mysteries in the weathercock.* But so much is surely due to ancient prejudice, that where there is no powerful reason to the contrary, the old distribution of parts ought to be adhered to. How many, from the want of these have found their piety damped, and have contracted an incurable aversion to modern churches!

But, to be more distinct:—

What I recommend upon a small scale is precisely what was done upon a large one at the rebuilding of St. Paul's, which, by the judicious adoption of the form of a cross, instead of becoming a heathen temple, remained a Christian cathedral. And whoever wishes to see the same reverence for antiquity in the form, united with unavoidable modernism in the manner, and that upon an imitable scale, may turn to Dr. Plott's two views of the churches of Ingestree and Okeover, in Staffordshire, restored in the reign of Charles II. In such erections, how much of the old effect is preserved by round arches, broken surfaces, and variety of light and shade!

The case of repairs is next to be considered.

Awakened by the remonstrances of their ecclesiastical superior, a parish discover that, by long neglect, the roof of their church is half rotten, the lead full of cracks, the pews falling down, the windows broken, the mullions decayed, the walls damp and mouldy. Here it is well if the next discovery be not the value of the lead. No matter whether this covering have or have not given an air of dignity and venerable peculiarity to the church for centuries. It will save a parish assessment.

However, the work of renovation proceeds: the stone tracery of the windows which had long shed their dim religious light is displaced, and with it all the armorial achievements of antiquity, the written memorials of benefactors, the rich tints and glowing drapery of saints and angels. In short, another Dowsing seems to have arisen. But, to console our eyes for these losses, the smart luminous modern sash is introduced; and if this be only pointed at

---

* This is no exaggeration. "Gallus supra ecclesiam positus prædicatores significat. Virga ferrea in quâ Gallus sedet rectum representat prædicantis sermonem, ut non loquatur ex spiritu hominis, sed Dei." But this is nothing to Durand's account of sand and gravel used in church-building. "Calx Charitas fervens est, quæ sibi conjungit sabulum— id est terrenum opus," &c. Yet is his work styled a Rationale!

top, all is well, for all is Gothic still.   Next are condemned the massy oaken stalls, many of which are capable of repair, and as many want none.   These are replaced by narrow, slender deal pews, admirably contrived to cramp the tall and break down under the bulky.   Next, the fluted woodwork of the roof, with all its carved enrichments, is plastered over.   It looked dull, and nourished cobwebs.   Lastly, the screens and lattices, which, from a period antecedent to the Reformation, had spread their light and perforated surfaces from arch to arch, are sawn away, and, in the true spirit of modern equality, one undistinguishing blank is substituted to separations which are yet canonical, and to distinctions which ought yet to be revered.

Whereas, if these works were conducted with a proper regard for antiquity, the failing parts restored on the same model, and with the same materials, as those which remain, and no feature of either concealed or removed, posterity would thank us, not only for transmitting to them with fidelity many venerable remains of ancient art, but those in a state more durable, and less likely to become burdensome to themselves, than the frail and unskilful substitutions of the present day.

It will not be long before the justice of these remarks comes to be acknowledged.

To the first style of church architecture in this and the adjoining districts I have allotted a duration of four centuries ; to the second, two and a half ; to the third it will be enough to assign a single century.

The long duration of the Norman architecture is to be ascribed to three causes—the narrow dimensions of the buildings themselves, the perpendicular pressure of the semicircular arches, and the bulk of the columns which sustain them.

But the pointed arch universally, and especially the broad, flat arch of Henry VIII.'s time, has a strong lateral pressure, and, being sustained on slender columns, has a perpetual tendency to throw them and the adjoining walls, in one direction or other, out of the perpendicular.*   It is to this cause, almost exclusively, that the decay of so many churches and chapels of that period which have failed within my recollection, is to be ascribed ; and of those which were enlarged at the same time from the old Norman structures I will venture to predict that, if left to themselves, the remains of the original building will long outlast the additions.

For my last opinion, that a single century is adequate to the probable duration of our modern churches, I have even now the support of fact.   Their walls are slight, and pervious to every shower; their roofs of slender deal timber, already bending under the pressure; and the ends of the beams rotting off, even in the first twenty years, from the cause already assigned.   The only church in Craven which is now actually rebuilding, or requires to be rebuilt, was completely restored in the modern style about eighty years since.

Let this prediction be remembered, and let it serve as a warning to parishes to repair their churches on the old model, but never, without extreme necessity, to pull them down.

The church of Arncliffe has two dependent chapels, Halton Gill and Hubberholm.   Of the antiquity of the former I know nothing more than that it is mentioned in Harrison's

---

* It was for this reason that the pointed arch introduced buttresses, the projection of which gradually increased as the arch became more obtuse.

"Description of Britain," A.D. 1577. It was rebuilt in 1636, but has no churchyard or interments.

[The chapel of Halton Gill, which is dedicated to St. John the Baptist, previous to 1848 consisted of a chapel with a massive open-timbered roof, and at the west end a bell-turret, and was dated 1632. At the west end the minister's house was connected with it, and was under the same roof. In 1848 it was rebuilt in the same form ; but the space occupied by the minister's house is now used as a school, with a portion parted off to form a vestry. Mr. A. B. Higham, of Wakefield, was the architect. The cost was borne by the three Misses Dawson, of Marshfield, and the church was consecrated on the 4th October, 1848.

CURATES OF THE CHAPEL OF HALTON GILL.

(As mentioned in the Registers.)

1631.	Nicholas Smith.
1673.	John Hargreaves, buried May 6.
1690.	Francis Bryer, of Halton Gill, and Agnes Lambert, of Kilnsay, married 22nd May.
1691.	—— (name illegible) of Francis Boyer or Bryan, clerk, baptised May 21.
1692.	Margaret, daughter of Francis Bryan, clerk, curate of Halton Gill, baptised Dec. 15th.
1694.	Christopher, son of Francis Brier, clerk, curate of Halton Gill, March 6th.
1711.	Mr. Tomson. Thomas, son of Mr. Tomson, curate of Halton Gill, baptised 5th Dec.
1714.	Humphrey Dickinson. Mary, daughter of Mr. Humphrey Dickinson, curate of Halton Gill, was baptised 29th Oct.
1716.	Elizabeth, daughter of Mr. Humphrey Dickinson, curate of Halton Gill, bapt. 13th Dec.
1722.	John Hogget, or Hogarth. Mr. Baldestone.
1737. 1739.	Miles Wilson.
1777.	Thomas Lindley. Vac. per mortem.
7 Sept. 1847.	Edwin Bettlestone, B.A. Vac. per resig.
17 Sept. 1866.	John Grisdale.

From Notes by the Rev. Canon Boyd.

[Henry Fawcett, Alderman of Norwich, in 1619 gave 10*l*. a year to the minister of Halton Gill, for teaching poor men's children, and reading services. This sum is paid as a rent-charge issuing out of an estate at Boughton, in the county of Norfolk, the property of Lord Suffield. William Fawcett, by will dated 27th April, 1630, reciting that Marmaduke Fawcett, his nephew, stood indebted to him in the sum of 630*l*., to be paid upon certain days, under an assignment of a lease for a long term of years of an estate at Upper or Over Hesleden therein mentioned, directed that towards the enlarging of the gift of his brother, Henry Fawcett, deceased, to the chapel of Halton Gill, the said Marmaduke Fawcett should be discharged of the said debt upon condition that, within two years of the testator's decease, he should make a sufficient assurance for the payment of 18*l*. 6*s*. 8*d*. a year—that is to say, 13*l*. 6*s*. 8*d*. *per annum* to a Master of Arts, or some other able and well qualified scholar, who should preach the Word of God, and catechise and instruct the younger sort of people of the town of Halton Gill, on the sabbath days, in the chapel of Halton Gill, and also instruct the children of the said parish on the week days, at the schoolhouse which he, the testator, had built for the purpose, in the rudiments of grammar and other learning, as a schoolmaster ought to do ; 1*l*. a year for two sermons—one to be preached in the forenoon of the 5th of November yearly, in the parish church of Arncliffe, and the other in the afternoon of the same day, in the chapel of Halton Gill—in remembrance of their deliverance from the Popish conspiracy of the Gunpowder Treason ; and 4*l*. a year, the remainder of the 18*l*. 6*s*. 8*d*., to the poor people of Litton Dale, in the parish of Arncliffe, to be distributed amongst them at the discretion of the minister and vestrymen of the said parish.

Soon after the testator's death the yearly sum of 18*l*. 6*s*. 8*d*. was charged by deed on an estate at Upper Hesledon, in the lordship of Litton ; but for a long time past an estate at the same place, consisting of a farmhouse and some acres of enclosed land, together with about 88 acres of waste land on Litton Moor, has been held by the curate of Halton Gill for the time being, on account of the charity, in substitution of the rent-charge.

A close of eight acres or thereabouts, in the township of Settle, and a rent-charge of 2*l*. 10*s*. a year, issuing out of a field in Halton called Stepton Field, are appropriated by the donation, as is understood, of Elizabeth Topfield, a daughter of the above-named William Fawcett, to the use of the curate of Halton Gill, and of poor persons of Halton Gill and Arncliffe—three-fifths being paid to the curate for a sermon on the 29th March yearly, and two-fifths for finding clothes for the poor people.—*Charity Commissioners' Report.*]

Among the singular characters of this country it will now give pain to no one if I notice Mr. Wilson, formerly curate of Halton Gill, and father of the late Rev. Edward Wilson, canon of Windsor.   He wrote a tract entitled " The Man in the Moon," which was seriously meant to convey the knowledge of common astronomy in the following strange vehicle :—A cobbler, Israel Jobson by name, is supposed to ascend first to the top of Penigent, and thence, as a second stage, equally practicable, to the moon ; after which he makes a tour of the whole solar system.   From this excursion, however, the traveller brings back little information which might not have been had upon earth, excepting that the inhabitants of one of the planets—I forget which—were made of pot-metal.   The work contains some other extravagances ; but the writer, after all, was a man of talents, and has abundantly shown that, had he been blessed with a sound mind and a superior education, he would have been capable of much better things.   If I had the book* before me, I could quote single sentences here and there which, in point of composition, rise to no mean degree of excellence.

Mr. Wilson had also good mechanical hands, and carved well in wood ; a talent which he applied to several whimsical purposes.   But his *chef d'œuvre* was an oracular head, like that of Friar Bacon and the disciple of the famous Escotillo,† with which he diverted himself and amazed his neighbours, till a certain reverend wiseacre threatened to complain of the poor man to his metropolitan as an enchanter.   After this the oracle was mute.

The chapel of St. Michael, of Hubberholm, bears marks of very high antiquity.‡ Several Norman arches remain entire, though the square piers of some of them were dressed away to slender octagons, when the chapel underwent a general repair, which seems to have been about the reign of Henry VIII.   The steeple is of the same period, if not still later. Over the entrance of the chancel is an entire and curious roodloft of oak, very handsomely wrought, and painted with broad red lines, like the screen of Skipton Church, and the roof of the nave at Bolton Abbey.

On the front of this work, towards the west, is the following inscription :—

𝕬𝖓𝖓𝖔 𝖉𝖔 𝕸° 𝕮𝕮𝕮𝕮 𝕷𝕼𝕵𝕵° 𝖍𝖔𝖈 𝖔𝖕𝖚𝖘 𝖊𝖗𝖆𝖙 𝕨𝖎𝖑𝖑𝖒𝖎 𝕵𝖆𝖐𝖊 𝖈𝖆𝖗𝖕𝖊𝖙.§

---

* It is rarely to be met with, having, as I am told, been industriously bought up by his family.   I have only seen one copy, and my recollection of what I read in it is not very particular.

† See " Don Quixote," b. iv. ch. 10.

‡ In the account of Henry Earl of Northumberland, relating to the Percy fee, anno 1502, is this entry :—

" In thannuitie of a Priest syngynge wᵗin Hobh'm chapell, in the same Forest of Langstroth dale, Xs.

"At this time Sir Thomas Tempest, of Bracewell, was steward and master forester of my Lord's lands in C'avyn, received an annual fee of XIII*l.* VI*s.* VIII*d.*

"John Ham'ton, Sqwyer, also recᵈ. (for what office it does not appear) VI*l.* XIII*s.* IV*d.*"   In the Act 29 Henry VIII. for the settling the Percy fee in Craven, it is provided, *inter alia,* that "John Norton, Squyre, and Richard Norton, his son, shall hold and enjoy for term of their lives, and the longer liver of them, one annuitie of XX*l.,* and also another yerely rent of XIII*l.* VI*s.* VIII*d.* for the executing the office of General Forestership of all the forests, parks, &c., of the Erle of N. in Yorkshire."   This connection brought on the ruin of the Nortons.

[§ Upon the screen the Percy Badge a fetter-lock within the horns of a crescent is twice carved, once reversed, there is also a plain annulet.]

The carpenter was very idly employed; for in that same year, 1558, Queen Mary's death put an end to the worship of images, and therefore to the use of rood-lofts in English churches.

This is a sequestered and interesting place, situated on the northern bank of the Wharf, shaded by tall trees on the east, and overhung by a steep and lofty wood beyond. I know few scenes better adapted to quiet and contemplation. [In 1875, on the 31st August, a violent storm split a magnificent sycamore into two parts. The girth at five feet from the ground was nineteen feet seven inches.*]

And when we take into the account, that nearly from the Conquest to the present day this humble edifice has been the only resort of the foresters of Longstrother for public worship, and the only deposit of their dead, that its foundation long preceded the stately piles of Fountains, Bolton, Kirkstall, and Sallay, and has much longer survived their fall, it is neither easy nor desirable to avoid a train of reflections on the instability of wealth or greatness, and the security which ever accompanies remote and unambitious indigence.

At Hubberholm there is a tradition of a flood, which inundated the churchyard, and left behind it many fish in the church. This is not absolutely incredible; but whoever observes the depth of the torrent beneath will have a lively idea of the devastation which must in that case have been committed on the plain and skirts of the valley.

The story probably refers either to the great inundation of 1686, mentioned under Kettlewell, or to one equally formidable which happened in September, 1673. †

In Arncliff 27 carucates made a knight's fee; a single exception to the general rule within the Percy fee, where the knight's fee was 12 carucates.

[The old chapel was entirely restored in 1863, under the direction of Ewan Christian of London. It consists of nave with two aisles; chancel without arch; low, square west tower; and south porch, dated 1696. The south arcade has four circular arches, built of rough stones, without the slightest dressing or moulding; the piers are also rough, but octagonal, with plain chamfered abaci. The north arcade has four arches; the three towards the west are pointed, resting on octagonal piers, but the fourth, in the chancel, is remarkably flat, springing from responds, and spanning twenty-two feet; its thrust is sustained by a very massive buttress from the east wall. The roofs are all covered with lead. The rood-screen and loft still remain; the loft has a railing on each side, with thirteen panels, pierced with rude Gothic tracery : upon the beam is carved the inscription and date as given above. The entrance to the loft was at the north-east angle, apparently by means of a ladder.

The font is early, and rudely carved with heads, fleurs-de-lis on steps, &c. On the bell is the legend, JHESUS BE OUR SPEED 1601.

The Registers date from 1660.

There are tablets to—

James Tennant, of Yockenthwaite, who died 7th October, 1769, in the 71st year of his age.

Margaret Tennant, sister to the above, she died 9th May, 1771, in the 83rd year of her age.

James Tennant, their son, who died 10th May, 1775, aged 14 years.

Jeffrey Tennant, of Yockenthwaite, Esq., died 5th Dec. 1825, aged 67.

[* The old house at Kirkgill, opposite the church, was the parsonage, it is now (1877) occupied by the parish clerk, and used as a public-house.]

† This is recorded in the parish register of Otley as follows :—"On the 11th day of this month there was a wonderful inundation of waters in the Northern parts. This river of Wharf was never known within the memory of man to be so big by a yard in height. It overturned Kettlewell, Burnsall, Barden, Ilkley, and Otley Bridges." The dates of the present bridges, which were rebuilt by the West Riding, prove the correctness of this account. Grassington Bridge appears to have stemmed the torrent.

Shield—Arg. on a chevron between 3 fleurs-de-lis sa. as many rams' heads erased of the field (*Ramsden*), impaling, arg. a lion ramp. within a double tressure flory and counter-flory gu. (*Dundas*).

John Charles Ramsden, eldest son of Sir John Ramsden, Bart., died 29th Dec. 1836, in the 49th year of his age.

John Jaques, of Cray, died 9th Nov. 1830, aged 36 years ; son of Leonard and Ellen Jaques of the same place.

Richard Foster, of Buckden, died 14th June, 1837, aged 71.

Also, Ann Foster, his widow, died 3rd Jan. 1860, aged 82.

Hubberholme is a perpetual curacy, value 110*l.* ; patron, the Vicar of Arncliffe. Some of the curates have been :—

10th July, 1727, *Henry Tennant,* A.B.

23rd Sept. 1765, *John Ibbetson.*

1838, *Thomas Lindley.*

13th Ap. 1847, *W. Richardson Metcalfe.*]

Beneath Arncliff, on the Skirfare, is Hawkswicke,* a word which requires no explanation. This was in very early times a mesne-manor of the Mauleverers; holden, I apprehend, of the Skipton fee; for as early as 1175, William, son of Helte de Mauleverer, the latter of whom was one of the witnesses to the donation of Kildwick to the priory of Bolton, gave to the abbey of Fountains one carucate here, called Gnip; and this grant was confirmed by Aaliza de Rumelli. It has now become impossible to explain how or when the distribution of the lands of Roger of Poitou took place between the houses of Percy and Rumelli. Gnip is probably a Danish word, for Gnipa † in the Islandic is *summitas montis.*

The last circumstance which I shall mention with respect to Hawkswic is extremely curious : William de Helte (by which I suppose is meant William son of Helte de Mauleverer), gave to the monks of Fountains the *firmatio* of his two bridges, one over Skirfare, the other over Werh, with a way of thirty feet wide between them. On this account I have to observe, first, that at this early period, or about 1175, there was a bridge in this neighbourhood over the Wharf, though it may be difficult to ascertain its site. It was evidently the property of this William, which renders it improbable that it was the same either with that of Coniston or Kettlewell, where he had no estates.

Secondly, the word *firmatio,* if I understand it, means rent ; and if this conjecture be right, it will follow, that the Mauleverers had built the two bridges in question, and imposed a toll upon them, which they first let to tenants, and then bestowed the profits upon the monks of Fountains. The idea was perhaps too rational, and implies too advanced a state of society for the twelfth century ; but I know not what other account can be given of the word *firmatio.*

The present lords of this village are the Duke of Devonshire and the devisee of the late John Tennant, Esq.

[* HAUKESWYK CUM OULECOTES.[1]—In eadem villis sunt VI car. terræ quæ tenentur de rege, et quælibet car. redd. per ann. ad finem prædictum III*d.* ob. q. ; unde summa est XI*d.* q.—Kirkby's " Inquest," A.D. 1284.

In the 9th Edward II., Willelmus de Haukeswyk, Rogerus de Hawkeswyk, and Johannes de Paryes (or Pereis) were Lords of the manor of Haukeswyk.—" Nomina Villarum."

In the old lead mines near this village a silver penny of Edward I. was found ; it is now in the possession of the Rev. Canon Boyd.]

† Runolphus Jonas, " Dict. Isl."

[¹ There is now no place of this name. Old Cote Moor extends from two to three miles N.W. of Hawkswick.]

I have purposely reserved to the last place in this account the transactions of the Percys and Cliffords, as chief lords of the fee, in connection with the parish of Arncliffe, to exhibit them in one view.

First, then, Richard de Percy gave Litton and Littondale to the monks of Fountains ; but this must be understood to except two oxgangs, and pasture for 300 sheep in this place, given by Agnes de Percy to Salley Abbey. No notice, however, is taken of this exception in the general confirmation of Richard I., which, in terms the most comprehensive, assures to the former house " Litton cum toto Littondale, et cum omnibus logiis et locis suis ib'm et cum totâ forestâ suâ de Gnoup et Dernbrook, et libertate omnium ferarum et avium ib'm, simul cum omnibus logiis et locis suis in eâdem forestâ." *

But the Percys appear to have allowed and contested these extravagant grants alternately, as devotion or self-interest happened to prevail ; for John, son of William de Percy, quit-claimed to Fountains Abbey all his right in the vale and forest of Litton, which was confirmed by Galfrid, son of Galfrid de Percy ; but long afterwards, Henry de Percy disputed this concession ; in consequence of which it was finally agreed, in 1294, that the said Henry should confirm all the grants of his ancestors in this place, but that the abbot and convent should release to him in return all kinds of wild beasts and birds of prey in Littondale, and that his chief forester should have the care of them. They also quit-claimed to him all their meadows and pastures in Bukkeden and elsewhere within the bounds of Longstrother, with the wild beasts of that chase ; and agreed to pay to the said Henry the sum of 600 marks in three years.†

It was evidently not the territorial rights, but those of the forest, about which this ancient baron was solicitous.

Seventeen years after this transaction, viz., 4 Edward II. [1310–11] the same Henry de Percy ‡ obtained a charter of free-warren within his demesnes of Arncliffe and Bukkeden; and died in the eighth year of the same reign completely reconciled, as it should seem, to the monks, for he was allowed to repose in the holy earth of Fountains.

From the time of this agreement the manorial and forest rights of Littondale and Longstrother were vested in the Percies till after the marriage of Margaret, daughter of the sixth Earl of Northumberland, with Henry, first Earl of Cumberland ; in consequence of which they were settled on Henry Lord Clifford, the issue of that match, 26th Henry VIII. [1534–5] and are now the property of his Grace the Duke of Devonshire, as representative of the last male line of the Cliffords.

Dr. Burton has with great exactness recited the donations of many mesne proprietors of lands here, in the twelfth and thirteenth centuries, to Fountains Abbey. From the original " Coucher Book" of that great house, which I have lately had an opportunity of examining,§ the following are extracted, as being of more interest and suggesting more reflections than the rest :—

* " Mon. Ang." in Fontanense Cœnobio.
† See the particulars in Dr. Burton's " Mon. Ebor." under Fountains.
‡ Dugdale's " Baronage," under Percy.
§ Let me be understood to mean, *in the Cotton Library, not in any private archives.*

"Thurstin de Arches d. & c. XVIII bov. in Erncleve, & præterea Borganes & Marescum & vasta loca ad vertendum. Test. Rad. presbytero de Ketelwell, Gwil. fil. Helte (de Mauleverer), & Hen. fra. ejus, & Herb. de Arches, & Hug. de Hertlinton, & Rad. f. Awdelm."

Borganes appear to be Bogs (perhaps from beonȝian, *vitare*) ; but I have not met the word in any etymologist.

Next—

"Wilymus f. Thurst. de Arches confirmat don. patris. Test. Joh. f. Edulph de Kilnsay, Hukemon f. Outhelf, Uckeman f. Antholin, Adam dec. de Ernecleve, Adam presb. Ivo senesc. Ric de Percy."

Ric. de Percy lived in the reigns of Richard I. and John; yet the proper names in Craven continued to be almost entirely Saxon.

Third—

"Wm. de Arches d. & c. 1 bov. quam emit de Elya de Kekeleswre, genero, decano."

Therefore this dean also was a married man.

Fourth—

"Wm. de Arches ded. dim. bov. cum corp. præsenti Wil'mi filii sui."

A moderate burial fee !

Lastly—

"Adam f. Ad. de Ghicleswic quietum clamavit red'm XV*d.* pro terris in Ernecleve, ad inveniendan velamina capitibus tineosorum qui sunt curandi ad portam."

Scald heads, like other cutaneous diseases, the offspring of filth and salted food, must then have been extremely common. But let us venerate the charity of the monks, who, in infirmaries purposely constructed near the gates of their houses, gratuitously exercised the arts of medicine and surgery on the most loathsome disorders.

About the end of Queen Mary's reign, or the beginning of Elizabeth's, the estates of Fountains Abbey, in Litton and Longstrothdale, were purchased from the Gresham family by the second Earl of Cumberland, who, in addition to his superiorities and forest rights, thus became possessed, excepting, perhaps, some trifling freeholds about Arncliff, of the whole parish, a tract not less than fifty square miles in extent. But these acquisitions, and many others, melted away in the hands of his two sons, among whose alienations I distinguish that of Hesseldene, including great part of Penigent, by Earl George, in 1604, for little more than 1100*l.*, and Greenfield, by Earl Francis, to Thomas Heber, of Marton, Esq. At Greenfield, the *forest* of Longstroth commences, and extends half a mile below Buckden ; but Longstroth*dale* extends a mile lower, and joins upon the manor of Kettlewell. All the forest is within the manor of Buckden, and all the hamlets within it are included under that township.

I have reason to think that the deer were finally destroyed in the latter end of the reign of Charles I.

In the year 1499 there were in Longstrothdale the following lodges, viz. Oughtershaw, consisting of 6 tenements ; Bekarmonth, of 4 tenements ; Greenfell, of 2 ; Depdale, of 7 ;

Yokenthwaite, of 6 ; Ramsgill, of 6 ; Midlemore, of 2 ; Kyrkgyll, of 4 ; Chapel, of 2 ; and Cray, of 4. The names of the old tenants were chiefly Calfherd (which gives the etymology of Calvert), Faldshagh (now Falshaw), Lodge, Forster, Jake, and Longstrothe ; of which the last were probably the immediate relatives of the celebrated Prior of St. John of Jerusalem.* The number of tenements, including Buckden, which contained 21, is 64, which, multiplied by 4½, gives a population of 288. The return for the same extensive tract, exactly three centuries after, was 280 ; a parity which implies a very settled state of manners and property in two distant periods. The entire rental of the Percy fee was 138*l.* 1*s.* 10*d.*, which in 1502 was conveyed from Cletop and Hubberholm to Petworth in Sussex, by four men on horseback, who were fourteen days on their journey forward and backward, and received each " 8*d*. per diem for his expenses."—" Blest paper credit ! "

I shall conclude this article and the work with the fragment of a very curious and ancient perambulation of the Percy fee, which, from the wild and romantic district which it traverses, and the singular as well as obsolete names by which the several boundaries are described, cannot but be highly gratifying to an antiquarian ear. Internal evidence will carry up this document to the reign of Richard II.

" These are the bounder between Longstroth' and Wencedale ; that is to say, first, from the Cold Keld Head of Cam to the height of Mosside, then to the midstake of the Wald, as hevyn water devides it, between Lord Percy,† *Duke of Braban,* of the Lo'pp of Langstroth and Wensladale. From the Midstake to a certaine Pyke there, and from thence to Piglerd hill, to the Midcause stone, then to the Gavel nabb and sic, lineallye to ye height of Setterynset, as the heaven and water divide it betwixt the foresaid Lord Pearcy and the Lord of Westmoreland,† of the forest of Langstrothdale and Bishopdale. From ye height of Setterynsett to Camfell End, to the Howrd house of Cam, to the Shorn crosse, to Ketelwell crosse, and from Ketelwell cross to a Keld Head in Wipartine close, and from that Keld Head to Crowne crosse, as heaven and water divide it betwixt the Lo'pp of Starbotten and Kettlewell. And from Crowne crosse to Litton crosse, from Litton crosse to the height of Swarthken, thence to Ulecross, thence to the hill of Penaygent and to Swarthgill ; from Swarthgill to the Meer Syke at ye West end of Greenfield Knot, and from the Meer Syke to Toghwoodshaw to Stanepapane, and from Stanepapane to the Cold Keld, as it falls into Lumbecke, betwixt the Lord Pearcy and the Lord Mowbray, as by ye feyth of ye men, and ye Wa'd' of ye Forest of Littondale ys ye afors'd L'd Pearcy. Waifs and strayes, and bloodwytes, and ye gift of ye office, bee ye Lord Pearcy. And the house of Fountains *pained* their waifes, and ye Lord shal hold a Court once a year at ye old *Wald* in bent of Litton, for all the forfeits afores'd."

On these " Cold Keld Heads " we have reached some of the highest ground in the island ; and looking southward far as the confines of the Peak, survey beneath our feet the three valleys of Craven, with all their boundaries of rock and fell, their scattered villages, rich pastures, and diversified landscapes. Farther, in the same direction, stretch the brown hills of "the ancient parish of Whalley," with their populous towns, descried through smoke, and their uniting streams gradually expanded into one great estuary, and mingling with the sea. These ample districts have now been exhausted in two successive works, by the labours of the same topographer. The point on which he stands, the elevation and almost unbounded prospect, are inspiring. He now turns his eye in another direction, and the valleys and plains of Richmondshire stretch like a map before him.

To the left is the Roman Bracchium, with its elevated summer camp. Beneath

[* See p. 575.]

† The Percies rarely used the style of Dukes of Brabant. But there is a chronological difficulty in this instrument, which I am unable to solve ; for the owner of the Percy fee is called Lord Pearcy, and that of Bishopdale the Lord of Westmoreland. Now Henry Lord Percy was created Earl of Northumberland 1st of Richard II. and Ralph Lord Nevile was not raised to the dignity of Earl of Westmoreland before the 21st of the same reign.—Dugdale's " Baronage " in Percy and Nevile.

appear the grey turrets of Nappay, while, bounding over the cataracts of Aysgarth, the Eure conducts him to another Bolton, pregnant with facts and recollections. Immediately beyond rise the proud towers of the Neviles at Middleham, and far to the north-east the Norman Keep of Richmond, begirt with its monastic accompaniments. In *that* vale to the east, the arches of Coverham distinctly present themselves. In *those* fertile meadows beneath, appear the fragments of Joreval, and Tanfield beyond, in whose church repose, beneath magnificent tombs, the Marmions of *real* history. Turning to the south-west, the "troublous Skell" leads him to the mighty carcase of Fountains, and to the more ancient and venerable foundation of Wilfred.

Time has been when such a scene might have inspired and dictated another Work. But the recollection of increasing years and declining health, together with the demands of duty in a most serious and important charge, checks at once the unseasonable impulse, and compels him to resign a History of Richmondshire * to some younger and more vigorous antiquary, on whom, were it in his power, he would willingly bestow whatever portion he may possess of two qualifications, henceforward of little value to himself, but indispensable to a true topographer, namely, perseverance and enthusiasm.

---

* Which has been suggested to the Author. From some future undertaking of a much less laborious nature, if life and leisure permit, he means not to preclude himself.

[Dr. Whitaker was, nevertheless, enabled to carry out his intention, and in 1823 published the "History of Richmondshire," in two folio volumes, illustrated with woodcuts and plates, many of which are from drawings by J. M. W. Turner, R.A.]

FINIS.

123 *Arms at Salley Abbey.*

4 *Arms of the same from Tong's Survey 1530.*

5 *Seal of Bolton Priory.*

6 *Seal of the 2.ᵈ Earl of Northumberland.*

7 *Arms of Kirkstall Abbey at Berholdswick Church.*

8 *Seal of Abbot Hugh de Mykelay & Counterseal of Kirkstall.*

10 *Seal of Cockersand Abbey relating to Milton.*

11 *Lady Ellénor Brandon.*

12 *Sir Ingram Clifford.*

13 *Seal of Isabella de Percy.*

14 *Seal of Hen: de Lacy Patron of Kirkstall.*

MISCELLANEOUS PLATE.

AUTOGRAPHS taken principally from the Evidences of the CLIFFORD FAMILY.

AUTOGRAPHS taken principally from the Evidences of the CLIFFORD FAMILY.

57

58

59

60 Daubeny

61 Br...

62 Dublin

63 T. Horton.

64

65

66 Esex

67 Bristol

68 Hen: Dover:

69

70

71 Howard

72 W. Cant:

73

74 Gul: London:

75

76

77 Salisbury

78

79 Goringe

80 Tho: Bromyn

81 Ed. Rishton.

82 Wm. Wintoun

83 George Monck

Longmate fc.

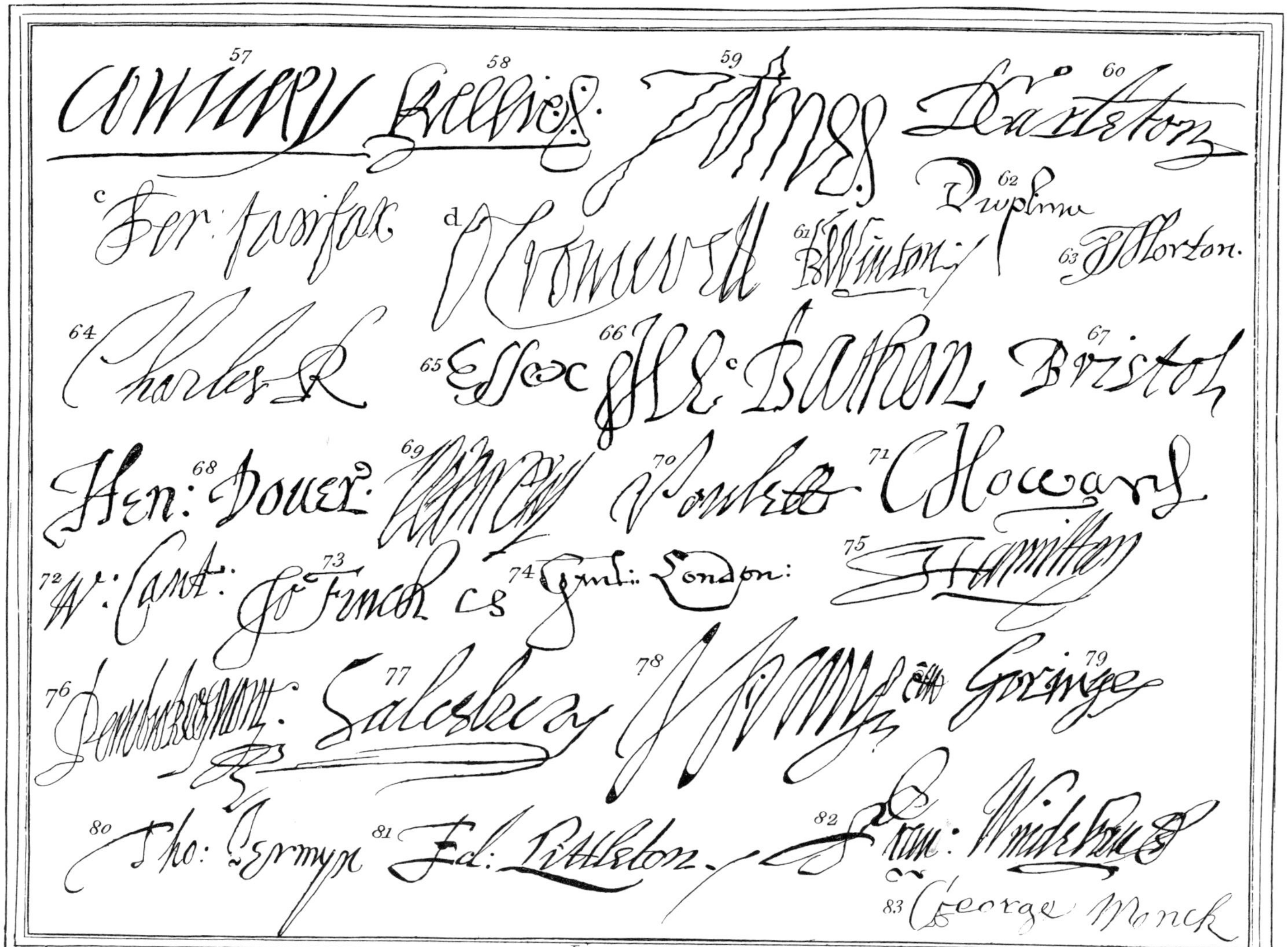

EXPLANATION of the three plates of AUTOGRAPHS.

1. The second Earl of Northumberland, A.D. 1441.
a. Paslew, the last Abbot of Whalley. [1507–1536].
2. Hammond, Abbot of Sallay. [1506–1527].
3. The third Earl of Derby, circ. 1537.
4. Major General Lambert.
5. Theophilus Earl of Suffolk. [Theophilus Howard, 1626–1640.]
6. Algernon tenth Earl of Northumberland. [1632–1668.]
7. Sir Andrew Carr, of Fernihurst, 1614.
8. Henry ninth Earl of Northumberland, 1614.
9. Henry second Earl of Cumberland, 1547.
10. Francis fourth Earl of Cumberland. [1605–1641.]
11. Anne Countess Dowager of Cumberland, 1579.
12. The Earl of Rothes, 1641.
13. George third Earl of Cumberland. [1569–1605.]
14. Robert Cecil, Earl of Salisbury. [1605–1612].
15. Henry Howard, Earl of Northampton, 1614.
16. Howard, Earl of Nottingham. [Query, which? there were three:—Charles Howard, 1596–1624; Charles Howard, 1624–1642; and Charles Howard, 1642–1681.]
b. Lady Anne Clifford, 1603.
17. Sir George Radcliff.
18. Earl of Marr.
19. Edward Lord Wotton. [1603–1604.]
20. Edward Earl of Worcester, 1625.
21. Edward Lord Zouch of Harringworth. [1571–1626.]
22. Sir Julius Cæsar, Master of the Rolls. [1614–1636.]
24. Sir Stephen Tempest of Broughton, Counsellor to George Earl of Cumberland, 1602.
25. Richard Viscount Dungarvon.
26. Carr, Earl of Somerset. [1613–1645.]
27. Archbishop Tobias Matthew. [Of York, 1606–28.]
28. Archbishop Abbot. [Of Canterbury, 1611–1623.]
29. Bishop Andrews. [Lancelot Andrewes: Bishop of Chichester, 1605–1609; then of Ely, 1609–1619; then of Winchester, 1619–1626.]
31. Lord Keeper Williams. [John Williams, Bishop of Lincoln, 1621–1625.]
32. James Stuart, Duke of Richmond. [1641–1655.]
33. Lord Mandevile, afterwards Earl of Manchester. [1620. Created Earl of Manchester, 1626.]
34. Henry Lord Clifford, afterwards the fifth Earl of Cumberland. [1628. Fifth earl in 1641.]
35. Lord Grandison. [Query, William Viscount Grandison, 1630–1643.]
36. The great Earl of Arundel.

38. Lord Keeper Coventry. [Sir Thomas Coventry, Lord High Chancellor, 1625–1640.]

40. Sir George Calvert.

41, 42. Ley, Earl of Marlborough, Lord Treasurer. [1626–1628. Lord High Treasurer in 1624–1625.]

43. William [Knollys] Viscount Wallingford. [1616–1626. Created Earl of Banbury, 1626.]

44. Hay, Earl of Carlisle. [Query, James Hay, Earl of Carlisle, 1622–1636, or his son, James, 1636–1660.]

45. Lord Treasurer Sir Richard Weston, afterwards Earl of Portland. [1633–1634. Lord High Treasurer, 1620; and again in 1624.]

46. The first Villiers Duke of Buckingham. [1623–1629.]

47. Philip [Herbert] Earl of Montgomery. [1605–1650.]

48. Edward [Sackville] Earl of Dorset. [1624–1652.]

49. Secretary [Sir John] Coke. [1625.]

50. Cecil, Earl of Exeter.

51. Neile, Bishop of Durham. [1617–1627.]

52. Dr. Laud, when Bishop of Bath and Wells. [1626–1628.]

53. William [Herbert] Earl of Pembroke. [There were three Earls of Pembroke of the name of William :—1551–1569; 1601–1630; 1669–74.]

54. Sir Humphrey May. [Master of the Rolls, 1629.]

55. Sir Robert Naunton. [Secretary of State, 1618.]

56. Rich, Earl of Hollande. [Query, Henry Rich, 1624–49, or Robert Rich, 1649–1675.]

57. Lord Conway, Secretary of State. [1625.]

58. Erskine, Earl of Kellie.

59. [George] Carew, Earl of Totnes. [1626–1629.]

60. Sir Dudley Carlton. [Secretary of State, 1630.]

61. Neile, when Bishop of Winchester. [1627–1632.]

65. The Earl of Essex, the Parliament's General.

66. Mawe, Bishop of Bath and Wells, 1628.

67. Digby, Earl of Bristol. [Query, John Digby, 1622–1653, or George Digby, 1653–1676.]

70. John Lord Powlet of Hinton. [There were three Johns in succession, from 1627 to 1680.]

72. Archbishop Laud. [Of Canterbury, 1633–1645.]

73. Lord Keeper [Sir John] Finch. [1640.]

74. Juxon, Bishop of London. [1633–1660.]

75. James first Duke of Hamilton.

76. Philip Earl of Pembroke.

77. Robert Cecil, a duplicate.

79. The Lord Goringe. [George Goring, 1628–1662.]

80. Sir Thomas Jermyn.

81. Lord Keeper [Sir Edward] Littleton. [1641.]

82. Secretary [Sir Francis] Windebank. [1632.]

These names having been entrusted to the engraver to arrange, I am sorry that so little attention has been paid to Chronology. Those which are not explained are either unknown to me, or too well known to my readers to require an explanation.

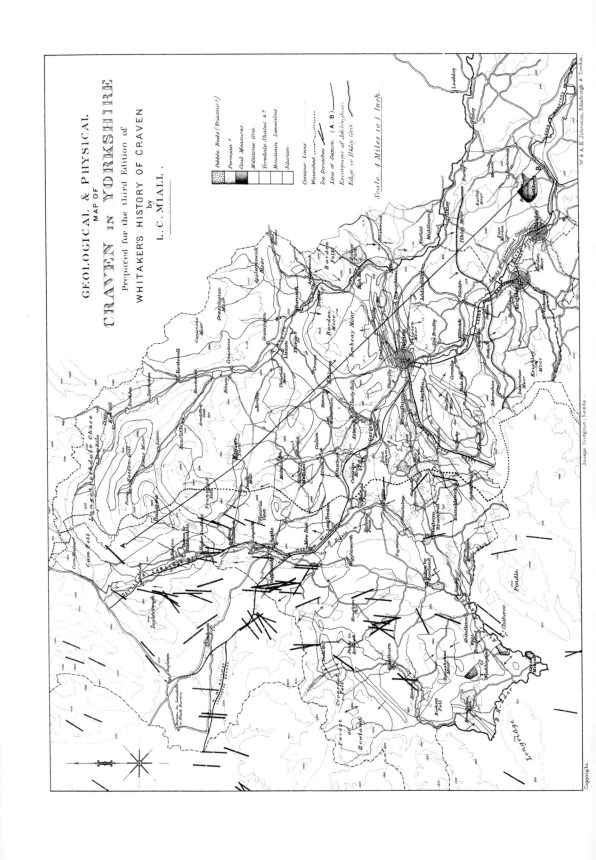

GEOLOGICAL & PHYSICAL
MAP OF
CRAVEN in YORKSHIRE
Prepared for the third Edition of
WHITAKER'S HISTORY OF CRAVEN
by
L. C. MIALL.

Pebble Beds (Triassic?)
Permian?
Coal Measures
Millstone Grit
Yoredale Shales &c.
Mountain Limestone
Silurian

Contour Lines
Watershed
Ice Scratches
Line of Section. (A. B)
Escarpment of Addingham:
Edge of Ilkley Grit

Scale. 4 Miles to 1 Inch.

W. & A. K. Johnston, Edinburgh & London.

Joseph Dodgson, Leeds.

Copyright.

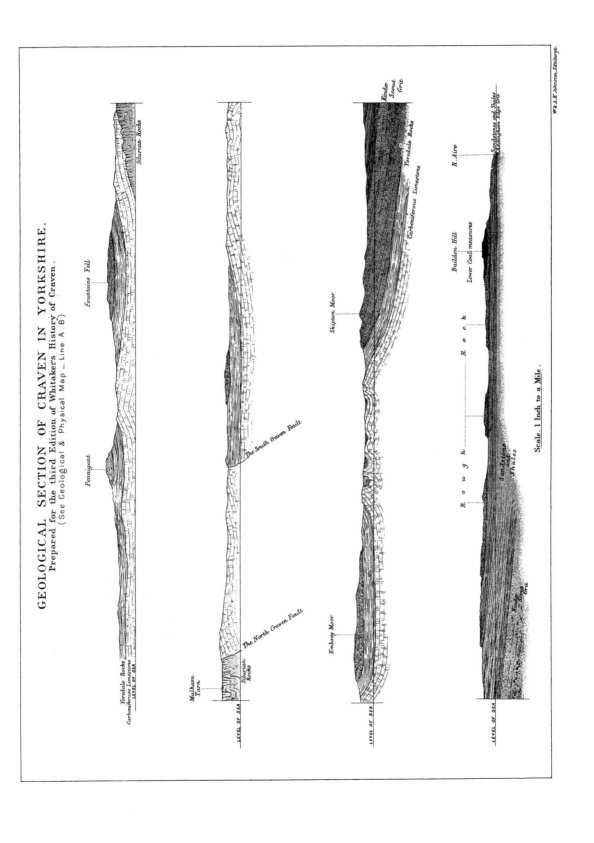

GEOLOGICAL SECTION OF CRAVEN IN YORKSHIRE.

Prepared for the third Edition of Whitaker's History of Craven.

(See Geological & Physical Map — Line A. B)

Scale. 1 Inch to a Mile.

W. & A. K. Johnston, Edinburgh.

THE

Geology Natural History and Pre-Historic Antiquities

of Craven in Yorkshire

BY

L. C. MIALL,

Professor of Biology in the Yorkshire College, and Curator of the Leeds Museum.

--------◆--------

 N setting forth the supplementary information respecting the geology, natural history, and pre-historic antiquities of Craven which the researches of the last sixty-six years have accumulated, the writer would best have consulted his own convenience by preparing a condensed tabular statement. Such an arrangement of the materials would prevent repetition and confusion, besides permitting the introduction of facts too insignificant for separate mention. But a treatise so dry and formal would ill recommend to any but professed students the natural objects of Craven or the memorials of its early tribes. Much, too, would on this plan remain untold which is entitled by its importance to a place in a discursive topographical work. The example of Whitaker himself, and the advantage of preserving in some degree the continuity of his history, plead on the same side. I have followed in the main a topographical arrangement, tracing the three rivers of Craven from their sources to the boundary of the district, and noticing in their order of occurrence those natural features and archæological relics which best deserve attention.

For detailed geological information, the works cited in the text, and particularly Phillips's "Geology of Yorkshire," may be consulted. The maps and memoirs of the Geological Survey include as yet very little relating to Craven. Dr. Windsor's "Flora Cravoniensis" (Manchester, 1873) contains the latest and most special catalogue of the plants. The pre-historic antiquities have not been treated in any connected memoir.

General Geological Features of Craven.

The more striking features which the rocks of Craven present have been selected for detailed description, each in its topographical connection. To those who approach the subject for the first time, the present condensed and general view may prove useful.

3 X

TABLE OF ROCKS.

Lower Coal Measures (Baildon).
Millstone Grit (Airedale).

Coarse Grit ⎱ Rough Rock. Flagstone ⎰	190 ft.
Shales	60 ft.
Sandstones and Shales ⎱ Addingham Edge Grit ⎬ Middle Grits. . . . . . Sandstones and Shales ⎰	750 ft.
Shales	700 ft.
Sandstone, in several beds, with intermediate shales (Kinder Scout Grit) . .	1,800 ft.

Yoredale Rocks (Penigent).

Thin Limestone	8 ft.
Shale	10 ft.
Grey Encrinital Limestone—Main Limestone	60 ft.
Sandstones, Shales, and Limestones	300 ft.

Mountain or Lower Scar Limestone; in Craven usually from 600 to 1,000 ft. thick, and
   nearly undivided. It is estimated to amount to 3,250 ft. between Sawley and Gisburn.[*]

Upper Silurian	3,000 ft. (?) visible.
Lower Silurian	10,000 ft. (?) visible.

The Silurian rocks form the natural floor to the Carboniferous rocks of Yorkshire. They are seen over a limited area in Ribblesdale and about Malham Tarn. The Silurian slates were greatly metamorphosed, upheaved, and denuded before the deposition of the Mountain Limestone.

In Craven the Mountain Limestone is nearly undivided. From 400 to 1,000 feet occur in one thick bed; above this, in the Yoredale Rocks of Phillips, are variable thin limestones. The greatest thickness of undivided limestone accessible to examination occurs near Kettlewell. Here we may suppose a deep but gently-shelving depression to have existed in the Carboniferous sea, favourable to the uninterrupted deposit of pure calcareous rock; while to the north, west, and south the greater thickness of argillaceous beds, and their variable succession, indicate comparatively shallow water. The base of the Mountain Limestone is exposed on Moughton Fell; near Crummack; at Norber; on Penigent; and in Gordale. It consists in some places of a few feet of conglomerate.

The Yoredale Rocks of Phillips constitute a group convenient for local use, but incapable of strict definition or of consistent application beyond narrow limits. With respect to their mode of origin, they imply shallow marine and estuarine conditions, and intervene chronologically, geographically, and physically between the continuous limestones and the fluviatile deposits of the Millstone Grit and Coal Measures.

The lower beds of the Millstone Grit (the Kinder Scout Grits) cover much of the high ground in Craven. South of Skipton a regular dip brings in the upper beds one after another, and the series is capped at Baildon by an outlier of the lower Coal Measures.

A small patch of Permian sandstone overlies the Carboniferous rocks below Waddow Hall, near Clitheroe,[†] and in Bashall Brook there is an exposure of a sandstone with a few quartz pebbles, supposed to be Triassic.[‡] The Waddow Hall section shows Permian

---

[*] R. H. Tiddeman, "Geology of the Burnley Coal Field," p. 14.
[†] *Ib.* p. 121.
[‡] *Ib.* p. 122.

rocks resting upon beds low in the Carboniferous series, and thus proves the great waste by denudation which occupied the interval (otherwise unrepresented in, at any rate, most British localities) between Carboniferous and Permian times. The beds removed at this point, subsequent to the local completion of the Carboniferous series, and prior to the deposition of the sandstone, amount, according to Mr. Tiddeman,[*] to at least 7,000 feet, leaving out the Coal Measures, which cannot be positively proved to have overlaid the spot. The high inclination of the Permian rocks (as also at Westhouse, near Ingleton), and their almost complete destruction, testify to later displacement and waste.

The original lie of the Carboniferous rocks of Craven has been greatly disturbed by the complex system of faults known collectively as the Craven Fault (see Map, Section, and pp. 604, 605). In South Craven a series of approximately parallel anticlinals, varying in direction from N.E.—S.W. to E.—W., brings up the limestone between the shales and grits of the Yoredale and Millstone Grit series, while these latter rocks are often thrown into synclinal basins or troughs.

Craven is, on the whole, thickly covered with glacial deposits, which within this area consist almost wholly of till—a tenacious clay containing scratched and subangular stones, local or travelled. In Airedale, but somewhat beyond the limits of Craven, gravelly and partially-stratified glacial deposits begin to appear, while south and east of Leeds all signs of an ice-sheet are scanty and obscure. The glacial till of Craven extends eastward as far as the vale of York, where it gives place to mounds of rounded pebbles, gravel, and sand, with indications in places of a stratified arrangement. The glacial striæ marked upon the map were noted or collected by Mr. Tiddeman.[†]

WHARFDALE.

Upper Wharfdale.—The sources of Wharf, like those of all the Craven rivers, lie among the hills in the north of the district, close to the dividing ridge which throws off the waters of Lancashire to the west, and those of Yorkshire to the east. From the wet and desolate moors of Dod Fell, Cam Fell, and Penigent many small rivulets spring, and unite on the eastern side of the watershed into two main streams. The more northerly of these bears the name of Wharf from its very beginning. It flows along the deep and secluded Langstrothdale, gradually sweeping southwards, and cutting its channel deeper and deeper through the rocks until it reaches the lower scar limestone about Oughtershaw. In Deepdale the scenery changes. The brown moors, ill-drained, clothed with heather, sedges, and moss, and strewn with grit boulders, separate a little on either hand, and disclose a narrow glen with precipitous rocks, bright green pastures, and scattered trees. Below Kettlewell the Wharf is joined by the Skirfare, descending from Littondale. Some four miles above the junction, in the valley of the tributary stream, lies the

---

[*] "Geol. of Burnley Coal Field," p. 122.   [†] *Geol. Journal*, vol. xxviii. p. 489 (1872).

beautiful village of Arncliffe.   Here may be found in perfection the rich flora of the
mountain limestone, varied by great differences of elevation and shelter.   The limestone,
which in Langstrothdale was exposed only towards the bottom of the valley, gradually
rises into the great white scars of Arncliffe Clowder, Hawkswick Clowder, Hard Flask,
and Kilnsey Crag.   It is probable from a comparison of measurements that near the
junction of the Wharf and the Skirfare the entire thickness of the limestone is penetrated
by the river, and that a section unobscured by alluvial deposits would expose Silurian slates
in the bed of the stream.*   Beyond this point the limestone sinks again, being apparently
carried down by a succession of throws which may represent the divisions of the Craven
Fault.   The Wharf flows through mountain limestone, without proved interruption, from
Deepdale to below Burnsall, and over the greater part of this distance the country to
the west, between the Wharf and the Aire, is overspread by the same rock.   On the
east, the millstone grit ranges of Great Whernside, Coniston Moor, and Grassington
overhang the river at no great distance.

Dowkerbottom Cave.—In the floor of this cave, whose situation is described in the text
of Whitaker, have been discovered numerous Romano-British relics, human skeletons,
bones of various recent animals, and a fragment of an antler of the extinct Irish elk.†   A
systematic re-examination of this and other ossiferous Craven caves would doubtless yield
important results.   The exploration of the Victoria Cave, near Settle, testifies to the rich
accumulation of ornaments, implements, and bones which may lie buried in the floor of an
obscure limestone cavern, while a special palæontological interest attaches to the determina-
tion of those pre-glacial and inter-glacial species of mammalia, whose remains, casually lodged
in caves and fissures, may have escaped destruction when the ice-sheet swept clear the
surface of the north of England.

Kilnsey Crag.—Close to the village of Kilnsey is a limestone cliff, rising directly to 170
feet, and at one point overhanging its base nearly forty feet.   When Professor Phillips wrote
his useful account of the " Rivers, Mountains, and Sea-Coast of Yorkshire," no doubt was
entertained that Kilnsey Crag, like Malham Cove and Giggleswick Scar, was an ancient
sea-cliff.‡   Geologists of a later date, succeeding to a rich inheritance of knowledge, of which
the chief share has been furnished by the labours of others, may, without taking to themselves any great share of merit, correct the natural but often mistaken hypotheses of the
founders of their science.   In not a few places we are tempted to qualify Professor Phillips'
statements as to the natural agents which have shaped the hills and valleys of Craven.   In
the case of these limestone cliffs, their occurrence at very different elevations, so that almost
every one would require a separate and long-maintained level of sea for its production, their
situation in remote winding valleys with a constant fall of level, and the universal absence of

---

* J. R. Dakyns, *Proc. W. R. Geol. Soc.*, N.S. vol. i. p. 159 (1877).

† " On the Geological and Archæological Contents of the Victoria and Dowkerbottom Caves in Craven."   By Henry
Denny, *Proc. W. R. Geol. Soc.* vol. iv. p. 45 (1860).   " Further Explorations in the Dowkerbottom Caves, in Craven," by
James Farrer, M.P.; with remarks by Henry Denny.   *Ibid.* vol. iv. p. 414 (1866).

‡ " The great inland cliffs, which are among the most striking phenomena of Yorkshire, only differ from sea-cliffs,
because the water no longer beats against them."—*Op. cit.* p. 11.

raised beaches, all require us to seek a denuding agent more appropriate to their production than the waste of the sea. The natural operations in daily exercise among the limestone hills of Craven supply an alternative explanation. Atmospheric waste—rain, streams, and frost each exerting an important and characteristic influence—is visibly at work, and we may, without exaggeration, affirm that here at least it has effaced the marks of previous marine denudation.

While we look to atmospheric waste as the cause of the rock-sculpture of Craven, it is not unimportant to consider the peculiar local conditions under which it has acted. The mountain limestone is a well-jointed rock, intersected by rectangular planes of division, which give the mass a tendency to break up into rectangular prisms. These joints, when freely exposed to the action of the weather, become enlarged, and produce the "helks" or prismatic columns so often seen on the edge of a limestone scar. When the beds of limestone are horizontal, or inclined at low angles, as is generally the case in Craven, the joints occupy a vertical position, and the rock, under suitable conditions of elevation and exposure, weathers to a vertical face, interrupted more or less by steps, according as the stratification locally overpowers the jointing. Frost is commonly in such cases the primary agent of denudation, and streams play the subordinate part of removing the fallen pieces. Where there is no stream powerful enough to clear the *débris*, we get "screes" at the base of the cliff—angular fragments, accumulated sometimes in such quantity as to bury the solid rock. Elsewhere the solvent power of water containing carbonic acid is conspicuous. A solid scar may be fretted away to a pile of fantastic pinnacles, or may retreat with immeasurable slowness, as film after film is dissolved by the rain. Instances might be cited of the excavation by surface-water of deep chasms with vertical and fluted sides. Still more numerous are the examples of precipitous ravines, whose existence is traced to the falling in of caverns hollowed out by subterranean rills.

The cliffs of the Craven hills are their noblest feature. In general, the limestone, like other well-bedded and well-jointed rocks, yields forms too definite and too often repeated to give pleasure. We miss the subtle curves and the ever-changing profiles of a hill-country carved out of volcanic or metamorphic rocks, and find, instead of the endless variety of the Highlands or Lake-country, a succession of flat-topped or rounded uplands intersected by abrupt gorges.

In some cases the great lines of ancient disturbance have produced marked features of the landscape. Though not often plainly traceable across the country, dislocations conspicuous to the eye are to be found more frequently than in most parts of England. Along the Craven Fault, as at Malham Cove, there are sheer cliffs almost directly on the line of upheaval. Elsewhere the cliff, while remaining vertical, has been wasted back far from the actual disruption. It is not impossible that at Kilnsey, too, a line of fault originally determined the existence of the crag, which has since receded by weathering to its present position.

Grassington Mines.—On Grassington Moor extensive and valuable veins of galena have long been worked. Unlike the mining-fields of North Yorkshire, which are almost restricted to the limestone, the productive veins at Grassington, Pateley Bridge, and Cononley chiefly traverse grit, plate and shale. The richest veins seem to be enclosed by cheeks of grit, or of grit on one side, and some other rock on the other. Where the cheeks become argillaceous or shaly, the lode usually breaks up, or falls to an inconsiderable thickness. Where the measures are much crushed by faults, as by a broken anticlinal, the lode is apt to split up into strings, and the galena is more or less converted into carbonate of lead. Minium, calamine, and pyromorphite (lead phosphate) are occasionally met with at Grassington, and native lead is said to have been found.*

In the "dowk," or non-metallic vein-stuff of Grassington Moor, numerous minute organisms have been detected by the close scrutiny of Mr. Charles Moore.† All the species cited in the subjoined list may be of Carboniferous age, and were in all probability already fossil when they were washed into the fissures. Rhætic and Liassic species, which are common, under similar circumstances, in the Mendips and South Wales, are rarely met with in the mineral veins of the North of England. The terrestrial and fluviatile forms (marked F in the list) present difficulties. Mr. Moore supposes that they are derived from a fresh-water Carboniferous limestone, but there is no direct evidence as to the existence of such a deposit. The species marked P are only known from their occurrence in mineral veins.

Seeds?
Plants, impressions on shale.
Nodosaria radicula, L.
—— sp.
Involutina polymorpha, Terquem.
—— *aspera*, Terq.
—— *nodosa*, Terq.
—— *vermiformis*, Brady (P.).
—— *incerta*, Brady (P.).
—— *recta*, Brady (P.).
—— *cylindrica*, Brady (P.).
Corals, sp.
Encrinites, sp.
Echinodermata, sp.
Echini, remains.
Serpula.
Serpulites.
Crustacea (fragment).
Bairdia plebeia, Reuss.
Beyrichia.
Cythere bilobata, Münst.
—— *nigrescens*, Baird.
—— *munda*.
—— *æqualis*, n. sp. (P.).
—— *intermedia*, Münst.
—— *fabulina*, J. & K.
—— *ambigua*, Jones.

Cythere Muensteriana, J. & K.
—— n. sp.
Leperdita Okeni, Münst.
Bryozoa, various sp.
Discina nitida, Phil.
Leptæna, sp.
Lingula, sp.
Terebratula hastata, Phil.
Thecidium?
Zellania? sp.
Bivalves, fragments.
Hydrobia, n. sp. (F., P.).
Lithoglyphus, sp. (F., P.).
Planorbis Mendipensis, Moore (F., P.).
Valvata anomala, Moore (F., P.).
Dentalium inornatum, McCoy.
Turbo, sp.
Cladodus, teeth.
Orodus, teeth.
Petalodus, teeth.
Psammodus, teeth.
Jaw of fish, portions.
Fish-scales.
Fish-vertebræ.
Conodonts.
Coal or coal-like shale.

Mountain Limestone of Thorpe.—Close to the old and half-deserted village of Thorpe, near Burnsall, the traveller cannot fail to remark the singular conical Limestone hills which range beneath the slightly higher Grit-edge of Rilston Moor. The Limestone is both contorted and faulted, so that it is not easy, in the absence of a detailed survey, to ascertain

* Stephen Eddy, " On the Lead-Mining Districts of Yorkshire," Report of British Association, 1858, ii. p. 167.
† " On Mineral Veins in Carboniferous Limestone," Brit. Assoc. Report, 1869, i. p. 371, &c.

its precise relation to the plateau of Millstone Grit. It is probable, however, that the line of junction is close to a line of fault. Here have been found workable veins of lead. Patches of the Limestone are extraordinarily rich in fossils, and the writer has gathered examples of the following rare species :—

Spirifera triangularis, Mart.	*Chonetes papilionacea*, Phil.
S. subconica, Mart.	*Cyrtina septosa*, Phil.
Spiriferina cristata, Schl.	*Lingula mytiloides*, Sow.
Retzia radialis, Phil.	*Murchisonia angulata*, Phil.
Productus ermineus, D. Kon.	*Turbo semisulcatus*, Phil.

The quarry at Cracoe Swinden, close to the coach-road between Skipton and Kettlewell, has also yielded many good fossils; among others :—

Griffithides globiceps, Port.	*P. tumida*, Phil.
Nautilus cariniferus, Sow.	*Metoptoma elliptica*, Phil.
Orthoceras reticulatum, Phil.	*Patella retrorsa*, Phil.
Goniatites intercostalis, Phil.	*Bellerophon Woodwardi*, Sow.
Pleurotomaria flammigera, Phil.	*Pecten interstitialis*, Phil.

The occurrence of fossils in the Mountain Limestone follows no general law of distribution which has hitherto been ascertained. The species seem to be mixed indiscriminately, and the rock proves barren or productive to the collector according as its texture is favourable or not to the preservation of organic remains. We may, however, occasionally trace the temporary predominance of a particular class of marine animals in a particular spot of the ancient Carboniferous sea. Thus, at Thorpe a densely-populated nest of *Productus giganteus* is found; a band rich in the same species occurs at Slaidburn, in Bolland, and is often met with at or near the top of the Lower Scar Limestone. A little patch of limestone near the calamine pits at Malham has yielded hundreds of trilobites (*Phillipsia gemmifera*); while the quarries about Clitheroe and Chatburn are rich in crinoidal heads, elsewhere very uncommon in the north of England.

Rilston Fell and Simon Seat.—The Kinder Scout Grits (see table on p. 4) occupy the high ground between Rilston and Burnsall, and extend continuously to Crookrise and Embsay Moor, where they are thrown off by the anticlinal of Skibeden. Over this tract they form a basin, and dip inwards on all sides. Across the Wharf we find the disposition of the same beds reversed in the hill known as Simon Seat. Here the grits occupy a dome, and dip away on all sides from the centre. On the summit of the hill the underlying shale is exposed, and a number of swallow-holes show that the limestone which composes the mass of the interior lies at no great distance from the surface.[*]

Sepulchral Barrow at Rilston.—Canon Greenwell remarks[†] that Craven abounds in remains of pre-historic times. Weapons and implements of stone and bronze have occurred at or near Rilston, and besides the sepulchral mound next to be described, barrows still exist in the neighbourhood. Some of these " yet remain unopened, but the greater number have been more or less destroyed by curiosity-hunters, without any note of their construction

---

[*] J. R. Dakyns, Brit. Assoc. Report, 1873, ii. pp. 78-9.   [†] " British Barrows," p. 374 (Oxford, 1877).

or contents having been preserved."   There are also many hill-terraces, supposed by Canon Greenwell to be "clearly of artificial origin."

A very interesting barrow was opened by Canon Greenwell at Scale House, near Rilston. It had been previously dug into, and the contents were disturbed and injured in consequence. The barrow was thirty feet in diameter and five feet high ; it was made of clay, and was encircled by a shallow trench.   "Immediately beneath the surface of the barrow, at the centre, there was a layer of flat stones, about six feet in diameter, carefully arranged. Under these stones the clay was firmly compacted, and rested upon a thin stratum of dark-coloured earthy matter, which was very fully charged with charcoal.   Beneath this again was a layer of finer clay, or rather of clay which appeared to have undergone a process of tempering. Below this finer clay, and carefully embedded in it, was an oaken coffin laid upon clay, and to some extent supported by a few stones, the whole being placed in a slight hollow sunk below the surface of the ground.   The coffin was formed of the trunk of an oak-tree split in two and then hollowed out.   It was $7\frac{1}{4}$ ft. long and 1 ft. 11 in. wide ; the trunk had been cut off at each end and then partially rounded, but on the outside no attempt at squaring or other workmanship had interfered with the natural surface of the timber.   The hollow within was 6 ft. 4 in. long and 1 ft. wide, roughly hewn out, and still showing the marks of the tool employed ; the ends inside were finished off square.   It was not possible to make out the precise nature of the tool which had been employed, but the appearances warranted the conclusion that it had been a narrow-edged metal implement.   The coffin was very much broken in consequence of the disturbance before mentioned ; it was, however, still sufficiently entire to allow its arrangement to be seen.   It was laid north and south, having the thicker end—where the head of the enclosed body had no doubt been placed—to the south.   The body had entirely gone to decay, and nothing was observed which might have formed a constituent part of it, except an unctuous whitish substance, which chemical analysis has proved to be of animal origin.   The corpse had been enveloped in a woollen fabric, enough of which remained to show that it had reached from head to foot.   It was very rotten, and partly on that account, and partly by reason of the infiltration of earth which had found its way into the coffin through the breakage occurring when the barrow was first opened, and which had become mixed up with the cloth, it was impossible to recover any but small pieces of it, or to prove whether the body had been laid in the grave in its ordinary dress or simply wrapped in a shroud.   It is on the whole probable that in this case, as in those of some tree-burials discovered in Denmark, the person had been interred in the dress worn by him in daily life, though perhaps it may be alleged that the absence of anything like a button or other fastening is rather against that view.   The material is now of a dark-brown colour due most likely to the tannin in the oak of the coffin ; whilst to the acid generated in the decaying wood, and set free by the percolation of water, is perhaps to be attributed the total disappearance of the bones.   There was nothing found in the coffin besides the woollen stuff; nor, with the exception of pieces of charcoal and some burnt earth, was anything met with foreign to the ordinary material of the rest of the barrow.

"In the absence of any associated articles in the coffin, or of potsherds or flints in the mound itself, it is difficult to assign a precise date or period to this remarkable burial.   But if we take the general shape and construction of the barrow into consideration, as also the encircling ditch, the presence of charcoal and other indications of burning, I see no reason for hesitating to refer it to the people whose usual custom it was to place the body of the dead person in a stone cist or in a grave within the barrow; merely supposing that in this and in a few other instances they departed from their ordinary practice in favour of a wooden receptacle. And when we compare this burial with some others found in this country, and with those which have occurred in Denmark, we can further have little doubt about attributing it to the time when bronze was in use for weapons and implements. The mode of interment in the hollowed trunk of a tree placed within a barrow is no doubt rare, although burials in cleft and hollowed trees placed in the ground without any superincumbent grave-mound are not so uncommon; many of these, however, are not to be referred to a very early period, and indeed probably belong to a time several centuries after the Christian era."

*Carboniferous Rocks of South Craven.**—The general arrangement of the Carboniferous rocks in this part of Craven may be illustrated by supposing them to have been subjected to pressure in two directions, which are approximately N.S. and E.W.† Two sets of folds have thus arisen, which cross at right angles, and produce by their intersection a well-marked basin and a well-marked dome. Beneath the escarpment of the Kinder Scout Grits on Burnsall, Thorpe, and Rilston Fells is a small exposure of the shales called by Phillips the Craven Shales, and ranked by him as equivalents of the Yoredale Rocks. On the southern edge of Embsay Moor the same beds are seen more completely, and here they are found to include two limestones. The shales occupy the comparatively low ground, which surrounds the limestone boss of Skibeden, and underlie Bolton Woods. On the steep river-bank opposite Bolton Woods we see them again in section. Immediately behind (that is, to the east of the river) a fault running N.E.—S.W., cuts off the shales, and the lower beds of the Millstone Grit form the high ground about Storriths and Bolton Park.

Crossing Rombald's Moor from Skipton to the S.E., we traverse in nearly regular succession all the beds of the Millstone Grit series. As a rule, the sandstones form conspicuous features along the sides and top of the moor, while the intermediate shales can be traced by the pastures of the lateral slopes, or by wet depressions overgrown with sphagnum moss at greater heights. The prevailing strike, which is nearly E.—W. at Skipton, gradually assumes a N.E.—S.W. direction as we go S.E. Ascending from Skipton, we first meet, on the edge of the moor, the so-called Yoredale Grit, which in this part of Yorkshire is merely a subordinate and variable division of the next member of the series. The more conspicuous sandstone above it, the Kinder Scout Grit of Derbyshire, forms the top of the ridge. It is here inclined to the S. at an angle of about 20°—a steep dip, which soon carries the rock down to the level of the river Aire. Near Cononley a fault, running across the valley, causes the beds to be repeated, and the Kinder Scout Grit

---

* See J. R. Dakyns on the "Geology of Keighley, Skipton, and Grassington," *Geol. Mag.* vol. iv. p. 346 (1877).
† See Prof. Hull on the "Relative Ages of the Leading Physical Features and Lines of Elevation of the Carboniferous District of Lancashire and Yorkshire," *Q. J. Geol. Soc.* vol. xxiv. pp. 323—335 (1868).

3 Y

reappears on Kildwick Moor, and forms the steeply-inclined sandstone shelf which slopes downwards to the village of Kildwick. A much divided and variable series of sandstones, flags, and shales, the Middle Grits, occupies the slopes about Silsden, and much of the lower ranges of Airedale as far as Shipley. On the other side of Rombald's Moor, the Middle Grits form the precipitous crags of Ilkley, Otley, and Bramhope. They may be conveniently studied above Sutton, along Addingham Edge, and in Holden Gill, near Silsden. The Rough Rock, the highest member of the Millstone Grit, rises to upwards of 1,300 feet on Rivock Edge, and ranges across the moor eastwards to the lower slopes of Otley Chevin. On Baildon Common it forms a conspicuous escarpment, and is extensively quarried. South of Shipley it appears as a low cliff at Windhill Crag, and is then cut off by a fault which brings against it the lower Coal Measures. On Baildon Hill and at Rawden are outliers of the Halifax Hard and Soft Beds, the lowest seams of the neighbouring coal-field.

Vegetation of the Millstone Grit.—The sandstones of the Millstone Grit are usually occupied by heather, coarse grasses, and such plants as love a peaty, ill-drained, and innutritious soil. Ericaceous shrubs, *Calluna vulgaris* (ling), *Erica tetralix, E. cinerea, Vaccinium myrtillus* (bilberry), are the predominant species. *Vaccinium vitis-idæa* and *V. oxyococcus* are found in a few places near Ilkley. *Empetrum nigrum* (crowberry) is often abundant. *Drosera rotundifolia* (sun-dew) and *Narthecium ossifragum* are found in swamps, while *Montia fontana* and *Stellaria uliginosa* fringe the rills. Of the grasses and sedges, *Juncus squarrosus, Scirpus cæspitosus, Eriophorum vaginatum, Festuca ovina, Nardus stricta,* and *Aira flexuosa* are the most characteristic. *Polygala vulgaris, Teucrium scorodonia, Sagina procumbens, Potentilla tormentilla, Rubus chamæmorus, Digitalis purpurea* (foxglove), *Galium verum, G. saxatile,* and *Myosotis versicolor* frequent the drier ground, or spring up where the heather has been cleared. Copses of oak fringe the moor; alders line the streams which flow down to the Aire and Wharf; the birch and rowan-tree are as plentiful at low elevations as the hazel and ash in the thickets of limestone hills. *Chrysosplenium, Caltha, Cardamine sylvatica, Parnassia, Crepis paludosa, Spiræa Ulmaria, Œnanthe crocata,* and *Equisetum Telmateia* haunt the wooded "gills." Many ferns are found: bracken among the heather; *Botrychium lunaria* locally on dry and stony edges; *Ophioglossum,* abundant. but hard to find, in the richer pastures; *Polypodium dryopteris, P. phegopteris, Lastræa recurva, and L. oreopteris* in the woods. *Lycopodium clavatum* and *L. alpinum* occur near Ilkley. The chief mosses are: *Sphagnum cymbifolium* and *acutifolium, Weissia controversa* and *cirrhata, Bartramia fontana, Seligeria recurvata, Ceratodon purpureus, Didymodon rubellus, Tortula subulata, Racomitrium aciculare* and *lanuginosum, Zygodon Mougeotii, Dicranum scoparium* and *heteromallum, Polytrichum commune, juniperinum* and *piliferum, Ptychomitrium polyphyllum, Hypnum cupressiforme, elegans, undulatum, loreum, denticulatum, splendens,* and *fluitans. Cetraria aculeata, Cladonia rangiferina* and *coccifera* are the common lichens of the heather; *Endocarpon smaragdulum, Biatora polytropa, Lecidea albo-cærulescens* and *contigua, Parmelia saxatilis, olivacea,* and *atra, Jungermannia Taylori* and *albicans* are also more or less characteristic.*

---

* I have found useful lists of Craven plants, and remarks on their distribution, in various papers and books by Mr. J. G. Baker and Dr. Carrington.

At considerable elevations the flora of the sandstones becomes very meagre. Thus the summit of Ingleborough presents only stunted plants of *Juncus squarrosus, Luzula campestris, Galium saxatile,* and *Festuca ovina (vivipara).*

The dull brown of a Grit moor, varied with pink when the heath is in bloom, distinguishes it at a glance from the short, fresh turf of the Mountain Limestone, thickly strewn with yellow pansies, orchids, and primroses. On some of the Craven hills the junction of a sandstone peak with a limestone plateau, or the opposition of a range of grits and shales to a limestone scar, can be detected at a distance of some miles, and by the colour no less certainly than by the form of the ground. In Charlotte Brontë's novels the Millstone Grit scenery is vividly described, in its beauty as in its desolateness; and the unimportant change of one word—sandstone for granite—renders the sketches of "Jane Eyre" faithful pictures of the moors of South Craven.

Pre-historic Remains on Rombald's Moor.—Several of the larger rocks on the moor above Ilkley exhibit the rude sculptures known as "cup-and-ring marks." Speculation has done what it can to elucidate these strange symbols, but as yet without the least success. It seems probable that they are of pre-historic antiquity: they are certainly of very wide distribution, and traceable on the rocks of many parts of Europe.* Casts of the Ilkley carvings, procured and given by Mr. John Holmes, are preserved in the Leeds Museum.

Local antiquaries have freely interpreted the more remarkable tumbled blocks of Rombald's Moor as Druidical remains,† and have even described as British huts the bell-pits excavated for working shallow coals on Baildon Common.‡ Pre-historic antiquities of a less disputable kind, barrows and stone circles, are to be found on the moor, and some of these have been dug out, but without the critical investigation which modern archæology exacts.

AIREDALE.

Malham Tarn.—The second Yorkshire river whose course we have to trace rises south of the Wharf, and in the midst of that Mountain Limestone area which the Wharf only reaches after it has traversed the greater part of Langstrothdale. One of the chief springs of the Aire is the water that escapes from Malham Tarn, loses itself within half a

---

* Stuart's "Sculptured Stones of Scotland;" Sir J. Y. Simpson, "Archaic Sculpturings," and *Proc. R. Soc. Ed.* vol. v. p. 52; George Tate, "Ancient British Sculptured Rocks of Northumberland" (*Trans. Berwickshire Naturalists' Club*, vol. v. p. 137); "Incised Markings on Stone," published by direction of Algernon Duke of Northumberland; Bateman's "Ten Years' Diggings," pp. 172, 178; Greenwell's "British Barrows," pp. 7, 341, 422; "Rambles on Rombald's Moor," by C. F. and W. G., part iii. (Wakefield, 1869).

† "Rambles on Rombald's Moor."

‡ Wardell in "Reliquiæ Antiquæ Eboracenses" (Leeds, 1855), p. 92. For an elaborate case of the same thing, see a paper by the Rev. S. F. Surtees, in *Proc. W. R. Geol. Soc.* (1870).

mile of its source in a fissure, and reappears at Aire Head. Another main feeder collects the waters of nameless subterranean streams, and emerges at the foot of Malham Cove. A third affluent rises north-east of the tarn, rushes through the wild cleft of Gordale, and joins the other streams below Malham.

It is not without surprise that the geologist acquainted with the jointed and fissured character of the Mountain Limestone of Craven sees a considerable body of water collected high up on the plateau of Malham Moor.* The shallow basin of the tarn is in reality excavated, not in the limestone but in Silurian slates, which are here exposed along a narrow strip of ground, bounded on the north by the base of the limestone, and on the south by the North Craven Fault, which carries the Silurian rocks and overlying limestone down several hundred feet. This exposure of the slates is greatly obscured by glacier-drift. The tarn is about a mile across, but nowhere exceeds fourteen feet in depth. Part even of this trifling depth is due to an artificial dam. It abounds in fish, the common yellow or brown trout of the Aire being taken in considerable numbers, and up to a good weight. The silver trout is less plentiful; perch are also found. It is plain, from the evidence collected by Whitaker, that the tarn has long been a fishing-ground, and that it was in 1175 already known and valued as such. Yet it is hard to suppose that it is naturally stocked, and that the fish made their way " by secret sluice" from the waters of the Aire, 600 feet below the tarn in vertical height, and distant more than a mile. The silver trout, besides, does not inhabit the Aire. Transport of ova may have been effected by such natural agents as aquatic birds, but most likely the tarn was stocked long ago by man. The trout present an unexplained peculiarity in the frequent decay of the gill-cover. About one in twenty of the silver trout, and one in thirteen of the yellow trout, have the gill-covers defective on one or both sides.†

Silurian Rocks and Mountain Limestone of Malham.—Underlying all the Carboniferous rocks of Craven are the Silurian slates, which are visible in Chapel-le-dale and Kingsdale near Ingleton, pass along the south-western base of Ingleborough, and are extensively exposed about Austwick, Wharfe, and Horton-in-Ribblesdale. Thence a narrow strip may be followed by Stainforth, Capon Hall, and Malham Tarn to Gordale. The denuded surface of the slates once formed a slightly irregular plane, upon which the solid limestones were deposited in ancient seas. The Craven Fault has disturbed and complicated this simple disposition. The slates are now cut off on the south by the North Craven Fault, which brings against them the Mountain Limestone, here lying between the two parallel faults, and sloping steeply to the south. The plane of junction is thus not only fractured but inclined in different directions. We find the visible base of the Carboniferous series rise from 800 feet above sea-level at Selside to 1,160 feet on Moughton Fell, and to upwards of 1,250 feet on Malham Moor. On Malham Moor the slate area varies in breadth from a few yards at Capon Hall to nearly a mile at the tarn. Eastwards it narrows again,

---

* " It is not the least curious circumstance about this place that, on a bottom so cleft and shattered, a basin should have been left capable of retaining a sheet of water not less than a mile in diameter—for such is Malham Tarn."—Whitaker, *ante*, p. 267.

† Information supplied by Walter Morrison, Esq., of Malham House, in 1868.

and is cut off immediately beyond Gordale. The area is much obscured by drift, and in two places only can the slates be fairly seen—viz., at Capon Hall and at Gordale. Here the Coniston Flags (Upper Silurian) appear with a steep dip S.S.W.*

Between the slates and the limestone an irregular conglomerate is often found, containing pebbles of Silurian rocks imbedded usually in the lowest beds of the limestone, but sometimes in a sandy matrix. This deposit is well seen at Thornton Force in Kingsdale, at Norber, at Austwick Beck Head, on Moughton Fell, at Capon Hall, in Gordale, and, farthest to the east, in a gorge about a mile and a quarter east of Gordale.

The Mountain Limestone about the sources of the Aire is massive and nearly undivided, reaching a thickness of 800 feet.

Craven Fault.—The regular sequence of the Carboniferous rocks in Craven is strikingly deranged by the extensive and complex dislocation known as the Craven Fault. At Ingleton the total displacement occasioned by two parallel and adjacent faults amounts, according to Phillips, to 3,000 feet; the real amount is probably greater. Further eastwards the faults begin to diverge. The northern branch crosses the Ribble at Stainforth, and is continued by Malham Moor to Gordale. The amount of throw diminishes towards Wharfdale, and the fault has not been detected beyond Threshfield. The southern primary branch passes south-east to Giggleswick, where it opposes the lower beds of the Millstone Grit to the Mountain Limestone. At Settle it divides. One line of dislocation, the Mid Craven Fault, turns sharply to the east, and may be traced along the hilly road which leads from Settle through Stockdale to Malham by the contrast in form and colour of the widely different rocks thus brought into contact. On the north the traveller sees the white scars of Attermire, the "helks" of fissured and weathered limestone, the close green turf, with the mountain pansy, the purple primrose, the rock-rose, and the ferns of a calcareous soil (*Cystopteris, Asplenium Trichomanes, Polypodium calcareum*). To the south are sombre fells covered with heather and long grasses (the Weets, Ryeloaf, Scosthrop Moor, &c.), rising out of a gently-undulating plain of rich meadows and pastures. Brook-sections immediately south of the fault reveal beds of sandstone and shale, with thin limestones, such as are not met with to the north until we get high upon Fountains Fell or Penigent. The Mid Craven Fault diminishes eastward; it has been traced as far as Pateley Bridge. The remaining division, or the South Craven Fault, follows the Aire to Skipton, and appears to be continuous with the faults which traverse the Skibeden valley between Skipton and Bolton. A less important branch may be traced along an east and west line between Airton and Winterburn.

Malham Cove is an escarpment of the limestone 285 feet high. This measurement will give by comparison some notion of the thickness of the Mountain Limestone, which is here about 800 feet. Some 200 feet of the limestone lie buried beneath the foot of the Cove.

Flora of Malham.—Malham has long been classic ground to the botanist, and the following short list of rare species will explain the eagerness with which Ray, Richardson,

---

* W. H. Dalton, *Proc. W. R. Geol. Soc.* N.S. vol. i. pp. 16—22 (1872).

Williselt, Lawson, and Robinson searched its rocks, and their frequent mention of it in books or letters :—

Thalictrum calcareum, Jord. Gordale.	*Primula farinosa*, L.
Trollius europæus,* L. Cove.	*Armeria maritima*, Willd. Stockdale.
Actæa spicata, L.† Cove, Malham Moor.	*Epipactis ovalis*, Bab. Gordale.
Thlaspi alpestre, L.‡ Malham Moor and Cove.	*E. palustris*, Sm. Above Gordale.
Hutchinsia petræa, Br. Awes Scar.	*Gymnadenia conopsea*, Br.
Cochlearia officinalis, L. ; var. *groenlandica*. Gordale, &c.	*Gagea lutea*, Ker. Cove.
Draba muralis, L.	*Carex curta*, Good. Tarn.
Helianthemum canum, Dun.	*C. intermedia*, Good. Tarn.
Geranium sanguineum, L. Cove.	*C. tertiuscula*, Good. Tarn.
Hippocrepis comosa, L. Cove and Tarn.	*C. limosa*, L. Tarn.
Potentilla verna, L. Tarn.	*Sesleria cærulea*, Scop. Cove, Gordale.
Potentilla alpestris, Hall. Gordale.	*Hordeum sylvaticum*, Huds. Cove.
Pyrus Aria, Sm. Cove.	*Polypodium calcareum*, Sm.
Ribes rubrum, var. *petræum*, Sm. Malham Moor.	*Polystichum Lonchitis*, Roth.
R. alpinum, L. Gordale.	*Asplenium viride*, Huds.
Galium pusillum, L. Above Gordale.	*Lycopodium selaginoides*, L.
Hieracium Gibsoni, Backh. Gordale.	*L. selago*, L.
Gentiana Amarella, L.	*Equisetum hyemale*, L. Cove.
Polemonium cæruleum,§ L. Gordale and Cove.	*Chara vulgaris*, L. Tarn and Cove.
Orobanche rubra, Sm. Tarn (Dr. Windsor).	*C. hispida*, L. Tarn.
Bartsia alpina, L. Gordale, Malham Moor.	*C. aspera*, W. Tarn.

Maritime and Boreal Plants of Craven.—The occurrence among the hills of Craven of certain maritime species, such as Scurvy-grass (*Cochlearia officinalis*), *Silene maritima*, Thrift (*Armeria maritima*), and *Plantago maritima*, suggests questions hardly ripe for solution. The distribution of these species in Yorkshire is here given in detail. Beyond Britain, all are arctic, alpine, and maritime ; occurring, that is to say, each in each habitat. The Scurvy-grass is found in Europe, Asia, and N. America ; *Silene maritima* in Europe alone ; the other two in congenial situations throughout the northern hemisphere. The Thrift extends along the Andes into Chili.

---

* "And now that I am speaking of local or provincial plants, give me leave to tell you that I think you labour under a mistake in thinking and asserting that few or no plants are peculiar to this or that shire. Be pleased to resolve me where *Calceolus Mariæ* [*Cypripedium calceolus*, L.], *Christophoriana* [*Actæa spicata*, L.], *Lysimachia lutea flore globoso* [*Trollius europæus*, L.], *Pentaphylloides fruticosa* [*Potentilla fruticosa*, L.], *Polygonatum floribus ex singularibus pediculis* [*Convallaria Polygonatum*, L.], *Pyrola folio mucronato serrato* [*Pyrola secunda*, L.], *Pyrola Alsines flore brasiliana* [*Trientalis europæa*, L.], *Ribes alpinus dulcis* [*Ribes alpinum*, L.], *Salix pumila montana folio rotundo* [*Salix herbacea*, L.], *Sedum alpinum Ericoides cæruleum* [*Saxifraga oppositifolia*, L.], *Sideritis arvensis latifolia hirsuta flo. luteo* [*Galeopsis dubia*, Leers.], *Thlaspi foliis Globulariæ* [*Thlaspi alpestre*, L.], *Lunaria vasculo sublongo intorto* [*Draba incana*, L.], and *Valeriana græca* [*Polemonium cæruleum*, L.], grow wild but in your own native county of Yorkshire."—Ray to Dr. Robinson, 1694. (?) All the plants quoted in this list have since been found elsewhere. The truly local plants of Malham (and of Craven) are *Hieracium Gibsoni*, a species of doubtful value, and the moss *Cinclidium stygium*, which has not been found in Britain except in the bog near Malham Tarn.

† "*Christophoriana*, Ger. [*Actæa spicata*, Linn.] among the shrubs by Malham Cove, Yorkshire."—Thomas Lawson to Ray, April 9, 1688.

‡ "I am sorry you have had soe much trouble in quest of *Thlaspi Globulariæ folio* [*T. alpestre*, Linn.], which grows upon all the heaps of earth that have been dug out of the old lead mines betwixt Malham and Settle ; and very often in the same places is to be met with *Alsine pusilla pulchro flore folio tenuissimo* [*Arenaria verna*, L.] ; but, except you know the plants perfectly well, you can scarce know them, except when in flower."—Richardson to Rauthmell, Sept. 2, 1737.

§ "And as for *Valeriana græca* [*Polemonium cæruleum*, L.], I have found that also in an unquestionable place this last week, both with a white flower, and also a blue one, viz., under Maulam Cove, a place so remarkable that it is one of the wonders of Craven."—Dr. Martin Lister to Ray, June 4, 1670.

Distribution in Yorkshire.

Cochlearia officinalis, L.—Common on the sea-coast; western hills, in many places, descending along the river-banks into the Vale of York.

Silene maritima, With.—Coatham salt-marshes; sandy ground near Redcar; rocks between Saltburn and Huntcliffe; Moughton Fell.

Armeria maritima, Willd.—Middlesborough and Coatham salt-marshes; Whitby; Woodhall lead-mines, near Askrigg, in Wensleydale, and along the stream running from them to the Ure; the Whey Sike in Teesdale; Stockdale, between Settle and Malham (on sandstone), where it was known to grow in the time of John Ray.*

Plantago maritima, L.—Common on the sea-coast. Seamerdale (in Wensleydale); Cronkley Scar, High Force and Winch Bridge (all in Teesdale); roadside between Grassington and Kilnsey, where it was noticed by Curtis in 1782.

It is still a question whether the inland range of these plants, or of some of them, is to be attributed to a preference for soil containing certain saline ingredients, or to that arctic and alpine tendency which is so strongly manifested in their distribution beyond Britain. The first alternative may be supported by such cases as the *Spergularia maritima*, found about the Cheshire salt-mines and the salt-springs of Auvergne and Dauphiné, or *Erodium maritimum, Rumex maritimus*, and *Scirpus maritimus*, at the foot of the Malverns. It would be necessary to prove, in order to make out the parallel, that the maritime species under consideration depend upon salt, or some such product of the soil; and further, that such ingredients, present perhaps in lead-washings or mineral veins, are invariably to be found in spots indicated by the presence of these plants.† As yet neither of these lemmas can be proved. On the other supposition—viz., that the Scurvy-grass, Thrift, and the rest, range hither as alpine or arctic plants, not as appropriators of a particular mineral substance—these cases would rank under the class of boreal species, which we proceed next to consider.

It may be well to caution any who propose to attack this problem that one and the same explanation may not be found to fit all the species enumerated; and further, that the question is complicated by obscure difficulties of specific identity—*e.g.*, whether *Armeria maritima* is the same as *A. alpina*. Direct experiment should be tried, in order to ascertain—1st, whether common salt, or any other substance not universally present in the soil, is necessary to the free growth of these species; 2nd, whether any such substance exists in recognisable quantity at the inland stations enumerated above.

An arctic flora occurs on the hills of Craven, as in the Highlands of Scotland, and in many other parts of the world far from the Arctic Circle, but of considerable elevation. The following are among the more typical species:—*Thalictrum alpinum*, L.; *Draba incana*, L.; *Saxifraga oppositifolia*, L.; *S. aizoides*, L.; *Sedum Rhodiola*, DC.; *S. villosum*,

---

* "Synopsis Stirpium Britannicarum" (1690).

† Mr. J. G. Baker notes ("Life of Charles Kingsley," vol. ii. p. 354) that "there are two other plants, not maritime, that, in the North of England, follow the lead-mines from stream-side to mountain-top—*Thlaspi alpestre* and *Arenaria verna*—the latter most plentiful." The whole letter from which this quotation is made should be read; it contains much good matter, of which I have made use in this place.

L.; *Ribes alpinum*, L.; *Rubus chamæmorus*, L. (cloudberry); *Dryas octopetala*, L.; *Potentilla alpestris*, Hall (*salisburgensis*, Haenke); *Bartsia alpina*, L.; *Salix herbacea*, L.; *Poa alpina*, L.; *Polystichum lonchitis*, Roth. (holly fern); and *Lycopodium selago*, L.* It seems at first sight easy to understand that increased altitude should compensate a comparatively low latitude; but it is to be remembered that Craven, like many other southern habitats of arctic species, is completely isolated from the polar regions by wide spaces of land and sea in which no arctic plants can live. We have thus to explain not merely the southern range of certain arctic species, but their transport across intervening areas of uncongenial climate. Allowance may be made for casual dispersal by the winds and waves, or by migrant birds, but the flora is too numerous to admit of such an explanation as complete. Oceanic islands, re-elevated coral-reefs, volcanic islets, and the population, at once scanty and mixed, which is found upon them after long ages of readiness for stray plants or animals, teach us how impotent is chance migration to explain the transport of a numerous and homogeneous flora. One of the most important generalisations from the facts of distribution may be given thus : Any noteworthy per-centage of species common to two areas means that the physical conditions necessary to the existence of such species extend, or have extended, simultaneously or successively, over the whole intervening space. These considerations lead us to believe that the boreal plants of Craven are remnants of an ancient arctic flora which occupied the British Isles within some part of the glacial period, when we know that the reindeer, glutton, and arctic fox, inhabited the north of England. Subsequent amelioration of the climate has, in this part of Europe, replaced the boreal species by plants native to temperate countries, and the remains of an arctic vegetation, far removed from their kindred, survive only on lofty and exposed hills. More striking instances of the same thing are furnished by the mountains of warm countries. The Himalayas,[†] the Pangerango mountain in Java,[‡] and the mountains of Abyssinia, exhibit an isolated northern flora. The plants of the Alps include species identical with those of Lapland, while the summit of the White Mountains, in New Hampshire, is occupied by the plants of Labrador. On the other hand, the Atlas Mountains and the Peak of Teneriffe, though both rise beyond the limit of vegetation, support no arctic vegetation—a striking and instructive exception. Unless we are prepared to admit that from the beginning everything has been pretty much what it is now, we seem obliged to suppose that the great gaps of distribution were anciently filled up, that arctic cold drove the plants of the far north into low latitudes, extending its influence across the high ground of Central Asia, and even imposing upon Java the plants of a temperate climate. When the temperature rose again, some of the migrants sought congenial climate by returning to the north, while others survived by ascending to considerable elevations.

Minerals and Fossils of Malham.—Near the Cove, on the bridle-road to Settle, are Calamine pits, which have been worked intermittently for many years. The Mountain Limestone of Malham yields many fossils, especially in the upper part. Trilobites occur in

---

* *Myosotis alpestris*, found on Micklefell, is to be noted as a similar example.
† Hooker, "Himalayan Journal."
‡ Wallace, "Malay Archipelago," vol. i. p. 118.

tolerable abundance close to the Calamine pits, but a practised eye is needed to discover them. Fossil corals lie in dense masses near the entrance to Gordale, and fragments are built into the walls hereabouts.

Geology of Airedale South of Malham.—South of Malham, the valley of the Aire is occupied by laminated bituminous and earthy Limestones, with partings of shale. No single section exposes any considerable proportion of these South Craven limestones; they are much faulted and contorted, besides being largely obscured by drift, so that their thickness can only be roughly guessed. The upper beds are probably seen in the quarries at and near Skipton, but we cannot certainly distinguish by lithological or palæontological tests the Upper from the Lower Mountain Limestone, and the evidence drawn from the lie of the rocks is incomplete. The South Craven limestones pass largely into shale in Bolland and around Clitheroe. It seems probable that we have in these limestones and shales representatives of part of the Yoredale Rocks of North Yorkshire, and of the upper part of the so-called Lower Scar Limestone of Great Whernside. The synclinals of Rilston Moor, Flasby, and Pinnow Pike are outliers of Kinder Scout Grit and Lower Millstone Grit shales, resting upon the South Craven limestones.

The intermediate limestones are thrown into many folds, of which the longest and most conspicuous have E.—W. axes. The contorted character of the rocks is well seen in the quarries of Thornton-in-Craven, Lothersdale, Skipton, and Draughton. Skipton limestone, known by its dark colour and numerous veins of calcite, can often be recognised in distant parts of Airedale, whither it has been transported by the river or by man. It is much used as road-metal, and as a flux in iron-smelting; it is also burned for lime. The larger veins of calcite mixed with baryte, which sometimes occur near Skipton, are now followed separately, and the spar, which was recently thrown upon the roads, is sold at a good price for the adulteration of white lead.

In the old quarry behind the village of Draughton, solid beds of limestone are bent without fracture into the figure of an inverted W. No better example of contortion could be desired to illustrate the three cardinal facts which every explanation must include—viz., the vast force engaged, its slow operation, and the presence during the crumpling of a great superincumbent mass, in this case of Upper Carboniferous rocks, since removed by denudation.

Ray Gill Quarries.—The quarries of Ray Gill, in Lothersdale, present other points of interest besides the contorted limestone and the thick veins of calcite and baryte. Here was lately (1874) disclosed, by quarrying, a cavity in the rock, which, though apparently surrounded by solid limestone, had formerly communicated with the surface by means of an open fissure. The upper part of the cleft is choked with glacial drift, in which are imbedded pebbles of local, and some few of distant rocks. A space clear of drift has been left, forty to fifty feet from the top, which the gradual removal of the face of the quarry is now fast diminishing (1876). In this space bones of the following animals have been found :—

Elephas antiquus.	*Rhinoceros leptorhinus.*
Hippotamus amphibius.	*Bos primigenius.*
Hyæna spelæa.	*Bison priscus.*

3 Z

The fauna is apparently of inter-glacial age, and the bones were probably introduced into the fissure either by the ice-sheet itself or by flowing water. From the sealing-up of the cleft by glacial drift we might conclude, if other evidence were not to be had, that the animals enumerated lived in Yorkshire in Pleistocene times, or before the close of the glacial period. The bulk of the remains are preserved in the Leeds Museum, to which they were contributed by Mr. E. G. Spencer and Mr. Tiddeman.

Geology of Airedale South of Skipton.—The succession of the Millstone Grit beds in Airedale has already been noticed. Below Skipton the valley presents few points of special interest beyond those which relate to stratigraphical geology. At Cononley, a vein of galena is worked in the Millstone Grit. Both cheeks are of flags and shale, and it is interesting to notice that here, where the limestone is distant, no organic remains occur in the "dowk" or vein-stuff. Mr. Charles Moore * says:—"I have not failed to detect them, more or less abundantly, except in one instance—in that of the Cononley Mine in the Airedale district." Baryte, witherite and fluor accompany the galena.

At Harden, on the grit edge which overlooks the village from the north, a natural cave has been formed, not, as in the case of the North Craven caves, by the solvent action of water and carbonic acid, but by the partial slipping of a great and irregular block of well-jointed sandstone from the edge of the cliff. The entrance is narrow, and not easily found. It is possible to wriggle for many yards along a tortuous and difficult passage, in which the crevice traverses the open joints, now vertical, now horizontal. After descending a step of about twenty feet, the bed of a subterranean stream is reached, in which are many rounded pebbles of local rocks. The cavern contains no ancient remains, and is interesting solely on account of the mode of its formation.

Above Bingley the valley of the Aire is occupied by beds of roughly stratified gravel and sand, which may be eskers heaped up by a stream debouching upon an ancient lake or arm of the sea. Some three miles lower down, the river takes a sharp turn, and quits the main valley. Instead of cutting through Hirst Wood, where the Midland Railway now passes, it bends sharply back, and after a second abrupt turn, flows through a confined gorge, which opens into the principal valley half a mile lower down. The railway-cutting in Hirst Wood exposes a great thickness of clay and rounded boulders. Putting the local facts together, it appears that the river-course was once nearly straight, but that by glacial deposit (apparently re-arranged by water), the channel became obstructed with drift. The stream was thus deflected, and forced to cut for itself a new course. This it did by channelling out the solid rock, and leaving the much looser obstruction comparatively untouched. South-east of the drift-mound—that is, down stream—we may still distinguish the ancient channel in the low and swampy ground, fringed by Hirst Wood on one side and Nab Wood on the other. It is possible that the damming-up of the Aire below Bingley facilitated the production of the eskers or mounds of rudely stratified drift at Marley.

---

* "Brit. Assoc. Report," 1869, p. 369.

RIBBLESDALE.

General Lie of the Rocks.—The Ribble, which rises beneath Cam Fell and Blea Moor, was, before the construction of the Settle and Carlisle Railway, rarely traced higher than Horton-in-Ribblesdale, where it flows between Ingleborough on the west and Penigent on the east. Here the Silurian slates which form the geological basis of Craven appear in the stream. They continue to reach the surface over an irregular area, which widens towards Settle, and sends out two expansions—a western round the base of Ingleborough, and an eastern (already traced, see p. 604), which stretches away continuously to Capon Hall, Malham Tarn, and Gordale. The slates occupy all the low ground from Selside to Stainforth, and rise to 1,160 feet above sea-level on Moughton Fell. Along their southern boundary they are cut off by the North Craven Fault.

The Mountain Limestone rests unconformably upon the slates, covering a wide space with its dry and fissured terraces and its white scars. Above the limestone the Yoredale Rocks and Kinder Scout Grit occupy the summits of Ingleborough, Penigent, Coska, and Fountains Fell. Between the North and Mid Craven Faults the limestone comes in at a lower level, and stretches from Ingleton to Wharfdale in a narrow slip, defined along nearly the whole of this distance of twenty miles by slate rocks to the north and Yoredale rocks to the south.

Silurian Rocks.—The Silurian rocks of Yorkshire are divisible into two groups, not very dissimilar lithologically, but unconformable, and containing few common fossils.* The lower series includes the Green Slates and Coniston Limestone—probable equivalents of the Caradoc beds; while the upper consists of the Coniston Flags and Grits (Upper Silurian). The lower series is visible in Chapel-le-dale and in the slate-quarries of Ingleton, at Horton, at Austwick Beck Head, where they lie in a sharp anticlinal running east and west, and around the village of Wharfe, where they are brought up by a parallel anticlinal, cut off on the north by a fault.

The Coniston Limestone is particularly well seen at Douk Gill, near Horton, at Wharfe Mill Dam, and at Wharfe Gill Dyke. An interval of time, during which upheaval and denudation went on, separated the formation of the Lower from that of the Upper Silurian series. This is shown by the fact that the Coniston Flags rest upon different members of the lower series, while the base of the Flags consists in some places of a conglomerate largely made up of fragments of the older beds. The Coniston Flags lie in a great synclinal, intermediate to the two anticlinals above-mentioned. This synclinal crosses Ribblesdale below Horton, and reappears in the adjacent Crummack valley, where the basin, somewhat shallower and more elevated than in Ribblesdale, is readily made out at a little distance. The Coniston Flags are divided by Prof. Hughes into four groups :—

---

* For many of the facts given in the following description of the Silurian rocks of Ribblesdale and the district I am indebted to an interesting and exact memoir on "The Break between the Upper and Lower Silurian Rocks of the Lake District, as seen between Kirkby Lonsdale and Malham, near Settle" (*Geol. Mag.* 1867, p. 346), by Prof. T. M'K. Hughes, whom I have also to thank for explaining the arrangement of the rocks to me on the ground.

1.　A conglomerate containing Lower Silurian pebbles, and resting unconformably upon Lower Silurian beds.　(Southwaite, Austwick Beck Head.)

2.　Soft, well-cleaved slates.　Thickness, probably several hundred feet.　(Bracken-bottom, Austwick Beck Head, Southwaite.)

3.　Tough grits, with subordinate beds of flags.　Thickness, about 1,000 feet.　(South of Horton, Bargh House, between Crummack and Southwaite.)

4.　Flags, with subordinate beds of grit (Coniston Flags proper).　Thickness, about 2,000 feet.　These slates are well seen in the quarries of Foredale and about Studfold on the opposite side of the valley.　Owing to the eastward fall of the synclinal axis, they do not reappear in the Crummack valley.

At the south end of Studfold Low Pasture the Coniston Flags are overlaid by a small patch of tough grits, which reach a thickness of about 1,200 feet on Casterton Fell, and are known in the Lake District as the Coniston Grits.　They do not reappear in Craven.

Professor Hughes gives the following lists of fossils.　Those printed in small capitals and followed by a note of stratigraphical distribution, have a special bearing upon the geological age of the containing rock :—

CONISTON LIMESTONE.

Halysites catenularia.
Heliolites.
PETRAIA ÆQUISULCATA (Caradoc).
Favosites fibrosus.
———— (two other species).
Encrinites.
Cystideans.
A phyllopod crustacean.
Calymene brevicapitata.
Cheirurus bimucronatus.
CYBELE VERRUCOSA (Caradoc, Lower Llandovery).
Illænus.
Lichas.
PHACOPS CONOPHTHALMUS (Caradoc).
Phacops, sp.
Remopleurides.
ATRYPA MARGINALIS (Caradoc, Lower Llandovery).
LEPTÆNA QUINQUECOSTATA (Llandeilo, Caradoc).

Leptæna sericea.
———— *transversalis.*
———— sp.
Lingula (two species ?).
ORTHIS ACTONIÆ (Llandeilo, Caradoc, Lower Llandovery).
———— BIFORATA (Llandeilo, Caradoc, Lower Llandovery).
Orthis calligramma.
———— *elegantula.*
ORTHIS FLABELLULUM (Caradoc).
———— PORCATA (Caradoc, Llandovery).
———— VESPERTILIO (Llandeilo, Caradoc).
Orthis sp.
Strophomena depressa.
Murchisonia (?).
Lituites (?).
Orthoceras.

All these are Caradoc fossils.

Above the Coniston Limestone, but conformable with it, is seen, at Southwaite and Norber, a series of slates with " ash-like beds " and bands of packed concretions.　Here occur—

PETRAIA SUBDUPLICATA, var. *crenulata* (Caradoc, Llandovery).
Encrinites.
PHACOPS APICULATUS (?).
———— OBTUSICAUDATUS (?) ⎱ Chiefly in
TRINUCLEUS CONCENTRICUS (Caradoc, ⎰ upper part.
　　Llandovery).

ORTHIS BIFORATA (Llandeilo, Caradoc, Lower Llandovery).
Orthis calligramma.
———— sp.
Strophomena depressa. ⎱ Abundant in
STROPHOMENA ALTERNATA (Caradoc). ⎰ lower part.
Strophomena, sp.
Orthoceras, &c.

All these are Caradoc fossils.

CONISTON FLAGS.

Favosites fibrosus.
ACTINOCRINUS PULCHER (Wenlock).
Graptolites Ludensis.
———— sp.
PTERINEA TENUISTRIATA (Ludlow).   [(Ludlow).
CARDIOLA INTERRUPTA (Upper Llandovery, Wenlock,

Lituites giganteus.
ORTHOCERAS PRIMÆVUM (Wenlock).
———— SUBUNDULATUM (Wenlock).
Orthoceras ventricosum (?).
Worm tracks, &c.

All these are Upper Silurian.

Swallow-holes and Caves.—Near Horton and Selside are many pits in the limestone, known locally as "pots." Chasms and caves abound in pure calcareous rocks, wherever they are hard and massive. We find them in the Mountain Limestone, not only of the North of England but of Somersetshire, Derbyshire, Belgium, Westphalia, Maine and Anjou, the Pyrenees and the Department of Aude, Virginia, and Kentucky. They occur in the Permian Limestones of Nottingham; in the Oolitic Limestones of Kirkdale, Franconia, Bavaria, and the Jura; in the Neocomian and Cretaceous Limestones of Périgord, Quercy, and Angoumois, Provence and Languedoc, Northern Italy, Sicily, Greece, Dalmatia, Carniola, and Turkey, Asia Minor and Palestine; in the Tertiary Limestones of Montpelier and Paris, and the Departments of Gard and Gironde.*

The flow of water through a well-jointed rock is, in most cases, the primary agent in the excavation of fissures, pot-holes, and caves. Water, unaided, is indeed a feeble wearing agent; but when rapid enough to bear along stones and sand, it can quickly enlarge its passage by the scour. If these simple physical conditions alone were in question, the form and extent of water-passages in Mountain Limestone would still differ from those in sandstone and shale, by reason of the greater tenacity and homogeneity of the rock. Falls of rock would be less frequent, and the stream would choke less readily. But there is another property of limestone far more important in this connection than its compactness. Water containing carbonic acid has the power of dissolving carbonate of lime. Wherever the acidulated water, or its vapour, can reach, the rock is either dissolved in films or etched and fretted away. Fallen blocks do not here, as in the water-passages of argillaceous rocks, crumble to clay or mud, but remain firm and angular until bit by bit they waste and disappear. High above the level of the stream, moisture laden with carbonic acid settles upon the roof of the cavity, and slowly corrodes it.

Evaporation of the water, or the mere escape of its carbonic acid, causes the calcareous matter to be thrown down, and thus a water-cave in limestone rocks is commonly ornamented with stalactites hanging from the roof, or stalagmitic films along the floor and sides.

Thirl Pot lies close to Horton, on the side of Penigent. It is a vertical chasm with an oval opening. The depth is not very great, and the descent can be made with or without ropes, through a narrow lateral cleft. It is said that a vein of galena, which may be seen to traverse the walls of Thirl Pot, furnished the lead for the roof of Horton Church. The stream at the bottom descends rapidly through the rock, and emerges in Douk Gill.

Thund Pot lies in the next field to Thirl Pot. It has a shelving mouth, and descends

---

* This list is taken, with unimportant alterations, from Professor Boyd Dawkins' "Cave-Hunting," p. 25.

at least two hundred feet before the stream is reached. This dangerous pit has not been explored fully.

Hellen Pot, on the Limestone plateau of Ingleborough, seems to have arisen by the falling in of part of the roof of a network of subterranean water-courses. One of these, the Long Churn Cavern, may be entered 150 yards north-west of the principal swallow-hole. The passage is not very difficult, and a small stream may be followed along its rough and precipitous descent through clefts, chambers lined with stalactites, water-falls and pools, until it plunges into the vertical pit of Hellen Pot, at about 100 feet from the surface. Other passages, some as yet unexplored owing to the depth of water, some dry, ramify from Long Churn Cavern. The open mouth of Hellen Pot is a fissure 100 feet long by 30 feet wide, grown with trees and ferns. A small rivulet empties itself into the chasm, and falls 198 feet clear. Ledges project from the side, and just below the entrance of the stream from Long Churn Cavern is a great fallen block, 10 feet long, which lies across the gulf. From the foot of the first vertical descent a passage may be followed along the bed of an underground stream. Waterfalls and rapids render the way difficult, but two parties have succeeded in reaching a distance of about 170 feet from the foot of the shaft of Hellen Pot. Here, in the darkness of a lofty chamber, a waterfall, said to be about 40 feet high, precipitates itself into a deep basin. The united streams disappear in a quiet, circling pool, at the end of the chamber, and upwards of 300 feet from the surface.

This formidable cavern was descended by Mr. Birkbeck and Mr. Metcalfe in 1847. The following year baulks of timber were laid across the top, and a much easier descent was made by means of a bucket and windlass. Mr. Birkbeck and eight others formed the exploring party. In 1870, a similar descent was made by Mr. Birkbeck and twelve others, of whom three were ladies.[*] The timbers still lie across the mouth, as if to invite further attempts.

Hellen Pot well illustrates the first formation and subsequent history of many a limestone cavern. There is the enlarging of fissures, the grinding away of the rock by a sand-bearing stream, the slow decay of the damp roof, and finally, the falling in of the top. "The two actions," says Professor Dawkins, "by which caves are hewn out of the calcareous rock are here seen in operation side by side. Below the level of the stream the rock is seen to be smoothed and polished by the mechanical action of the material swept down by the current. Above the water-level the sides of the cave are honeycombed and eaten into the most fantastic and complex shapes, the resultant surface bearing small points and keen knife-edges of stone that stand out in relief, and mark the less soluble portions of the rock. This is due to the chemical effect of the carbonic acid in the water percolating through the strata. . . . The floor of the pot and the cave was strewn with masses of limestone, rounded by the action of the streams, and the water-channels were smoothed, and grooved, and polished, in a most extraordinary way, by the silt and stones carried along by the current. Some of the layers of limestone were jet-black, and others were of a light fawn-colour, and as the strata were nearly horizontal, the alternation of colours gave a peculiarly

---

[*] An account of this descent is given by Professor Boyd Dawkins in his "Cave-Hunting," p. 41. A narrative of the earlier explorations of Hellen Pot is contained in Howson's "Guide to Craven."

striking effect to the walls. Beneath each waterfall was a pool, more or less deep, and here and there in the bed of the stream were holes, drilled in the rock by stones whirled round by the force of the water. High up, out of the present reach of the water, were old channels, which had evidently been water-courses before the pot and cave had been cut down to their present level. In the sides of the pot there are two vertical grooves, reaching very nearly from the top to the bottom, which are unmistakably the work of ancient waterfalls. There was no stalactite [in the further passages], but everywhere the water was wearing away the rock and enlarging the cave." *

Katnot Cave, Brow Gill Cave, Birkwith Cave, Jackdaw Hole, Sel Gill, and a hundred unnamed caverns and swallow-holes, pierce the limestone floors of Ingleborough and Penigent on the Ribblesdale side. The more extensive and famous caves of Clapham and Weathercote lie beyond the limits of Craven.

Victoria Cave, Settle.—The range of Limestone Scars in which the Victoria Cave opens, lies north of the Attermire Rocks, and a mile and a quarter N.E. of Settle. The cave faces S.S.W., about 1,450 feet above the sea, and 900 feet above the Ribble, which is about a mile distant. From the mouth of the cave the eye ranges over an extensive landscape of green pastures, through which the Ribble and Lune wander. At greater elevations are the brown moors of Bolland, and the white rocky terraces of Ingleborough, Moughton, and Penigent. The Lake Hills bound the view northwards, and Pendle Hill to the south.

Here the Victoria Cave was discovered by Mr. Joseph Jackson, of Settle, in 1837. It was explored by him and others in a desultory way, but with many curious results, until, in 1870, a committee of the local gentry, subsequently assisted by the British Association, undertook to dig out the cave systematically.

The floor of the cave when first examined gave abundant proof of habitation by man at different times, some of them very remote. In the superficial or Romano-British layer have been found coins of Trajan (98–117), Tetricus (267–272); Gallienus (260–268); Constantine II. (337–343); Constans (337–350); and three base coins, cast in imitation of the minimi of Tetricus. With these were two harp-shaped bronze fibulæ, a split-ring fibula, a brooch of bronze, made by soldering together two circular plates, and stamped with a regular trifoliate, spiral pattern (the so-called Celtic scroll), enamelled fibulæ of late Celtic manufacture, fibulæ plated with silver bracelets, pins, a Roman key, knife-blades, a spear-head, and a scent-box perforated with four holes. There were also pins, studs, buttons, and knife-handles of bone, carved spoon-shaped bone fibulæ, glass beads, stone pot-boilers, hearthstones, black, white, and red Samian pottery. Bones associated with these relics have been identified as belonging to the red deer, roebuck, Celtic short-horn (*Bos longifrons*) sheep or goat, pig, horse, badger, fox, and dog.

Beneath the Romano-British layer, towards the mouth of the cave, lay a thickness of loose fragments of fallen stones, to the amount of five or six feet, imperfectly cemented by stalagmite. Remains of pre-historic antiquity occur beneath this loose talus. Here was found a bone harpoon with double barbs, a sculptured bone bead, and three flint flakes. To the

* " Cave-Hunting," pp. 42, 45.

same (Neolithic) horizon are referred a rude leaf-shaped flint found in 1874, and a small adze of melaphyre ground to a neat cutting-edge. Strong testimony supports the ascription of the adze to the Victoria Cave, but it is perfectly similar in form, size, and material to Polynesian tools, while no strictly comparable implement has been recorded from European soil. Bones of the brown bear, horse, Celtic shorthorn, and red deer have been found in the Neolithic layer.

The Romano-British and Neolithic deposits extended over nearly the whole surface of the middle and the left-hand principal chamber. When they were formed, the right-hand chamber was almost entirely choked up by still more ancient accumulations.

These are divisible into three layers—the Upper Cave-earth, the Laminated Clay, and the Lower Cave-earth. Far within the cave, the laminated clay ceases, and the upper cave-earth lies directly upon the lower. Mr. Tiddeman describes these deposits in the following terms :—

"In their physical aspect, the upper and lower cave-earth have much in common. They both consist of large and small angular blocks of limestone, intermingled with a stiff buff clay, occasional beds of stalagmite, and fallen blocks of stalactite. The limestone and stalactite have undoubtedly fallen from the roof. The stalagmite has formed upon the floor from time to time, when circumstances have been favourable. In the upper bed much of the clay seems to be derived from the laminated clay beneath, worked up and re-deposited by water, or *puddled* by the animals whose bones are found in it ; certainly where bones have occurred in the surface of this clay, it has lost its characteristic finely-bedded structure, and is simply homogeneous. A good deal of this homogeneous clay has probably been washed down through fine crevices in the roof by little runnels during wet weather, although at present certainly all water that drops from the roof seems to be well filtered. In the lower cave-earth, between the blocks of limestone, little chinks have been filled in with laminated clay, which is possibly of the same age, and deposited under identical circumstances, with the great mass of it above—the conditions necessary for this only being a pre-existing chink and a crack leading to it, wide enough to permit water to trickle through it, bearing the finest impalpable mud." *

The intermediate stratum of laminated clay presents certain difficulties of interpretation. It is of great but irregular thickness (twelve feet in one place), tolerably free from mixture with other deposits, and consists of a multitude of thin films of clay, such as would result from the subsidence of an intermittent, muddy stream. It extends at least 70 feet from the entrance. Mr. Tiddeman offers the explanation of a flow of water derived from the daily melting of a glacier. It will be seen further on that the existence of a sheet of ice at the mouth of the cave may possibly be required by another set of facts. The laminated clay is perhaps due to this cause, but other equally valid interpretations could be framed. Finely-stratified layers are occasionally found in boulder-clay, and this makes for Mr. Tiddeman's view ; but Professor Dawkins points out that they are also being formed at the present time at the bottom of pools in many caves, such as that of Ingleborough. There are no features of the laminated clay which imperatively require the glacier supposition,† and, perhaps, none which refute it. An intermittent, earth-laden flow of water is implied, and there is more than one way of accounting for its former existence.

The bones yielded by the older and the newer cave-earth are extremely numerous.

---

* *Proc. W. R. Geol. Soc.* N.S. vol. i. pp. 83, 84 (1875).

† Mr. Tiddeman calls attention to the existence of a few glaciated boulders in its upper layers. The Rev. W. H. Crosskey, who has had much experience of similar clays, and has carefully washed some of the laminated clay of the Victoria Cave for organisms, reports that it is in all respects similar to the laminated glacial clays of the West of Scotland, except that it contains no foraminifera.

They may be conveniently studied in the museum of Giggleswick School, where are also preserved the more recent human ornaments and tools disinterred from the Victoria Cave. In the appended table the fauna is enumerated, so as to facilitate the verification of the general statements and inferences which succeed. The supposed characteristic older ("Pleistocene," or "quaternary") animals are marked *. The absence of the cave-lion, *Felis leo*, var. *spelæa*, is noteworthy.

	Victoria Cave, Older Cave Earth.	Victoria Cave, Newer Cave Earth.	Fissure at Lothersdale.	Wortley, nr. Leeds.	Now extinct.	Now extinct in Britain.
Man...	?	?				
Hyæna crocuta, var spelæa (Cave Hyæna)	×		×			×
Ursus arctos (Brown Bear)	×	×				×
Ursus ferox (Grizzly Bear)	×	×				×
Ursus spelæus (Cave Bear)	×				×	×
Canis lupus (Wolf)		×				×
Canis vulpes (Fox)	×	×				
Meles taxus (Badger)		×				
Elephas antiquus ...	×		×	?	×	×
Equus caballus (Horse) ...	?	×				
Rhinoceros leptorhinus	×				×	×
Bison priscus	×		×		×	×
Bos primigenius	×		×	×		
Sus scrofa (Pig)		×				
Cervus elaphus (Red Deer)	×	×				
Cervus megaceros (Irish Elk)		?			×	×
Cervus tarandus (Reindeer)	×	×				×
Hippopotamus amphibius	×		×	×		×

The presence of man in the lower cave-earth of the Victoria Cave was supposed to be vouched for by a fragmentary fibula, determined as human, after a long and minute investigation, by Professor Busk. This identification is now withdrawn, and Professor Busk states that he "should not himself be inclined to rest or to base the existence of Pre-Glacial Man on a fragment of bone like that, about which it is impossible that some doubt should not exist." *

Mr. Tiddeman, speaking of the species marked * in the table, remarks that—

"There are two very marked species, the hippopotamus and the hyæna, which point to a very warm climate ; of the remainder, the elephant and the rhinoceros, of species both extinct, may be considered, from their frequent companionship with the hippopotamus, and, as Prof. Dawkins points out, from their range, to have also lived in warm countries. The rest are all either adaptable to a wide range of climate, or of temperate proclivities. Upon the whole, then, we have an assemblage of species which require, or could live in, a tolerably warm climate. Arctic species are entirely absent. This state of things must have lasted a long time, but higher in the section the bones become more scarce, the more tropical animals are wanting. The bear, the fox, and the ox, are scattered about at rare intervals ; eventually these vanish, and about twenty feet above the busy-looking hyæna floor we come upon the base of the laminated clay, interbedded with an occasional layer of stalagmite, but without a trace of any living thing. We work our way up through it, and find near the top of it some well-scratched boulders, and we look out at the cave mouth, and seeing the rubbish left by a vanished glacier, we naturally ask—Do not these represent the coming events which cast their cold shadows before them, and first drove from the district the tropical animals, and then those of greater powers of endurance?" †

* *Q. J. Geol. Soc.* vol. xxxiii. p. 610 (1877).   † *Proc. W. R. Geol. Soc.* N.S. vol. i. pp. 88, 89.

4 A

Prof. Boyd Dawkins contests this view.   He considers that a mixed fauna is universal in British bone-caves, and enumerates the species,

"Some of which are extinct, such as the mammoth, the woolly rhinoceros and Irish elk. Others are now living in temperate climates, such as the horse and bison ; others in hot countries, such as the spotted hyæna and the lion ; while one, the reindeer, which is very abundant, is now only living in the cold region of the north. This mixed fauna is one which is to be met with universally in the bone-caves of this country, and with one exception, that of Baume in the Jura, in those also of France, Germany, Switzerland, and Belgium.

"In some caves in this country, such as Kirkdale, Victoria, and Raygill, in Yorkshire, and in those of Cefn near St. Asaph, and in those of the Mendip Hills, we find the hippopotamus associated with the remains of the above-mentioned species, while in others we meet with northern forms, such as the lemming, lagomys, arctic fox, and glutton, in like association. In the caves of Auvergne, Professor Lartet detected musk sheep along with the same forms, an arctic animal found in this country in the river strata along with the mixed fauna above-mentioned. The species composing this mixed fauna occur in the caves of Britain in the closest possible relation to each other. In none do we find the southern group of animals in one situation and the northern in another ; but they are found mingled together either just as they were left by the hyænas or by palæolithic man, or as they were introduced by a stream, or by the falling in of animals into swallow-holes, as the case may be.

" On this point the experience of Buckland and Falconer is amply confirmed by my own. Nor is the reputed case of the Victoria Cave an exception, in which a southern fauna with hyæna, rhinoceros, and hippopotamus is stated by Mr. Tiddeman to be met with below the horizon of reindeer. While the exploration was under my charge, the reindeer was determined from the stratum in question, in 1872, and published in the British Association Report for that year, which apparently has been overlooked in the succeeding reports. It is not to be seen in the collection from the cave in the Giggleswick Grammar School. The same intimate association of northern and southern forms is observable in a large number of river-strata, as may be seen by my lists published in 1869 (*Quarterly Journal Geological Society*, p. 199)." [*]

At the mouth of the cave the explorers found it necessary to remove a great thickness of talus or rock-*débris*, which had fallen, bit by bit, from the overhanging cliff. This attained in places a depth of twenty feet. Beneath the talus a line of boulders was unexpectedly struck. The boulders were well scratched, and consisted of large and small fragments of Silurian Grit, Mountain Limestone, Mountain Limestone Conglomerate, and Millstone Grit. They lay in a stratum of no great thickness, dipping away from the entrance, and resting against the edge of the lower cave-earth.

When these boulders had been imperfectly cleared, various opinions were expressed as to the mode of their deposition. Professor Boyd Dawkins [†] puts the case thus :—

"They may be the constituents of a lateral moraine *in situ*, as Mr. Tiddeman suggests, or they may merely be derived from the waste of boulder-clay which has dropped from a higher level. The latter view seems to me to be most likely to be true, because some of the boulders have been deprived of the clay in which they were imbedded, and are piled on each other with empty space between them, the clay being carried down to a lower level and re-deposited. Their position, however, on the edges of the cave-earth, implies, in any case, that they had been dropped after its accumulation."

We shall see that questions of importance turn upon the exact mode in which the boulders were dropped into their present position. To the suggestion that they were not left where we now find them by the ice-sheet, but have fallen from the cliff subsequently, Mr. Tiddeman replies : [‡]—

" 1. The boulders lie at the base of all the screes, which are nineteen feet thick, and no other boulders occur throughout that whole thickness.

" 2. The cliff immediately above the cave is quite free from boulders for a considerable distance.

" 3. The screes (talus) are allowed to be the result of the destruction of the cliff above by atmospheric agencies, and, as they lie above all the boulders, must have fallen subsequently. Even now the boulders lie so close beneath the cliff that it would be barely possible for them to fall from it into their present position. But if we could restore to the cliff all the limestone screes lying above the boulders, such a fall would be quite impossible.

" 4. The extent of the glacial deposits now exposed is so great, covering an area of 1,200 square feet or more, that it is impossible that they can be a mere chance accumulation of boulders."

[*] *Journ. Anthr. Inst.*, Nov. 1877.
[†] " Cave-Hunting," p. 121.
[‡] *Proc. W. R. Geol. Soc.* N.S. vol. i. p. 87 (1875).

The writer can testify to the correctness of these statements, and considers it a fair, though not incontestable inference, that the boulders were brought to the mouth of the cave directly by moving ice. It must be admitted that the hypothesis is tenable, not so much by reason of its own strength, as from the absence of substantial alternatives.

We may infer, from the facts already summarised, that many mammals now extinct existed in Yorkshire during Pleistocene times; that the deposit in which their bones lie was covered up—a stratum containing no trace of life, and possibly of glacial origin (the laminated clay)—while the exposed edges of the ossiferous cave-earth were thickly strewn with travelled, and doubtless ice-borne, boulders. It seems fair to conclude that the fauna of the lower cave-earth of the Victoria Cave is of glacial or pre-glacial age—that, at any rate, it inhabited Yorkshire before the ice-sheet had finally disappeared.

The table on p. 617, when illustrated by a few cognate facts, gives independent evidence in support of these positions. In the river-gravels of England we find all the species represented in the lower cave-earth of the Victoria Cave, and, with these, rude flint implements—indubitable signs of coeval man. But when we examine the surface of the ground in the north of England, the river-gravels, with their bones and palæolithic flint implements, disappear, and we find in their place thick and widespread deposits of till or unstratified boulder-clay. The locality nearest to the barren area in which remains of the old fauna have been found in a river-valley is Wortley, near Leeds, where bones of the hippopotamus, elephant, and urus (*Bos primigenius*) have occurred. The absence of signs of the old fauna over the glacial area is both well ascertained and significant. It leaves us still a choice of conclusions. They are absent, either because they never existed there, or because, having once existed, they have been swept away. In deciding between these alternatives, the Lothersdale fissure (p. 609) and the Victoria Cave demand attention. Here we find well within the glacial area, in the one case a few, in the other many, characteristic species of the old fauna. These two exceptional cases of preservation prove the ancient existence of the Pleistocene fauna within the glacial area, and lead to the conclusion that its total absence in river-beds or surface-deposits immediately to the north of Leeds must be explained by the direct action of the ice-sheet, sweeping clear the open country, and sparing the fragmentary remains only where sealed up within rocky chambers.

But on this question also, it is but just to hear the other side. Professor Dawkins says—

"The distribution also of the mammalia is urged in support of the view that palæolithic man is not of post-glacial age, and therefore either inter- or pre-glacial. There are certain areas in Britain in which the marks of recent glaciation are the freshest, and in which the fauna of the caves and river-beds is conspicuous by its absence. This is taken to prove that originally the animal remains were distributed alike over the mountains of Wales, Scotland, and Cumberland, and the high grounds of the North generally, and that they have been removed from those areas by the extension of the ice. The view which I advanced in 1871 (*Popular Science Review*, and 'Cave Hunting,' 1874) still seems to me a better explanation of the facts, that the non-glacial lowlands were inhabited by the animals, *while* the ice covered the glaciated areas, in the second ice or glacier period.

* * * * * * * * * * *

"The physical changes of the glacial period are so little understood even in such a limited area as Britain, that they are a fertile subject for discussion among geologists. Even if they were thoroughly mastered, it seems to me that they would offer no means of testing the age of palæolithic man in non-glaciated areas, or those in which the majority of the ossiferous caves and river-strata are to be found. The glacial period, further, is not a hard and fast line dividing one fauna from another. The classification by means of ice is one thing, and the classification by means of animals is quite a different thing."*

* *Journ. Anthr. Inst.* Nov. 1877.

To sum up so intricate a controversy would be no easy task while some cardinal facts (such as the presence of the reindeer in the older deposits of the cave) are still in question. We must wait for further investigation before making up our minds, and this furnishes an additional plea for adequate public support of the explorations now carried on with diligence and care under Mr. Tiddeman's direction.*

Flora of the Mountain Limestone.—The sharp definition of the calcareous rocks of Settle from the argillaceous or sandy rocks, the great vertical range (from 400 to 2,200 feet above sea-level), and the occurrence of both calcareous and non-calcareous rocks under like conditions of elevation, exposure, temperature, and moisture, render it peculiarly interesting to study here the local distribution of plants. For similar reasons the comparative frequency of certain diseases (phthisis, cancer, goître) supposed to prevail upon some geological areas with greater intensity than elsewhere, might be investigated more usefully here than in almost any other part of England.

The botanical species which show a marked preference for the Mountain Limestone are—

PHANEROGAMIA.

Thalictrum minus, L.
Actæa spicata, L.
Trollius europæus, L.
Thlaspi alpestre, L.
Draba incana, L.
——— *muralis*, L.
Arabis hirsuta, Br.
Cardamine Impatiens, L.
Hutchinsia petræa, Br.
Reseda Luteola, L.
Helianthemum vulgare, Gärtn.
Viola hirta, L.
—— *lutea*, Huds.
Arenaria verna, L.
Geranium sanguineum, L.
Hippocrepis comosa, L.
Potentilla verna, L.
——— *alpestris*, Hall.
Dryas octopetala, L.
Rubus saxatilis, L.
Rosa Sabini, Woods.
—— *villosa*, L.
Poterium Sanguisorba, L.
Ribes petræum, Sm.
—— *alpinum*, L.
Saxifraga oppositifolia, L.
Silaus pratensis, Besser.
Galium sylvestre, Poll.
——— *montanum*, Vill.
——— *boreale*, L.
Scabiosa Columbaria, L.
Hieracium Gibsoni, Backh.
——— *crocatum*, Fries.

Hieracium cæsium, Backh.
——— *vulgatum*, var. *rubescens*, Backh.
——— *pallidum*, Backh.
Crepis succisæfolia, Tausch.
Carlina vulgaris, L.
Carduus nutans, L.
Gentiana Amarella, L.
——— *campestris*, L.
Polemonium cœruleum, L.
Bartsia alpina, L.
Orobanche rubra, Sm.
Origanum vulgare, L.
Primula farinosa, L.
Epipactis ovalis, Bab.
Cypripedium Calceolus, L.
Gymnadenia Conopsea, Br.
Polygonatum officinale, All.
Carex fulva, Good.
Sesleria cærulea, Scop.
Festuca sylvatica, Vill.
Brachypodium pinnatum, Beauv.
Avena pratensis, var. *alpina*, Sm.
Aira cristata, Pers.
Melica nutans, L.

FILICES.

Polypodium calcareum, Sm.
Cystopteris fragilis, Bernh.
Lastrea rigida, Desv.
Polystichum Lonchitis, Sw.
Scolopendrium vulgare, Sm.
Asplenium viride, Huds.

---

* The most convenient and generally useful notices of the Victoria Cave are to be found in Professor Boyd Dawkins' "Cave-Hunting," and in Mr. Tiddeman's "Work and Problems of the Victoria Cave Exploration," cited above.

CHARACEÆ.

Chara vulgaris, L.
—— *flexilis*, L.
—— *hispida*, L.
—— *aspera*, W.

HEPATICÆ.

Jungermannia incisa, Schrad.
—————— *echinata*, Tayl.

MUSCI.

Weissia verticillata, Brid.
Seligeria pusilla, B. & S.
Anacalypta lanceolata, C. Müll.
Trichostomum mutabile, Br.
———————— *rigidulum*, Sm.
———————— *flexicaule*, C. Müll
Tortula fallax, Hed. var. *brevifolia*.
—— *tortuosa*, W. & M.
Cinclindotus fontinaloides, Beauv.
Encalypta ciliata, Hed.
———— *rhabdocarpa*, Schwaeg.
———— *streptocarpa*, Hed.
Schistidium apocarpum, Hed.
Orthotrichum cupulatum, Hoff.

Orthotrichum anomalum, Bruch.
———————— *tenellum*, Bruch.
———————— *stramineum*, Hornsch.
———————— *crispum*, Brid.
———————— *Lyellii*, Hook.
Bryum Zierii, Dicks.
Mnium cuspidatum, Hed.
—— *orthorhynchum*, Brid.
—— *serratum*, Brid.
Cinclidium stygium, Wahl.
Funaria Mühlenbergii, Schw.
Bartramia calcarea, B. & S.
—— *Œderi*, Swartz.
Cylindrothecium Montaguei, Br.
Leskea Sprucei, Br.
—— *moniliformis*, Wils.
—— *subrufa*, Wils.
Hypnum crassinervum, Tayl.
———— *Teesdalei*, Dicks.
———— *tenellum*, Dicks.
———— *catenulatum*, Brid.
———— *delicatulum*, L.
———— *rugosum*, Ehr.
———— *commutatum*, Hed.
———— *molluscum*, Hed.
———— *incurvatum*, Schrad.
———— *depressum*, Br.
Neckera crispa, Hed.

Many lists of the Lichens of Craven have been drawn up, but until the classification of this class is put upon a better footing than at present, it seems almost useless to give a catalogue of the species of the Mountain Limestone. Lichenologists are slow to accept Schwendener's views as to the nature and life-history of these plants, but until the questions raised by him are fairly answered, we can hardly use or quote the specific names now current.*

Bolland.—In the vale of Hodder an anticlinal axis running north-east brings up the limestone about Whitewell and Slaidburn. Parallel to the main axis are smaller folds, in which lie the contorted limestones of Sykes and Whitendale. Yoredale shales form the slopes which surmount the limestones, while the summits of Croasdale Fell, Bolland Knots, Browsholme Moor, and Birkett Fell, which on every side but the south-west shut in the upper part of the vale of Hodder, are composed of Millstone Grit. The upper part of Bolland, which alone enters Craven, is of less interest to the geologist or naturalist than the Trough of Bolland and the western bend of the Hodder. The panorama from Bolland Knots should, however, be noted as one of the finest views in the deanery.

———————————

Craven has been diligently searched for two centuries. The older race of English botanists—John Ray, Thomas Williselt, and Dr. Richardson—loved its woods and fields.

———————————

* The distribution of plants in Yorkshire has been thoroughly handled by Mr. J. G. Baker, formerly of Thirsk, now of Kew, whose book on "North Yorkshire," and other less elaborate writings, hold out an excellent example to local naturalists. I am indebted to Mr. Baker for many useful facts, and for others to Dr. Carrington, who formerly explored the botany, and especially the cryptogamic botany, of Craven with much diligence.

Here Martin Lister gathered minerals and fossils, and elaborated notions which, crude as they were, entitle him nevertheless to an honourable place among the founders of geology.   In later days Phillips applied the new-discovered principles of stratigraphical geology to the Mountain Limestone of Craven, and earned thereby much of his early fame.   Side by side with these honoured names may be ranked others, less familiar to the public ear, but hardly less esteemed among students.   In our own day, and down to the present moment, Craven has continued to offer in its fields and caves and rocks a wide and varied area for the collection of natural facts.   It seems at times as if all the most significant phenomena had been noted; it is hard to find unbroken ground, and the duller or more desponding are prone to shrink from active research into the easier though less productive path of antiquarian natural history.   But we may rest assured that the field is as wide as ever, that its fertility is inexhaustible, and that fresh facts will to the end of time reward the seeing eye and the attentive mind.

POSTSCRIPT.

I HAVE to thank several geological friends for help in the preparation of this chapter. Some of my obligations have been already noticed in their places.   Mr. J. R. Dakyns, of the Geological Survey, has furnished additions and corrections.   Mr. R. H. Tiddeman, of the Geological Survey, has revised the manuscript, and supplied many details for the map. It will be seen that I have made free use of Mr. Tiddeman's published papers, especially of those which record the results of his zealous, careful, and important work at the Victoria Cave.   My colleague, Prof. A. H. Green, has prepared the geological section across Craven, and I have further benefited by his revision of the proofs.

CATALOGUE OF THE RARER PLANTS

GROWING IN CRAVEN, IN THE COUNTY OF YORK.

[Compiled for Dr. Whitaker by SAMUEL HAILSTONE, Esq., of Bradford.]

"These are thy glorious works, Parent of Good,
Almighty!"   MILTON.

AUCTORES CITATI.

Flo. Brit. Flora Britannica. Auctore Jacobo Edwardo Smith, M.D. Societatis Linnæanæ Præside, &c. Tom. I. II. III.
Huds. Gulielmi Hudsoni Flora Anglica.
With. Withering's Arrangement of British Plants, 1796, 8vo.
Eng. Bot. English Botany, or Coloured Figures of English Plants, 8vo.
Raii Syn. Joannis Raii Synopsis Methodica Stirpium Britannicarum, 8vo. 1724.
Dill. Historia Muscorum (Joannis Jacobi Dillenii), 4to. 1741.
Ach. Prod. Lichenographiæ Suecicæ Prodromus, Auctore Erik Achario, M.D. &c. 1798.
Bolt. Fil. Filices Britannicæ, by James Bolton, of Halifax, 2 vols. 4to.

MONANDRIA MONOGYNIA.

CHARA VULGARIS. *Flo. Brit.* 4.
C. HISPIDA. *Ib.* 5.
 Var. C. tomentosa. *Huds.* 398. *With.* 2. nec Linn.
 In the brook which runs from Malham Tarn before it falls into the ground.

DIANDRIA MONOGYNIA.

CIRCÆA LUTETIANA. *Flo. Brit.* 13.
 Moist hedges and woods.
VERONICA MONTANA. *Flo. Brit.* 21.
 In Ravenroyd Wood, near Bingley.
VERONICA SCUTELLATA. *Flo. Brit.* 21.
 In boggy places, upon Rumbald's Moor, near Helwick.
PINGUICULA VULGARIS. *Flo. Brit.* 27. *Eng. Bot.* 70.
 Gordale. Near the watering-trough by the road-side at Hawcliffe turnpike.

TRIANDRIA MONOGYNIA.

SCHŒNUS COMPRESSUS. *Flo. Brit.* 44. *Eng. Bot.* 791.
 Plentifully adjoining to the rivulet between Malham Tarn and the Cove.

SCIRPUS CÆSPITOSUS. *Flo. Brit.* 49.
 Upon most of the high moors.
S. LACUSTRIS. *Flo. Brit.* 52.
 Eshton and Giggleswick Tarns.
ERIOPHORUM VAGINATUM. *Flo. Brit.* 58.
 Frequent upon peat moors.
E. POLYSTACHION. *Flo. Brit.* 59. *Trans. Lin. Soc.* vol. ii. 289.
 Near Malham Tarn.
E. ANGUSTIFOLIUM. *Flo. Brit.* 59.
 Common upon the moors.

DIGYNIA.

MILIUM EFFUSUM. *Flo. Brit.* 75.
 Bingley Woods.
AIRA CRISTATA. *Flo. Brit.* 83.
 Settle Rock. *Mr. Hustler.*
MELICA NUTANS. *Flo. Brit.* 92.
 Helks Wood, by Ingleton. Woods about Settle.
SESLERIA CŒRULEA. *Flo. Brit.* 94. Cynosurus cœruleus. *Huds.* 59.
 Upon the rock at Settle. Crevices of the Limestone Rocks at the foot of Ingleborough. *Dr. Stokes.*
 Upon the rocks at the Strid, near Bolton.

POA AQUATICA. *Flo. Brit.* 95.
  In the Leeds and Liverpool Canal, between Stockbridge
  and Silsden.
P. SUBCŒRULEA. *Eng. Bot.* 1004, var. P. Pratensis. *Knapps.*
  Gram. Brit. tab. 118.   Poa humilis. *Flo. Brit.* 1387.
P. NEMORALIS. *Flo. Brit.* 106.
  In the woods about the Strid.
FESTUCA OVINA. *Flo. Brit.* 113. v. Fes. tenuifolia. Sibth.
  44. *With.* 155.
F. VIVIPARA. *Flo. Brit.* 114. Fes. ovina B. *Spec. plant.*
  108. (Var. 4.) *With.* 152.
  On Ingleborough, Ryeloaf, &c.
F. BROMOIDES. *Flo. Brit.* 117.
  Bellbank Wood, near Bingley.
BROMUS PINNATUS. *Flo. Brit.* 137. *Trans. Lin. Soc.*
  4 vol. 301. Festuca pinnata. *With.* 158.
  Under the walls of Skipton Castle.
AVENA PRATENSIS. *Flo. Brit.* 141.
  About Skipton.

TETRANDRIA MONOGYNIA.

SCABIOSA COLUMBARIA. *Flo. Brit.* 171.
  About Skipton.
ASPERULA ODORATA.
  Plentifully in the hedges and woods about Bingley.
A. CYNANCHICA. *Flo. Brit.* 172. *Eng. Bot.* 33.
  About Malham.
GALIUM SAXATILE. *Flo. Brit.* 175. G. procumbens. *With.*
  187.
GALIUM PUSILLUM. *Flo. Brit.* 177. *Eng. Bot.* 74.
  In plenty about Malham.
G. BOREALE. *Flo. Brit.* 180. *Eng. Bot.* 105.
  Upon the rocks at the Strid.
PLANTAGO MEDIA. *Flo. Brit.* 183.
  About Skipton, Thornton, &c.
P. MARITIMA. v. *Huds.* 64.
  Mountains near Settle. *Mr. Teesdale.*

TETRAGYNIA.

POTAMOGETON DENSUM. *Flo. Brit.* 194.
  Giggleswick Tarn.

PENTANDRIA MONOGYNIA.

ANCHUSA SEMPERVIRENS. *Flo. Brit.* 215. *Eng. Bot.* 45.
  By the road-side between Settle and Ingleton. *Mr.*
  Teesdale.
PRIMULA FARINOSA. *Flo. Brit.* 224. *Eng. Bot.* 6.
  Covering whole meadows with a fine pinky colour about
  Conistone and other parts of Craven. *Mr. Caley, in*
  Withering.
  The British flora cannot boast many more beautiful
  productions than this elegant Primula, which adorns
  the rills and wet pastures most abundantly in the
  romantic neighbourhood of Malham.
MENYANTHES TRIFOLIATA. *Flo. Brit.* 225.
  In the bogs upon Rumbald's Moor, near Helwick, in the
  parish of Bingley.
LYSIMACHIA NEMORUM. *Flo. Brit.* 228. *Eng. Bot.* 527.
  In woods.

ANAGALLIS TENELLA. *Flo. Brit.* 230. *Eng. Bot.* 530.
  In a bog on the right of the road leading between the
  Vicarage and Greenhill near Bingley.
CONVOLVULUS SEPIUM. *Flo. Brit.* 233.
  Skipton, &c.
POLEMONIUM CŒRULEUM. *Flo. Brit.* 234. *Eng. Bot.* 14.
  "Found by Dr. Lister in Carlton Beck, in the falling
  of it into the river Aire ; but more plentifully both
  with a blue flower and a white one about Malham
  Cove, a place so remarkable that it is esteemed one of
  the wonders of Craven. It grows there in a wood on
  the left hand of the water as you go to the Cove from
  Malham, plentifully ; and also at *Cordil*, or the Wern,
  a remarkable Cove, where comes out a great stream
  of water near the said Malham." *Raii Syn.* 288.
  Above the Cascade at Gordale.
CAMPANULA LATIFOLIA. *Flo. Brit.* 236.
  Between Clapham and Settle.
JASIONE MONTANA. *Flo. Brit.* 241.
VIOLA HIRTA. *Flo. Brit.* 244. *With.* 260.
  Amongst the Limestone Rocks, on the common above
  Gordale, in going from thence towards the Tarn.
V. PALUSTRIS. *Flo. Brit.* 246.
  In Ravenroyd Wood, near Bingley, in a boggy place on
  the left of the footpath.
CHIRONIA CENTAURIUM. *Flo. Brit.* 257. *Eng. Bot.* 417.
  Gentiana Centaurium. *Spec. Plan.* 332 ; and *Huds.*
  102.
  In barren places about Eshton, &c.
EUONYMUS EUROPÆUS. *Flo. Brit.* 262.
  Skirethorn Wood.

DIGYNIA.

GENTIANA PNEUMANANTHE. *Flo. Brit.* 285.   Gentiana
  palustris angustifolia. *Raii Syn.* 274.
  A quarter of a mile beyond Clapham, in the field going
  the middle way to Ingleton. *Ray.*
G. AMARELLA. *Flo. Brit.* 287. *Eng. Bot.* 236.
  About Gordale, *below* the waterfall. *Mr. Wood, in*
  Withering. About Settle, *Mr. Hustler.*
G. CAMPESTRIS. *Flo. Brit.* 288. *Eng. Bot.* 237.
  Amongst the high rocks *above* the waterfall at Gordale.
  Mr. Wood, in Withering.
  I have found G. Amarella among these rocks, but not the
  Campestris. *S. H.*
HYDROCOTYLE VULGARIS. *Flo. Brit.* 290.
  In swampy ground upon Rumbald's Moor, and upon
  Cottingley Moor, in the parish of Bingley.
SANICULA EUROPÆA. *Flo. Brit.* 291.
  About Gill, Greenberfield, and in the woods about
  Bingley.
PEUCEDANUM SILAUS. *Flo. Brit.* 305.
  Gargrave.
MEUM ATHAMANTICUM. *Flo. Brit.* 308. Æthusa meum.
  Sys. Veg. edit. 14, 287. *With.* 305.
  In the mountainous parts of the West Riding, sparingly.
  Teesdale.
OENANTHE CROCATA. *Flo. Brit.* 319.
  On the side of the canal between Silsden and Bingley,
  and by the turnpike [gate at Hawcliffe near
  Steeton.

SCANDIX ODORATA. *Flo. Brit.* 323.
In the meadows between Morton and Rishforth, certainly a native. *Dr. Richardson.*
Growing very plentifully in the meadows, and upon the sides of the brook near Glusburn, certainly wild.

TETRAGYNIA.

PARNASSIA PALUSTRIS. *Flo. Brit.* 340. *Eng. Bot.* 82.
About Skipton, Settle, &c., in boggy places, and at Gordale.

HEXAGYNIA.

DROSERA ROTUNDIFOLIA. *Flo. Brit.* 346. *Eng. Bot.* 867.
Upon Gilstead Moor, near Bingley.

HEXANDRIA MONOGYNIA.

ALLIUM CARINATUM. *Flo. Brit.* 357.
This I observed on the scars of the mountains near Settle. *Ray.* Among rocks at Conystone and Kilnsey. *Curtis.*
ORNITHOGALUM LUTEUM. *Flo. Brit.* 362. *Eng. Bot.* 21.
Under Malham Cove. *Mr. Wood, in With.*
CONVALLARIA MAJALIS. *Flo. Brit.* 370.
In moist woods in Craven. *Mr. Caley, in With.*
C. POLYGONATUM. *Flo. Brit.* 371.
Fissures of rocks near Wharf, Settle, and Skipton. Helks Wood. *Mr. Teesdale.* Sykes Wood. *Mr. Caley.*

POLYGYNIA.

ALISMA PLANTAGO. *Flo. Brit.* 400.
In the dam belonging to the mill at Bracewell.

HEPTANDRIA MONOGYNIA.

TRIENTALIS EUROPÆA. *Flo. Brit.* 406. *Eng. Bot.* 15.
On Rumbald's Moor, about a mile above Helwick, in a flat boggy place on the left of the road leading to Otley.
Invenit T. Willisel, ad orientalem extremitatem Rumbald's Meer, prope Helwick, in comitatu Eboracensi, loco paludoso inter juncos. *Raii Syn.* 286.

OCTANDRIA MONOGYNIA.

EPILOBIUM ANGUSTIFOLIUM. *Flo. Brit.* 409.
Ingleborough. *Pennant.* Among the rocks above Gordale.
E. ALPINUM. *Flo. Brit.* 419. *With.* 368.
Near Settle. *Mr. Teesdale.*
VACCINIUM VITIS IDÆA. *Flo. Brit.* 415.
Upon Rumbald's Moor, in the parish of Bingley.
V. OXYCOCCOS. *Flo. Brit.* 416.
In boggy places upon Rumbald's Moor, near Helwick, &c.

TRIGYNIA.

POLYGONUM AMPHIBIUM. *Flo. Brit.* 423. *Eng. Bot.* 436.
In the Leeds and Liverpool Canal, near Silsden, and in dams and pools near Skipton.

4 B

POLYGONUM VIVIPARUM. *Flo. Brit.* 428. *Eng. Bot.* 669.
In a moist spot of ground a little below the Culms near Horton in Craven. *Mr. Bingley, in Eng. Bot.*

TETRAGYNIA.

PARIS QUADRIFOLIA. *Flo. Brit.* 431. *Eng. Bot.* 7.
In the woods about Bingley, and particularly near Rishforth.
ADOXA MOSCHATELLINA. *Flo. Brit.* 432.
Bellbank Wood, near Bingley.

DECANDRIA MONOGYNIA.

PYROLA ROTUNDIFOLIA. *Flo. Brit.* 444. *Eng. Bot.* 213.
Mr. Tenant's Wood, near Kilnsey. *Curtis.* I am apprehensive that this plant has been taken for P. minor, and that this habitat applies to the latter. Vide *Flo. Brit.* 445. *S. H.*
P. MINOR. *Flo. Brit.* 444. *Eng. Bot.* 158.
Near Clapham. *Teesdale and Withering.*

DIGYNIA.

SAXIFRAGA UMBROSA. *Flo. Brit.* 449. *Eng. Bot.* 663.
On a rocky bank near a rivulet half a mile west of Mrs. Foster's house, in Hestleton Gill, betwixt Arncliffe and Horton. *Mr. Bingley, in Eng. Bot.*
Reddins Gill, near Keighley. *Mr. Knowlton.*
S. OPPOSITIFOLIA. *Flo. Brit.* 449. *Eng. Bot. tab.* 9.
Ingleborough.
S. AIZOIDES. *Flo. Brit.* 452. *Eng. Bot. tab.* 39. S. autumnalis. *Huds.* 180.
Ingleborough.
S. GRANULATA. *Flo. Brit.* 453.
About Malham Cove plentifully.
S. TRIDACTYLITES. *Flo. Brit.* 454.
Upon the walls and buildings at Barnoldswick, Coatshall, &c. Common in Craven, but rare in Lancashire. *Mr. Caley, in With.*
S. HYPNOIDES. *Flo. Brit.* 457.
About Gordale and Malham, and plentifully on the rocks at the Tarn.

TRIGYNIA.

STELLARIA NEMORUM. *Flo. Brit.* 473.
In Ravenroyd Wood near Bingley.
ARENARIA VERNA. *Flo. Brit.* 481. A. Saxatilis. *Huds. ed.* 1. 168. Var. 3. A. laricifolia. *With.*
On the Malham Road above Settle. *Mr. Hustler.*
Mountains about Settle. *Teesdale. Ray.*
At the Strid above Bolton Park. *S. H.*
About the Ebbing and Flowing Well beyond Giggleswick, in plenty. *Bolt.*
A. LARICIFOLIA. Var. 3. *Flo. Brit.* 482.
About the lead-mines at the bottom of Ingleborough towards Horton and Ribblesdale. *Bolt. MSS.* 1768.

PENTAGYNIA.

SEDUM TELEPHIUM. *Flo. Brit.* 485.
In a small glen on the right of the road as you turn to go over the fields to Gordale from Malham.

S. VILLOSUM. *Flo. Brit.* 488.
  On the moist rocks about Ingleborough Hill, as you go
  from the hill towards Horton in Ribblesdale, in
  ground where peat is got in great plenty. *Raii Syn.*
  270. In et juxta montem Hinklehaw prope Settle.
  Dr. Richardson.
  Close by Wethercoat Cave, at the foot of Ingleborough.
  Mr. Woodward, in With.
  At Settle. *Mr. Hustler.*
SPERGULA NODOSA. *Flo. Brit.* 503.
  Plentifully in the moist ground below Gordale, bogs
  about Settle. *Curtis, in With.*
  Malham Cove. *Mr. Hustler.*

DODECANDRIA MONOGYNIA.

LYTHRUM SALICARIA. *Flo. Brit.* 510.
  In the fields adjoining to the river at Steeton, and upon
  the edges of the canal there.

ICOSANDRIA MONOGYNIA.

PYRUS ARIA. *Flo. Brit.* 534. Cratægus aria. *With.* 458.
  Grass Wood, and Dib, near Coniston.
SPIRÆA FILIPENDULA. *Flo. Brit.* 535.
  Near Skipton.
ROSA VILLOSA. *Flo. Brit.* 538.
  Grass Wood near Kilnsey. *Curtis.* In the Craven
  part of Yorkshire. *Mr. Wood, in Withering.*
RUBUS IDÆUS. *Flo. Brit.* 541.
  Bingley Woods.
RUBUS SAXATILIS. *Flo. Brit.* 544.
  In the north-west part of Yorkshire. *Ray*, 261. Woods
  about Settle and Ingleton. *Curtis.* In the wood
  beyond the Strid at Bolton.
R. CHAMŒMORUS. *Flo. Brit.* 545.
  Ingleborough and Hinclehaugh near Settle. *Ray.*
  Sides of the highest mountains about Settle and
  Ingleton.
POTENTILLA VERNA. *Flo. Brit.* 550.
  Giggleswick, near the Ebbing and Flowing Well.
GEUM RIVALE. *Flo. Brit.* 555.
  Settle, Ingleton, Gargrave, &c.
DRYAS OCTOPETALA. *Flo. Brit.* 555. *Eng. Bot.* 431.
  Arncliffe Clowder, near Kilnsay. *Curtis.* Near Settle.
  Dr. Fell. Stonecliffe in Littondale. *Mr. Wood, in
  With.*
COMARUM PALUSTRE. *Flo. Brit.* 556.
  Giggleswick Tarn. In a bog called Maud's Stable, upon
  Cottingley Moor, in the parish of Bingley.

POLYANDRIA MONOGYNIA.

ACTÆA SPICATA. *Flo. Brit.* 562.
  In dumetis infra Malham Cove juxta murum Aquilonem
  versus prope rupes, ubi Fraxini juniores crescunt,
  reperiuntur hujus plantæ nonnullæ. *Dr. Richardson.*
  Raii Syn. 262. In a wood near Clapham. Upon
  Ingleborough. *Mr. Woodward.* And in the fissures
  of the very curious natural pavement of limestone at
  the foot of it. *Dr. Stokes.*
  I found it growing among the limestone rocks in passing
  over the common from Gordale to Malham Tarn.

CHELIDONIUM MAJUS. *Flo. Brit.* 563.
  Bolton Abbey, &c.
CISTUS HELIANTHEMUM. *Flo. Brit.* 575.
  Plentiful about Malham, &c.

PENTAGYNIA,

AQUILEGIA VULGARIS. *Flo. Brit.* 578.
  Upper part of Girling Trough near Conistone. Kilnsey.
  Curtis.

POLYGYNIA.

THALICTRUM MINUS. *Flo. Brit.* 584.
  Plentiful under the waterfall at Gordale. Abundantly
  at Malham and Settle. *Ray.* Kilnsey. *Curtis.*
TROLLIUS EUROPÆUS. *Flo. Brit.* 597.
  Moist woods about Settle. *Curtis.* About Malham
  Tarn.

DIDYNAMIA GYMNOSPERMIA.

GALEOPSIS VERSICOLOR. *Flo. Brit.* 630. *Eng. Bot.* 667.
  G. cannabina. *With.* 529.
  Amongst corn in the fields about Bingley and
  Keighley.
G. LADANUM. *Flo. Brit.* 628.
  Settle. *Mr. Hustler.*
GALEOBDOLON LUTEUM. *Flo. Brit.* 631.
  In Bellbank Wood, near Bingley.
ORIGANUM VULGARE. *Flo. Brit.* 639.
  Skipton.
THYMUS SERPYLLUM. *Flo. Brit.* 640.
  Var. serpyllum vulgare *hirsutum. Raii Syn.* 231.
  Malham Tarn, Skipton, &c.

ANGIOSPERMIA.

SCROPHULARIA AQUATICA. *Flo. Brit.* 663.
  In Lord Thanet's Canal at Skipton.

TETRADYNAMIA SILICULOSA.

DRABA INCANA. *Flo. Brit.* 678.
  About Settle. *Curtis.*
D. MURALIS. *Flo. Brit.* 679.
  Arnbar Scar near Arncliff, Littondale. *Curtis.* A little
  below Malham Cove. *Mr. Caley.* On the sides of
  the mountains in several parts of Craven. *Raii Syn.*
  On Malham Cove. *Mr. Hustler.*
THLASPI ALPESTRE. *Flo. Brit.* 686.
  Pastures about the Ebbing and Flowing Well at
  Giggleswick. Also in many places of the moun-
  tainous pastures between Settle and Malham. *Raii
  Syn.* Growing with Arenaria verna, near Settle.
  Curtis.
COCHLEARIA OFFICINALIS. *Flo. Brit.* 688,
  Var. C. Groenlandica. *With.* 573, *nec Linn.*
  Ingleborough Hill. *Mr. Teesdale.*
C. ARMORACIA. *Flo. Brit.* 690.
  Upon the banks of Skipton Beck and in Bolland in
  Craven. *Raii Syn.*

SILIQUOSA.

CARDAMINE IMPATIENS. *Flo. Brit.* 697.
About Settle. *Mr. Hustler.* Giggleswick Scar.
CARDAMINE AMARA. *Flo. Brit.* 699.
Crosshills, near Kildwick. *Mr. Hustler.*
ERYSIMUM PRÆCOX ? *Flo. Brit.* 707.
I insert this rare plant upon the authority of my much esteemed, much valued, and ever to be lamented friend William Hustler, Esq., who brought me a specimen from the neighbourhood of Settle, but the precise place I have forgot.
CHERIANTHUS FRUTICULOSUS. *Flo. Brit.* 709. C. Cheiri. *With.* 586.
Bolton Abbey, Skipton Castle, &c.
TURRITIS HIRSUTA. *Flo. Brit.* 716.
Common about Skipton, Bolton Abbey, &c. Settle.

MONADELPHIA PENTANDRIA.

ERODIUM MOSCHATUM. *Flo. Brit.* 728. Geranium moschatum. *With.* 609.
Gargrave. *Mr. Hustler.*

DECANDRIA.

GERANIUM PHÆUM. *Flo. Brit.* 729.
In woods about Settle and Ingleton. *Teesdale.* About Clapham. *With.* Beckfoot Lane, near Bingley.
G. SYLVATICUM. *Flo. Brit.* 731.
About Settle and Ingleton. *Teesdale.* Plentifully in the woods about Bolton Abbey.
G. LUCIDUM. *Flo. Brit.* 733.
G. PYRENAICUM. *Flo. Brit.* 735.
On the bank of the river Aire between Bingley and Keighley. *Huds.* I have not been able to find this plant in this place.
G. SANGUINEUM. *Flo. Brit.* 738.
At Gordale.

DIADELPHIA HEXANDRIA.

FUMARIA CLAVICULATA. *Flo. Brit.* 752.
Bingley Woods and Hawcliffe Wood near Steeton.

DECANDRIA.

GENISTA ANGLICA. *Flo. Brit.* 756.
Upon Rumbald's Moor above Morton.
ANTHYLLIS VULNERARIA. *Flo. Brit.* 759.
In Craven. *Mr. Caley.* Malham.
VICIA SYLVATICA. *Flo. Brit.* 768.
Malham. *Woodward, in Withering.*
HIPPOCREPIS COMOSA. *Flo. Brit.* 777.
Limestone rocks about Malham, Settle, Giggleswick, Kilnsay, and Wharf.

POLYADELPHIA POLYANDRIA.

HYPERICUM MONTANUM. *Flo. Brit.* 803.
Near Ingleton.
H. HIRSUTUM. *Flo. Brit.* 804.
At the foot of Ingleborough, near to Hirtle Pot, and in many other places in Craven.

SYNGENESIA POLYGAMIA EQUALIS.

TRAGOPOGON PRATENSIS. *Flo. Brit.* 812.
About Settle, Giggleswick, &c.
PRENANTHES MURALIS. *Flo. Brit.* 821.
About Bingley. In the Springs, Skipton, and about Malham.
HIERACIUM MURORUM. *Flo. Brit.* 830.
Bolton Abbey.
Var. B. Hieracium macrocaulon hirsutum folio rotundiore. *Raii Syn.* 169.
Gordil. *Dr. Richardson.*
H. PALUDOSUM. *Flo. Brit.* 831.
Ravenroyd Wood, near Bingley.
In pratis humidis et juxta rivulos Craveniæ montosos abundat. *D. Richardson, in Syn. Raii,* 166.
H. VILLOSUM. *Flo. Brit.* 833.
Near Meer Gill, at the foot of Ingleborough.
HYPOCHÆRIS MACULATA. *Flo. Brit.* 840.
Near Ottermine Cave. Settle. Malham Cove. *Eng. Bot.* 225.
SERRATULA TINCTORIA. *Flo. Brit.* 845.
Malham Cove.
CARDUUS HETEROPHYLLUS. *Flo. Brit.* 853. C. helenioides. *With.* 702.
Coppice near Giggleswick, in Skirrith Wood, and in the pastures about Bordley, near Malham.
CARLINA VULGARIS. *Flo. Brit.* 857.
Near Clapham, Giggleswick, &c.

POLYGAMIA SUPERFLUA.

GNAPHALIUM DIOICUM. *Flo. Brit.* 869.
Ingleborough, Gilstead Moor, near Bingley.
ERIGERON ACRE. *Flo. Brit.* 877.
Bingley Locks.
TUSSILAGO HYBRIDA. *Flo. Brit.* 879.
Near the River Wharf between Ilkley and Skipton.
SENECIO SARACENICUS. *Flo. Brit.* 887.
About Clapham and Ingleton. *Huds.*
S. TENUIFOLIUS. *Flo. Brit.* 884.
Gargrave.
SOLIDAGO VIRGAUREA. *Flo. Brit.* 889.
γ. S. cambrica. *With.* 728.
On the rocky precipice on the summit of Ingleborough to the north-west. *Mr. Woodward, in Withering.*

GYNANDRIA DIANDRIA.

SATYRIUM ALBIDUM. *Flo. Brit.* 929.
Moist meadows about Malham. *Ray.*
OPHRYS CORDATA. *Flo. Brit.* 933.
On Ingleborough. On Rumbald's Moor near Helwick.
O. MUSCIFERA. *Flo. Brit.* 937.
Near Settle. *Mr. Hustler.*
CYPRIPEDIUM CALCEOLUS. *Flo. Brit.* 941.
About Arncliffe, Kilnsay, Litton, and Kettlewell. In Helks Wood by Ingleborough. *Raii Syn.* But I believe it is now nearly eradicated there by the rapacity of collectors.
SERAPIAS LATIFOLIA. *Flo. Brit.* 942.
B. helleborine altera atro rubente flore. *Raii Syn.* 383.
On the sides of mountains about Malham and Settle.

S. ENSIFOLIA. *Flo. Brit.* 945.
    Woods at Settle and Ingleton.   Helks Wood.
S. RUBRA. *Flo. Brit.* 946.
    About Clapham and Ingleton.   *Huds.*

MONOECIA TRIANDRIA.

CAREX DIOICA. *Flo. Brit.* 963.
    Rumbald's Moor near Helwick.
C. CURTA. *Flo. Brit.* 967.   C. brizoides.   *Huds.*
    Plentiful on Rumbald's Moor near Helwick.
C. TERETIUSCULA. *Flo. Brit.* 977.
    Abundant in Salterforth Moss.
C. DISTANS. *Flo. Brit.* 992.
    Giggleswick Tarn.   *Curtis.*
C. VESICARIA. *Flo. Brit.* 1005.
    Salterforth Moss.
C. AMPULLACEA. *Flo. Brit.* 1006.
    Giggleswick Tarn.   Rumbald's Moor, near Helwick.

POLYANDRIA.

POTERIUM SANGUISORBA. *Flo. Brit.* 1025.
    Plentiful about Skipton, Thornton, &c.

DIOECIA DIANDRIA.

SALIX HELIX. *Flo. Brit.* 1040.   S. monandra.   *With.* 45.
    About Thornton, Broughton, and by the canal side
    between Skipton and the latter place.
S. TRIANDRA. *Flo. Brit.* 1044.
S. AMYGDALINA. *Flo. Brit.* 1045.
S. PENTANDRA. *Flo. Brit.* 1046.
S. MYRSINITES. *Flo. Brit.* 1054.
    On the slope of a high hill between Kilnsay and Arn-
    cliffe.   *Curtis.*
S. HERBACEA. *Flo. Brit.* 1056.
    Ingleborough.   *Pennant, Teesdale.*
S. RETICULATA. *Flo. Brit.* 1057.
    On the rocks on the uppermost part of Ingleborough,
    on the north side, and on Whernside over against
    Ingleborough on the other side the subterraneous
    river.   *Ray.*

OCTANDRIA.

RHODIOLA ROSEA. *Flo. Brit.* 1082.
    On a rock on the summit of Ingleborough to the north-
    west.   *Mr. Woodward.*

MONADELPHIA.

TAXUS BACCATA. *Flo. Brit.* 1086.
    In a truly wild state, growing out of the clefts of the
    rocks on Giggleswick Scar and Gordale.

CRYPTOGAMIA. FILICES.

EQUISETUM HYEMALE. *Flo. Brit.* 1105.
    Skipton and other parts of Craven.   *With.*
OSMUNDA LUNARIA. *Flo. Brit.* 1107.
    Near Settle, Meer Bank by Sykes Wood, in Ingleton.
O. REGALIS. *Flo. Brit.* 1108.
    Near Keighley.

LYCOPODIUM CLAVATUM. *Flo. Brit.* 1108.
    Plentiful upon Rumbald's Moor.
L. SELAGINOIDES. *Flo. Brit.* 1109.
    Upon the Moor before you come to the Tarn from Mal-
    ham in abundance.
L. SELAGO. *Flo. Brit.* 1111.
    Near the top of Ingleborough.
L. ALPINUM. *Flo. Brit.* 1112.
    Near the top of Ingleborough and other high hills in
    that part of the county.   Upon Rumbald's Moor.
POLYPODIUM VULGARE. *Flo. Brit.* 1113.
    γ. P. vulgare lobis proliferis.   *Bolt. Fil. t.* 2. *f.* 5. *b.*
    In a wood near Bingley.   *Dr. Alexander.*
P. PHEGOPTERIS. *Flo. Brit.* 1116.
    In the woods about the Strid, near Bolton.
P. DRYOPTERIS. *Flo. Brit.* 1116.
    Bingley Woods, and particularly in those south of St.
    Ives.
P. CALCAREUM. *Flo. Brit.* 1117.   P. dryopteris.   Var.
    With. 781.   *Bolt. Fil.* 53. tab. 1.
    White Scars near Ingleton.
ASPIDIUM LONCHITIS. *Flo. Brit.* 1118.   Polypodium lon-
    chitis.   *With.* 773.
    Near Bingley.   *Huds, edit.* 1. but I believe the Poly-
    podium aculeatum has been taken for this plant, and
    that Hudson's habitat is an error.
A. ACULEATUM. *Flo. Brit.* 1122.   Polypodium aculeatum.
    With. 777, and *Huds.* 459.
    Plentiful in Bellbank Wood and the other woods about
    Bingley.
A. DILATATUM. *Flo. Brit.* 1125.   Polyp. cristatum.   *With.*
    778.
    Bingley, Keighley, &c.
ASPLENIUM TRICHOMANES. *Flo. Brit.* 1126.
    Skipton Castle.
        B. trichomanes foliis eleganter incisis.   *Dill. in Raii*
        Syn. 120.
    Ingleborough Hill.
A. VIRIDE. *Flo. Brit.* 1127.
    On Ingleborough.   Plentiful in the crevices of the
    limestone rocks about Malham.   On walls and rocks
    about Settle.
        Var. B.   A. Trichomanes ramosum.   *Bolt. Fil.* 25.
        tab. 2. fig. 3.   *Raii Syn.* 119.
    On Ingleborough and on limestone rocks in the
    neighbourhood of Settle and Ingleton.
A. SEPTENTRIONALE. *Flo. Brit.* 1129.   Acrostichum sep-
    tentrionale.   *With.* 764.
    On Ingleborough.
A. LANCEOLATUM. *Flo. Brit.* 1132.
    On a wall in the village of Wharf.   *Bolt. Fil.* 31.
    Bolton must have made a mistake in referring to the
    village of Wharf, as there is no such place : what
    village he meant I cannot even guess.
SCOLOPENDRIUM VULGARE. *Flo. Brit.* 1133.   Asplenium
    scolopendrium.   *With.* 766.
    Plentiful in Bellbank Wood, and at the foot of the wall
    as you enter Skipton Castle.
S. CETERACH. *Flo. Brit.* 1134.   Asp. Ceterach.   *With.* 766.
    Rocks about the Tarn at Malham, where it was ob-
    served by Ray.
PTERIS CRISPA. *Flo. Brit.* 1137.   Osmunda crispa.   *Huds.*
    450.
    Ingleborough.

CYATHEA FRAGILIS. *Flo. Brit.* 1139. Polypodium fragile. *With.* 779.

Malham Cove, Gordale, &c.

Var. B. Polypodium rhœticum. *With.* 780.

Gordale.

HYMENOPHYLLUM TUNBRIDGENSE. *Flo. Brit.* 1141. Trichomanes Tunbridgense. *With.* 781.

On the rock called Foal Foot on Ingleborough Hill.

Var. B. Trichomanes pyxidiferum. *Bolt. Fil.* 56. *tab.* 30.

Bellbank Wood, near Bingley, at the head of a remarkable spring. *Ray.* In a little dark cavern under a dripping rock in the same wood. *Bolt.*

Mr. Teesdale also found this rare plant in September, 1782, in the same place as mentioned by Ray, but it is not now to be found, and I suspect has been extirpated by the rapacity of those who do not deserve the name of botanists.

CRYPT. MUSCI.

ANDRÆA ALPINA. *Flo. Brit.* 1179. Jungermannia alpina. *With.* 882. *Dill.* 506. *t.* 73. *f.* 39.

Ingleborough.

GRIMMIA APOCARPA. *Flo. Brit.* 1200. Bryum apocarpum. *With.* 809.

On trunks of trees and rocks.

DICRANUM SCOPARIUM. *Flo. Brit.* 1201. Mnium scoparium. *With.* 799.

In woods.

D. GLAUCUM. *Flo. Brit.* 1216. Mnium glaucum. *With.* 801.

Bellbank Wood; but I never detected it in fruit.

D. ADIANTOIDES. *Flo. Brit.* 1234. Hypnum adiantoides. *With.* 844.

Springs and wet woods.

TORTULA RIGIDA. *Flo. Brit.* 1249. Bryum rigidum. *With.* 813.

On Ingleborough.

NECKERA CRISPA. *Flo. Brit.* 1273. Hypnum crispum. *With.* 847. *Eng. Bot.* 617.

On rocks and trunks of trees in the woods about the Strid.

HYPNUM UNDULATUM. *Flo. Brit.* 1294. *Eng. Bot.* 1181.

In Bingley Woods. Dr. Smith in "English Botany" observes that it rarely produces fructifications. I cannot say I have found the fruit so rare.

HYPNUM PROLIFERUM. *Flo. Brit.* 1297. *With.* 853.

Plentiful in Bellbank Wood.

H. MOLLUSCUM. *Flo. Brit.* 1335. *Eng. Bot.* 1327. H. crista-castrensis. *With.* 854.

Upon the rocks about Gordale.

FONTINALIS SQUAMOSA. *Flo. Brit.* 1337. *With.* 788.

In the brook which runs from the Tarn to the Cove at Malham. *Mr. Mellor.*

BARTRAMIA POMIFORMIS. *Flo. Brit.* 1340. Bryum pomiforme. *With.* 822.

Woods and fissures of rocks.

B. FONTANA. *Flo. Brit.* 1342. Mnium fontanum. *With.* 799.

Bogs and wet places.

BRYUM HORNUM. *Flo. Brit.* 1360. Mnium hornum. *With.* 804.

In shady woods.

POLYTRICHUM COMMUNE. *Flo. Brit.* 1372.

Bogs, &c.

P. ATTENUATUM. *Flo. Brit.* 1373. *Eng. Bot.* 1198.

In turfy bogs.

CRYPT. HEPATICÆ.

JUNGERMANNIA SINUATA. *Dill.* 74. *With.* 869.

Very plentiful at the head of Elm Cragg Well, in Bell Bank, near Bingley.

This is one of those proliferous plants which seldom form fructifications; and Mr. Wood, in *Withering,* suspects the fructification of this plant had never been found in England; but in April, 1801, I was so fortunate as to detect a plant in fruit in this place.

J. PINGUIS. *Dill.* 74. *Eng. Bot.* 185.

Bell Bank, near Bingley.

J. ASPLENOIDES. *Dill.* 69. 5. 6. *With.* 870.

Bell Bank. Springs behind Skipton Castle.

J. VITICULOSA. *Dill.* 69. 7. *With.* 873.

Malham Cove.

J. BIDENTATA. *Dill.* 70. 11. *With.* 871.

Bingley Woods.

J. NEMOROSA. *Dill.* 71. *With.* 875.

Bingley Woods.

MARCHANTIA POLYMORPHA. *With.* 884.

Bingley Locks.

TARGIONIA HYPOPHYLLA. *Eng. Bot.* 287. *With.* 883.

Near Keighley. *Mr. Knowlton.*

CRYPT. ALGÆ.

LEPRARIA ANTIQUITATIS. Lichen antiquitatis. *Ach. Prod.* 5. *With. vol.* 4. *p.* 3.

Upon walls and limestone rocks about Malham.

L. FLAVA. *Eng. Bot.* 1350. Lichen flavus. *Ach. Prod.* 6.

Upon trunks of trees.

LEPRARIA ALBA. *Eng. Bot.* 1349. Lichen albus. *Ach. Prod.* 7.

Rocks, trees, mosses, &c. Gordale.

VERRUCARIA.

LICHEN PERTUSUS. *Ach. Prod.* 17. *With. vol.* 4. 15.

On the bark of trees and upon stones.

L. HYMENIUS. *Ach. Prod.* 80.

On a young ash-tree in the springs behind Skipton Castle.

OPEGRAPHA.

L. VULGATUS. *Ach. Prod.* 21. L. rugosus. *With.* 4.

Bark of trees.

L. SCRIPTUS. *Ach. Prod.* 25.

Bark of trees.

VARIOLARIA.

L. FAGINEUS. *Ach. Prod.* 27.

Trunks of trees, and particularly the beech.

URCEOLARIA.

L. HOFFMANNI. *Ach. Prod.* 31. L. rupicola. *With.* 13.

Walls about Skipton Castle.

L. SCRUPOSUS. *Ach. Prod.* 32.
  On walls and stones.
L. CINERIUS. *Ach. Prod.* 32. *Eng. Bot.* 820.
  Walls beyond Skipton Castle.
L. GEOGRAPHICUS. *Ach. Prod.* 33.
  On rocks.
L. EXANTHEMATICUS. *Ach. Prod.* 35. *Act. Lin. Soc. tom.*
  1. *tab.* 4. *fig.* 1. *Eng. Bot.* 1184.
  This rare lichen I found upon the limestone rocks
  passing from Gordale to Malham Tarn.

PATELLARIA.

L. PARELLUS. *Ach. Prod.* 35. *With.* 17.
  Rocks, walls, and stones.
L. TARTAREUS. *Ach. Prod.* 37.
  Plentiful upon rocks and walls about Bingley.
L. CERINUS. *Ach. Prod.* 40. *With.* 24. *Eng. Bot.* 627.
  On the trunks of trees, Bingley Woods.
L. AURANTIACUS. *Ach. Prod.* 44. L. flavorubescens.
  With. 15.
  On the bark of trees and upon stones about Skipton.
L. HÆMATOMMA. *Ach. Prod.* 45. *Eng. Bot.* 486.
  Var. L. coccineus. *Eng. Bot.* 223.
  Upon rocks in Holden Wood, near Silsden.
L. DISPERSUS. *Ach. Prod.* 49.
  Limestone walls.
LICHEN VERNALIS. *Ach. Prod.* 51.
  Bark of trees.
L. ULMI. *Ach. Prod.* 54. L. marmoreus. *Eng. Bot.* 739.
  Upon rocks near Gennetts Cave, at Malham.
L. SULPHUREUS. *Ach. Prod.* 58. *Eng. Bot.* 1186.
  Upon walls about Malham.
L. CALCARIUS. *Ach. Prod.* 60.
  Limestone walls about Gargrave, Eshton, Airton, &c.
L. LAPICIDA. *Ach. Prod.* 61. L. concentricus. *Trans.*
  Lin. Soc. vol. 2. *Eng. Bot.* 206.
  Walls about Broughton.
L. PARASEMUS. *Ach. Prod.* 64.
  Upon the trunks of trees in the springs behind Skipton
  Castle.
L. SANGUINARIUS. *Ach. Prod.* 65.
  Upon stones.
L. SILACEUS. *Ach. Prod.* 66. *Eng. Bot.* 1118.
  Crinah Bottom, Ingleborough.
L. TEPHROMELAS. *Ach. Prod.* 67. L. ater. *With.* 18.
  Eng. Bot. 949.
  Walls about Malham, &c.
L. IMMERSUS. *Ach. Prod.* 70. *Eng. Bot.* 193.
  Rocks, walls, and stones, about Malham.
L. QUERNEUS. *Eng. Bot.* 485.
  Upon oaks and other trees in Holden Wood.
L. CALVUS. *Ach. Prod.* 72. *Eng. Bot.* 948.
  Rocks at Malham and Ingleborough.

BŒOMYCES.

L. ERICETORUM. *Ach. Prod.* 91. *Eng. Bot.* 372.
  On turfy heaths.
L. BYSSOIDES. *Ach. Prod.* 82. *Eng. Bot.* 373.
  On rotten wood, stones, heaths, &c. Plentiful in Beck-
  foot Lane, near Bingley.

PSOROMA.

L. NIGER. *Ach. Prod.* 92.
  Upon limestone walls about Malham.
L. CANDELARIUS. *Ach. Prod.* 92.
  Stones, walls, and trunks of trees.
L. VESICULARIS. *Ach. Prod.* 94. L. cœruleo-nigricans.
  Eng. Bot. 1139.
  Gordale.
L. CRASSUS. *Ach. Prod.* 97. *Huds.* 530. L. cartilagineus.
  With. 29.
  About Malham.

PLACODIUM.

LICHEN SYMPAGEUS? *Ach. Prod.* 105. L. flavicans?
  With. L. murorum? *Ach. Prod.* 101.
  Limestone walls about Bank Newton, &c.

IMBRICARIA.

L. INCURVUS. *Ach. Prod.* 107. *Eng. Bot.* 1375. L. multi-
  fidus. *Dicks.* and *With.*
  Malham Tarn, upon the rails by the canal side at
  Broughton.
L. STELLARIS. *Ach. Prod.* 111. *With.* 31.
  Bark of trees.
L. AIPOLIUS. *Ach. Prod.* 112.
  Trunks of old ash-trees, &c.
L. PULVERULENTUS. *Ach. Prod.* 112. Var. 2d. L. stellaris.
  With. 31.
  On sycamore, lime, and willow-trees.
L. OMPHALODES. *Ach. Prod.* 114. *With.* 34. *Eng. Bot.*
  604.
  Rocks and stones.
L. SAXATILIS. *Ach. Prod.* 115. *Eng. Bot.* 603.
  Rocks and stones. Holden Wood.
L. PHYSODES. *Ach. Prod.* 115. *Eng. Bot.* 126.
  Bark of trees.
L. CAPERATUS. *Ach. Prod.* 119. *Eng. Bot.* 654.
  On stones, rocks, trees, pales, &c.
L. PARIETINUS. *Ach. Prod.* 121.
  Common on walls, stones, houses, and trees.
L. OLIVACEUS. *Ach. Prod.* 121.
  On the bark of trees.

COLLEMA.

L. MARGINALIS. *Ach. Prod.* 127. *With.* 34.
  On walls near Settle.
L. HYDATERPUS. *Ach. Prod.* 129. L. fluviatilis. *With.*
  and *Huds.*
  On stones in the river which comes from under Malham
  Cove.
L. FASCICULARIS. *Ach. Prod.* 129. *Eng. Bot.* 1162.
  On walls about Malham.
L. LACERUS. *Ach. Prod.* 133. L. tremelloides. *With.* 72.
  On the ground and upon walls mixed with mosses about
  Skipton, Malham, and most parts of Craven.

ENDOCARPON.

L. MINIATUS. *Ach. Prod.* 141. *With.* 66. *Eng. Bot.* 593.
  Upon rocks in a deep glen on the right hand as you
  pass to Gordale from Malham.

LICHEN COMPLICATUS. *Ach. Prod.* 142. L. miniatus. var. 2. of Lightfoot.
Upon stones in the river under Malham Cove.

LOBARIA.

L. PULMONARIUS. *Ach. Prod.* 152. *With.* 54. *Eng. Bot.* 572.
Upon the trunks of trees in the woods about the Strid, near Bolton.
L. PERLATUS. *Ach. Prod.* 153.
Upon the trunks of trees.

PELTIDEA.

L. HORIZONTALIS. *Ach. Prod.* 160.
Bingley and Steeton Woods.
L. CANINUS. *Ach. Prod.* 160.
In moist shady places upon the ground.
L. APTHOSUS. *Ach. Prod.* 161. *With.* 70.
Ingleborough Hill and other places.
L. POLYDACTYLUS. *Ach. Prod.* 162. *With.* 69.
Rumbald's Moor near Helwick. *Richardson* and *Dillenius.*
L. SACCATUS. *Ach. Prod.* 165. *With.* 67.
About the mouth of Yordas Cave in ingleborough. *Dr. Smith.* Gordale.

PLATISMA.

L. GLAUCUS. *Ach. Prod.* 167.
Beckfoot Lane, near Bingley.

PHYSCIA.

L. ISLANDICUS. *Ach. Prod.* 170. *With.* 54.
Ingleborough.
L. TENELLUS. *Ach. Prod.* 172. *With.* 56.
On the bark of trees and upon stones.
L. CILIARIS. *Ach. Prod.* 173. *With.* 55.
On trees and stones.
L. FURFURACEUS. *Ach. Prod.* 173.
Stones and trees about Skipton and various other places.
L. PRUNASTRI. *Ach. Prod.* 174.
Trees.
L. FRAXINEUS. *Ach. Prod.* 175.
Upon oak and ash trees.

LICHEN FASTIGIATUS. *Ach. Prod.* 175.
L. CALICARIS. *Ach. Prod.* 176.
L. FARINACEUS. *Ach. Prod.* 177.
Upon trees.

SCYPHOPHORUS.

L. ALCICORNIS. *Ach. Prod.* 184. *Eng. Bot.* 1392. L. foliaceus. *With.*
Gordale.
L. PYXIDATUS. *Ach. Prod.* 186.
L. COCIFERUS. *Ach. Prod.* 187.
L. DEFORMIS. *Ach. Prod.* 189.
In shady places upon the earth, among moss, &c.

CLADONIA.

L. UNCIALIS. *Ach. Prod.* 201.
L. RANGIFERINUS. *Ach. Prod.* 202.
Heaths, woods, &c.
L. SPINOSUS. *Ach. Prod.* 205.
Ravenroyd Wood, near Bingley.

SPHAEROPHORUS.

L. GLOBIFERUS. *Ach. Prod.* 210.
Rocks and stones.
L. FRAGILIS. *Ach. Prod.* 211. *Eng. Bot.* 114.
Rocks in the woods near St. Ives in the parish of Bingley; and, though it is observed in *Eng. Bot.* to be very rarely found in fructification, I have very frequently observed it in that state even in the driest seasons.

SETARIA.

L. JUBATUS. *Ach. Prod.* 219.
Rocks and trees in Bingley Woods and Beckfoot Lane.
L. CHALYBEIFORMIS. *Ach. Prod.* 220.
Rocks in woods near St. Ives.

USNEA.

L. FLORIDUS. *Ach. Prod.* 224.
L. hirta. *With. Huds.*
Upon oak, beech, elm, &c. in Bingley Woods.

OBSERVATION.

EPIMEDIUM ALPINUM, *Eng. Bot.* 438, is said by *Dr. Richardson*, in *Blackstone* 19, to grow in Bingley Woods. I believe the Doctor was imposed upon, for it certainly is not now to be found there, nor do I believe it to be indigenous to this country.

CATALOGUE OF MINERALS

FOUND IN CRAVEN, BY W. E. SHEFFIELD, ESQ.

COPPER, &c., ORE OF.

COPPER PYRITES. Copper combined with Iron and sulphur.

MARTIAL PYRITES. Sulphur combined with Iron, with Baroselenite Foliated and Crystallised, found in a mine at Beggarmans, to the north-west of Buckden.

LEAD, ORES OF.

GALENA. Lead combined with Sulphur, the common blue Lead Ore.

LEAD mineralised by Oxygen and Carbonic Acid, the White Lead Ore. Crystallised and compact.

There are many mines in this part of Yorkshire which produce the above varieties of Lead Ore in considerable quantities ; the Liberties of Buckden, Starbottom, Kettlewell, Coniston, Grassington, Hebden, &c. &c., but the White Lead Ore has been raised in greatest quantities in the Liberties of Buckden and Grassington.

GREEN LEAD ORE, Phosphorated Lead Ores, I have discovered in very small quantity on Grassington Moor.*

ZINC, ORES OF.

CALAMINE, Lapis Calaminaris, Zinc mineralised by Oxygen, with or without Carbonic Acid. Compact and stalactitical, raised in considerable quantities in the Liberties of Arncliffe, Kettlewell, and several others in that neighbourhood ; and at Malham, Lord Ribblesdale's Liberty. There is also found at or near Malham, an Oxide of Zinc, in form of a white powder ; some of it is rich ; this has not been met with in any other part of England that I know of.

COAL.

A thin bed of Coal is found on Grassington Moor and other places in that neighbourhood.

The above-mentioned Ores are accompanied in the Vein with Baroselenite (Cank of some), Calcareous Spar, or Carbonate of Lime and Quartz, &c.

---

* " I myself know two places in Craven, in the West Riding of Yorkshire, where formerly good Silver Ore hath been gotten ; the one is a place called Brungill Moor, in the parish of Slaidburn, where between 50 and 70 years since Sir Bevis Bulmer got good store of Silver Ore that held about 67 pound *per* ton, as Walter Basby, an expert Essay or Test Master, who was at least a person of 76 years of age, and had, as an expert Artist, been in the time of King James sent to the Emperor of Russia to settle the standard of his coin, where he remaining divers years, and going down to the borders of Tartaria to view the Mines there, was taken prisoner by the Tartars, and after redeemed by the Russian Emperor, and sent over into England, where after about the year 1655 he was again brought down by some Londoners that then had a Patent for Mines. But they being then neither of free purses to follow such a work, nor of skill or government fit to follow such an enterprize, they at last deserted the poor old man, whom I entertained for three quarters of a year, and got some of the Ore picked forth of the old rubbish of the works that Sir Bevis Bulmer had left, and caused him to make several trials, &c. The other place was within the Township of Rimington, in the parish of Gisburne in Craven, in a field called Skelkorn belonging to one Mr. Pudsey, an antient Esquire, and owner of Bolton Hall juxta Bowland, who in the reign of Queen Elizabeth, did get there good store of Silver Ore, and converted it to his own use, or rather coined it, as many do believe, there being many shillings marked with an escalop, which the people of the Country call Pudsey's shillings to this day. It yielded in the ton about 26 pounds."

Webster's " History of Metals," pp. 21, 22, Ed. 1671.

INDEX.

4 C

THE END.

CASSELL, PETTER & GALPIN, BELLE SAUVAGE WORKS, LONDON, E.C.

DIRECTIONS TO THE BINDER.

SEPARATE PEDIGREES,

To be guarded, and placed as follows: